CORRECTION SYMBOLS IN ALPHABETICAL ORDER

Boldface numbers and letters refer to chapters and sections of the handbook.

ab	Faulty abbreviation, **28**		no ⌃	Comma not needed, **21j**
ad	Misuse of adjective or adverb, **9**		no ¶	No new paragraph needed, **3**
agr	Error in agreement, **8**		num	Error in use of numbers, **29**
ap	Apostrophe needed or misused, **23**		p	Error in punctuation, **20–25**
appr	Inappropriate diction, **31a**		. ? !	Period, question mark, exclamation point, **20**
awk	Awkward construction		⌃	Comma, **21**
bib	Error in bibliography form, **35d-2**		;	Semicolon, **22**
ca	Error in case form, **6**		⌄	Apostrophe, **23**
cap	Use capital letter, **26**		" "	Quotation marks, **24**
cit	Missing source citation or error in form of citation, **36i**		: — ( ) [ ] . . . /	Colon, dash, parentheses, brackets, ellipsis mark, slash, **25**
coh	Coherence lack			new paragraph, **3**
con	Be more concis			graph not coherent, **3b**
co-ord	Co-ordination r faulty, **16a**			graph not developed, **3c**
cs	Comma splice,			graph not unified, **3a**
d	Error in diction,			ctive passive voice, **8d**
dev	Inadequate development, **1, 3c**		ref	Error in pronoun reference, **12**
div	Incorrect word division, **30**		rep	Unnecessary repetition, **31c-2**
dm	Dangling modifier, **14f**		rev	Revise or proofread, **2**
emph	Emphasis lacking or faulty, **18**		shift	Inconsistency, **13**
exact	Inexact word, **31b**		sp	Misspelled word, **34**
fn	Error in footnote form, **36i-2**		spec	Be more specific, **3c, 4e**
frag	Sentence fragment, **10**		sub	Subordination needed or faulty, **16b**
fs	Fused sentence, **11c**		t	Error in verb tense, **7e–f**
gl/us	See Glossary of Usage, p. 732		t seq	Error in tense sequence, **7f**
gr	Error in grammar, **5–9**		trans	Transition needed, **3b–6, 3e**
hyph	Error in use of hyphen, **34d**		var	Vary sentence structure, **19**
inc	Incomplete construction, **15c–e**		vb	Error in verb form, **7a–d**
ital	Italicize (underline), **27**		w	Wordy, **31c**
k	Awkward construction		ww	Wrong word, **31b-1**
lc	Use lower-case letter, **26f**		//	Faulty parallelism, **17**
log	Faulty logic, **4b-4**		#	Separate with a space
mixed	Mixed construction, **15a–b**		⌒	Close up the space
mm	Misplaced modifier, **14a–e**		ℬ	Delete
mng	Meaning unclear		∾	Transpose letters or words
ms	Error in manuscript form, **App. A**		x	obvious error
			∧	Something missing, **15e**
no cap	Unnecessary capital letter, **26f**		??	Manuscript illegible or meaning unclear

THE
LITTLE, BROWN
HANDBOOK

First Canadian Edition

H. Ramsey Fowler
Memphis State University

Jane E. Aaron
Parsons School of Design/
The New School for Social Research

Deane E. D. Downey
Trinity Western University

Barbara H. Pell
Trinity Western University

gage EDUCATIONAL PUBLISHING COMPANY
A DIVISION OF CANADA PUBLISHING CORPORATION
TORONTO ONTARIO CANADA

Canadian Cataloguing in Publication Data

Main entry under title:

The Little, Brown handbook

1st Canadian edition.
ISBN 0-7715-5756-6

1. English language—Grammar—1950-
2. English language—Rhetoric.   I. Fowler, H.
Ramsey (Henry Ramsey).

PE1112.L58   1990   808′.042   C90-093785-8

Cover Design: Michael van Elsen Design Inc.

ISBN: 0-7715-**5756-6**

 2 3 4 5 6 7   JD   96 95 94 93 92

Printed and bound in Canada

Preface to First Canadian Edition

For a number of years we had both admired and used successive editions of *The Little, Brown Handbook*. Like many of our Canadian teaching colleagues, we appreciated this handbook for its well-known strengths: its comprehensiveness; the logic and accessibility of its organization; the clarity of its examples; its lucid, no-nonsense style; the abundance of its practical student exercises; and its helpful marking system. We had really only one major criticism of the textbook and that was the virtually total absence of things Canadian—a regrettable limitation in a textbook that was being used quite widely in colleges and universities throughout Canada.

The first Canadian edition embodies our efforts to correct this situation. It reflects our conviction that a Canadian edition of this fine handbook, in the course of instructing students in the fundamentals of written expression, should also foster in those students a greater awareness of and appreciation for their country's geography, history, literature, and rich cultural diversity.

Although we have been working on this project since 1986, the first Canadian edition is based on the fourth edition of *The Little, Brown Handbook*, which appeared in the Spring of 1989. The main features of that fourth edition's extensive improvements over the 1986 third edition are described in the accompanying "Preface for Instructors." We have reason to believe that the changes we have effected are among the most extensive ever made in a Canadian edition of an American handbook on English composition, grammar, punctuation, and usage. In addition to the more obvious changes in geographical place names and measurements, we have replaced with Canadian content (including about 60 quotations from some of Canada's best-known creative writers and journalists) the vast majority of explicit references to U.S. history, literature, and unique elements of that country's social and political structures. With respect to spelling, we of course were obliged to preserve American spellings as used in quoted material, both Canadian and otherwise, in that the use of American spellings is a practice currently observed by many Canadian periodicals and publishing houses. For a description of the current rather complicated state of affairs as to what constitutes orthodox practice in Canadian spelling, see Chapter 34.

One of our major revisions was the replacement of Pat Lucas's extensive first, revised, edited, and final drafts of an essay on The Renaissance Center in Detroit (in Chapters 1 and 2) with similar drafts of an authentic student essay by Lisa MacDonald on the National Gallery of

Canada. This essay is referred to and/or analysed several times throughout the book. Similarly, a research paper by Deborah Wiebe on British Columbia's entry into Confederation, substantially prepared for in Chapter 36 and reproduced verbatim in Chapter 37, replaces the sample research paper by Ann Wiess on the Declaration of Independence. In addition, Mark Shannon's paper on women executives, also discussed and presented in Chapters 36 and 37, has been revised and updated to reflect Canadian as well as American experience. Similar modifications and additions have been made in the student sociology essay entitled "An Assessment of Dating Violence on Campus" in Chapter 38. The discussion of research methods and materials in Chapters 35 and 36 has been updated as well as expanded to include Canadian reference and resource materials.

Only one significant deletion without replacement has been made. Because of space limitations, it was deemed necessary to relegate the Glossary of Grammatical Terms to the *Instructor's Manual*, which has been produced as a separate volume. The very handy guide to correction symbols and plan of the entire book, which appear at the end of the book, have been preserved.

We acknowledge with sincere appreciation the support and encouragement of several of our colleagues at Trinity Western, including Elsie Holmes, Ken Davis, Don Page, and Bob Burkinshaw, as well as the assistance of T.W.U. librarians Rick Wiebe and Ted Goshulak. Program co-ordinator Janet Turner, editorial services manager Darleen Rotozinski, and editors June Trusty and Julie Canton are also worthy of mention for their helpful work at Gage's end of the process.

To our spouses, Margaret and Archie, goes our heartfelt appreciation for their tolerance, encouragement, patience—and occasional browbeating—as they urged us to bring this lengthy project to a conclusion. Lisa MacDonald and Deborah Wiebe made significant contributions by their essays on the National Gallery and B.C.'s entry into Confederation respectively, and we are very grateful for their fine work on our behalf.

Throughout this project we have attempted to be modestly patriotic without being mindlessly parochial or immoderately nationalistic. By incorporating periodic encounters with aspects of Canadian literary, cultural, historical, and geographical experience, we hoped to relieve the occasional tedium of examining such topics as composition techniques, grammar and punctuation orthodoxy, research paper methodology, and so forth. While we are indebted to the many sources of those insights and perspectives, all infelicities and excesses in that regard are aspects of this edition for which we take full responsibility.

Deane E. D. Downey
Barbara H. Pell
Department of English
Trinity Western University
Langley, British Columbia

Preface for Instructors

Adapted from U.S. fourth edition

The changes in the fourth edition of *The Little, Brown Handbook* are paradoxically both few and numerous. The book continues to serve a dual function as both a text for composition classes and a reference for writers, distinguished by its comprehensiveness, clarity, accessibility, and an organization that places the writing process up front. But within this context myriad revisions and additions keep pace with changes in the teaching and learning of composition. The most significant of these alterations make the handbook even more convenient as a reference, introduce critical thinking and academic writing, and expand and refine the discussions of the writing process and the research paper.

Undoubtedly the most conspicuous change in the fourth edition is the brightened design, conceived to be functional as well as handsome. Headings are easier to find and read; exercises are more distinct; and crucial material is more accessible in the eighty-three screened boxes. These boxes extend a popular feature of the previous edition, the two-page guide to punctuation. New this time are four summary/index charts that pull together all the book's information on nouns, pronouns, verbs and verbals, and modifiers; a comprehensive guide to handling quotations; and seventy-seven other summaries, indexes, diagrams, and checklists encompassing everything from the writing situation to patterns of parallelism to the uses of the comma. Intended for quick reference, these boxes supplement rather than replace more detailed text discussions, providing students with two levels of explanation.

Throughout the handbook, new chapters and sections respond to a changing composition curriculum and the changing needs of students. Chapter 4, formerly devoted mainly to persuasive writing, has been broadened to encompass critical thinking, reading, and writing. It emphasizes writing summaries as an aid to analysis, discusses inference and other aspects of reasoning, and explains how to read as well as how to write an argument. Chapter 38, all new, treats writing in the disciplines, introducing students to the demands and rewards of academic writing and outlining the methods, goals, and concerns of the humanities (with an emphasis on literature), the social sciences, and the natural and applied sciences. The chapter provides four sample papers (including literary analyses both with and without secondary sources), complete models and explanations of the documentation style in psychology (APA), and highlights of a style commonly used in the sciences (CBE).

Instructors concerned with the writing process will appreciate the expansions in Chapters 1 and 2, especially in invention (including clustering), audience, organization (including tree diagrams, drafting, and writing a title).

vii

As before, examples in these chapters come from the work-in-progress of several students, including one student's complete first, revised, edited, and final drafts. A new Appendix B on word processing adapts the process outlined in Chapters 1 and 2 as the context for specific, practical advice on using a computer to write and revise.

The material on the research paper is also much strengthened. Although it continues to treat research writing as a process, it is divided into three chapters (35–37) for easier access to bibliographic models and other practical information. New sections advise students on planning and scheduling a long-term research project and on conducting interviews as primary research. Boxes frame such reference aids as a model schedule, indexes to the book's bibliographic and parenthetical-reference forms, and a list of verbs for introducing quotations. The discussion of paraphrasing and summarizing is fuller and is now followed by the former appendix on avoiding plagiarism, with a new exercise. A new student paper on women in management illustrates all stages of research writing and appears in final form with extensive annotations. As before, an analytical paper is also included.

These substantial revisions in the handbook are complemented by innumerable smaller adjustments. Among the other additions are a treatment of narrative and descriptive paragraphs (3c-2), guidance on double negatives (9f), a discussion of sexist and other biassed language (31a-8), and detailed instructions for typing punctuation (Appendix A). Editing has affected nearly every page, producing tighter explanations and clearer examples. The exercises in all the chapters that typically received the hardest use—case, verbs, fragments, commas, and the like—now consist entirely of connected discourse on subjects as diverse as computerized music and humour in business. As before, paragraph-format exercises conclude most chapters.

Supplements

The changes in the fourth edition have their equal in an extensive package of supplements. These supplements may be used in conjunction with *The Little, Brown Handbook*, First Canadian Edition. A new essay on contemporary approaches to teaching writing joins chapters on designing a composition course, evaluating student writing, and collaborative learning. New with this edition is word-processing software with extensive documentation: *PFS:Write* for the Apple and *PFS:Professional Write* for the IBM and compatibles, accompanied by the text/workbook *Composing with PFS:Write/PFS: Professional Write*, by Rosalie Hewitt and Vicky T. Miller, Northern Illinois University; and *MacWrite* for the Macintosh, accompanied by *MacWrite and the Writing Process*, by Mark Coleman, State University of New York at Potsdam.

Other supplements in this large package are an answer key to the handbook, available to students at an instructor's option; a student manual for peer evaluation; a collection of essays; a collection of student research papers; videotapes of the PBS television series *The Story of English*, with an accompanying study guide; a compilation of ideas for teaching writing; a set of transparency masters; a poster-size correction chart; a competency profile test bank; two sample CLAST tests; and diagnostic tests. Information on any of the supplements may be obtained from the publisher.

Acknowledgments

Dozens of instructors contributed thoughtful, detailed, and constructive comments based on their classroom experiences with students and with handbooks. We thank Christopher Baker, Lamar University; James E. Barcus, Baylor University; Glynn Baugher, Frostburg State University; Lynn Beene, University of New Mexico; Ethel L. Bonds, Virginia Western Community College; John Briggs, University of California, Riverside; Sally J. Bright, Tulsa Junior College; Harry M. Brown, Midwestern State University; Sara L. Brown, Tulsa Junior College; Wayne A. Buchman, Rose State College; Betsy R. Burke, Columbus State Community College; Santi Buscemi, Middlesex County College; Sylvia Cara-Monica, Clark County Community College; Barbara Carr, Stephen F. Austin State University; Margaret L. Carter, Bradley University; Betty Clement, Paris Junior College; Suzanne Clepper, Tarrant County Junior College; Paul Cohen, Southwest Texas State University; Mark Coleman, State University of New York, Potsdam; Thomas A. Copeland, Youngstown State University; Pat Coward, Bowling Green State University; Richard Cox, Abilene Christian University; Mary Ann Dazey, Mississippi State University; John T. Dever, Thomas Nelson Community College; Norbert Elliot, East Texas State University; G. Dale Gleason, Hutchinson Community College; Craig M. Goad, Northwest Missouri State University; D. Wayne Gunn, Texas A & I University; Iris Rose Hart, Santa Fe Community College; Milton Hawkins, Del Mar College; Vicki L. Hill, Southern Methodist University; Con Hood, Southwestern Oklahoma State University; Maurice Hunt, Baylor University; Vanessa Furse Jackson, Bowling Green State University; Judy Kaplow, William Rainey Harper Community College; Helen E. Kaufmann, Parkland College; Philip M. Keith, St. Cloud State University; Joanne Little, Pima Community College; Daniel T. Lochman, Southwest Texas State University; Larry R. Long, Harding University; Helen M. Loschky, Lincoln University; Helen Maloney, Tidewater Community College; Michael Meyer, University of Connecticut; Sandra Nagy, Arizona State University; Christopher O'Hearn, Los Angeles Harbor College; Blakeney J. Richard, Texas A & I University; Brad Rogharr, Weber State College; Robert Ross, Southern Methodist University; Bea Sandlin, Scottsdale Community College; Adeline Skillman, Essex County College; John F. Slater, University of Wyoming; Barbara Sloan, Santa Fe Community College; Louise Z. Smith, University of Massachusetts, Boston; M. Clare Sweeney, Arizona State University; Marc E. Tappmeyer, Southwest Baptist University; Richard F. Thompson, Northern Virginia Community College; Noel Toups, Nicholls State University; William J. Vande Kopple, Calvin College; George Van Devender, Hardin-Simmons University; Sue Fisher Vaughn, University of Rhode Island; and Laura W. Zlogar, University of Wisconsin at River Falls.

We extend special appreciation to several instructors who contributed text as well as ideas to the fourth edition: Kathleen S. Cain, Merrimack College; Mary E. McGann, Rhode Island College; Leonard J. Rosen, Bentley College; and William Van Pelt, University of Wisconsin at Milwaukee. Special thanks also to Andrew Christensen for insightful suggestions and to those responsible for producing this handsome edition: the book editor, Andrea Cava; the copy editor, Roberta H. Winston; the designer, Patricia Girvin Dunbar; the artist, Lyrl Ahern; and the editorial assistants, Dorothy Paschal and Susan McIntyre. As in previous editions, we again happily acknowledge a great debt to Robert A. Schwegler, University of Rhode Island, and Richard S. Beal, professor emeritus at Boston University, for their advice and support.

Preface for Students: Using This Book

Adapted from U.S. fourth edition

A handbook is a comprehensive reference guide to the essential information in a field or discipline, whether it is stamp collecting, home maintenance, or chemistry. *The Little, Brown Handbook* is no exception. A basic resource for English composition, grammar, and usage, it can serve you as a text and reference book for writing not only in a composition course but also in other courses and outside college. Mastery of the principles and conventions discussed in this book will not by itself make you a good writer; for that, you need to care about your work at every level from conceiving a topic to spelling words. But learning how to use the handbook and then referring to it as the need arises will give you the means to say *what* you want in the *way* you want. The following pages tell you about the book's organization and store of information, the ways of locating that information, and the standard of usage recommended.

The handbook's organization and coverage

An overview of the handbook's contents appears at the end of the book. The first four chapters discuss larger elements of composition—the essay and the paragraph. Chapters 1 and 2 describe and illustrate the writing process, from choosing a topic through considering an audience and generating and organizing ideas to revision. Chapter 3 treats composing and revising paragraphs. And Chapter 4 discusses critical thinking and writing, including how to read and write an argument. The principles discussed in these chapters are basic to everything that follows in the handbook, so you may want to read and digest them even if they are not assigned.

You may also want to read Chapter 5, which presents the system of English grammar. Though much of the material will be familiar to you, the chapter will repay your attention because it shows that the grammar of English is more than just a hodgepodge of rules, and it provides background for the fourteen chapters that follow. After Chapter 5 are four charts that summarize the information in these later chapters about nouns, pronouns, verbs and verbals, and modifiers. Then each chapter treats a principle or convention of grammatical correctness (Chapters 6 to 9), clarity (Chapters 10 to 15), or effectiveness (Chapters 16 to 19). Your instructor may discuss some or all of these chapters in class or may suggest that you consult specific chapters when you encounter problems.

Chapters 20 to 25 of the handbook describe the current conventions of punctuation. Punctuation is also discussed in earlier chapters, but these separate chapters bring together all the conventions for each mark. Preceding Chapter 20 is a chart showing the rules and options for the marks that cause the most confusion, even for experienced writers. If you aren't sure how to punctuate a sentence you are working on, this chart can suggest the alternatives. Another chart, in Chapter 24, shows all your options when you are quoting others, including what punctuation to use and where to put it. Chapters 26 to 30 present the conventions of mechanics—capitalization, abbreviations, italics (or underlining), numbers, and word division. Whether or not you are assigned these chapters, you should think of them as resources to consult continually for advice on specific questions.

Chapters 31 to 34 deal with words. Chapter 31, which discusses the principles guiding effective word choice, is intended to help you express your meaning exactly and concisely. Chapter 32 introduces the features and uses of any desk dictionary. Chapters 33 and 34 suggest ways in which you can develop your vocabulary and master the complexities of English spelling.

The last chapters of the handbook treat specific kinds of writing. Chapters 35–37 trace the process of writing and documenting a research paper for which you consult books and periodicals on some issue or question. Chapter 38 discusses writing in the various academic disciplines, such as literature, psychology, and biology. Chapter 39 provides specific advice on writing essay examinations for college courses. And Chapter 40 explains and illustrates basic business writing: the letter of complaint or request, the job application and résumé, and the memorandum.

The handbook concludes with two appendixes, a glossary, and an index. Appendix A describes a widely accepted standard for preparing a manuscript. Appendix B offers practical advice on writing and revising with a word processor. The Glossary of Usage provides brief notes on troublesome or confusing words and expressions that plague writers at all levels of experience. And finally, the index contains an entry for every principle, convention, and term discussed in the book as well as many specific words and phrases that you may need to look up.

Throughout the handbook screened boxes contain information that is especially important or that writers tend to seek often, such as a checklist for revising a paper or the uses and misuses of the apostrophe. Like the charts described above, these boxes can be used for quick reference. Further explanation can generally be found in the adjacent text.

Finding information in the handbook

The Little, Brown Handbook provides a wealth of specific information—what form of a verb to use, how to express an idea concisely, whether to punctuate with a comma or a semicolon, whether to capitalize a word, how to arrange the title page of a paper, and so on. The handbook also provides many ways of locating such information quickly. When you seek information on your own, you can check the guide to useful lists and summaries inside the front cover; you can refer to the table of contents at the end of the book or immediately after this preface; or you can refer to the index. The table of contents shows all the book's parts, chapters, and main sections within chapters. The sections are labelled with letters (*a*, *b*, and so on). These letters and the corresponding chapter numbers (for instance, 9d or 12a) also appear before the appropriate convention or guideline in the text itself, and they are printed as tabs on the sides of the pages. Thus you can find a section heading in the contents and thumb the book until you arrive at its number and letter on the side of the page. If you are uncertain of what to look for and need a more detailed guide to the book's contents, consult the index.

Your instructor may mark your papers using heading numbers and letters, symbols, or written comments. Pages 72–76 show a student essay marked in all three ways. If your instructor marks your paper with, say, 10a, you can refer to the contents to learn that you have made an error involving a sentence fragment. If you need further information to correct the error, you can then refer to the text by finding the appropriate page number or by locating 10a in a tab on the side of the page, as described in the preceding paragraph. If your instructor uses a symbol such as *frag* to mark your paper, you can find out how to correct the error by referring to the alphabetical list of symbols at the beginning of the book. Using this guide, you would be directed by the symbol *frag* to Chapter 10 on sentence fragments. The symbols also appear in the tabs at the sides of the pages. The best way to find specific handbook sections from your instructor's written comments is to consult the index. Look up the term used by your instructor and scan the subentries under it until you find one that seems to describe the error you have made. Then turn to the page number given.

The handbook's recommended usage

The Little, Brown Handbook describes and recommends the conventions of standard written English—the written language common to business and the professions. Written English is more conservative than spoken English in matters of grammar and usage, and a great many words, phrases, and constructions that are widely spoken remain unaccepted in careful writing.

When clear distinctions exist between the language of conversation and that of careful writing, the handbook provides examples of each and labels them *spoken* and *written*. When usage in writing itself varies with the level of formality intended, the handbook labels examples *formal* and *informal*. When usage is mixed or currently changing, the handbook recommends that you choose the more conservative usage because it will be acceptable to all readers.

If you follow the guidelines discussed in this handbook, your writing will be clearer and more demanding of serious attention than it might otherwise have been. Remember, however, that adhering to established conventions is but a means to the real achievement and reward of writing: communicating your message effectively.

Contents

PART 1

The Whole Paper and Paragraphs

CHAPTER 1

Developing an Essay

As varied as they may seem, most of the papers you write in college or university share certain characteristics. Whether you describe a physics experiment, compare two data-processing systems, analyse a short story, examine the causes of a historical event, argue against acid rain, or relate a personal experience, you are writing an essay, a non-fiction composition that analyses and interprets a topic, offering your view of it. An essay may address almost any subject and may range in length from a page to twenty or more pages. In it you present ideas and information, selected and arranged to reinforce your perspective, in a way that gains and holds the attention of readers and leaves them with a sense that you have said something worthwhile.

From the moment you begin working on an essay until you make the last correction on the final draft, you are continually discovering and deciding: exploring possible topics, finding what you have to say about the topic you choose, selecting a suitable arrangement for your material, and experimenting with paragraphs, sentences, and words to capture meaning. No one can tell you what discoveries you may make or what the right decisions may be, for these depend entirely on your topic and what you aim to do with it. But your work as a writer can be guided by an understanding of how other writers think about writing and what procedures they find helpful. These are the subjects of this chapter and the next.

1a The writing situation and the writing process

All writing occurs in a context that simultaneously limits and clarifies the writer's choices. Most obviously, context includes the nature of the assignment, the assigned length, and the deadline. But context can also be seen as the **writing situation**. In all essay writing, the writer aims to communicate something about a subject to a particular audience of readers. The three elements (writer, subject, audience) interact continuously throughout the development, drafting, and revision of a piece of writing, with the writer balancing his or her view, the demands of the subject, and the needs, interests, and expectations of the audience. As we will see throughout this chapter, the nature of the elements and their relative importance change with each new writing task, but the elements are always present. Asking for each task what your subject is, who your audience is, and how you want to present yourself and your subject to that audience can help you define and make choices.

Sometimes the writing situation is clearly defined from the start. Imagine, for instance, that you are assigned a report on an experiment in your physics course, a report expected to show your instructor that you have mastered scientific observation and the principles studied in the course. In this case, your subject, your audience and its expectations, and the way you should present yourself are predefined for you by the assignment. For other writing tasks, however, the writing situation may be left to you to define. Suppose, for instance, that your composition instructor asks you to write an essay relating a significant learning experience. You will have to determine what experience to relate as well as how you want to present yourself and your experience, and you may be required to select your audience and determine its needs and expectations.

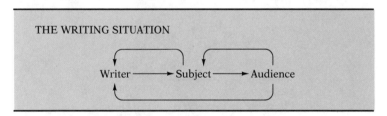

THE WRITING SITUATION

Writer ⟶ Subject ⟶ Audience

Understanding the writing situation is an important part of the **writing process**—the term for all the activities, mental and physical, that go into writing what eventually becomes a finished piece of work. Even for experienced writers, the process is usually messy, which is one reason that it is sometimes painful. Though we get a sense of ease and orderliness from, for example, a well-crafted magazine article, we can safely assume that the writer had to work hard to achieve this result, suffering frustration when ideas would not come, struggling to express half-formed thoughts, shaping and reshaping the same paragraph to make a point convincingly.

While engaged in the writing process, a writer continually alternates between a wide and a narrow focus—opening up the mind to take in new information and then closing in on a single idea to shape and refine it, seeking the general picture and then filling in the specific details. This alternating pattern continues through a sequence of overlapping stages: *developing* or *planning*, the stage of exploring ideas, gathering information, developing a central theme, and organizing material; *drafting*, the stage of expressing and connecting ideas; and *revising*, the stage of rethinking and improving the structure, content, and style.

Aside from the widening and narrowing of focus and the rough division into stages, there is no *one* writing process: no two writers proceed in the same way, and even an individual writer adapts his or her process to the task at hand. Still, most experienced writers rely on a bundle of procedures that have consistently helped them with the activities involved in writing: finding a topic (section 1b), defining a purpose and identifying an audience (1c), developing the topic (1d), grouping ideas (1e), considering the audience (1f), developing a thesis (1g), organizing (1h), and drafting, revising, and editing (Chapter 2). As you encounter difficulties with any of these activities in the course of writing, you can experiment with the procedures suggested until you find one or more that work for you. With experience, as you

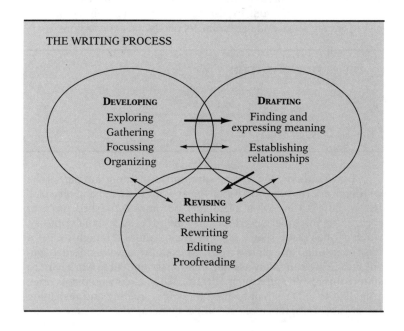

THE WRITING PROCESS

DEVELOPING
Exploring
Gathering
Focussing
Organizing

DRAFTING
Finding and
expressing meaning

Establishing
relationships

REVISING
Rethinking
Rewriting
Editing
Proofreading

complete a variety of assignments and try a variety of procedures, you will develop your own basic writing process.

Periodically in this chapter and the next you will see examples of how one student worked from an assignment to a finished essay by drawing on some of the procedures discussed. Occasionally, examples of other students' work will also be introduced to illustrate other approaches. These students' writing situations are not yours, and their solutions to writing problems may not work for you. But following their progress should supplement what you learn on your own about the difficulties and the rewards of writing.

EXERCISE 1

Recall several writing experiences that you have had in the past—a letter you had difficulty writing, an essay you enjoyed, an all-nighter spent happily or miserably on a term paper, and so on. What do these experiences reveal to you about writing, particularly your successes and problems with it? For instance:

> Do you like to experiment with language?
> Do you prefer writing to specific assignments rather than general ones?
> Are some kinds of writing easier than others?
> Do you have trouble getting ideas or expressing them?
> Do you worry about grammar and spelling?
> Do your readers usually understand what you mean?

Write these thoughts down as the first entry in a continuing journal or log in which you track your new experiences as a writer. As you complete writing assignments for your composition course and other courses, keep adding to the journal, noting especially which procedures seem most helpful to you. Your aim is to discover your feelings about writing so that you can develop a dependable writing process of your own.

1 b   Discovering and limiting a subject

Many writers (including experienced ones) encounter their first stumbling block in finding a subject to write about or in finding a way to make an assigned subject their own. Sometimes an appropriate subject or a unique angle may come to you with little effort, but when it does not, you can try one of the approaches discussed in this section.

TECHNIQUES FOR DISCOVERING A SUBJECT

1. Pursue your interests and experiences (1b-1).
2. Keep a journal (1b-2).
3. Observe your surroundings (1b-3).
4. Read (1b-4).
5. Freewrite (1b-5).
(See also p. 14, "Techniques for Developing a Topic.")

---

1   **Pursuing your interests and experiences**

To discover an essay subject when one is not assigned, review your own experiences, interests, and curiosities. Look for a subject you already know something about or have been wondering about, such as some issue at your school or in your community. Recall something you have discussed with others recently, perhaps an event in your family's history or a change in relations between men and women. Consider what you have read or have seen at the movies or on television: for instance, a shocking book, a violent or funny movie, a television commercial. Run your mind over the reading and class discussions in your courses to discover an idea or situation that intrigues you or that you can apply to your own experience—perhaps a social issue such as homelessness or a psychological issue such as diagnosis of depression. Think about things that make you especially happy, such as a hobby, or especially angry, such as the behaviour of your neighbours. Examine your own or others' dislikes and preferences to identify any that you would like to understand better. The goal is to think of a subject that sparks your imagination and stimulates your mind. If you care about your subject, then writing will be more interesting for you, and what you write will be more likely to interest readers.

If you are assigned a general subject, as often happens in college and university courses, then your goal is to discover your special interests within the boundaries of the assignment. For instance, if you are assigned a comparison-and-contrast essay on two people you know, then you will need to think of two people—friends, relatives, teachers—whose similarities or differences you find striking. If you are assigned a history essay on, for example, Sir John A. Macdonald as the first prime minister of Canada, you will need to review the reading you have done for the course and your notes from lectures and discussions to find an aspect of that subject that you'd like to know more about—perhaps Macdonald's nationalist policies or the achievements of his government.

2   Keeping a journal

Many writers record their thoughts and observations in a **journal**, a diary that is concerned more with ideas than with day-to-day events. *Journal* comes from the Latin for "daily," and many journal keepers do write faithfully every day; others make entries less regularly, when the mood strikes or an insight occurs or they have a problem to work out. Journal keepers often become dependent on the process for the writing practice it gives them and the concentrated thought it encourages. Usually for the same reasons, teachers of writing and other subjects sometimes require students to keep journals.

Whether you keep a journal on your own or by request, it can provide many ideas for writing. When you need to invent an essay topic or find a way into an assigned topic, review your journal entries for observations and connections you may have forgotten or been unaware of. A thought you recorded months ago about a chemistry experiment may be just what you need for direction on a research paper. Two long-ago entries about arguments with your brother may suggest a psychology paper on sibling relations.

3   Observing your surroundings

Sometimes you can find a good subject by looking around you, not in the half-conscious way most of us move from place to place in our daily lives but deliberately, all senses alert. On a bus, for instance, are there certain types of passengers? What seems to be on the driver's mind? On campus, which buildings stand out? Are bicycle riders and pedestrians at peace with each other? At a movie, do the viewers seem well suited to the film? Does one particular type of viewer eat popcorn?

To get the most from observation, you should have a notebook and pen or pencil handy for notes and sketches. If you have a camera, you may find that the lens sees things your unaided eyes do not notice. (When observing or photographing people, though, keep some distance, take photographs quickly, and avoid staring. Otherwise, your subjects will feel uneasy.) Back at your desk, study your notes, sketches, or photographs for oddities or patterns that you'd like to explore further.

4 Reading

Even when your assignment does not require reading, you can mine newspapers, magazines, and books for writing subjects. People often read passively, absorbing content like blotters, not interacting with it. To read for ideas, you will need to be more active, probing text and illustrations with your mind, nurturing any sparks they set off. Perhaps an article on a jazz trumpeter reminds you of your own experiences playing the trumpet. Or perhaps an editorial on financing community colleges makes you wonder how primary and secondary schools are financed. In either case you have the seed of a subject.

If your general subject is assigned—public art or corporate public relations, perhaps—then your reading will obviously be focussed on material that deals with the subject. (Chapter 35 includes lists of general references and periodical indexes for most subjects. See 35c.) An article on changes in public art may raise interesting questions about how corporations are using art. A book on public relations may suggest looking at corporate annual reports as tools of public relations.

NOTE: Whenever you use the information or ideas of others in your writing, you must acknowledge your sources in order to avoid the serious offense of plagiarism. (See 36d.) If a writer's ideas merely suggest a direction for you, you need not acknowledge the source. But if you actually present any of those ideas in your final paper, then you must also acknowledge the sources. (See 36h and 36i for how to acknowledge sources.)

5 Freewriting

Another way to find a subject is to write your way into it: write without stopping for a certain amount of time (perhaps ten minutes) or to a certain length (one page, for example). The goal of this **freewriting** is to bypass the part of your mind that doesn't want to write or can't think of anything to write and to let words themselves suggest other words. *What* you write is not important; that you *keep* writing is. Don't stop, even if that means repeating the same words until new words come. Don't go back to reread, don't censor ideas that seem dumb or repetitious, and above all don't stop to edit: grammar, punctuation, spelling, and the like are irrelevant at this stage.

In the physical act of freewriting, you may gain access to ideas you were unaware of. The following is an example of freewriting done to come up with a subject for writing.

dev
1b

> Write to write. Seems pretty obvious, also weird. What to gain by writing? never anything before. Writing seems always—always— Getting corrected for trying too hard to please the teacher, getting corrected for not trying hard enuf. Frustration, nail biting, sometimes getting carried away making sentences to tell stories, not even true stories, *esp.* not true stories, *that* feels like creating something. Writing just pulls the story out of me. The story lets me be someone else, gives me a disguise.

In this rough sample the student has broken through his resistance to writing to realize that he enjoys fiction writing for the sense of creation and disguise it gives him. He seems to have learned something about himself and to have given himself a general subject at the same time. (For a discussion and example of freewriting done to discover ideas when you already have a subject, see pp. 15–16.)

6	Limiting the subject

An assigned subject or one you find by a method described above is likely to be quite general—for instance, summer jobs, provincial aid to universities, two friends, the achievements of Sir John A. Macdonald, or corporations and art. You could begin developing such a subject right away, generating the ideas and details that will eventually form the substance of the essay. But sooner or later you might run into trouble because these subjects are too broad to be covered thoroughly and interestingly in the few pages often specified in college writing assignments.

It takes experience and often some actual drafting to gauge whether a subject is too broad for the space and time allowed. You need to be able to provide ample specific information—facts, examples, sensory details, and so on—to support the subject fully so that readers understand and appreciate what you have to say. For example, as the first prime minister of Canada, Sir John A. Macdonald was responsible for Confederation, the building of a transcontinental railroad, and the National Policy of protective tariffs on imports. A careful examination of all these achievements, including the pros and cons of each action, could conceivably take a whole book. A short essay would have to deal with a much smaller area, one specific achievement or controversy. The examples on the next page illustrate how this and other broad subjects can be scaled down to one of several manageable **topics**—limited, specific essay subjects.

BROAD SUBJECTS	SPECIFIC TOPICS
Macdonald's achievements as prime minister	Macdonald as a nation builder Macdonald and the Canadian Pacific Railway Macdonald's National Policy
Summer jobs	Kinds of summer jobs for unskilled workers How to find a summer job What a summer job can teach
Provincial aid to college and university students	Which students should be entitled to provincial aid Kinds of provincial aid available to students Why the provincial government should (or should not) aid students
Two friends	How _____ and _____ are alike despite their differences Why _____ and _____ don't like each other The different roles of _____ and _____ as friends

These specific topics are just a few of the possible approaches to the corresponding broad subjects, and they suggest the problems that might result from trying to cover the full range of ideas implied by any of the subjects. The much narrower area defined by each specific topic could, however, be covered both clearly and interestingly in a limited space. (The essay on pp. 78–79 illustrates how a student developed the specific topic of what a summer job can teach into a focussed and reasonably well-detailed essay.)

You may find that you need to do some planning and writing, exploring different facets of the general subject and pursuing your specific interests, before you hit on the best topic. And the topic you select may require further narrowing or may shift subtly or even dramatically as you move through the writing process. Still, the earlier you can narrow your subject to a specific topic, the more focussed your subsequent work will be, so it's worthwhile to push yourself soon after you have your subject to limit its scope.

EXERCISE 2

Use one or more of the techniques discussed in the preceding section to come up with three or four subjects for writing. Or take three or four of the following general subjects and use one or more techniques to make them your own.

1. immigration
2. the environment
3. community politics
4. working
5. professional sports
6. academic courses
7. success
8. science

EXERCISE 3

Narrow each of the broad subjects from Exercise 2 to one or more specific topics suitable for a brief essay of two or three pages (500 to 750 words). What aspect of the subject interests you most? What aspect can you discuss most effectively, using enough specific information to convey your perspective to your readers?

EXERCISE 4

For each of the following general subjects, provide at least one specific topic that interests you and that you think you could cover well in a brief essay of two or three pages.
1. music, dance, painting, drama, or some other art form
2. automobile safety
3. relations between parents and children
4. relations between the sexes
5. travel

1c   Defining a purpose and identifying an audience

Purpose

A writer's **purpose** is his or her chief reason for communicating something about a topic to a particular audience. *Purpose* thus includes all three elements of the writing situation: writer, topic, and audience. It ties together both the specific context in which the writer is working and the goal the writer hopes to achieve.

THE PURPOSES FOR WRITING

1. To entertain readers
2. To express yourself
3. To explain something to readers (exposition)
4. To persuade readers to accept or act on your opinion (argumentation)

dev

1 c

Most writing you do will have one of four main purposes. Occasionally, you will *entertain* readers or *express yourself*—your feelings or beliefs—to readers. More often you will *explain* something to readers or *persuade* readers to respect and accept, and sometimes even act on, your opinion. These purposes often overlap in a single essay, but usually one predominates. That dominant purpose will demand an emphasis on one of the three elements of the writing situation. When you write mainly to express yourself, for instance, *you* predominate. In contrast, when you write mainly to persuade or entertain readers, *they* predominate. And when you write mainly to explain, the *topic* predominates. Always, though, the other two elements also help determine what and how you write.

Most academic and business writing has the primary purpose of explaining or persuading. Writing that is mainly explanatory is often called **exposition** (from a Latin word meaning "to explain or set forth"). Almost any topic is suitable for exposition, from how to pitch a knuckle ball to why you want to major in business to the implications of a new discovery in computer science. It is the kind of writing encountered most often in newspapers, magazines, and textbooks; and it is the kind of writing this book concentrates on. (Expository essays appear on pp. 72–76 and 79–80.) Writing that is primarily persuasive is often called **argumentation**. A newspaper editorial favouring city council reform, a magazine article urging mandatory seat-belt use in all provinces, student papers recommending more required courses or opposing legalized abortion—all these are argumentative essays. (Chapter 4 discusses argumentation in some detail and provides an illustrative essay.)

Often a writing assignment will specify or imply your purpose: when assigned a report on a physics experiment, for instance, you know the purpose is to explain; when assigned an editorial presenting a case for or against expanding your school's health facilities, you know the purpose is to persuade. If the assignment leaves your purpose up to you, then try to define it soon after you have your topic, to give yourself some direction. You may not be successful: sometimes writers do not discover their purpose until they begin drafting. Or you may find that your initial sense of purpose changes as you move through the writing process. Nevertheless, if you are able to define a purpose early, it can set a preliminary course for you to follow and help you recognize changes in your thinking when they occur.

Audience

While you are defining your purpose for writing, you may also be identifying who your readers will be and why they will be reading your work. As discussed above, the two are closely linked, with purpose establishing a certain relation of writer to topic and audience. Like purpose, audience is often specified or implied in a writing assignment: when you write an editorial for the student newspaper favouring expansion of the university health facilities, your audience is fellow students, who will be reading the paper for information of general and personal interest; when you write a report on a physics experiment, your audience is your physics instructor, who will be reading to evaluate your competence and see if you need help. If no particular audience is specified or implied, then, as with purpose, you are free to decide whom you want to address: your classmates? your boss? those who drive cars?

This sense of your readers tells you something about how you need to treat your topic: for example, your fellow students will expect you to treat the subject of health facilities non-technically and to outline the benefits of the proposed expansion for them. A sense of audience can also help you discover ideas about your topic by making your purpose more concrete. The realization that you want to address an essay on bicycle riding to car drivers could direct you to a persuasive purpose and ideas about drivers' carelessness toward riders.

In the earliest stages of the writing process, many writers find it inhibiting to think much more specifically than this about the traits and views of their audience. Most of the discovery activities covered in the previous section and the next one will work best when you concentrate on pulling ideas out of yourself and expanding your mental horizons rather than on people "out there." It is important to give your audience detailed consideration, but we will postpone the guidelines for doing so until later in the writing process (see 1f).

EXERCISE 5

For each of the following topics, suggest both a likely purpose for an essay on the topic (entertainment, self-expression, explanation, persuasion) and a possible audience to which the essay could be addressed.
1. why study of a foreign language should be required in university
2. four kinds of rock music
3. the place where I feel most relaxed
4. a vacation that was a comedy of errors
5. how to find a trusty automobile mechanic

EXERCISE 6

For each of the following general subjects, write down four specific topics, each one suitable for a brief essay written with a different purpose (entertainment, self-expression, explanation, persuasion).

For each topic and purpose, identify an audience that might be interested in such an essay.

Example:

General subject: sports

Topics: (1) Football training as torture (entertainment; students who don't play football). (2) Learning by losing (self-expression; composition course classmates). (3) How to avoid injury during weight training (explanation; fellow weight trainers). (4) Why the school should build a new athletic facility (persuasion; school administrators).

1. music
2. Saturday night
3. work

4. television
5. driving

EXERCISE 7

To begin developing a brief essay of your own, select a topic that has particular interest for you. (The topic may come from your answers to Exercise 3 or 4 on p. 11 or to Exercise 6.) Define a purpose for your essay, and decide what kind of essay will best suit your topic and purpose.

1d   Developing the topic

As you limit a subject, define a purpose, and identify the audience for writing, you make choices and, at least temporarily, close options. To develop the topic—to generate the ideas and information that will help you achieve your purpose—you open up again within a narrower field. You probe the topic to discover implications, possibilities, and relations not considered before.

Sometimes ideas will tumble forth on paper, especially if your topic is very familiar or personal. But when they do not, you may need a technique for freeing them. Anything that starts your mind working is appropriate: if you like to make drawings or take pictures,

---

TECHNIQUES FOR DEVELOPING A TOPIC

1. Freewrite with a focus (1d-1).
2. Make a list, or brainstorm (1d-2).
3. Cluster (1d-3).
4. Read with a focus (1d-4).
5. Ask the journalist's questions (1d-5).
6. Use the patterns of development (1d-6).
(See also p. 6, "Techniques for Discovering a Subject.")

for instance, then try it. The following pages describe varied strategies that writers find helpful, some of which follow from the strategies for finding a subject (see 1 b). Whatever strategy or strategies you
used, do your work in writing, not just in your head. Not only will
your ideas be retrievable, but the act of writing will aid your concentration and lead you to fresh, sometimes surprising, insights.

dev

1d

1 Focussed freewriting

In **focussed freewriting** you start with your topic and write
without stopping for, perhaps, fifteen minutes or one full page. As
with freewriting for a subject (see 1b-5), you push to bypass mental
blocks and self-consciousness, not debating what to say or editing
what you've written. With focussed freewriting, though, you let the
physical act of writing take you into and around your subject.

An example of focussed freewriting can be found in the work of
a student, Lisa MacDonald, whose writing process we will follow in
this chapter and the next. In a composition course, MacDonald and
her classmates were given the following assignment: "Write an essay
of 600–800 words on any topic of current interest or debate in
Canada." For MacDonald, choosing a subject was easy because she
turned to her first academic interest and future profession: architecture. Narrowing this broad subject to a specific topic also presented
little problem, since she immediately thought of the most significant
architectural construction in Canada in recent years—the new
National Gallery of Canada—and the controversy surrounding its
style. (The photograph of the National Gallery will help you follow

The National Gallery of Canada

McDonald's thinking.) Since she had visited it in Ottawa recently and been very impressed, she decided to write an essay on the National Gallery for her instructor. To get started, MacDonald tried freewriting for fifteen minutes to generate ideas:

> Safdie's purpose in design of National Gallery of Canada? Great contrast between public and private areas—large, grand reception areas and small, intimate galleries. Wide variety of styles in each room—attempt to suit architecture of each individual gallery to particular collection on display—personal, intimate quality. Use of natural light—art not contained in artificial, impersonal spaces—displayed in an open atmosphere—onlooker can relate. Private, intimate spaces. Not distancing onlookers—involving them in the art. Neutrality of gallery architecture—allowing art itself to dominate. Grand facade—imposing columns and striking glass pavilions—fits stately grandeur of the capital's architecture. Extensive use of glass creates impression of openness and invitation—inviting those on the outside to look in. Exterior appears imposing, but not intimidating. Exterior similar principle to interior—displaying art to reveal beauty and majesty without appearing unapproachable—shared intimacy.

With this freewriting, MacDonald generated several promising ideas, especially the connections between the architect's purpose and the wide variety of styles, between the architecture and the art, and between the art and the people. As we'll see on pages 20–22, she pursued these ideas further using another discovery technique.

2   Making a list

Like focussed freewriting, list-making requires opening yourself to everything that seems even remotely connected to your topic, without concern for order or repetition or form of expression. You can let your topic percolate for a day or more, recording thoughts on it whenever they occur. (For this approach to work, you need to keep a notebook and pen or pencil with you at all times.) Or, in a method more akin to freewriting, you can **brainstorm** the topic—that is, focus intently on the topic for a fixed amount of time (perhaps fifteen minutes), pushing yourself to list every idea and detail that comes to mind. Like freewriting, brainstorming requires turning off your internal editor so that you keep moving ahead instead of looping back to correct what you have already written.

A list of ideas and details made while brainstorming might look something like the following one. The student's topic is what a summer job can teach—one of the specific topics derived earlier from the general subject of summer jobs.

> summer work teaches—
>> how to look busy while doing nothing
>> how to avoid the sun in summer
>> seriously: discipline, budgeting money, value of money
> which job? fast-food outlet cashier? baby-sitter? mail-room clerk?
> mail room: how to sort mail into boxes: this is learning??
> how to survive getting fired—humiliation, outrage
> Mrs. King! the mail-room queen as learning experience
> the shock of getting fired: what to tell parents, friends?
> Mrs. K was so rigid—dumb procedures
> initials instead of names on the mailboxes—confusion!
> Mrs. K's anger, resentment: the disadvantages of being smarter than your boss
> the odd thing about working in an office: a world with its own rules for how to act
> what Mr. D said about the pecking order—big chick (Mrs. K) pecks on little chick (me)
> probably lots of Mrs. Ks in offices all over—offices are all barnyards
> Mrs. K a sad person, really—just trying to hold on to her job, preserve her self-esteem
> a job can beat you down—destroy self-esteem, make you desperate enough to be mean to other people
> how to preserve/gain self-esteem from work??
> Mrs. K had to call me names to protect herself—I forced her into a corner
> if I'd known about the pecking order, I would have been less show-offy, not so arrogant

This informal list jumps around quite a bit, but toward the end the student focusses on what she learned about office politics from working as a mail-room clerk. Thus list-making helps her both refine her topic and discover what she thinks about it.

3   Clustering

A technique similar to freewriting and list-making is **clustering**. As developed by the writer and teacher Gabriele Lusser Rico, clustering also draws on free association and rapid, unedited work but combines writing and non-linear drawing. When clustering, you radiate outward from a centre point, your topic. When an idea occurs, you pursue its implications in a branching structure until all possibilities seem to be exhausted. Then you do the same with other

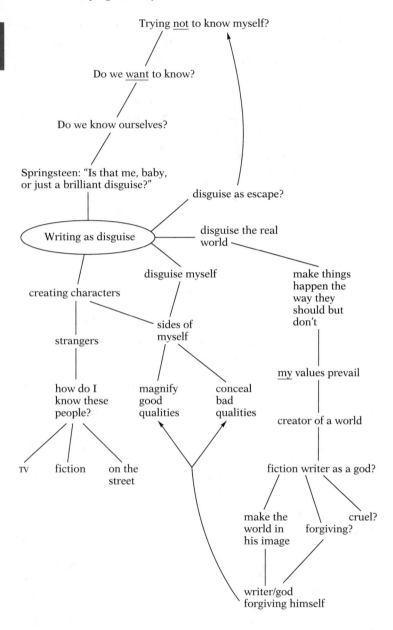

ideas, staying open to possibilities and connections, continuously branching out or drawing arrows.

The example of clustering above shows how a student

used the technique for ten minutes to expand on the topic of creative writing as a means of disguise, an idea he arrived at through freewriting (see p. 8). Though the student ventured into several dead ends, he also came to the interesting possibility (lower right) that the fiction writer is like a god who forgives himself by creating characters that represent his good and bad qualities. With such a start, the student next began a draft of his paper. If he had felt the need to develop ideas further, he could have tried another diagram or another strategy such as focussed freewriting.

4   Focussed Reading

Reading magazines, newspapers, and books can help you find or narrow a subject for writing (see 1b-4) and can help you develop your topic. Unless the topic draws exclusively on your own observations and experiences, reading can introduce you to ideas you hadn't considered or can help you expand on what you already know. Often, of course, an assignment will require reading, and essays on literary works as well as research papers demand reading. But even when reading is not required by the assignment, it can help you develop a topic by providing opinions, facts, and examples and by stimulating your own thinking. Although MacDonald's essay was not a research assignment, she read about the National Gallery in a recent issue of *The Canadian Architect*. Being aware of the danger of plagiarism, she was careful to acknowledge any ideas from other sources which she incorporated into her essay. (See note below.) (See 35c for library research techniques that you can use to locate readings on your topic.)

When you read to discover information or to respond to the author's ideas, do so with a pen or pencil in hand and (unless the material is yours to mark up) with a pad of paper by your side. Then you will be able to keep notes on what you read and—more importantly—on what the reading makes *you* think. Writing while reading leads you to participate actively in the process, not just passively. (See also Chapter 4 on reading critically.)

NOTE: To avoid the serious offence of plagiarism, you must acknowledge all ideas and information that you borrow from others' writings and present in your final paper. See 36d on how to avoid plagiarism, and see 36h and 36i on how to acknowledge sources.

5   Using the journalist's questions

Asking yourself a set of questions about your topic—and writing out the answers—can help you look at the topic objectively and see fresh possibilities in it. Asking questions can also provide some structure to the development of ideas.

One such set of questions is that posed by a journalist with a story to report:

> *Who was involved?*
> *What happened and what were the results?*
> *When did it happen?*
> *Where did it happen?*
> *Why did it happen?*
> *How did it happen?*

These questions can also be useful in probing an essay topic, especially if your purpose is to entertain or to explain by telling a story from your experience or from history or by examining causes and effects. (See also pp. 22 and 43.) For instance, the student writing about a summer job as a mail-room clerk could use the journalist's questions to isolate the important people involved, the main events and their order, and the possible causes of the events. Similarly, if you decided to explain the dynamics of a single-parent, single-child family, the questions would lead you to consider the characteristics of the two people, the ways they interact, and the possible causes and effects of their style of interaction.

6 Using the patterns of development

Also useful for probing a topic and at the same time providing some structure for developing ideas is a set of questions derived from the **patterns of development**. These patterns—such as narration, illustration, definition, and comparison and contrast—are ways we think about and understand a vast range of subjects, from our own daily experiences to the most complex scientific theories, and they also serve as strategies for writing about these subjects. As you will see later in this chapter and then in Chapter 3, the patterns of development can provide an organization for an essay (see pp. 41–43) and a means of introducing information in a paragraph (see pp. 107–16, where the patterns are illustrated with paragraph-length examples). Here, Lisa MacDonald's further work on her essay about the National Gallery of Canada will show how the patterns can open up the possibilities in a topic.

How did it happen? In **narration** the writer develops the topic as a story, with events usually arranged chronologically (as they occurred in time); for instance, an exciting hockey game, or the steps leading to a war. Lisa MacDonald thought narration would be most useful if she decided to provide background information on the history of the National Gallery between its founding in 1880 and the completion of the present building. But she decided that this would be a digression from her present topic. (Another student's narrative essay appears on pp. 78–79.)

How does it look, sound, feel, smell, taste? This question opens up the possibilities of **description**, the use of sensory details to give a clear impression of a person, place, or thing: a friend, a favourite room, a building. Thinking of the National Gallery, MacDonald realized that she could rely heavily on description to portray and characterize the building.

How can it be illustrated or supported? The pattern of **illustration or support** suggests development with one or more examples of the topic (one couple's efforts to adopt a child, for example, or three television soap operas) or with the reasons for believing or doing something (three reasons for majoring in English, four reasons for driving defensively). When MacDonald asked this question, she quickly saw that her freewriting (p. 16) suggested connections among the architecture and the art and the people which she must explore by providing examples of, and reasons for, these connections.

What is it? What does it encompass, and what does it exclude? These questions lead to development by **definition**: specifying what the topic is and is not to give a precise sense of its meaning. For MacDonald the questions suggested an essay defining the philosophy of art of the National Gallery. But since this discussion would digress from the topic, she decided to mention it only briefly as it related to her essay on the building.

What are its parts or characteristics? Or what groups or categories can it be sorted into? These questions derive from the related patterns of **division** and **classification**—dividing a singular subject such as a short story into its parts (characters, setting, plot, and so on) or classifying a plural subject such as automobiles into groups or classes (subcompact, compact, and so on). When MacDonald considered these questions, she concluded that she might divide the building into its parts—exterior and interior, public spaces and private galleries—to illustrate its characteristics.

How is it like, or different from, other things? The pattern of **comparison and contrast** suggests development by pointing out the similarities and differences between ideas, objects, people, places, and so on: the differences between two similar computer systems, for instance, or the similarities between two political candidates from different parties. For MacDonald this question opened up an approach to her topic that her freewriting had not: she could compare the National Gallery with traditional galleries such as the

Louvre. (Another student's comparison-and-contrast essay appears on pp. 79–80.)

Is it comparable to something that is in a different class but more familiar? This question leads to **analogy**, an extended comparison of unlike subjects. Analogy is often used to explain a topic that may be unfamiliar to readers (for instance, the structure of a government) by reference to a familiar topic (the structure of a family). From an article in *The Canadian Architect*, MacDonald obtained a helpful answer to this question: an analogy between the National Gallery and a microcosmic city. She would be careful, of course, to acknowledge her source in her essay.

What are its causes or its effects? With the pattern of **cause-and-effect analysis**, the writer explains why something happened or what its consequences were or will be, or both: the causes of cerebral palsy, the effects of a Supreme Court decision, the causes *and* effects of a gradual change in the climate. In asking this question, Mac-Donald foresaw that her essay on the National Gallery would attempt to explain the effects of the building on the visitor, but otherwise cause-and-effect analysis did not seem useful.

How does it work or how do you do it? This question prompts a **process analysis**—an explanation of how the topic occurs naturally or how it is accomplished: the growth of a plant, the making of a robot, the writing of an essay. Of all the pattern questions, this is the one in which MacDonald saw the least potential. A narrative of how the National Gallery evolved might include stages in a process (such as the workings of the Canada Museums Construction Corporation), but MacDonald abandoned this approach because she lacked enough information and interest to pursue it.

As the examples of MacDonald's interest indicate, more than one of these questions are likely to seem promising, and several may in fact play a role in the development of an essay. After considering each question, MacDonald determined that her essay would primarily be a description of the National Gallery but would include other patterns (a common occurrence in essays). She also expected to divide the building into parts, explore the analogy between the gallery and a city, and explain the effects of the building on visitors by use of some examples and reasons. The questions also helped her to discard some interesting ideas (the history of the National Gallery and its philosophy of art) that she realized would distract from her intended focus. Even when you are assigned an essay in a specific pattern, other patterns will almost inevitably prove useful to develop certain ideas or to organize certain categories of information. (For further discussion of how the patterns may combine in an essay, see 3e, pp. 127–29.)

EXERCISE 8

Experiment with freewriting (p. 15), brainstorming (p. 17), or clustering (p. 18) on the topic you chose in Exercise 7 (p. 14) for your essay-in-progress; or start anew with one of the following topics. Write or draw for at least ten minutes without stopping to edit. When you finish, examine what you have written for ideas and relationships that could help you develop the topic.

1. a shopping mall or other centre or building
2. a restaurant
3. borrowing (or lending) money
4. prejudice in my hometown
5. the academic grading system
6. pigeons
7. a country music singer
8. a television show
9. a brother or a sister
10. an awkward or embarrassing moment
11. a radio personality
12. hockey strategies
13. shyness
14. parties
15. patriotism

EXERCISE 9

Continuing from the preceding exercise, generate further ideas on the topic by writing answers to each of the questions derived from the patterns of development (pp. 20–22). Give the closest consideration to the questions that seem most promising. Which pattern might you use for the overall development of your essay, and which other patterns might you use to introduce or organize ideas within the overall pattern?

EXERCISE 10

If you feel that the topic from Exercises 8 and 9 should be developed further, try reading about it or asking the journalist's questions (p. 20). Subsequent exercises leading you through the writing process will be based on the ideas you generate in Exercises 8–10.

1e Grouping ideas

After developing ideas about your topic, you may need to organize the ideas to see what you have. This procedure is not the same as organizing the essay itself, although the relationships and patterns you discover in your ideas may prove useful later (see 1h, p. 38). Rather, at this point in your thinking and writing you apply order to ideas so that connections, distinctions, hierarchies, overlaps and gaps will become apparent. Grouping ideas helps you control and understand your topic. It helps you see your central theme and how specific ideas fit into it.

To group ideas, you need to distinguish between general and specific ideas and to see the connections between ideas. **General** and **specific** refer to the number of instances or objects included in a group signified by a word. *Plant*, for example, is general because it encompasses all kinds of plants; *rose* is specific because it refers to a certain kind of plant. But *general* and *specific* are actually relative terms—that is, something is one or the other only in relation to something else. Thus, *plant* is general in relation to *rose*, but it is specific in relation to the broader category of *life form*. And *rose* is specific in relation to *plant*, but it is general in relation to the smaller category of *Rosa acicularis* (Alberta's floral emblem), which is itself

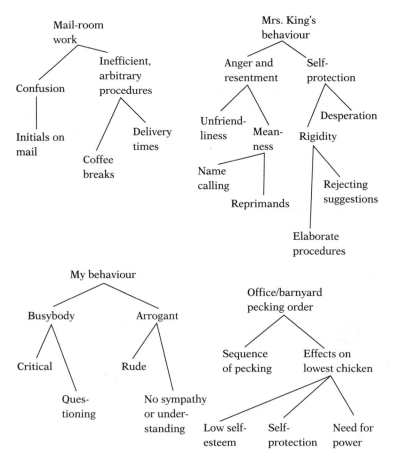

general in relation to the singular category of *Uncle Ben's prize-winning* Rosa acicularis.

When you group your ideas, subordinate the more specific ideas to the more general ones. At the same time, respect the meaning of your ideas so that your hierarchies are not jumbled—so that you don't end up with *rose* subordinated to the more general category of *animal*.

One technique for sorting ideas is the **tree diagram**, in which ideas and details branch out in increasing specificity. On the opposite page is a tree diagram that was prepared from the earlier list of ideas on a summer job (p. 17), which helped the student focus on what she learned about office politics. Each main part of the four-part diagram represents a different general idea about the summer-job experience. Notice that the diagram helped the student to drop irrelevant ideas from her earlier list. In addition, the structure of the diagram showed where she needed more details (such as effects of the office pecking order).

Some writers use a simple list with indentions and perhaps dashes—a kind of rough outline—to accomplish the same purpose. Lisa MacDonald prepared such a list from her notes on the National Gallery:

National Gallery—variety of styles
   –great contrast between public and private spaces
      –grandeur vs. intimacy
      –large vs. small
      –striking vs. neutral
      –impersonal vs. personal
Nat. Gall.—exterior
   –architect's consciousness of creating an exterior which fits
    in with the stately grandeur of a capital
      –grand facade
      –imposing columns
      –striking glass pavilions which dominate exterior
   –but even exterior creates sense of openness and invitation
    with extensive use of glass
      –inviting those on outside to look in, participate
      –result that exterior appears imposing but not intimidating, forbidding
   –exterior anticipates philosophy of internal design
      –preserving the dignity and stature of the art without
      distancing it from the viewer
Nat. Gall.—interior
   –each gallery space designed to complement and blend in
    with particular works BUT design never overbearing,
    always subdued, leaning toward neutrality
      –focus on the art itself

–creating sense of intimacy with, and involvement in,
   the art
–each room a new world in which the art is the centre
–personal quality of design
–use of natural light
   –avoids sense of artificiality
   –art not hidden away in a tomb, but open and accessible
   –creates feeling that galleries are part of the real world
–sense of participation of art in life also conveyed through
   layout of building as microcosm of a city
   –places for people to gather and talk—entrance pavilion
      and Great Hall
   –places for people to relax, meditate, be restful—court-
      yards
   –thoroughfares by which people move from one area to
      another—Colonnade and Galleria
   –separate buildings, each with its own entrance and
      atmosphere
   –small, intimate rooms, each adapted to suit the works it
      contains
   –choice of flexibility rather than rigidity
   –creates intimacy with art rather than distancing the
      viewer from it
Comparison with traditional galleries (e.g., the Louvre)
   –long, cold, impersonal halls
      –formality
      –alienation
   –artificial lighting

In forming these groups of ideas and details, MacDonald isolated several approaches to her topic: the variety of styles; the parts of the building (exterior and interior); the comparison of the National Gallery with traditional art galleries. The groups of ideas led her to see that her main focus was that the variety of architectural styles—both exterior and interior—in the National Gallery illustrated a philosophy that art should be accessible to people. The comparison with more traditional galleries seemed underdeveloped for lack of information and potentially distracting from her main interest. Thus, by grouping her ideas, MacDonald discovered how she wanted to focus her essay, and with that focus she could also make early decisions about what *not* to cover.

EXERCISE 11

For your essay-in-progress, use a tree diagram or a list to group the ideas you generated in Exercises 8, 9, and 10 (p. 23) into general categories. Delete, add, or modify ideas as necessary to reflect your thinking at this new stage.

1f Considering the audience

As we saw earlier, the basic purpose of all essay writing is to *communicate ideas and information to readers*. Readers are your audience. If they do not understand what they read or do not react the way you want, then you may be at fault. The chances are good that you have not considered carefully enough what the audience must be told in order to understand and to react appropriately.

You will probably consider your audience to some extent from the start of the writing process—when, for an obvious example, you decide not to write on macroeconomic theory for your music history teacher—and a sense of your audience can help you refine your purpose, as we saw in 1c. But at some point while you are developing an essay, it's important to make your readers your primary concern.

QUESTIONS ABOUT AUDIENCE

1. Why are readers going to read my writing? Will they expect information, opinion, entertainment, self-expression, or some combination?
2. What do I want readers to know or do after reading my work, and how should I make that clear to them?
3. What characteristic(s) do readers share? For instance:

   > age or gender
   > occupation: students, part-time workers, professional colleagues, etc.
   > social or economic role: adults, children, car buyers, potential employers, etc.
   > economic or educational background
   > political, religious, or moral beliefs and values
   > hobbies or activities

4. How will the characteristic(s) of readers influence their attitudes toward my topic?
5. What do readers already know and *not* know about my topic? How much do I have to tell them?
6. If my topic involves specialized language, how much should I use and define?
7. What ideas, arguments, or information might surprise readers? excite them? offend them? How should I handle these points?
8. What misconceptions might readers have of my topic or my approach to the topic? How can I dispel these misconceptions?
9. What role and tone should I assume? What role do I want readers to play?

As you know from your own experience as a reader, anyone who begins a text has needs and expectations. Readers require clarity and a certain interest—qualities that prove the writer's commitment to make reading easier. Readers also require a clear structure, a certain kind and amount of information, and a sense of who the writer is. Many academic disciplines prescribe some of these needs and expectations; thus Chapter 38 discusses the special concerns of writing in the arts and humanities, social sciences, and natural applied sciences. But even in these fields, the writer must make many choices based on audience. In other areas where the conventions of structure and presentation are vaguer, the choices are even more numerous. The box entitled "Questions About Audience" on the preceding page contains questions that can help you define and make these choices.

1   Using specific information

When you write, you use specific information to gain and keep the attention of your readers and to guide them to accept your conclusions or opinions. This information may be concrete details, facts, examples, or any other evidence that makes your ideas clear or supports your assertions. And your selection of information must suit what you know of the background of your audience: its familiarity with your topic, its biases, and its special interests.

Consider the student who needs money. He writes two letters, one to his parents and another to his school's Office of Student Aid. First he writes to his parents:

> Well, I did it again. Only two weeks into a new semester, and I'm broke already. But you know I needed a sweater, and besides, book prices have just skyrocketed and I've got this Canadian history course that almost broke the bank all by itself ($70 for books!). Oh, and I've met this really great girl (more later). So anyway, I'm pretty low on cash right now and am going to need another $50 to make it through the rest of the month. This should be the last time I have to ask for money, though. Starting next week I'm going to work part-time at a restaurant—doing some short-order cooking and general kinds of work—so if you want your money back. . . .

Then he writes to the Office of Student Aid:

> I am writing to request a short-term loan of $50 for bill consolidation and for other personal reasons. Starting in ten days, I will be employed for ten hours per week, as a cook, at Better Burgers, 315 North Main Street. Thus I will be able to repay the loan easily within the required three-month limit. I understand that if I fail to make any payment. . . .

The two letters make the same request, but they contain very different information. In the first letter the student chooses details that he believes his parents will relate to: he's "broke already" and not, apparently, for the first time; he needed new clothes; he's serious enough about his studies to pay large sums for his books; he has a new girlfriend; he's not specific about his job. In the second letter he chooses details that will reassure the administrators of student aid: he omits any mention of his purchases, his girlfriend, and other personal details; he explains where he will be working and for precisely how many hours each week; he stresses the certainty of repayment; he proves he knows the regulations—the "three-month limit" and the penalties for non-payment. If, by accident, the student mailed the second letter to his parents, they might be mystified or amused. And if he mailed the first letter to the Office of Student Aid, the recipients might deny his request.

The questions in the "Questions About Audience" box lead you to analyse both the general orientation of your readers and their specific position on your topic, and that analysis can help you decide how best to approach them.

2 | Deciding on an appropriate role and tone

Besides deciding what information your audience needs, you should also consider how you want to present yourself and your topic to readers—that is, how you want them to perceive both you and your attitude toward your topic. One way to make this decision is to think of yourself, as writer, playing a role in relation to the reader. The possible roles are many and varied, including, for instance, storyteller, portrait painter, lecturer, guide, reporter, advocate, and inspirer. The choice of a role for yourself will depend partly on your purpose—on whether you intend primarily to express yourself, entertain, explain, or persuade—and partly on how you feel about your topic and expect your readers to feel about it. As you write your essay, the role you choose will help determine *what* you say and also the *way* you say it—your **tone**. Tone in writing is like tone of voice in speaking: words and sentence structures on the page convey some of the same information about attitude as pitch and volume in the voice.

Conceived broadly, tone may be informal or formal, as illustrated by the student's two requests for money. In the first letter, the student's tone is informal, personal. His sentences are typical of conversation: loose, and full of the second-person pronoun *you*, contractions (*I've, I'm*), and casual expressions like *really, pretty, so anyway*. His paragraph is loosely structured, introducing subjects like the new girlfriend as they occur to him and burying the most important point, the request for money, in the middle. The student's purpose is as much to entertain his parents as to persuade them to lend him money. He plays the role of a still scatterbrained but always lovable and almost responsible son—a role he expects his parents to appreciate. In contrast, the second letter is written in a much more formal tone. The student's words (*bill consolidation, employed, per week, thus*) are formal and serious. He avoids *you* and contractions. His carefully constructed sentences (*Thus I will be able to repay the loan easily within the required three-month limit*) would sound stiff in most conversation. The paragraph is tightly structured. The student's purpose is strictly to persuade the school administrators to lend him money, and he assumes the role—serious, responsible adult—that he believes his readers expect.

As these examples suggest, different roles and tones are appropriate for different topics, purposes, and audiences. You have the widest range of choice when your purpose is entertainment or self-expression and when you can assume your audience is sympathetic. Then your attitude toward your topic may lead you to play any role from comedian to tragic figure, adopting any tone from teasing to solemn. For other purposes, one or more elements of the writing situation, in addition to your own attitude, are likely to narrow your choices. In business reports and memos, for instance, clarity and conciseness take precedence over self-expression, and formality of tone tends to increase with the rank and number of readers being addressed.

Most writing you do for your college or university courses will demand an academic role and tone. You will be expected to present yourself as a serious and competent student of the subject on which you are writing, one who possesses at least a basic understanding of the discipline's research methods, vocabulary, and principles and who can write clearly. Befitting such a role, the tone of most academic writing is somewhat formal and impersonal. The following, for instance, is a passage from a student's psychology paper:

> One technique for heightening the emotional appeal of advertisements is "colour engineering." Adding colour to an advertisement or product can increase sales despite the fact that the colour serves no practical purpose. For example, until the 1920s fountain pens were made of hard, black rubber. When coloured pens were introduced, sales rose dramatically.

Such straightforward writing allows considerable room for you to express your attitudes by your choice of words and sentence structures. Consider the effect of small changes in the second sentence above:

New colour in an advertisement or product can boost sales even when the colour serves no other purpose.

The brisker tone and the idea of the writer it conveys still fall within the range of academic writing. As you gain experience with such writing, you will develop the flexibility to write in your own voice while also respecting the conventions of the various disciplines.

3 | Writing for a general audience—or for your instructor

What do you do when you are not writing exclusively for your parents or the Office of Student Aid—when, in other words, you don't know much about your audience? From compositions assigned to be written for your classmates to bulletins inviting film-society subscriptions, much of the writing you do will be for a **general audience**—"general" because it includes people of diverse backgrounds and interests. General audiences read newspapers and magazines such as *Maclean's*. These readers are sceptical and easily distracted, but they are also curious and thoughtful. They may not share all your interests, but they can understand and appreciate anything you write, as long as it is specific, clear, honest, and fresh. They will expect you to explain any specialized terms you use and to support any assertions you make with ample details, examples, and reasons. Further, they will expect you to present yourself as thoughtful and competent, the master of your information and a careful writer. An appropriate tone may range from light-hearted to grave, depending on the topic and writing situation, but a moderate and assured tone midway between the extremes of informality and formality will almost always work.

Of course, much of your academic writing may have only one reader besides you: the instructor of the course you are writing for. In a composition course your instructor is likely to read your work as the representative of a general audience and respond to it in the additional role of helpful critic (see 2e). That means you should not assume specialized interest in or knowledge of your topic, nor should you expect the patience and tolerance of a doting parent who fills in what his or her child can't or won't express. If something about your topic would need to be said to a classmate or a reader of your local newspaper, say it clearly and carefully. For example, MacDonald has decided to describe the National Gallery in enough detail to create a clear picture for a reader who is not familiar with it, and she also plans to write objectively in a semi-formal tone.

As discussed in the previous section, most writing for the academic disciplines such as literature, psychology, business, and chemistry is not really addressed to a general audience but to a specialized audience of practitioners of the discipline, represented by your instructor. If you are writing a paper on the economic background of the War of 1812 for a Canadian history course, you can assume your instructor's familiarity with the key events, players, and published interpretations. Your job is to show your own command of them and their relevance to your topic while assuming an appropriate academic role and tone and, as you would for any reader, being specific, clear, and concise.

EXERCISE 12

Analyse the content and tone of each of the following paragraphs. What do the writer's choice of information and selection of words and sentence structures indicate about his or her role, attitude toward the subject, and intended audience?

1. Canadians essentially don't want to be bothered. They will leave to others in Tehran and Kabul a form of government involvement that means burning down buildings and, if necessary, cabinet ministers. The Canadian way is to write a letter to the editor. Five years after becoming the first prime minister from a working-class background, The Ego That Walks Like a Jaw has learned a very useful lesson. It is that the reason Mackenzie King ruled so long was that he was so purposely dull that we forgot about him. Let him run the government. While we went about our more interesting lives.   —ALLAN FOTHERINGHAM, "Cromwell Rules in the Nation's Capital"

2. All air bags [in automobiles] work in essentially the same way. First, a sensor detects a sudden decrease in speed and triggers the device. The sensitivity of the sensor is such that no normal driving situation, such as abruptly slamming on the brakes at highway speeds or hitting another car while parking, will trigger it: an impact equivalent to hitting a wall at a speed of at least 12 miles an hour is required to set it off. Then a powdered chemical, sodium azide, is electrically ignited, and produces a quick burst of nitrogen gas to inflate a fabric bag. Nitrogen is a harmless gas that constitutes 78 percent of the air we breathe, but sodium azide can be poisonous and is therefore carefully sealed in the air-bag cannister until used. The bag can inflate within 1/25th of a second, then deflates again within seconds.   —DAVID L. CHANDLER, "Air Bags—Life-Saving and Unavailable"

EXERCISE 13

To practise considering an audience, choose one of the following topics and ask the questions in the "Questions About Audience" box on page 27 for each audience specified. Decide on four points you would make, the role you would assume, and the tone you would adopt for each audience. Then write a paragraph for each based on your decisions.

1. the effects of smoking: for elementary school students and for adult smokers
2. your opinion of welfare: for someone who is on welfare and for someone who is not and who opposes it
3. the advantages of a summer camp: for a prospective camper and for his or her parents
4. why your neighbours should remove the wrecked truck from their yard: for your neighbours and for your community zoning board
5. the beauty of a snowfall: for someone who has never experienced snow and for someone who hates it

EXERCISE 14

Continuing from the groups of ideas that you prepared in Exercise 11 (p. 26), use the "Questions About Audience" on page 27 to determine as much as you can about the probable readers of your essay-in-progress. Evaluate your groups of ideas to ensure that they include the specific information your readers need. Decide what role you want to assume and what tone may best convey your attitude toward your topic.

1g   Developing the thesis

Most essays are focussed on and controlled by a single main idea that the writer wants to communicate to readers—a central point to which all the general statements and specific information of the essay relate. This main idea, called the **thesis**, encompasses the writer's attitude toward the topic and purpose in writing.

Sometimes your thesis may be apparent to you very early in the writing process: you may have chosen your topic in the first place because you had an idea about it that you wanted to communicate. At other times you may need to write and rewrite before a central, controlling idea emerges. Still, it's wise to try to pin down your thesis once you have a sense of your purpose, your attitude, your audience, and the information you will use. Then the thesis can help keep you focussed throughout the rest of the writing process, or it can serve as a point of reference so that you recognize changes in intention or direction if they occur.

1   Conceiving the thesis sentence

A good way to develop your thesis is to frame it in a **thesis sentence**. The thesis sentence gives you a vehicle for expressing your thesis at an early stage, and eventually it or a revised version may be placed in the introduction of your final essay as a signal to your readers.

As an expression of the thesis, the thesis sentence serves two crucial functions and one optional one, as shown in the box below.

FUNCTIONS OF THE THESIS SENTENCE

1. It narrows the topic to a single idea that you want readers to gain from your essay.
2. It asserts something about the topic, conveying your purpose, your opinion, and your attitude.
3. It *may* provide a concise preview of how you will arrange your ideas in the essay.

The following are some examples of topics and corresponding thesis sentences that fulfil the first two and, in one case, the third of these functions.

TOPIC	THESIS SENTENCE
1. Why there should be a policy of universal accessibility to Canadian universities and community colleges	If Canada hopes to compete economically among the industrialized nations, post-secondary education must be accessible for any student who qualifies academically.
2. The effects of strip-mining	Strip-mining should be tightly controlled in this region to reduce its pollution of water resources, its permanent destruction of the land, and its devastating effects on people's lives.
3. A terrible moving experience	The surest way to lose good friends is to enlist their help in a move from one fourth-floor walk-up apartment to another.

4. My city neighbourhood	The main street of my neighbourhood contains enough variety to make almost any city dweller feel at home.
5. Macdonald's National Policy	Macdonald introduced the National Policy of tariffs in 1879 to protect Canadian manufacturing interests, primarily against American imports.
6. The dynamics of single-parent families	In families consisting of a single parent and a single child, the boundaries between parent and child often disappear so that the two interact as siblings or as a married couple.
7. What public relations is	Although most of us are unaware of the public relations campaigns directed at us, they can significantly affect the way we think and live.

All of these thesis sentences serve the first two functions listed above: they state a single idea about the topic, and the assertion conveys information about the writer's stand on the topic. (Sentence 2 also serves the third function of previewing the main supporting ideas and their order.) We know from these sentences what each writer's primary purpose is: persuasion in the first two, entertainment in the third, and explanation in the last four. In addition, these sentences not only state opinions but also reveal something of the writers' attitudes, including strong feelings and a sense of urgency (sentences 1 and 2), a groaning good humour (3), pride (4), objectivity (5 and 6), and caution (7).

2 **Writing and revising the thesis sentence**

When you set out to draft a thesis sentence, ask yourself what central idea emerges from the work you have done so far, how you can frame that idea as an assertion about your topic, and how you can convey your purpose and attitude in that assertion. Answering all these questions in a sentence usually requires more than one attempt, sometimes over one or more drafts of the essay. But the thinking required can help you discover potentially serious problems, such as that you're trying to write about three ideas, not one.

Lisa MacDonald went through a common procedure in writing and revising her thesis sentence on the National Gallery. First she turned her topic into an assertion:

> The National Gallery of Canada illustrates a variety of architectural styles.

This sentence reflected MacDonald's intention to examine the controversial variety of styles in the National Gallery. However, it conveyed nothing specific about those styles or the fact that they represented the purpose and philosophy of the architect. When she recognized this omission, she rewrote the sentence:

> The National Gallery of Canada illustrates a philosophy of architecture in which stately grandeur is tempered with personal intimacy.

This sentence was better, but MacDonald still needed to make clear what this philosophy of architecture is and what its connection is with the art and the people in it. She tried again:

> The National Gallery of Canada illustrates a philosophy of architecture in which stately grandeur is tempered with personal intimacy to present the art which it houses as real and accessible rather than distant and intimidating.

With this sentence MacDonald felt she had drafted an assertion that encompassed all her ideas and supporting details. Though she knew the sentence might require further revision, she felt it was adequate to help her for the time being.

When you are writing and revising your thesis sentence, check to be sure it fulfils the following requirements set out in the box below.

REQUIREMENTS OF THE THESIS SENTENCE

1. Does it make an *assertion* about your topic?
2. Does it convey your *purpose*, your *opinion*, and your *attitude*?
3. Is it *limited* to an assertion of only one idea?
4. Is the assertion *specific*?
5. Is the sentence *unified* in that the parts relate to each other?

The following are other examples of thesis sentences revised to meet these requirements.

ORIGINAL

People should not go on fad diets. [A vague statement that needs limiting with one or more reasons: what's wrong with fad diets?]

Televised sports are different from live sports. [A general statement that needs to be made more specific: how are they different, and why is the difference significant?]

Seat belts can save lives, but now car makers may be required to install air bags. [Not unified: how do the two parts of the sentence relate to each other?]

REVISED

Fad diets can be dangerous when they deprive the body of essential nutrients or rely on excessive quantities of potentially harmful foods.

Although television cannot transmit all the excitement of being in a crowd during a game, its close-ups and slow-motion replays more than compensate.

If drivers more often used life-saving seat belts, the car makers might not be required to install air bags.

dev

1g

EXERCISE 15

Evaluate the following thesis sentences, considering whether each one is sufficiently limited, specific, and unified. Rewrite the sentences as necessary to meet these goals.

1. Travelling on a tight budget can be educational.
2. Aggression usually leads to violence, injury, and even death, and we should use it constructively.
3. Control of acid rain is essential.
4. One evening of a radio talk show amply illustrates both the appeal of such shows and their silliness.
5. Good manners make our society work.
6. City people are different from country people.
7. Television is a useful baby-sitter and an escape for people who do not want to think about their own problems.
8. I liked Canadian history in high school, but I do not like it in university.
9. We are encouraged to choose a career in community college, but people change jobs frequently.
10. Drunken drivers, whose perception, co-ordination, and reaction time are impaired, should receive mandatory suspensions of their licences.

EXERCISE 16

Write limited, specific, and unified thesis sentences for three of the following topics. Each of your sentences should convey the purpose given in parentheses and your own attitude.

1. why (or why not) major in business (*persuasion*)
2. a frustrating experience (*self-expression*)
3. why cable television should be free (*persuasion*)
4. how an old house or apartment is better than a new one (or vice versa) (*explanation*)
5. the sounds of the city or country (*self-expression or entertainment*)
6. how to care for a plant (*explanation*)
7. why students attend community college or university (*explanation*)
8. how a rumour spreads (*explanation*)
9. why divorce laws should be tougher (or looser)(*persuasion*)
10. a disliked person (*explanation*)

EXERCISE 17

Continuing from Exercise 14 (p. 33), write a limited, specific, and unified thesis sentence for your essay-in-progress.

1h   Organizing the essay

An effective essay has a recognizable shape—an arrangement of parts that guides readers, helping them see how ideas and details relate to each other and contribute to the whole. If readers can't see a clear order in your material or how each new idea or piece of information develops your thesis, they will have difficulty understanding you and they may mistrust what you say.

Writers sometimes let an effective organization emerge over one or more drafts. But many writers find that organizing ideas to some extent before drafting can provide a helpful sense of direction, as a map can help a driver negotiate a half-familiar system of roads. If you feel uncertain about the course your essay should follow or have a complicated topic with many parts, devising a shape for your material can clarify your options.

1   Arranging the parts of an essay

Most essays share a basic shape consisting of an introduction, a body, and a conclusion. The introduction draws readers into the world of the essay, stating the topic and often the thesis sentence. It makes a commitment that the rest of the essay fulfils. The conclusion generally gives readers something to take away from the essay—a summary of ideas, for instance, or a suggested course of action. (Both introductory and concluding paragraphs are discussed with other special kinds of paragraphs in 3d, pp. 120–25.) The body of the essay is its centre, the part offering ideas and supporting details, examples, and reasons to develop the thesis and thus fulfil the commitment of the introduction. In an essay of two or three pages, the body may contain three to five substantial paragraphs, each presenting and supporting a part of the thesis.

The organization of the body of your essay will depend on your topic, your purpose, and your sense of what your readers need and expect from you. In almost any writing situation, at least one of the organizing schemes listed in the box below will be appropriate. These schemes are so familiar that readers expect them and look for them. Thus the schemes both help you arrange your material and help readers follow you.

SCHEMES FOR ORGANIZING IDEAS IN AN ESSAY

1. Space
2. Time
3. Emphasis

General to specific	Decreasing familiarity
Specific to general	Increasing complexity
Increasing importance (climactic)	

4. Pattern of development

Narration	Comparison and contrast
Description	Analogy
Illustration or support	Cause-and-effect analysis
Definition	Process analysis
Division and classification	

Organizing by space or time

Two organizational schemes—spatial and chronological—grow naturally out of the topic. A **spatial organization** is especially appropriate for expository essays that describe a place, an object, or a person. Following the way people normally survey something, you move through space from a chosen starting point to other features of the subject. Describing a friend, for instance, you might begin with his shoes and move upward or begin with his face and move downward. If, instead, you moved from hands to face to shoes to arms, your arrangement might be less effective because your readers would have to work harder to stay with you. The following thesis sentence suggests that the writer might move in space from one end of the street to the other.

> The main street of my neighbourhood contains enough variety to make almost any city dweller feel at home.

To illustrate variety, the writer can provide details of the shops, apartment buildings, and people encountered along the street.

A **chronological organization** reports events as they occurred in time, usually from first to last. This pattern, like spatial organization, corresponds to readers' own experiences and expectations. It suits expository essays in which you recount a historical or more recent sequence of events or explain a process from beginning to end (for instance, how to run a marathon). And it suits the retelling of more personal stories for the purpose of self-expression or entertainment. In an essay developed from the following thesis sentence, the author would probably proceed chronologically through the event, emphasizing the difficulties and the effects they had on his friends.

> The surest way to lose good friends is to enlist their help in a move from one fourth-floor walk-up apartment to another.

A chronological organization structures the essay on pages 78–79. This is the essay on a summer job for which we earlier saw a list of ideas (p. 17) and a tree diagram (p. 24).

Organizing for emphasis

Several other organizational schemes do not so much grow out of the topic as they are imposed on it to aid readers' understanding and achieve a desired emphasis. Two of these depend on the distinction between the general and the specific as discussed on page 24. The **general-to-specific scheme** is common in expository and argumentative essays that start with a general discussion of the main points and then proceed to specific examples, facts, or other evidence. The following thesis sentences forecast expository and argumentative essays with general-to-specific organizations:

> In families consisting of a single parent and a single child, the boundaries between parent and child often disappear so that the two interact as siblings or as a married couple.

> If Canada hopes to compete economically among the industrialized nations, post-secondary education must be accessible to any student who qualifies academically.

Following from the first sentence, the body of the essay might first discuss generally the dynamics of the families in question and then provide specific examples of the two forms of interaction. Following the second sentence, the body of the essay might first elaborate on the basic argument and then provide the supporting data.

In some expository or argumentative essays, a **specific-to-general scheme** can arouse readers' interest in specific examples or other evidence, letting the evidence build to more general ideas. The following thesis sentence could be developed in this way.

> Most of us are unaware of the public relations campaigns directed at us, but they can significantly affect the way we think and live.

The writer might devote most of the essay to a single specific example of a public relations campaign, showing how it influenced people without their knowledge. Then he could explain more generally how the example typifies public relations campaigns.

The other ways of organizing for emphasis draw on different principles for arranging material. In a **climactic organization**, ideas unfold in order of increasing drama or importance to a climax. For example, the following thesis sentence lists three effects of strip-mining in order of their increasing severity, and the essay would cover them in the same order.

> Strip-mining should be tightly controlled in this region to reduce its pollution of water resources, its permanent destruction of the land, and its devastating effects on people's lives.

As this example suggests, the climactic organization aids argumentation by leaving readers with the most important point freshest in their minds. In exposition such an arrangement can create suspense and thus hold readers' attention.

Expository essays can also be arranged in variations of the climactic pattern. An essay on learning to play the guitar might proceed from **most familiar to least familiar**, that is, from simply plucking strings and sliding the hand up and down the instrument's neck, which most people have seen, to the less familiar styles of picking and chording. Similarly, an essay on various computer languages might proceed from **simplest to most complex**, so that the explanation of each language provides a basis for readers to understand the more difficult one following.

Using a pattern of development

Each of the patterns of development discussed as a discovery strategy on pages 20–22 also suggests at least one overall structure for an essay. If you have been assigned or have chosen a pattern as a way to develop your essay, it can help you arrange your material, almost always in combination with one of the organizational schemes already discussed. (See 3c, pp. 107–16, for paragraph-length examples of each pattern.)

In **narration** the arrangement is almost always chronological, with events arranged as they occurred in time. When writing a narrative, you will probably want to manipulate the sequence of events for emphasis or interest, extending some significant events to minute-by-minute replays, collapsing less significant events to mere summary. (See the narrative essay on pp. 78–79 for an example.) In addition, you may want to alter the sequence, using flash-backs to recall earlier events or forecasting later events.

For **description** of a person, place, or thing, the organization is usually spatial, beginning at one point and surveying others in an orderly way such as near to far or top to bottom. A description of a country lane could move from one end to the other, describing the sights, sounds, and smells as they are encountered.

Using **illustration or support**, you list examples or reasons, or you expand on a single example. You can arrange the individual examples or reasons or the details of the single example in the way that seems most appropriate. For instance, you might arrange several examples in climactic order for an essay arguing that the children's television program *Sesame Street* displays subtle sexism. Or you might arrange a single example chronologically for an essay explaining how one episode of the local evening news illustrates a tendency to downplay serious news in favour of trivial stories.

Using **definition** to specify the precise meaning of a word, object, or concept, you will usually differentiate the topic from other things in its class and then fill in the special characteristics of the topic itself. In an essay defining *soap opera*, for instance, you might first differentiate the soap opera from other television dramas (other members of its class) and then extend the definition with examples of the distinguishing features, arranged in the way most appropriate for emphasis.

Division (separating something into its parts) and **classification** (sorting many things into groups or classes) lead you to list and detail the parts or classes of your topic, which you further arrange for maximum emphasis. In a division essay pointing out the unvarying format of local evening news shows, you might cover the most obvious regular segments first (headline news, weather, sports) and then turn to the less obvious regular segments (police-and-fire story and human-struggle story). In a classification essay sorting soap opera characters into groups, you might arrange the groups in order of increasing complexity—perhaps from consistently evil characters to consistently wholesome characters to good-hearted but weak characters whose behaviour is inconsistent.

In **comparison and contrast** and **analogy**, similar patterns specifying the similarities and differences between topics, you usually follow one of two basic organizational schemes: (1) you discuss each topic separately, covering all the pertinent features of one and then all the pertinent features of the other; or (2) you discuss the topics side by side, comparing them feature for feature. A comparison of the attitudes toward defence spending revealed by the network news programs might follow the first scheme, with each network being examined separately. The second scheme might work for an analogy between wild cards in poker and good-hearted but weak characters in soap operas, showing how both cause sudden realignments among players. Both topics would be examined under each comparable feature. In either scheme, the specific features can be arranged in any order that achieves the desired emphasis.

The pattern of **cause-and-effect analysis** also usually leads you to one of two organizations, depending on whether you are examining why something happened or what its consequences were or will be: (1) you first explain an effect and then examine its causes; or (2) you first explain a cause or causes and then examine the actual or possible effects. The first scheme would suit an essay explaining why television game shows are popular; the second scheme would suit an essay arguing that television news makes viewers impatient for quick solutions to complex problems. The causes or effects themselves may be arranged in order of their occurrence (chronologically) or of their importance or complexity.

The final pattern, **process analysis**, is almost always organized chronologically, as the steps in the process actually occur. In a process essay explaining how to improve one's chances of winning a television game show, for instance, you would present the sequence of steps involved in preparing for the show and playing the game on the air.

2 Outlining

When you have chosen an overall organization for your essay, you may find it helpful to work it out in an outline, a blueprint showing what you will cover and where. Some writers rarely use an outline, and some use one primarily during revision to check the underlying structure of a draft (see p. 57). But writers who do use some form of preliminary outline during planning find that it helps them see potential problems—flaws in organization, gaps or overlaps in coverage, unwanted digressions—and then helps guide the actual drafting. (For these reasons, writing teachers often encourage or require students to experiment with outlining.)

Any of the following types of outlines can be useful. Keep in mind, though, that while the thought you give an outline can be very productive, you may not be able to anticipate changes that drafting will demand. Think of the outline as an aid, not a taskmaster.

Using a scratch or informal outline

For many essays, especially those with a fairly straightforward structure, a simple listing of ideas and perhaps their support may provide adequate direction for your writing. A **scratch outline** lists the key points of the paper in the order they will be covered. The following is Lisa MacDonald's scratch outline for her essay on the National Gallery.

THESIS SENTENCE

The National Gallery of Canada illustrates a philosophy of architecture in which stately grandeur is tempered with personal intimacy to present the art which it houses as real and accessible rather than distant and intimidating.

SCRATCH OUTLINE

Contrast of public and private spaces
Exterior as reflection of atmosphere and philosophy of interior
    design
Personal, individual quality of each gallery
Making art real—natural light and city-like plan

MacDonald put more into this outline than its simplicity might indicate. From her rough groups of ideas (pp. 25–26), she followed through on her earlier decision to omit a lengthy comparison with traditional galleries (she integrates a brief mention at one point instead). And for clarity, she sorted the features of the gallery into three main groups. With this much thought, such a scratch outline may be all you need to begin drafting. Sometimes, though, it may prove to be too skimpy a guide, and you may want to use it as a preliminary to a more detailed outline. Indeed, MacDonald used her scratch outline as a base for a detailed formal outline that gave her an even surer sense of direction (see p. 46).

An **informal outline** is usually more detailed than a scratch outline, including key points and the evidence for them. As we saw on pages 39–40, the thesis of the essay about a neighbourhood street suggests a spatial organization. In an informal outline the writer set up topic headings that would correspond to separate paragraphs of her essay, and she added the features of the street.

THESIS SENTENCE

The main street of my neighbourhood contains enough variety to make almost any city dweller feel at home.

INFORMAL OUTLINE

The beginning of the street
  high-rise condominium occupied by well-to-do people
  ground floor of building: an art gallery
  across the street: a delicatessen
  above the delicatessen: a tailor's shop, a camera-repair shop, a
    lawyer's office
The middle of the street
  four-storey brick apartment buildings on both sides
  at ground level: an Italian bakery and a Japanese restaurant
  people sitting on steps
  children playing ball on sidewalks
The end of the street
  a halfway house for drug addicts
  a boarding house for retired men
  a discount drugstore
  an expensive department store
  a wine shop
  another high-rise condominium

Using a tree diagram

In addition to its use for grouping ideas, the branching tree diagram described and illustrated on pages 24–25 can be a helpful preliminary and guide to drafting. You isolate your main ideas as if for a scratch outline and, under them, array supporting points and then details. If you have already used such a diagram for grouping ideas, then a revision or extension of it may serve you at the later stage. Or you can begin one now. In either case, the diagram can serve the functions of any detailed outline: provide a map and warn of gaps, overlaps, and digressions. Further, because the tree diagram can be supplemented and extended almost indefinitely, it is easy to alter for new ideas and arrangements discovered during drafting and revision.

Using a formal outline

For complex topics requiring complex arrangements of ideas and support, you may want or be required to construct a **formal outline**, either before you begin drafting or afterward, as a check on what you have done (see p. 57). More rigidly arranged and more detailed than a scratch or informal outline, a formal outline not only lays out main ideas and their support but also shows the relative importance of all the essay's elements and how they connect with each other.

On the basis of her scratch outline (p. 44), Lisa McDonald prepared the following formal outline for her essay on the National Gallery:

THESIS SENTENCE

The National Gallery of Canada illustrates a philosophy of architecture in which stately grandeur is tempered with personal intimacy to present the art which it houses as real and accessible rather than distant and intimidating.

FORMAL OUTLINE

I. Contrast between public and private spaces
   A. Large/grand spaces vs. small/intimate spaces
   B. Striking quality vs. neutral quality
II. Exterior as reflecting interior in atmosphere and philosophy
   A. Stately grandeur befitting national building
   B. Extensive use of glass creating openness and invitation
III. Galleries with personal, individual qualities
   A. Variety of styles for each collection
   B. Small, intimate rooms
      1. Focus on the art
      2. Closeness to the art
IV. Interior making art real
   A. Use of natural light
      1. Sense of openness
      2. Relation to real life
   B. City-like plan
      1. Sense of familiarity and comfort
      2. Sense of freedom and interaction

In this formal outline, MacDonald refined her thinking even further, describing the principal philosophical aspects of the interior (sections I, III, and IV) and their reflection in the exterior (section II) and arranging her evidence under each point. Though she knew her outline might change as she drafted and revised her essay, she was satisfied that it solved some problems and would provide a course for her to follow until new issues arose.

MacDonald's outline illustrates not only the potential value of outlining but also several principles of outlining that can help ensure completeness, balance, and clear relationships. (These principles largely depend on distinguishing between the general and the specific. See p. 24.)

1. So that the outline both clarifies the order of ideas and details and indicates their relative importance, all its parts are systematically indented and numbered or lettered: Roman numerals (I, II, III) for primary divisions of the essay; indented capital

letters (A, B) for secondary divisions; further indented Arabic numerals (1, 2) for principal supporting examples. A level of detail below the Arabic numbers would be indented further still and labeled with small letters (a, b). Each succeeding level contains more specific information than the one before it.

2. The outline divides the material into several groups. An uninterrupted listing of ideas like the one following would indicate a need for tighter, more logical relationships among ideas. (Compare this example with sections III and IV of MacDonald's actual outline.)

   III. The Galleries
      A. Variety of styles for each collection
      B. Small, intimate rooms
      C. Focus on art
      D. Closeness to art
      E. Use of natural light
      F. Sense of openness
      G. Relation to real life
      H. City-like plan
      I. Sense of familiarity and comfort
      J. Sense of freedom and interaction

3. Within each part of the outline, distinct topics of equal generality appear in parallel headings (with the same indention and numbering or lettering). In the following example, points B and C are more specific than point A, not equally general, so they should be subheadings 1 and 2 under it.

      A. Small, intimate rooms
      B. Focus on the art
      C. Closeness to the art

4. All subdivided headings in the outline break into at least two parts because a topic cannot logically be divided into only one part. The following example violates this principle.

      A. Stately grandeur
         1. Befitting national building

   Any single subdivision should be combined with the heading above it (as the example is in Section IIA of MacDonald's outline), matched with another subdivision that is missing, or rechecked for its relevance to the heading that precedes it.

5. All headings are expressed in parallel grammatical form. MacDonald's is a topic outline, in which each heading consists of a noun plus modifiers. In a sentence outline all headings are expressed as full sentences (see 36e and pp. 619–620 for discussion and an example). Compare the mixture of forms at the top of the next page with section IVA of MacDonald's actual outline.

    A. Use of natural light
      1. Creates a sense of openness
      2. Realistic

6. The outline covers only the body of the essay, omitting the introduction and the conclusion. The beginning and the ending are important in the essay itself, but you need not include them in the outline unless you are required to do so or anticipate special problems with their organization.

PRINCIPLES OF THE FORMAL OUTLINE

1. Labels and indentions indicate order and relative importance.
2. Sections and subsections reflect logical relationships.
3. Topics of equal generality appear in parallel headings.
4. Each subdivision has at least two parts.
5. Headings are expressed in parallel grammatical form.
6. The introduction and conclusion may be omitted (though not, of course, from the essay).

---

3   Checking for unity and coherence

In conceiving your organization, devising and checking your outline, and writing your essay, you should be aware of two qualities of effective writing that relate to organization: unity and coherence. An essay has **unity** if all its parts support the thesis sentence and relate to each other. It has **coherence** if readers can see the relations and move easily from one thought to the next. A unified and coherent outline will not necessarily guide you to a unified and coherent essay. Much depends on how you specify connections in sentences and paragraphs, and the very process of specifying connections may lead you to see different relations and arrangements from those suggested by the outline. Still, checking your outline for unity and coherence will help you spot and solve obvious problems and thus perhaps avoid unnecessary distractions during drafting.

To check your outline for unity, ask whether each primary division is relevant to the thesis sentence and whether, within major sections of the outline, each example or detail supports the main idea of that section. Don't be too hard on your information at this stage: you may find a way to use an apparently wayward idea or example while drafting. But do cut anything that is clearly irrelevant and likely to sidetrack you during drafting.

To check your outline for coherence, ask whether your arrangement of material suits both your purpose and your readers' needs and whether readers are likely to recognize the shape of your material. You may see a clear need to rearrange parts of your outline.

The unity and coherence of an essay begin in its paragraphs, so the two are treated in greater detail in Chapter 3 (see 3a and 3b).

EXERCISE 18

Choose three of the following topics and list four to six specific points for each one. Then arrange the ideas using the organizational scheme given in parentheses, unless a different scheme seems more appropriate for your material.

1. a festive or depressing place (*spatial*)
2. my view of what happens after death (*chronological or climactic*)
3. why parking facilities for commuting students should be expanded (*specific to general*)
4. ways to release frustration or tension (*illustration*)
5. the meaning of success or failure (*definition*)
6. the parts of a religious service, a twelve-speed bicycle, a camera, or a baseball (*division*)
7. kinds of self-help books, students on campus, joggers, part-time jobs, or teachers (*classification*)
8. the differences or similarities between two television sitcoms, grandparents, newspapers, magazines, or cars (*comparison and contrast*)
9. the causes or effects of an accident, quitting smoking, playing a sport, or cheating (*cause-and-effect analysis*)
10. how to make a great dessert, take a photograph, make a triple play in baseball, train a dog, or study for an examination (*process analysis*)

EXERCISE 19

Revise the following outline so that it adheres to the principles of the formal outline given on pages 46–48. Use the thesis sentence as a guide to appropriate divisions in the outline.

THESIS SENTENCE

Strip-mining should be tightly controlled in this region to reduce its pollution of water resources, its permanent destruction of the land, and its devastating effects on people's lives.

FORMAL OUTLINE

I. Effects of strip-mining in this region
   A. Causes of water pollution
      1. Soil acids are leached by rainwater.
      2. Run-off of acids into streams
   B. Disappearance of fish
   C. Poisoning of water supply
   D. Appearance of hills caused by mining
      1. Scarring
      2. Vegetation is destroyed.
   E. Erosion of the land
      1. Topsoil removed
      2. Mud slides are very common.
   F. Elimination of people's forms of recreation
   G. Health problems
      1. Polluted water causes illness.
   H. Destruction of people's farmland and homes
      1. Acid soil
      2. Mud slides
   I. Inadequate compensation for destruction of farmland and homes

II. Possible controls on strip-mining
   A. Regulate mining techniques.
      1. To limit erosion
      2. Limitations on pollution
   B. Mining companies should be required to replace topsoil.
      1. Restore vegetation to prevent erosion
   C. Compensation for destruction of farmland and homes
      1. Cash payments
      2. Rebuilding

EXERCISE 20

Continuing from Exercise 17 (p. 38), choose an appropriate organization for your essay-in-progress. Then, to discover whether and to what extent an outline can help you plan and draft an essay, prepare a tree diagram or a scratch, informal, or formal outline, as specified by your instructor.

CHAPTER 2

Drafting and Revising the Essay

The separation of drafting and revising from the planning activities discussed in Chapter 1 is somewhat artificial because the stages almost always overlap during the writing process. But gradually for some writers, more distinctly for others, the primary goal shifts during the writing process from gathering and shaping information to forming connected sentences and paragraphs in a draft and then restructuring and rewriting the draft.

2a Writing the first draft

Just as they vary in every other part of the writing process, writers vary in the way they draft. At one extreme is the writer who essentially drafts and revises at the same time, getting each unit of thought right before going on to the next. At the other extreme is the writer who plunges on until ideas are exhausted, rarely or never stopping to reread and rewrite. Neither of these styles is preferable, nor is any style between the extremes, except as it suits the writer. But all effective drafting styles share a common characteristic: the writers do not transcribe fully formed, coherent, and polished thoughts into words but strive to find and convey their meaning through the act of writing.

Because of its uncertainties, drafting can be off-putting. Many experienced writers as well as inexperienced ones find elaborate ways of avoiding the blank page or screen: arranging shelves, checking office supplies, washing hairbrushes, napping, lunching with friends. Such procrastination may actually help you if you let ideas for writing simmer at the same time. At some point, though, enough is enough: the deadline looms; you've got to get started. If the blankness still stares back at you, try one of the techniques listed in the box below.

WAYS TO START DRAFTING

1. Read over what you've already written—notes, outlines, and so on—and immediately start your draft with whatever comes to mind.
2. Freewrite. (See 1d-1).
3. Write scribbles or type nonsense until usable words start coming.
4. Pretend you're writing to a friend about your topic.
5. Conjure up an image that represents your topic—a physical object, a facial expression, two people arguing over something, a giant machine gouging the earth for a mine, whatever. Describe that image.
6. Skip the opening and start in the middle. Or write the conclusion.
7. Write a paragraph on what you think your essay will be about when you finish it.
8. Using your outline, divide your essay into chunks—one for the introduction, another for the first example or reason, and so on. Start writing the chunk that seems most eager to be written, the one you understand best or feel most strongly about.

You should find some momentum once you've started writing. Then, unless you already have a different drafting style that works for you, try to be as fluid as possible. A degree of spontaneity will allow your attitudes toward your topic to surface naturally in your sentences. And, more important, it will make you receptive to ideas and relationships you have not seen before. Your thesis sentence and an outline can help keep you moving by reminding you of your planned purpose, organization, and content; but they should not constrain you from exploring new ideas or even developing a new thesis if that is where your writing leads you. If you feel hampered by your preliminary materials, put them aside until you need them or use them to check your draft when you've finished it.

To keep a draft flowing, skip over sticky spots. If you can't find the right word, leave a blank. If an idea suddenly pops up out of nowhere but doesn't seem to fit where you are in the draft, jot it down on a separate sheet of paper or write it in anyway and underline or bracket if for later attention. Periodically, you will probably need to stop and reread portions of your draft to see where you are and to recapture momentum. If this rereading turns up serious problems, you may need to resolve them before continuing or at least make marginal notes about them. But resist being too self-critical or wondering what your readers will think: there is occasion enough for that in revision. Also resist the urge to improve style, word choice, grammar, punctuation, spelling, and the like. These are not unimportant matters, but you should save them for a later draft, after you have resolved larger issues of purpose, content, and structure. Tinkering with them during the first draft may distract you from the more important issues, and the time and energy spent may be wasted because substantial additions, cuts, and rearrangements often remove old flaws and introduce new ones.

To accommodate these later changes, write or type your first draft on only one side of the paper, leave wide margins, and double- or triple-space all lines. Then you will find it easy to change words or whole sentences and to cut the draft apart and rearrange it without tedious recopying or retyping.

For a brief essay, a first draft written fairly fluidly is likely to take at least an hour or two. Set aside the time, and work in a place where you are not likely to be interrupted. If interruptions are unavoidable, as they probably will be for longer essays, jot a note before leaving the draft about what you expect to do next. Then when you return you can pick up where you left off.

Lisa MacDonald's first draft of her essay on the National Gallery of Canada appears below. She retyped the completed draft in order to have a clean copy for revision.

First draft

Title?

Since it's opening in May 1988, many critics

have questioned the purpose and intention behind

what has been described as the mixed architectural

style of the new National Gallery of Canada. The

National Gallery of Canada illustrates a philosophy

of architecture in which stately grandeur is tem-

pered with personal intimacy to present the art

which it houses as real and accessible rather than distant and intimidating.

The public spaces in the art gallery, those areas in which people gather to meet and talk, are what one would expect in one of the major buildings of the capital region; designed with a formal grandeur that is breath-taking, the architect himself describes the Great Hall as having a "great sense of ceremony." These spaces are in direct contrast to the smaller and more subdued galleries. While the public areas are spectacular with their soaring ceilings and vast expanse of glass the individual galleries, with there neutral quality, conveys a sense of intimacy and informality. Through a variety of architectural styles, all types of human interaction are provided for within the same structure.

The atmosphere and architectural philosophy of the galleries is evident in the exterior design of the National Gallery. Through his use of simple lines, accented with a series of imposing columns, Safdie has produced as edifice with the stately grandeur befitting a building of national importance. Yet, at the same time, what might have been a forbidding facade is relieved by the vast expanse of glass along the south elevation from the eye-catch-

ing entrance pavilion to the magnificent Great Hall.
Such an extensive use of glass creates a sense of
openness an invitation, making the National Gallery
appear from the outside imposing but not
intimidating.

The galleries themselves are adapted to suit
each of the collections housed in the National
Gallery: the European and American Collection, the
Contemporary Collection and the Canadian Collection.
The rooms which house these collections have been
individually desinged to reflect the period and
style of the works displayed, this creates a harmony
between the art and the architecture. Rather than
producing long, cold halls, common in traditional
art galleries such as the Louvre, Safdie creates
smaller rooms in which the architecture, reflecting
the qualities of the art itself, evokes a sense of
unity which is in turn conveyed to the onlooker.
Yet, even though the style and design of each gallery changes as one wanders from collection to collection, the architecture is never intrusive or distracting, but only serves to focus the onlooker's
attention onto the art itself. Thus, the architect
creates a sense of unity and intimacy between the
art and the onlooker.

rev
2a

Safdie's design not only evokes an atmosphere of intimacy within the National Gallery but also one of reality. Through his extensive use of natural light within the rooms, let in through sky-lights, the artificial and tomb-like atmosphere so common in museums and art galleries is dispelled, replaced by a feeling of openess and familiarity. With this new atmosphere of light and freedom, the art ceases to be regarded as artifacts that are confined within a dim musty mausoleum, and takes on a new aspect as something having some relevance to real life. This sense of reality, creating a harmony between the art and those who observe it, is perpetuated in the overall structure of the building. The floor plan, seen as a microcosm of a city, containing public meeting areas (the entrance pavilion and Great Hall), major thorough-fares (the Colonnade and the Galleria), individual buildings (the collection galleries), and even gardens for rest and relaxation (the garden and water courtyards). This concept provides an element of comfort and familiarity to the visitor, providing for all levels of anticipated interaction within the structure. In this way, the architect has aleviated those feelings of discomfort and repression that tend to pervade the conventional

```
gallery, and produces a building which inspires

those within it with a sense of freedom and

familiarity.

    This approach to architecture, creating a

structure which is impressive yet approachable,

reflects the approach to art which the National

gallery is attempting to project.
```

EXERCISE 1

Compare MacDonald's draft with the last step in her planning (her formal outline) on page 46. Where has the act of drafting led her to rearrange her information, add or delete material, or explore new ideas?

EXERCISE 2

Prepare a draft of the essay you began in Chapter 1. Use your thesis sentence (Exercise 17, p. 38) and your outline (Exercise 20, p. 50) as guides, but don't be unduly constrained by them. Concentrate on opening up options, not on closing them down.

2b Revising the first draft

Revision literally means "re-seeing"—looking anew at ideas and details, their relationships and arrangement, the degree to which they work or don't work for the thesis. While drafting, you have been focussed inwardly, concentrating on pulling your topic out of yourself. In revising, you look out to your readers, trying to anticipate how they will see your work. You examine your draft as a pole-vaulter or dancer would examine a videotape of his or her performance, or as you might examine a photograph of yourself.

Obtaining the needed distance for revision can be difficult, even for experienced writers. The following are three techniques that may help you.

1. Take a break after finishing the draft to pursue some other activity. A few hours may be enough; a whole night or day is preferable. The break will clear your mind, relax you, and give you some objectivity.

2. Ask someone to read and react to your draft. Many writing instructors ask their students to submit their first drafts so that the instructors and, often, the other members of the class can serve as an actual audience to help guide revision. (See also 2e on benefiting from criticism.)

3. Outline your draft. A formal outline, especially, with its careful structure and many possible levels of detail, can show where organization is illogical or support is skimpy. (See 1h-2 for a discussion of outlining.)

CHECKLIST FOR REVISION

1. Does the body of the essay carry out the purpose and central idea expressed by the thesis sentence (1c, 1g)? Is the reason for writing apparent, not only in the thesis sentence but also throughout the essay (1f)? If the body of the essay does not carry out the thesis sentence, is the problem more with the thesis sentence (because it does not reflect a new and better direction in the draft) or with the body (because it wanders)?

2. Are there adequate details, examples, or reasons to support each of the ideas (1d)? Will (or do) readers need more information at any point to understand the meaning or appreciate the point of view (1f)?

3. Is the essay unified (1h-3)? Does each paragraph and sentence relate clearly to the thesis sentence?

4. Is the essay coherent (1h-3)? Are the relationships within and among its parts apparent? Will (or can) readers see the shape of the essay, its overall organization?

5. Does the tone of the writing convey a clear and appropriate attitude toward the topic and convey the role assumed (1g-2)? Is the tone appropriate for the purpose and audience? Is it consistent throughout the essay?

6. Is each paragraph in the body unified (3a), coherent (3b), and well developed (3c)?

7. Does the title state or hint at the essay's scope and approach? Will (or does) the introduction engage and focus readers' attention (3c-1)? Will (or does) the conclusion provide readers with a sense of completion (3c-2)?

Strictly speaking, revision includes editing—refining the manner of expression to improve clarity or style or to correct errors. In this chapter, though, revision and editing are treated separately to stress their differences: in revision you deal with the underlying meaning and structure of your essay; in editing you deal with its surface. Often it is tempting to skip the fundamental work of revision and move directly to editing the first draft. But the resulting essay, though perhaps superficially correct, may not show you at your best and may be flawed in ways that will negatively affect readers' responses. You can avoid the temptation to substitute editing for revision and prevent them from interfering with each other by making at least two separate drafts beyond the first: a revised one and then an edited one (p. 65).

rev

2b

Set aside at least as much time to revise your essay as you took to draft it. Plan on going through the draft several times to answer the questions in the "Checklist for Revision" box and to resolve any problems. (If you need additional information on any of the topics in the checklist, refer to the handbook sections given in parentheses.) Note that the checklist can also help you if you have been asked to comment on another writer's draft.

A note on titling your essay

One operation that could fall either with revision or with editing—could in fact occur at any time during the writing process—is titling your essay. Sometimes a title may be obvious as soon as your topic is clear to you. At other times you may find yourself straining for a title when everything else is finished to your satisfaction. If you haven't considered a title before, though, the revision stage is a good time to do so because attempting to sum up your essay in a phrase can focus your attention sharply on your topic, purpose, and audience.

The following are some suggestions for titling an essay.

1. A **descriptive title** is almost always appropriate and is often expected for academic writing. It announces the topic clearly, accurately, and as briefly as possible. For Lisa MacDonald's essay, "The Architectural Philosophy of the National Gallery of Canada" would be an appropriate title. Other examples: "Images of Victimization in *Surfacing*"; "An Experiment in Small-Group Dynamics"; "Conflicts in Federal-Provincial Relations in the 1970s."

2. A **suggestive title**—the kind often found in popular magazines—may be appropriate for more informal writing. The title MacDonald finally chose, "Art, Architecture, and Interaction," conveys her main interests but not her precise topic, thereby pulling readers into the essay to learn more. A source for such a title may be a familiar phrase, a fresh image, or a significant expression from the essay itself.

3. A title tells readers how big the topic is. For MacDonald's essay, the title "The National Gallery" or "Architectural Style" would be deceptively broad, whereas "Glass Windows" or "Natural Light for Art" would be deceptively narrow.

4. A title should not restate the assignment or the thesis sentence, as in "Why the National Gallery Has a Variety of Architectural Styles."

For more information on essay titles, see 12c-1 (appropriate reference to the title in the opening sentence of the paper), 26b (capitalizing words in a title), and Appendix A2-d (the format of a title in the final paper).

When Lisa MacDonald returned to her first draft after half a day, questions like those in the revision checklist revealed several problems. Though she felt that the purpose and main idea expressed in her thesis sentence had held up well throughout the draft, she realized that she had not organized and developed her ideas as well as possible. As happens to most writers in the process of drafting, MacDonald's own need to get her ideas down had taken precedence over her sense of her readers' needs for clarity and fullness.

In revising her draft, MacDonald made some stylistic changes directly on the copy, but she also considerably developed the introduction and conclusion, and she changed the position of one paragraph. Her revision begins after the following explanation of the principal changes, which are keyed to the revision by numbers.

1. With a suggestive title, MacDonald hoped to signal her main interests and engage readers without giving the whole essay away.

2. MacDonald expanded the previous abrupt introduction to explain more clearly the central concern of her essay and to lead into her thesis sentence more coherently.

3. MacDonald moved the third paragraph to a position just before the conclusion to achieve a clearer movement in space: having established the basic contrast in styles, she then moves from the intimate galleries, to the overall interior lighting and structure, to the exterior of the building (the paragraph which she moved). This organization is also more logical since she can now establish her central point about "the atmosphere and architectural philosophy of the galleries" before she notes that these are reflected in the exterior of the building.

4. The introduction of details about the specific art collections housed in the galleries distracted from her main concern with the architecture, so MacDonald cut the digression.

5. MacDonald realized that her abrupt conclusion, while restating her thesis, needed expansion to summarize for her readers the complex connections between the architecture, the art, and the viewer which she had explored in this essay.

rev
2b

Revised first draft

Art, Architecture, and Interaction   1
~~Title~~

    Since it's opening in May 1988, many critics   2

have questioned the purpose and intention behind

what has been described as the mixed architectural

style of the new National Gallery of Canada.

In his design for Ottawa's newest national
edifice, architect Moshe Safdie has combined
a wide variety of styles to create a building
in which large, extravagant public areas
are juxtaposed with small, intimate
galleries. While the lack of uniformity
has puzzled many observers, the architectural
design merely reflects the diversity of art
it is intended to house, and the wide
variety of purposes for which it is intended.

The National Gallery of Canada illustrates a philos-

ophy of architecture in which stately grandeur is

tempered with personal intimacy to present the art

which it houses as real and accessible rather than

distant and intimidating.

    The public spaces in the art gallery, those

areas in which people gather to meet and talk, are

what one would expect in one of the major buildings

of the capital region; designed with a formal grandeur that is breath-taking, the architect himself
describes the Great Hall as having a "great sense
of ceremony." These spaces are in direct contrast
to the smaller and more subdued galleries. While the
public areas are spectacular with their soaring
ceilings and vast expanse of glass the individual
galleries, with there ~~neutral quality~~, conveys a *quiet harmony of architecture and art*
sense of intimacy and informality. Through a variety
of architectural styles, all types of human interaction are provided for within the same structure.

3

The atmosphere and architectural philosophy of
the galleries is evident in the exterior design of
the National Gallery. Through his use of simple
lines, accented with a series of imposing columns,
Safdie has produced as edifice with the stately
grandeur befitting a building of national importance. Yet, at the same time, what might have been a
forbidding facade is relieved by the vast expanse of
glass along the south elevation from the eye-catching entrance pavilion to the magnificent Great Hall.
Such an extensive use of glass creates a sense of
openness an invitation, making the National Gallery
appear from the outside imposing but not
intimidating.

move to becom ¶5

~~The galleries themselves are adapted to suit~~ 4

~~each of the collections housed in the National~~

~~Gallery: the European and American Collection, the~~

~~Contemporary Collection and the Canadian Collection.~~

The rooms which house ~~these~~ *the National Gallery's art* collections have been

individually desinged to reflect the period and

style of the works displayed, this creates a harmony

between the art and the architecture. Rather than

producing long, cold halls, common in traditional

art galleries such as the Louvre, Safdie creates

smaller rooms in which the architecture, reflecting

the qualities of the art itself, evokes a sense of

unity which is in turn conveyed to the onlooker.

Yet, ~~even though the style and design~~ *although* of each gal-

lery changes ~~as one wanders~~ from collection to col-

lection, (the architecture) *it* is never intrusive or dis-

tracting, but only serves to focus the ~~onlooker's~~ *visitor's*

attention onto the ~~art itself.~~ *works displayed.* Thus, the architect

creates a sense of unity and intimacy between the

art and the ~~onlooker.~~ *individual.*

Safdie's design not only evokes an atmosphere

of intimacy within the National Gallery but also one

of reality. Through his extensive use of natural

light within the rooms, let in through sky-lights,

the artificial and tomb-like atmosphere so common in

museums and art galleries is dispelled, replaced by
a feeling of openess and familiarity. With this new
atmosphere of light and freedom, the art ceases to
be regarded as artifacts that are confined within a
dim musty mausoleum, and takes on a new aspect as
something having some relevence to real life. This
sense of reality, creating a harmony between the art
and those who observe it, is perpetuated in the
overall structure of the building. The floor plan *can be*
seen as a microcosm of a city, Containing public
meeting areas (the entrance pavilion and Great
Hall), major thorough-fares (the Colonnade and the
Galleria), individual buildings (the collection galleries), and even gardens for rest and relaxation
(the garden and water courtyards), ~~This concept pro-~~
~~vides an element of~~ (comfort and familiarity) ~~to the~~
it provides
~~visitor, providing~~ for all levels of anticipated
activity   *with*
~~interaction~~ within the structure. In this way, the
aleviates
architect ~~has aleviated~~ those feelings of discomfort
inhibition
and ~~repression~~ that ~~tend to~~ pervade the conventional
producing   *embraces*
gallery, ~~and produces~~ a building which ~~inspires~~
visitors   *atmosphere of casual*
~~those within it~~ with ~~a sense of freedom and~~
graciousness.
~~familiarity~~.

This approach to architecture, creating a
structure which is impressive yet approachable,   5

reflects the approach to art which the National gal-

lery is attempting to project. Just as the architecture conveys a sense of both dignity and intimacy, so too the art should be viewed as having the capacity to not only inspire awe in the individual but also to communicate on a personal level. By creating an atmosphere of intimacy between the art and the visitor, the architecture preserves the power of the art without making it inacesible. Thus, in designing an architecture which is in harmony with the works and people within it, Moshe Safdie invites the visitor to participate in the artistic process which is embodied in the works rather than to remain distant and aloof as a mere spectator.

EXERCISE 3

Compare MacDonald's revised draft with her first draft on pages 53–57. Based on the discussion of her intentions for revision (pp. 60–61), can you see the reasons for most of her changes? Do you think she identified and solved all the significant problems in her first draft? If not, where would you suggest further revisions, and why?

EXERCISE 4

Revise your own first draft from Exercise 2 (p. 57). Use the checklist for revision on page 58 as a guide. Concentrate on purpose, content, and organization, leaving smaller problems for the next draft.

2c   Editing the second draft

Editing for style, sense, and correctness may come second to more fundamental revision, but it is far from unimportant. A carefully developed, interesting essay will still affect readers negatively if the writer appears oblivious to or careless about awkwardness, repetition, incorrect grammar, misleading punctuation, misused or mis-spelled words, and similar problems.

When you have revised your first draft, recopy, retype, or print out the revision so that you can read it easily and have plenty of room for changes. Then as you read the new draft, try to imagine yourself encountering it for the first time, as a reader will. The responses of a friend or relative can help you gain this perspective, as can the comments of your writing instructor and classmates if you share your work in class. Or you can read the draft aloud, perhaps into a tape recorder, listening for awkward rhythms, repetitive sentence patterns, and missing or clumsy transitions. When reading aloud or silently, be careful to read what you actually see on the page, not what you may have intended to write but didn't.

In your editing, work for clarity and a smooth movement among sentences as well as for correctness. Use the questions in the "Checklist for Editing" to guide your editing. (As in the earlier revision checklist, chapter numbers in parentheses indicate where you can look in the handbook for more information.) Note that the checklist can also serve as a guide if you are commenting on another writer's paper.

In response to these questions and her own sense of clarity and effectiveness, Lisa MacDonald edited the second draft of her essay as follows.

CHECKLIST FOR EDITING

1. Are the sentences grammatical? Do they avoid errors in case (6), verb form (7), agreement (8), and adjectives and adverbs (9)?
2. Are the sentences clear? Do they avoid sentence fragments (10), comma splices and fused sentences (11), errors in pronoun reference (12), shifts (13), misplaced or dangling modifiers (14), and mixed or incomplete constructions (15)?
3. Are the sentences effective? Do they use subordination and co-ordination (16) and parallelism (17) appropriately? Are they emphatic (18) and varied (19)?
4. Is the use of commas, semicolons, colons, periods, and other punctuation correct (20–25)?
5. Are the sentences mechanically correct in the use of capitals, italics, abbreviations, numbers, and hyphens (26–30)?
6. Does diction conform to standard usage (31a)? Are the denotations and connotations of words clear and appropriate, and does the writing avoid triteness (31b)? Is the writing concise (31c)?
7. Are the words spelled correctly (34)? Are there typographical errors (which tend to be repeated on multiple drafts done on a word processor or computer)?

Edited second draft

        Art, Architecture, and Interaction
                its
Since ~~it's~~ opening in May 1988, many critics

have questioned the purpose and intention behind

what has been described as the mixed architectural

style of the new National Gallery of Canada. In his

design, ~~for Ottawa's newest national edifice,~~ archi-

tect Moshe Safdie has combined a wide variety of
                                            imposing
styles to create a building in which large, ~~extrava-~~

~~gant~~ public areas are juxtaposed with small, inti-

mate galleries. While the lack of uniformity has

puzzled many observers, the architectural design,
in fact,   *designed*
~~merely~~ reflects the diversity of art it is ~~intended~~

to house, and the wide variety of purposes for which

it is intended. The National Gallery of Canada

illustrates a philosophy of architecture in which

stately grandeur is tempered with personal intimacy

to present the art which it houses as real and

accessible rather than distant and intimidating.
                        of
    The public spaces ~~in~~ the art gallery, ~~those~~

~~areas in which people gather to meet and talk, are~~

~~what one would expect in one of the major buildings~~
                        have been
~~of the capital region,~~ designed with a formal gran-
    appropriate to their use as reception
deur~~, that is breath-taking, the architect himself~~
areas and places of assembly.
~~describes the Great Hall as having~~ a "great sense

~~of ceremony."~~ These spaces are in direct contrast
to the smaller and more subdued ~~galleries~~ *gallery rooms*. While the
public areas are spectacular, with their soaring
ceilings and vast expanse of glass, the individual
galleries, with ~~there~~ *their* quiet harmony of architecture
and art, conveys a sense of intimacy and informality. Through a variety of architectural styles, all
types of human *and artistic* interaction are provided for within
the same structure.

The rooms which house the National Gallery's
art collections have been individually designed to
reflect the period and style of the works displayed,
this creates a harmony between the art and the
architecture. Rather than producing long, cold
halls, common in traditional art galleries such as
the Louvre, Safdie creates smaller rooms in which
the architecture, reflecting the qualities of the
art itself, evokes a sense of unity which is in turn
conveyed to the onlooker. Yet, although the architecture of each gallery changes from collection to
collection, it is never intrusive or distracting,
but only serves to focus the visitor's attention
onto the works displayed. Thus, the architect
creates a sense of unity and intimacy between the
art and the individual.

rev
2c

Safdie's design not only evokes an atmosphere of intimacy within the National Gallery but also one of reality. Through his extensive use of natural light, ~~within the rooms, let in through sky-lights,~~ the artificial and tomb-like atmosphere so common in museums and art galleries is dispelled, replaced by a feeling of openness and ~~familiarity~~ *unpretentiousness*. With this new atmosphere of light and ~~freedom~~ *unrestraint*, the art ceases to be regarded as *an* artifacts that ~~are~~ *is* confined within a dim musty mausoleum, and takes on a new aspect as something ~~having some~~ *which might have* relevence ~~to real~~ *in contemporary* life. This ~~sense of reality~~ *perception of art as real and vital*, creating a harmony between the art and those who observe it, is perpetuated in the overall structure of the building. The ~~floor plan~~ *design* can be seen as a microcosm of a city.[1] Containing public meeting areas (the entrance pavilion and Great Hall), major thorough-fares (the Colonnade and the Galleria), individual buildings (the collection galleries), and even gardens for rest and relaxation (the garden and water courtyards), it provides for all ~~levels~~ *varieties* of anticipated activity within the structure with comfort and familiarity. In this way, the architect al*l*eviates those feelings of discomfort and

[1] "Building Appraisal: The National Gallery of Canada, Ottawa," *The Canadian Architect* June 1988: 30.

inhibition that pervade the conventional gallery,
producing a building which embraces visitors with ~~an~~
atmosphere of casual graciousness.

The atmosphere and architectural philosophy of
the galleries ~~is~~ *are also* evident in the exterior design of
the National Gallery. Through his use of simple
lines, ~~accented with~~ *punctuated by* a series of imposing columns,
Safdie has produced a~~s~~ *n* edifice with the stately
grandeur befitting a building of national impor-
tance. ~~Yet.~~ A~~t~~ the same time, *however,* what might have been
a forbidding façade is relieved by the vast expanse
of glass along the south elevation from the eye-
catching entrance pavilion to the magnificent Great
Hall. Such an extensive use of glass creates a sense
of openness an~~d~~ invitation, ~~making~~ *so that,* the National Gallery appear~~s~~ [from the outside] imposing but not
intimidating.

This approach to architecture, ~~creating~~ *producing* a
structure which is impressive yet approachable,
reflects the approach to art which the National Gallery is attempting to project. Just as the architec-
ture conveys a sense of both dignity and ~~intimacy.~~ *familiarity,*
so too the art should be viewed as having the capac-
ity to not only inspire awe in the individual but
also to communicate on a personal level. By creating

```
an atmosphere of intimacy between the art and the

visitor, the architecture preserves the power of the
                                    S
art without making it inaccesible. Thus, in design-
                                  ^
ing an architecture which is in harmony with the

works and people within it, Moshe Safdie invites the

visitor to participate in the artistic process which

is embodied in the works, rather than to remain dis-

tant and aloof as a mere spectator.
```

EXERCISE 5

Use the "Checklist for Editing" (p. 66) and your own sense of your essay's needs to edit the revised draft you prepared in Exercise 4 (p. 65).

2d Proofreading and submitting the final draft

After editing your essay, recopy, retype, or print it once more for submission to your instructor. Follow the guidelines in Appendix B or the wishes of your instructor for an appropriate manuscript form. Be sure to proofread the final essay several times to spot and correct errors. To increase the accuracy of your proofreading, you may need to experiment with ways to keep yourself from relaxing into the rhythm of your prose. Try reading the paper aloud and very slowly, distinctly pronouncing exactly what you see. Or try placing a ruler under each line as you read it. Or try reading the essay backward, beginning with the last sentence and moving toward the beginning, examining each sentence as a separate unit. This last technique will help keep the content of your writing from distracting you in your search for errors.

Lisa MacDonald's final essay, along with her instructor's comments, follows. The instructor points out the strengths she sees in the essay as well as the flaws remaining in it. She uses a combination of written comments, correction symbols (see the first page of this handbook), and correction codes (the last two pages).

Final draft with instructor's comments

Art, Architecture, and Interaction

Since its opening in May 1988, many critics

have questioned the purpose and <u>intention</u> behind *w* 31c

what has been described as the mixed architectural

style of the new National Gallery of Canada. In his

design, architect Moshe Safdie has combined a wide

variety of styles to create a building in which

large, imposing public areas are juxtaposed with

small, intimate galleries. While the lack of uni-

formity has puzzled many observers, the architec-

tural design, in fact, reflects the diversity of art

it is designed to house, and the wide variety of

purposes for which it is intended. The National

Gallery of Canada illustrates a philosophy of archi- *Good thesis sentence*

tecture in which stately grandeur is tempered with

personal intimacy to present the art which it houses

as real and accessible rather than distant and

intimidating.

The public spaces of the art gallery have been

designed with a formal grandeur appropriate to their

use as reception areas and <u>places of assembly.</u> These *w*

spaces are in direct contrast to the smaller and

more subdued gallery rooms. While the public areas

are spectacular, with their soaring ceilings and *agr*

vast expanse of glass, the individual <u>galleries.</u> *—note verb on next page* with their quiet harmony of architecture and art,

conveys a sense of intimacy and informality. Through

a variety of architectural styles, all types of

human and artistic interaction are provided for

within the same structure.

The rooms which house the National Gallery's

art collections have been individually designed to

reflect the period and style of the works displayed

ref 12c this creates a harmony between the art and the

architecture. Rather than producing long, cold

halls, common in traditional art galleries such as

the Louvre, Safdie creates smaller rooms in which

the architecture, reflecting the qualities of the

art itself, evokes a sense of unity which is in turn

conveyed to the onlooker. Yet, although the archi-

tecture of each gallery changes from collection to

collection, it is never intrusive or distracting,

but only serves to focus the visitor's attention

onto the works displayed. Thus, the architect

creates a sense of unity and intimacy between the

art and the individual.

Safdie's design not only evokes an atmosphere

of intimacy within the National Gallery but also one

of reality. Through his extensive use of natural

light, the artificial and tomb-like atmosphere so

common in museums and art galleries is dispelled,

rev
2d

cs //a
subordinate
by using a
verbal phrase
16b

//

rev 2d

replaced by a feeling of openness and unpretentious-

ness. With this new atmosphere of light and unres-

traint, the art ceases to be regarded as an artifact

that is confined within a dim musty mausoleum and   ∧21f

takes on a new aspect as something which might have

sp relevence in contemporary life. This perception of

art as real and vital, creating a harmony between

the art and those who observe it, is perpetuated in

the overall structure of the building. The design

Good development of analogy. can be seen as a microcosm of a city. Containing →*move down*

It's from the article, right? You need to make clearer that clearer by moving the footnote numeral to the end of the analogy. public meeting areas (the entrance pavilion and

Great Hall), major thoroughfares (the Colonnade and *no hyph*

the Galleria), individual buildings (the collection

galleries), and even gardens for rest and <u>relaxation</u>   *w*

(the garden and water courtyards), (it) provides for   *ref (could be clearer what this pronoun refers?)*

all varieties of anticipated activity within the

structure with comfort and familiarity. In this way,

the architect alleviates those feelings of discom-

fort and inhibition that pervade the conventional

gallery, producing a building which embraces visi-

tors with an atmosphere of casual graciousness.

The atmosphere and architectural philosophy of

the galleries are also evident in the exterior

[1] "Building Appraisal: The National Gallery of
Canada, Ottawa." <u>The Canadian Architect</u> June 1988: 30.

design of the National Gallery. Through his use of
simple lines, punctuated by a series of imposing
columns, Safdie has produced an edifice with the   *meaning?*
stately grandeur befitting a building of national
importance. At the same time, however, what might   *in what way?*
have been a forbidding façade is relieved by the
vast expanse of glass along the south elevation from
the eye-catching entrance pavilion to the magnificent Great Hall. Such an extensive use of glass
creates a sense of openness and invitation, so that,
from the outside, the National Gallery appears   *This ¶ is not as clear as your*
imposing but not intimidating.   *others. See 3c*

   This approach to architecture, producing a
structure impressive yet approachable, reflects the
approach to art which the National Gallery is
attempting to project. Just as the architecture conveys a sense of both dignity and familiarity, so too
the art should be viewed as having the capacity to
// not only inspire awe in the individual but also to
communicate on a personal level. By creating an
atmosphere of intimacy between the art and the visitor, the architecture preserves the power of the art
without making it inaccessible. Thus, in designing
an architecture which is in harmony with the works
and people within it, Moshe Safdie invites the   *Effective Conclusion*

rev

2d

visitor to participate in the artistic process which

is embodied in the works, rather than to remain dis-

tant and <u>aloof</u> as a mere spectator.   *w*

> Your analysis of the connections between the architecture of the National Gallery, the art within it, and the visitors to it is very effective. Your writing is clear and coherent; the essay is well organized and the ideas are well developed.
>
> In revising, see what you can do to clarify the details of the fifth ¶. Also correct the errors noted. Reading Chapter 17 on parallelism could help you avoid faulty parallelism (// in ¶s 3, 5) in your future work. Although your writing style is elegant, you have a tendency toward wordiness and redundant repetitions (*w*-see 31c).

EXERCISE 6

Proofread the following passage, using any of the techniques discussed on p. 71 to bring errors into the foreground. There are ten errors in the passage: missing and misspelled words, typographical errors, and the like. If you are in doubt about any spellings, consult a dictionary.

Becuase natural light can damage sensitive works art, ultraviolet filtering glass has been used in gallry skylights and windows. Inner courtyards an walkways such as the Colonnade enjoy stronger natural light; the vast glass surfaces in these public space are treated with heet-reflecting coatings and double-glazed to prevent condensation There air supply systems, and those serving restarant and kitchen, are isolated from systems supplying air to the art conservation and display areas.

EXERCISE 7

To become familiar with the symbols and codes of this handbook, revise MacDonald's essay wherever her instructor has used a symbol or code to mark a problem.

EXERCISE 8

Prepare the final draft of the essay you have been working on throughout Chapters 1 and 2. Proofread carefully and correct all errors before submitting your essay for review.

2e. Benefiting from criticism

Almost all the writing you do in university or community college will generate responses from an instructor. In writing courses you may submit early drafts as well as your final paper, and your readers may include your classmates as well as your instructor. In any case your readers will act as counsellors and editors to help you see both virtues and flaws in your work and to sharpen your awareness of readers' needs. Listen closely to what they say, and try not to become defensive. Repeated practice in working from ideas to essay, along with information on the writing process offered by your instructor and classmates, can help you become a more efficient writer. Attentive responses to the comments of critical readers can help you become a more capable writer.

To increase the benefit from readers' comments, always consider them seriously and, if they seem appropriate, revise your work in response to them, whether or not you are required to do so. Consult your instructor, a classmate, or the appropriate sections of the handbook if you need additional help. (See "Using This Book," p. xi, for a guide to the handbook.) In addition, keep track of problems that recur in your work so that you can give them special attention in revisions and new essays. In this way your learning on one assignment will inform your work on the next one.

One device for tracking recurring problems is a chart like the one below, with a vertical column for each assignment (or draft) and

	Assignment			
Problems	1	2	3	4
not enough details for readers (1f)	✓	✓		✓
unity—wanders away from thesis (1h)	✓			
parallelism (17)	✓✓	✓	✓	
agreement (8a)	✓		✓	✓
comma splice (11)	✓✓	✓	✓	

a horizontal row for each of the weaknesses that others and you yourself note on your essays. The handbook section is noted for each problem, and check marks in the boxes indicate how often the problem occurred in each essay. The chart also provides a convenient place to keep track of words you misspell so that you can master their spellings.

EXERCISE 9

Carefully read the following student essays, and answer these questions about each one: (1) What is the writer's purpose? (2) How well does the thesis sentence convey the purpose? What assertion does the thesis sentence make? How specific is the sentence? How well does it preview the writer's ideas and organization? (3) What organization does the writer use? Is it clear throughout the essay? (4) What details, examples, and reasons does the writer use to support his or her ideas? Where is supporting evidence skimpy? (5) Who do you think constitutes the writer's intended audience? What role does the writer seem to be assuming? What does the tone reveal about the writer's attitude toward the topic? (6) How successful is the writer in making you care about the topic and his or her views of it?

Working in the Barnyard

Until two months ago I thought summer jobs occupied time and helped pay the next year's tuition but otherwise provided no useful training. Then I took a temporary job in a large government department. Two months taught me a very valuable lesson about how people work together.

Last May I was hired by the personnel office of the department to fill in for vacationing workers in the mail room. I had seven co-workers and a boss, Mrs. King. Our job was to sort the huge morning and afternoon mail shipments into four hundred slots, one for every employee in the department. Then we delivered the sorted mail out of grocery carts that we wheeled from office to office along assigned corridors, picking up outgoing mail as we went along. Each mail delivery took an entire half-day to sort and deliver.

My troubles began almost as soon as I arrived. Hundreds of pieces of mail were dumped on a shallow table against a wall of mail slots. I was horrified to see that the slots were labelled not with people's names but with their initials—whereas the incoming letters, of course, contained full names. Without thinking, I asked why this was a good idea, only to receive a sharp glance from Mrs. King. So I repeated the question. This time Mrs. King told me not to question what I didn't understand. It was the first of many such exchanges, and I hadn't been on the job a half-hour.

I mastered the initials and the sorting and delivery procedures after about a week. But the longer I worked at the job, the more I saw how inefficient all the procedures were, from delivery routes to times for coffee breaks. When I asked Mrs. King about the procedures, however, she always reacted the same way: it was none of my business.

I pestered Mrs. King more and more over the next seven weeks, but my efforts were fruitless, even counter-productive. Mrs. King began calling me snide names. Then she began picking on my work and singling me out for reprimands, even though I did my best and worked faster than most of the others.

Two months after I had started work, the personnel manager called me in and fired me. I objected, of course, calling up all the deficiencies I had seen in Mrs. King and her systems. The manager interrupted to ask if I had ever heard of the barnyard pecking order: the top chicken pecks on the one below it, the second pecks on the third, and so on all the way down the line to the lowliest chicken, whose life is a constant misery. Mrs. King, the manager said, was that lowliest chicken at the bottom of the pecking order in the department's management. With little education, she had spent her entire adult life building up her small domain, and she had to protect it from everyone, especially the people who worked for her. The arbitrariness of her systems was an assertion of her power, for no one should doubt for a moment that she ruled her little roost.

I had a month before school began again to think about my adventure. At first it irritated me that I should be humiliated while Mrs. King continued on as before. But eventually I saw how arrogant, and how unsympathetic, my behaviour had been. In my next job, I'll learn the pecking order before I become a crusader, *if* I do.

—A Student

The Canadian Character

An attempt to summarize the national character of any population might seem somewhat trite; human nature is far too colourful and varied to be classified according to international boundaries. Nevertheless, certain stereotypes do emerge when countries observe each other and remark on their differences. One can easily call to mind such classic images as the philosophical and inscrutable Chinese, the suave and sexy French, the always neutral Swiss, or the volatile and wildly gesticulating Italian. Yet determining the typical character of so wide and diverse a country as Canada is very difficult. While one recognizes the many cultural and regional traits within it, one can hardly synthesize all characteristics together and name the final product a typical Canadian.

The image which Canada itself has presented to the world has varied over time. Originally, Canada was represented in the mind of the world by the faithful Mountie. Honest, forthright, and stalwart, this character trekked through the wilderness in the pursuit of justice and "always got his man." Of late, however, the Mountie has given ground to the backwoods charm of the Mackenzie brothers: "Take off, eh?" Rustic and uncouth, swilling beer, and sporting their toques, this amiable pair perpetuate the image of Canada as a wild and untamed outpost of the British Empire, whose inhabitants are friendly but backward.

The perception which Canadians have of themselves has been largely formed as a negation: "We are NOT Americans!" Overshadowed by their strident, flag-waving neighbour to the south, Canadians have long struggled to establish their own identity as separate from that of Americans. Thus, they take pride in their many cultural and historical differences. While the United States had to fight for independence from Britain, Canada made the transition to nationhood relatively smoothly and without bloodshed. Ironically, one of the few conflicts waged on Canadian soil, the War of 1812, resulted from the refusal of Canadians to be forcibly "freed" from British tyranny by the crusading Americans. Carefully avoiding the extremism of its rather violent and pugnacious neighbour, Canada plays a moderate role in both domestic and international politics and has gained a favourable international reputation as a peaceful country for its prominent role in the United Nations' peacekeeping forces.

At home, regionalism generally determines the Canadian's perception of national character, each area of the country remarking on the foibles of the others. Thus, such stereotypes arise as the poverty-stricken Newfoundlander, boorish and slow-witted ("How many Newfies does it take to change a light bulb?"), the middle-class WASP from southern Ontario to whom respectability and conformity mean everything, and the lotus-eater of the West Coast who has earned his province the title, British California. Yet it seems typical of all regions to underrate both themselves and their country. This self-conscious pessimism, rarely observed by the world but painfully obvious to Canadians themselves, is characterized by the Canadian restraint in matters of patriotism and national pride. Canadians secretly long to sing their national anthem at hockey games as proudly and boisterously as the Americans sing theirs, but they will never have the courage of national conviction to do so.

It seems, therefore, that the Canadian national character can only be described in negative, or at best neutral, terms. Kindly but unassertive, moderate and self-deprecating, Canadians can best be identified in their efforts to dissociate themselves from their imperious neighbour, the United States. But then, it must be remembered that a Canadian is writing this essay. Would this portrayal of Canadian character be different if it had been written by, perhaps, an American?   —A STUDENT

CHAPTER 3

Composing Paragraphs

Whatever our purpose in writing and whatever our subject, we normally write in **paragraphs**, groups of related sentences set off by a beginning indention. In the process of composing paragraphs and revising them, we work toward two complementary goals: to give full expression to our ideas and to help readers follow and appreciate our train of thought. For the writer, paragraphing provides a way to break down complex ideas into manageable parts, discuss each part separately and completely, and relate each part to the central theme or thesis of the essay. For readers, paragraphing focusses attention on one idea at a time and provides the mixture of general statements and specific information needed to understand meaning.

The following paragraph provides a fairly simple illustration of how the paragraph aids the writer and the reader.

Like lessons of this sort, those about the north are taught by precept and example, but also, more enjoyably, by cautionary nasty tale. There is death by blackfly, the one about the fellow who didn't have his shirt cuffs tight enough in the spring and undressed at night only to find he was running with blood, the ones about the lost travellers who bloated up from too many bites and who, when found, were twice the size, unrecognizable, and dead. There is death from starvation, death by animal, death by forest fire; there is death from something called "exposure," which used to confuse me when I heard about men who exposed themselves: why would they intentionally do anything that fatal? There's death by thunderstorm, not to be sneered at: on the open lake, in one of the excessive northern midsummer thunderstorms, a canoe or a bush plane is a vulnerable target. The north is full of Struwwelpeter-like stories about people who didn't do as they were told and got struck by lightning. Above all, there are death by freezing and death by drowning. Your body's heat-loss rate in the water is twenty times that in air, and northern lakes are cold. Even in a life jacket, even holding on to the tipped canoe, you're at risk. Every summer the numbers pile up. —MARGARET ATWOOD, *"True North"*

The thesis of the essay in which this paragraph appears is that the north represents the Canadian unconscious—mystery and fear. Atwood begins the paragraph with a general statement that relates to her thesis. That statement leads her directly to eight examples— evidence of the cautionary tales cited in her thesis. She keeps herself and the reader focussed on her general statement by repeating the word "death" and by using a repetition or variation of "there is death" at the beginning of all the examples. She sticks to the same idea throughout the paragraph and develops it with plenty of specific details. Atwood's paragraph illustrates the three characteristics of most effective paragraphs, which are set out in the box below.

QUALITIES OF EFFECTIVE PARAGRAPHS

1. **Unity:** the paragraph adheres to one idea. (See 3a.)
2. **Coherence:** the parts of the paragraph relate clearly to each other. (See 3b.)
3. **Development:** the idea of the paragraph is well supported with specific evidence such as details, facts, examples, and reasons. (See 3c.)

These are three qualities of an effective essay as well (see 1f and 1h), but it is mainly through paragraphs that they are achieved. Thus they are the subjects of the first three sections of this chapter. A fourth section, 3d, treats introductions, conclusions, and other kinds of paragraphs that serve special functions in essays. And a final section, 3e, discusses how paragraphs work together in the whole essay.

3a Maintaining paragraph unity

Since readers expect a paragraph to explore one idea, they will be alert for that idea and will patiently follow its development. In other words, they will seek and appreciate paragraph **unity**, clear identification and clear elaboration of one idea and of that idea only. If readers' attention is not rewarded and they must shift their focus from one idea to another and perhaps back again, their confusion or frustration will impede their understanding and acceptance of the writer's meaning.

In an essay the thesis sentence often announces the main idea as a commitment to readers (see 1g). In a paragraph a **topic sentence** often alerts readers to the essence of the paragraph by stating the central idea and expressing the writer's attitude toward it. Like the thesis sentence, the topic sentence is a commitment to readers, and the rest of the paragraph delivers on that commitment. In Atwood's paragraph on the north, the topic sentence or commitment is sentence 1: the author states generally that lessons about the north are taught by cautionary tales. The next seven sentences fulfil the commitment with specific examples of northern dangers. The last sentence invites us to consider the number of people who have ignored these warnings.

In the body of an essay each paragraph is likely to treat one part of the essay's thesis sentence; the topic sentences simply elaborate on parts of the thesis. A topic sentence will not, of course, guarantee a unified paragraph, any more than a thesis sentence guarantees a unified essay. The next several sections explain how to write unified paragraphs controlled by strong topic sentences.

1   **Focussing on the central idea**

Atwood's paragraph on the north works because it follows through on the topic sentence. The sentences after the topic sentence do not stray off to other subjects, such as enjoyable aspects of travel in the north or the personal northern travel experiences of the author herself. Instead, each one helps us better understand the writer's central idea.

The following paragraph, in contrast, begins to lose its way in sentence 5.

> Professional wrestling satisfies viewers' needs for heroic strug-   1
> gle. The confrontation between men like "Angel Boy" Johnson   2
> and "Dirty Dan" Hogan—each one costumed to reflect his nick-
> name—may seem absurd, not heroic. But the absurdity   3
> removes the contest from reality, so that the wrestlers are like
> characters in a fairy tale who symbolize good and evil. We know   4
> the action is all (or mostly all) staged, yet that unreality
> increases the symbolism of the contest. There is also staged   5
> action in TV crime shows. The action *seems* real, so we begin to   6
> care about who wins or loses. The shootings and other violence   7
> usually do not offend us but seem justified and even necessary.
> Of course, crime shows are even more violent than professional   8
> wrestling.

By the end of this paragraph, the author seems to have forgotten his commitment (stated in sentence 1) to show how professional wrestling satisfies viewers' needs for heroic struggle. At sentence 5 he becomes distracted by the staged action in TV crime shows, returning to wrestling only weakly in the last sentence.

The writer might have kept on track and produced a more unified paragraph if he had been more careful to relate every sentence both to the sentence before it and to the central idea of the topic sentence. In sentences 2–4 the writer does establish these relationships, discussing the absurdity and symbolism of wrestling. In sentence 5, however, when he shifts to TV crime shows, the writer leaves behind both the central idea and the more specific notions of absurdity and symbolism. From then on he loses his thread and, in the process, his readers.

Compare the disunified paragraph with the following revision, noting especially how the writer uses the new sentences 5–7 to develop his explanation.

Professional wrestling satisfies viewers' needs for heroic struggle. 1 The confrontation between men like "Angel Boy" Johnson 2 and "Dirty Dan" Hogan—each one costumed to reflect his nickname—may seem absurd, not heroic. But the absurdity 3 removes the contest from reality, so that the wrestlers are like characters in a fairy tale who symbolize good and evil. We know 4 the action is all (or mostly all) staged, yet that unreality increases the symbolism of the contest. Watching "Angel Boy" 5 and "Dirty Dan" grab, twist, and hurl each other, we are watching good struggle against evil and freedom struggle against repression. It becomes important who wins or loses, so that 6 every hammerlock has significance. Such a struggle—ending, 7 of course, with "Angel Boy" victorious—renews our faith in the rightness of the world.   —A STUDENT

Depending on his purpose, the writer may develop the deleted comparison with TV crime shows in a separate paragraph, or he may omit it altogether.

Writers often follow the central idea in the topic sentence with a **clarifying or limiting sentence**. Such a sentence can help the writer maintain unity by providing a sharper, clearer focus for the paragraph; and it can help the reader by providing a more precise sense of the writer's idea. In the following paragraph, for instance, sentence 2 clarifies and limits what the writer means in her topic sentence (sentence 1) about the inconsistent attitude toward computer intelligence.

Another inconsistency in *2001: A Space Odyssey* is the attitude 1 toward computer intelligence. The filmmakers apparently 2 could not decide whether they wanted to present the shipboard computer, HAL, as self-governed and therefore dangerous or as human-governed and therefore controllable. In his name, the 3 fact that he is a *he* (not an *it*), his soft, slightly menacing voice, and his control over the spaceship, HAL seems human and more than human, with a mind of his own. When he starts murdering 4

crew members, the filmmakers seem to be saying that computer
intelligence can be dangerously independent: the nightmare of
the appliance taking vengeance on its users. Yet eventually the   5
one surviving crew member disconnects HAL's circuits to make
him harmless. Then the message seems to be that HAL is, after   6
all, just a machine under human control. In the end, it is not   7
clear whether the filmmakers fear artificial intelligence or not.

—A STUDENT

2   Placing the topic sentence

The topic sentence of a paragraph (along with any limiting or
clarifying sentence) and its supporting details may be arranged
variously, depending on how the writer wants to direct readers'
attention and on how complex the central idea is. The most common
positions for the topic sentence are discussed below.

Topic sentence at the beginning

In the most familiar arrangement—illustrated by all the paragraphs examined so far—the topic sentence comes first, then sometimes a clarifying or limiting sentence, then the supporting information. This arrangement can help the writer maintain paragraph unity
because the topic sentence provides a guide for selecting details in
the rest of the paragraph. For readers the topic-first model establishes an initial context in which all the following details can be
understood. Look again at the paragraphs on pages 81 and 83 to see
how easily we readers relate each detail or example back to the point
made in the first sentence.

The topic-first model is common not only in expository paragraphs, such as those above, but also in argumentative paragraphs,
such as the following one. Here the author first states his opinion and
then provides the information to support it.

Enough. Canadians, as a people, are no better and no worse   1,2
than anyone else. We were slavers in the eighteenth and early   3
nineteenth centuries, and our treatment of minorities, from
Indians to Jehovah's Witnesses, is only marginally different   4
from that of the Americans. We have staged some of the bigger
and more bloody-minded riots on the continent, from the
Bytown Riots of the 1840s ("Them Bytown days was fightin'
days") to the Kenora race riots of 1974. We have not only passed,   5
but applauded, viciously repressive legislation, and our gun
laws, to take only one example of wrong-headed self-
congratulation, are in fact looser and dumber than those in
most U.S. states.   —WALTER STEWART, *But Not in Canada*

Topic sentence following transitional sentence

In many paragraphs the opening sentence serves as a transition or bridge for the preceding paragraph, simultaneously pointing back to the previous idea and forward to a new one. The topic sentence is then often the second sentence, with the remaining sentences providing the support. In the following paragraph, for example, the first, transitional sentence refers to the assertion in the author's preceding paragraph that science is taught as if it does not undergo change. Sentence 2 is the topic sentence.

> And, of course, it [science] is not like this at all. In real life, every [1,2] field of science is incomplete, and most of them—whatever the record of accomplishment during the last 200 years—are still in their very earliest stages. In the fields I know best, among the life [3] sciences, it is required that the most expert and sophisticated minds be capable of changing course—often with a great lurch—every few years. In some branches of biology the mind- [4] changing is occurring with accelerating velocity. Next week's issue of any scientific journal can turn a whole field upside [5] down, shaking out any number of immutable ideas and installing new bodies of dogma. This is an almost everyday event in [6] physics, in chemistry, in materials research, in neurobiology, in genetics, in immunology.
> —LEWIS THOMAS, "The Art of Teaching Science"

If a writer is making a significant change in direction, the transition from a preceding paragraph may require more than one sentence or even a separate short paragraph (see 3d–3). Even for very slight changes, however, writers frequently use words or phrases to link paragraphs so that readers see the progression of ideas. For instance, in the paragraph on computer intelligence (p. 84) the word *another* creates a bridge from the preceding paragraph. Brief links like this one are discussed in more detail in the next section (see 3b–3 and 3b–6).

Topic sentence at the beginning and in the middle

When the central idea of a paragraph requires fairly extensive support or breaks naturally into two parts, the topic sentence may be divided between the beginning and middle of the paragraph, with each part developed separately. Often the two parts compare two subjects or, as in the following paragraph, examine different sides of an issue.

> So far the only bright side [to nuclear war] I can come up with— [1] at least the only one I can sanely recommend—is the certainty that, in a nuclear war, the perpetrators will also die. In fact, [2]

since they are no doubt somewhat better prepared for it than we are, the likelihood is that they will die more slowly, and with a more agonizingly clear awareness of what's happened, than the rest of us. But even this prospect gives me only cold comfort. I 3,4 have never understood those bereaved parents who, as is occasionally reported to us, find it in their hearts to rejoice at the execution of their child's killer. The thought of the Pentagon 5 brass stumbling in terror through a darkened bunker or of the Kremlin leadership preparing to wash down their cyanide pills with shots of Stolichnaya does not, I am afraid, begin to compensate.

—BARBARA EHRENREICH, "Finding the 'Bright Side' to Nuclear War"

In this paragraph sentences 1 and 3 together form the central idea of the paragraph: the one bright side of nuclear war is not very comforting. In this case the paragraph is simple enough not to need an opening statement of the whole idea to tie the parts together. In more complex paragraphs, however, the opening sentence may state the entire idea briefly before it is divided. Such an opening sentence can keep the paragraph from breaking in half and also help the writer ensure that the two parts are, in fact, closely related.

Topic sentence at the end

In some paragraphs the central idea may be stated at the end, after supporting sentences have made a case for the general statement. Since this model leads the reader to a conclusion by presenting all the evidence first, it can prove effective in argumentation. And because the point of the paragraph is withheld until the end, this model can be dramatic in exposition as well. For example, all the details in the following paragraph about the sale of land in Regina by the railway lead up to and support the idea stated in sentence 7.

In Regina, the railway's interests were identical with those of the 1 government, which was also in the land business. Under the 2 terms of the contract, the CPR had title to the odd-numbered sections along the right of way, save for those originally ceded to the Hudson's Bay Company. In Regina and in several other 3 important prairie towns, the government and the CPR pooled their land interests, placed them under joint management, and agreed to share the profits equally. That summer the railway, in 4 order to raise funds, agreed to sell an immense slice of its land— five million acres—to a British-Canadian syndicate, the Canada North-West Land Company, for $13,500,000. The syndicate's 5 job was to manage townsite sales in forty-seven major communities, including Moose Jaw, Calgary, Regina, Swift Current, and Medicine Hat. The railway was to receive half of the net 6

proceeds of these townsite sales. Thus, in Regina, one quarter of   7
the land profits went to the railway, one quarter to the land
company, and one half to the government.
                                        —PIERRE BERTON, *The Last Spike*

Expressing the central idea at the end of the paragraph does not
eliminate the need to unify the paragraph. The idea in the topic
sentence must still govern the selection of all the preceding details.

Topic sentence at the beginning and the end

Sometimes the central idea may be stated at the beginning of
the paragraph and then restated at the end. Generally, the first
sentence provides a context for the supporting information, and the
last sentence provides an elaboration or summary of that information. For example:

The Liberals failed in English-speaking Canada. If the nation   1,2
were to survive, it had to be anchored in both English- and
French-speaking Canada, and a *modus vivendi* had to be established between the two. The Liberals failed to recognize that the   3
real danger to nationalism lay in the incipient continentalism of
English-speaking society, rather than in any Quebec separa-
tism. Their economic policies homogenized the culture of   4
Ontario with that of Michigan and New York.
                                        —GEORGE GRANT, *Lament for a Nation*

This model, like the previous one, will not work if the writer
tries to make the last sentence rescue a disunified paragraph. To be
effective, the final statement must reflect some development in the
sentences preceding it.

Central idea not stated

Occasionally, a paragraph's central idea will be stated in the
previous paragraph or will be so obvious that it need not be stated at
all. The following paragraph, about Montrealers "taking the Two and
Twenty" in the late seventies, has no explicit topic sentence.

The other way of escaping from the city westwards towards   1
lovely Ontario is the older highway, which is really an extension
of Sherbrooke Street and Saint James Street, going by the name   2
of Highway 2/20. It is the shortest way into exile, crossing the
bridge where the Ottawa flows into the St. Lawrence—historic
meeting-place—and leading on to the Ontario border just east
of Lancaster. One can imagine Jesus, Mary and Joseph making   3
their way along 2/20 with mule and saddlebags, in either direction. Much depends upon which province is to be imagined as   4
Egypt.   —HUGH HOOD, *Tony's Book*

The effectiveness of this paragraph rests on the power of details to describe Highway 2/20. Thus a stated central idea—such as "English-speaking Montrealers moved out of the city with mixed feelings"—not only would weaken the paragraph but would contradict its intention. Nevertheless, the central idea is clearly implied.

Paragraphs in descriptive writing (like the preceding one) and in narrative writing (relating a sequence of events) often lack stated topic sentences. But producing a paragraph without a topic sentence does not release the writer from the need to unify the paragraph. Each paragraph should have a central idea, and its details should develop that idea.

¶ un

3a

EXERCISE 1

What is the central idea of each paragraph below? In what sentence or sentences is it expressed?

1. Advocates of the rights of animals have sabotaged research 1 laboratories that experiment with animals, physically pre- vented seal hunters from killing seals, freed caged animals from commercial fur farms, harassed whaling vessels, released animals from zoos, and hindered hunters in their search for prey. In search of public support for their point of view, they 2 have taken advertisements and distributed printed fliers and vivid photographs that give graphic examples of how animals are sometimes inhumanely treated. Such acts represent the 3 philosophy of a growing number of people in this and other countries who believe nonhuman animals are sentient creatures that can feel pain, are aware of their plight, and, like humans, have certain rights.
—Bayard Webster, "Should Vivisection Be Abolished?"

2. Though they do not know why the humpback whale sings, 1 scientists do know something about the song itself. They have 2 measured the length of a whale's song: from a few minutes to over half an hour. They have recorded and studied the variety 3 and complex arrangements of low moans, high squeaks, and sliding squeals that make up the song. And they have learned 4 that each whale sings in its own unique pattern.   —A Student

3. The two most expressive things about him were his mouth 1 and the pockets of his jacket. By looking at his mouth, one could 2 tell whether he was plotting evil or had recently accomplished it. If he was bent upon malevolence, his lips were all puckered 3 up, like those of a billiard player about to make a difficult shot. After the deed was done, the pucker was replaced by a delicate, 4 unearthly smile. How a teacher who knew anything about boys 5 could miss the fact that both expressions were masks of Satan I'm sure I don't know. Wallace's pockets were less interesting 6

than his mouth, perhaps, but more spectacular in a way. The   7
side pockets of his jacket bulged out over his pudgy haunches
like burro hampers. They were filled with tools—screwdrivers,   8
pliers, files, wrenches, wire cutters, nail sets, and I don't know
what else. In addition to all this, one pocket always contained a   9
rolled-up copy of *Popular Mechanics*, while from the top of the
other protruded *Scientific American* or some other such magazine. His breast pocket contained, besides a large collection of   10
fountain pens and mechanical pencils, a picket fence of drill
bits, gimlets, kitchen knives, and other pointed instruments.
When he walked, he clinked and jangled and pealed.   11
                                          —RICHARD ROVERE, "Wallace"

EXERCISE 2

The following paragraphs contain ideas or details that do not
support their central ideas. Identify the topic sentence in each
paragraph and delete the unrelated material.

1. In the northern part of the province, some people still live   1
much as they did a century ago. They use coal- or wood-burning   2
stoves for heating and cooking. Their homes do not have elec-   3
tricity or indoor bathrooms or running water. The towns can't   4
afford to put in sewers or power lines, because they don't receive
adequate funding from the government. Beside most homes   5
there is a garden where fresh vegetables are gathered for can-
ning. Small pastures nearby support livestock, including cattle,   6
pigs, horses, and chickens. Most of the people have cars or   7
trucks, but the vehicles are old and beat-up from travelling on
unpaved roads.

2. Most people don't realize how difficult it is to work and go to   1
school at the same time. If you want to make good grades but   2
need to pay your own way, the burdens are tremendous. I work   3
in an office sixteen hours a week. Each term I have to work out a   4
tight schedule that will let me take the courses I want and still be
at work when I'm needed. I like the job. The people there are   5,6
pleasant, and they are eager to help me learn. In the end my job   7
will be good training for the kind of managerial position I hope
to have some day, because I'm gaining useful experience in
office procedures and working with people. It's hard for me to   8
have a job and go to school, but when I graduate, both will make
me more employable.

EXERCISE 3

Develop the following topic sentence into a unified paragraph by
using the relevant information in the statements below it. Delete

each statement that does not relate directly to the topic, and then rewrite and combine sentences as appropriate.

TOPIC SENTENCE

Mozart's accomplishments in music seem remarkable even today.

Wolfgang Amadeus Mozart was born in 1756 in Salzburg, Austria.
He began composing music at the age of five.
He lived most of his life in Salzburg and Vienna.
His first concert tour of Europe was at the age of six.
On his first tour he played harpsichord, organ, and violin.
He published numerous compositions before reaching adolescence.
He married in 1782.
Mozart and his wife were both poor managers of money.
They were plagued by debts.
Mozart composed more than six hundred musical compositions.
His most notable works are his operas, symphonies, quartets, and piano concertos.
He died at the age of thirty-five.

EXERCISE 4

Develop three of the following topic sentences into detailed and unified paragraphs.

1. Fans of country music (or rock music, classical music, jazz) come in [number] varieties.
2. My high school was an ugly (or attractive or homely or whatever) building.
3. Words can hurt as much as sticks and stones.
4. Professional sports have (or have not) been helped by extending the regular season with championship playoffs.
5. Working for good grades can interfere with learning.

3b Achieving paragraph coherence

A paragraph is unified if it holds together—if all its details and examples support the central idea. A paragraph is **coherent** if readers can see *how* the paragraph holds together without having to puzzle out the writer's reasons for adding each new sentence. Each time readers must pause and reread to see how sentences relate to each other, they lose both comprehension and patience.

Coherent paragraphs convey relations in many ways, and we will look at each one in detail. First, however, we will examine what makes a paragraph, like the following one, incoherent.

> The ancient Egyptians were masters of preserving dead people's 1
> bodies by making mummies of them. Mummies several 2
> thousand years old have been discovered nearly intact. The skin, 3
> hair, teeth, finger- and toenails, and facial features of the mum-
> mies were evident. It is possible to diagnose the diseases they 4
> suffered in life, such as smallpox, arthritis, and nutritional
> deficiencies. The process was remarkably effective. Sometimes 5,6
> apparent were the fatal afflictions of the dead people: a middle-
> aged king died from a blow on the head, and polio killed a child
> king. Mummification consisted of removing the internal 7
> organs, applying natural preservatives inside and out, and then
> wrapping the body in layers of bandages.

This paragraph seems to be unified: it sticks to the topic of mummifi-cation throughout. But the paragraph is hard to read. It jumps back and forth between specific details about features, diseases, and causes of death (sentences 3, 4, 6) and general statements about mummies' intactness (sentence 2), the effectiveness of the process (sentence 5), and the process itself (sentence 7). All the sentences seem disconnected from each other, so that the paragraph lurches instead of gliding from point to point.

The paragraph as it was actually written is much clearer.

> The ancient Egyptians were masters of preserving dead people's 1
> bodies by making mummies of them. Basically, mummification 2
> consisted of removing the internal organs, applying natural
> preservatives inside and out, and then wrapping the body in
> layers of bandages. And the process was remarkably effective. 3
> Indeed, mummies several thousand years old have been discov- 4
> ered nearly intact. Their skin, hair, teeth, finger- and toenails, 5
> and facial features are still evident. Their diseases in life, such as 6
> smallpox, arthritis, and nutritional deficiencies, are still diag-
> nosable. Even their fatal afflictions are still apparent: a middle- 7
> aged king died from a blow on the head; a child king died from
> polio.   —A STUDENT

This paragraph contains the same information and the same number of sentences as the previous one, but now we have no difficulty moving from one sentence to the next, seeing the writer's intentions, understanding the writer's meaning. The initial broad assertion (the topic sentence) is the same, but now the writer responds to the expectations it creates with two more specific statements: first (in sentence 2) he defines the process of making mummies; then (in sentence 3) he notes why the Egyptians were masters of the process (because the process was remarkably effective). Sentence 3 automati-cally leads us to expect an explanation of how the process was effective, and in sentence 4 the writer proceeds to tell us: ancient mummies have been discovered nearly intact. "How intact?" we want to know. And again the writer responds to our expectation: we can make out features (sentence 5), diseases (sentence 6), and even fatal afflictions (sentence 7).

¶ coh
3b

The writer has thus responded to our expectations for content, and he has arranged his sentences in a familiar, general-to-specific organization. In addition, he has linked sentences effectively, so that each either grows out of or aligns with the one before. Here is the paragraph marked up to show these connections.

CENTRAL IDEA

The ancient Egyptians were masters of preserving dead people's bodies by making mummies of them. *EXPLANATION* Basically, mummification consisted of removing the internal organs, applying natural preservatives inside and out, and then wrapping the body in layers of bandages. *EXPLANATION* And the process was remarkably effective. Indeed, mummies several thousand years old have been discovered nearly intact. *SPECIFIC EXAMPLES* Their skin, hair, teeth, finger- and toenails, and facial features are still evident. Their diseases in life, such as smallpox, arthritis, and nutritional deficiencies, are still diagnosable. Even their fatal afflictions are still apparent: a middle-aged king died from a blow on the head; a child king died from polio.

1
2
3
4
5
6
7

Circled and connected words repeat or restate key terms or concepts. Boxed words link sentences and clarify relationships. Underlined and connected phrases are in parallel grammatical form to reflect their parallel content.

Though some of the connections in this paragraph may have been added in revision, the writer probably attended to them while drafting as well. Not only superficial coherence but also an underlying clarity of relationships can be achieved by tying each sentence to the one before—generalizing from it, clarifying it, qualifying it, adding to it, illustrating it. As we saw just above, each sentence in a paragraph creates an expectation of some sort in the mind of the reader, a question such as "How was a mummy made?" or "How intact are the mummies?" or "What's another example?" When the writer recognizes these expectations and tries to fulfil them, readers are likely to understand relationships without struggle.

The next pages discuss organization, parallelism, repetition and restatement, use of pronouns, consistency, and transitional expressions—all techniques used together to achieve coherence while both drafting and revising.

1   Organizing the paragraph

The paragraphs on mummies illustrate an essential element of coherence: information must be arranged in an order that readers can follow easily and that corresponds to their expectations. The common organizations for paragraphs correspond to those for entire essays (see 1h–1). Here we will examine the arrangements by space, by time, and for emphasis. The patterns of development, each suggesting its own arrangement, will be examined in the next section (p. 101).

Organizing by space or time

A paragraph organized **spatially** focusses readers' attention on one point and scans a person, object, or scene from that point. The movement may be from top to bottom, from side to side, from a farther point to a closer one, or from a closer point to a farther one. Donald Hall follows the last pattern in the following paragraph.

> Across the yard, between the cow barn and the road, was a 1
> bigger garden which was bright with phlox and zinnias and
> petunias. Beyond was a pasture where the color changed as the 2
> wild flowers moved through the seasons: yellow and orange
> paint brushes at first, then wild blue lupines and white Queen
> Anne's lace, and finally the goldenrod of August. Mount Kear- 3
> sarge loomed over the pasture in the blue distance, shaped like a
> cone with a flattened point on top. We sat on the porch and 4
> looked at garden, field, and mountain.
> —DONALD HALL, *String Too Short to Be Saved*

Since a spatial organization parallels the way people actually look at a place for the first time, it conforms to readers' expectations. The spatial relationships can be further clarified with explicit signals, such as Hall's *Across* and *between* (sentence 1), *beyond* (2), and *over* (3). The writer may place a topic sentence at the beginning of the paragraph, may (like Hall) pull the scene together at the end, or may omit a topic sentence and let the details speak for themselves.

Another familiar way of organizing the elements of a paragraph is **chronologically**—that is, in order of their occurrence in time. In a chronological paragraph, as in experience, the earliest events come first, followed by more recent ones.

> There is no warning at all—only a steady rising intensity of the 1
> sun's light. Within minutes the change is noticeable; within an 2
> hour, the nearer worlds are burning. The star is expanding like a 3
> balloon, blasting off shells of gas at a million miles an hour as it
> blows its outer layers into space. Within a day, it is shining with 4
> such supernal brilliance that it gives off more light than all the
> other suns in the Universe combined. If it had planets, they are 5
> now no more than flecks of flame in the still-expanding shells of
> fire. The conflagration will burn for weeks before the dying star 6
> collapses back into quiescence
>   —ARTHUR C. CLARKE, "The Star of the Magi"

Like spatial paragraphs, chronological paragraphs can be almost automatically coherent because readers are familiar with progressions of events. The writer can help readers by signalling the order of events and the time that separates them, as Clarke does with the phrases and words *Within minutes* and *within an hour* (sentence 2), *Within a day* (4), *now* and *still* (5), and *before* (6). Like Clarke's, a chronological paragraph may lack a topic sentence when the idea governing the sequence is otherwise clear.

Organizing for emphasis

Whereas the spatial or chronological organization is almost dictated by the content of the paragraph, other organizational schemes are imposed on paragraphs to achieve a certain emphasis. These imposed organizations are also familiar to readers.

In the **general-to-specific** scheme the topic sentence generally comes first and then the following sentences become increasingly specific. The paragraph on mummies (p. 93) illustrates this organization: each sentence is either more specific than the one before it or at the same level of generality. The following paragraph is a more straightforward illustration.

> Perhaps the simplest fact about sleep is that individual needs for 1
> it vary widely. Most adults sleep between seven and nine hours, 2
> but occasionally people turn up who need twelve hours or so,
> while some rare types can get by on three or four. Rarest of all 3
> are those legendary types who require almost no sleep at all;
> respected researchers have recently studied three such people.
> One of them—a healthy, happy woman in her seventies—sleeps 4
> about an hour every two or three days. The other two are men in 5
> early middle age, who get by on a few minutes a night. One of 6

them complains about the daily fifteen minutes or so he's forced to "waste" in sleeping.

—LAWRENCE A. MAYER, "The Confounding Enemy of Sleep"

After the general statement of his topic sentence, the author moves from common and less common sleep patterns (sentence 2) to the rarest pattern (sentence 3) and (in the remaining sentences) to particular people.

In the **specific-to-general** organization the elements of the paragraph build to a general conclusion. Such is the pattern of the next paragraph.

> It's disconcerting that so many college women, when asked how   1
> their children will be cared for if they themselves work, refer
> with vague confidence to "the day care center" as though there
> were some great amorphous kiddie watcher out there that the
> state provides. But such places, adequately funded, well run,   2
> and available to all, are still scarce in this country, particularly
> for middle-class women. And figures show that when she takes   3
> time off for family-connected reasons (births, child care), a
> woman's chances for career advancement plummet. In a job   4
> market that's steadily tightening and getting more competitive,
> these obstacles bode the kind of danger ahead that can shatter
> not only professions, but egos. A hard reality is that there's not   5
> much more support for our daughters who have family-plus-
> career goals than there was for us; there's simply a great deal
> more self- and societal pressure.
>
> —JUDITH WAX, *Starting in the Middle*

The author first states a common belief (sentence 1) and two reasons why it is a misconception (sentence 2 and 3). Then she explains the implications, first specifically (sentence 4) and then generally (sentence 5). The last sentence is the topic sentence of the paragraph.

When the details of a paragraph vary in significance, they can be arranged in a **climactic** order, from least to most important or dramatic. The following paragraph builds to a climax, saving the most dramatic example for last.

> Nature has put many strange tongues into the heads of her   1
> creatures. There is the frog's tongue, rooted at the front of the   2
> mouth so it can be protruded an extra distance for nabbing prey.
> There is the gecko lizard's tongue, so long and agile that the   3
> lizard uses it to wash its eyes. But the ultimate lingual whopper   4
> has been achieved in the anteater. The anteater's head, long as it   5
> is, is not long enough to contain the tremendous tongue which   6
> licks deep into anthills. Its tongue is not rooted in the mouth or
> throat: it is fastened to the breastbone.
>
> —ALAN DEVOE, "Nature's Utmost"

Similar to the organizations discussed so far are those which arrange details according to readers' likely understanding of them. In discussing the virtues of the CBC, for instance, you might proceed from **most familiar to least familiar**, from a well-known program your readers have probably seen to less well-known programs they may not have seen. Or in defending the right of government employees to strike, you might arrange your reasons from **simplest to most complex**, from the employees' need to be able to redress grievances to more subtle consequences for employer-employee relations.

2   Using parallel structures

Another way to achieve coherence, although not necessarily in every paragraph, is through **parallelism**—the use of similar grammatical structures for similar elements of meaning within a sentence or among sentences. (See Chapter 17 for a detailed discussion of parallelism.) Parallel structures help tie together the last three sentences in the paragraph on mummies (p. 93). In the following paragraph the parallel structures of *It is the* and *Democracy is the* link all sentences after the first one; and parallelism also appears within many of the sentences (for instance, *hole in the stuffed shirt* and *dent in the high hat* in sentence 4). The author, writing during World War II, was responding to a request from the Writer's War Board for a statement on the meaning of democracy.

> Surely the Board knows what democracy is. It is the line that forms on the right. It is the don't in Don't Shove. It is the hole in the stuffed shirt through which the sawdust slowly trickles; it is the dent in the high hat. Democracy is the recurrent suspicion that more than half of the people are right more than half of the time. It is the feeling of privacy in the voting booths, the feeling of communion in the libraries, the feeling of vitality everywhere. Democracy is the score at the beginning of the ninth. It is an idea which hasn't been disproved yet, a song the words of which have not gone bad. It's the mustard on the hot dog and the cream in the rationed coffee. Democracy is a request from a War Board, in the middle of a morning in the middle of a war, wanting to know what democracy is.
>
> —E. B. WHITE, *The Wild Flag*

(marginal line numbers: 1,2 3,4 5 6 7,8 9 10)

3   Repeating or restating words and word groups

Since every unified paragraph has only one topic, that topic is bound to recur in many of the sentences. In fact, repeating or restating key words or word groups is an important means of achieving paragraph coherence and of reminding your readers what the topic is. In the following paragraph, also by E. B. White, the repetition of *poets/poet* and *clearer/clear* ties the sentences together and stresses the important words of the paragraph.

"I wish poets could be clearer," shouted my wife angrily from the   1
next room. Hers is a universal longing. We would all like it if the   2,3
bards would make themselves plain, or we think we would. The   4
poets, however, are not easily diverted from their high mysterious ways. A poet dares be just so clear and no clearer; he   5
approaches lucid ground warily, like a mariner who is determined not to scrape his bottom on anything solid. A poet's   6
pleasure is to withhold a little of his meaning, to intensify by
mystification. He unzips the veil from beauty, but does not   7
remove it. A poet utterly clear is a trifle glaring.   8

—E. B. WHITE, "Poetry"

White's paragraph also includes some restatements of his key
words: *bards* for *poets* and *plain* and *lucid* for *clear*. Such restatements or **synonyms**—words with similar meaning—figure promi-
nently in the following paragraph.

Since the industrial revolution work has been rearranged and   1
much of the satisfaction has been rationalized out. Very few   2
workers have a chance to set their own task. Jobs have been   3
divided and subdivided so that each person performs a single
operation upon a continuous flow of parts or papers. Increas-   4
ingly the worker is denied not only the chance to set his own
task but even the chance to finish the task someone else sets for
him. The jobs are so fragmented that few workers can feel they   5
are helping to make a car or to issue an insurance policy. They   6
are merely repeating the same few motions, the same simple
calculations over and over throughout a lifetime of labor.

—BARBARA GARSON, *All the Livelong Day*

The writer's repetitions and restatements both bind her sentences
together and ensure that readers perceive her central idea, the seg-
menting of workers' jobs. *Work* (sentence 1) becomes a *task* (2, 4),
jobs (3, 5), *labor* (6). *Workers* and *the worker* (2, 4, 5) become *each
person* (3), *him* (4), *they* (5, 6). The work has been *rearranged* (1),
divided and subdivided (3), *fragmented* (5). It consists of *a single
operation* (3), *the same few motions, the same simple calculations* (6).

Though planned repetition can be effective, careless or excessive repetition weakens prose. See 31c.

4   **Using pronouns**

The previous examples illustrate yet another device for achieving paragraph coherence: the use of pronouns like *it, him, his,* and
they. **Pronouns** refer to and function as nouns (see 5a–2) and thus
can help relate sentences to each other. In the following paragraph
the pronouns *he, him,* and *his* indicate that the patient is still the
subject while enabling the writer to avoid repeating *the patient* or *the
patients.*

The experience is a familiar one to many emergency-room 1
medics. A patient who has been pronounced dead and unex- 2
pectedly recovers later describes what happened to him during
the moments—sometimes hours—when his body exhibited no
signs of life. According to one repeated account, the patient feels 3
himself rushing through a long, dark tunnel while noise rings in
his ears. Suddenly, he finds himself outside his own body look- 4
ing down with curious detachment at a medical team's efforts to
resuscitate him. He hears what is said, notes what is happening 5
but cannot communicate with anyone. Soon, his attention is 6
drawn to other presences in the room—spirits of dead relatives
or friends—who communicate with him nonverbally. Gradually 7
he is drawn to a vague "being of light." This being invites him to 8
evaluate his life and shows him highlights of his past in pano-
ramic vision. The patient longs to stay with the being of light but 9
is reluctantly drawn back into his physical body and recovers.
—KENNETH L. WOODWARD, "Life After Death?"

The pronouns in this paragraph give it coherence, in part
because they refer clearly to a noun. The opposite effect will occur if
the reader cannot tell exactly what noun a pronoun is meant to refer
to (see Chapter 12).

5   Being consistent

Being consistent is the most subtle way to achieve paragraph
coherence because readers are aware of consistency only when it is
absent. Consistency (or the lack of it) occurs primarily in the person
and number of nouns and pronouns and in the tense of verbs (see
Chapter 13). Although some shifts will be necessary because of
meaning, inappropriate shifts will interfere with a reader's ability to
follow the development of ideas. The writers of the following paragraphs destroy coherence by shifting person, number, and tense,
respectively.

SHIFTS IN PERSON

An enjoyable form of exercise is modern dance. If *one* wants to 1,2
stay in shape, *you* will find that dance tones and strengthens
most muscles. The leaping and stretching *you* do also improves 3
a person's balance and poise. And *I* found that *my* posture 4
improved after only a few months of dancing.

SHIFTS IN NUMBER

Politics is not the activity for everyone. It requires quickness 1,2
and patience at the same time. A *politician* must like speaking to 3
large groups of people and fielding questions without having
time to think of the answers. *Politicians* must also be willing to 4

compromise with the people *they* represent. And no matter how 5
good *a politician* is, *they* must give up on becoming popular with
all constituents. It isn't possible. 6

SHIFTS IN TENSE

I *am developing* an interest in filmmaking. I *tried* to take courses 1,2
that relate to camera work or theatre, and I *have read* books
about the technical and artistic sides of movies. Though I *would* 3
have liked to get a job on a movie set right away, I *will* probably
continue my formal education and training in filmmaking after
college. There simply *aren't* enough jobs available for all those 4
who *wanted* to be in films but *have* no direct experience.

6 Using transitional expressions

In addition to the methods for achieving coherence discussed
above, writers also rely on specific words and word groups to connect
sentences whose relationships may not be instantly clear to readers.
Sometimes the omission of these words or word groups will make an
otherwise coherent paragraph choppy and hard to follow, as the next
paragraph shows.

Medical science has succeeded in identifying the hundreds of 1
viruses that can cause the common cold. It has discovered the 2
most effective means of prevention. One person transmits the 3
cold viruses to another most often by hand. An infected person 4
covers his mouth to cough. He picks up the telephone. His 5,6
daughter picks up the telephone. She rubs her eyes. She has a 7,8
cold. It spreads. To avoid colds, people should wash their hands 9,10
often and keep their hands away from their faces.

This paragraph is unified and fundamentally coherent because
the sentences do seem related to each other. However, it is choppy to
read, and we can only guess at the precise relationships spelled out by
the italicized words below:

Medical science has *thus* succeeded in identifying the hundreds 1
of viruses that can cause the common cold. It has *also* discov- 2
ered the most effective means of prevention. One person 3
transmits the cold viruses to another most often by hand. *For* 4
instance, an infected person covers his mouth to cough. *Then* he 5
picks up the telephone. *Half an hour later*, his daughter picks up 6
the *same* telephone. *Immediately afterward*, she rubs her eyes. 7
Within a few days, she, too, has a cold. *And thus* it spreads. To 8,9,10
avoid colds, *therefore*, people should wash their hands often and
keep their hands away from their faces. —A STUDENT

Now the paragraph is smoother and clearer because the writer added
connections that tell us precisely what to make of each sentence.

The linking words and word groups are called **transitional expressions**. They state relationships clearly and thus enhance paragraph coherence. The box below presents a partial list of these expressions, arranged by the functions they perform.

¶ coh
3b

TRANSITIONAL EXPRESSIONS

To add or show sequence

again, also, and, and then, besides, equally important, finally, first, further, furthermore, in addition, in the first place, last, moreover, next, second, still, too

To compare

also, in the same way, likewise, similarly

To contrast

although, and yet, but, but at the same time, despite, even so, even though, for all that, however, in contrast. in spite of, nevertheless, notwithstanding, on the contrary, on the other hand, regardless, still, though, yet

To give examples or intensify

after all, an illustration of, even, for example, for instance, indeed, in fact, it is true, of course, specifically, that is, to illustrate, truly

To indicate place

above, adjacent to, below, elsewhere, farther on, here, near, nearby, on the other side, opposite to, there, to the east, to the left

To indicate time

after a while, afterward, as long as, as soon as, at last, at length, at that time, before, earlier, formerly, immediately, in the meantime, in the past, lately, later, meanwhile, now, presently, shortly, simultaneously, since, so far, soon, subsequently, then, thereafter, until, until now, when

To repeat, summarize, or conclude

all in all, altogether, as has been said, in brief, in conclusion, in other words, in particular, in short, in simpler terms, in summary, on the whole, that is, therefore, to put it differently, to summarize

To show cause or effect

accordingly, as a result, because, consequently, for this purpose, hence, otherwise, since, then, therefore, thereupon, thus, to this end, with this object

(For a discussion of transitional sentences and paragraphs, see pp. 86 and 125, respectively.)

7 Combining devices to achieve coherence

The devices we have examined for achieving coherence rarely appear in isolation in effective paragraphs. As any example in this chapter shows, writers usually combine sensible organization, parallelism, repetition, pronouns, consistency, and transitional expressions to help readers follow the development of ideas. And the devices also figure, naturally, in the whole essay (see 3e).

EXERCISE 5

Which of the organizational schemes discussed on pages 94–97 has been used in each of the following paragraphs?

1. The losing animal in a struggle saves itself from destruction by an act of submission, an act usually recognized and accepted by the winner. In some cases, for instance, the loser presents to its rival a vulnerable part of its body such as the top of the head or the fleshy part of the neck. The central nervous system of the winner recognizes the "meaning" of the presentation, and the instinct to kill is inhibited. Typical of this natural pattern is the behavior of two wolves in combat. As soon as one of the animals realizes it cannot win, it offers its vulnerable throat to the stronger wolf; instead of taking advantage of the opportunity, the victor relents, even though an instant earlier it had appeared frantic to reach the now proffered jugular vein.
—RENÉ DUBOS, "Territoriality and Dominance"

2. While French Canada remained under its somewhat uncertain destiny for ten years after the conquest, Nova Scotia was being opened up for settlement and was assuming its characteristic form of a British, in places a Scottish, province. A few settlers came to Pictou County in 1667; then, in 1772, a whole shipload of Highlanders, landing with kilts (forbidden in Scotland since Prince Charlie's rebellion), skean-dhu, and broadswords, the woods loud with the bag-pipes. Other Scots settled on the Gulf of St. Lawrence coast, later New Brunswick. Lumber and ship-building sprang into life. The great pines of Longfellow's "forest primeval" furnished masts for the British navy, 108 feet long, three feet through at the butt and worth £136 each. The Irish came also, 500 of them to Colchester in 1766 and others to Cumberland County, with Yorkshire Methodists to balance their exuberance. Cape Breton by 1765 had enough settlers to rank it as a county, with two members in the Halifax Assembly. Thus was set on maritime Canada the stamp it has never lost—its homeward look, its industry of the woods and the sea.
—STEPHEN LEACOCK, *Canada*

3. One must descend to the basement and move along a confus- 1
ing mazelike hall to reach it. Twice the passage seems to lead 2
against a blank wall; then at last one enters the brightly lighted
auditorium. And here, finally, are the social workers at the 3
reception desks; and there, waiting upon the benches rowed
beneath the pipes carrying warmth and water to the floors
above, are the patients. One sees white-jacketed psychiatrists 4
carrying charts appear and vanish behind screens that form the
improvised interviewing cubicles. All is an atmosphere of hur- 5
ried efficiency; and the concerned faces of the patients are
brightened by the friendly smiles and low-pitched voices of the
expert workers. One has entered the Lafargue Psychiatric 6
Clinic.   —RALPH ELLISON, *Shadow and Act*

4. There are three reasons, quite apart from scientific con- 1
siderations, that mankind needs to travel in space. The first 2
reason is the need for garbage disposal: we need to transfer
industrial processes into space, so that the earth may remain a
green and pleasant place for our grandchildren to live in. The 3
second reason is the need to escape material impoverishment:
the resources of this planet are finite, and we shall not forego
forever the abundant solar energy and minerals and living space
that are spread out all around us. The third reason is our 4
spiritual need for an open frontier: the ultimate purpose of
space travel is to bring to humanity not only scientific discoveries and an occasional spectacular show on television but a real
expansion of our spirit.
                    —FREEMAN DYSON, "Disturbing the Universe"

EXERCISE 6

After the topic sentence (sentence 1), the sentences in each paragraph below have been deliberately scrambled to make the paragraph incoherent. Using the topic sentence and other clues as
guides, rearrange the sentences in each paragraph to form a well-
organized, coherent unit.

1. The animal is an eating machine, even if it is not always 1
hungry. It *must* chaw continually with its chisel-like teeth or it 2
will perish. Trees up to forty-two inches in diameter have been 3
felled by these determined lumber-rats, their heads tilted as they
chew against the grain, spitting out the chips. The incisors can 4
chop their way through a six-inch tree in five minutes. Its four 5
self-sharpening incisors, coated with bright orange enamel, can
grow up to a length of seven inches and if not worn down by
constant gnawing will eventually pierce the beaver's skull.
                    —PETER NEWMAN, *Company of Adventurers*

2. Because that settlement and that land were my first and for 1
many years my only real knowledge of this planet, in some
profound way they remain my world, my way of viewing. I am 2

always unable to argue this point effectively. My eyes were   3
formed there. The town of my childhood could be called bizarre,   4
agonizingly repressive or cruel at times, and the land in which it
grew could be called harsh in the violence of its seasonal
changes. All I can say is—well, you really have to live there to   5
know that country. Towns like ours, set in a sea of land, have   6
been described thousands of times as dull, bleak, flat, uninteresting. I have had it said to me that the railway trip across   7
Canada is spectacular, except for the prairies, when it would be
desirable to go to sleep for several days, until the ordeal is over.
Never dull. But never merely flat or uninteresting.   8,9
         —MARGARET LAURENCE, "Where the World Began"

EXERCISE 7

Study the paragraphs in Exercise 1 (pp. 89–90) for the authors' use
of various devices to achieve paragraph coherence. Look especially
for parallel structures and ideas, repetition and restatement, pronouns, and transitional expressions.

EXERCISE 8

The paragraph below is incoherent because of inconsistencies in
person, number, or tense. Identify the inconsistencies and revise
the paragraph to give it coherence.

I rebel against the idea of males always being the sole family   1
provider. For me to be happy, I needed to feel useful, and so I   2
work to support myself and my daughter. I did not feel that it is   3
wrong for one to be a housewife while a man supports your
household, but that way is not for me. I enjoy the business   4
world, and I have been pleased with my job. Working, I make   5
enough now to support the two of us, and I know that when I
graduate, I will be able to earn even more. I can do very well as   6
my own provider.

EXERCISE 9

Transitional expressions have been removed from the following
paragraph at the numbered blanks. Fill in each blank with an
appropriate transitional expression (1) to contrast, (2) to intensify,
and (3) to show effect. Consult the list on page 101 if necessary.
All over the country people are swimming, jogging, weight-
lifting, dancing, walking, playing tennis—doing anything to keep

fit. __(1)__ this school has consistently refused to construct and equip a fitness center. The school has __(2)__ refused to open existing athletic facilities to all students, not just those playing organized sports. __(3)__ students have no place to exercise except in their rooms and on dangerous public roads.

EXERCISE 10

Write a coherent paragraph from the following information, combining and rewriting sentences as necessary. First, begin the paragraph with the topic sentence given and arrange the supporting sentences in a climactic order. Then combine and rewrite the supporting sentences, helping the reader see connections by introducing parallelism, repetition and restatement, pronouns, consistency, and transitional expressions.

TOPIC SENTENCE

Hypnosis is far superior to drugs for relieving tension.

SUPPORTING INFORMATION

Hypnosis has none of the dangerous side effects of the drugs that relieve tension.

Tension-relieving drugs can cause weight loss or gain, illness, or even death.

Hypnosis is non-addicting.

Most of the drugs that relieve tension do foster addiction.

Tension-relieving drugs are expensive.

Hypnosis is inexpensive even for people who have not mastered self-hypnosis.

EXERCISE 11

Develop three of the following topic sentences into coherent paragraphs. Organize your information by space, by time, or for emphasis, as seems most appropriate. Use parallelism, repetition and restatement, pronouns, consistency, and transitional expressions to link sentences.

1. Of all my courses, _____ is the one that I think will serve me best throughout life.
2. The movie (or book) had an exciting plot.
3. Although we Canadians face many problems, the one we should concentrate on solving first is _____ .
4. The most dramatic building in town is the _____ .
5. Children should not have to worry about the future.

3c Developing the paragraph

A paragraph may be both unified and coherent but still be skimpy, unconvincing, or otherwise inadequate. The following paragraph is unified and coherent: it adheres to the topic of bad television commercials, and the relations among sentences are apparent. But it is not an effective paragraph.

> Despite complaints from viewers, television commercials aren't   1
> getting any more realistic. Their makers still present idealized   2
> people in unreal situations. And the advertisers also persist in   3
> showing a version of male-female relationships that can't exist
> in more than two households. What do the advertisers know   4
> about us, or about how we see ourselves, that makes them
> continue to plunge millions of dollars into these kinds of com-
> mercials?

Sentences 2 and 3 create expectations in our minds: we anticipate that the writer will give examples of commercials showing idealized people and unrealistic male-female relationships. But our expectations are disappointed because the paragraph lacks **development**, completeness. It does not provide enough information for us to evaluate the writer's assertion in sentence 1.

A well-developed paragraph always provides the specific information that readers need and expect in order to understand you and to stay interested in what you say. Often you may develop and arrange this information according to a particular pattern that is determined by your topic and what you want to say about it.

1 Using specific information

If they are sound, the general statements you make in any writing will be based on what you have experienced, observed, read, and thought. Readers will assume as much and will expect you to provide the evidence for your statements. They need details, examples, and reasons—the heart of paragraph development—to understand and appreciate your meaning.

The following is the actual version of the paragraph discussed above. Notice how the added descriptions of commercials (in italics) turn a sketchy paragraph into an interesting and convincing one.

> Despite complaints from viewers, television commercials aren't   1
> getting any more realistic. Their makers still present idealized   2
> people in unreal situations. *Friendly shopkeepers stock only their*   3
> *favourite brand of toothpaste or coffee or soup. A mother cleans*   4
> *and buffs her kitchen floor to a mirror finish so her baby can play*

on it. A rosy-cheeked pregnant woman uses two babies, two 5
packaged diapers neatly dissected, and two ink blotters to demon-
strate one diaper's superior absorbency to her equally rosy-cheeked
and pregnant friend. The advertisers also persist in showing a 6
version of male-female relationships that can't exist in more
than two households. *The wife panics because a meddlesome* 7
neighbour points out that her husband's shirt is dirty. Or she fears 8
for her marriage because her finicky husband doesn't like her
coffee. What do the advertisers know about us, or about how we 9
see ourselves, that makes them continue to plunge millions of
dollars into these kinds of commercials?   —A STUDENT

In this paragraph the writer has recognized that sentences 2 and 6
create expectations for supporting examples, and she has duly
responded to these expectations. Whereas the general statements
merely *tell* us about the commercials, the detailed examples *show*
them to us.

2   **Using a pattern of development**

Sometimes you may have difficulty developing an idea, or you
may not see the most effective way to shape the information you
have. Then you can use one of the patterns of paragraph development
that correspond to patterns of essay development discussed on pages
20–22 and 41–43. Experienced writers use these patterns all the time,
often unconsciously. Inexperienced writers can ask themselves a
series of questions about an idea that will suggest how to develop it
and how to organize the supporting information.

How did it happen?

Asking how something happened leads to **narration**, the retelling of a sequence of events, usually in the order of their occurrence
(that is, chronologically). The paragraph by Arthur C. Clarke on page
95 narrates the stages of a star's death. Here is another narrative
paragraph in which events occupy not weeks but moments. The
author's larger concern is contemporary language such as "sharing
feelings" that reduces complex human interactions to formulas.

Years ago, my husband and I rented a summer place in which 1
we found ourselves surrounded by a tightly knit community
that seemed to be speaking some common and slightly alien
language. One night, at a party, one of these neighbors com- 2
plained about the Moonie encampment around the corner and
my husband—whose unconscious must surely have known
what his conscious mind was slower to suspect—said that the
Moonies weren't half so bad as . . . and he mentioned an espe-

cially strident human-potential group then receiving a good deal of publicity and notoriety. As a hush fell over the room, it 3 dawned on us that the language we'd been puzzling over all summer was the language of that same group. No one breathed 4 until at last our host turned to my husband and said, "Thank you for sharing that with us."

—FRANCINE PROSE, "Therapy Clichés"

As this paragraph illustrates, a narrative usually does not correspond to real time but collapses transitional or background events (as in sentence 1) and then expands the events of particular interest (2–4). In addition, writers often rearrange events, as when they simulate the workings of memory by briefly flashing back to an earlier time.

How does it look, sound, feel, smell, taste?

Detailing the sensory qualities of a person, place, or thing is the act of **description**. You use concrete and specific words to evoke in readers your own experience of the subject. Some description is **subjective**: the writer filters the subject through his or her biases and emotions. In Donald Hall's subjective description on page 94, the *bright* garden and the mountain that *loomed in the blue distance* indicate Hall's feelings about these physical features of his environment.

In contrast to subjective description, journalists and scientists often favour description that is **objective**, conveying the subject without bias or emotion. As the following example from a psychology paper illustrates, the writer of objective description tries to record all relevant sensory data as specifically as possible without interpretation.

The two toddlers, both boys, sat together for half an hour in a 1 3-m^2 room with yellow walls (one with a two-way mirror for observation) and a brown carpet. The room was unfurnished 2 except for two small chairs and about two dozen toys. The boys' 3 interaction was generally tense. They often struggled physically 4 and verbally over several toys, especially a large red beach ball and a small wooden fire engine. The larger of the two boys often 5 pushed the smaller away or pried his hands from the desired object. This larger boy never spoke, but he did make grunting 6 sounds when he was engaging the other. In turn, the smaller boy 7 twice uttered piercing screams of "No!" and once shouted "Stop that!" When he was left alone, he hummed and muttered to 8 himself. —A STUDENT

How can it be illustrated or supported?

Some ideas can be developed simply by **illustration or support**—supplying detailed examples or reasons. The writer of the paragraph on television commercials (pp. 106–07) developed her idea with several specific examples of each general statement. You can also supply a single extended example, as the author of the following paragraph does to illustrate his assertion (sentence 1) about cultural differences in the ways people communicate.

> One of my earliest discoveries in the field of intercultural com- 1
> munication was that the position of the bodies of people in
> conversation varies with the culture. Even so, it used to puzzle 2
> me that a special Arab friend seemed unable to walk and talk at
> the same time. After years in the United States, he could not 3
> bring himself to stroll along, facing forward while talking. Our 4
> progress would be arrested while he edged ahead, cutting
> slightly in front of me and turning sideways so we could see
> each other. Once in this position, he would stop. His behavior 5, 6
> was explained when I learned that for the Arabs to view the
> other person peripherally is regarded as impolite, and to sit or
> stand back-to-back is considered very rude. You must be 7
> involved when interacting with Arabs who are friends.
> —EDWARD T. HALL, *The Hidden Dimension*

The details of this example are arranged in a rough chronological sequence. In a paragraph containing several examples, a climactic organization is often effective; see the paragraph by Alan Devoe on page 96 for an example.

Sometimes you can develop a paragraph by providing your reasons for stating a general idea. Such is the method used in the following paragraph.

> It is time to defend the welfare state—taxes, bureaucrats, rules 1
> and regulations—the whole thing. Not only because it actually 2
> helps people who need help and subsidizes and enables a range
> of socially valuable activities: it does all that, and all that has to
> be done. There is another, and ultimately a more important, 3
> reason for defending the welfare state. It expresses a certain 4
> civil spirit, a sense of mutuality, a commitment to justice.
> Without that sense, no society can survive for long as a decent 5
> place to live—not for the needy, and not for anyone else.
> —MICHAEL WALZER, "The Community"

Sentences 2, 4, and 5 provide reasons for the general assertion in sentence 1. As is often the case in such paragraphs, the reasons are arranged in a climactic order. (For another example, see the paragraph by Freeman Dyson in Exercise 5, p. 103.)

¶ dev

3c

What is it? What does it encompass, and what does it exclude?

Asking "What is it?" leads to development by **definition**— saying what something is and is not, specifying the characteristics that distinguish it from the other members of its class. You can easily define concrete, non-controversial terms in a single sentence: *A knife is a cutting instrument* (its class) *with a sharp blade set in a handle* (the characteristics that set it off from, say, scissors or a razor blade). But defining a complicated, abstract, or controversial topic often requires extended explanation (see 4d-2), and you may need to devote a whole paragraph or even an essay to it. Such a definition may provide examples to identify the subject's characteristics. It may also involve other methods of development discussed below, such as division (separating things into their parts), classification (combining things into groups), or comparison and contrast.

The following is a paragraph developed by definition. It is from an essay asserting that "quality in product and effort has become a vanishing element of current civilization."

> In the hope of possibly reducing the hail of censure which is   1
> certain to greet this essay (I am thinking of going to Alaska or
> possibly Patagonia in the week it is published), let me say that
> quality, as I understand it, means investment of the best skill
> and effort possible to produce the finest and most admirable
> result possible. Its presence or absence in some degree charac-   2
> terizes every man-made object, service, skilled or unskilled
> labor—laying bricks, painting a picture, ironing shirts, practic-
> ing medicine, shoemaking, scholarships, writing a book. You do   3
> it well or you do it half-well. Materials are sound and durable or   4
> they are sleazy; method is painstaking or whatever is easiest.
> Quality is achieving or reaching for the highest standard as   5
> against being satisfied with the sloppy or fraudulent. It is hon-   6
> esty of purpose as against catering to cheap or sensational
> sentiment. It does not allow compromise with the second-rate.   7
> —BARBARA TUCHMAN, "The Decline of Quality"

To explain just what she means by *quality*—the key word of her essay—the author first provides a general definition (sentence 1) and then refines it with examples of the range of activities in which quality may figure (2), followed by a list of the characteristics that distinguish quality from non-quality (3–7). In this paragraph the sentences after the first move roughly from specific to general, but an arrangement by increasing specificity, importance, or complexity often works in definition as well.

What are its parts or characteristics? Or what groups or categories can it be sorted into?

Separating a single thing into its parts is the activity of **division** (also called **analysis**). Using division, you might examine a family by dividing it into its individual members—mother, father, daughter, son. Grouping many things according to their similarities is the activity of **classification**. Using classification to describe families, you might examine family structures in various cultures—matriarchal, patriarchal, nuclear, extended, and so on. Division and classification are so closely related that writers often combine them in developing an idea, a paragraph, or an essay. Thus in describing the family you might first classify the types and then divide each type into the separate roles of the individual family members.

In the following paragraph the writer divides a small portion of a daily newspaper into its parts, giving the technical name for each part.

> A typical daily newspaper compresses considerable informa- 1
> tion into the top of the first page, above the headlines. The most 2
> prominent feature of this space, the newspaper's name, is called
> the *logo* or *nameplate*. Under the logo and set off by rules is a 3
> line of small type called the *folio line*, which contains the date of
> the issue, the volume and issue numbers, copyright informa-
> tion, and the price. To the right of the logo is a block of small 4
> type called a *weather ear*, a summary of the day's forecast. And 5
> above the logo is a *skyline*, a kind of advertisement in which the
> paper's editors highlight a special feature of the issue.
>
> —A STUDENT

Division always begins with a single object or concept; in the preceding paragraph it is a segment of a newspaper's front page. The task is then to identify and explain the distinct elements that constitute the object or concept. The elements might be arranged spatially as they are above, or in order of importance or complexity.

In the following paragraph the writer classifies parents.

> In my experience, the parents who hire daytime sitters for their 1
> school-age children tend to fall into one of three groups. The 2
> first group includes parents who work and want someone to be
> at home when the children return from school. These parents 3
> are looking for an extension of themselves, someone who will
> give the care they would give if they were at home. The second 4
> group includes parents who may be home all day themselves but
> are too disorganized or too frazzled by their children's demands
> to handle child care alone. They are looking for an organizer 5
> and helpmate. The third and final group includes parents who 6
> do not want to be bothered by their children, whether they are

home all day or not. Unlike the parents in the first two groups,   7
who care for their children whenever and however they can,
these parents are looking for a permanent substitute for
themselves.   —A STUDENT

The groups in this paragraph are arranged in a climactic order, but
complexity or familiarity may also serve to organize a classification.
This paragraph also illustrates several principles of classification.
First, the subject being classified is plural (parents), in contrast to the
singular subject of division. Second, the classes or groups are alike in
at least one basic way: all hire sitters for their children. And third, the
classes do not overlap, as would parents who work and parents who
don't because both groups include some uncaring and some caring
parents.

How is it like, or different from, other things?

Asking about similarities and differences leads to **comparison
and contrast**. The two may be used separately or together to develop
an idea or to relate two or more things. In the following paragraph
the author contrasts a man's and a woman's relationships to the
house in which they live.

A house is all right for a man to work in. He brings his work into   1,2
the house, a place is cleared for it; the house rearranges itself as
best it can around him. Everybody recognizes that his work   3
exists. He is not expected to answer the telephone, to find things   4
that are lost, to see why the children are crying, or to feed the
cat. He can shut his door. Imagine (I said) a mother shutting her   5,6
door, and the children knowing she is behind it; why, the very
thought of it is outrageous to them. A woman who sits staring   7
into space, into a country that is not her husband's or her
children's is likewise known to be an offense against nature. So a   8
house is not the same for a woman. She is not someone who   9
walks into the house to make use of it, and will walk out again.
She is the house; there is no separation possible.   10
        —ALICE MUNRO, "The Office"

This paragraph illustrates one of two common ways of organizing a comparison and contrast: **subject-by-subject**, with the two
subjects discussed separately, first one and then the other. The next
paragraph illustrates the other common organization: **point-by-
point**, with the two subjects discussed side by side and matched
feature for feature.

This emphasis on the unfairness of language to women is   1
misplaced. We should be erasing all bias from language, and   2
that means bias against men as well. If a female pilot should not   3
be stigmatized as an "aviatrix," then a male pilot should not be
stigmatized as a "fly-boy." If it is unfair to label women as   4

"witches," then it is equally unfair to label men as "cads." If a   6
woman should not be called a "dog," then a man should not be
called a "nerd" or a "wimp." If it demeans the homeless woman
to call her a "baglady," then it also demeans the homeless man to
call him a "bum."   —A STUDENT

The most effective comparisons show similarities between subjects usually perceived as different, such as the words used for
women and men in the preceding paragraph. Contrasts, however, are
most effective when they show differences between subjects usually
perceived as similar, such as the two attitudes toward "the house"
illustrated in Munro's paragraph.

Is it comparable to something that is in a different class but more familiar?

Whereas we draw comparisons and contrasts between elements in the same general class (basketball players, words), we link
elements in different classes with a special kind of comparison called
analogy. Most often in analogy we illuminate or explain an unfamiliar, complex, abstract class of things with a familiar and concrete
class of things. In the following paragraph the author develops
an analogy between writing style (abstract) and a distance runner
(concrete).

> The good style is the lean style. Like a good distance runner, it   1,2
> hasn't an ounce of excess fat anywhere on it. And like the good   3
> distance runner, it moves without excess motion. Its arms don't   4
> flail out in all directions; they swing easily at the sides in a
> beautiful economy of effort. A good style has the same grace and   5
> beauty in its motion as a good athlete because there's nothing
> wasted. Everything is there for a purpose.   6
> —LAURENCE PERRINE, "Fifteen Ways to
> Write Five Hundred Words"

In the next paragraph the author draws an analogy between the
weather and human combat.

> In an age all too familiar with war the yearly cycle of the weather   1
> is well imagined in terms of combat. It is a war in which a   2
> stronghold or citadel sometimes beats off assault after assault.
> More often the battle-line shifts quickly back and forth across   3
> thousands of miles—a war of sudden raids and swift counterat-
> tacks, of stern pitched battles, of deep forays and confused
> struggles high in the air. In the Northern Hemisphere the   4
> opponents are the Arctic and the Tropics, North against South.
> Uncertain ally to the South—now bringing, now withdrawing   5
> aid—the sun shifts among the signs of the zodiac. And the chief   6
> battle-line is known as the Polar Front.
> —GEORGE R. STEWART, *Storm*

What are its causes or its effects?

When you analyse why something happened or what is likely to happen, then you are determining causes and effects. **Cause-and-effect analysis** is especially useful in writing about social, economic, or political events or problems, as the next paragraphs illustrate. In the first, the author looks at the causes of Japanese collectivism.

> The *shinkansen* or "bullet train" speeds across the rural areas of Japan giving a quick view of cluster after cluster of farmhouses surrounded by rice paddies. This particular pattern did not develop purely by chance, but as a consequence of the technology peculiar to the growing of rice, the staple of the Japanese diet. The growing of rice requires the construction and maintenance of an irrigation system, something that takes many hands to build. More importantly, the planting and the harvesting of rice can only be done efficiently with the cooperation of twenty or more people. The "bottom line" is that a single family working alone cannot produce enough rice to survive, but a dozen families working together can produce a surplus. Thus the Japanese have had to develop the capacity to work together in harmony, no matter what the forces of disagreement or social disintegration, in order to survive.
>
> —WILLIAM OUCHI, *Theory Z: How American Business Can Meet the Japanese Challenge*

In sentences 1, 2, and 6 Ouchi specifies an effect: the Japanese live close together and work in harmony. The middle sentences explain the conditions that caused this effect: the Japanese depend heavily on rice, and growing rice demands collective effort.

Cause-and-effect paragraphs tend to focus either on causes, as Ouchi's does, or on effects, as the next paragraph does.

> The War of 1812 thus tended to bring British North America together and strengthened the bond with Britain. Any common feelings among the colonists, however, were largely directed against the United States. This anti-American spirit was still a narrow basis on which to build a Canadian nationalism. Anti-Americanism was particularly evident in Upper Canada. Further American settlement was largely prevented there, and American settlers already in the province were in danger of persecution—the Loyalists' case in reverse—if their declarations of British sentiments were not loud enough. Nevertheless, on the whole these reactions to the strain of the War of 1812 were understandable; and not an extreme price to pay for the survival of British North America.
>
> —J. M. S. CARELESS, *Canada: A Story of Challenge*

How does it work?

When you explain how something works, you explain the steps in a **process**. Paragraphs developed by analysing a process are usually organized chronologically or spatially, as the steps in the process occur. Some process analyses tell the reader how to do something. For example:

> Car owners waste money when they pay a mechanic to change 1
> the engine oil. The job is not difficult, even for someone who 2
> knows little about cars. All one needs is a wrench to remove the 3
> drain plug, a large, flat pan to collect the draining oil, plastic
> bottles to dispose of the used oil, and fresh oil. First, warm up 4
> the car's engine so that the oil will flow more easily. When the 5
> engine is warm, shut it off and remove its oil-filler cap (the
> owner's manual shows where this cap is). Then locate the drain 6
> plug under the engine (again consulting the owner's manual for
> its location) and place the flat pan under the plug. Remove the 7
> plug with the wrench, letting the oil flow into the pan. When the 8
> oil stops flowing, replace the plug and, at the engine's filler hole,
> add the amount and kind of fresh oil specified by the owner's
> manual. Pour the used oil into the plastic bottles and take it 9
> to a waste-oil collector, which any garage mechanic can
> recommend.   —A STUDENT

Other process analyses explain how a process is done or how it works in nature. The following paragraph, for example, explains how an island of mangrove trees begins "from scratch."

> Nor can a tree live without soil. A hurricane-born mangrove 1,2
> island may bring its own soil to the sea. But other mangrove 3
> trees make their own soil—and their own islands—from
> scratch. These are the ones which interest me. The seeds germi- 4,5
> nate in the fruit on the tree. The germinated embryo can drop 6
> anywhere—say, onto a dab of floating muck. The heavy root end 7
> sinks; a leafy plumule unfurls. The tiny seedling, afloat, is on its 8
> way. Soon aerial roots shooting out in all directions trap debris. 9
> The sapling's networks twine, the interstices narrow, and water 10
> calms in the lee. Bacteria thrive on organic broth; amphipods 11
> swarm. These creatures grow and die at the tree's wet feet. The 12,13
> soil thickens, accumulating rainwater, leaf rot, seashells, and
> guano; the island spreads.   —ANNIE DILLARD, "Sojourner"

Combining patterns of development

Whatever pattern you choose as the basis for developing a paragraph, other patterns may also prove helpful. We have seen combined patterns often throughout this section: Tuchman uses contrast to define *quality* (p. 110); Munro uses examples to contrast male and female attitudes toward "the house" (p. 112); Perrine uses analogy to define a good writing style (p. 113).

As we will see in 3e, the paragraphs within an essay inevitably will be developed with a variety of patterns, even when one controlling pattern develops and structures the entire essay.

3 | Checking length

The average paragraph contains between 100 and 150 words, or between four and eight sentences. These numbers are averages, of course. The actual length of a paragraph depends on its topic, the role it plays in developing the thesis of the essay, and its position in the essay. Nevertheless, very short paragraphs are often inadequately developed; they may leave readers with a sense of incompleteness. And very long paragraphs often contain irrelevant details or develop two or more topics; readers may have difficulty sorting out or remembering ideas.

When you are revising your essay, reread the paragraphs that seem very long or very short, checking them especially for unity and adequate development. If the paragraph wanders, cut everything from it that does not support your main idea (such as sentences that you might begin with *By the way*). If it is underdeveloped, supply the specific details, examples, or reasons needed, or try one of the methods of development we have discussed here.

EXERCISE 12

The following paragraphs are not well developed. Analyse them, looking especially for general statements that lack support or leave questions in your mind. Then rewrite one into a well-developed paragraph, supplying your own concrete details or examples.

1. One big difference between successful and unsuccessful   1
teachers is the quality of communication. A successful teacher   2
is sensitive to students' needs and excited by the course subject.
In contrast, an unsuccessful teacher seems uninterested in   3
students and bored by the subject.

2. Gestures are one of our most important means of communi-   1
cation. We use them instead of speech. We use them to supple-   2,3
ment the words we speak. And we use them to communicate   4
some feelings or meanings that words cannot adequately
express.

3. Children who have been disciplined too much are often easy   1
to spot. Their behaviour toward adults may reflect the harsh   2
treatment they have received from adults. And their behaviour   3
toward other children may be uncontrolled.

EXERCISE 13

¶ dev
3c

Identify the pattern or patterns of development in each of the
following paragraphs. Where does the author supply specific information to achieve development?

1. St. Asaph's is episcopal. As a consequence it has in it and 1,2
about it all those things which go to make up the episcopal
church—brass tablets let into its walls, blackbirds singing in its
elm trees, parishioners who dine at eight o'clock, and a rector
who wears a little crucifix and dances the tango.

. . . .

    There could be no greater contrast with Mr. Fareforth Fur- 3
long [the rector of St. Asaph's] than the minister of St. Osoph's
the Rev. Dr. McTeague, who was also honorary professor of
philosophy at the university. The one was young, the other was 4
old; the one could dance, the other could not; the one moved
about at church picnics and lawn teas among a bevy of disciples
in pink and blue sashes; the other moped around under the trees
of the university campus, with blinking eyes that saw nothing
and an abstracted mind that had spent fifty years in trying to
reconcile Hegel with St. Paul, and was still busy with it. Mr. 5
Furlong went forward with the times; Dr. McTeague slid quietly
backwards with the centuries.

              —STEPHEN LEACOCK, "The Rival Churches of
                      St. Asaph and St. Osoph"

2. I am a Canadian, and a birthright one, in spite of the unin- 1
formed xenophobe who recently, in an issue of *Canadian
Dimension*, denounced me as a "former Englishman." When I 2
try to set out the reasons why I take pleasure in this fact, I find
myself at first evoking eloquent vaguenesses. The land attracts 3
me, of course; I feel a swell of emotion coasting in over the great
muddy fan of the Fraser from Japan with the mountains rim-
ming the horizon, or sailing up the St. Lawrence with the
northern lights pulsating over the starboard sky. I know of no 4
city, among the hundreds I have passed through or lived in in
Europe, Asia, Africa, and the Americas, which I would sooner
make my place of constant return than Vancouver, whose combination of sea, mountain, and pearly light seems to be inimita-
ble. And as I look forward to the day, a week ahead, when I shall 5
start on a long meandering drive across the country from Pacific
to Atlantic, I feel a habitual excitement mounting at the prospect of those prodigal vastnesses—mountains—then plains—
then lakes, all enough for a dozen normal lands—and the great
river at the end, duplicating the great river at the beginning,
with Montreal as a crown of human vitality and blessed with
dozen-landed disunity.

              —GEORGE WOODCOCK, "Various Americas"

3. A dying person may pass through five separate attitude ¹
stages, according to the psychiatrist Elisabeth Kübler-Ross. In ²
the first stage, denial, the patient ignores symptoms of illness
and refuses to accept diagnosis and sometimes even treatment.
Then, in a stage of anger, the patient feels outraged at the ³
injustice of dying. A stage of bargaining may follow, when the ⁴
patient tries to make an exchange with the hospital staff or his
or her family or God for a little more time. Then the patient may ⁵
enter a period of depression that comes when he or she realizes
that everything is soon to be finished, that life is almost over.
And finally, the dying person may feel acceptance of death, a ⁶
quiet resignation to the power of death.   —A STUDENT

4. In American society there exist people classified by encyclo- ¹
pedia salesmen as "mooches." Mooches can be generally ²
defined as people who like to buy the product; they see the
encyclopedia salesman as the bearer of a rare and desirable gift.
Mooches are people whose incomes and occupational levels ³
exceed their educational attainments; persons whose income is
in the middle-middle range but whose education doesn't exceed
high school, or may not even attain that level. Without educa- ⁴
tion, mooches cannot have professional status, although they
might make as much money as a professional; consequently,
mooches try to assume professionalism by accruing what they
think are indications of professional status. A conspicuously ⁵
displayed set of encyclopedias tells the mooch's friends that he
can afford to consume conspicuously, that he values a highly
normative product over creature comforts, and that he provides
for the long-range benefit of his protectorate. The mooch asso- ⁶
ciates all these characteristics with professional persons. For ⁷
him, then, encyclopedias function as easily interpreted profes-
sional-status indicators.
            —LYNN M. BULLER, "The Encyclopedia Game"

EXERCISE 14

Write a well-developed paragraph on one of the following ideas or
an idea of your own. Or take an underdeveloped paragraph from
something you have written and revise it. Be sure your paragraph is
unified and coherent as well as adequately developed with specific
information.

1. how billboards blight (or decorate) the landscape
2. why you like (or don't like) poetry
3. a place where you feel comfortable (or uncomfortable)
4. an unusual person you know
5. an instance of unusual kindness or cruelty

EXERCISE 15

Identify an appropriate pattern or patterns for developing a paragraph on each of the following topics. (Choose from narration, description, illustration or support, definition, division or classification, comparison and contrast, analogy, cause-and-effect analysis, and process analysis.)

1. the influences of a person's biorhythms or astrological sign on his or her behaviour
2. a typical situation comedy on television
3. tuning an engine
4. rock music and country music
5. why read newspapers
6. what loyalty is
7. the picture of aliens shown by a recent science-fiction movie
8. dancing as pure motion, like a kite in the wind
9. an especially vivid moment in your life
10. the kinds of fans at a hockey game (or a game in some other sport)

EXERCISE 16

Write a paragraph about a topic from Exercise 15, using the development pattern you chose in that exercise. Or if you prefer, choose a topic of your own and develop it with one of the patterns discussed in the text. Be sure the paragraph is also unified and coherent.

EXERCISE 17

Write nine unified, coherent, and well-developed paragraphs, each one developed with a different pattern. Draw on the topics provided here or in Exercise 15. Or choose your own topics.

1. *Narration*
   an experience of public
      speaking
   a disappointment
   leaving home
   waking up

2. *Description (objective or subjective)*
   your room
   a crowded or deserted
      place
   a food
   an intimidating person

3. *Illustration or support*
   why study
   having a headache
   the best sports event
   usefulness (or uselessness)
      of a self-help book

4. *Definition*
   humour
   an adult
   fear
   authority

5. *Division and classification*

the segments of a
television news show
factions in a campus
controversy
styles of playing poker
parts of a barn

6. *Comparison and contrast*

driving a friend's car and
driving your own car
AM and FM radio
announcers
high school and university
football
movies on TV and in a
theatre

7. *Analogy*

paying taxes and giving
blood
religious beliefs and a
building's foundation
graduating from high
school and being
released from prison

8. *Cause-and-effect analysis*

connection between
tension and anger
causes of failing a course
connection between credit
cards and debt
causes of a serious
accident

9. *Process analysis*

preparing for a job
interview
making a cabinet
protecting your home from
burglars
making a jump shot

3d Writing special kinds of paragraphs

Several kinds of paragraphs do not always follow our guidelines for unity, coherence, development, and length because they
serve special functions. These are the essay introduction, the essay
conclusion, the transitional or emphatic paragraph, and the paragraph of spoken dialogue.

1 Opening an essay

Most essays open with a paragraph that draws readers from
their world into the writer's world. An opening paragraph should
focus readers' attention on the topic and arouse their curiosity about
what the writer has to say. It should be concise. It should specify what
the writer will discuss and what his or her attitude is. It should be
sincere. And it should be interesting without misrepresenting the
content of the essay that follows.

¶
3d

SOME STRATEGIES FOR OPENING PARAGRAPHS

1. State the subject.
2. Use a quotation.
3. Relate an incident.
4. Create an image.
5. Ask a question.
6. State an opinion.
7. Make a historical comparison or contrast.

The safest kind of introduction opens with a statement of the essay's general subject, clarifies or limits the subject in one or more sentences, and then, in the thesis sentence, asserts the point of the essay (see 1g). This is the pattern in the following paragraph, which introduces an essay on the Canadian Charter of Rights and Freedoms.

> Nobody ever called Pierre Trudeau a supporter of the American [1] way of life, but it has recently become clear that in a strange and unexpected way he presided over the Americanization of Canada. It has been commonplace for a long time to say that our [2] major political institutions have been growing steadily closer to those of the United States: the concentration of power in the person of the prime minister has often and justly been called "presidential," and our political parties—with their flamboyant and expensive leadership conventions, their opinion polling, and their TV advertising—have slavishly copied the American models, often bringing in hired American experts to tell them how to do it. It might be argued, however, that these are simply [3] modern practices and techniques, made inevitable by the growth of government and mass communications. But the prin- [4] ciple that Trudeau brought us with the Canadian Charter of Rights and Freedoms is absolutely and intrinsically American and reaches back to the roots of the U.S. Constitution in the eighteenth century. It is the principle that judges know better [5] than politicians what is good for everyone.
>   —ROBERT FULFORD, "Charter of Wrongs"

The writer's first sentence introduces his subject. The next sentence elaborates on the subject by introducing examples that are well known. The third sentence is a bridge to the writer's specific purpose. The fourth sentence states the thesis explicitly, and the final sentence clarifies it. The following is another example of this form of introductory paragraph.

> Can your home or office computer make you sterile? Can it [1, 2] strike you blind or dumb? The answer is: probably not. Never- [3, 4] theless, reports of side effects relating to computer use should be examined, especially in the area of birth defects, eye

complaints, and postural difficulties. Although little conclusive   5
evidence exists to establish a causal link between computer use
and problems of this sort, the circumstantial evidence can be
disturbing.   —THOMAS HARTMANN, "How Dangerous
Is Your Computer?"

Several other types of introductions can be equally effective, though they are sometimes harder to invent and control. One kind begins with a quotation that leads into the thesis sentence.

"It is difficult to speak adequately or justly of London," wrote   1
Henry James in 1881. "It is not a pleasant place; it is not   2
agreeable, or cheerful, or easy, or exempt from reproach. It is   3
only magnificent." Were he alive today, James, a connoisseur of   4
cities, might easily say the same thing about New York or Paris
or Tokyo, for the great city is one of the paradoxes of history. In   5
countless different ways, it has almost always been an unpleas-
ant, disagreeable, cheerless, uneasy and reproachful place; in
the end, it can only be described as magnificent.   —*Time*

Another kind of introduction opens by relating an incident or creating an image that sets the stage for the thesis.

Canada is pink. I knew that from the map I owned when I was   1,2
six. On it, New York was green and brown, which was true as far   3
as I could see, so there was no reason to distrust the map
maker's portrayal of Canada. When my parents took me across   4
the border and we entered the immigration booth, I looked
excitedly for the pink earth. Slowly it dawned on me: this   5
foreign, "different" place was not so different. I discovered that   6
the world in my head and the world at my feet were not the
same.   —ROBERT ORNSTEIN, *Human Nature*

An introduction may also start with a question, as in the earlier paragraph by Thomas Hartmann, or with an opinion, preferably a startling one that will grab the reader's attention.

Caesar was right. Thin people need watching. I've been watch-   1, 2,3
ing them for most of my adult life, and I don't like what I see.
When these narrow fellows spring at me, I quiver to my toes.   4
Thin people come in all personalities, most of them menacing.   5
You've got your "together" thin person, your mechanical thin   6
person, your condescending thin person, your tsk-tsk thin per-
son. All of them are dangerous.   7
—SUZANNE BRITT JORDAN, "That Lean and Hungry Look"

A historical comparison or contrast may make an effective introduction when some background to the essay topic is useful, as in this essay on Santa Claus.

The modern version of him first took shape in New York City in 1822. He was very small indeed at that date, an elf in fact, who fitted with ease into the narrowest chimney stack. He flew through the air in a sleigh full of toys, drawn by reindeer who could land on rooftops. His clothes, which covered him from head to foot in fur, were understandably begrimed with soot. He was a heavy smoker. —MARGARET VISSER, "No, Virginia"

An effective introductory paragraph need not be long, as the following opener shows.

I've often wondered what goes into a hot dog. Now I know and I wish I didn't. —WILLIAM ZINSSER, *The Lunacy Boom*

When writing and revising an introductory paragraph, avoid the approaches listed in the "Opening Paragraphs to Avoid" box. These are likely to bore readers or make them question your sincerity or control.

OPENING PARAGRAPHS TO AVOID

1. Don't simply mark time with vague generalities or repetition and then rely entirely on your thesis sentence to get moving. You may have needed a warm-up paragraph to start drafting, but your readers can do without it.
2. Don't start with "The purpose of this essay is . . . ," "In this essay I will . . . ," or any similar flat announcement of your intention or topic.
3. Don't refer to the title of the essay in the first sentence—for example, "This is my favourite activity" or "This is an interesting problem."
4. Don't start with "According to Webster . . . " or a similar phrase leading to a dictionary definition. A definition can be an effective springboard to an essay, but this kind of lead-in has become dull with overuse.
5. Don't apologize for your opinion or for inadequate knowledge of your subject with "I'm not sure if I'm right, but I think . . . ," "I don't know much about this, but . . . ," or similar lines.

---

2 Closing an essay

Most essays end with a closing statement or conclusion, a signal to readers that the writer has not simply stopped writing but has actually finished. The conclusion completes the essay, bringing it to a climax while assuring readers that they have understood the writer's intention. Usually set off in its own paragraph, the conclusion may consist of a single sentence or a group of sentences. It may summarize the evidence presented in the essay, restate the thesis with a fresh emphasis, suggest a course of action, ask a question, strike a note of hope or despair, introduce a startling fact, quote an authority, or tell an anecdote.

SOME STRATEGIES FOR CLOSING PARAGRAPHS

1. Summarize the paper.
2. Echo the introduction.
3. Create an image.
4. Use a quotation.
5. Give a symbolic or powerful fact or other detail.
6. Recommend a course of action.

The following paragraph concludes the essay on the Charter of Rights and Freedoms, which was introduced on page 121. The writer both summarizes his essay and echoes his introduction.

> Trudeau recognized, rightly, that there are elected politicians who can—out of stupidity or lust for power—turn into dictators. He set out to save us from them. Instead, he created a whole new class of potential dictators. The Charter was the great legal project of Trudeau's generation; undoing it may turn out to be the great legal project of the generation following him.
> —ROBERT FULFORD, "Charter of Wrongs"

Maxine Hong Kingston uses a different technique—a vivid image—to conclude an essay on her aunt, a suicide by drowning.

> My aunt haunts me—her ghost drawn to me because now, after fifty years of neglect, I alone devote pages of paper to her, though not origamied into houses and clothes. I do not think she always means me well. I am telling on her, and she was a spite suicide, drowning herself in the drinking water. The Chinese are always very frightened of the drowned one, whose weeping ghost, wet hair hanging and skin bloated, waits silently by the water to pull down a substitute.
> —Maxine Hong Kingston, "No Name Woman"

In the following paragraph, the author concludes an essay on environmental protection with a statement of opinion and, in the last sentence, a call for action.

> Until we get the answers, I think we had better keep on building power plants and growing food with the help of fertilizers and

such insect-controlling chemicals as we now have. The risks are well known, thanks to the environmentalists. If they had not created a widespread public awareness of the ecological crisis, we wouldn't stand a chance. But such awareness by itself is not enough. Flaming manifestos and prophecies of doom are no longer much help, and a search for scapegoats can only make matters worse. The time for sensations and manifestos is about over. Now we need rigorous analysis, united effort and very hard work.   —PETER F. DRUCKER, "How Best to Protect the Environment"

These three paragraphs illustrate ways of avoiding several pitfalls of conclusions.

CLOSING PARAGRAPHS TO AVOID

1. Don't simply restate your introduction—statement of subject, thesis sentence, and all. Presumably the paragraphs in the body of your essay have contributed something to the opening statements, and it's that something you want to capture in your conclusion.
2. Don't start off in a new direction, with a subject different from or broader than the one your essay has been about.
3. Don't conclude more than you reasonably can from the evidence you have presented. If your essay is about your frustrating experience trying to clear a parking ticket, you cannot reasonably conclude that *all* local police forces are too tied up in red tape to be of service to the people.
4. Don't apologize for your essay or otherwise cast doubt on it. Don't say, "Even though I'm no expert," or "This may not be convincing, but I believe it's true," or anything similar. Rather, to win your readers' confidence, display confidence.

---

3   **Using short transitional or emphatic paragraphs**

A short paragraph of a sentence or two may direct readers' attention to a turn in an essay or emphasize an idea that has been or will be developed. A transitional paragraph, because it is longer than a word or phrase and set off by itself, moves a discussion from one point to another more slowly or more completely than does a single transitional expression (3b-6) or even a transitional sentence attached to a paragraph (3a-2).

¶
3d

These, then, are the causes of the current expansion in hospital facilities. But how does this expansion affect the medical costs of hospital insurance?

The conclusion would seem to be obvious. To be sure, however, we must look at a few other facts.

So the debates were noisy and emotion-packed. But what did they accomplish? Historians agree on at least three direct results.

Use transitional paragraphs rarely—only to shift reader's attention when your essay makes a significant turn. A paragraph like the one below betrays a writer who is stalling; it does not redirect the flow but stops it altogether.

Now that we have examined these facts, we can look at some others that are equally important to an examination of this issue.

A short, emphatic paragraph gives unusual stress to an important idea, in effect asking the reader to pause and consider before moving on.

In short, all those who might have taken responsibility ducked it, and catastrophe was inevitable.

4 Writing dialogue

When recording a conversation between two or more people, start a new paragraph for each person's speech. The paragraphing establishes for the reader the point at which one speaker stops talking and another begins.

Now that they are out of world affairs and back where they started, Peter Frazier's wife says, "Everybody else did well in the international thing except us."

"You have to be crooked," he tells her.

"Or smart. Pity we weren't."

—Mavis Gallant, "The Ice Wagon Going Down the Street"

Though dialogue appears most often in fictional writing (the source of the example above), it may occasionally freshen or enliven narrative or expository essays. (For guidance in using quotation marks and other punctuation in dialogue, see 24c.)

EXERCISE 18

Analyse the introductory and concluding paragraphs in the first and final drafts of the student essay in Chapter 2, pages 53–57 and 72–76. What is wrong with the first-draft paragraphs? Why are the final-draft paragraphs better? Could they be improved still further?

3e Linking paragraphs in the essay

Paragraphs do not stand alone but contribute to a larger piece of writing. Each unified, coherent, and well-developed paragraph adds something to a unified, coherent, and well-developed essay (see Chapter 1).

In a two- to four-page essay each paragraph between the introductory and concluding ones will develop and support a part of the essay's central idea, its thesis. The devices for achieving paragraph coherence—organization, transitional expressions, and the like—will also link paragraphs in a coherent whole. And the patterns for developing paragraphs—definition, division, and so on—will suit the needs of individual paragraphs in the larger context of the essay. Thus the paragraph patterns may or may not reflect the overall pattern of the whole essay, and they may vary from one paragraph to the next.

The following essay illustrates the way effective paragraphs can contribute to an effective essay.

A hyperactive committee member can contribute to efficiency. A hyperactive salesperson can contribute to profits. But when a child is hyperactive, people—even parents—may wish he had never been born. To understand hyperactivity in children, we can visualize a collage of the thoughts, feelings, and attitudes of those who must cope with the problem: doctors, parents, even the child himself. 1

The first part of our collage is the doctors. In their terminology the word *hyperactivity* is short for H-LD, a hyperkinesis-learning disability syndrome. They apply the word to children who are "abnormally or excessively busy." But doctors do not fully understand the problem and thus differ over how to treat it. For example, some recommend special diet; others, behaviour-modifying drugs; and still others, who do not consider hyperactivity to be a medical problem, a psychiatrist for the entire family. The result is a merry-go-round of tests, confusion, and frustration for the parents and the child. 2

As the parent of a hyperactive child, I can say what the word *hyperactivity* means to the parents who form the second part of the collage. It means a worry that is deep and enduring. It means a despair that is a companion on dark and sleepless nights. It means a fear that is heart-twisting and constant, for the hyperactive child is most destructive toward himself. It means a mixture of frustration, guilt, and anger. And finally, since there are times when that anger goes out of control and the child is in danger from the parent, it means self-loathing. 3

The weight of hyperactivity, however, rests not on the doctors or the parents but on the child. For him is reserved the final and darkest part of our collage because he is most affected. 4

From early childhood he is dragged from doctor to doctor, is attached to strange and frightening machines, and is tested or discussed by physicians, parents, neighbours, teachers, peers. His playmates dislike him because of his temper and his unwillingness to follow rules; and even his pets fear and mistrust him, for he treats them erratically, often hurting them without meaning to. As time goes on, he sees his parents more and more often in tears and anger, and he knows that he is the cause. Though he is highly intelligent, he does poorly when he enters school because of his short attention span. He is fond of sports and games but never joins the other children on the playground because he has an uncontrollable temper and poor co-ordination. By the time he reaches age seven or eight, he is obsessed with one thought: "Mama," my son asks me repeatedly, "why do I have do be hyperactive?"

At last the collage is completed, and it is dark and sombre.   5 *Hyperactivity*, as applied to children, is a word with uncertain, unattractive, and bitter associations. But the picture does have a bright spot, for inside every hyperactive child is a loving, trustful, calm person waiting to be recognized.   —A STUDENT

The overall pattern of development in this essay is division or analysis: the writer examines the human elements involved in hyperactivity. In addition, the writer creates an analogy, comparing those involved to the pieces in a collage. The essay's basic organization is climactic or general to specific, proceeding from the general notions of the seemingly distant doctors to the more specific and poignant experiences of a single child. Within this general scheme, however, each paragraph follows the course required by its topic and the writer's purpose. For instance, having shown in paragraph 2 that doctors do not agree on what hyperactivity is, the writer develops paragraph 3 by defining the word as she sees it. And she develops paragraph 4 by analysing the effects of hyperactivity on the one most harmed by it, the child himself. This paragraph also follows a chronological organization in tracing the child's experiences.

Despite the varied organizational schemes and patterns of development in her paragraphs, the writer guides us smoothly and steadily from one paragraph to the next. She recalls the promise of the thesis sentence, a three-part collage, in the topic sentence of every succeeding paragraph. She links paragraphs with transitional words to remind us where we are in the essay: *first* (paragraph 2), *second* (3), *however* and *final* (4), *at last* (5). The entire first sentence of paragraph 4 is a transition from the earlier paragraphs. The writer repeats the key words of the essay, *collage* and *hyperactive* or *hyperactivity*, in the first or second sentence of every paragraph. At the end of paragraph 2, on doctors, she looks ahead to the next two paragraphs, on parents and the child. In the conclusion she echoes the distinction, first made in the introduction, between the useful hyperactivity of adults and the destructive hyperactivity of children. The combination of these techniques produces a tightly woven analysis that readers can easily understand.

¶
3e

EXERCISE 19

Analyse the ways in which paragraphs combine in the three student essays in Chapter 2, pages 72, 78, and 79. With what techniques, if any, does each writer link paragraphs to the thesis sentence and to each other? Where, if at all, does the writer seem to stray from the thesis or fail to show how paragraphs relate to it? How would you revise the essays to solve any problems they exhibit?

EXERCISE 20

Analyse the following paragraphs for unity, coherence, and development. For each paragraph, identify the central idea (even if it is not stated explicitly), the organizational scheme, the devices used to achieve coherence, and the pattern or patterns of development.

1.   If it is the very essence of life you seek, visit Japan. The wine   1,2
is served piping hot in the tiniest thimble bowls, and it is better
than gulping beakers of cold sauterne. Some of the finest Japa-   3
nese sculptures are no larger than a walnut and can be worn as
the tassel to one's belt. In the Japanese dance, one tightly   4
controlled gesture stands for an entire routine, and in the
theater the merest corner of handkerchief pressed to the eye
symbolizes unbearable grief.
            —JAMES MICHENER, "Why I Like Japan"

2.   To feel used is to have a sense of something of ours being   1
taken away. But it is more than that. To feel used is to feel that   2,3
our services have been separated from ourselves. It is a sense of   4
the violation of our central worth, as though we ourselves are
important to the other individual only because we are a vehicle
for supplying the stuff that he desires. It may be most graphic   5
and evident when what he desires is a material or physical
thing—our money or our possessions—but we are equally
offended when what is taken or used is our intelligence, our
creativity, our companionship, or our love.
            —WILLARD GAYLIN, "Feeling Used"

3.   As more products and services become available to consu-   1
mers, their quality and effectiveness seem to decline. To avoid   2
unnecessary frustration and expense, consumers should be well
informed before buying products and services. First, they   3
should shop around, hunting among dealers for the best quality,

¶
3e

price, and service available. Second, they should consult guides, 4
such as *Consumer Reports*, that are published by non-profit
product-testing services. Finally, they should refuse to accept 5
oral promises, demand to see relevant contracts and warranties,
and decline to sign or accept any document they do not fully
understand.   —A STUDENT

4.   We may extend this conclusion for hearts to a general state- 1
ment about the pace of life in small versus large animals. Small 2
animals tick through life far more rapidly than large animals—
their hearts work more quickly, they breathe more frequently,
their pulse beats much faster. Most importantly, metabolic rate, 3
the so-called fire of life, increases only three-fourths as fast as
body weight in mammals. To keep themselves going, large 4
mammals do not need to generate as much heat per unit of body
weight as small animals. Tiny shrews move frenetically, eating 5
nearly all their waking lives to keep their metabolic fire burning
at the maximal rate among mammals; blue whales glide majes-
tically, their hearts beating the slowest rhythm among active,
warm-blooded creatures.
                                    —STEPHEN JAY GOULD, *The Panda's Thumb*

5.   Shortly after World War II, decades of investigation into the 1
internal workings of the solids yielded a new piece of electronic
hardware called a transistor (for its actual invention, three
scientists at Bell Laboratories won the Nobel Prize). Transis- 2
tors, a family of devices, alter and control the flow of electricity
in circuits; one standard rough analogy compares their action
to that of faucets controlling the flow of water in pipes. Other 3
devices then in existence could do the same work, but transis-
tors are superior. They are solid. They have no cogs and wheels, 4,5
no separate pieces to be soldered together; it is as if they are
stones performing useful work. They are durable, take almost 6
no time to start working, and don't consume much power.
Moreover, as physicists and engineers discovered, they could be 7
made very small, indeed microscopic, and they could be produced cheaply in large quantities.
                                  —TRACY KIDDER, *The Soul of a New Machine*

CHAPTER 4

Critical Thinking and Writing

Critical thinking—the ability to read (or listen) objectively, to analyse, and finally to argue a position—is a fundamental activity of academic life. In most contexts, thinking critically involves both reading *and* writing. For example, to determine the validity of an argument, you must first understand—objectively and accurately— the main points of that argument; and a good way to reach that understanding is to write a summary. Or as a critical reader you will identify and challenge questionable logic used in an argument, and as a writer of arguments you will use this same knowledge to avoid faulty reasoning. Being an accomplished critical reader *and* writer are flip sides of the same coin. When you learn to do one well, you need only apply what you've learned to do the other equally well.

Critical thinking and writing are associated with certain inter-related skills that are discussed in this chapter: summarizing a passage; reasoning effectively; evaluating an argument; and writing an argument.

4a Summarizing

A great deal of the writing you do in college or university is based on reading that you use in some way—perhaps as evidence for your assertions, as background information, or as the subject of your evaluation. To use reading, you need to understand the author's main points and be prepared, if the occasion requires, to restate these points objectively. The most efficient way to reach and demonstrate this understanding is to write a **summary**: a distillation of the author's text to its main points, in your own words.

4a

The essence of summary is *conciseness, objectivity,* and *completeness*: your goal is to state in as few words as possible the main thrust of a passage. When you need to summarize a few paragraphs or a brief article, your summary should be no longer than one-quarter the length of the original passage. For longer texts, such as chapters of books or whole books, your summary should be quite a bit shorter in proportion to the original.

The following paragraph begins the first chapter in a book on civil disobedience. As you read the paragraph, think how you would summarize it.

> The life of every civilized community is governed by rules. Neither peace of mind for the present nor intelligent planning for the future is possible for men who either live without rules or cannot abide by the rules they have. Making rules for the community, and enforcing

---

TWO TECHNIQUES FOR WRITING SUMMARIES

SUMMARIZING BRIEF TEXTS (ten pages or fewer)

1. Write a one-sentence summary of every paragraph.
2. Formulate a single sentence that summarizes the whole. (Look at the author's own summary—a thesis or topic sentence—as a guide.)
3. Write a full paragraph (or more, if needed): begin with the overall-summary sentence and follow it with the paragraph-summary sentences.
4. Rewrite and rearrange the paragraph as needed to make it clear and concise, to eliminate repetition and relatively minor points, and to provide transitions (see 3b-6). The final version should be a unified and coherent whole.

SUMMARIZING LONGER TEXTS (eleven pages or more)

1. Outline the text. Break it down into its component sections—groups of paragraphs focussed on a common topic—and list the main supporting points for each section. (A formal outline may help. See 1h-2.)
2. Write a one- or two-sentence summary of each section.
3. Formulate a single sentence to summarize the whole, looking to the author's thesis sentence or topic sentences as a guide.
4. Write a full paragraph (or more, if needed): begin with the overall-summary sentence and follow it with the section-summary sentences.
5. Rewrite and rearrange the paragraph as needed to make it clear and concise, to eliminate repetition and relatively minor points, and to provide transitions (see 3b-6). The final version should be a unified and coherent whole.

them, is the job of government. No community can be truly civilized, therefore, without an effective and reasonably stable government. That is why the international community, whose rules are few, often broken, and badly enforced, is largely an uncivilized community, while within the many nation states may be found every degree of community order, from the chaotic to the overorganized. An established government, providing and maintaining an effective system of laws, is certainly not by itself a sufficient condition of happy human life, but it is, with few exceptions, a necessary condition of such life.

—Carl Cohen, *Civil Disobedience*

Writing a concise, objective, and complete one-sentence summary of such a paragraph could easily take a couple of attempts. Here's one:

Draft summary

Carl Cohen claims that communities—both national and international—must be governed by rules if they are to be civilized.

But this sentence makes no mention of two important points in the middle and end of Cohen's paragraph: the role of governments in establishing and enforcing rules, and the relationship between civilized communities and the possibility of one's leading a "happy human life." A revision corrects the problem:

Revised summary

Carl Cohen claims that a community becomes civilized only when it is led by an effective, stable government that can establish and enforce rules—and in so doing create the possibility for "happy human life."

Because a summary distils information, no summary will retain all the detail of an original passage. Your job as a critical reader and as a writer of summary is to identify an author's important points, distinguishing them from the less important.

Note: When you write a summary, remember to identify your source both with a text reference (see p. 600) and in your list of works cited (see p. 598). You may also choose to introduce the summary with the name of the author and some information on his or her credentials. For example:

In her essay "Wealth and Elected Power," Sheila Doland argues against what she has identified as a dangerous recent trend: a candidate's needing to be exceedingly wealthy in order to mount a credible race for high elected office (20–22).

For more on introducing summaries in your papers, see page 594.

4a

EXERCISE 1

Read and reread the passage below, and follow the instructions after it.

In Europe the clock very early became a *public* machine. 1
Churches expected communicants to assemble regularly and
repeatedly for prayers, and flourishing cities brought people
together to share a life of commerce and entertainment. When
clocks took their places in church steeples and town belfries,
they entered on a public stage. There they proclaimed themselves to rich and poor, awakening the interest even of those
who had no personal reason to mark the hours. Machines that
began as public instruments gradually became some of the most
widely diffused private instruments. But instruments that
began their lives in private might never become diffused into the
wants and needs of the whole community. The first advertisement for the clock was the clock itself, performing for new
publics all over Europe.

No self-respecting European town would be without its 2
public clock, which tolled all citizens together to defend, to
celebrate, or to mourn. A community that could focus its
resources in a dazzling public clock was that much more a
community. The bell tolled for all and each, as the poet John
Donne noted in 1623, and the tolling of the community's bells
was a reminder that "I am involved in mankind."

Many communities, even before they had organized sew- 3
age disposal or a water supply, offered the town clock as a public
service. In due course each citizen wanted his own private
clocks—first for his household, then for his person. When more
people had their private timepieces, more other people needed
timepieces to fulfill their neighbors' expectations at worship, at
work, and at play.

All the while, the clock was being secularized—another 4
way of saying it was being publicized. The first European
clocks, as we have seen, alerted cloistered monks for their
regular prayers, but when the clock moved into the church
steeple and then into the town belfry, it moved out to a secular
world. This larger public soon required the clock for the whole
schedule of daily life. In Europe the artificial hour, the machine-
made hour, took the calculations of time out of the calendar-
universe, out from the penumbra of astrology, into the bright
everyday light. When steam power, electric power, and artificial
illumination kept factories going around the clock, when night
was assimilated into day, the artificial hour, the clock-marked
hour became the constant regimen for everyone. The story of
the rise of the clock in the West, then, is the story of new modes
and widening arenas of publicity.

—DANIEL J. BOORSTIN, *The Discoverers*

1. From the following lists, choose the one sentence for each paragraph that best summarizes the paragraph. Explain why the two remaining sentences are inappropriate summaries. Recall that a good summary is concise, complete, and objective.

4a

Paragraph 1

a) Found in the churches and town squares of Europe, clocks were at first public machines that announced events of communal interest; but once displayed, they gradually gained value as private machines.

b) The invention of the clock, once introduced to the public, inevitably corrupted townspeople, who all too easily allowed a machine to dominate their lives.

c) Clocks were first used in churches to call people to prayer and were later moved to public settings in order to announce events of community interest, such as markets and entertainment. Once on public display, clocks became instruments desired by private individuals. Had their first use been private, one suspects that their *public* use would never have grown widespread.

Paragraph 2

a) It was a mark of civic pride for European towns to have a grand, publicly displayed clock that could summon citizens for communal needs—such as defence, celebration, or mourning—and remind all who heard the hourly tolling that individuals exist in a community, and that each person (as John Donne wrote) is "involved in mankind."

b) European townspeople placed great stock in impressing one another and visitors with the grandness of their public clocks.

c) European townspeople were proud of their public clocks, for clocks summoned individuals to a common cause and reminded them that they were interdependent.

Paragraph 3

a) Some early communities foolishly built public clocks before securing adequate water or arranging for the disposal of sewage, an attitude which explains perfectly the lamentable hygiene of those times.

b) The highly valued town clock after a time became an instrument desired by private citizens, whose increasing reliance on the "hourly" organization of the day created an ever greater demand for timepieces.

c) After a time, townspeople required private clocks.

Paragraph 4

a) The clock, both public and private, was perfectly suited to the advancements of the modern age and soon came to organize everyday life.

b) The advent of steam power and electric power, along with electric light, enabled unscrupulous factory owners to force day labourers into extending their "hours," or clock-time at the job, into the night.

c) Uses of the clock grew increasingly secular—moving from the church, originally, to the town belfry, to the home, and finally to the factory, at which point the "machine-made hour" (as opposed to the natural cycles of sun, moon, and stars) came to organize everyday life.

2. Now write your own one-sentence summary of the entire passage on clocks. Following this sentence, place the four sentences you have chosen as appropriate summaries of the separate paragraphs. Rewrite and rearrange the sentences as needed to achieve clarity, to eliminate repetition, and to ensure a smooth final draft.

EXERCISE 2

Read the passage below carefully, and follow the instructions after it to plan and write your own summary.

The whole art world of the Indian was completely and 1 irrevocably upset by the appearance of the white man. This strange new person came in several waves, each exerting a different influence. Initially, the explorer brought little and took little; he perhaps levied the least toll.

But hard on his heels came the trader, eager to introduce 2 new things in exchange for local resources. Moreover, what he had to give—cloth, metal, decorative materials—made the greatest single change in Indian art. With metal knives, carving could be done more efficiently; with new cloth, new garment designs were possible; and with the decorative materials such as dyestuffs and glass beads, a whole new world of applied ornament was opened.

Many new decorative materials were used in old ways— 3 this is especially true of beads, which were applied more or less as the older porcupine quills had been. Careful examination of beadwork and quillwork will reveal the debt the one owes the other in style, technique, and execution.

Next came the missionary, whose whole purpose in life was 4 to influence. By and large, this had a less happy effect on Indian art; there was no sensitivity to or interest in native aesthetic abilities, and little tolerance for a differing mode of life. The demand for conformity tended to bring about a loss of freedom of expression in many arts, and Indian religious art in particular suffered at the hand of the incoming non-believers.

Mission schools, notably the French convents in Canada, established new design styles, as the young girls were taught to copy European models of the period. This occurred at a time when garment decoration was elaborately florid, which happened to fit in nicely with the curvilinear art so popular with the aboriginal artist. From this set of circumstances evolved an art form still in use today in the Eastern Woodlands region. [5]

The settler's arrival was of more concern, since it brought a more lasting influence. The household possessions which these newcomers brought with them included many readily usable items which the Indian was quick to adopt. These articles affected art sizes, shapes, forms, and, to some extent, techniques. One example will suffice—the wealthy settler who brought along a few prized Oriental rugs then in vogue started a chain reaction he little suspected. These patterns seem to have made their way into Sioux beadwork, and became popular as "Indian design" when they were taken East with the Buffalo Bill shows. Eventually they turned up in Navajo weaving, after traders gave these patterns out to the weavers, convinced that the beadwork design would make rugs salable in the East. [6]

—FREDERICK J. DOCKSTADER, *Indian Art in America*

1. What effects did the various "waves" of white men have on Indian art? State the effects of each wave in a sentence.
2. Follow the first of the two recommended techniques for writing a summary (see p. 132). Restate concisely, completely, and objectively the content of these six paragraphs. Your summary should be roughly one hundred words.
3. Compare your summary with that of a classmate. In principle, two summaries of the same passage should include the same information. Is this the case? If not, why?

EXERCISE 3

Choose a ten- to twelve-page article, essay, or chapter from a book, and write a summary by following the second technique given on page 132. Work on a passage that at least one other student is also summarizing, and compare your results.

4b Effective reasoning

In order to write an accurate summary of Dockstader's passage on Indian art, one needs to make an inference. Recall the following sentence by Dockstader:

> By and large, this [the missionaries' purpose of influencing] had a less happy effect on Indian art; there was no sensitivity to or interest in native aesthetic abilities, and little tolerance for a differing mode of life.

Dockstader's views on the value of Indian art are not stated directly here; rather, they are *implied* and must be *inferred* by the reader. What are the author's views? If Indian art was art that missionaries showed "no sensitivity" toward and if the art displayed "aesthetic abilities" that the missionaries did not appreciate, then—and here is the inference—Indian art in itself was valuable and worth preserving in its native form. An **inference** is a conclusion based on available evidence. Though the conclusion is not stated directly, the reader feels justified in attributing it to the author. The logical method that allows such an attribution is induction; its opposite is deduction. These methods figure not only in our reading and our formal writing but also in our everyday activities, as the following example demonstrates.

You want to buy a reliable used car. In thinking of what kind of car to buy, you follow specific steps of reasoning. (1) You consider your friends' experiences with used cars: one has had to spend a lot of money to repair her used Volkswagen; another has complained that his used Ford handles badly; and three others have raved about their used Toyotas. (2) You recall an article in *Consumer Reports* rating Toyota high among used cars. (3) You conclude that Toyota is the most reliable used car. So far your reasoning is **inductive**. You have made a series of specific observations about the reliability of different used cars. And you have induced, or inferred, from those observations the generalization that Toyota is the most reliable used car. The **generalization** is based on the assumption that what is applicable in one set of circumstances (your friends' experiences, *Consumer Reports'* tests) is or will be applicable as well in a similar set of circumstances (your own experiences). Having thus reasoned inductively, you then proceed with **deductive** reasoning, from the generalization to specific circumstances. You start with a generalization you believe to be true (Toyota is the most reliable used car) and apply it to particular circumstances (you want to buy a reliable used car) in order to reach a conclusion (you want to buy a used Toyota).

As this example demonstrates, induction and deduction are fundamental to our thought. They derive from our experience of the world as coherent (with one event related to another) and not fragmented. We activate these reasoning processes effortlessly and habitually in the daily business of living. We employ them more consciously in organizing essays and paragraphs from specific to general (inductively) and from general to specific (deductively). (See 1h-1 and 3b-1.) And we can use induction and deduction methodically in

QUESTIONS TO ASK ABOUT YOUR OWN
AND OTHERS' REASONING

1. Has the writer (meaning you, if you are the writer) reasoned inductively or deductively, and to what effect? (See 4b-1 and 4b-2.)
2. Has the writer faced the questions implied by his or her assertions? (See 4b-3.)
3. Has the writer avoided faulty reasoning? (See 4b-4.)

reasoning about complex ideas—whether in what we read or in what we write. As a *reader,* you will need to determine the effectiveness of the author's reasoning. As a *writer*, you will want to present your own views as reasonably and thus convincingly as possible.

1 Inductive reasoning

Induction is the dominant method of reasoning in two situations: generalizing from observations and attributing a cause to a set of observed circumstances.

We saw an example of generalizing from observations in the identification of a reliable used car. In another case you might observe that few students attend showings of the school film society, which presents only serious foreign films; that your university friends seem to prefer science-fiction, adventure, and horror movies; and that a magazine article says these three kinds of entertainment films are most popular with people under twenty-five. From these observations you infer that most university students prefer entertainment movies. The more students you talk to and the more you read about the subject, the more certain you can be that your generalization is true.

Attributing a cause to circumstances is essentially the same process as generalizing from observations. You and your friends, and presumably most students, prefer science-fiction, adventure, and horror movies, which entertain you and offer relief from studying. The president of the student film society, however, programs only weighty foreign films, and few students attend. From these observations you conclude that the president is unaware of students' needs and preferences. True, with a little imagination you could also conclude that the president knows students' preferences but is determined to ignore them because she is a snob. You could even conclude that she is ignoring them because she wants to learn foreign languages. But the conclusion you do draw is the simplest because it adheres to the available evidence: the president does not demonstrate awareness of students' preferences. And the simplest explanation of cause, based exclusively on the evidence, is usually more reasonable than the more elaborate one for which supporting facts must be invented.

The more evidence a writer has, the more likely it is that his or her generalizations are valid, but absolute certainty is not possible. Instead, the goal is reasonableness: sound conclusions based on sound evidence.

EXERCISE 4

Study the following facts and then evaluate each of the numbered conclusions after them. Which of the generalizations are reasonable given the evidence, and which are not? Why?

> Between the 1971 and 1981 national census, the population of Canada increased 12.8 percent to 24 343 810.
>
> The percentage increase from 1961 to 1971 was 18.3 percent.
>
> The population of Alberta increased 37.4 percent between 1971 and 1981.
>
> The population of Nova Scotia increased only 7.4 percent between 1971 and 1981.

1. Between 1971 and 1981 the population of Canada continued to grow at the same rapid rate as in the 1960s.
2. During the 1970s the population of Alberta increased five times more than the population of Nova Scotia.
3. Canadians prefer to live in the climate of the Prairies rather than in the climate of the Maritimes.

2 Deductive reasoning

You reason deductively when you use some assertions to arrive at others. As when you determined that you should buy a used Toyota, in deduction you apply generalizations or conclusions that are accepted as true to slightly different but similar situations or issues. For example, if you know that all male members of your psychology class are on the football squad, and André is in your psychology class, then you conclude that André must be on the football squad. This group of three statements constitutes a **syllogism**, two premises stating facts or judgments that together lead to a conclusion.

1. *Premise*: English papers containing sentence fragments receive poor grades.
2. *Premise*: Your English paper contains sentence fragments.
3. *Conclusion*: Your English paper will receive a poor grade.

The first premise states a generalization that was already arrived at by induction. The second premise states a specific case of the generalization. The conclusion derives logically from the two premises.

Though it is rarely laid out as neatly as in the preceding syllogism, deductive reasoning underlies many arguments you read or write. The force of such arguments depends on the reliability of the premises and the care with which they are applied in drawing new conclusions. Two common sources of difficulty with deduction are unstated premises and overstated premises.

Many deductive arguments depend on **unstated premises**—that is, the basic premise is not explicitly stated but is understood. For instance:

> Ms. Chang has worked with drug addicts for fifteen years, so she should know a great deal about their problems. [Unstated premise: Anyone who has worked fifteen years with drug addicts knows about their problems.]

> As student council president, Jordan will have to deal with conflicting demands from all sides. [Unstated premise: A student council president must deal with conflicting demands.]

Problems arise when the unstated premise is wrong or unfounded, as in the following sentences.

> Since Jane Lightbow is a senator, she must make a lot of money for doing nothing. [Unstated premise: All senators receive a lot of money for doing nothing.]

> Now that Sally Matlock's father is in jail, Sally will become a behaviour problem. [Unstated premise: All children whose fathers are jailed become behaviour problems.]

As these sentences show, you must be alert to the logic of deductive reasoning when you read or write. Examine basic premises, especially when they are implied.

The second common problem in deduction, **overstated premises**, results from the difficulty in making a generalization that will apply to all instances, since ordinarily we must base any generalization on only a few instances. When such generalizations are premises in a deductive argument, they must contain or imply limiting words such as *some, many*, and *often* rather than absolute words such as *all, no one, never*, or *always*. Compare the difference in reasonableness in the following pairs of sentences.

log

4b

OVERSTATED	Parents are *always* too busy to help their children solve problems.
MODIFIED	Parents are *often* too busy to help their children solve problems.
OVERSTATED	Movie theatre ushers *are* a thing of the past; one *never* sees them in cinema complexes.
MODIFIED	Movie theatre ushers *may be* a thing of the past; one *rarely* sees them in cinema complexes.

Even when a premise sounds reasonable, it still must be supportable. For instance, modifying the unstated assumption about Sally Matlock might result in this sentence:

Now that Sally Matlock's father is in jail, Sally *may* become a behaviour problem. [Unstated premise: *Some* children whose fathers are jailed become behaviour problems.]

But it does not necessarily follow that Sally is one of the "some." The sentence, though logical, is not truly reasonable unless evidence demonstrates that Sally is potentially a behaviour problem.

EXERCISE 5

Supply the element needed to complete each of the following syllogisms.
1. a) Cigarette smokers risk lung cancer.
   b)
   c) Therefore, cigarette smokers risk death.
2. a) The challenging courses are the good ones.
   b) Biology is a challenging course.
   c)
3. a)
   b) That child receives no individual attention.
   c) Therefore, that child learns slowly.
4. a) Discus throwers develop large pectoral muscles.
   b)
   c) Therefore, Warren has large pectoral muscles.
5. a)
   b) Enrolments will certainly decline.
   c) Therefore, the school will close.

EXERCISE 6

At least one of the following assertions is reasonable, but the others either generalize from inadequate evidence or depend on faulty or overstated assumptions. Circle the number preceding any sentence that seems reasonable, and explain what is wrong with each of the others.

1. Since capital punishment prevents murder, it should be the mandatory sentence for all murderers.
2. The mayor opposed pollution controls when he was president of a manufacturing company, so he may not support new controls or vigorously enforce existing ones.
3. The only way to be successful in Canada is to make money, because Canadians measure success by income.
4. Keeping the library open until midnight has caused the increase in late-night crime on the campus.
5. Government demands so much honesty that we should not leave it to lawyers and professional politicians.

3 | Facing the question

Reasoning is likely to go awry if the writer does not directly face the questions implied by his or her statements. In an argument, for instance, the thesis usually centres on an issue or question: Should the risk of accident in a nuclear plant be lowered further? Is free trade with the United States beneficial to the Canadian economy? Will the Meech Lake Accord weaken national social programs? An effective argument faces the central issue squarely. It answers the question by stating relevant opinions about it and supporting those opinions with facts. But facing the question can be difficult. It is often easier to oversimplify complex issues or to argue superficially about them than it is to grapple with all the evidence. Sometimes, too, a favoured opinion dies hard, though the evidence fails to support it. These circumstances can cause two common faults: begging the question (also called circular reasoning) and ignoring the question through inappropriate emotional appeals.

Begging the question

A writer **begs the question** by treating an opinion that is open to question as if it were already proved or disproved. (In essence, the writer begs readers to accept his or her ideas from the start.) For example, a writer begs the question when arguing that the expenses of the school library should be reduced by cutting subscriptions to useless periodicals. Without supplying the necessary evidence, the writer asserts that at least some of the library's periodicals are useless and then uses that unproved assertion to support the proposal.

The following sentence begs the question in a slightly different way.

Teenagers should be prevented from having abortions because they would not become pregnant in the first place if they weren't allowed to terminate their "mistakes."

The writer assumes—and asks us to agree—that the option of having an abortion leads teenagers to unwanted pregnancies; therefore, removing the option of abortion will remove the problem of pregnancy. But how can we agree when we still have no proof for the fundamental assertion? The writer has merely substituted one debatable assumption for another.

Ignoring the question

Appeals to readers' emotions are common in effective arguments, as we will see in 4c-2. But such appeals must be relevant and must supplement rather than substitute for facts, examples, and other evidence. If they do not, they obscure or **ignore the question**.

Writers sometimes ignore the question with **appeals to readers' fear, pity, or sense of decency**.

By electing Martha Jovic to the city council, you will prevent the city's economic collapse. [Trades on people's fears: Can Jovic single-handedly prevent economic collapse?]

She should not have to pay taxes because she is an aged widow with no friends or relatives. [Appeals to people's pity: Should age and loneliness, rather than income, determine a person's tax obligation?]

Dr. Bowen is an honest man because he attends church regularly and participates in community activities. [Appeals to people's sense of decent behaviour: Are churchgoers and community participants necessarily honest?]

Sometimes writers ignore the question by appealing to readers' sense of what other people believe or do. One approach is **snob appeal**, inviting readers to accept an assertion in order to be identified with others they admire.

As any literate person knows, James Joyce is the best twentieth-century novelist. [But what qualities of Joyce's writing make him a superior novelist?]

The business community's support for the prime minister proves that the prime minister is doing a good job. [What has the prime minister actually accomplished?]

A similar tactic invites readers to accept an assertion because everybody else does. This is the **bandwagon approach**.

As everyone knows, marijuana use leads to heroin addiction. [What is the evidence?]

No one in this town would consider voting for him. [What is the basis for judging him?]

Yet another diversion involves **flattery** of readers, in a way inviting them to join in a conspiracy.

Since you are thoughtful and perceptive, you know how corrupt the politicians are. [What is the evidence of corruption?]

We all understand campus problems well enough to see the disadvantages of such a backward policy. [What are the disadvantages of the policy?]

All these assertions resort to appeals having nothing to do with the issues they raise. A careless reader might be momentarily swayed by such appeals, but a careful reader is more likely to be put off by the writer's evasion.

One final kind of inappropriate emotional appeal addresses *not* the pros and cons of the issue itself but the real or imagined negative qualities of the people who hold the opposing view. This kind of argument is called **ad hominem**, Latin for "to the man."

We need not listen to her arguments against abortion because she has five children. [Her having children does not necessarily discredit her views on abortion.]

One of the scientists has been treated for emotional problems, so his pessimism about nuclear war merits no attention. [Do the scientist's previous emotional problems invalidate his current views?]

You'll recognize most of these tricks for ignoring the question from advertising and political campaigns. Are your children's teeth cavity-free? Is your kitchen floor as spotless as your neighbour's? Are you the only person who does not eat a certain brand of cereal? Is that candidate as incompetent as his opponent says? You should be wary of these pitches in what you read and hear, for they betray carelessness at best, dishonesty at worst. And you should avoid these tactics in your own writing. Readers are unlikely to be persuaded by them, and their presence in your work could cause readers to mistrust everything else you say.

EXERCISE 7

Identify the question implied by each of the following assertions, and evaluate the writer's effectiveness in facing the question.

1. Many women are bored with their lives because their jobs are tedious.

2. Steven McRae spends too much time making himself look good to be an effective spokesman for the student body.
3. Teenagers are too young to be allowed to use birth control.
4. Giving nuclear capability to emerging nations is dangerous because they will probably use it to wage war.
5. Our souls are immortal because they are not made of matter and thus are indestructible.

EXERCISE 8

Leaf through a magazine or watch television for half an hour, looking for advertisements that attempt to sell a product not on the basis of its worth but by snob appeal, flattery, or other inappropriate appeals to emotions. Be prepared to discuss the advertiser's techniques.

4 Spotting faulty reasoning

Some kinds of faulty inductive and deductive reasoning—errors called **fallacies**—are common in all sorts of writing. Like begging or ignoring the question, these fallacies weaken what you read and what you write.

Hasty generalization

A **hasty generalization** is based on too little evidence or on evidence that is unrepresentative (see 4e). For example:

Because it trains one for work, business is the only major worth pursuing. [Other majors train one for work, and other students may have different goals.]

When attendance is down and the team is losing, the basketball coach should be fired. [The sentence does not allow for other influences on the team's performance.]

A variation of the hasty generalization involves the use of absolute words such as *all*, *always*, *never*, and *no one* when your evidence cannot support such terms and what you really mean is *some*, *sometimes*, *rarely*, and *few* (see the overstated and modified assertions on p. 142).

Another common hasty generalization is the **stereotype**, a conventional and oversimplified characterization of a group of people. The ideas that the French are good lovers, the British reserved, and the Italians emotional are stereotypes. When you apply such a characterization to an individual Frenchman or Briton or Italian, you extend a prejudice, an opinion based on insufficient or unexamined evidence (see p. 159). Here are several other stereotypes: *People who live in cities are unfriendly. Torontonians are snobbish. Women are emotional. Men are less expressive than women.* (See also 31a-8 on sexist and other biassed language.)

Oversimplification

A frequent fallacy in writing is **oversimplification** of the relation between causes and their effects. The fallacy (sometimes called the **reductive fallacy**) often involves linking two events as if one caused the other directly, whereas the causes may be more complex or the relation may not exist at all. For example:

> Poverty causes crime. [If so, then why do people who are not poor commit crimes? And why aren't all poor people criminals?]

> The better a school's athletic facilities are, the worse its academic programs are. [The sentence assumes a direct cause-and-effect link between athletics and scholarship.]

Post hoc fallacy

Related to oversimplification of cause and effect is the fallacy of assuming that because *A* preceded *B*, then *A* must have caused *B*. This fallacy is called in Latin *post hoc, ergo propter hoc,* meaning "after this, therefore because of this," or the ***post hoc* fallacy** for short.

> In the two months since he took office, Mayor Holcomb has allowed crime in the city to increase 2 percent. [The increase in crime is no doubt attributable to conditions existing before Holcomb took office.]

> The town council erred in permitting the adult bookstore to open, for shortly afterward two women were assaulted. [It cannot be assumed without evidence that the women's assailants visited or were influenced by the bookstore.]

Either/or fallacy

In the **either/or fallacy** (also called **false dilemma**) you assume that a complicated question has only two answers, one good and one bad, both bad, or both good.

> City policemen are either brutal or corrupt.

> Either we increase health care funding or thousands of people will die.

Like the illustrations for the previous fallacies, these sentences over-simplify complex issues and relations to make the writer's perspective seem convincing. But no careful reader would be fooled. Many city policemen are neither brutal nor corrupt. And allowing people to die is not necessarily the only alternative to increased health care funding.

Non sequitur

A **non sequitur** occurs when no logical relation exists between two or more connected ideas. In Latin *non sequitur* means "it does not follow." In the following sentences the second thought does not follow from the first.

> If high school English were easier, fewer students would have trouble with the university English requirement. [Presumably, if high school English were easier, students would have *more* trouble.]

> Kathleen Newsome has my vote for mayor because she has the best-run campaign organization. [Shouldn't one's vote be based on the candidate's qualities, not the campaign organization's?]

False analogy

An **analogy** is a comparison between two essentially unlike things for the purpose of definition or illustration. (See also 1d-6 and 3c-2.) In arguing by analogy, a writer draws a likeness between things on the basis of a single shared feature and then extends the likeness to other features. But analogy can only illustrate a point, never prove it. It can trick one into assuming that because things are similar in one respect, they *must* be alike in other respects. The following is an example of this fallacy, which is called **false analogy**.

> The non-human primates such as chimpanzees and gorillas care for their young, clean and groom each other, and defend themselves and sometimes the group from attack. Why, then, must the human primates go so much further—unemployment insurance, child care, welfare, hospital insurance, and so on—to protect the weak? [Taken to its logical extreme, this analogy would lead us to ask why we speak to each other when gorillas do not.]

EXERCISE 9

The following sentences exemplify the fallacies discussed in the text. Determine what is wrong with each sentence, and then revise it to make it more logical.

1. A successful marriage demands a maturity that no one under twenty-five possesses.
2. Students' persistent complaints about the grading system prove that it is unfair.
3. World War I was caused by the assassination of Archduke Ferdinand.
4. People watch television because they are too lazy to talk or read or because they want mindless escape from their lives.
5. Working people are slaves to their corporate masters: they have no freedom to do what they want, and they can be traded to other companies.
6. The stories about welfare chiselers show that the welfare system supports only shirkers and cheats.
7. Mountain climbing is more dangerous than people think: my cousin has fainted three times since he climbed Mount Revelstoke.
8. Racial tension is bound to occur when people with different backgrounds are forced to live side by side.
9. The free-trade agreement with the United States will eventually destroy our national identity.
10. She admits to being an atheist, so how can she be a good philosophy teacher?

EXERCISE 10

Evaluate the following brief essay for its effectiveness in persuading you (or any reader) to accept the writer's argument. Look especially for sound or unsound inductive or deductive reasoning, begged or ignored questions, overstated assumptions, and fallacies.

Let's Hear It for Asphalt

The truly disadvantaged students on this campus are the commuters. We pay our money and work hard for our degrees, yet we can never find places to park our cars. Commuters are regularly treated as second-class citizens compared with resident students. But nowhere is the discrepancy more noticeable than in the parking situation.

The fact is that there aren't enough parking spaces for half the cars on campus. Students are lucky to make their classes at all after driving around for hours looking for a place to park their cars. If parking were easier, students would get better grades, and the school administrators would probably have the higher enrolments they're so desperate for.

The most maddening thing is that we have to pay good money for parking tickets on top of tuition and everything else. The money probably goes toward a new faculty office building or residence or one of the other building projects that eat up what little parking space there is. Meanwhile, we commuters are pushed farther and farther away from the centre of campus. But then why should the rich folks in charge of things care what happens to a few struggling students, some with families to support, who seek to better themselves?

The commuting students are like the Jews wandering in the wilderness. We need homelands for our cars and freedom from persecution by campus cops.

4c   Understanding the construction of arguments

Reading and writing arguments, a large part of what you do in school, can test all your critical skills. As a reader of arguments, you seek to understand, to determine validity, and to respond. You expect to have your views challenged, and you evaluate the validity of that challenge. As a writer of arguments, you work to offer a compelling, sound logic and ample evidence in hopes of changing the reader's views or behaviour. The previous sections on writing summaries and reasoning effectively can help you to do these things well. This section and the next two address argumentation more specifically.

Whether you are reading an argument or trying to construct one, the knowledge involved is much the same. Use the "Checklist for Reading or Writing an Argument" to help you evaluate any argument, including your own.

1   The general and the specific

In conversation with friends who trust your judgment, you might gain their acceptance of a general statement, such as *That movie is boring*, without supplying any supporting evidence. In a narrative essay you might gain readers' acceptance of the significance of an event by providing plentiful concrete details, without stating the significance outright. In argumentation, however, you cannot expect readers to accept you opinions unless you state them and provide the evidence to back them up. Nor should you, as a reader, accept the views of anyone who does not make a plain case and offer specific supporting evidence for it. An argumentative essay must present both general statements, or **assertions**, and the evidence to support those assertions. Neither is effective without the other. (We will discuss the kinds of assertions and evidence in detail in 4d and 4e.)

4c

CHECKLIST FOR READING OR WRITING AN ARGUMENT

1. What appeals does the writer (meaning you, if you are the writer) make to the reader? Emotional? Rational? A combination of the two? Are the appeals appropriate? (See 4c-2.)
2. Has the writer anticipated and responded to reasonable objections? (See 4c-3.)
3. What combination of fact, opinion, and belief constitutes the writer's assertions? Has the author defined the key terms of the assertions? (See 4d-1 and 4d-2.)
4. Has the writer supported the assertions with varying and appropriate kinds of evidence (i.e., facts, examples, expert opinions)? Is the evidence accurate, relevant, representative, and adequate? (See 4e-1 and 4e-2.)
5. Has the writer reasoned inductively or deductively? Is the reasoning effective? (See 4b-1 and 4b-2.) Has the writer faced the question? (See 4b-3.) Has the writer avoided faulty reasoning? (See 4b-4.)

Most effective arguments state the central assertion of the essay in a thesis sentence (see 1g) so that readers understand the writer's purpose and know what they are supposed to agree with. The body of the essay then demonstrates the validity of the thesis by breaking it down into other assertions. Each assertion may be the topic sentence of a paragraph (see 3a), with the remainder of the paragraph consisting of the evidence for the assertion—the facts, examples, and so on that make the assertion true.

2 | **Appeals to reason and emotion**

In Chapter 1 we discussed the way details and tone can gain readers' interest and support in any kind of writing (see 1f). Argumentation presents a special challenge to the writer because the aim is to affect, often to change, the way readers think and feel about a subject. Readers approached for this reason are also challenged to remain open to new ideas and evidence and yet not submit to sheer manipulation of their thoughts and feelings.

In forming convictions about arguable issues—capital punishment, acid rain, defence spending, the best location for a new town dump—we generally interpret the factual evidence through the filter of our values, beliefs, tastes, desires, and feelings. Mayor Jones may object to placing the new town dump in a particular wooded area because the facts suggest that the site is not large enough and that prevailing winds will blow odours back through the town. But Mayor

4c

Jones may also have fond memories of playing in the wooded area as a child, feelings that colour his interpretation of the facts and strengthen his conviction that the dump should be placed elsewhere. His conviction is partly rational, because it is based on evidence, and partly emotional, because it is also based on feelings.

Most effective arguments combine **rational appeals** to readers' capacities for reasoning logically from evidence to a conclusion with **emotional appeals** to readers' beliefs and feelings. The following three passages, all expressing the same view on the same subject, illustrate how either a primarily rational or a primarily emotional appeal may be weaker than an approach that uses both.

RATIONAL APPEAL

In its report the commission expresses too strong a concern for the public image of nuclear power. The commission regards the Howe nuclear plant as now "safe," with the risk of accident "an acceptably low 3 in 10 000 per year." Yet it maintains that the general public may not accept the experts' judgments of safety. To "strengthen public faith in nuclear power," the commission calls for additional safety precautions to achieve a "slight" further reduction in risk, to 1 in 10 000. The report does not address the high cost of these additional precautions or how the financially unstable plant is to pay for them.

EMOTIONAL APPEAL

The commission is clearly more intent on improving the public image of nuclear power than on making this much-needed source of energy available for public use. In recommending additional and totally unnecessary safety precautions at the Howe nuclear plant, the commission shows blind unconcern that a minor improvement in public image might be gained at the expense of the plant's being shut down for good.

RATIONAL AND EMOTIONAL APPEALS

In its report the commission reveals itself to be more intent on improving the public image of nuclear power than on making this much-needed source of energy available for public use. The commission regards the Howe nuclear plant as now "safe," with the risk of accident "an acceptably low 3 in 10 000 per year." Yet it worries that the general public may not accept the experts' judgments of safety. To "strengthen public faith in nuclear power," the commission calls for additional safety precautions to achieve a "slight" further reduction in risk, to 1 in 10 000. The report does not acknowledge that these unnecessary precautions would be prohibitively expensive, especially for a plant that is already financially unstable. Apparently the commission is unconcerned that a minor

4c

improvement in public image might be gained at the expense of the plant's being shut down for good.

Notice the differences in these three passages. The first one emphasizes the evidence that supports the claim of the first sentence: the current risk, the desired risk, and the omissions from the report. The writer appeals to readers' reason by making an arguable assertion and then providing the facts to back it up; but he fails to address readers' feelings on the issue. The second passage emphasizes the writer's interpretation of the facts: merely to improve the public image of nuclear power, the commission requires unnecessary safety precautions that will jeopardize the availability of nuclear power. The writer appeals to readers' emotions—to their desire for more plentiful energy supplies, their receptiveness to nuclear energy, and even their distaste for public relations ploys—but he fails to provide supporting evidence. The third passage combines both kinds of appeal. Thus it gives readers both a rational and an emotional basis for accepting the writers' view that the commission is willing to sacrifice nuclear power out of concern for public relations alone, not for actual safety.

As the third passage illustrates, an appeal to emotion is a way to establish common ground between the writer and the reader. Writers use emotional appeals to demonstrate that they share with readers beliefs and desires that can and should influence the interpretation of the facts. For such an appeal to be successful, however, it must be appropriate for the audience and the argument. An appeal is inappropriate for the *audience* when it misjudges readers' actual feelings. The writer of the third passage assumed that his readers would want nuclear power to supplement other energy supplies. If, instead, his readers feared nuclear power, finding even a minimal risk too high, then he would fail to convince them that the commission's concerns were misplaced.

An appeal is inappropriate for the *argument* when it raises emotional issues that are irrelevant to the assertions and the evidence. For example, the writer of the third passage might have tried to bolster his case by stating that one member of the commission was once an executive with the regional natural-gas company. But the statement would be inappropriate on at least two counts: it would attack a member of the commission rather than the report of the entire commission; and the attack would be based on the unproved assumption that the member's past employment invalidated his current judgment. As a writer, you want to avoid inappropriate appeals. As a reader, you are justified in challenging a writer who makes inappropriate appeals. See pages 143–45 for further examples of inappropriate appeals.

4c

3 Anticipation of objections

By definition, an arguable issue has more than one side: however well supported a case is and however strongly the writer believes in it, others can marshal their own evidence to support a different view or even several different views. Some of these others are likely to be in any reading audience. But even readers who have no preconceptions about a subject will suspect that the one side presented in an argument is but *one* side. When a writer ignores the opposition or pretends that none exists, readers are justified in finding the resulting argument less sound than the writer claims and even in considering the argument dishonest.

As a reader, then, you may decide whether to agree or disagree with a writer partly on the basis of how he or she handles possible objections. As a writer, you need to acknowledge opposing views forthrightly, grant any validity they may have, and demonstrate why, despite their validity, the opposing views are less compelling than your own. The student who wrote the following paragraph took this approach.

> The administration argues against increasing the meagre budget of the French department on the grounds that the French courses now offered are underenrolled. It is true that the first-year courses have few students, and some upper-level courses have had to be cancelled. But the Dean is missing the point. The issue is not that demand determines supply but that supply encourages demand. If the French department had the money to improve the language labs, hire more professors, and offer a full and varied program of courses, the students would respond in large numbers, instead of seeking their degrees in French at other better-equipped institutions.

The writer first acknowledges the possible truth of the administration's arguments. Then he shows that the Dean fails to address the central issue, the viability of the French program.

4 A sample argument

The following student essay illustrates the principles discussed so far in this section. As you read the essay, look especially for general assertions and supporting evidence and for rational and emotional appeals.

A Year for Canada

Among the social problems in Canada today two are particularly troubling. One is the tendency of people to see those with different moral, reli-

Introduction: identification of problems

gious, social, economic, and political views as "the enemy"—absolutely wrong, even somewhat less than human. The other is the tendency to see government not as the resolver of such differences—the place where compromises are hammered out—but as the chief problem itself, either too intrusive or not responsive enough, depending on one's point of view. The loss of respect and sympathy for the "other guy" and the loss of faith in government are depriving us of a sense of community—of belonging to, sharing in, and contributing to our country. One step toward restoring this sense of community could be achieved by requiring a year of government service from each citizen.

Thesis: a proposal for a solution

A program of mandatory government service might be set up as follows. On finishing high school or reaching age eighteen, all young adults would be expected to spend one year working for the government (local, provincial, or federal). The service might be with the military, but it could also be with social service agencies, hospitals, schools, national parks, data processing centres, road maintenance departments, or any other government group. Program participants would be paid the minimum wage and would work full-time throughout the year. There would be no deferments or exemptions from service, except possibly for severe economic hardship or mental or physical disability.

Explanation of the proposal

This program could substantially reduce the present polarization in our society. In keeping with the Canadian multicultural and mosaic heritage, the program would be a great integrator: male and female, rich and poor, urban and rural—all would serve together. Participants would be exposed to others whose cultures, backgrounds, experiences, and values were previously unknown or misunderstood. They would become more aware and tolerant of diversity, more sympathetic toward "different" people, more respectful of different views.

Support for the proposal: first advantage

In addition to learning about each other, the participants would also learn first-hand about their government. They would see for themselves the huge variety of services that we expect our government to deliver, from keeping roads free of litter to providing health care. In many jobs they would come face to face with the people who benefit from government services—the middle-class homeowner, the school-aged child, the disabled senior citizen, the impoverished mother of five. In short, participants would see the many ways in which their government serves them and others. And that experience could turn their cynicism about government into healthy appreciation and respect.

Support for the proposal: second advantage

The participants would gain personally as well. The year of service would expose them to a broad range of career options, both in and out of government. They would gain some of the exper-

Support for the proposal: third advantage

4c

ience and information necessary to discover their talents and interests and to make realistic and appropriate decisions about further education and eventual career paths. They would also acquire marketable skills that would give them a boost in whatever work they chose. On a less practical level, participants would begin to see themselves as belonging and contributing to the larger community of which they were a part. Such awareness would reduce the sense of isolation and frustration that often disturbs young adults.

The proposal for a mandatory year of government service is bound to meet at least two objections. First, the young adults who would be affected might not want to give up a year of their lives. However, since everyone else in their age group would be making the same sacrifice, they would not be at any disadvantage. And with public education, the young adults could be made to take pride in their sacrifice and service. The second major objection would be cost: with budget deficits already weakening our economy, how can we possibly afford such as program? Granted, the program would cost money in its initial stages, as the administrative machinery was set in motion and the low-level government employees being displaced by participants were retrained for jobs outside government. Eventually, however, the program could save money because the participants, receiving minimum wage, would cost less to do the same work now performed by relatively highly paid government employees. Furthermore, the government labour force would grow temporarily when participants began serving but before existing employees had been retrained and moved out. With a larger labour force, government could do many things it now cannot do because of inadequate labour, such as plant trees in logging areas, give individual attention to disadvantaged children, and help the elderly with daily living. The money would be well spent.

Responses to probable objections

Despite its personal and monetary costs, a program of mandatory government service would be enormously beneficial to Canada. Its young people would learn to work together creatively, despite their differences, to resolve problems. And instead of seeing their government as something *other* than themselves, a faceless giant either too intrusive or too unresponsive to be worth its cost, they would see it as an integral part of their lives.

Conclusion: summary of how the plan would solve the problems identified in the introduction

—A STUDENT

EXERCISE 11

Analyse the construction and effectiveness of the preceding essay by answering the following questions.

1. Where does the writer make general assertions related to her thesis sentence, and where does she provide examples or other evidence to support the assertions?

4c

2. Where does the writer appeal primarily to reason, and where does she appeal primarily to emotion? What specific beliefs, values, and desires of readers does the writer appeal to?
3. What objections to her plan does the writer anticipate? What reasons does she give for dispensing with them?
4. How effective do you find this argument? To what extent do you agree with the writer about the problems identified in her introduction? To what extent does she convince you that her plan is desirable and workable and would solve those problems? Does she fail to anticipate any major objections to her plan?
5. Write a formal evaluation of "A Year for Canada." First summarize the writer's views. Then respond to those views by answering the questions posed in item 4, above.

EXERCISE 12

Identify each sentence below either as a general assertion in need of support or as possible evidence for some general assertion.

1. Drugs and alcohol are particularly dangerous for someone with a family history of substance abuse.
2. Revenue Canada estimates that perhaps half of all taxpayers do not report all their income.
3. The city jail is so overcrowded that cells intended for two inmates now house three or four.
4. The university's policy of open admissions has benefited economically and educationally disadvantaged students.
5. Whatever her motivation, Ms. Horne has succeeded in refocussing employees' attention and energy on achieving corporate goals.

EXERCISE 13

Identify each sentence below either as a rational appeal or as an emotional appeal.

1. Only complacency, indifference, or selfishness could allow us to ignore these people's hunger.
2. As the data collected by the researchers demonstrate, a mandatory sentence for impaired driving can lead to a reduction in alcohol-related car accidents.
3. The broadcasters themselves accept that children's television is a fair target for regulation.
4. Anyone who cherishes life in all its diversity could not help being appalled by the mistreatment of laboratory animals.
5. Many experts in constitutional law have warned that the rule violates the Charter of Rights and Freedoms.

4d

4d Testing assertions

As we saw in the preceding section, assertions are fundamental to an argument. Though an assertion must generally be well supported for readers to accept it fully, the likelihood of acceptance can be improved or diminished by the nature of the assertion and its degree of concreteness or abstraction.

1 Fact, opinion, belief, and prejudice

Most statements we hear, read, or make in speaking and writing are assertions of fact, opinion, belief, or prejudice. In argumentation the usefulness and acceptability of an assertion depends partly on which of these categories it falls into.

A **fact** is verifiable—that is, one can determine whether it is true. It may involve numbers or dates: *The football field is 110 yards long. World War II ended in 1945*. Or the numbers may be implied: *The earth is closer to the sun than Saturn is. The cost of medical care is rising*. Or the fact may involve no numbers at all: *The city council adjourned without taking a vote. The Senate vetoed the bill*. The truth of the fact is beyond argument if one can assume that measuring devices or records or memories are correct. Facts provide crucial support for the assertions of an argument. But because they are inarguable, they do not make worthwhile assertions by themselves.

An **opinion** is a judgment *based* on facts, an honest attempt to draw a reasonable conclusion from evidence. For example, you know that hundreds of thousands of people go without proper food and lodging because they can't afford it, and so you form the judgment that governments should increase welfare payments even though it would cost millions of dollars. This opinion expresses a viewpoint. It is arguable because the same facts might lead another reasonable person to a different opinion (for instance, that governments simply can't afford higher welfare payments, even if people must suffer). And the opinion is potentially changeable: with more evidence you might conclude that the problems of welfare recipients could be solved by other means than increased payments.

The thesis of an argument is always an opinion, and other, more specific opinions generally form the backbone of the argument supporting the thesis. By themselves, however, opinions do not make arguments. A writer must always let readers know what the evidence is and how it has led to each opinion, and readers must always satisfy themselves that the writer has fulfilled this responsibility. (See 4e on evidence.)

4d

An opinion is not the same as a **belief**, a conviction based on cultural or personal faith, morality, or values. Statements such as *Capital punishment is legalized murder* and *The primary goal of government should be to provide equality of opportunity for all* are often called opinions because they express viewpoints. Unlike opinions, however, such beliefs are not based on facts and other evidence. They cannot be disproved by facts or even contested on the basis of facts. Thus they should not serve as the thesis of an argument because they, like facts, are inarguable. However, as we saw in the earlier discussion of emotional appeals, statements of belief can be effective in argumentation if readers share the writer's feelings. For instance, a writer might support an argument that governments should increase welfare payments not only with facts demonstrating the need but also with the assertion that a nation cannot be just while hundreds of thousands of its citizens suffer needlessly. If you as the reader agree with this assertion, you will probably be more open to other parts of the writer's argument.

One kind of assertion that has no place in argumentation is **prejudice**, an opinion based on insufficient or unexamined evidence: *Women are bad drivers. Fat people are jolly. Teenagers are irresponsible.* Unlike a belief, a prejudice is testable: it can be contested and disproved on the basis of facts. Very often, however, we form prejudices or accept them from others—parents, friends, the communications media—without questioning their meaning or testing their truth. At best, they are thoughtless oversimplifications: *some* women are bad drivers, but so are *some* men. At worst, assertions of prejudice reflect a narrow-minded view of the world. Writers who display prejudice are not likely to win the confidence and agreement of readers. Readers who accept prejudice are not thinking critically. (See also 31a-8 on avoiding sexist and other biassed language.)

2   Defined terms

In any argument, but especially in arguments about abstract ideas, clear and consistent definition of terms is essential. In the following assertion the writer is not clear about what she means by *justice*.

> Over the past few decades justice has deteriorated so badly that it almost does not exist anymore.

We can't tell what the writer is asserting because we don't know what *justice*, the crucial term of the sentence, means to her. The word is abstract; it does not refer to anything specific or concrete and in fact

4d

has varied meanings. The eight definitions in the *Gage Canadian Dictionary* include "fair dealing" and "the administration of law." When the writer specifies her meaning, her assertion is much clearer.

> If by *justice* we mean treating people fairly, punishing those who commit crimes, and protecting the victims of those crimes, then justice has deteriorated badly over the past few decades.

Of course, we need to see how this writer supports her assertion before we can accept it, but at least we now understand her definition of *justice*.

Highly abstract words such as *justice*, *equality*, *success*, and *maturity* may require an entire paragraph of definition if they are central to an argument. See Chapter 3, page 110, for more on definition and a paragraph defining the abstract word *quality*.

EXERCISE 14

Identify the assertions of fact, opinion, belief, and prejudice in the following paragraph.

Cigarette advertising has already been banned from television and radio, and the federal government is fully justified in now banning it from newspapers, magazines, and billboards, as well as from cultural and sports sponsorships. Numerous research studies have linked smoking with disease and death, and it is simply wrong to advertise a health- and life-threatening activity. Nevertheless, the major tobacco companies continue to spend more than $500 million per year advertising their products. In sharp contrast, the federal government and health organizations such as the Canadian Cancer Society spend perhaps $100 million per year on programs and advertisements designed to educate the public about the dangers of smoking. Clearly, these efforts cannot begin to counterbalance the onslaught of the tobacco companies' messages that smoking gives a person romance, beauty, fun, and happiness. And even if there were more balance in what the public is told about smoking, people who smoke are so mindless that they would ignore the warnings and heed only the sales pitches.

EXERCISE 15

The following paragraph fails to define important words clearly enough for us to pin down the meaning intended. Identify the undefined terms and revise the paragraph as you see fit to eliminate the problems.

The best solution to current problems is one we don't hear of very often: self-sufficiency. If we were more self-sufficient, we would not have to rely so much on scarce resources to satisfy basic needs. Sure, some of us play at gardening, sewing, and other skills, but very few of us try to free ourselves of the grocery store's vegetables or the department store's clothes. If we were more self-sufficient, we would be more secure because independence ultimately creates a bond between individuals.

4e Weighing evidence

As we saw in Chapters 1 and 3, evidence is crucial in any kind of writing to make readers understand meaning and to engage their interest. In argumentation, however, evidence must do even more: it must demonstrate to readers the validity of the writer's opinions. A clear and reasonable assertion will open readers' minds to evidence. But if the evidence is then inadequate or questionable, readers should and probably will reject the assertion, and the writer's cause will be at least partly and perhaps wholly lost. In the following sections we will look at the kinds of evidence used in argumentation and then at the criteria for evaluating such evidence.

1 Kinds of evidence

Writers draw on several kinds of evidence to support their assertions. One discussed already is **facts**, statements whose truth is subject to verification (see p. 158).

Quebec is almost three times the size of France.

By law, seat belts must be worn in a majority of the provinces.

Facts employing numbers are **statistics**.

Of those polled, 62 percent stated a preference for a flat tax.

In 1987 there were 85 000 men and women in the full-time Canadian Armed Forces and approximately 22 000 in the reserves.

The average Canadian household consists of 3.1 persons.

Another kind of evidence is **examples**, specific instances of the point being made, including historical precedents. The following passage uses a personal anecdote as partial support for the assertion in the first sentence.

4e

Besides broadening students' knowledge, required courses can also introduce students to possible careers that they otherwise would have known nothing about. Somewhat reluctantly, I enrolled in a psychology course to satisfy the social science requirement. But what I learned in the course has led me to consider becoming a clinical psychologist instead of an engineer.

A third kind of evidence is **expert opinions**, the judgments formed by authorities on the basis of their own examination of the facts. In the following passage the writer cites the opinion of an expert to support the assertion in the first sentence.

Despite tremendous advancements in our century, science is powerless, by itself, to solve the world's escalating problems of overpopulation and environmental destruction. Dr. David Suzuki, a well-known geneticist from the University of British Columbia who has fostered public awareness of the relation between science and society, maintains that "solutions to the environmental crisis will not come from science but will be political and socio-economic."

As this passage illustrates, a citation of expert opinion is generally accompanied by a reference to the expert's credentials. (See also 36f-2, p. 594.)

2 The reliability of evidence

To support assertions and convince readers, evidence must be reliable—that is, it must be accurate, relevant, representative, and adequate.

Accurate evidence is drawn from trustworthy sources, quoted exactly, and presented with the original meaning unchanged. In researching an essay in favour of free trade, for instance, you might consult statistics provided by the Canadian Labour Congress as well as those provided by the Canadian Manufacturers' Association to ensure that your evidence is sound from both perspectives. In quoting a source, be careful to preserve the author's true meaning, not just a few words that happen to support your argument. For instance, you would distort the writer's meaning if you quoted only the first sentence in the following passage as evidence of the positive effect of television.

Television can be an effective force for education and understanding, for appreciation of people and their troubles and accomplishments. But it assumes that role so rarely that we have only fleeting glimpses of the possibilities. We know better the dull-witted, narrow-minded fare that monopolizes the set from one year to the next.

Not just opinions but also facts and examples may be misinter-
preted or distorted. Suppose you were reading an argument for
extending a three-year-old law allowing the police to stop vehicles
randomly as a means of apprehending drunk drivers. If the author
cited statistics showing that the number of drunk-driving accidents
dropped in the first two years of the law, but failed to note that the
numbers rose back to the previous level in the third year, then the
evidence would be distorted and thus inaccurate. You or any reader
would be justified in questioning the entire argument, no matter how
accurate the rest seemed.

Relevant evidence comes from sources with authority on a
topic and relates directly to the point the writer is making. Unless
your uncle is a recognized expert on the Canadian Security Intelligence Service (CSIS), or unless you can establish his authority, his
opinion of whether the CSIS threatens the civil rights of Canadians is
not relevant to your paper on the subject. If your aunt is a member of
the town council, however, her views may very well be relevant
evidence in an essay on how a new shopping mall will hurt the town
merchants.

Representative evidence reflects the full range of the sample
from which it is said to be drawn. For instance, in an essay arguing
that residences should stay open during school holidays, a writer
might cite the opinions of the school's 10 000 students. But that
writer would mislead you and other readers if, on the basis of a poll
among her roommates and residence neighbours, she reported as
evidence that "the majority of students favour leaving the residences
open." A few residents could not be said to represent the entire
student body, particularly the non-resident students. To be representative, the poll would have to survey many more students in propor-
tions that reflect the numbers of resident and non-resident students
on campus.

Adequate evidence is plentiful and specific enough to support
a writer's assertions. To convince readers of an opinion, a writer must
tell them what information it is based on. If you are writing an essay
about animal abuse, you cannot hope to win over your readers solely
with statements like *Too many animals are deliberately injured or
killed by humans every year*. You need to supply facts instead of the
vague *too many*. How many animals are injured? How many die? You
need to specify the conditions under which animals are injured or
killed. And you need to demonstrate that the actions are deliberate,
perhaps with examples of animal abuse. Adequate, well-selected
evidence is crucial to an effective argument.

As a writer, you are responsible for the accuracy, relevance,
representativeness, and adequacy of your evidence. As a reader, you

should be alert to these qualities (or their absence) and sensitive to how the quality and quantity of evidence affects your responses.

4e

EXERCISE 16

Supply at least two pieces of evidence—examples from your own experience or facts or expert opinions from other sources—to support each of the following general assertions.

1. A university education is too costly (or is a good value for the money).
2. _____ is a television program (or movie or book) that should be a model for all entertainment aimed at adolescents (or children or parents).
3. _____ is a good teacher (or employer, doctor, or politician).
4. Canadians are energy spendthrifts.
5. Driver education makes one a better driver.

EXERCISE 17

Locate the statements of evidence in the following passages, and evaluate each one against the four criteria of accuracy, relevance, representativeness, and adequacy.

1. Our lakes and forests are being destroyed by acid rain. For example, many groves of maple trees have died. My minister says there are several lakes where fish can't survive. Are we a country that does not care enough about its resources to conserve them?

2. Crime is out of control in this city. Three months ago my parents' house was burglarized. The thieves stole their food processor and their vibrating bed as well as their television and stereo. Then a month ago my roommate had her pocket picked on the subway. And last week I saw a confused old man trying to describe to the police how muggers had stolen his wallet and his groceries as he walked home from the corner market.

PART II

Grammatical Sentences

CHAPTER 5

Understanding Sentence Grammar

Grammar describes how language works. Many people who write well would have difficulty explaining in grammatical terms how their sentences work. But when something goes wrong in a sentence, a knowledge of grammar helps in recognizing the problem and provides a language for discussing it.

Grammar can help us understand sentences even if we don't know the meaning of all the words in the sentence.

The rumfrum biggled the pooba.

We don't know what that sentence means. But we can infer that something called a *rumfrum* did something to a *pooba*. He (or she, or it) *biggled* it, whatever that means. We know this because we understand the basic grammar and word order of simple English sentences. We understand that this sentence seems like *The boy kicked the ball* or *The student passed the test*. As in those sentences, a single word following *the* names something; words with *-ed* endings usually denote action of some sort, especially when they fall in patterns like *the rumfrum biggled*; and the word groups beginning with *the* and *that*, coming after words like *biggled*, usually name something that receives the action indicated.

In the sense that we understand *The rumfrum biggled the pooba*, we can understand more complex sentences such as the following:

The stintless rumfrums biggled the jittish poobas who were kerpesting the gloots.

We don't know what *stintless* and *jittish* mean, but we do know that they describe *rumfrums* and *poobas*, respectively, and that the *poobas were kerpesting* (doing something to) *the gloots*, probably more than one *gloot*. We understand these relations among the words because we recognize structures that recur in everyday talking and writing. Each statement is a **sentence**, the basic unit of writing.

5a   Understanding the basic sentence

The basic grammar of sentences consists of the kinds of words that compose them, the functions of those words, the patterns on which sentences are built, and the ways those patterns can be expanded and elaborated. Understanding basic grammar can help you create clear sentences that effectively relate your ideas.

1   Identifying subjects and predicates

Most sentences make statements. First they name something; then they make an assertion about or describe an action involving that something. These two sentence parts are the **subject** and the **predicate**.

Subject	Predicate
Amanda	took the money to the bank.
Leroy	rode his bicycle down the middle of the street.
All the members of my family	were churchgoers from their earliest years.

2   Identifying the basic words: nouns and verbs

If we study the following five simple sentences, we find that they consist almost entirely of two quite different kinds of words.

Subject	Predicate
The earth	trembled.
The earthquake	destroyed the city.
The result	was chaos.
The government	sent the city aid.
The citizens	considered the earthquake a disaster.

In these sentences the words *earth, earthquake, government,* and *citizens* name things; in contrast, the words *trembled, destroyed,* and *sent* express actions. These two groups of words work in different ways. We can have one *citizen* or many *citizens,* but we cannot have one or more *destroyeds.* If we drop the *-ed* from *destroyed,* we change the time of the action. But we cannot add *-ed* to *citizen* and have *citizened.* The word *citizen* just doesn't work that way.

gr
5a

Grammar reflects these differences by identifying **parts of speech** or **word classes.** Except for the words *the* and *a,* which simply point to and help identify the words after them, our five sentences consist of two parts of speech: **nouns,** words that name; and **verbs,** words that express an action or an occurrence or a state of being. These are the basic words in English; without them we cannot form even the simplest sentences. The nouns and verbs in our sample sentences appear below.

NOUNS	VERBS
earth	trembled
earthquake	destroyed
result	was
government	sent
citizens	considered
city	
chaos	
aid	
disaster	

We can identify nouns and verbs both by their meanings and by their forms.

Nouns

MEANING

Nouns name. They may name a person (*Glenn Gould, Jacques Cartier, astronaut*), a thing (*chair, book, airplane*), a quality (*pain, mystery, simplicity*), a place (*city, Ottawa, ocean, Red Sea*), or an idea (*reality, peace, success*). Whatever exists or can be thought to exist has a name. Its name is a noun.

FORM

Almost all nouns that name countable things add an *-s* to distinguish between the singular, meaning "one," and the plural, meaning "more than one": *earthquake, earthquakes; city, cities; citizen, citizens.* A few nouns form irregular plurals: *man, men; child, children; goose, geese.* Nouns also form a possessive by adding *-'s:*

citizen, citizen's; city, city's; father, father's. This possessive form shows ownership (*Sheila's books*) and source (*Auden's poems*) as well as some other relationships.

Some nouns in our sample sentences—*chaos* and *earth*—do not usually form plurals. These words belong to a subgroup called **mass nouns**. They name something that is not usually countable, such as *sugar, silver*, and *gravel*; or they name qualities, such as *courage, fortitude*, and *anger*. Other important groups of nouns not illustrated in our sentences are **proper nouns** such as *Ann, Cairo*, and *Fraser River*, which name specific people, places, and things; and **collective nouns** such as *army, family*, and *herd*, which name groups.

gr
5a

THE PARTS OF SPEECH

(For more information, consult the sections or pages in parentheses.)

Nouns name persons, places, things, ideas, or qualities: *Champlain, girl, North Saskatchewan River, coastline, Koran, table, strife, happiness*. (See opposite page and Guide to Nouns, p. 207.)

Pronouns usually substitute for nouns and function as nouns: *I, you, he, she, it, we, they, myself, this, that, who, which, everyone*. (See p. 171 and Guide to Pronouns, p. 208.)

Verbs express actions, occurrences, or states of being: *run, bunt, inflate, become, be*. (See p. 170 and Guide to Verbs and Verbals, p. 209.)

Adjectives describe or modify nouns or pronouns: *gentle, small, helpful*. (See p. 177 and Guide to Modifiers, p. 211.)

Adverbs describe or modify verbs, adjectives, other adverbs, or whole groups of words: *gently, helpfully, almost, really, someday*. (See p. 177 and Guide to Modifiers, p. 211.)

Prepositions relate nouns or pronouns to other words in a sentence: *about, at, down, for, of, with*. (See 5c-1.)

Conjunctions link words, phrases, and clauses. **Co-ordinating conjunctions** and **correlative conjunctions** link words, phrases, or clauses of equal importance: *and, but, or, nor; both . . . and, not only . . . but also, either . . . or*. (See 5d-1.) **Subordinating conjunctions** introduce subordinate clauses and link them to main clauses: *although, because, if, whenever*. (See 5c-4.)

Interjections express feeling or command attention, either alone or in a sentence: *hey, oh, darn, wow*. (See 20e, 21c-4.)

NOUNS WITH *THE*, *A*, and *AN*

Nouns are often preceded by *the* or *a* (*an* before a vowel sound: *an apple*). These words are usually called **articles**, but they may be described as **noun markers** since they always indicate that a noun will soon follow.

Verbs

MEANING

Verbs express an action (*bring, change, grow*), an occurrence (*become, happen*), or a state of being (*be, seem*).

FORM

Almost all verbs change form to indicate a difference between present and past time. To show past time, most verbs add *-d* or *-ed* to the form listed in the dictionary: *They play today. They played yesterday.* Some verbs indicate past time irregularly: *eat, ate; begin, began.* (See 7a.)

All verbs except *be* and *have* add *-s* or *-es* to their dictionary forms when their subjects are singular nouns or singular pronouns such as *he, she*, and *it*: *The bear escapes. It escapes. The woman begins. She begins.* When their subjects are plural nouns or pronouns, verbs retain their dictionary forms: *The bears escape. The women begin.* The *-s* forms of *be* and *have* are *is* and *has*; and *are* is the form of *be* with plural subjects. (See Chapter 7, pp. 223–25, for a fuller discussion of verb forms.)

HELPING VERBS

The dictionary form of all verbs can combine with the words *do, does, did, can, could, may, might, will, would, shall, should*, and *must*: *could run, may escape, must help.* These words are called **helping verbs** or **auxiliary verbs**. They and a few others combine with special forms of verbs to make verb phrases such as *will be running, might have escaped*, and *could have been helped*. (See Chapter 7, pp. 224 and 230.)

A note on form and function

In different sentences an English word may serve different functions, take correspondingly different forms, and belong to different word classes. For example, *aid* functions as a noun in the sentence *The government sent the city aid.* But in *The government aids the city*, the word *aid* functions as a verb, taking the characteristic *-s* ending of a verb with a singular subject, *government*. In *The light burns*, the word *light* functions as a noun; but in *The lanterns light the path*, the word *light* functions as a verb. Because words can function in different ways, we must always determine how a particular word works in a sentence before we can identify what part of speech it is. The *function* of a word in a sentence always determines its part of speech in that sentence.

Pronouns

Before looking at the five basic sentence patterns in English, we need to look at a third group of words, the pronouns.

> Susanne enlisted in the Air Force. *She* leaves for her training in two weeks. Susanne is one of the people *who* took advanced physics in high school.

Most **pronouns** substitute for nouns and function in sentences as nouns do. In the sentences above, the pronoun *she* substitutes for *Susanne*, and the pronoun *who* substitutes for *people*.

Pronouns fall into several subclasses depending on their form or function. **Personal pronouns** refer to a specific individual or to individuals. They are *I*, *you*, *he*, *she*, *it*, *we*, and *they*. **Indefinite pronouns**, such as *everybody* and *some*, do not substitute for any specific nouns, though they function as nouns (*Everybody likes Archie*). **Demonstrative pronouns**, including *this*, *that*, and *such*, identify or point to nouns (*This is the computer she used*). The **relative pronouns** *who*, *which*, and *that* relate groups of words to nouns or other pronouns (*Jim spoke to the boys who broke the window*). Intensive and reflexive pronouns have different functions but the same form: a personal pronoun plus *-self* (*himself*, *yourself*). **Intensive pronouns** emphasize a noun or other pronoun (*She herself asked the question*). **Reflexive pronouns** indicate that the sentence subject also receives the action of the verb (*You might hurt yourself*). Finally, **interrogative pronouns**, including *who*, *which*, and *what*, introduce questions (*Who will come to the concert?*).

The personal pronouns *I*, *he*, *she*, *we*, and *they* and the relative pronoun *who* change form depending on their function in the sentence. (For a discussion of these form changes, see Chapter 6.)

EXERCISE 1

Identify the subject and the predicate of each of the following sentences. Then use each sentence as a model to create a sentence of your own.

Example:
An important scientist spoke at convocation.

SUBJECT	PREDICATE
An important scientist	spoke at convocation.

The hungry family ate at the restaurant.

1. The leaves fell.
2. October ends soon.
3. The orchard owners made apple cider.
4. They examined each apple carefully before using it.
5. More than a hundred people will buy cider at the roadside stand.

EXERCISE 2

In the following sentences identify all words functioning as nouns with *N*, all words functioning as verbs with *V*, and all pronouns with *P*.

Example:

We took the tour through the museum.

   P   V   N   N
We took the *tour* through the *museum.*

1. The trees died.
2. They caught a disease.
3. The disease was a fungus.
4. It ruined a grove that was treasured.
5. Our great-grandfather planted the grove in the last century.

EXERCISE 3

Identify each of the following words as a noun, as a verb, or as both. Then create sentences of your own, using each word in each possible function.

Example:

fly
Noun and verb.
The *fly* sat on the meat loaf. [noun] The planes *fly* low. [verb]

1. wish	5. spend	8. company
2. tie	6. label	9. whistle
3. swing	7. door	10. glue
4. mail		

---

3   **Forming sentence patterns with nouns and verbs**

The five sample sentences introduced earlier reappear below with an *N* over each noun and a *V* over each verb.

       N   V
1. The earth trembled.

       N   V   N
2. The earthquake destroyed the city.

      N   V   N
3. The result was chaos.

       N   V   N N
4. The government sent the city aid.

     N   V   N   N
5. The citizens considered the earthquake a disaster.

These five sentences typify the five basic patterns on which we build all our sentences, even the most complex. The subjects of the sentences are similar, consisting only of a noun and an article or marker. But each predicate is different because the relation between the verb and the remaining words is different. The five patterns are diagrammed below. The following discussion examines each pattern in turn.

gr
5a

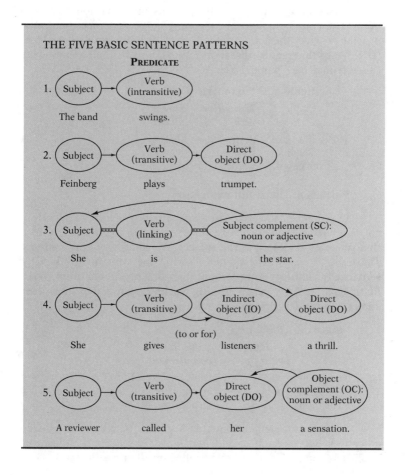

THE FIVE BASIC SENTENCE PATTERNS

PREDICATE

1. Subject → Verb (intransitive)

The band   swings.

2. Subject → Verb (transitive) → Direct object (DO)

Feinberg   plays   trumpet.

3. Subject ⋯ Verb (linking) ⋯ Subject complement (SC): noun or adjective

She   is   the star.

4. Subject → Verb (transitive) → Indirect object (IO) → Direct object (DO)

(to or for)

She   gives   listeners   a thrill.

5. Subject → Verb (transitive) → Direct object (DO) → Object complement (OC): noun or adjective

A reviewer   called   her   a sensation.

Pattern 1: The earth trembled.

In the simplest pattern the predicate consists only of the verb. Verbs in this pattern do not require following words to complete their meaning and thus are called **intransitive** (from Latin words meaning "not passing over").

SUBJECT	PREDICATE
	Intransitive verb
The earth	trembled.
Mosquitoes	buzz.
We	have been swimming.

Pattern 2: The earthquake destroyed the city.

In sentence 2 the predicate consists of a verb followed by a noun. The noun completes the meaning of the verb identifying who or what receives the action of the verb. This noun is a **direct object** (DO). Verbs that require direct objects to complete their meaning are called **transitive** ("passing over").

SUBJECT	PREDICATE	
	Transitive verb	*Direct object*
The earthquake	destroyed	the city.
The man	stubbed	his toe.
The people	wanted	peace.

Pattern 3: The result was chaos.

In sentence 3 the predicate also consists of a verb followed by a single noun. But here the verb *was* serves merely to introduce a word that renames or describes the subject. We could write the sentence *The result = chaos*. The noun following the verb in this kind of sentence is a **subject complement** (SC), or a **predicate noun**. Verbs in this pattern are called **linking verbs** because they link their subjects to the description that follows.

SUBJECT	PREDICATE	
	Linking verb	*Subject complement*
The result	was	chaos.
Jenn	is	an engineer.
The man	became	an accountant.

Subject complements in this sentence pattern may also be adjectives, words such as *tall* and *hopeful* (see 5b-1). Adjectives serving as complements are often called **predicate adjectives**.

SUBJECT	PREDICATE	
	Linking verb	*Subject complement*
The result	was	chaotic.
The house	seemed	expensive.

Pattern 4: The government sent the city aid.

In sentence 4 the predicate consists of a verb followed by two nouns. The second noun is a direct object, identifying what was sent. But the first noun, *city*, is different. This noun is an **indirect object** (IO), identifying to or for whom or what the action of the verb is performed. The direct object and indirect object refer to different things, people, or places.

SUBJECT	PREDICATE		
	Transitive verb	*Indirect object*	*Direct object*
The government	sent	the city	aid.
Neighbours	gave	the dog	a bone.
The boys	asked	their teacher	a question.
George	tossed	me	an apple.

Pattern 5: The citizens considered the earthquake a disaster.

In sentence 5 the predicate again consists of a verb followed by two nouns. But in this pattern the first noun is a direct object and the second noun renames or describes it. Here the second noun is an **object complement** (OC).

SUBJECT	PREDICATE		
	Transitive verb	*Direct object*	*Object complement*
The citizens	considered	the earthquake	a disaster.
The manager	made	him	an assistant.
The class	elected	Joan O'Day	president.
We	declared	her	the winner.

Notice that the relation between a direct object and an object complement is the same as that between a subject and a subject complement in pattern 3. Just as the subject complement renames or describes a subject, so an object complement renames or describes a direct object. And just as we can use either nouns or adjectives in pattern 3, so we can use either nouns or adjectives as object complements in this last pattern.

SUBJECT	PREDICATE		
	Transitive verb	*Direct object*	*Object complement*
The citizens	considered	the earthquake	disastrous.
The results	proved	Sweeney	wrong.
Success	makes	some people	nervous.

gr

5a

These five sentence patterns are the basic frameworks for most written English sentences. However long or complicated a sentence is, one or more of these basic patterns forms its foundation. A question may change the order of the subject and verb (*Is she a doctor?*), a command may omit the subject entirely (*Be quiet!*), and the order of the parts may be different in some statements (see 5e), but the same basic sentence parts will be present or clearly understood.

EXERCISE 4

In the following sentences, identify each verb as intransitive, transitive, or linking. Then identify each direct object (DO), indirect object (IO), subject complement (SC), and object complement (OC).

Example:
Children give their parents both headaches and pleasures.
Give is a transitive verb.

Children give their *parents* both *headaches* and *pleasures*.
(IO) (DO) (DO)

1. Many people find the movie offensive.
2. The car stalled.
3. I lost my dry-cleaning ticket.
4. The building is unusual.
5. Marie calls her boyfriend a genius.
6. The dentist's bill was five hundred dollars.
7. I read my brother *Charlotte's Web*.
8. Then I bought him his own copy.
9. The counterfeiter was a child.
10. The magician showed the audience his tricks.

EXERCISE 5

Create sentences by using each of the following verbs in the pattern indicated. You may want to change the form of the verb.

Example: give (S–V–IO–DO)

Sam gave his brother a birthday card.

1. laugh (S–V)
2. elect (S–V–DO–OC)

3. steal (S–V–DO)
4. catch (S–V–DO)

5. bring (S–V–IO–DO)
6. seems (S–V–SC)
7. call (S–V–DO–OC)

8. become (S–V–SC)
9. buy (S–V–IO–DO)
10. study (S–V)

5b   Expanding the basic sentence with single words

We have been studying simple sentences and their basic structures. But most of the sentences we read, write, or speak are more complex and also more informative and interesting. Most sentences contain one or more of the following: (1) modifying words; (2) word groups, called phrases and clauses; and (3) combinations of two or more words or word groups of the same kind. These sentence expanders are the subjects of this and the next two sections.

1   Using adjectives and adverbs

The simplest expansion of sentences occurs when we add modifying words to describe or limit the nouns and verbs. Modifying words add details.

Recently, the earth trembled.
The earthquake *nearly* destroyed the *old* city.
The *federal* government *soon* sent the city aid.

The added words do not all act the same way. *Old* and *federal* modify nouns, but *recently*, *nearly*, and *soon* do not. We don't speak of a *recently earthquake* or a *soon government*. Nor do we say *old sent*. We are dealing with two different parts of speech. **Adjectives** (such as *old*, *federal*, *heartless*, *friendly*) describe or modify nouns and pronouns. **Adverbs** (such as *recently*, *nearly*, *soon*, *never*, *always*) describe the action of verbs and also modify adjectives, other adverbs, and whole groups of words.

We cannot always identify adjectives and adverbs by their form. Although an *-ly* ending often signals an adverb, many adverbs—*never* and *always*, for example—have a different form. Moreover some adjectives end in *-ly*: in *likely candidate* and *lovely breeze*, *likely* and *lovely* clearly modify nouns and are thus adjectives. Therefore, to determine whether a word is an adjective or an adverb, we must identify the word or words it modifies.

Adjectives modify only nouns and pronouns. Adverbs may modify verbs, but they may also modify adjectives and other adverbs: *extremely unhappy* (adverb-adjective); *bitterly cold* (adverb-adjective); *very quickly* (adverb-adverb). Adverbs may also modify whole sentences or groups of words within a sentence. In *Unfortunately, we have no money*, for example, *unfortunately* modifies the whole sentence that follows it. In *She ran almost to the end of the street*, the adverb *almost* modifies *to the end of the street*.

Adverbs usually indicate where, when, how, or to what extent, as in the following sentences.

gr
5b

> Send all the mail *here*. [*Here* is *where* the mail is to be sent.]
>
> Fred will arrive *tomorrow*. [*Tomorrow* is *when* Fred will arrive.]
>
> Jeremy answered *angrily*. [*Angrily* is *how* Jeremy answered.]
>
> We are *completely* satisfied. [*Completely* indicates *to what extent* we are satisfied.]

Adjectives and adverbs appear in three forms distinguished by degree. The **positive degree** is the basic form, the one listed in the dictionary: *good, green, angry; badly, quickly, angrily*. The **comparative** form indicates a greater degree of the quality named by the word: *better, greener, angrier; worse, more quickly, more angrily*. The **superlative** form indicates the greatest degree of the quality named: *best, greenest, angriest; worst, most quickly, most angrily*. (For further discussion of the forms and uses of comparatives and superlatives, see 9e.)

EXERCISE 6

Identify the adjectives and adverbs in the following sentences. Then use each sentence as a model for creating a sentence of your own.

Example:

The *red* barn sat uncomfortably among *modern* buildings.
    ADJ   ADV   ADJ
The *red* barn sat *uncomfortably* among *modern* buildings.

The little girl complained loudly to her busy mother.

1. The icy rain created glassy patches on the roads.
2. Happily, children played in the slippery streets.
3. Fortunately, no cars ventured out.
4. Wise parents stayed indoors where they could be warm and dry.
5. The dogs slept soundly near the warm radiators.

EXERCISE 7

Change each of the following adjectives into an adverb, and change each adverb into an adjective. Then write one sentence using the adjective and another using the adverb.

Example:
sorrowful: *sorrowfully.*
Her expression was *sorrowful.*
David watched *sorrowfully* as the firefighters removed the charred remains of his furniture.

1. skilful	5. fortunately	8. painfully
2. wisely	6. bluntly	9. stupid
3. new	7. happy	10. sturdy
4. bright		

2   Using other words as modifiers

We have already observed that a particular word may function sometimes as a noun, sometimes as a verb. Similarly, nouns and special forms of verbs may sometimes serve as modifiers of other nouns. In combinations such as *office buildings, Thanksgiving prayer,* and *shock hazard,* the first noun modifies the second. In combinations such as *singing birds, corrected papers,* and *broken finger,* the first word is a verb form modifying the following noun. (These modifying verb forms are discussed in more detail in 5c-2.) Again, the part of speech to which we assign a word always depends on its function in a sentence.

EXERCISE 8

Use each of the following verb forms to modify a noun in a sentence of your own.

Example:
smoking
Only a *smoking cigar* remained.

1. scrambled	5. painted	8. ripened
2. twitching	6. written	9. known
3. rambling	7. charging	10. driven
4. typed		

EXERCISE 9

To practise expanding the basic sentence patterns with single-word modifiers, combine each group of sentences below into one sentence. You will have to delete and rearrange words.

Example:
The speaker told us the facts. The speaker told us calmly.
The facts were terrifying.
The speaker *calmly* told us the *terrifying* facts.

1. A painting hung on a wall. The painting was religious. The wall was wooden.
2. The clock ticked. The clock was big. It was a wall clock. It ticked noisily.
3. The parents comforted their children. The parents were departing. The children were nervous.
4. The house sheltered people. The people were homeless. The house was abandoned.
5. Children leave toys. The children are growing. They leave the toys behind. The toys are many. The toys are broken.
6. The car is a Chevrolet. The car is wrecked. The car is silver.
7. We bought our father a knife. We bought the knife recently. It is for carving.
8. The doors open. The doors are brass. They open inward.
9. The oceans are deep. The oceans contain fish. The fish are peculiar.
10. The boy drank the water. The boy was hiccupping. He drank the water quickly.

5c   Expanding the basic sentence with word groups

We have seen that nouns and verbs are the basic words of our language. Naming and asserting, they are all we need to build the basic sentence patterns. Adjectives and adverbs are the simplest modifiers, permitting us to qualify or limit nouns and verbs. But most sentences we read or write contain whole word groups that *serve* as nouns and modifiers. Such word groups enable us to combine several bits of information into one sentence and to make the relations among them clear. Consider the following sentence:

> When the ice cracked, the skaters, fearing an accident, sought safety at the lake's edge.

The skeleton of this sentence—the basic subject and predicate—is *The skaters sought safety*. The sentence pattern is subject (*skaters*), verb (*sought*), and direct object (*safety*). But attached to this skeleton are three other groups of words that add related information. Each word group could itself be stated as a basic sentence pattern: *The ice cracked. The skaters feared an accident. The lake's edge was safe.* In the sample sentence, however, each of these statements is reduced to something less than a sentence and then is inserted into the basic pattern *The skaters sought safety.* The reduced constructions are phrases and clauses.

A **phrase**, such as *at the lake's edge* or *fearing an accident*, is a group of related words that lacks either a subject or a predicate or both. A **clause**, in contrast, contains both a subject and a predicate. Both *The skaters sought safety* and *When the ice cracked* are clauses, though only the first can stand alone as a sentence. We will examine the various kinds of phrases and clauses in the following sections.

1 **Using prepositional phrases**

Prepositions are connecting words. Unlike nouns, verbs, and modifiers, which may change form according to their meaning and use in a sentence, prepositions never change form. We use many prepositions with great frequency.

COMMON PREPOSITIONS

about	beneath	in spite of	round
above	beside	instead of	since
according to	between	into	through
across	beyond	like	throughout
after	by	near	till
against	concerning	next to	to
along	despite	of	toward
along with	down	off	under
among	during	on	underneath
around	except	onto	unlike
as	except for	out	until
aside from	excepting	out of	up
at	for	outside	upon
because of	from	over	with
before	in	past	within
behind	in addition to	regarding	without
below	inside		

A preposition always connects a noun, a pronoun, or a word group functioning as a noun to another word in the sentence: *Robins nest in trees.* The noun, pronoun, or word group so connected (*trees*) is the **object of the preposition**. The preposition plus its object and any modifiers is a **prepositional phrase**.

PREPOSITION	OBJECT
of	spaghetti
on	the surface
with	great satisfaction
upon	entering the room
from	where you are standing

Prepositions normally come before their objects. But sometimes the preposition comes after its object, particularly in speech.

What do you want to see him *about*?
They know the *town* we are *from*.

Prepositional phrases usually function as adjectives (modifying nouns) or as adverbs (modifying verbs, adjectives, or other adverbs). As modifiers, they add details that make sentences clearer and more interesting for readers.

PREPOSITIONAL PHRASES AS ADJECTIVES

Terry is the boy *in the pink shirt*. [Phrase describes *boy*.]

Life *in a lumber camp on Vancouver Island* was an opportunity *for adventure*.

[*In a lumber camp* describes *life*; *on Vancouver Island* describes *lumber camp*; and *for adventure* describes *opportunity*.]

PREPOSITIONAL PHRASES AS ADVERBS

She had driven steadily *for four hours from Calgary*. [Both phrases describe *driven*.]

Our Great Dane, Joshua, buries his bones *behind the garage*. [Phrase describes *buries*.]

Occasionally, prepositional phrases also function as nouns, though rarely in writing.

PREPOSITIONAL PHRASE AS NOUN

Across the river is too far to go for ice cream. [Phrase functions as sentence subject.]

Punctuating prepositional phrases

Since a prepositional phrase lacks a subject and a predicate, it should not be punctuated as a complete sentence. If it is, the result is a **sentence fragment**:

FRAGMENT   Toward the sun.

The phrase must be attached to another group of words containing both a subject and a predicate:

REVISED   The plane turned *toward the sun*.

See Chapter 10 for a full discussion of how to recognize and revise sentence fragments.

A prepositional phrase that introduces a sentence is set off with punctuation, usually a comma, unless it is short (see 21b).

According to the newspaper and other sources, the Senate has finally passed the bill.

In 1918 World War I finally ended.

A prepositional phrase that interrupts or concludes a sentence is *not* set off with punctuation when it restricts the meaning of the word or words it modifies (see 21c).

gr
5c

Nothing *about him* surprises me.
We saw her riding *in Sandy's car*.

When an interrupting or concluding prepositional phrase does *not* restrict meaning, but merely adds information to the sentence, then it *is* set off with punctuation, usually a comma or commas (see 21c).

The Senate, *according to the newspaper and other sources*, has finally passed the bill.

The Senate has finally passed the bill, *according to the newspaper and other sources*.

As all the preceding examples illustrate, a preposition and its object are not separated by a comma (see 21j-1).

EXERCISE 10

Identify the prepositional phrases in the following passage. Indicate whether each phrase functions as an adjective or as an adverb, and name the word that the phrase modifies.

Example:

After an hour I finally arrived at the home of my professor.

ADV PHRASE   ADV PHRASE   ADJ PHRASE
After an hour I finally arrived *at the home* *of my professor*
[*After an hour* and *at the home* modify *arrived*; *of my professor* modifies *home*.]

The woman in blue socks ran from the policeman on horseback. She darted down Bates Street and then into the bus depot. At the depot the policeman dismounted from his horse and searched for the woman. The entrance to the depot and the interior were filled with travellers, however, and in the crowd he lost sight of the woman. She, meanwhile, had boarded a bus on the other side of the depot and was riding across town.

EXERCISE 11

To practise writing sentences with prepositional phrases, combine each pair of sentences below into one sentence that includes one or two prepositional phrases. You will have to add, delete, and rearrange words. Some items have more than one possible answer.

> *Example:*
> I will start working. The new job will pay the minimum wage.
> I will start working *at a new job for the minimum wage.*

1. A doctor first discovered the cure. Toronto was where the doctor lived.
2. A young couple bought the house. The couple had two small children. The house cost little money.
3. The lawyer accepted the case. She had no hesitation.
4. The band members held a party. They invited one hundred people.
5. We are required to write the exam. We must use pencil and white paper.
6. The interview continued. Two hours was the time it took.
7. Jan received a glass paperweight. An unknown admirer gave it.
8. They took a long walk. They followed the stream and crossed the bridge.
9. The wagging tail toppled the lamp. The tail belonged to the dog.
10. Everyone attended the lecture. Only Vicky and Pierre did not go.

2 Using verbals and verbal phrases

Verbals are special verb forms like *smoking* or *hidden* or *to win* that can function as nouns (*smoking is dangerous*) or as modifiers (*the hidden money, the urge to win*). Verbals *cannot* stand alone as the complete verb in the predicate of a sentence. For example, *The man smoking* and *The money hidden* are not sentences but sentence fragments (see 10a). Any verbal must combine with a helping verb to serve as the predicate of a sentence: *The man was smoking. The money is hidden*.

Because verbals cannot serve alone as sentence predicates, they are sometimes called **non-finite verbs** (in essence, they are "unfinished"). **Finite verbs**, in contrast, can make an assertion or express a state of being without a helping verb (they are "finished"). Either of two tests can distinguish finite and non-finite verbs.

TESTS FOR FINITE AND NON-FINITE VERBS (VERBALS)

TEST 1: Does the word require a change in form when a third-person subject changes from singular to plural?

    Yes.   Finite verb: *It sings. They sing.*

    No.   Non-finite verb (verbal): *bird singing, birds singing.*

TEST 2: Does the word require a change in form to show the difference in present, past, and future?

    Yes.   Finite verb: *It sings. It sang. It will sing.*

    No.   Non-finite verb (verbal): *The bird singing is/was/will be a robin.*

gr
5c

There are three kinds of verbals: participles, gerunds, and infinitives.

Participles

All verbs have two participle forms, a present and a past. The **present participle** consists of the dictionary form of the verb plus the ending *-ing*: *beginning, completing, hiding*. The **past participle** of most verbs consists of the dictionary form plus *-d* or *-ed*: *believed, completed*. Some common verbs have an irregular past participle: *begun, hidden*. (See 7a.)

Both present and past participles function as adjectives to modify nouns and pronouns.

> The *freezing* rain made the roads dangerous. [modifies *rain*]
> The *exhausted* miners were rescued. [modifies *miners*]
> Oliver found his *filing* job *boring*. [Both participles modify *job*.]
> *Disgusted*, he quit that night. [modifies *he*]

Gerunds

Gerund is the name given to the *-ing* form of the verb when it serves as a noun.

> Unfortunately, *studying* always bored Nick. [sentence subject]
> His sister Olga hated *swimming*. [object of *hated*]
> Both Nick and Olga preferred *loafing* to *working*. [*Loafing* is the object of *preferred*; *working* is the object of *to*.]
> Their principal occupation was *loafing*. [subject complement]

Present participles and gerunds can be distinguished *only* by their function in a sentence. If the *-ing* form functions as an adjective (*a teaching degree*), it is a present participle. If the *-ing* form functions as a noun (*Teaching is difficult*), it is a gerund.

Infinitives

The **infinitive** is the *to* form of the verb, the dictionary form preceded by the infinitive marker *to: to begin, to hide, to run*. Infinitives may function as nouns, adjectives, or adverbs.

He plans *to go*. [The infinitive functions as a noun, the object of *plans*.]

He is the man *to elect*. [The infinitive functions as an adjective, modifying *man*.]

Some physics problems are difficult *to solve*. [The infinitive functions as an adverb, modifying *difficult*.]

Verbal phrases

Participles, gerunds, and infinitives—like other forms of verbs—may take subjects, objects, or complements, and they may be modified by adverbs. The verbal and all the words immediately related to it make up a **verbal phrase**. With verbal phrases, we can create concise sentences packed with information.

PARTICIPIAL PHRASES

Like participles, **participial phrases** always serve as adjectives, modifying nouns or pronouns.

Chewing his pencil steadily, Dick stared into the air. [modifies *Dick*]

He was frustrated by the paper *lying before him*. [modifies *paper*]

Defeated by the same blank paper earlier in the day, Dick knew he must somehow write something. [modifies *Dick*]

GERUND PHRASES

Gerund phrases, like gerunds, always serve as nouns.

Eating an entire lemon pie for lunch was easy for Wesley. [sentence subject]

His mother was annoyed at *his eating the whole pie*. [Object of preposition *at*. *His* is the subject of the gerund; see 6h.]

But she had hidden a second pie because she anticipated *his doing it*. [object of *anticipated*]

INFINITIVE PHRASES

Infinitive phrases may serve as nouns, adjectives, or adverbs.

To lie repeatedly is *to deny reality*. [Both phrases function as nouns, the first as the sentence subject and the second as a subject complement.]

We wanted *him to go*. [The phrase functions as a noun, the object of *wanted*. *Him* is the subject of the infinitive; see 6f.]

Saul's is the best place *to eat pancakes*. [The phrase functions as an adjective, modifying *place*.]

Frank jogged *to keep himself fit*. [The phrase functions as an adverb, modifying *jogged*.]

Jack was too young *to understand the story*. [The phrase functions as an adverb, modifying *young*.]

gr
5c

NOTE: When an infinitive or infinitive phrase serves as a noun after verbs such as *hear*, *let*, *help*, *make*, *see*, and *watch*, the infinitive marker *to* is omitted: *We all heard her (to) tell the story*.

Punctuating verbals and verbal phrases

Like prepositional phrases, verbal phrases punctuated as complete sentences are sentence fragments. A complete sentence must contain a subject and a finite verb (p. 185).

FRAGMENT	*Treating* the patients kindly.
REVISED	*She treats* the patients kindly.

See Chapter 10 on sentence fragments.

A verbal or verbal phrase serving as a modifier is almost always set off with a comma when it introduces a sentence (see 21b).

To pay her tuition, she worked at two jobs.
Breathing evenly, the cat lay asleep on the rug.

A modifying verbal or verbal phrase that interrupts or concludes a sentence is *not* set off with punctuation when it restricts the meaning of the word or words it modifies (see 21c).

The boy *selling hot dogs* is my brother.
She worked at two jobs *to pay her tuition*.

When an interrupting or concluding verbal modifier does *not* restrict meaning, but merely adds information to the sentence, it *is* set off with punctuation, usually a comma or commas (see 21c).

The cat, *breathing evenly*, lay asleep on the rug.
The cat lay asleep on the rug, *breathing evenly*.

gr
5c

EXERCISE 12

The following sentences contain participles, gerunds, and infinitives as well as participial, gerund, and infinitive phrases. First identify each verbal or verbal phrase. Then indicate whether it is used as an adjective, an adverb, or a noun.

Example:

Laughing, the talk-show host prodded her guest to talk.

ADJ   ADV
Laughing, the talk-show host prodded her guest *to talk*.

1. Isolated in the bush, Susanna Moodie learned to provide for her family.
2. She is self-confident enough to laugh at her own faults.
3. Sliding and slipping, they moved across the ice to greet their friends.
4. Eating at a nice restaurant is a relaxing way to end a hectic week.
5. To fly was one of humankind's recurring dreams.
6. Because of the dwindling water supply, the remaining vacationers decided to leave for another campground.
7. The periodic firing of the rifle kept the hungry wolves at bay.
8. The train moved too fast for us to enjoy the countryside.
9. Three misbehaving children ruined our attempt to stage a play in the elementary school.
10. After missing rehearsal three times in a row, I received a call from the conductor.

EXERCISE 13

To practise writing sentences with verbals and verbal phrases, combine each pair of sentences below into one sentence. You will have to add, delete, change, and rearrange words. Each item has more than one possible answer.

Example:

My father took pleasure in mean pranks. For instance, he hid my neighbours' cat.

My father took pleasure in mean pranks such as *hiding the neighbours' cat*.

1. The sound grew louder. It swelled as the airplanes approached.
2. Florists import flowers from all over the world. In this way they manage to sell tulips in December.
3. The highway leads into the town. It is lined with fast-food restaurants.
4. The ancient Greeks gave their children cheese. The cheese rewarded good behaviour.
5. The islands of Japan form a thousand-mile-long archipelago. The archipelago lies mostly in the temperate zone.

6. Lee knew she had lost the race. She was falling far behind the other runners.
7. The letter had been opened by mistake. It was lying on the table.
8. Children shop in supermarkets with their parents. This is an early experience that almost all children share.
9. I must get a job. I must support myself.
10. They discovered a box of old money. They were cleaning the cellar.

gr
5c

3 **Using absolute phrases**

Absolute phrases consist of a noun or pronoun and a participle, plus any modifiers.

The parade passed by slowly, *the bands blaring, the crowds shouting*.

The old tree stood alone, *its trunk stripped and rotting*.

Their work nearly finished, the men rested.

These phrases are called *absolute* (from a Latin word meaning "free") because they have no specific grammatical connection to any word in the rest of the sentence. Instead, they modify the entire rest of the sentence, adding information or clarifying meaning.

Notice that absolute phrases, unlike participial phrases, always contain a subject. Compare the following.

The large man *standing before me* turned to speak. [participial phrase modifying *man*, the sentence subject]

A large man having moved in front of me, I could see nothing. [absolute phrase having its own subject, *A large man*, and modifying the rest of the sentence]

We often omit the participle from an absolute phrase when it is some form of *be* such as *being* or *having been*.

Sammy watched intently, *his mouth (being) wide open*.

Punctuating absolute phrases

Absolute phrases are always set off from the rest of the sentence with punctuation, usually a comma or commas (see 21d).

Its finish waxed and buffed, the car looked almost new.
The car, *its finish waxed and buffed*, looked almost new.
The car looked almost new, *its finish waxed and buffed*.

gr

5c

EXERCISE 14

To practise writing sentences with absolute phrases, combine each pair of sentences below into one sentence that contains an absolute phrase. You will have to add, delete, change, and rearrange words.

Example:

The flower's petals wilted. It looked pathetic.

Its petals wilted, the flower looked pathetic.

1. Her face turned pale. She stared at the woman ahead of her.
2. The steelworkers called a strike. The factory was closed down.
3. We were forced to cancel the annual picnic. The funds had run out.
4. The thief stood before the safe. His fingers twitched eagerly.
5. The swimmer rose again to the surface. Her arms thrashed.

4   **Using subordinate clauses**

As we noted earlier, a **clause** is any group of words that contains both a subject and a predicate. There are two kinds of clauses, and the distinction between them is important. A **main** or **independent clause** can stand alone as a sentence: *The sky darkened.* A **subordinate** or **dependent clause** is just like a main clause *except* that it begins with a subordinating word: *when the sky darkened.* *When* and other subordinating words such as *because, if, who,* or *that* express particular relationships between the clauses they introduce and the main clauses to which they are attached. Clauses that have been subordinated can *never* stand alone as sentences (see the discussion of punctuation on p. 193). The following examples show the differences between the two kinds of clauses.

TWO MAIN CLAUSES

The chair is expensive. We cannot buy it.

FIRST CLAUSE SUBORDINATED

Because the chair is expensive, we cannot buy it.

TWO MAIN CLAUSES

I met a man. He was selling boa constrictors.

SECOND CLAUSE SUBORDINATED

I met a man *who was selling boa constrictors*.

We use two kinds of subordinating words to connect subordinate clauses with main clauses. The first kind is **subordinating conjunctions** or **subordinators**. They always come at the beginning of subordinate clauses. Like prepositions, subordinating conjunctions are few and never change form in any way.

COMMON SUBORDINATING CONJUNCTIONS

after	because	in order that	than	when
although	before	now that	that	whenever
as	even if	once	though	where
as if	even though	rather than	till	whereas
as long as	if	since	unless	wherever
as though	if only	so that	until	while

The second kind of connecting word is the **relative pronoun**. It also introduces a subordinate clause and links it with an independent clause.

RELATIVE PRONOUNS

which	what	who (whose, whom)
that	whatever	whoever (whomever)

Like subordinating conjunctions, relative pronouns link one clause with another. But unlike subordinating conjunctions, relative pronouns also usually act as subjects or objects in their own clauses, and two of them (*who* and *whoever*) change form accordingly (see 6g).

Subordinate clauses function as adjectives, adverbs, and nouns and are described as adjective, adverb, or noun clauses according to their use in a particular sentence. Only by determining its function in a sentence can we identify a particular clause.

ADJECTIVE CLAUSES

Adjective clauses modify nouns and pronouns, providing necessary or helpful information about them. They usually begin with the relative pronouns listed in the "Relative Pronouns" box, although a few adjective clauses begin with *when* or *where* (standing for *in which*, *on which*, or *at which*). The relative pronoun is the subject or object of the clause it begins. The clause ordinarily falls immediately after the noun or pronoun it modifies.

My family still lives in the house *that my grandfather built*. [modifies *house*]

Dale is the girl *who always gets there early*. [modifies *girl*]

My yellow Volkswagen, *which I bought seven years ago*, has travelled 78 000 kilometres. [modifies *Volkswagen*]

There comes a time *when each of us must work*. [modifies *time*]

gr

5c

ADVERB CLAUSES

Like adverbs, adverb clauses modify verbs, adjectives, other adverbs, and whole groups of words. They usually tell how, why, when, where, under what conditions, or with what result. They always begin with subordinating conjunctions.

Calvin liked to go *where there was action*. [modifies *go*]

Elaine is friendlier *when she's talking on the telephone*. [modifies *friendlier*]

Because he did not study, Donald failed. [modifies *failed*]

She came as quickly *as she could*. [modifies *quickly*]

An adverb clause can often be separated from the word it modifies. In both of the following sentences, the adverb clause modifies *ended*.

The game ended *before he had a chance to play*.
Before he had a chance to play, the game ended.

NOUN CLAUSES

Noun clauses function as subjects, objects, and complements in sentences. They begin either with relative pronouns or with the words *when*, *where*, *whether*, *why*, and *how*. Unlike adjective and adverb clauses, noun clauses *replace* a word (a noun) within a main clause; therefore, they can be difficult to identify.

The lecture pleased the audience. [*The lecture* is the sentence subject.]

What the lecturer said pleased the audience. [The noun clause replaces *The lecture* as the sentence subject.]

The following are some typical noun clauses.

Everyone knows *what a panther is*. [object of *knows*]

Whoever calls the station first will win two tickets to the Bruce Cockburn concert. [subject of sentence]

They thought about *whether they could afford the trip*. [object of preposition *about*]

ELLIPTICAL CLAUSE

A subordinate clause that is grammatically incomplete but clear in meaning is an **elliptical clause** (*ellipsis* means "omission"). The meaning of the clause is clear because the missing element can be supplied from the context. Most often the elements omitted are the relative pronouns *that*, *which*, and *whom* from adjective clauses or the predicate from the second part of a comparison.

Thailand is among the countries (*that* or *which*) *he visited*.
Ellen dances better *than Martha* (*dances*).

Other typical elliptical clauses are as follows.

> *When (she was) only a child*, Julia saw a great grey owl.
>
> *Though (they are) rare south of Canada*, great grey owls sometimes appear in Massachusetts.

Punctuating subordinate clauses

gr
5c

Subordinate clauses punctuated as complete sentences are sentence fragments. Though a subordinate clause contains a subject and a predicate and thus resembles a complete sentence, it also contains a subordinating word that makes its meaning dependent on a main clause.

FRAGMENT	Because the door was ajar.
REVISED	The door was ajar.
REVISED	I overheard *because the door was ajar*.

See Chapter 10 on sentence fragments.

A subordinate clause serving as an adverb is almost always set off with a comma when it introduces a sentence (see 21b).

> *Although the project was almost completed*, it lost its funding.

A modifying subordinate clause that interrupts or concludes a main clause is *not* set off with punctuation when it restricts the meaning of the word or words it modifies (see 21c).

> The woman *who spoke* is a doctor.
> The project lost its funding *because it was not completed on time*.

When an interrupting or concluding subordinate clause does *not* restrict meaning, but merely adds information to the sentence, it *is* set off with punctuation, usually a comma or commas (see 21c).

> The woman, *who is a doctor*, cares for her invalid father.
> The project lost its funding, *although it was almost completed*.

EXERCISE 15

Identify the subordinate clauses in the following sentences. Then indicate whether each is used as an adjective, an adverb, or a noun. If the clause is a noun, indicate its function in the sentence.

> *Example:*
> The article explained how one could build an underground house.
>
> > NOUN
> The article explained *how one   could build an underground house*. [object of *explained*]

1. They were not interested in what the tour guide said.
2. The auctioneer opened the bidding once everyone was seated.
3. Whenever the economy is uncertain, people tend to become anxious.
4. Whoever wants to graduate must pass all the required courses.
5. I knew the ending would be unhappy when the main character started falling apart.
6. That Stefanie has not gone to university is a disappointment to her parents.
7. Ever since she was a small child, they have saved money for her education.
8. Stefanie decided, though, that she wanted to work a year or two before university.
9. Until she makes up her mind, Stefanie's education money is collecting interest.
10. Her parents are the kind who let their children think for themselves.

EXERCISE 16

To practise writing sentences with subordinate clauses, combine each pair of the following main clauses into one sentence. Use either subordinating conjunctions or relative pronouns as appropriate, referring to the lists on page 191 if necessary. You will have to add, delete, and rearrange words. Each item has more than one possible answer.

Example:
She did not have her bicycle wrenches with her. She could not change her bicycle tire.

Because she did not have her bicycle wrenches with her, she could not change her bicycle tire.

1. The phone lines went dead. Earlier a fire destroyed much of the central office.
2. Taxpayers should understand something. Revenue Canada does not make exceptions.
3. The critic reviewed the Frank Capra movie. It was playing at the revival theatre.
4. He is an accountant. He rarely makes mistakes.
5. We came to the gate. We had first seen the deer tracks there.
6. Someone is fickle. This person cannot be relied on.
7. The town council cancelled the new playground. Then small children demonstrated in the streets.
8. Those dogs have a master. He gives them equal discipline and praise.
9. The basketball team has had a losing season. The team still shows promise.
10. He did not bother to undress for bed. He was too tired.

5 Using appositives

An **appositive** is a word or word group that renames the word or word group before it. (The word *appositive* derives from a Latin word that means "placed near to" or "applied to.") The most common appositives are nouns that rename other nouns.

> Her sister *Jean* attends law school. [noun as appositive]
>
> Bizen ware, *a dark stoneware*, has been produced in Japan since the fourteenth century. [noun phrase as appositive]
>
> His first love, *racing stock cars*, was his last love. [gerund phrase as appositive]

All appositives can replace the words they refer to: *A dark stoneware has been produced in Japan. Racing stock cars was his last love.*

Appositives are often introduced by words and phrases such as *or, that is, such as, for example,* and *in other words*.

> Kangaroos, opossums, and wombats are all marsupials, *that is, mammals that carry their young in external abdominal pouches.*
>
> Jujitsu, *or judo,* is based on the principle that an opponent's strength may be used to defeat him or her.

Although most appositives are nouns that rename other nouns, they may also be and rename other parts of speech.

> All papers should be proofread carefully, that is, *checked for spelling, punctuation, and mechanics.* [The appositive defines the verb *proofread*.]

Noun appositives can always be stated as clauses with some form of the verb *be*.

> Bizen ware, *(which is)* a dark stoneware, has been produced in Japan since the fourteenth century.

Thus appositives are economical alternatives to adjective clauses containing a form of *be*.

Punctuating appositives

Appositives punctuated as complete sentences are sentence fragments (see Chapter 10). Correcting such fragments generally involves connecting the appositive to the main clause containing the word referred to.

> **FRAGMENT**   An exceedingly tall man with narrow shoulders.
>
> **REVISED**   I stood next to a basketball player, *an exceedingly tall man with narrow shoulders.*

An appositive is *not* set off with punctuation when it restricts the meaning of the word it refers to (see 21c).

> The verb *howl* comes from the Old English verb *houlen*.

When an appositive does *not* restrict the meaning of the word it refers to, it *is* set off with punctuation, usually a comma or commas (see 21c).

> *An aged elm*, the tree was struck by lightning.
> The tree, *an aged elm*, was struck by lightning.
> Lightning struck the tree, *an aged elm*.

A non-restrictive appositive is sometimes set off with a dash or dashes, especially when it contains commas (see 25b-2).

> Three people—*Will, Carolyn, and Tom*—objected to the new procedure.

A concluding appositive is sometimes set off with a colon (see 25a-1).

> Two principles guide the judge's decisions: *justice and fairness*.

EXERCISE 17

To practise writing sentences with appositives, combine each pair of sentences into one sentence that contains an appositive. You will have to delete and rearrange words. Some items have more than one possible answer.

Example:
The largest land animal is the elephant. The elephant is also one of the most intelligent animals.

The largest land animal, *the elephant*, is also one of the most intelligent animals.

1. The poet is an egocentric boor. He is rarely invited to read.
2. The part of King Lear is played by William Hutt. Lear was the tragic hero.
3. The tapestry depicted a unicorn. That is the fabled horselike animal with one horn.
4. Cactus growing attracts patient people. It is a hobby with no immediate rewards.
5. The most popular professional sports pay their players well. They are hockey, football, baseball, and basketball.
6. Sir Charles G. D. Roberts was a writer of animal stories. He was also a famous poet.
7. The house was a five-room log structure. It was bought by a neighbourhood group.
8. English adopted many words for animals from the Algonquin Indians. These are words such as *moose, opossum*, and *raccoon*.
9. Jerry's aim in life is to avoid all productive labour. His aim will surely change when his parents stop supporting him.

10. Their Beatles memorabilia occupied a room in their base-
    ment. The memorabilia consisted of records, photographs,
    posters, and T-shirts.

5d   Compounding words, phrases, and clauses

gr
5d

We have seen how to modify the nouns and verbs of the basic
sentence patterns and how to use word groups in place of single
nouns and modifiers. Here we examine how to combine words and
word groups that are closely related and parallel in importance.

Simone spent the afternoon in the park. Her father spent the
afternoon in the park.
Simone and her father spent the afternoon in the park.

Kurt was tired. He was sick. He was depressed.
Kurt was *tired, sick, and depressed.*

Brenda went to the drugstore. She bought some vitamins. She
returned as soon as possible.
Brenda *went to the drugstore, bought some vitamins, and returned
as soon as possible.*

In the first pair of examples the two different subjects, *Simone* and
her father, become a **compound subject**, thus avoiding repetition of
the same predicate in two sentences. In the second pair of examples
the three adjective complements become a **compound complement**
(*tired, sick, and depressed*) that describes the common subject *Kurt*
after the common linking verb *was*. And in the last pair of examples
the three different predicates become a **compound predicate**
(*went . . . , bought . . . , and returned . . .*) with the common subject
Brenda. In every example *and* joins the parts.

1   Using co-ordinating conjunctions and correlative conjunctions

The word *and* is a **co-ordinating conjunction**. Like prepositions and subordinating conjunctions, co-ordinating conjunctions
are few and do not change form.

CO-ORDINATING CONJUNCTIONS			
and	nor	for	yet
but	or	so	

The co-ordinating conjunctions *and*, *but*, *nor*, and *or* always connect words or word groups of the same kind—that is, two or more nouns, verbs, adjectives, adverbs, phrases, subordinate clauses, or main clauses.

> Henrik *or* Ingrid will have to go.
> The chair was unfashionable *but* charming.
> Alison worked every day *and* partied every evening.
> He studied day and night, *but* he could not pass the course.

The conjunctions *for* and *so* cannot connect words, phrases, or subordinate clauses, but they can connect main clauses. *For* may also function as a preposition (*a present for the girls*). When it functions as a conjunction, it indicates cause. *So* indicates result.

> Tanya stayed home, *for* she had work to do.
> Senyo was tired, *so* he went to bed early.

The word *yet* often functions as an adverb (*She has not left yet*), but it can also function as a co-ordinating conjunction. Like *but*, it indicates contrast.

> He tended the goldfish carefully, *yet* it died.

Some conjunctions pair up with other words to form **correlative conjunctions**.

COMMON CORRELATIVE CONJUNCTIONS

both . . . and	neither . . . nor
not only . . . but also	whether . . . or
not . . . but	as . . . as
either . . . or	

> *Both* Simone *and* her father went to the park.
> The basketball is *either* on the shelf *or* in the closet.
> The class stood *neither* when he arrived *nor* when he left.
> We consume energy *not only* when awake *but also* when asleep.

Punctuating compounded words, phrases, and clauses

Unless they form a series of three or more, words, phrases, and subordinate clauses that are connected by a co-ordinating conjunction are *not* separated by commas (see 21j-2).

> The *boys and girls* segregated themselves.
> The cat jumped *off the roof and into the tree*.
> The robbery occurred *after I left but before Jim arrived*.

When two *main* clauses are joined into one sentence with a co-ordinating conjunction, a comma precedes the conjunction (see 21a).

> The test was difficult, *but* I think I did well.

When two main clauses are joined *without* a co-ordinating conjunction, they must be separated with a semicolon to avoid the error called a **comma splice** (see 11a).

gr

5d

> The joke was not funny; it was insulting.

The semicolon sometimes separates two main clauses joined by a co-ordinating conjunction when the clauses are long or contain commas (see 22c). The semicolon *always* separates two main clauses related by a conjunctive adverb (see the next section).

In a series of three or more items, commas separate the items, with *and* usually preceding the last item (see 21f-1).

> The curtains were mostly white with splotches of pink, yellow, *and* brown.

Semicolons sometimes separate the items in a series if they are long or contain commas (see 22d).

The comma also separates co-ordinate adjectives (those which modify a noun or pronoun equally) when the adjectives are not joined a co-ordinating conjunction (see 21f-2).

> *Wet*, *slick* roads made driving dangerous.

The comma does *not* separate adjectives when the one nearer the noun is more closely related to it in meaning (see 21f-2).

> She gave the teacher a *large red* apple.

2   Using conjunctive adverbs

One other kind of connecting word, called a **conjunctive adverb**, relates only main clauses, not words, phrases, or subordinate clauses.

Unlike co-ordinating and subordinating conjunctions, conjunctive adverbs do not bind the two clauses into a grammatical unit. Rather, as adverbs, they describe the relation of the *ideas* in two clauses. Compare the following examples.

> The game was exciting; *consequently*, we stayed to the end.
> The game was exciting, *and* we stayed to the end.
> *Because* the game was exciting, we stayed to the end.

In the first sentence the conjunctive adverb *consequently* describes how the second independent statement relates to the first, but it does not form the two statements into a grammatical unit. In the second sentence the co-ordinating conjunction *and* does join the two main clauses into a unit. In the third sentence the subordinating conjunction *because* reduces the first clause from a main clause to an adverb modifier.

gr

5d

COMMON CONJUNCTIVE ADVERBS

accordingly	furthermore	moreover	similarly
also	hence	namely	still
anyway	however	nevertheless	then
besides	incidentally	next	thereafter
certainly	indeed	nonetheless	therefore
consequently	instead	now	thus
finally	likewise	otherwise	undoubtedly
further	meanwhile		

A simple test can distinguish a conjunctive adverb from a co-ordinating or subordinating conjunction. Because a conjunctive adverb is an adverb, it can be moved from where it appears to elsewhere in the clause.

> The game was long and boring; *however*, we stayed to the end.
> The game was long and boring; we stayed, *however*, to the end.
> The game was long and boring; we stayed to the end, *however*.

In contrast, co-ordinating and subordinating conjunctions cannot be moved. For example, we would not write *we stayed to the end but* or *the game although was long and boring*.

These differences among conjunctive adverbs, co-ordinating conjunctions, and subordinating conjunctions are important because they determine very different punctuation between clauses. (See the discussion of punctuation below.)

NOTE: Just as some words may serve as nouns, verbs, or modifiers depending on their function in a sentence (see pp. 170 and 179), so some connecting words may have more than one use. *After*, *before*, *until*, and some other words may be either prepositions or subordinating conjunctions. Some prepositions, such as *behind*, *in*, and *outside*, can serve also as adverbs, as in *He trailed behind*. Most relative pronouns are used also as interrogative pronouns to ask questions: *What time is it? Who left?* And some conjunctive adverbs, particularly *however*, may also serve simply as adverbs in sentences such as *However much it costs, we must have it*. Again, the part of speech of a word depends on its function in a sentence.

Punctuating sentences containing conjunctive adverbs

Because the two main clauses related by a conjunctive adverb remain independent units, they must be separated by a semicolon (see 22b). If they are separated by a comma, the result is a **comma splice**.

COMMA SPLICE	We hoped for sunshine, *instead*, we got rain.
REVISED	We hoped for sunshine; *instead*, we got rain.

gr
5d

See Chapter 11 for a full discussion of comma splices.

A conjunctive adverb is almost always set off from its clause with a comma or commas.

No one was injured; *however*, the car was totalled.
No one was injured; the car, *however*, was totalled.
No one was injured; the car was totalled, *however*.

The comma or commas are optional with some one-syllable conjunctive adverbs (especially *hence*, *now*, *then*, and *thus*) and are not used with a few others when they appear inside or at the ends of clauses.

Interest rates rose; *thus* real estate prices declined.

All the performances were sold out; the play *therefore* made a profit.

We hoped for sunshine; we got rain *instead*.

EXERCISE 18

To practise compounding words, phrases, and clauses, combine each pair of sentences below into one sentence that is as short as possible without altering meaning. Use an appropriate connecting word of the type specified in parentheses, referring to the lists on pages 197–98 and page 200 if necessary. You will have to add, delete, and rearrange words, and you may have to change or add punctuation.

Example:
The encyclopedia had some information. It was not detailed enough. (*conjunctive adverb*)

The encyclopedia had some information; *however*, it was not detailed enough.

1. Arthur Erickson was an influential architect. Many consider him the leading Canadian architect of the twentieth century. (*conjunctive adverb*)
2. The new model is more powerful than the old. It is heavier and less portable. (*co-ordinating conjunction*)
3. Steve did not have an education degree. He did not have teaching experience. (*correlative conjunction*)

4. Physics is a difficult subject. It is an enjoyable subject. (*co-ordinating conjunction*)
5. The cheerleaders missed the bus. The backup centre also missed the bus. (*co-ordinating conjunction*)
6. Politicians cannot be shy people. They must be outgoing. (*conjunctive adverb*)
7. The newspaper publishes interesting feature articles. It publishes feeble editorials. (*co-ordinating conjunction*)
8. My mother attended Sir Frederick Banting Secondary School. My mother-in-law also attended Sir Frederick Banting Secondary School. (*correlative conjunction*)
9. The news stories from Uganda were censored. They were out of date because the censor had held on to them for so long. (*conjunctive adverb*)
10. The crocuses were blooming. There were no other signs of spring. (*co-ordinating conjunction*)

5e   Changing the usual order of the sentence

So far, all the examples of basic sentence grammar have been similar: the subject of the sentence comes first, naming the performer of the predicate's action, and the predicate comes second. This arrangement of subject and predicate describes most sentences that occur in writing, but we need to look briefly at four other kinds of sentences that alter this basic pattern.

1   Forming questions

We form questions in one of several ways. We may invert the normal subject-verb arrangement of statements:

The dog is barking. Is the dog barking?

We may use a question word such as *how*, *what*, *who*, *when*, *where*, *which*, or *why*:

What dog is barking?

Or we may use some combination of the two methods:

Why is the dog barking?

In each case a question mark signals that the sentence is a question.

2 Forming commands

We construct commands even more simply than we construct questions: we merely delete the subject of the sentence, *you*.

Open the window.   Eat your spinach.
Go to the store.   Leave me alone.

3 Writing passive sentences

In any sentence that uses a transitive verb—that is, in any sentence where the verb takes an object—we can move the object to the position of the subject and put the subject in the predicate. The result is a **passive sentence**, using the **passive voice** of the verb rather than the **active voice**. (See also Chapter 7, pp. 241–43.)

Greg *wrote* the paper. [active voice]

The paper *was written* by Greg. [passive voice]

A passive sentence is so called because its subject does not perform or initiate the action indicated by the verb. Rather, the subject *receives* the action. In passive sentences the verb is always a phrase consisting of some form of the verb *be* and the past participle of the main verb (*paper was written*, *exams are finished*). The prepositional phrase specifying the subject of the active verb (the actor) may be omitted entirely if the actor is unknown or unimportant: *The house was flooded*.

(See 7h and 18d concerning overuse of the passive voice.)

4 Writing sentences with postponed subjects

The subject follows the predicate in two sentence patterns that are not questions, commands, or passive sentences. In one pattern the normal word order is reversed for emphasis: *Then came the dawn. Up walked Henry*. This pattern occurs most often when the normal order is subject–intransitive verb–adverb. Then the adverb moves to the front of the sentence while subject and predicate reverse order.

A second kind of sentence with a postponed subject begins with either *it* or *there*, as in the following:

        V   S
There will be eighteen people attending the meeting.

   V   S
It was surprising that Vander Zalm was nominated.

The words *there* and *it* in such sentences are **expletives**. Their only function is to postpone the sentence subject. Expletive sentences are common, but they can be unemphatic because they add words and delay the sentence subject. Usually, the normal subject-predicate order is more effective: *Eighteen people will attend the meeting. Vander Zalm's nomination was surprising.* (See also 18e and 31c-3.)

EXERCISE 19

Form a question and a command from the following noun and verb pairs.

> *Example:*
>
> split, wood
>
> *Did* you *split* all this *wood*?
> *Split* the *wood* for our fire.

1. water, boil
2. music, stop
3. table, set
4. roll, dice
5. telephone, use

EXERCISE 20

Rewrite each passive sentence below as active, and rewrite each expletive construction to restore normal subject-predicate order. (For additional exercises with the passive voice and with expletives, see pp. 243, 354, and 487.)

1. The music for "O Canada" was written by Calixa Lavallée.
2. The tarragon was added to the stew by the chef.
3. The football was thrown by the quarterback to the wide receiver.
4. It is uncertain whether microwave ovens are dangerous.
5. There was an audience of nearly ten thousand at the outdoor concert.

5f   Classifying sentences

We describe and classify sentences in two different ways: by function (statement, question, command, exclamation, and so forth) or by structure. Four basic sentence structures are possible: simple, compound, complex, and compound-complex.

1   Writing simple sentences

Simple sentences consist of a single main clause. The clause may contain phrases, and the subject, the verb, and its objects may be compound; but the sentence is simple as long as it contains only one complete main clause and no subordinate clause.

> Last July was unusually hot.
>
> In fact, both July and August were very hot months.
>
> The summer drought made farmers leave the area for good or reduced them to bare existence. [two predicates but only one subject]

2 Writing compound sentences

A **compound sentence** consists of two or more main clauses. The clauses may be joined by a co-ordinating conjunction and a comma, by a semicolon alone, or by a conjunctive adverb and a semicolon.

> Last July was hot, but August was even hotter.
>
> The hot sun scorched the land to powder; the lack of rain made the soil untillable.
>
> The government later provided assistance; consequently, the remaining farmers gradually improved their lot.

3 Writing complex sentences

A sentence is **complex** if it contains one main clause and one or more subordinate clauses.

> Rain finally came, although many had left the area by then. [main clause, then subordinate clause]
>
> When the rain came, people rejoiced. [subordinate clause, then main clause]
>
> Those who remained were able to start anew because the government came to their aid. [main clause containing subordinate clause, then another subordinate clause]

Notice that length does not determine whether a sentence is complex or simple; both kinds can be short or long.

4 Writing compound-complex sentences

A **compound-complex sentence** has the characteristics of both the compound sentence (two or more main clauses) and the complex sentence (at least one subordinate clause).

> Even though government aid finally came, many people had already been reduced to poverty, and others had been forced to

leave the area. [subordinate clause, then main clause, then another main clause]

Some of the farmers who had left the area moved back gradually to their original homes, but several years passed before the land became as fertile as before. [main clause containing subordinate clause, then another main clause, then another subordinate clause]

EXERCISE 21

Mark the main clauses and subordinate clauses in the following sentences. Identify each sentence as simple, compound, complex, or compound-complex.

Example:

The police began patrolling more often when crime in the neighbourhood increased.

‾‾‾‾‾‾‾‾‾‾ MAIN ‾‾‾‾‾‾‾‾‾‾
Complex: The police began patrolling more often

‾‾‾‾‾‾‾‾‾ SUBORDINATE ‾‾‾‾‾‾‾‾‾
when crime in the neighbourhood increased.

1. The Canadian Authors Association first presented the Governor General's Literary Awards in 1936.
2. The Canada Council, in 1959, undertook to award the prizes for literature in English and French.
3. Although the awards have been controversial from time to time, they are the most important literary prizes in Canada.
4. The police strike lasted a week, but no robberies occurred in that time.
5. Even though hockey has supplanted lacrosse as our national sport, many young people still play the ancient game, and they seem to enjoy it.

EXERCISE 22

Combine each of the following groups of simple sentences to produce the kind of sentence specified in parentheses. You will have to add, delete, change, and rearrange words.

Example:

The traffic passed her house. It never stopped. (*complex*)
The traffic that passed her house never stopped.

1. Dinner was tasty. It did not fill us up. (*compound*)
2. The storm was predicted to be fierce. It passed by quickly. (*complex*)
3. The musical notes died away. Then a strange object filled the sky. (*complex*)
4. The wolves were afraid. They feared the fire. (*simple*)
5. We wanted the rumours to stop. We hoped for that. They did not. (*compound-complex*)

GUIDE TO NOUNS

Summary and index of information in this book (consult sections or pages in parentheses).

Description of nouns

Nouns as sentence subjects (5a-1, 5a-2)

Nouns as direct and indirect objects (5a-3), object complements (5a-3), objects of prepositions (5c-1), appositives (5c-5), modifiers (9g)

Classes of nouns: proper, common, collective, count, mass, concrete, abstract (5a-2)

Forms of nouns: subjective and objective case (p. 213), possessive case (23a), and plural (34b-6)

Other structures serving as nouns: gerunds and gerund phrases (5c-2), infinitives and infinitive phrases (5c-2), subordinate clauses (5c-4)

Conventions regarding nouns

FORMS OF NOUNS

Possessive forms: *boy's* vs. *boys'*; *Park's* vs. *Parks's* vs. *Parkses'* (23a)

Possessives before gerunds: *Nguyen's writing is clear*. (6h)

Plurals of nouns and compound nouns: *dish, dishes; child, children; mother-in-law, mothers-in-law* (34b-6)

NOUNS AND OTHER SENTENCE PARTS

Agreement of subjects and verbs: *The* <u>towel was</u> *wet. The* <u>towels were</u> *wet*. (8a)

Agreement of antecedents and pronouns: *The* <u>children</u> *surrounded* <u>their</u> *father*. (8b)

Grammatical fit between subjects and predicates (avoiding mixed grammar): *In the supervision of others is the best preparation for a management career.*——*The* <u>supervision</u> *of others* <u>is</u> *the best preparation for a management career*. (15a)

Fit in meaning of subjects and predicates (avoiding faulty predication): *The use of the airwaves is the ideal medium for campaigning.*——*The* <u>airwaves are</u> *the ideal medium for campaigning*. (15b)

CLARITY AND EFFECTIVENESS

Nouns as modifiers (avoiding overuse): *adult education grants workshop*——*workshop on grants for adult education* (9g)

Consistency in subjects and the voice of verbs: *Tony woke suddenly, but his eyes were kept shut.*——*Tony woke suddenly, but* <u>he kept his eyes shut</u>. (13c)

gr

GUIDE TO PRONOUNS

Summary and index of information in this book (consult sections or pages in parentheses).

Description of pronouns

Pronouns as substitutes for nouns (5a-2, 8b)

Pronouns as subjects, objects, complements, appositives, modifiers (pp. 213–15)

Case forms of pronouns: subjective, objective, possessive (pp. 213–15)

Person, number, and gender of personal pronouns (8b)

Classes of pronouns: personal, relative interrogative, demonstrative, reflexive, intensive, reciprocal, indefinite (5a-2)

Conventions regarding pronouns

FORMS OF PRONOUNS

Subjective case for subjects and subject complements: *You and I can talk. It was she.* (6a)

Objective case for objects: *Ken gave me a dog. He gave her to me.* (6b)

We or *us* with nouns: *We drivers like highways. Many of us drivers like highways.* (6c)

Case in appositives: *Two drivers, she and Nell, won the award. The province rewarded two drivers, her and Nell.* (6d)

Case after *than* or *as*: *Nell likes Buddy more than (she likes) him. Nell likes Buddy more than he (likes Buddy).* (6e)

Objective case for subjects and objects of infinitives: *We invited him to meet her.* (6f)

Who vs *whom*: *Who can predict whom he will ask?* (6g)

Possessives before gerunds: *his working* (6h)

Possessive forms of personal pronouns: *hers* (not *her's*); *theirs* (not *their's*) (23b)

Possessive pronouns vs. contractions: *its* vs. *it's*; *your* vs. *you're*; *their* vs. *they're* (23c)

PRONOUNS AND OTHER SENTENCE PARTS

Agreement of pronoun subjects and verbs: *Neither he nor they are late. Everybody is finished.* (8a)

Agreement of pronouns and antecedents: *Everybody finished his/her/his or her paper. Lisa or Maria left her notebook.* (8b)

Reference of pronouns to antecedents (avoiding unclear or remote reference): *The first act of the play seemed weak, but then it improved.*—→*The first act of the play started weakly but then improved.* Or: *Though the first act was weak, the play then improved.* (12a–12f)

GUIDE TO VERBS AND VERBALS

Summary and index of information in this book (consult sections or pages in parentheses).

Description of verbs and verbals

Verb as sentence predicate (5a-1, 5a-2, 5a-3)
Transitive, intransitive, and linking verbs (5a-3)
Forms of verbs: infinitive, past tense, past participle, present participle, -s form (pp. 223–25)
Regular vs. irregular verbs (7a)
Finite vs. non-finite verbs (5c-2)
Helping (auxiliary) verbs (pp. 224, 230)
Tense of verbs: present, past, future, etc. (pp. 231–33)
Mood of verbs: indicative, imperative, subjunctive (pp. 238–41)
Voice of verbs: active and passive (pp. 241–42)
Verbals and verbal phrases: participles, gerunds, infinitives (5c-2)

Conventions regarding verbs and verbals

FORMS AND TENSES OF VERBS

Principal parts of common irregular verbs: e.g., *begin*, *began*, *begun*; *run*, *ran*, *run* (7a)
Sit vs. *set* and *lie* vs. *lay* (7b)
Needed *-s* and *-ed* endings: *He asks/asked too much.* (7c)
Needed helping verbs: *He is asking too much.* (7d)
Present tense (*runs*) and perfect tenses (*has/had/will have run*) (7e)
Sequence of tenses: e.g., *We would like to have gone* vs. *We would have liked to go.* (7f)
Subjunctive mood: *I wish I were there.* (7g)

VERBS AND OTHER SENTENCE PARTS

Agreement of verbs and subjects: *The guests are here. Nobody is missing.* (8a)
Unseparated verb phrases and infinitives: *They had before long agreed to voluntarily surrender.*——*Before long they had agreed to surrender voluntarily.* (14e)
Grammatical fit between subjects and predicates (avoiding mixed grammar: *By saving is how they could buy a car.*——*By saving, they could buy a car.* (15a)
Fit in meaning of subjects and predicates (avoiding faulty predication): *The reason is because they were frugal.*——*The reason is that they were frugal.* (15b)

(*continued*)

gr

GUIDE TO VERBS AND VERBALS *(continued)*

PROBLEMS WITH VERBALS

Verbs required in complete sentences (avoiding sentence fragments with verbals): *Rain falling silently.*⟶*Rain fell silently.* (10a, 10c)

Clear and logical modifiers (avoiding dangling modifiers): *Flying home, her thoughts remained behind.*⟶*As she flew home, her thoughts remained behind.* (14f)

PUNCTUATION WITH VERBALS

Commas after introductory verbal modifiers: *Struggling for air, the climbers reached the summit.* (21b)

Commas to set off non-restrictive verbal modifiers: *The climbers, struggling for air, reached the summit.* (21c)

CLARITY AND EFFECTIVENESS

Active rather than passive voice: *Hands were raised by the students.*⟶*The students raised their hands.* (7h)

Consistency in voice: *Before you tighten the bolts, the car should be lowered to the ground.*⟶*Before you tighten the bolts, you should lower the car to the ground.* (13c)

Consistency in tense: *The hero escapes, but he was captured.*⟶*The hero escapes, but he is captured.* (13b)

Consistency in mood: *Unscrew the bolts, and then you remove the wheel.*⟶*Unscrew the bolts, and then remove the wheel.* (13b)

Strong rather than weak verbs (avoiding wordiness): *The book is a depiction of family strife.*⟶*The book depicts family strife.* (31c-3)

gr

GUIDE TO MODIFIERS

Summary and index of information in this book (consult the sections or pages in parentheses).

Description of modifiers

Functions of adjectives: modifying nouns and pronouns (p. 258)
Functions of adverbs: modifying verbs, adjectives, other adverbs, phrases, and clauses (p. 258)
Forms of adjectives and adverbs: positive, comparative, superlative (9e)
Irregular adjectives and adverbs (9e-2)
Other structures serving as modifiers: nouns (9g); prepositional phrases (5c-1); participles and participial phrases (5c-2); infinitives and infinitive phrases (5c-2); subordinate clauses (5c-4)

Conventions regarding modifiers

DISTINCTIONS BETWEEN ADJECTIVES AND ADVERBS

Adverbs (not adjectives) to modify verbs, adjectives, adverbs: *Susan writes well* (not *good*). (9a)
Adjectives after linking verbs, adverbs to modify other verbs: *I feel bad. She sings badly.* (9b)
Adjectives to modify objects, adverbs to modify verbs: *We believed him honest. We treated him honestly.* (9c)

FORMS OF ADJECTIVES AND ADVERBS

Short vs. *-ly* forms of adverbs: *slow* vs. *slowly* (9d)
Comparatives and superlatives: *steady, steadier/more steady, steadiest/most steady* (9e-1); *good/well, better, best* (9e-2); *most steadiest—→most steady* (9e-3); *the bigger of two* and *the biggest of three* (9e-4); *most unique—→unique* (9e-5)

MODIFIERS AND OTHER SENTENCE PARTS

Clear placement of modifiers: *We waited for the rain to stop in a doorway.—→We waited in a doorway for the rain to stop.* (14a–14e)
Clear and logical modifiers (avoiding dangling modifiers): *Watching the rain, our hands and feet froze.—→As we watched the rain, our hands and feet froze.* (14f)

PUNCTUATION AND MECHANICS WITH MODIFIERS

Commas after most introductory modifiers: *Happily, we have friends.* (21b)
Commas to set off non-restrictive modifiers: *Ellen, who is our best friend, checks in every day.* (21c)

(continued)

gr

211

GUIDE TO MODIFIERS (*continued*)

PUNCTUATION AND MECHANICS WITH MODIFIERS (*continued*)

Commas to set off absolute phrases: *Her workday finished, she calls us*. (21d)

Commas for co-ordinate adjectives: *She is a steady, reliable friend.* (21f-2)

Commas with conjunctive adverbs: *Traffic was bad; we left, however, before it could get worse.* (5d-2, 22b)

Semicolons between clauses related by conjunctive adverbs: *We did not leave right away; instead, we waited for Ellen.* (11b, 22b)

Capital letters for proper adjectives: *Indian tea; Buddhist chant* (26d)

Figure vs. words for numbers: *327* vs. *twenty-three* (29a)

Hyphens in compound adjectives and numbers: *well-spoken words* vs. *words well spoken* (34d-1); *thirty-two minutes* (34d-2)

CLARITY AND EFFECTIVENESS

Clear negation (avoiding double negatives): *They don't want no interruptions.——→They don't want any interruptions. Or: They want no interruptions.* (9f)

Nouns as modifiers (avoiding overuse): *business managers spreadsheet analysis seminar——→seminar on spreadsheet analysis for business managers* (9g)

Complete and logical comparisons: *The value of friendship is greater than money.——→The value of friendship is greater than the value of* (or *that of*) *money.* (15d)

CHAPTER 6

Case of Nouns and Pronouns

Case is the form of a noun or pronoun that shows the reader how it functions in a sentence—that is, whether it functions as a subject, as an object, or in some other way. The pronouns *I, we, he, she, they,* and *who* have separate forms for three cases: subjective, possessive, and objective. Most other pronouns and all nouns have only two case forms, subjective and possessive, with the subjective form serving all functions except that of the possessive. The case forms are summarized in the "Case Forms of Nouns and Pronouns" box. Since only *I, we, he, she, they,* and *who* change form for each case, we will focus on these pronouns in this chapter.

The **subjective form** is used when a pronoun is the subject of a sentence, the subject of a clause, the complement of a subject, or an appositive identifying a subject. (See 5a and 5c.)

SUBJECT OF SENTENCE

She and *I* skied three days last week.
They tried to save the house.

SUBJECT OF SUBORDINATE CLAUSE

Give the money to the kids *who* cleaned up the house.
He is the man *who* I thought would win.

SUBJECT OF UNDERSTOOD VERB

Sarah has more money than *he* (has).
I am not as smart as *she* (is).

SUBJECT COMPLEMENT

The editors of the paper were *he* and *I*.
They assumed it was *I*.

APPOSITIVE IDENTIFYING SUBJECT.

Only two members, Susan and *I*, went to the jazz festival.

CASE FORMS OF NOUNS AND PRONOUNS

	SUBJECTIVE	**POSSESSIVE**	**OBJECTIVE**
NOUNS	boy	boy's	boy
	Jessie	Jessie's	Jessie

PERSONAL PRONOUNS

Singular

1st person	I	my, mine	me
2nd person	you	your, yours	you
3rd person	he	his	him
	she	her, hers	her
	it	its	it

Plural

1st person	we	our, ours	us
2nd person	you	your, yours	you
3rd person	they	their, theirs	them

RELATIVE AND INTERROGATIVE PRONOUNS

who	whose	whom
whoever	—	whomever
which, that, what	—	which, that, what

INDEFINITE PRONOUNS

everybody	everybody's	everybody

The **objective form** is used when a pronoun is the direct or indirect object of a verb or verbal, the object of a preposition, the subject of an infinitive, or an appositive identifying an object (see 5a and 5c).

OBJECT OF VERB

Lisa likes both Tom and *him*.
The woman *whom* they elected was experienced.
The exam gave *him* a headache.

OBJECT OF PREPOSITION

Most of *us* hated to get up.
I didn't know *whom* they laughed at.

OBJECT OF VERBAL

Electing *her* was easy. [object of gerund]

Having elected *her*, the committee adjourned. [object of past participle]

Mary ran to help *him*. [object of infinitive]

SUBJECT OF INFINITIVE

We invited *them* to eat with us.
They asked *me* to speak.

APPOSITIVE IDENTIFYING OBJECT

The judge fined both defendants, Joe and *her*.

The **possessive form** of a pronoun is used before nouns and gerunds.

BEFORE A NOUN

His sisters needed *our* bicycles.

BEFORE A GERUND

Their flying to Halifax was my suggestion.

In addition, the possessive forms *mine, ours, yours, his, hers,* and *theirs* (and only those forms) may be used without a following noun, in the position of a noun.

IN NOUN POSITIONS

Hers is the racket on the table.
The blue car is *mine* (*ours, yours, his, theirs*).

(For the possessive forms of nouns, see 23a.)

6a   Use the subjective case for all parts of compound subjects and for subject complements.

In compound subjects use the same pronoun form you would use if the pronoun stood alone as a subject.

SUBJECTS

Yvonne and *I* left, but *Bill* and *he* stayed.
After *she* and *I* left, the fight started.

If you are in doubt about the correct form, try each part of the subject in a separate sentence: *Joan left. I left.* Therefore, *Joan and I left.*

A pronoun following the forms of the verb *be* (*am, is, are, was, were*) is a subject complement (see 5a-3). Since it renames the subject, the pronoun is in the subjective case.

6b

SUBJECT COMPLEMENTS

The ones who paid the bill were *you* and *I*.
It was *she* whom the premier finally appointed.

Sentences like these may sound stilted because expressions such as *It's me* and *It was her* are common in speech. In writing, unless you seek special emphasis, use the more natural order: *You and I were the ones who paid the bill. The premier finally appointed her.*

6b Use the objective case for all parts of compound objects.

In compound objects use the same pronoun form you would use if the pronoun stood alone as an object.

OBJECTS OF VERBS

We wanted to invite Larry and *her*. [direct object]
The coach gave *her* and *me* a lecture. [indirect object]

OBJECTS OF PREPOSITIONS

Marty gave presents to *Gloria* and *me*.
The gift was divided between *him* and *me*.

If you are in doubt about the correct form, try each part of the object in a separate sentence: *We wanted to invite Larry. We wanted to invite her.* Therefore, *We wanted to invite Larry and her.*

EXERCISE 1

From the pairs in parentheses, select the appropriate subjective or objective pronoun(s) for each of the following sentences.

Example:

"Between you and (*I*, *me*)," the salesman said, "this deal is a steal."

"Between you and *me*," the salesman said, "this deal is a steal."

1. Jody and (*I*, *me*) had been hunting for jobs.
2. The best employees at our old company were (*she*, *her*) and (*I*, *me*), so (*we*, *us*) expected to find jobs quickly.
3. One company did offer jobs to both (*she*, *her*) and (*I*, *me*).
4. After (*she*, *her*) and (*I*, *me*) had discussed the offers with several people, however, (*we*, *us*) both decided to decline.
5. The jobs did not seem appropriate for (*we*, *us*) if (*we*, *us*) wanted to become management trainees.
6. That left (*she*, *her*) with only one offer and (*I*, *me*) with none.

7. Between (*she, her*) and (*I, me*) the job search had lasted two months, and still it had barely begun.
8. Slowly, (*she, her*) and (*I, me*) stopped sharing leads.
9. It was obvious that Jody and (*I, me*) could not be as friendly as (*we, us*) had been.
10. Sadly, money seemed to mean more to (*she, her*) and (*I, me*) than our friendship.

ca

6d

6c Use the appropriate case when the plural pronouns *we* and *us* occur with a noun.

The case of the first-person plural pronoun used with a noun depends on the use of the nouns.

Freezing weather is welcomed by *us* skaters. [*Skaters* is the object of the preposition *by*.]

We skaters welcome freezing weather. [*Skaters* is the subject of the sentence.]

6d In appositives the case of a pronoun depends on the function of the word it describes or identifies.

The class elected representatives, Debbie and *me*. [*Representatives* is the object of the verb *elected*, so the words in the appositive, *Debbie and me*, take the objective case.]

Two representatives, Debbie and *I*, were elected. [*Representatives* is the subject of this sentence, so the words in the appositive, *Debbie and I*, take the subjective case.]

If you are in doubt about case in an appositive, try the sentence without the word the appositive identifies: *The class elected Debbie and me*; *Debbie and I were elected*.

EXERCISE 2

From the pairs in parentheses, select the appropriate subjective or objective pronoun for each of the following sentences.

Example:

Convincing (*we, us*) women to vote yes on this issue will be difficult.

Convincing *us* women to vote yes on this issue will be difficult.

1. Obtaining enough protein is important to (*we, us*) vegetarians.
2. Instead of obtaining protein from meat, (*we, us*) vegetarians get our protein from other sources.
3. Jeff claims to know only two vegetarians, Helena and (*he, him*), who avoid all animal products, including milk.
4. Some of (*we, us*) vegetarians eat fish, which is a good source of protein.
5. (*We, Us*) vegetarians in my family, my parents and (*I, me*), drink milk and eat fish.

6e **The case of a pronoun after *than* or *as* in a comparison depends on the meaning.**

When we use *than* and *as* in comparisons, we often do not complete the clauses they introduce: *Joe likes spaghetti more than (he likes) ravioli*. Without the words in parentheses, this sentence is clear because it can have only one sensible meaning. But in *Annie liked Ben more than Joe*, we cannot tell whether *Annie liked Ben more than (she liked) Joe* or *Annie liked Ben more than Joe (liked him)*.

When such sentences end with a pronoun, the case of the pronoun indicates what words have been omitted. When the pronoun is subjective, it must serve as the subject of the omitted verb.

Annie liked Ben more than *he* (liked Ben).

When the pronoun is objective, it must serve as the object of the omitted verb.

Annie liked Ben more than (she liked) *him*.

Be careful to choose the pronoun form that fits your meaning.

6f **Use the objective case for pronouns that are subjects or objects of infinitives.**

SUBJECT OF INFINITIVE

We wanted Gail and *her* to win the bowling tournament. [*Gail and her* is the compound subject of the infinitive *to win*.]

OBJECT OF INFINITIVE

They expect to meet *him*. [*Him* is the object of the infinitive *to meet*.]

6g The form of the pronoun *who* depends on its function in its clause.

1 At the beginning of questions use *who* if the question is about a subject, *whom* if it is about an object.

To determine the form of *who* at the beginning of a question, construct an answer to the question, using a personal pronoun in the answer. The case of the pronoun in the answer will indicate the required case of *who* in the question.

(*Who, Whom*) left the freezer door open? *She* left it open. Therefore, *Who* left the freezer door open?

(*Who, Whom*) does one ask? One asks *him*. Therefore, *Whom* does one ask?

(*Who, Whom*) is the pizza for? It is for *them*. Therefore, *Whom* is the pizza for?

In speech the subjective case *who* is commonly used whenever it is the first word of a question, regardless of whether it is a subject or an object. But writing requires a distinction between the forms.

SPOKEN *Who* should we blame?

WRITTEN *Whom* should we blame? [object of verb *blame*]

2 In subordinate clauses use *who* and *whoever* for all subjects, *whom* and *whomever* for all objects.

The case of a pronoun in a subordinate clause depends on its function in the clause, regardless of whether the clause itself functions as a subject, an object, or a modifier. (See 5c-4.)

Give the clothes to *whoever* needs them. [*Whoever* is the subject of *needs*. The entire clause *whoever needs them* is the object of the preposition *to*.]

I don't know *whom* the mayor appointed. [*Whom* is the object of *appointed*: *the mayor appointed whom*. The whole clause *whom the mayor appointed* is the object of the verb *know*.]

Whom he appointed is not my concern. [Again, *whom* is the object of *appointed*. This time the clause is the subject of the sentence.]

Larry is the man *whom* most people prefer. [*Whom* is the object of *prefer*: *people prefer whom*. The clause *whom most people prefer* modifies the noun *man*.]

If you have trouble determining which form to choose, rewrite the subordinate clause as a separate sentence, substituting a personal pronoun for the *who* form. The form of the personal pronoun will be the same as the required form of *who*. For instance:

> I remember (*who, whom*) was sitting on the sofa. *He* was sitting on the sofa. Therefore, I remember *who* was sitting on the sofa.

> The manager hired the woman (*who, whom*) his boss recommended. His boss recommended *her*. Therefore, the manager hired the woman *whom* his boss recommended.

NOTE: Don't let expressions such as *I think* and *she says* confuse you when they come between the subject *who* and its verb.

> He is the man *who* I think *was* on duty yesterday. [*Who* is the subject of *was*, not the object of *think*.]

> I asked the mechanic *who* Barbara said *was* her friend. [*Who* is the subject of *was*, not the object of *said*.]

To choose between *who* and *whom* in such constructions, delete the interrupting phrase: *I asked the mechanic who was her friend.*

EXERCISE 3

From the pairs in parentheses, select the appropriate form of the pronoun in each of the following sentences.

> *Example:*
> My mother asked me (*who, whom*) I was going out with.
> My mother asked me *whom* I was going out with.

1. The school administrators suspended Jurgen, (*who, whom*) they suspected of setting the fire.
2. Jurgen had been complaining to other custodians, (*who, whom*) reported him.
3. He constantly complained of unfair treatment from (*whoever, whomever*) happened to be passing in the halls, including pupils.
4. "(*Who, Whom*) here has heard Mr. Jurgen's complaints?" the police asked.
5. "(*Who, Whom*) did he complain most about?"
6. His co-workers agreed that Jurgen seemed less upset with the staff or students, most of (*who, whom*) he did not even know, than with the building itself.
7. "He took out his aggressions on the building," claimed one co-worker (*who, whom*) often witnessed Jurgen's behaviour.
8. "He cursed and kicked the walls and (*whoever, whomever*) he saw nearby."

9. The co-worker thought that Jurgen might have imagined people (*who*, *whom*) instructed him to behave the way he did.
10. "He's someone (*who*, *whom*) other people can't get next to," said the co-worker.

EXERCISE 4

Combine each pair of sentences below into one sentence that contains a clause beginning with *who* or *whom*. Be sure to use the appropriate case form. You will have to add, delete, and rearrange words. Each item may have more than one possible answer.

Example:

David is the candidate. We think David deserves to win.
David is the candidate *who* we think deserves to win.

1. Some children have undetected hearing problems. These children may do poorly in school.
2. They may not hear important instructions and information from teachers. Teachers may speak softly.
3. Classmates may not be audible. The teacher calls on those classmates.
4. Some hearing-impaired children may work harder to overcome their handicap. These children get a lot of encouragement at home.
5. Some hearing-impaired children may take refuge in fantasy friends. They can rely on these friends not to criticize or laugh.

6h | **Ordinarily, use the possessive form of a pronoun or noun immediately before a gerund.**

A **gerund** is the -*ing* form of the verb (*running, sleeping*) used as a noun (see 5c-2). Like nouns, gerunds are commonly preceded by possessive nouns and pronouns: *her marriage* (noun), *her marrying* (gerund), *our vote* (noun), *our voting* (gerund).

He disapproved of *their* exercising. [Compare *their exercise*.]
Jo's failing in history surprised us. [Compare *Jo's failure*.]

Notice the difference between the gerund and the present participle. Both have the same -*ing* form. But whereas the gerund serves as a subject or object, the participle serves as an adjective.

We often met *John* coming home late. [*Coming home late* is a participial phrase modifying *John*.]

> *John's* coming home late worried us. [*Coming home late* is a gerund phrase serving as the subject of *worried*.]

The case of a noun or pronoun before the *-ing* form of a verb can subtly influence the meaning of a sentence.

> We noticed *Ann* driving. [The emphasis is on *Ann*, who happened to be driving when she was noticed. *Driving* is a participle.]
>
> We noticed *Ann's* driving. [The emphasis is on Ann's activity—her driving. *Driving* is a gerund.]

Note that a gerund usually is not preceded by the possessive when the possessive would create an awkward construction.

> **AWKWARD**   We heard a rumour about everybody's on the team wanting to quit.
>
> **LESS AWKWARD**   We heard a rumour about everybody on the team wanting to quit.
>
> **BETTER**   We heard a rumour that everybody on the team wants to quit.

ca
6h

EXERCISE 5

Correct all inappropriate case forms in the following paragraph, and explain the function of each case form.

Mike and I arrived at the campground just after sunset. The manager, whom we thought looked like a movie star, was naturally reluctant to let we ruffians in, but eventually she showed us to a tiny campsite. When we unpacked the tent, Mike and me discovered that we were missing two tent pegs. Searching in the dark, Mike managed to find some sturdy sticks to use as pegs, and between he and I we managed to set up the tent. But Mike was apparently more tired than me, because he didn't drive his pegs deeply enough into the ground. Several hours later, when him and me had finally dozed off, the tent collapsed on top of us. Us yelling at each other woke the people in the next campsite, who were even less amused than us by our plight. We piled everything into the car as fast as possible and took off down the road for a motel.

CHAPTER 7

Verb Forms, Tense, Mood, and Voice

VERB FORMS

All verbs except *be* have five basic forms. The first three forms—infinitive, past tense, and past participle—are the verb's **principal parts**. The **infinitive** (sometimes called the **plain form**) is the dictionary form of the verb. It is the form we use when the verb's action occurs in the present and the subject is a plural noun or the pronoun *I, we, you,* or *they*.

> We *live* in the city.
> Examinations *frighten* me.
> They *go* downtown.

The **past-tense form** indicates that the verb's action occurred in the past. It is usually formed by adding *-d* or *-ed* to the infinitive, although for some irregular verbs it is formed in other ways (see 7a).

> We *lived* in the city.
> Examinations *frightened* me.
> They *went* downtown. [Irregular verb]

VERB FORMS

INFINITIVE: close, run
PAST TENSE: closed, ran
PAST PARTICIPLE: closed, run
PRESENT PARTICIPLE: closing, running
-*s* FORM: closes, runs

The **past participle** is the verb form we use with *have, has,* or *had* (*have climbed, had opened*); with a form of *be* in the passive voice (*was created*; see 7h); and by itself to modify nouns and pronouns (*sliced bread*). Except for some irregular verbs (see 7a), the past participle is the same as the past-tense form.

> We have *lived* in the city.
> Examinations have *frightened* me.
> They had *gone* downtown. [Irregular verb]

In addition to the three principal parts, all verbs have two other forms, a present participle and an -*s* form. We form the **present participle** by adding -*ing* to the verb's infinitive, as in *acting, eating, living, studying.* The present participle can modify nouns and pronouns (*boiling water, the girl driving*); and, as a gerund, the same form functions as a noun (*Running exhausts me*). In addition, the present participle may combine with forms of the verb *be* (*am, is, are, was* and *were*) to indicate continuing action: *is buying, was finishing, were swimming.*

The -**s form** of the verb is the one ending in -*s* or -*es* (*begs, lives, is, has*). We use it when the verb's action occurs in the present and the subject is third-person singular—that is, a singular noun (*dog, Harry*), a singular indefinite pronoun (*everybody, someone*), or the personal pronoun *he, she,* or *it.*

> The dog *begs*.   Everybody *is* asleep.
> Harry *lives* in town.   She *has* a car.

The verb *be* has eight forms rather than the five forms of most other verbs. In addition to its infinitive *be*, its present participle *being*, and its past participle *been*, *be* has three distinct forms in the present tense and two in the past tense.

	I	*he, she, it*	*we, you, they*
PRESENT TENSE	am	is	are
PAST TENSE	was	was	were

Helping verbs, also called **auxiliary verbs**, combine with a verb's infinitive, present participle, or past participle to indicate time and other kinds of meaning, as in *can run, was sleeping, had been eaten.* These combinations are **verb phrases** (see also 7d). Since the infinitive, present participle, or past participle in any verb phrase always carries the principal meaning, it is sometimes called the **main verb**.

Some helping verbs—*shall* and *will*; *have, has,* and *had*; *do, does,* and *did*; and the forms of *be* (*am, is, are, was, were, been,* and *being*)—combine with main verbs to indicate time and voice (see pp. 231 and 241).

I *will go*.	The doors *were opened*.
She *had run*.	The child *was awakened*.
Sylvia *did* not *want* grapes.	They *have been seen*.

Helping verbs such as *can, could, may, might, must, ought, shall, should, will,* and *would* combine with main verbs to indicate necessity, obligation, permission, possibility, and other conditions.

She *can write*.	You *must go*.
I *should study*.	I *might come*.

The two kinds of helping verbs sometimes work together to create complex verb phrases.

You *might have told* me.
I *may be sleeping*.
You *ought to have eaten*.

vb

7a

7a Use the correct form of regular and irregular verbs.

As indicated above, most verbs are **regular**; that is, they form their past tense and past participle by adding *-d* or *-ed* to the infinitive.

INFINITIVE	**PAST TENSE**	**PAST PARTICIPLE**
live	lived	lived
act	acted	acted

Since the past tense and past participle are created simply by adding to the infinitive and since the two are identical, the forms of regular verbs do not often cause problems in speech and writing (but see 7c).

Some verbs, however, do not follow the pattern of regular verbs. About two hundred English verbs are **irregular**; that is, they form their past tense and past participle in some irregular way. We have to learn the parts of the verbs by memorizing them, just as we learn new words.

Most irregular verbs form the past tense and the past participle by changing an internal vowel.

INFINITIVE	**PAST TENSE**	**PAST PARTICIPLE**
begin	began	begun
come	came	come

Some irregular verbs change an internal vowel and add an *-n* in the past participle.

INFINITIVE	**PAST TENSE**	**PAST PARTICIPLE**
break	broke	broken
draw	drew	drawn

Some irregular verbs have the same form in both the past tense and the past participle or in all three forms.

INFINITIVE	PAST TENSE	PAST PARTICIPLE
sleep	slept	slept
let	let	let

vb

7a

Check a dictionary if you have any doubt about a verb's principal parts. The form listed there is the infinitive. If no other forms are listed, the verb is regular; that is, both the past tense and the past participle add *-d* or *-ed* to the infinitive (*agree, agreed; sympathize, sympathized; talk, talked*). If the verb is irregular, the dictionary will list the infinitive, the past tense, and the past participle in that order (*speak, spoke, spoken; go, went, gone*). If the dictionary gives only two forms (as in *hear, heard* or *think, thought*), then the past tense and the past participle are the same.

The following list includes the most common irregular verbs. (When a principal part has two possible forms, as in *dove* and *dived*, both are included.) Look over this list to find verbs whose parts you are unsure of. Then spend some time memorizing the parts and trying them in sentences.

PRINCIPAL PARTS OF COMMON IRREGULAR VERBS

INFINITIVE	PAST TENSE	PAST PARTICIPLE
arise	arose	arisen
become	became	become
begin	began	begun
bid	bade, bid	bidden, bid
bite	bit	bitten, bit
blow	blew	blown
break	broke	broken
bring	brought	brought
burst	burst	burst
buy	bought	bought
catch	caught	caught
choose	chose	chosen
come	came	come
cut	cut	cut
dive	dived, dove	dived
do	did	done
draw	drew	drawn
dream	dreamed, dreamt	dreamed, dreamt
drink	drank	drunk
drive	drove	driven
eat	ate	eaten
fall	fell	fallen

Infinitive	Past tense	Past participle
find	found	found
flee	fled	fled
fly	flew	flown
forget	forgot	forgotten, forgot
freeze	froze	frozen
get	got	got, gotten
give	gave	given
go	went	gone
grow	grew	grown
hang (suspend)	hung	hung
hang (execute)	hanged	hanged
hear	heard	heard
hide	hid	hidden
hold	held	held
keep	kept	kept
know	knew	known
lay	laid	laid
lead	led	led
leave	left	left
let	let	let
lie	lay	lain
lose	lost	lost
pay	paid	paid
prove	proved	proved, proven
ride	rode	ridden
ring	rang	rung
rise	rose	risen
run	ran	run
say	said	said
see	saw	seen
set	set	set
shake	shook	shaken
shrink	shrank, shrunk	shrunk, shrunken
sing	sang	sung
sink	sank, sunk	sunk
sit	sat	sat
slide	slid	slid
speak	spoke	spoken
spring	sprang, sprung	sprung
stand	stood	stood
steal	stole	stolen
swim	swam	swum
take	took	taken
tear	tore	torn
throw	threw	thrown
wear	wore	worn
write	wrote	written

vb

7a

EXERCISE 1

For each irregular verb in parentheses, supply either the past tense or past participle, as appropriate, and identify the form you used.

> *Example:*
> Though we had (*hide*) the cash box, it was (*steal*).
> Though we had *hidden* the cash box, it was *stolen*. [two past participles]

1. The world population has (*grow*) by two-thirds of a billion people in less than a decade.
2. Recently it (*break*) the 5-billion mark.
3. Experts have (*draw*) pictures of a crowded future.
4. They predict that the world population may have (*slide*) up to as much as 16 billion by the year 2100.
5. Though the food supply (*rise*) in the last decade, the share to each person (*fall*).
6. At the same time the water supply, which had actually (*become*) healthier over the previous century, (*sink*) in size and quality.
7. The number of animal species on earth (*shrink*) by 20 percent.
8. Changes in land use (*run*) nomads and subsistence farmers off the land.
9. Yet all has not been (*lose*).
10. Recently human beings have (*begin*) to heed these and other problems and to explore how technology can be (*drive*) to help the earth and all its populations.

7b Distinguish between *sit* and *set* and between *lie* and *lay*.

The principal parts of *sit* and *set* and of *lie* and *lay* are easy to confuse. The following are the forms of the four verbs.

INFINITIVE	PAST TENSE	PAST PARTICIPLE
sit	sat	sat
set	set	set
lie	lay	lain
lay	laid	laid

Sit and *lie*, as in *Sit down* and *Lie down*, mean "be seated" and "recline," respectively. They are both **intransitive verbs**: they cannot take objects. *Set* and *lay*, as in *Set the eggs down carefully* and *Lay the floor boards there*, mean "put" or "place". They are **transitive verbs** and usually take objects. (See 5a-3.)

> Angela *lies* down every afternoon. [no object]
> Carter *laid* the plans on the table. [*Plans* is the object of *laid*.]
> The dog *sits* by the back door. [no object]
> Mr. Flood *set* the jug down roughly. [*Jug* is the object of *set*.]

EXERCISE 2

Choose the correct verb from the pair given in parentheses and then supply the past tense or past participle, as appropriate.

> *Example:*
> After I washed all the windows, I (*lie, lay*) down the squeegee and then I myself (*lie, lay*) down for a nap.
> After I washed all the windows, I *laid* down the squeegee and then I myself *lay* down for a nap.

1. Last Christmas, Jay (*lie, lay*) in bed all day with a fever.
2. When he awoke, Millard (*sit, set*) up in his chair, picked up the fallen book, and (*sit, set*) it on the table.
3. The spider (*sit, set*) in its web and (*lie, lay*) in wait for its prey.
4. After she had (*sit, set*) the table, she (*lie, lay*) a cloth over it.
5. Joan's wallet had (*lie, lay*) in the street for two days.

7c   Use the -s and -ed forms of the verb when they are required.

Some English dialects use the infinitive of the verb instead of the -*s* form that is required by standard English whenever the subject is third-person singular and the verb's action occurs in the present.

> The roof *leak* (*leaks*).   Nobody *have* (*has*) a car.
> Harry *live* (*lives*) in town.   She *be* (*is*) happy.
> He *don't* (*doesn't*) care.

In sentences like these, standard English requires the forms in parentheses.

Some dialects also omit the -*ed* or -*d* ending from the past tense or past participle of regular verbs when the ending is not clearly pronounced.

> We *bag* (*bagged*) groceries.   I bought a *use* (*used*) book.
> He was *suppose* (*supposed*)   Gloria has *ask* (*asked*) for help.
>   to call.

In standard English, however, the -*ed* and -*d* ending is required for regular verbs whenever (1) the verb's action occurred in the past (*we bagged*); (2) the past participle functions as a modifier (*used books*); and (3) the past participle combines with a form of *be* or *have* (*were supposed, has asked*).

EXERCISE 3

In the following sentences, supply the correct form of each verb in parentheses. Be careful to include -*s* and -*ed* (or -*d*) endings where they are needed for standard English.

A teacher sometimes (*ask*) too much of a student. In high school I was once (*punish*) for being sick. I had (*miss*) some school, and I (*realize*) that I would fail a test unless I had a chance to make up the class work. I (*discuss*) the problem with the teacher, but he said I was (*suppose*) to make up the work while I was sick. At that I (*walk*) out of the class. I (*receive*) a failing grade then, but it did not change my attitude. Today I still balk when a teacher (*make*) unreasonable demands or (*expect*) miracles.

vb

7d

7d   Use helping verbs when they are required.

Helping verbs combine with the infinitives, present participles, and past participles of verbs to indicate time and other kinds of meaning (see p. 224). In some English dialects the helping verb is omitted:

> The owl (*is*) *hooting*.   Sara (*has*) *been* at home.
> I (*have*) *taken* French.   That (*would*) *be* awful.

However, standard English requires the helping verbs in these sentences and in others like them.

Often, the omission of a helping verb creates an incomplete sentence, or **sentence fragment**, because a present participle (*hooting*) or an irregular past participle (*taken, been*) cannot stand alone as the only verb in a sentence (see Chapter 10).

> FRAGMENTS   Few people *smoking*. The toy *broken*.
> REVISED   Few people *were smoking*. The toy *was broken*.

Smoking and *broken* are **non-finite**, or "unfinished," verbs: they can modify other words, but they cannot serve as sentence predicates. Only a **finite**, or "finished," verb can serve as a sentence predicate, and to be made finite a non-finite verb must be combined with a helping verb. (See p. 184 for additional discussion of finite and non-finite verbs.)

EXERCISE 4

Add helping verbs in the following sentences where they are needed for standard English.
1. The floors squeak loudly, and we been meaning to repair them.
2. The essay written by a woman who earned a degree in biology and worked as a laboratory technician.
3. They expected that the play be cancelled because of poor attendance.

4. Joey complaining that his course load leaves him no time for running, and he talking about dropping physics.
5. Most of the harsh words spoken at the meeting been left out of the minutes.

TENSE

Tense is the attribute of a verb that shows the time of the verb's action in relation to the time at which the writer writes or the speaker speaks. The table on the next two pages shows all the tense forms for a regular and an irregular verb in the active voice. (See pp. 241–43 on voice.)

The **simple tenses** indicate that an action or state of being is present, past, or future relative to the speaker or writer. The present tense uses the verb's infinitive (*work*, *write*), or, for third-person singular subjects, its *-s* form (*he works*, *she writes*). The past tense uses the verb's past-tense form (*worked*, *wrote*). The future tense uses the helping verb *will* or *shall* and the verb's infinitive. (See the "Glossary of Usage" section of this text, p. 745, for the distinction between *will* and *shall*.)

The **perfect tenses** indicate that an action was or will be completed before another time or action. (The term *perfect* derives from the Latin *perfectus*, meaning "completed.") The perfect tenses consist of the verb's past participle (*worked*, *written*) preceded by a form of the helping verb *have*.

All verbs also have a set of **progressive forms**, sometimes called the **progressive tense**, which indicate continuing (therefore progressive) action. The progressive uses the *-ing* form of the verb plus a form of *be* (*is working*, *were writing*). Regular and irregular verbs do not differ.

We use the helping verb *do* (*does*) or its past tense *did*, together with the infinitive of the verb, in asking questions, making negative statements, and showing emphasis.

> *Does* he *write* every day? [question]
> He *did* not *write* every day. [negation]
> He *does write* every day. [emphasis]

7e Use the appropriate tense to express your meaning.

For native speakers of English, the selection of an appropriate verb tense usually presents few problems. Most errors in tense are

t
7

TENSES OF A REGULAR AND AN IRREGULAR VERB (ACTIVE VOICE)

	SINGULAR	**PLURAL**
SIMPLE TENSES		
Present		
1st person	I work/write	we work/write
2nd person	you work/write	you work/write
3rd person	he/she/it works/writes	they work/write
Past		
1st person	I worked/wrote	we worked/wrote
2nd person	you worked/wrote	you worked/wrote
3rd person	he/she/it worked/wrote	they worked/wrote
Future		
1st person	I will work/write	we will work/write
2nd person	you will work/write	you will work/write
3rd person	he/she/it will work/write	they will work/write
PERFECT TENSES		
Present perfect		
1st person	I have worked/written	we have worked/written
2nd person	you have worked written	you have worked/ written
3rd person	he/she/it has worked/ written	they have worked/ written
Past perfect		
1st person	I had worked/written	we had worked/written
2nd person	you had worked/ written	you had worked written
3rd person	he/she/it had worked written	they had worked/ written
Future perfect		
1st person	I will have worked/ written	we will have worked/ written
2nd person	you will have worked/ written	you will have worked/ written
3rd person	he/she/it will have worked/written	they will have worked/ written
PROGRESSIVE TENSES		
Present progressive		
1st person	I am working/writing	we are working/writing
2nd person	you are working/writing	you are working/writing
3rd person	he/she/it is working/ writing	they are working/ writing

(continued)

PROGRESSIVE TENSES *(continued)*

Past progressive

1st person	I was working/writing	we were working/writing
2nd person	you were working/writing	you were working/writing
3rd person	he/she/it was working/writing	they were working/writing

Future progressive

1st person	I will be working/writing	we will be working/writing
2nd person	you will be working/writing	you will be working/writing
3rd person	he/she/it will be working/writing	they will be working/writing

Present perfect progressive

1st person	I have been working/writing	we have been working/writing
2nd person	you have been working/writing	you have been working/writing
3rd person	he/she/it has been working/writing	they have been working/writing

Past perfect progressive

1st person	I had been working/writing	we had been working/writing
2nd person	you had been working/writing	you had been working/writing
3rd person	he/she/it had been working/writing	they had been working/writing

Future perfect progressive

1st person	I will have been working/writing	we will have been working/writing
2nd person	you will have been working/writing	you will have been working/writing
3rd person	he/she/it will have been working/writing	they will have been working/writing

t
7e

---

actually errors in verb form like those discussed in the preceding sections—misusing the principal parts of irregular verbs, omitting, *-d* or *-ed* endings, and omitting helping verbs. Still, errors in tense do sometimes occur, so it is a good idea to edit your work carefully to ensure that the tenses of verbs accurately express your meaning.

Any problems in verb tense are most likely to occur with some special uses of the present tense and with the perfect tenses.

1   **Observe the special uses of the present tense.**

The present tense generally indicates action occurring at the time of speaking, as in *She understands what you mean* or *From here I see the river and the docks*. It is also used in several special situations.

TO INDICATE HABITUAL OR RECURRING ACTION

Abby *goes* to Montreal every Friday.
The store *opens* at ten o'clock.

TO STATE A GENERAL TRUTH

The mills of the gods *grind* slowly.
The earth *is* round.

TO DISCUSS THE CONTENT OF LITERATURE, FILMS, AND SO ON (see also pp. 668–69)

When Anne *arrives* at Green Gables, she *is* a surprise to everyone.
In that article the author *examines* several causes of crime.

TO INDICATE FUTURE TIME

Our friends *arrive* the day after tomorrow.
Ted *leaves* in the next half-hour.

(Notice that in sentences like the last two, time is really indicated by *the day after tomorrow* and *in the next half-hour*.)

2   **Observe the uses of the perfect tenses.**

The perfect tenses generally indicate an action completed before another specific time or action. The present perfect tense also indicates action begun in the past and continued into the present.

PRESENT PERFECT

Hannah *has fed* the dog, so we can go. [The action is completed at the time of the statement.]

Hannah *has* always *fed* the dog. [The action began in the past but continues now.]

PAST PERFECT

Hannah *had fed* the dog by the time we were ready. [The action was completed before another past action.]

FUTURE PERFECT

Hannah *will have fed* the dog a thousand times by the end of the month. [The action was begun in the past and will be completed by a specified time in the future.]

She *will have fed* the dog at least another seven hundred meals by this time next year. [The action begins now or in the future and will be completed by a specified time in the future.]

7f   Use the appropriate sequence of verb tenses.

The term **sequence of tenses** refers to the relation between the verb in a main clause and the verbs or verbals in subordinate clauses or verbal phrases (see 5c). The tenses need not be identical as long as they reflect changes in actual or relative time. For example, in the sentence *He had left before I arrived* the past tense *arrived* is in normal sequence with the past perfect *had left*. The principal conventions governing tense sequence are discussed below. (For a discussion of tense shifts—changes *not* required by meaning—see 13b.)

1   Generally, the verb in a subordinate clause may be in any tense required by meaning.

As long as the tense of the verb in the main clause is neither past nor past perfect (see 7f-2 below), the tense in the subordinate clause need only reflect your meaning. In the following sentences all the verb forms follow a clear and natural sequence, though the tenses in main and subordinate clauses are different.

Mike *knows* that Susan *visited* Regina. [Mike's present knowledge is about something that happened in the past, Susan's visit.]

Mike *has known* all along that Susan *will visit* Regina. [Mike's knowledge began in the past and continues; Susan's going to Regina lies in the future.]

Susan *will explain* to Mike why she *changed* her plans. [The explanation lies in the future, but the change of plans occurred at some time in the past.]

Note that any change of tense between a main and a subordinate clause must be logical. The sentence *My family always keeps pets because we liked them* does not seem logical because *liked* indicates that the liking is past and thus is not a reason to keep pets in the present.

2 The verb in a subordinate clause must be past or past perfect if the verb in the main clause is past or past perfect.

The past or past perfect tense in a main clause refers to an action already completed (*smiled, had smiled*). Since the meaning of a subordinate clause depends on that of the main clause, the verb in the subordinate clause must also be completed and thus past or past perfect.

> We *talked* for a long time after we *returned* home. [Since the talking took place in the past, the return home must also have occurred in the past. The past perfect *had returned* would also indicate that the return occurred at a time before the past talking. But the present *return* or the future *will return* would make no sense in the sentence.]

> My friend *had left* before I *arrived*. [The past perfect *had left* indicates that the friend's leaving occurred earlier than the past arrival.]

EXCEPTION: When a subordinate clause expresses a general truth such as *The earth is round*, use the present tense even though the verb of the main clause is in the past or past perfect tense.

> I never *realized* that many marriages *are* genuinely happy.

3 Observe the appropriate tense sequence with infinitives.

The tense of an infinitive is determined by the tense of the verb in the predicate. The **present infinitive** is the verb's plain form preceded by *to* (see 5c-2). It indicates action *at the same time* as or *later* than that of the verb.

> I *went to see* a Stanley Cup playoff game last year. [The going and the seeing occurred at the same time in the past.]

> I *want to see* a Stanley Cup playoff game this year. [The wanting is present; the seeing is still in the future.]

> I *would have liked to see* (not *to have seen*) the other Stanley Cup playoff games last year. [The present infinitive indicates the same past time as *would have liked*.]

The verb's **perfect infinitive** consists of *to have* followed by the past participle, as in *to have talked, to have won*. It indicates action *earlier* than that of the verb.

Denise *would like* (not *would have liked*) *to have heard* Gwendolyn MacEwen read her poetry. [The liking occurs in the present; the hearing would have occurred in the past.]

The election *was thought to have been rigged*. [The rigging of the election occurred before the thinking about it.]

| **4** | **Observe the appropriate tense sequence with participles.** | **t seq** **7f** |

Like the tense of an infinitive, the tense of a participle is determined by the tense of the verb in the predicate. The present participle shows action occurring *at the same time* as that of the verb.

> *Driving* across Canada, he *was astonished* by the vast spaces. [The driving and the astonishment occurred in the same past time.]

The past participle and the present perfect participle show action occurring *earlier* than that of the verb.

> *Exhausted* by overwork, Sheila *remained* at home for two weeks. [The exhaustion occurred before Sheila remained home.]
>
> *Having lived* all his life in the country, he *is frightened* by cities. [Life in the country preceded the fear of cities.]

EXERCISE 5

Revise the following sentences so that the sequence of verb tenses is appropriate. If a sentence is already correct as given, circle the number preceding it. Some items have more than one possible answer.

Example:

Jean had hoped to have been elected.
Jean had hoped *to be elected*.

1. A recent history of hospitals describes how changes in medicine and in our society have fostered increasing dependence on hospitals.
2. Until well into the nineteenth century, hospitals were mainly places to house the desperately sick who have been poor and alone.
3. The sick in hospitals usually received little professional care and usually improved, if at all, simply because time has elapsed.
4. As doctors learned more about infectious diseases, they also decided that the hospital was the best place to have trained young doctors and to have conducted medical research.

5. Tending the wounded in the Crimean War, the British nurse Florence Nightingale then campaigned for hospital improvements and training of nurses.
6. Surgeons increasingly believed that to have performed their work properly required a hospital setting.
7. In addition, doctors of all kinds saw hospitals as places to improve their knowledge and to gain new patients.
8. Having learned to depend heavily on hospitals, Canadians soon find that the services were very expensive.
9. After Saskatchewan initiates hospital insurance, the Canadian government in 1958 has begun to share the cost with the provinces.
10. By 1961, all provinces are providing federally assisted hospital insurance to their residents.

EXERCISE 6

The tenses in each of the following sentences are in correct sequence. Change the tense of one verb as instructed in parentheses. Then change the tense of infinitives, participles, and other verbs as necessary to restore correct sequence. Some items have more than one possible answer.

Example:

He will call when he reaches his destination. (*Change will call to called.*)

He called when he *reached* (or *had reached*) his destination.

1. Diaries that Adolf Hitler is supposed to have written have surfaced in Germany. (*Change have surfaced to had surfaced.*)
2. Many people believe that the diaries are authentic because a well-known historian has declared them so. (*Change believe to believed.*)
3. However, the historian's evaluation has been questioned by other authorities, who call the diaries forgeries. (*Change has been questioned to was questioned.*)
4. They claim, among other things, that the paper is not old enough to have been used by Hitler. (*Change claim to claimed.*)
5. Eventually, the doubters will win the debate because they have the best evidence. (*Change will win to won.*)

MOOD

Mood in grammar is a verb form that indicates the writer's or speaker's attitude toward what he or she is saying. The **indicative mood** states a fact or opinion or asks a question.

They *need* our help. [opinion]
Marie *works* only on Saturday. [fact]
Why *does* she *work* on Saturday? [question]

The **imperative mood** expresses a command or gives a direction. It omits the subject of the sentence, *you*.

> *Work* hard. [command]
> *Turn* right at the light. [direction]

vb
7g

The **subjunctive mood** expresses a requirement, a suggestion, or a desire, or states a condition that is contrary to fact (that is, imaginary or hypothetical).

> Her father urged that she *work* only on Saturdays. [suggestion]
>
> Rules require that applications *be* in writing. [requirement]
>
> I wish that I *swam* better. [desire]
>
> He could have the job if he *were* harder working. [present condition contrary to fact]
>
> The movie would have been more interesting if the lead actor *had been* tougher. [past condition contrary to fact]

With all subjects the subjunctive uses only the infinitive of the verb for suggestions and requirements (*work*, *be*). For desires and present conditions contrary to fact, the subjunctive uses the past tense of the verb (*swam*) or, for *be*, the past-tense form *were*. For past conditions contrary to fact, the subjunctive uses the past perfect (*had known*, *had been*). With conditions contrary to fact, notice that the verb in the main clause also expresses the imaginary or hypothetical with the helping verb *could* (*could have*) or *would* (*would have been*).

(For a discussion of keeping mood consistent within and among sentences, see 13b.)

7g   Use the subjunctive verb forms appropriately.

Although in the past English used distinctive subjunctive verb forms in many contexts, such forms appear now only in two kinds of constructions and in a few idiomatic expressions.

1   Use the subjunctive in contrary-to-fact clauses beginning with *if* or expressing desire.

If I *were* you, I would see a doctor.

If you *saw* a doctor, the rash would disappear.
I wish Jeannie *were* my doctor.

NOTE: The indicative form *was* (*I wish Jeannie was my doctor*) is common in speech and in some informal writing, but the subjunctive *were* is usual in formal English.

Not all clauses beginning with *if* express conditions contrary to fact. In the sentence *If Andreas is out of town, he hasn't heard the news*, the verb *is* is correct because the clause refers to a condition presumed to exist.

2 **Don't use *would* or *could* in the *if* clause of a conditional statement.**

As discussed above, the helping verb *would* or *could* appears in the main clause of a sentence expressing a condition contrary to fact. The helping verb does *not* appear in the subordinate clause beginning *if*.

> **NOT**   I would have called if I *would have* known.
>
> **BUT**   I would have called if I *had* known.

3 **Use the subjunctive in *that* clauses following verbs that demand, request, or recommend.**

Verbs such as *ask, insist, urge, require, recommend*, and *suggest* often precede subordinate clauses beginning with *that* and containing the substance of the request or suggestion. The verb in such *that* clauses should be in the subjunctive mood.

> The psychologist urged that the patient *be released*.
> The law required that he *report* weekly.
> Julie's mother insisted that she *stay* home.
> Instructors commonly ask that papers *be finished* on time.

NOTE: These constructions have widely used alternative forms that do not require the subjunctive, such as *The law required him to report weekly* or *Julie's mother insisted on her staying home*.

4 **Use the subjunctive in some set phrases and idioms.**

Several English expressions commonly use the subjunctive.

For example:

> *Come* rain or *come* shine.
> *Be* that as it may.
> The people *be* damned.

EXERCISE 7

Revise the following sentences with appropriate subjunctive verb forms.

> *Example:*
> I would help the old man if there was a way I could reach him.
> I would help the old man if there *were* a way I could reach him.

1. The audience would have walked out if the performance would have been any worse.
2. The letter requests that we are patient.
3. If I was a rich man, I would still clip coupons from the paper.
4. The syllabus requires that each student writes three papers and takes two essay tests.
5. I wish the lighting in the office was better because my eyes are strained.

VOICE

Verbs that take objects (transitive verbs) can show whether their subjects are acting or are acted upon. In the **active voice** the subject names the actor.

> *David wrote* the paper.
> *The regulations require* a deposit.

In the **passive voice** the subject names the object or receiver of the action. The actor may be named in a prepositional phrase or omitted.

> *The paper was written* by David.
> *A deposit is required* by the regulations.
> *A deposit is required.* [actor omitted]

The passive voice of a verb always consists of the appropriate form of the helping verb *be* plus the past participle of the main verb. Other helping verbs may also be present.

> Senators *are appointed* by the Governor-in-Council.
> Jerry *has been given* complete freedom.

To change a sentence from active to passive voice, we convert the direct object or the indirect object of the verb into the subject of the verb.

ACTIVE	We *gave* Jerry complete freedom.
PASSIVE	Jerry *was given* complete freedom. [Indirect object becomes subject.]
PASSIVE	Complete freedom *was given* (to) Jerry. [Direct object becomes subject.]

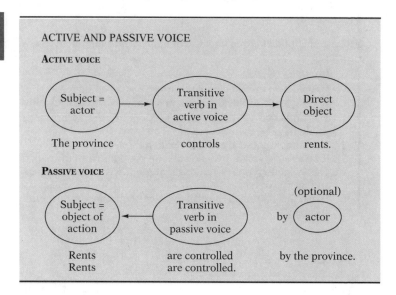

To change a sentence from passive to active voice, we convert the verb's subject into a direct or an indirect object and substitute a new subject for the previous one.

PASSIVE	Sally *was bitten* by Jamie's dog.
ACTIVE	Jamie's dog *bit* Sally.
PASSIVE	The statement *was read* at a press conference.
ACTIVE	The company's representative *read* the statement at a press conference.

7h Generally, prefer the active voice. Use the passive voice when the actor is unknown or unimportant.

Because the passive omits or de-emphasizes the actor (the performer of the verb's action), it can deprive writing of vigour and is often vague or confusing. The active voice is usually stronger, clearer, and more forthright.

> **WEAK PASSIVE**   The exam was thought by us to be unfair because we were tested on material that was not covered in the course.
>
> **STRONG ACTIVE**   We thought the exam unfair because it tested us on material the course did not cover.

pass

7h

The passive voice is useful in two situations: when the actor is unknown and when the actor is unimportant or less important than the object of the action.

> Ray Appleton *was murdered* after he returned home. [The murderer is presumably unknown, and in any event Ray Appleton's death is the point of the sentence.]
>
> In the first experiment acid *was added* to the solution. [The person who added the acid, perhaps the writer, is less important than the fact that acid was added. Passive sentences are common in scientific writing.]

Except in such situations, however, you should prefer the active voice in your writing. (See 18d and 13c-3 for additional cautions against the passive voice.)

EXERCISE 8

To practise using the two voices of the verb, convert the following sentences from active to passive or from passive to active. (In converting from passive to active, you may have to add a subject for the new sentence.) Which version of each sentence seems more effective, and why? (For additional exercises with the passive voice, see pp. 204, 354, and 487.)

Example:

The aspiring actor was discovered in a nightclub.

A *talent scout discovered* the aspiring actor in a nightclub.

1. When the Eiffel Tower was built in 1889, it was thought by the French to be ugly.
2. At that time many people still resisted industrial technology.
3. The tower's naked steel construction epitomized this technology.
4. Beautiful ornament was expected to grace fine buildings.
5. Further, the tower could not even be called a building because it had no solid walls.

EXERCISE 9

Circle all the verbs and verbals in the following paragraph and correct their form, tense, or mood if necessary.

For centuries the natives of Melanesia, a group of islands laying northeast of Australia, have practise an unusual religion. It began in the eighteenth century when European explorers first have visited the islands. The natives were fascinated by the rich goods or "cargo" possessed by the explorers. They saw the wealth as treasures of the gods, and cargo cults eventually had arisen among them. Over the centuries some Melanesians turned to Christianity in the belief that the white man's religion will bring them the white man's treasures. During World War II, American soldiers, having arrived by boat and airplane to have occupied some of the islands, introduced new and even more wonderful cargo. Even today some leaders of the cargo cults insist that the airplane is worship as a vehicle of the Melanesians' future salvation.

CHAPTER 8

Agreement

Agreement is the correspondence in form between subjects and verbs and between pronouns and their **antecedents**, the nouns or other pronouns they refer to. Agreement helps readers understand the relations between elements in a sentence. The aspects of agreement are explained on the next page.

Subjects and verbs agree in number and in person.

Sarah often *speaks* up in class. [Both subject and verb are in the third-person singular form.]

Even though *we understand, we* still *dislike* it. [Both subjects and verbs are in the first-person plural form.]

Pronouns and their antecedents agree in person, number, and gender.

Claude resented their ignoring *him*. [Both the pronoun *him* and its antecedent *Claude* are masculine and third-person singular.]

The *dogs* stand still while *they* are judged. [The pronoun *they* and its antecedent *dogs* are both third-person plural.]

8a Make subjects and verbs agree in number.

Most subject-verb agreement problems arise when endings are omitted from subjects or verbs, when the subject is not clearly singular or plural, or when words come between subject and verb and blur their relationship. The conventions in the "Aspects of Agreement" box cover these and other situations that affect subject-verb agreement.

ASPECTS OF AGREEMENT

PERSON

1st person, the speaker(s): *I, we*
2nd person, the person(s) spoken to: *you*
3rd person, the person(s) or thing(s) spoken about: *he, she, it, they*;
  nouns; indefinite and relative pronouns

NUMBER

Singular, one: *I, you, he, she, it*; nouns naming one; indefinite and
  relative pronouns referring to plural nouns and pronouns
Plural, more than one: *we, you, they*; nouns naming more than one;
  indefinite and relative pronouns referring to plural nouns and
  pronouns

GENDER

Masculine: *he*; nouns naming males; indefinite and relative pronouns referring to males
Feminine: *she*; nouns naming females; indefinite and relative pronouns referring to females
Neuter: *it*; nouns naming places, things, qualities, and ideas; indefinite and relative pronouns referring to same

---

1 **Use the verb ending -*s* or -*es* with all third-person
singular subjects. Use the noun ending -*s* or -*es* to make
most nouns plural.**

Adding -*s* or -*es* to a noun usually makes the noun *plural*,
whereas adding -*s* or -*es* to a present-tense verb makes the verb
singular. Thus if the subject noun is plural, it will end in -*s* or -*es* and
the verb will not. If the subject is singular, it will not end in -*s* and the
verb will.

SINGULAR	**PLURAL**
The boy eats.	The boys eat.
The bird soars.	The birds soar.

The only exceptions to these rules involve the nouns that form
irregular plurals, such as *child/children*; *woman/women*. The irregular plural still requires a plural verb: *The children play*.

Writers often omit -*s* and -*es* endings from nouns or verbs
because they are not pronounced clearly in speech (as in *asks* and
lists) or because they are not used regularly in some English dialects.
However, the endings are required in standard English.

NON-STANDARD	Daniella *resist* any kind of change.
STANDARD	Daniella *resists* any kind of change.
NON-STANDARD	Their *action* demand a response.
STANDARD	Their *actions* demand a response.

Remember that the verb *be* is irregular. In the present tense we use *is* with *he*, *she*, *it*, and singular nouns (*tree is*) and *are* with all plurals (*trees are*). In the past tense we use *was* with *he*, *she*, *it*, and singular nouns (*tree was*) and *were* with all plurals (*trees were*). (See Chapter 7, pp. 224 and 229, for more on these verb forms.)

agr

8a

NOTE: In a verb phrase (verb plus helping verb), the helping verb sometimes reflects the number of the subject and sometimes does not: *The car does run*; *The cars do run*; *The car/cars will run*. The verb itself (*run*) does not change in any way.

2   **Subject and verb should agree even when other words come between them.**

When the subject and verb are interrupted by other words, particularly nouns, then agreement errors may result from connecting the verb to the nearest noun instead of the actual subject.

A calendar of courses and requirements often *baffles* (not *baffle*) students. [The verb must agree with the subject, *calendar*, not the nearer word *requirements*.]

The profits earned by the cosmetic industry *are* (not *is*) high. [The subject is *profits*, not *industry*.]

NOTE: Phrases beginning with *as well as*, *together with*, *along with*, *in addition to*, and similar expressions do not change the number of the subject.

The premier, as well as his advisers, *has* (not *have*) agreed to attend the protest rally.

If you really mean *and* in such a sentence, you can avoid awkwardness by using it. Then the subject is compound, and the verb should be plural: *The premier and his advisers have agreed to attend*.

3   **Subjects joined by *and* usually take plural verbs.**

Two or more subjects joined by *and* usually take a plural verb, whether one or all of the subjects are singular.

Atwood and Purdy *are* her favourite poets.
The dog, the monkey, the children, and the tent *were* in the car.

EXCEPTIONS: When the parts of the subject form a single idea or refer to a single person or thing, then they take a singular verb.

> Avocado and bean sprouts *is* my favorite sandwich.
> The winner and new champion *was* in the shower.

When a compound subject is preceded by the adjective *each* or *every*, then the verb is usually singular.

> At customs, every box, bag, and parcel *is* inspected.
> Each man, woman, and child *has* a right to be heard.

But when a compound subject is *followed* by *each*, the verb is plural.

> The man and the woman each *have* different problems.

4   **When parts of a subject are joined by *or* or *nor*, the verb agrees with the nearer part.**

When all parts of a subject joined by *or* or *nor* are singular, the verb is singular; when all parts are plural, the verb is plural.

> Neither the teacher nor the student *knows* the answer.
> The rabbits or the woodchucks *have eaten* my lettuce.

Problems with subjects joined by *or* or *nor* occur most often when one part of the subject is singular and the other plural. In that case the verb should agree with the subject part closer to it. To avoid awkwardness in such sentences, place the plural part closer to the verb.

> **AWKWARD**   Neither the players nor the coach *was* on time.
>
> **IMPROVED**   Neither the coach nor the players *were* on time.

The same problem arises when the subject consists of nouns and pronouns of different person requiring different verb forms: *neither Jim nor I*, *either he or you*. In this case, too, the verb agrees with the part of the subject nearer to it.

> Neither Jim nor I *am* late.
> Either she or you *are* late.

Since observing this convention often results in awkwardness, avoid the problem altogether by rewording the sentence.

> **AWKWARD**   Either she or you *are* late.
>
> **IMPROVED**   Either she *is* late, or you *are*.

5   **Generally, use singular verbs with indefinite pronouns.**

An **indefinite pronoun** is one that does not refer to a specific person or thing.

COMMON INDEFINITE PRONOUNS			
all	each	neither	one
any	either	nobody	some
anybody	everybody	none	somebody
anyone	everyone	no one	someone
anything	everything	nothing	something

agr
8a

Most indefinite pronouns are singular in meaning (they refer to a single unspecified person or thing), and they take singular verbs.

Something *smells*.   Neither *is* right.

A few indefinite pronouns like *all*, *any*, *none*, and *some* may be either singular or plural in meaning. The verbs you use with these pronouns depend on the meaning of the nouns or pronouns they refer to.

All of the money *is* reserved for emergencies. [*All* refers to the singular noun *money*, so the verb is singular.]

When the men finally arrive, all *go* straight to work. [*All* refers to the plural noun *men*, so the verb is plural.]

6 **Collective nouns take singular or plural verbs depending on meaning.**

A **collective noun** has singular form but names a group of individuals or things—for example, *army*, *audience*, *committee*, *crowd*, *family*, *group*, *team*. When used as a subject, a collective noun may take a singular or plural verb, depending on the context. When considering the group as one unit, use a singular verb.

The group *agrees* that action is necessary.
Any band *sounds* good in that concert hall.

But when considering the group's members as individuals who act separately, use the plural form of the verb.

The old group *have* gone their separate ways.
The band *do* not agree on where to play.

NOTE: Even when the plural verb form is properly used, as in these examples, it often sounds awkward. For this reason you may prefer to rephrase such sentences with plural subjects, as in *The members of the old group have gone their separate ways*.

The collective noun *number* may be singular or plural. Preceded by *a*, it is plural; preceded by *the*, it is singular.

A number of my friends *have* decided to live off campus.
The number of people in debt *is* very large.

7 The verb agrees with the subject even when the normal word order is inverted.

Inverted subject-verb order occurs in questions.

Is voting a right or a privilege? [*Voting* is the subject; *is* is the verb. Compare *Voting is a right or a privilege*.]

Are Madigan and Harris married? [*Madigan and Harris* is the compound subject; *are* is the verb. Compare *Madigan and Harris are married*.]

Inverted subject-verb order also occurs in expletive constructions beginning with *there* or *it* and a form of *be* (see 5e-4).

There *are* too many students in that class. [*Students* is the subject; *are* is the verb. Compare *Too many students are in that class*.]

After many years there *is* finally peace in that country. [*Peace* is the subject; *is* is the verb. Compare *Peace is in that country*.]

In expletive constructions, *there is* may be used before a compound subject when the first element in the subject is singular.

There *is* much work to do and little time to do it.

Word order may sometimes be inverted for emphasis. The verb still agrees with its subject.

From the mountains *comes* an eerie, shimmering light.

8 A linking verb agrees with its subject, not the subject complement.

When a linking verb is followed by a subject complement, make the verb agree with its subject, the first element, not with the noun or pronoun serving as a subject complement (see 5a-3).

Henry's sole support *is* his mother and father. [The subject is *support*.]

Henry's mother and father *are* his sole support. [The subject is *mother and father*.]

9 When used as subjects, *who*, *which*, and *that* take verbs that agree with their antecedents.

The relative pronouns *who*, *which*, and *that* do not have different singular and plural forms. When one of these pronouns serves as a subject, its verb should agree with the noun or other pronoun that the relative pronoun refers to (its antecedent).

Mayor Garber ought to listen to the people who *work* for her. [*Who* refers to the plural *people*, so the verb is plural.]

Jane is the person who usually *solves* our problems. [*Who* refers to the singular *person*, so the verb is singular.]

Agreement problems often occur with relative pronouns when the sentence includes *one of the* or *the only one of the* before the pronoun.

Roberts is one of the teachers who *give* difficult tests. [*Who* refers to the plural *teachers*. Several teachers give difficult tests; Roberts is one of them.]

Roberts is the only one of the teachers who *has* paid attention to me. [*Who* refers to *one*. Among the teachers only one, Roberts, has paid attention.]

10 **Nouns with plural form but singular meaning take singular verbs.**

Some nouns with plural form (that is, ending in *-s*) are usually regarded as singular in meaning. They include *athletics*, *economics*, *mathematics*, *measles*, *news*, *politics*, *physics*, and *statistics*.

After so long a wait, the news *has* to be good.
Statistics *is* required of psychology majors.

Measurements and figures ending in *-s* may also be singular when the quantity they refer to is a unit.

Three years *is* a long time to wait.
Three-fourths of her library *consists* of reference books.

These words and amounts are plural in meaning when they describe individual items rather than whole groups or whole bodies of activity or knowledge.

The statistics *prove* him wrong. [*Statistics* refers to facts, individual items.]

Two-fifths of the cars on the road *are* unsafe. [The cars are unsafe separately.]

11 **Titles and words named as words take singular verbs.**

When your sentence subject is the title of a corporation or a work (such as a book or a movie) or a word you are defining or describing, the verb should be singular even if the title or the word is plural.

Hakada Associates *is* a new firm.
The Stone Angel remains one of her favourite books.
Folks is a colloquial word for *people*.

EXERCISE 1

Revise the verbs in the following sentences as needed to make subjects and verbs agree in number. If the sentence is already correct as given, circle the number preceding it.

Example:

Each of the job applicants *type* sixty words per minute.
Each of the job applicants *types* sixty words per minute.

1. Weinstein & Associates are a consulting firm that try to make business people laugh.
2. Statistics from recent research suggests that humour relieves stress.
3. Reduced stress in businesses in turn reduce illness and absenteeism.
4. Reduced stress can also reduce friction within an employee group, which then work together more productively.
5. In special conferences held by one consultant, each of the participants practise making the others laugh.
6. "Isn't there enough laughs within you to spread the wealth?" the consultant asks his students.
7. The consultant quotes Casey Stengel's rule that the best way to keep your management job is to separate the underlings who hate you from the ones who have not decided how they feel.
8. Such self-deprecating comments in public is uncommon among business managers, the consultant says.
9. Each of the managers in a typical firm take the work much too seriously.
10. The humorous boss often feels like the only one of the managers who have other things in mind besides profits.
11. One consultant to many companies suggest cultivating office humour with practical jokes such as a rubber fish in the water cooler.
12. When employees or their manager regularly post cartoons on the bulletin board, office spirit usually picks up.
13. When someone who has seemed too easily distracted is entrusted with updating the cartoons, his or her concentration often improves.
14. In the face of levity, the former sourpuss becomes one of those who hides bad temper.
15. Every one of the consultants caution, however, that humour has no place in life-affecting corporate situations such as employee layoffs.

8b **Make pronouns and their antecedents agree in person and number.**

The **antecedent** of a pronoun is the noun or other pronoun it refers to. The antecedent usually comes before the pronoun that refers to it, but it may follow the pronoun.

Every *dog* in that kennel has received *its* shots. [*Dog* is the antecedent of *its*.]

Having received *their* tax bills, the *home-owners* worried about payment. [*Home-owners*, the subject of the main clause, is the antecedent of *their* in the introductory phrase.]

As these examples show, a pronoun agrees with its antecedent in gender (masculine, feminine, neuter), person (first, second, third), and number (singular, plural) (see p. 246 for an explanation of these terms). Since pronouns derive their meaning from their antecedents, pronoun-antecedent agreement is essential for the reader to understand what you are saying.

1 **Antecedents joined by *and* usually take plural pronouns.**

Two or more antecedents joined by *and* usually take a plural pronoun, whether one or all of the antecedents are singular.

My adviser and I can't co-ordinate *our* schedules.
Their argument resolved, George and Jennifer made up.

EXCEPTIONS: When the compound antecedent refers to a single idea, person, or thing, then the pronoun is singular.

The athlete and scholar forgot both *his* javelin and *his* books.

When the compound antecedent follows *each* or *every*, the pronoun is singular.

Every girl and woman took *her* seat.

2 **When parts of an antecedent are joined by *or* or *nor*, the pronoun agrees with the nearer part.**

When the parts of an antecedent are connected by *or* or *nor*, the pronoun should agree with the part closer to it.

Steve or Karl should have raised *his* hand.

Either consumers or car manufacturers will have *their* way.

Neither the student nor the elderly people will retrieve *their* deposits from that landlord.

When one subject is plural and the other singular, as in the last example, the sentence will be awkward unless you put the plural subject second.

AWKWARD   Either the dogs or the cat will have to be returned to the shop *it* came from.

REVISED   Either the cat or the dogs will have to be returned to the shop *they* came from.

3 Generally, use a singular pronoun when the antecedent is an indefinite pronoun.

Indefinite pronouns such as *anybody* and *something* refer to persons or things in general rather than to a specific person or thing (see p. 249 for a list). Most indefinite pronouns are singular in meaning. When these indefinite pronouns serve as antecedents to other pronouns, the other pronouns are singular.

Everyone on the team had *her* own locker.
Each of the boys likes *his* teacher.

Using a singular pronoun to refer to an indefinite pronoun may result in an awkward sentence when the indefinite pronoun clearly means "many" or "all."

AWKWARD   After everyone left, I shut the door behind *him*.

In speech we commonly avoid such awkwardness with a plural pronoun: *After everyone left, I shut the door behind them.* In writing, however, you should rewrite the sentence.

REWRITTEN   After *all the guests* left, I shut the door behind *them*.

The generic *he*

The meaning of an indefinite pronoun often includes both masculine and feminine genders, not one or the other. The same is true of other indefinite words such as *child, adult, individual*, and *person*. In such cases we traditionally use *he* (or *him* or *his*) to refer to the antecedent. But many people see the so-called **generic *he*** (or generalized *he*) as excluding females. Thus many writers now avoid using *he* in these situations by rewriting their sentences.

ORIGINAL	Everyone had *his* book in class.
BROADER	Everyone had *his* or *her* book in class. [Overused, this option can be wordy or awkward.]
PLURAL	*All the students* had *their* books in class. [This option can be used frequently without creating awkwardness.]

In speech we often solve the problem of the generic *he* by combining a plural pronoun with an indefinite pronoun, as in *Everyone brought their books to class*. But many readers view this construction as wrong, so it should be avoided in writing.

For more on avoiding gender bias in writing, see 31a-8.

agr
8b

4 **Collective noun antecedents take singular or plural pronouns depending on meaning.**

Collective nouns such as *army*, *committee*, *family*, *group*, and *team* have singular form but may be referred to by singular or plural pronouns, depending on the meaning intended. When you are referring to the group as a unit—all its members acting together—then the pronoun is singular.

> The committee voted to disband *itself*.
> The team attended a banquet in *its* honour.

When you are referring to the individual members of the group, the pronoun is plural.

> The audience arose quietly from *their* seats.
> The old group have gone *their* separate ways.

The last example demonstrates the importance of being consistent in verb use as well as pronoun choice when assigning a singular or plural meaning to a collective noun (see also 8a-6).

INCONSISTENT	The old group *has* gone *their* separate ways.
CONSISTENT	The old group *have* gone *their* separate ways.

EXERCISE 2

Revise the following sentences so that pronouns and their antecedents agree in person and number. Some items have more than one possible answer. Try to avoid the generic *he* (see p. 254), and if you change the subject of a sentence be sure to change verbs as necessary for agreement. If the sentence is already correct as given, circle the number preceding it.

Example:
Each of the Boudreaus' children brought their laundry home at Thanksgiving.

Each of the Boudreaus' children brought *his or her* laundry home at Thanksgiving. *Or: All* of the Boudreaus' children brought *their* laundry home at Thanksgiving.

1. Almost any child will quickly astound observers with their capabilities.
2. Despite their extensive research and experience, neither child psychologists nor parents have yet figured out how children work.
3. Of course, the family has a tremendous influence on the development of a child in their midst.
4. Each of the members of the immediate family exerts their own unique pull on the child.
5. Other relatives, teachers, and friends can also affect the child's view of the world and themselves.
6. Genetics and physiology also strongly influence the development of children, but it may never be fully understood.
7. The psychology community often cannot agree in its views of whether nurture or nature is more important in a child's development.
8. Another debated issue is whether the child's emotional development or their intellectual development is more central.
9. Just about everyone has their strong opinion on these issues, often backed up by evidence.
10. Neither the popular press nor scholarly journals devote much of their space to the wholeness of the child.

EXERCISE 3

In the following sentences subjects agree with verbs, and pronouns agree with antecedents. Make the change specified in parentheses after each sentence, and then revise the sentence as necessary to maintain agreement. Try to avoid the generic *he* (see p. 254). Some items have more than one possible answer.

Example:
The student attends weekly conferences with her teacher. (*Change The student to Students.*)
Students *attend* weekly conferences with *their* teacher.

1. Recently, one psychologist has published his ideas about the entire process of child development. (*Change one psychologist to some psychologists.*)
2. This theory meshes social and intellectual development and illuminates the connection between them. (*Change This theory to These theories.*)

3. Stanley Greenspan, a child psychiatrist, proposes that children proceed through stages in their first ten years. (*Change children to the child.*)
4. Each stage integrates emotions and cognition, and it prepares the way for following stages. (*Change Each stage to The stages.*)
5. In the first stage, for example, the child learns some self-regulation as a means of protecting himself from overstimulation. (*Change the child to children.*)
6. But self-regulation also helps the child organize his immediate experience, so it serves a cognitive purpose for him as well. (*Change the child to children.*)
7. At a much later stage, around age nine, children identify strongly with adults of the same sex and imitate their roles and behaviours. (*Change children to the child.*)
8. Children also become preoccupied with their peers at this stage and begin to seek relationships. (*Change Children to The child.*)
9. Yet the child's interaction with peers is often guided by strict rules, indicating that it has a cognitive function. (*Change interaction to interactions.*)
10. The child is organizing experience that is abstract and complex, not just immediate and concrete as in infancy. (*Change experience to experiences.*)

agr

8

EXERCISE 4

Revise the sentences in the following paragraph to correct errors in agreement between subjects and verbs or between pronouns and their antecedents.

Everyone has their favourite view of professional athletes. A common view is that the athletes are like well-paid children who have no real work to do, have no responsibilities, and simply enjoy the game and the good money. But this view of professional athletes fail to consider the gruelling training the athletes have to go through to become professionals. Either training or competing lead each athlete to take risks that can result in their serious injury. The athletes have tremendous responsibility to the team they play on, which need to function as a unit at all times to win their games. Most athletes are finished as active team players by the age of forty, when he is too stiff and banged-up to go on. Rather than just listening to any of the people who criticizes professional athletes, everyone interested in sports need to defend the athletes. They take stiff physical punishment so neither the sports fanatic nor the casual observer are deprived of their pleasure.

CHAPTER 9

Adjectives and Adverbs

Adjectives and adverbs are modifiers that describe, restrict, or otherwise qualify the words to which they relate.

FUNCTIONS OF ADJECTIVES AND ADVERBS

Adjectives modify nouns: *serious* student
pronouns: *ordinary* one

Adverbs modify verbs: *warmly* greet
adjectives: *only* three people
adverbs: *quite* seriously
phrases: *nearly* to the edge of the cliff
clauses: *just* when we were ready to leave
sentences: *Fortunately*, she is now employed.

Many of the most common adjectives are familiar one-syllable words such as *good, bad, strange, true, false, large, right,* and *wrong.* Many others are formed by adding endings such as *-al, -able, -ful, -less, -ish, -ive,* and *-y* to nouns or verbs: *optional, fashionable, beautiful, fruitless, selfish, expressive, dreamy.*

Most adverbs are formed by adding *-ly* to adjectives: *badly, strangely, falsely, largely, beautifully, selfishly.* But note that we cannot depend on *-ly* to identify adverbs, since some adjectives also end in *-ly* (*fatherly, lonely, silly*) and since some common adverbs do not end in *-ly* (*always, forever, here, not, now, often, quite, then, there*). Thus the only sure way to distinguish between adjectives and adverbs is to determine how an individual word functions in its sentence. If a word modifies a noun or pronoun, it is an adjective; if it modifies a verb, an adjective, another adverb, or an entire word group, it is an adverb.

Don't use adjectives to modify verbs, adverbs, or other adjectives.

Adjectives modify only nouns and pronouns. Using adjectives instead of adverbs to modify verbs, adverbs, or other adjectives is non-standard.

NON-STANDARD	They took each other *serious*.
STANDARD	They took each other *seriously*.
NON-STANDARD	Jenny read the book *easy*.
STANDARD	Jenny read the book *easily*.

The adjectives *good* and *bad* often appear where standard English requires the adverbs *well* and *badly*.

NON-STANDARD	Playing *good* is the goal of practising baseball.
STANDARD	Playing *well* is the goal of practising baseball.
NON-STANDARD	The band played *bad* last night.
STANDARD	The band played *badly* last night.

Although in informal speech the adjective forms *real* and *sure* are often used in place of the adverb forms *really* and *surely*, formal speech and writing require the *-ly* adverb form.

INFORMAL	After a few lessons Dan drove *real* well.
FORMAL	After a few lessons Dan drove *really* well.
INFORMAL	I *sure* was shocked by his confession.
FORMAL	I *surely* was shocked by his confession.

Use an adjective after a linking verb to modify the subject. Use an adverb to modify a verb.

A **linking verb** is one that links, or connects, a subject and its complement: *They are golfers* (noun complement); *He is lucky* (adjective complement). (See also 5a-3.) The verbs most often used as linking verbs are forms of *be* and verbs associated with our five senses (*look*, *sound*, *smell*, *feel*, *taste*), as well as a few others (*appear*, *seem*, *become*, *grow*, *turn*, *prove*, *remain*). But some of these verbs may or may not be linking, depending on their meaning in the sentence. When the word after the verb modifies the subject, the verb is linking and the word should be an adjective. When the word modifies the verb, however, it should be an adverb.

Hallie felt *bad* after she lost the race. [Adjective *bad*, meaning "ill" or "unhappy," modifies *Hallie*.]

She had lost the race *badly*. [Adverb *badly* modifies *had lost*.]

The evidence proved *conclusive*. [Adjective *conclusive* modifies *evidence*.]

The evidence proved *conclusively* that the defendant was guilty. [Adverb *conclusively* modifies *proved*.]

9c After a direct object, use an adjective to modify the object and an adverb to modify the verb.

If the direct object of a verb is followed by a word that modifies the verb, the word must be an adverb: *She repeated the words angrily.* If, in contrast, the direct object is followed by a word that modifies the object itself (an object complement), that word must be an adjective: *Campus politics made Martin angry.* (See also 5a-3.) You can test whether a modifier should be an adjective or an adverb by trying to separate it from the direct object. If you can separate it, it should be an adverb: *She angrily repeated the words.* If you cannot separate it, it is probably an adjective.

The instructor considered the student's work *thorough*. [The adjective can be moved in front of *work* (*student's thorough work*), but it cannot be separated from *work*.]

The instructor considered the student's work *thoroughly*. [The adverb can be separated from *work*. Compare *The instructor thoroughly considered the student's work*.]

9d When an adverb has a short form and an *-ly* form, distinguish carefully between the forms.

Some adverbs have two forms, one with an *-ly* ending and one without. These include the following:

cheap, cheaply	loud, loudly	sharp, sharply
high, highly	near, nearly	slow, slowly
late, lately	quick, quickly	wrong, wrongly

With some of these pairs the choice of form is a matter of idiom, for the two forms have developed entirely separate meanings.

He went *late*.   Winter is drawing *near*.
Lately he has been eating more.   Winter is *nearly* here.

In other pairs the long and short forms have the same meaning. However, the short forms generally occur in informal speech and writing. The -*ly* forms are preferable in formal writing.

ad

9d

INFORMAL	Drive *slow*.
FORMAL	The funeral procession moved *slowly* through town.
INFORMAL	Jones wants to get rich *quick*.
FORMAL	Leung became rich *quickly* when she invested in the stock market.

EXERCISE 1

Identify the adjectives and adverbs in the following sentences, and determine what part of speech each one modifies. Then compose a sentence of your own that parallels each sentence.

Example:

The angry man shouted loudly and moved inside.

The *angry* man shouted *loudly* and moved *inside* .

The *hungry* child cried *plaintively* and fussed *about*.

1. The weary tourists slowly filed into the large grey bus.
2. During the rapid descent through the thick clouds, passengers muttered tensely among themselves.
3. Everyone in the class answered the hardest question wrong.
4. He was such an exciting person that everyone felt bad when he left.
5. As the Ferris wheel slowly turned, raising him higher in the air, he became increasingly ill.

EXERCISE 2

Revise the following sentences to make adjectives modify nouns and pronouns and to make adverbs modify verbs, adjectives, and other adverbs. If any sentence is already correct as given, circle the number preceding it.

Example:

The announcer warned that traffic was moving very slow.
The announcer warned that traffic was moving very *slowly*.

1. I was real surprised when Marcel and Madeleine bought a Porsche.
2. If you take your lessons more serious, you will improve faster.

3. That perfume smelled similarly to my mother's.
4. Thinking about the accident, Brian felt bad.
5. After playing poor for six games, the hockey team finally had a game that went good.

9e Use the comparative and superlative forms of adjectives and adverbs appropriately.

Adjectives and adverbs can show different degrees of quality or amount with the endings *-er* and *-est* or with the words *more* and *most* (to compare upward) or *less* and *least* (to compare downward). Most modifiers have three forms. The **positive form** is the dictionary form and simply describes without comparing.

> a *big* book
> spoke *forcefully*

The **comparative form** compares the thing modified with one other thing.

> a *bigger* book
> spoke *more* (or *less*) *forcefully*

The **superlative form** compares the thing modified with two or more other things.

> the *biggest* book
> spoke *most* (or *least*) *forcefully*

1 When word length or sound requires, use *more* and *most* instead of the endings *-er* and *-est*.

For downward comparisons, all adjectives and adverbs use *less* for the comparative (*less open*) and *least* for the superlative (*least successfully*). For upward comparisons, most one-syllable adjectives and adverbs and many two-syllable adjectives take the endings *-er* and *-est*: *red, redder, reddest; lucky, luckier, luckiest; fast, faster, fastest*.

Many two-syllable adjectives can either add *-er* and *-est* or use the words *more* and *most*: *steady, steadier* or *more steady, steadiest* or *most steady*. The use of *more* or *most* tends to draw the comparison out and so places more emphasis on it.

Using *more* and *most* is the only way to form the comparative and superlative for adjectives of three or more syllables and for most adverbs of two or more syllables (including nearly all ending in *-ly*): *beautiful, more beautiful, most beautiful; often, more often, most often; sadly, more sadly, most sadly*.

If you are in doubt about how to form a comparative or superlative, consult a dictionary. If the degrees can be formed with the ending *-er* and *-est*, the dictionary will give those forms. Otherwise, use *more* and *most*.

2   **Use the correct form of irregular adjectives and adverbs.**

The irregular modifiers change the spelling of their positive form to show comparative and superlative degrees.

DEGREES OF IRREGULAR ADJECTIVES AND ADVERBS

POSITIVE	COMPARATIVE	SUPERLATIVE
Adjectives		
good	better	best
bad	worse	worst
little	little, less	littlest, least
many } some } much }	more	most
Adverbs		
well	better	best
badly	worse	worst

3   **Don't use double comparatives or double superlatives.**

A doubled comparative or superlative combines the *-er* or *-est* ending with the word *more*, *most*, *less*, or *least*. It is redundant and should be avoided.

> He was the *wisest* (not *most wisest*) man I ever knew.
> My sister gets privileges because she's *older* (not *more older*).

4   **In general, use the comparative form for comparing two things and the superlative form for comparing three or more things.**

> She was the *taller* of the two girls. [Comparative]
> Of all those books, *Colony to Nation* is the *best*. [Superlative]

In conversation the superlative form is often used even though only two things are being compared: *When two people argue, the angriest one is usually wrong*. But the distinction between the forms should be observed in writing.

> **5** **In general, don't use comparative or superlative forms for modifiers that cannot logically be compared.**

Adjectives and adverbs that cannot logically be compared include *perfect, unique, dead, impossible,* and *infinite*. These words are absolute; that is, they are not capable of greater or lesser degrees because their positive form describes their only state. Although they can be preceded by adverbs like *nearly* or *almost* that mean "approaching," they cannot logically be modified by *more, most, less,* or *least* (as in *most perfect*). This distinction is sometimes ignored in speech, but it should always be made in writing.

NOT	He was the *most unique* teacher we had.
BUT	He was a *unique* teacher.

EXERCISE 3

Write the comparative and superlative forms of each of the following adjectives or adverbs. Then use all three forms in sentences of your own.

Example:

heavy: heavier (comparative), heaviest (superlative)

The barbells were too *heavy* for me. The magician's trunk was *heavier* than I expected. Lyle Smith was the *heaviest* person on the team.

1. badly
2. great
3. lively
4. steady

5. some
6. often
7. good

8. well
9. elegant
10. understanding

EXERCISE 4

Revise the following sentences so that the comparative and superlative forms of adjectives and adverbs are appropriate for formal usage.

Example:

Attending classes full-time and working at two jobs was the most impossible thing I ever did.

Attending classes full-time and working at two jobs was *impossible* (or *the hardest thing I ever did*).

1. Brad is the smallest of the two boys.
2. That is the most saddest story I have ever heard.
3. Of the two major problems with nuclear power plants—waste disposal and radiation leakage—radiation leakage is the most terrifying.
4. If I study hard, I should be able to do more better on the next economics test.
5. Working last summer as an assistant to my member of Parliament was one of the more unique experiences I have ever had.

9f   Avoid double negatives.

A **double negative** is a construction in which two negative words such as *no*, *none*, *neither*, *barely*, *hardly*, or *scarcely* cancel each other out. For instance, in *Cecily did not feel nothing*, the negatives *not* and *nothing* in essence produce a positive: the sentence asserts that Cecily felt other than nothing, or something. For the opposite meaning, one of the negatives must be eliminated or changed to a positive: *She felt nothing* or *She did not feel anything*.

FAULTY   We could *not hardly* hear the speaker. *None* of her ideas *never* made it to the back of the room.

REVISED   We could *hardly* hear the speaker. *None* of her ideas made it to the back of the room.

REVISED   We could *not* hear the speaker. Her ideas *never* made it to the back of the room.

9g   Avoid overuse of nouns as modifiers.

We often use one noun to modify another. For example:

| father figure | shoe box | child care |
| flood control | truth serum | security guard |

Carefully conceived, such phrases can be both clear and concise: *security guard* seems preferable to *guard responsible for security*. But overuse of noun modifiers can lead to flat, even senseless, writing. To avoid awkwardness or confusion, observe two principles. First, prefer possessives or adjectives as modifiers.

NOT   Glenn took the *province* law *society* exams to become a lawyer.

BUT   Glenn took the *provincial* law *society's* exams to become a lawyer.

Second, use only short nouns as modifiers and use them only in two-
or three-word sequences.

> **CONFUSING**   Minimex maintains a *plant employee relations improvement program.*
>
> **REVISED**   Minimex maintains a *program* for *improving relations* among *plant employees.*

EXERCISE 5

Revise the following sentences so that they conform to formal usage of adjectives and adverbs as described in this chapter. If a sentence is already correct as given, circle the number preceding it.

Example:

Of the three books in the trilogy, the third is the better.
Of the three books in the trilogy, the third is the *best*.

1. She batted real well this season, but she didn't field good enough to make the all-star team.
2. It was the most totally perfect apartment we saw.
3. All three candidates claimed to be the more responsive.
4. Todd felt strangely the next day, and he was sure his exam would go bad.
5. The cat stalked its prey careful and quiet.
6. That argument sounds too illogical to take serious.
7. The university administration student absenteeism policy was controversial.
8. Marco could not barely remember his older brother.
9. He remained firm, refusing to give in even though we asked him nicely.
10. One can buy a tape player cheap, but the cheap players rarely work good or last long.

PART III

Clear Sentences

CHAPTER 10

Sentence Fragments

A **sentence fragment** is part of a sentence that is set off as if it were a whole sentence by an initial capital letter and a final period or other end punctuation. Unlike a complete sentence, a sentence fragment lacks a subject or a verb or both, or it is a subordinate clause not attached to a complete sentence.

FRAGMENT	The sign leaning against the wall. [The word group lacks a verb.]
FRAGMENT	Feeling sick. [The word group lacks both a subject and a verb.]
FRAGMENT	When it is time. [The word group is a subordinate clause.]

COMPLETE SENTENCES VS. SENTENCE FRAGMENTS

A complete sentence

1. contains a subject and a verb (*Candy is sweet*);
2. *and* is not a subordinate clause (beginning with a subordinating conjunction such as *because* or *whereas* or a relative pronoun such as *who* or *that*).

A sentence fragment

1. lacks a verb (*The horse running away*);
2. *or* lacks a subject (*And ran away*);
3. *or* is a subordinate clause not attached to a complete sentence (*Because it was confused*).

Although writers occasionally use fragments deliberately and effectively (see 10e), readers perceive most fragments as serious errors because they are distracting or confusing. (Before proceeding with this chapter, you may find it helpful to review 5a and 5c on sentences and clauses.)

10a **Test your sentences for completeness, and revise any fragments.**

The following three tests will help you determine whether a word group punctuated as a sentence is actually a complete sentence. If the word group does not pass *all three* tests, it is a fragment and needs to be revised.

frag
10a

Test 1: Find a verb.

Look for a verb in the group of words. If you do not have one, the word group is a fragment.

> **FRAGMENT**   Four years of study and then graduation. [The group contains no verb. Compare a complete sentence: *Four years of study* <u>precede</u> *graduation*.]

To function as the verb in a complete sentence, any verb form you find must be a **finite verb**, one that is capable of making an assertion without the aid of a helping verb. (See also 5c-2.) A finite verb changes form at least once to show the difference in present, past, and future time. Verbals such as *working* and *to work* do not change and thus are not finite verbs.

	FINITE VERBS	**VERBALS IN FRAGMENTS**
PRESENT	The riveters *work*.	The riveters *working*.
PAST	The riveters *worked*.	The riveters *working*.
FUTURE	The riveters *will work*.	The riveters *working*.

A finite verb in the present tense also changes form when the subject changes from singular to plural. A verbal does not.

	FINITE VERBS	**VERBALS IN FRAGMENTS**
SINGULAR	The riveter *works*.	The riveter *working*.
PLURAL	The riveters *work*.	The riveters *working*.

Fragments like those above require change in the verbal or the addition of a helping verb to become complete sentences.

FRAGMENT   The statue standing by the door [Compare a complete sentence: *The statue is* (or *was* or *will be*) *standing by the door*.]

FRAGMENT   The skies having darkened. [Compare a complete sentence: *The skies have* (or *had* or *will have*) *darkened*.]

Test 2: Find a subject.

If you find a finite verb, look for its subject by asking who or what performs the action or makes the assertion of the verb. The subject will usually come before the verb. If there is no subject, the word group is a fragment unless it is a command.

frag

10a

FRAGMENT   And closed the door quietly. [The word group lacks a subject and is not a command. Compare complete sentences: *And he closed the door quietly. And close the door quietly*.]

Test 3: Look for a subordinating word.

If you find a finite verb and its subject, look for a subordinating conjunction (*although*, *because*, *when*, and so on) or a relative pronoun (*who*, *whoever*, *which*, *that*). These words almost always signal subordinate clauses, which do not express complete, independent thoughts and must be attached to main clauses. (See 5c-4.)

FRAGMENT   As the plane lifted from the runway. [The word group contains a finite verb, *lifted*, and a subject, *plane*. But the subordinating conjunction *as* reduces the word group to a subordinate clause, so the thought is incomplete. Compare a complete sentence: *The plane lifted from the runway*.]

FRAGMENT   The plane that he had missed. [The word group contains two possible subjects, *plane* and *he*, and a finite verb, *had missed*. But the verb is in a subordinate clause beginning with *that*, so the thought about the plane is incomplete. Compare a complete sentence: *The plane that he had missed took off*.]

If the word group begins with *how*, *who*, *whom*, *whose*, *which*, *where*, *when*, *what*, or *why*—words that may introduce either subordinate clauses or questions—the group is a fragment unless it is attached to a complete main clause or asks a question.

FRAGMENT	When she goes to the office. [The word group contains a finite verb, *goes*, and a subject, *she*. But it begins with *when* and does not ask a question. Compare complete sentences: *She goes to the office. When does she go to the office?*]

Revising sentence fragments

Almost all sentence fragments can be corrected in one of two ways, the choice depending on the importance of the information in the fragment. First, the fragment can be made into a complete sentence. This method gives the information in the fragment the same importance as that in other complete sentences.

frag

10a

FRAGMENT	The baboon waited for his challenger. *Poised for combat.*
REVISED	The baboon waited for his challenger. *He was* poised for combat.
FRAGMENT	He stared at the woman. *Who had once been his wife.*
REVISED	He stared at the woman. *She* had once been his wife.

Once the fragment is corrected, it can be punctuated as a separate sentence (as in the preceding examples), or it can be separated from another main clause with a semicolon (see 22a).

FRAGMENT	She hesitated briefly. *Then blurted out her idea.*
REVISED	She hesitated briefly; then *she* blurted out her idea.

The second method of correcting a fragment is to combine it with a main clause. This method subordinates the information in the fragment to the information in the main clause.

FRAGMENT	The baboon waited for his challenger. *Poised for combat.*
REVISED	The baboon, poised for combat, waited for his challenger.

In this example, commas separate the inserted phrase from the rest of the sentence because the phrase does not restrict the meaning of any word in the main clause but simply adds information (see 21c). When a phrase or subordinate clause *does* restrict the meaning of a word in the main clause, a comma or commas do not separate the two elements.

FRAGMENT	He stared at the woman. *Who had once been his wife.*
REVISED	He stared at the woman who had once been his wife.

Sometimes a fragment may be combined with the main clause using a colon or a dash (see 25a and 25b, respectively).

FRAGMENT	His sculptures use four materials. *Wood, iron, plastic, and paper.*
REVISED	His sculptures use four materials: wood, iron, plastic, and paper.
FRAGMENT	*A shortage of money, the illness of her father, a fear of failure.* These were her reasons for dropping out of school.
REVISED	A shortage of money, the illness of her father, a fear of failure—these were her reasons for dropping out of school.

frag

10a

EXERCISE 1

Apply the tests for completeness to each of the following word groups. If a word group is a complete sentence, circle the number preceding it. If it is a sentence fragment, revise it in two ways: by making it a complete sentence, and by combining it with a main clause written from the information given in other items.

Example:

And could not find his money.

The word group has a verb (*could . . . find*) but no subject.

Revised into a complete sentence: And *he* could not find his money.

Combined with a new main clause: *He was lost* and could not find his money.

1. In an interesting article about vandalism against works of art.
2. The motives of the vandals varying widely.
3. Those who harm artwork are usually angry.
4. But not necessarily at the artist or the owner.
5. For instance, a man who hammered at Michelangelo's *Pietà*.
6. And knocked off the Virgin Mary's nose.
7. Because he was angry at the Roman Catholic Church.
8. Which knew nothing of his grievance.
9. Although many damaged works can be repaired.
10. Usually even the most skilful repairs are forever visible.

10b Don't set off a subordinate clause as a sentence.

Subordinate clauses contain both subjects and verbs, but they always begin with a subordinating conjunction (*although*, *because*, *if*, and so on) or a relative pronoun (*who*, *which*, *that*). (See 5c-4). Subordinate clauses cannot stand alone as complete sentences.

To correct a subordinate clause set off as a sentence, combine it with the main clause or remove or change the subordinating word to create a main clause.

frag
10b

Fragment	Many pine trees bear large cones. *Which appear in August.* [The fragment is a subordinate clause modifying *cones*.]
Revised	Many pine trees bear large cones, which appear in August. [The subordinate clause is combined with the main clause.]
Revised	Many pine trees bear large cones. *They* appear in August. [Substituting *They* for *Which* makes the fragment into a complete sentence.]
Fragment	The decision seems fair. *Because it considers all parties.*
Revised	The decision seems fair because it considers all parties.
Revised	The decision seems fair. It considers all parties.

EXERCISE 2

Correct any sentence fragment below either by combining it with a main clause or by making it a main clause. If an item contains no sentence fragment, circle the number preceding it.

Example:

Jujitsu can be an excellent form of self-protection. Because it enables one to overcome an opponent without the use of weapons.

Jujitsu can be an excellent form of self-protection because it enables one to overcome an opponent without the use of weapons.

1. In the nineteenth century chemists began synthesizing perfume oils. Which previously could be made only from natural sources.
2. After Medieval Crusaders returned from the East. European perfumers began using animal oils as well as plant oils in their mixtures.

3. The most popular animal oil for perfume today is musk. Although some people dislike its heavy, sweet odour.
4. Musk oil goes a long way. Because of its pungency very little is needed to make a strong perfume.
5. Synthetic musk oil would help conserve a certain species of deer. Whose gland is the source of musk.

10c Don't set off a verbal phrase or a prepositional phrase as a sentence.

A **verbal phrase** consists of an infinitive (*to choose*), a past participle (*chosen*), or a present participle or gerund (*choosing*) together with any objects and modifiers it may have (see 5c-2). Verbal phrases cannot serve as the verbs in complete sentences. Fragments consisting of verbal phrases are most easily corrected by combining them with the main clauses they are related to. Verbal phrases can be converted into main clauses only by rewriting.

> **FRAGMENT** He backed closer and closer to the end of the diving board. *At last falling into the water.*
>
> **REVISED** He backed closer and closer to the end of the diving board, at last falling into the water. [The phrase is combined with the main clause.]
>
> **REVISED** He backed closer and closer to the end of the diving board. At last *he fell* into the water. [The phrase is made into a complete sentence by changing *falling* to the verb *fell* and by adding the subject *he*.]

A **prepositional phrase** consists of preposition (such as *in*, *on*, *to*, and *with*) together with its object and modifier (see 5c-1). A prepositional phrase cannot stand alone as a complete sentence. It may be combined with a main clause or rewritten as a main clause.

> **FRAGMENT** More than anything else, I wanted to get away from the heat. *To someplace cooler.*
>
> **REVISED** More than anything else, I wanted to get away from the heat to someplace cooler. [The phrase is combined with the main clause.]
>
> **REVISED** More than anything else, I wanted to get away from the heat. *I longed for* someplace cooler. [With a new subject and verb, *I longed for*, the phrase becomes a complete sentence.]

EXERCISE 3

Correct any sentence fragment below either by combining it with a main clause or by rewriting it as a main clause. If an item contains no sentence fragment, circle the number preceding it.

> *Example:*
>
> A hobby can contribute to a fulfilling life. Engaging one in activities outside work.
>
> A hobby can contribute to a fulfilling life, engaging one in activities outside work.

1. Deliberately scenting the air. It is a behaviour that originated in prehistory.
2. Some sources say that the custom arose as an attempt to cover up the smell of burning flesh. During sacrifices to the gods.
3. The sacred use of perfume survives. In the incense burned during religious services.
4. Perfumes became religious offerings in their own right. Being expensive to make, they were highly prized.
5. The earliest historical documents from the Middle East record the use of fragrances. Not only in religious ceremonies but on the body.
6. The Egyptians, Greeks, and Romans used fragrance extravagantly. Applying different scents to hair, arms, feet, and clothing.
7. To smell like several open perfume bottles. This was apparently desirable in earlier centuries.
8. The interest in perfume fell with Rome. For hundreds of years the Catholic Church forbade personal use of fragrance.
9. The Crusaders returned to Europe between the eleventh and fourteenth centuries. Bearing exotic scents from the Near and Far East.
10. Spreading rapidly throughout the continent. Perfume once again adorned human bodies.

frag

10d

| **10d** | **Don't set off any other word group as a sentence if it lacks a subject or a verb or both.** |

Besides subordinate clauses and verbal and prepositional phrases, several other word groups are often mistakenly punctuated as complete sentences—especially nouns plus their modifiers, appositives, and parts of compound predicates.

We often follow a noun with a phrase or subordinate clause that modifies the noun. No matter how long the noun and its modifier are, they cannot stand alone as a sentence.

Fragments	*People waving flags and cheering. Lined the streets for the parade.*
Revised	People waving flags and cheering lined the streets for the parade. [The two fragments are combined into one sentence.]
Fragment	*Japanese Canadians who were interned during World War II.* They may finally be compensated.
Revised	Japanese Canadians who were interned during World War II may finally be compensated. [The fragment replaces *They* as the modified subject of the main clause.]

frag

10d

Appositives are nouns, or nouns and their modifiers, which rename or describe other nouns (see 5c-5). They cannot stand alone as sentences.

Fragment	When I was a child, my favourite adult was an old uncle. *A retired sea captain who always told me long stories of wild adventures in faraway places.*
Revised	When I was a child, my favourite adult was an old uncle, a retired sea captain who always told me long stories of wild adventures in faraway places. [The appositive is combined with the main clause.]

Compound predicates are predicates made up of two or more verbs and their objects, if any. A verb or its object cannot stand alone as a sentence.

Fragment	Pat worked all day. *And danced at night.*
Revised	Pat worked all day and danced at night. [The fragment, part of the compound predicate *worked . . . and danced*, is combined with the main clause.]
Fragment	If his friends were in trouble, Henry always offered them much advice. *But no real help.*
Revised	If his friends were in trouble, Henry always offered them much advice but no real help. [The fragment, part of the compound object of *offered*, is combined with the main clause.]

Note: Beginning a sentence with a co-ordinating conjunction such as *and* and *but* can lead to a sentence fragment. Check every sentence you begin with a co-ordinating conjunction to be sure it is complete.

| EXERCISE 4

Correct any sentence fragment below either by combining it with a main clause or by rewriting it as a main clause. If an item contains no sentence fragment, circle the number preceding it.

>   *Example:*
>   Lynn graduated from university in 1987. But did not begin working until 1990.
>   Lynn graduated from university in 1987 but did not begin working until 1990.
>   Lynn graduated from university in 1987. But *she* did not begin working until 1990.

1. Human beings who perfume themselves. They are not much different from other animals.
2. Animals as varied as insects and dogs release *pheromones*. Chemicals that signal other animals.
3. The chemicals sometimes repel other animals. But more often they perform a sexual function by attracting a member of the opposite sex.
4. Human beings have a diminished sense of smell. And do not consciously detect most of their own species' *pheromones*.
5. The human substitute for *pheromones* may be perfumes. Especially musk and other fragrances derived from animal oils.

frag

10e

10e Be aware of the acceptable uses of incomplete sentences.

A few word groups lacking the usual subject-predicate combination are incomplete sentences, but they are not fragments because they conform to the expectations of most readers. They include exclamations (*Oh no!*); questions and answers (*Where next? To Moncton.*); and commands (*Move along. Shut the window.*). Exclamations and questions and answers occur most often in speech or in writing that records speech; commands occur in speech and in written directions. Another kind of incomplete sentence, which occurs in special situations, is the transitional phrase (*So much for the causes, now for the results. One final point.*).

Professional writers sometimes use incomplete sentences that *are* sentence fragments when they want to achieve a special effect. Such fragments appear more in informal than in formal writing. Unless you are experienced and thoroughly secure in your own writing, you should avoid all fragments and concentrate on writing clear, well-formed sentences.

EXERCISE 5

Break each of the following sentences at the vertical line, and then add, delete, or change words and punctuation as necessary to produce two *complete* sentences.

> *Example:*
>
> Classes may not resume after vacation | because the school has run out of money.
>
> Classes may not resume after vacation. The school has run out of money.

1. When the Prime Minister came to town, | plain-clothes RCMP officers were everywhere.
2. They concealed themselves in the woods | surrounding the outdoor theatre where the Prime Minister was to speak.
3. They stopped pedestrians to question them | and even to open any bags or parcels.
4. Suspicious-looking in dark glasses and sober suits, | they stood erect on street corners.
5. Their presence gave a sinister cast to the event, | which was supposed to be a celebration.

EXERCISE 6

Revise the following paragraph to eliminate sentence fragments by combining them with main clauses or rewriting them as main clauses.

Hiring Steele as the manager of the hockey team was a stupid move. Or a very clever manoeuvre. Depending on whether one is thinking like a fan or like the team's owner. Fans claim it was stupid. Because Steele is hard to get along with and unfair. They say he is also a poor manager. Failing to make the best use of the team's talents. And creating friction among the players. But the team's owner may have had a good reason for hiring such a manager. Some people think the owner hired Steele only temporarily. In order to make the team less attractive to unfriendly buyers. Who have been threatening a hostile takeover of the team. Hiring Steele could have been intended to prevent the takeover. And in the long run save the team. Not ruin it.

frag
10

CHAPTER 11

Comma Splices and Fused Sentences

When two or more main clauses appear consecutively, readers expect them to be clearly separated from each other in one of four ways:

1. With a period:

   The ship was huge. Its mast stood nine metres high.

2. With a semicolon:

   The ship was huge; its mast stood nine metres high.

3. With a comma preceding a co-ordinating conjunction that joins the clauses and specifies the relation between them:

   The ship was huge, *and* its mast stood nine metres high.

4. Occasionally with a colon when the second clause explains the first (see 25a):

   The ship was huge: its mast stood nine metres high.

Two problems commonly occur in punctuating consecutive main clauses. One is the **comma splice**, in which the clauses are joined (or spliced) *only* with a comma instead of a comma and co-ordinating conjunction or instead of a period, semicolon, or colon.

COMMA SPLICE

The ship was huge, its mast stood nine metres high.

The other problem is the **fused sentence** (also called a **run-on sentence**), in which no punctuation or co-ordinating conjunction appears between the clauses.

FUSED SENTENCE

The ship was huge its mast stood nine metres high.

POSSIBLE SOURCES OF COMMA SPLICES AND FUSED SENTENCES

1. Balanced negative and positive clauses:

   SPLICE   Monique is not a nurse, she is a doctor.

   REVISED   Monique is not a nurse; she is a doctor.

2. Amplification or illustration in the second clause:

   FUSED   She did well in university she had a 3.9 average.

   REVISED   She did well in university: she had a 3.9 average.

3. Conjunctive adverb in the second clause (see 11b):

   SPLICE   She had intended to become a biologist, *however*, she switched to medicine.

   REVISED   She had intended to become a biologist; *however*, she switched to medicine.

4. Same subject in both clauses:

   FUSED   Virginia is an internist *she* practises in Saskatoon.

   REVISED   Virginia is an internist. *She* practises in Saskatoon.

5. An attempt to link related ideas or to smooth choppy sentences:

   SPLICE   She is very committed to her work, she devotes almost all her time to patient care.

   REVISED   *Because* she is very committed to her work, she devotes almost all her time to patient care.

Like sentence fragments (see Chapter 10), comma splices and fused sentences are serious errors because they generally force the reader to reread for sense. They also suggest that the writer has been careless or does not understand the structure of a sentence.

COMMA SPLICES

Separate two main clauses with a comma *only* when they are joined by a co-ordinating conjunction.

A comma cannot separate main clauses unless they are linked by a co-ordinating conjunction (*and, but, or, nor, for, so, yet*). Readers expect the same sentence to continue after a comma. When they find themselves reading a second sentence before they realize they have finished the first, they may have to reread to understand the writer's meaning.

> COMMA SPLICE   Rain had fallen steadily for sixteen hours, many basements were flooded.

> COMMA SPLICE   Cars would not start, many people were late for work.

EXCEPTION: Experienced writers sometimes use commas between very brief main clauses that are grammatically parallel.

> He's not a person, he's a monster.

However, many readers view such punctuation as incorrect. Unless you are certain that your readers will not object to the comma in a sentence like this one, separate the clauses with periods or semicolons, as described below.

You have four main options for correcting a comma splice. The option you choose depends on the relation you want to establish between the clauses.

REVISING COMMA SPLICES

1. Make the clauses into separate sentences.
2. Insert an appropriate co-ordinating conjunction after the comma between clauses.
3. Insert a semicolon between clauses.
4. Subordinate one clause to the other.

Making separate sentences

Revising a comma splice by making separate sentences from the main clauses will always be correct.

> Rain had fallen steadily for sixteen hours. Many basements were flooded.

The period is not only correct but preferable if the ideas expressed in the two main clauses are only loosely related.

> COMMA SPLICE   Chemistry has contributed much to our understanding of foods, many foods such as wheat and beans can be produced in the laboratory.

> REVISED   Chemistry has contributed much to our understanding of foods. Many foods such as wheat and beans can be produced in the laboratory.

Inserting a co-ordinating conjunction

When the ideas in the main clauses are closely related and equally important, you may choose to correct a comma splice by inserting the appropriate co-ordinating conjunction immediately after the comma to join the clauses.

Cars would not start, *and* many people were late for work.

COMMA SPLICE	He had intended to work all weekend, his friends arrived Friday and stayed until Sunday.
REVISED	He had intended to work all weekend, *but* his friends arrived Friday and stayed until Sunday.

CS
11a

Notice that the relation indicated by a co-ordinating conjunction can be complementary (*and*), contradictory (*but*, *yet*), causal (*for*, *so*), or alternate (*or*, *nor*).

Many people were late for work, *for* cars would not start.

People were late for work, *or* they stayed home to pump out flooded basements.

Using a semicolon

If the relation between the ideas expressed in the main clauses is very close and obvious without a conjunction, you can separate the clauses with a semicolon. (See also 11b.)

Rain had fallen steadily for sixteen hours; many basements were flooded.

COMMA SPLICE	Rhoda and Nate were more than close friends, they were inseparable.
REVISED	Rhoda and Nate were more than close friends; they were inseparable.

Subordinating one clause

When the idea in one clause is more important than that in the other, you can express the less important idea in a phrase or a subordinate clause. (See p. 191 for a list of subordinating conjunctions.)

After rain had fallen steadily for sixteen hours, many basements were flooded. [The addition of the subordinating conjunction *After* reduces the first sentence to a subordinate clause indicating time.]

After sixteen hours of steady rain, many basements were flooded. [The clause is reduced to a prepositional phrase.]

Subordination is often more effective than forming separate sentences because it defines the relationship between ideas more precisely.

COMMA SPLICE	The examination was finally over, Becky felt free to enjoy herself once more.
REVISED	The examination was finally over. Becky felt free to enjoy herself once more. [Both ideas receive equal weight.]
IMPROVED	*When* the examination was finally over, Becky felt free to enjoy herself once more. [Emphasis on the second idea.]
COMMA SPLICE	The house was for sale, the price was reasonable.
REVISED	The house was for sale. The price was reasonable.
IMPROVED	The house was for sale at a reasonable price.

11b   Use a period or semicolon to separate main clauses related by conjunctive adverbs.

Conjunctive adverbs are modifiers such as *consequently*, *however*, *nevertheless*, *then*, and *therefore* (see p. 200 for a more complete list). Conjunctive adverbs frequently relate main clauses, and then the clauses must be separated by a period (forming two separate sentences) or by a semicolon (see 22b). The conjunctive adverb is also generally set off by a comma or commas.

COMMA SPLICE	Many Canadians refuse to give up unhealthful habits, consequently our medical costs are higher than necessary.
REVISED	Many Canadians refuse to give up unhealthful habits. Consequently, our medical costs are higher than necessary.
REVISED	Many Canadians refuse to give up unhealthful habits; consequently, our medical costs are higher than necessary.

Unlike co-ordinating and subordinating conjunctions, conjunctive adverbs do not join two clauses into a grammatical unit but merely describe the way the clauses relate in meaning. Also unlike conjunctions, which must be placed between the word groups they join (co-ordinating) or at the beginning of the word group they introduce (subordinating), conjunctive adverbs may usually be moved from one place to another in the clause (see 5d-2). No matter where in the clause a conjunctive adverb appears, however, the clause must be separated from another main clause by a period or a semi-colon.

COMMA SPLICE

The increased time devoted to watching television is not the only cause of the decline in reading ability, it is one of the important causes.

COMMA AND CO-ORDINATING CONJUNCTION

The increased time devoted to watching television is not the only cause of the decline in reading ability, *but* it is one of the important causes.

SUBORDINATING CONJUNCTION

Although the increased time devoted to watching television is not the only cause of the decline in reading ability, it is one of the important causes.

PERIOD AND CONJUNCTIVE ADVERB

The increased time devoted to watching television is not the only cause of the decline in reading ability. *However*, it is one of the important causes.

SEMICOLON AND CONJUNCTIVE ADVERB

The increased time devoted to watching television is not the only cause of the decline in reading ability; *however*, it is one of the important causes.

The increased time devoted to watching television is not the only cause of the decline in reading ability; it is, *however*, one of the important causes.

The increased time devoted to watching television is not the only cause of the decline in reading ability; it is one of the important causes, *however*.

EXERCISE 1

Correct each comma splice below in *two* of the following ways: make separate sentences of the main clauses; insert an appropriate co-ordinating conjunction after the comma; substitute a semicolon for the incorrect comma; or subordinate one clause to another. If an item contains no comma splice, circle the number preceding it.

   Example:

   Carolyn still had a headache, she could not get the child-proof cap off the aspirin bottle.

Carolyn still had a headache *because* she could not get the child-proof cap off the aspirin bottle. [subordination]

Carolyn still had a headache, *for* she could not get the child-proof cap off the aspirin bottle. [co-ordinating conjunction]

1. Money has a long history, it goes back at least as far as the earliest records.
2. Many of the earliest records concern financial transactions, indeed, early history must often be inferred from commercial activity.
3. Every known society has had a system of money, though the objects serving as money have varied widely.
4. Sometimes the objects have had real value, in modern times, however, their value has been more abstract.
5. Cattle, fermented beverages, and rare shells have served as money, each one had actual value for the society.
6. As money, however, these objects acquired additional value because they represented other goods.
7. Today money may be made of worthless paper, it may even consist of a bit of data in a computer's memory.
8. We think of money as valuable, only our common faith in it makes it valuable.
9. That faith is sometimes fragile, consequently, currencies themselves are fragile.
10. Economic crises often shake the belief in money, such weakened faith helped cause the Great Depression of the 1930s.

fs

11 c

FUSED SENTENCES

  Don't combine two main clauses without using an appropriate connecter or punctuation mark between them.

When two main clauses are joined without a word to connect them or a punctuation mark to separate them, the result is a **fused sentence**, sometimes called a **run-on sentence**. Fused sentences can rarely be understood on first reading, and they are never acceptable in standard written English.

FUSED   Many people would be lost without television they would not know how to amuse themselves.

FUSED   Our foreign policy sometimes differs from that of our closest allies it annoys them.

Fused sentences may be corrected in the same ways as comma splices (see 11a).

fs
11c

REVISING FUSED SENTENCES

1. Make the clauses into separate sentences.
2. Insert a comma and an appropriate co-ordinating conjunction between clauses.
3. Insert a semicolon between clauses.
4. Subordinate one clause to the other.

SEPARATE SENTENCES

Our foreign policy sometimes differs from that of our closest allies. It annoys them. [The two main clauses are made into separate sentences.]

COMMA AND CO-ORDINATING CONJUNCTION

Our foreign policy sometimes differs from that of our closest allies, and it annoys them. [The two main clauses are separated by a comma and a co-ordinating conjunction.]

SEMICOLON

Our foreign policy sometimes differs from that of our closest allies; it annoys them. [The two main clauses are separated by a semicolon.]

SUBORDINATING CONJUNCTION

Because our foreign policy sometimes differs from that of our closest allies, it annoys them. [*Because* subordinates the first clause to the second.]

EXERCISE 2

Revise each of the following fused sentences in *two* of the four ways shown in the preceding section.

> *Example:*
> Tim was shy he usually refused invitations.
> Tim was shy, *so* he usually refused invitations.
> *Because* Tim was shy, he usually refused invitations.

1. Throughout history money and religion were closely linked there was little distinction between government and religion.
2. The head of state and the religious leader were often the same person all power rested in one ruler.
3. These powerful leaders decided what objects would serve as money their backing encouraged public faith in the money.
4. Coins were minted of precious metals the religious overtones of money were then strengthened.
5. People already believed the precious metals to be divine their use in money intensified its allure.

EXERCISE 3

Combine each following pair of sentences into one sentence without creating comma splices or fused sentences. Combine sentences by supplying a comma and co-ordinating conjunction, supplying a semicolon, or subordinating one clause to the other. You will have to add, delete, or change words as well as punctuation.

Example:

The sun sank lower in the sky. The colours gradually faded.

As the sun sank lower in the sky, the colours gradually faded. [The first clause is subordinated to the second.]

1. The exact origin of paper money is unknown. It has not survived as coins, shells, and other durable objects have.
2. Scholars disagree over where paper money originated. Many scholars believe it was first used in Europe, however.
3. Perhaps goldsmiths were also bankers. Thus they held the gold of their wealthy customers.
4. The goldsmiths probably gave customers receipts for their gold. These receipts were then used in trade.
5. The goldsmiths were something like modern-day bankers. Their receipts were something like modern-day money.
6. The goldsmiths became even more like modern-day bankers. They began issuing receipts for more gold than they actually held in their vaults.
7. Today's bankers owe more to their customers than they actually have in reserve. They keep enough assets on hand to meet reasonable withdrawals.
8. In economic crises bank customers sometimes fear the loss of their money. Consequently, they demand their deposits.
9. Depositors' demands may exceed a bank's reserves. The bank may collapse.
10. The government now regulates banks to protect depositors. Bank failures are less frequent than they once were.

cs, fs

11

EXERCISE 4

Identify and revise the comma splices and fused sentences in the following paragraph.

A good way to meet new people during the summer is to take evening courses, many community colleges, high schools, and adult-education centres offer them. They attract different kinds of people who share common interests. Last summer in my woodworking class I met a woman who was also interested in colonial chairs we have been touring antique shows ever since. This summer in my singing class I met several people who enjoy folk music as much as I do, we have gone to numerous concerts together, we are planning a trip to the Vancouver Folk Festival. If I had not attended evening classes, I would not have met these new friends, they have enriched my life.

CHAPTER 12

Pronoun Reference

A **pronoun** such as *it* or *they* derives its meaning from its **antecedent**, the noun it substitutes for. Therefore, a pronoun must refer clearly and unmistakably to its antecedent in order for the sentence containing the pronoun to be clear. A sentence such as *Darryl told Kevin he was not invited* is not clear because the reader does not know whether *he* refers to Darryl or to Kevin.

Whether a pronoun and its antecedent appear in the same sentence or in adjacent sentences, you should be certain their relation is clear. One way to achieve clarity is to ensure that pronoun and antecedent agree in person and number (see 8b). The other way is to ensure that the pronoun refers unambiguously to a single, close, specific antecedent.

12a Make a pronoun refer clearly to one antecedent.

A pronoun may, of course, refer to two or more nouns in a compound antecedent, as in *Gagnon and Vachon pooled their resources and became partners*. But when either of two nouns can be a pronoun's antecedent, the reference will not be clear.

CONFUSING	The men removed all the furniture from the room and cleaned *it*. [Does *it* refer to the room or to the furniture?]
CLEAR	The men removed all the furniture from the room and cleaned *the room* (or *the furniture*).
CLEAR	After removing all the furniture from it, the men cleaned the room.
CLEAR	The men cleaned all the furniture after removing it from the room.

PRINCIPAL CAUSES OF UNCLEAR PRONOUN
REFERENCE

1. More than one possible antecedent (12a):

CONFUSING   To keep birds from eating seeds, soak *them* in
blue food colouring.

CLEAR   To keep birds from eating seeds, soak *the seeds*
in blue food colouring.

2. Antecedent too far away (12b):

CONFUSING   Employees should consult with their
supervisor *who* require personal time.

CLEAR   Employees *who* require personal time should
consult with their supervisor.

3. Antecedent only implied (12c):

CONFUSING   Many children begin reading on their own by
watching television, but *this* should be
discounted in education policy.

CLEAR   Many children begin reading on their own by
watching television, but *such self-instruction*
should be discounted in education policy.

See also 12d, 12e, and 12f.

ref
12a

Clarifying pronoun reference may require simply replacing the
pronoun with the appropriate noun, as in the first revision in the box
above. But to avoid repetition, you may want to restructure the
sentence so that the pronoun can refer to only one possible antecedent, as in the second and third revisions.

Sentences that report what someone said, using verbs like *said*
or *told*, often require direct rather than indirect quotation.

CONFUSING   Oliver told Bill that he was mistaken.

CLEAR   Oliver told Bill, "I am mistaken."

CLEAR   Oliver told Bill, "You are mistaken."

NOTE: Avoid the awkward device of using a pronoun followed
by the appropriate noun in parentheses.

WEAK   Mary should help Joan, but *she* (*Joan*) should help
herself first.

IMPROVED   Mary should help Joan, but *Joan* should help
herself first.

12b	Place a pronoun close enough to its antecedent to ensure clarity.

When the relative pronoun *who, which,* or *that* introduces a clause that modifies a noun, the pronoun generally should fall immediately after its antecedent to prevent confusion (see also 14b).

Confusing	Jody found a dress in the attic *that* her aunt had worn. [Her aunt had worn the attic?]
Clear	In the attic Jody found a *dress that* her aunt had worn.

Even when only one word could possibly serve as the antecedent of a pronoun, the relationship between the two may still be unclear if they are widely separated.

Confusing	Dawson, where my grandmother grew up, was once the scene of a mad gold rush with fortune seekers, motion picture theatres, dance halls, noisy saloons, and dirt streets. When I was a child, *she* often retold the stories she had heard of those days. [*She* can sensibly refer only to *grandmother,* but the pronoun is too far from its antecedent to be clear.]
Clear	Dawson, where my grandmother grew up, was once the scene of a mad gold rush with fortune seekers, motion picture theatres, dance halls, noisy saloons, and dirt streets. When I was a child, *my grandmother* often retold the stories she had heard of those days. [The noun is repeated for clarity.]

The confusing separation of pronoun and antecedent is most likely to occur in long sentences and, as illustrated by the preceding example, in adjacent sentences within a paragraph.

EXERCISE 1

Rewrite the following sentences to eliminate unclear pronoun reference. If you use a pronoun in your revision, be sure that it refers to only one antecedent and that it falls near enough to its antecedent to ensure clarity.

Example:

Saul found an old gun in the rotting shed that was just as his grandfather had left it.

In the rotting shed Saul found an old gun that was just as his grandfather had left it.

1. Mrs. Krieger telephoned her daughter often when she was away.
2. The picture on the cover of the novel is disturbing; one expects it to be more gruesome than it is.
3. Two brothers had built the town's oldest barn, which over the years had served as a cow barn, a blacksmith shop, and a studio for artisans. However, no one could remember their names.
4. Laurence played a piece on the piano that dated from the seventeenth century.
5. Since Colson was operating the rented backhoe that ran over Mrs. Gibb's fence, he is responsible for the damage it suffered.
6. If your pet cheetah will not eat raw meat, cook it.
7. My father and his sister have not spoken for thirty years because she left the family when my grandfather was ill and never called or wrote. But now he is thinking of resuming communication.
8. There is a difference between the heroes of today and the heroes of yesterday: they have flaws in their characters.
9. Jan held the sandwich in one hand and the telephone in the other, eating it while she talked.
10. Tom told his brother that he was in trouble with their grandparents.

12c Make a pronoun refer to a specific antecedent rather than to an implied one.

As a rule, the meaning of a pronoun will be clearest when it refers to a specific noun or other pronoun. When the antecedent is not specifically stated but is implied by the context, the reference can only be inferred by the reader.

1 Use *this*, *that*, *which*, and *it* cautiously in referring to whole statements.

The most common kind of implied reference occurs when the pronoun *this*, *that*, *which*, or *it* refers to a whole idea or situation described in the preceding clause, sentence, or even paragraph. Such reference, often called **broad reference**, is acceptable only when the pronoun refers clearly to the entire preceding clause. In the following sentence, *which* could not possibly refer to anything but the whole preceding clause.

> I can be kind and civil to people, *which* is more than you can.
> —GEORGE BERNARD SHAW

But if a pronoun might possibly confuse a reader, you should recast the sentence to avoid using the pronoun or to provide an appropriate noun.

CONFUSING   I knew nothing about economics, *which* my instructor had not learned. [*Which* could refer to *economics* or to the whole preceding clause.]

CLEAR   I knew nothing about economics, *a fact* my instructor had not learned.

CLEAR   I knew nothing about economics *because* my instructor knew nothing about it.

CONFUSING   The faculty members reached agreement on a change in the requirements, but *it* took time. [Does *it* refer to reaching agreement or to the change?]

CLEAR   The faculty members agreed on a change in the requirements, but *arriving at agreement* took time.

CLEAR   The faculty members reached agreement on a change in the requirements, but *the change* took time to implement.

CONFUSING   The American invaders misunderstood the Canadians' loyalties and miscalculated their readiness for war. *This* gave the Canadians the advantage in 1812. [Does *This* refer to the whole preceding sentence, to the misunderstanding alone, or to the miscalculation alone?]

CLEAR   The American invaders misunderstood the Canadians' loyalties and miscalculated their readiness for war. *Their misunderstanding and miscalculation* gave the Canadians the advantage in 1812.

ref
12c

2 Don't use a pronoun to refer to a noun implied by a modifier.

Adjectives, nouns used as modifiers, and the possessives of nouns or pronouns make unsatisfactory antecedents. Although they may imply a noun that could serve as an antecedent, they do not supply the specific antecedent needed for clarity.

WEAK   In the Finance Minister's speech *he* outlined plans for tax reform.

REVISED   In *his* speech *the Finance Minister* outlined plans for tax reform.

WEAK	Liz drove a red car; *it* was her favourite colour.
REVISED	Liz drove a red car because *red* was her favourite colour.
REVISED	Liz drove a car *that was red*, her favourite colour.

3 Don't use a pronoun to refer to a noun implied by some other noun or phrase.

WEAK	Lorne talked at length about entrepreneurship, although he had never been *one*.
REVISED	Lorne talked at length about entrepreneurship, although he had never been *an entrepreneur*.
WEAK	Gérard was bitten by a rattlesnake, but *it* was not serious.
REVISED	Gérard was bitten by a rattlesnake, but *the bite* was not serious.

ref

12d

4 Don't use part of a title as an antecedent in the opening sentence of a paper.

The title of a paper is entirely separate from the paper itself, so a pronoun cannot be used to refer to the title. If you open a paper with a reference to the title, repeat whatever part of the title is necessary for clarity.

TITLE	How to Row a Boat
NOT	*This* is not as easy as it looks.
BUT	*Rowing a boat* is not as easy as it looks.

12d Avoid the indefinite use of *it* and *they*. Use *you* only to mean "you, the reader."

In conversation we commonly use expressions such as *It says in the paper* or *In Newfoundland they say*. But such indefinite use of *it* and *they* is inappropriate in writing. The constructions are not only unclear but wordy.

| WEAK | In Chapter 4 of this book *it* describes Alexander Graham Bell's invention of the telephone. |
| REVISED | In Chapter 4 of this book *the author* describes Alexander Graham Bell's invention of the telephone. |

WEAK	In the average television drama *they* present a false picture of life.
REVISED	The average television *drama* presents a false picture of life.

Using *you* with indefinite reference to people in general is also well established in conversation: *You can tell that my father was a teacher*. The indefinite *you* frequently occurs in informal writing, too. And in all but very formal writing, *you* is acceptable when the meaning is clearly "you, the reader," as in *You can learn the standard uses of pronouns*. But the context must be appropriate for such a meaning. Consider this example:

INAPPROPRIATE	In the fourteenth century *you* had to struggle simply to survive. [Clearly, the meaning cannot be "you, the reader."]
REVISED	In the fourteenth century *one* (or *a person* or *people*) had to struggle simply to survive.

ref
12f

12e Avoid using the pronoun *it* more than one way in a sentence.

We use *it* idiomatically in expressions such as *It is raining*. We use *it* to postpone the subject in sentences such as *It is true that more jobs are available to women today*. And, of course, we use *it* as a personal pronoun in sentences such as *Adrienne wanted the book, but she couldn't find it*. All these uses are standard, but two of them in the same sentence can confuse the reader.

CONFUSING	When *it* is rainy, shelter your bicycle and wipe *it* often. [The first *it* is idiomatic; the second refers to *bicycle*.]
REVISED	*In rainy weather*, shelter your bicycle and wipe *it* often.

12f Be sure the relative pronouns *who*, *which*, and *that* are appropriate for their antecedents.

The relative pronouns *who*, *which*, and *that* commonly refer to persons, animals, or things. *Who* refers most often to persons but may also refer to animals that have names.

Travis is the boy *who* leads the other boys into trouble.
Their dog Wanda, *who* is growing lame, has difficulty running.

Which refers to animals and things.

> The Orinoco River, *which* is approximately 2600 km long, flows through Venezuela into the Atlantic Ocean.

That refers to animals and things and occasionally to persons when they are collective or anonymous.

> The jade tree *that* my grandmother gave me suddenly died.
> Infants *that* walk need constant tending.

(See also 21c-1 for the use of *which* and *that* in non-restrictive and restrictive clauses.)

The possessive *whose* generally refers to people but may refer to animals and things to avoid awkward and wordy *of which* constructions.

ref
12f

> The book *whose* binding broke had been my father's. [Compare *The book of which the binding broke had been my father's.*]

EXERCISE 2

Many of the pronouns in the following sentences do not refer to specific, appropriate antecedents. Revise the sentences as necessary to make them clear.

Example:

In Jasper National Park they have moose, elk, and bighorn sheep.

Moose, elk, and bighorn sheep live in Jasper National Park.

1. Bertha Wilson has been a Supreme Court Justice since 1982, when she was the first woman appointed to it.
2. Ever since I read a book on the Buddhists' beliefs, I've been thinking of becoming one.
3. In impressionist paintings they used colour to imitate reflected light.
4. Six or seven bearskin rugs decorated the rooms of the house, and Russell claimed to have killed them.
5. In Japan they are very loyal to the companies they work for.
6. Borduas was a painter that worked primarily in oils.
7. In my weight-training class, the instructors advise you to leave two or three days between workouts.
8. The play was supposed to open the first week in March, but because of casting problems this did not happen.
9. We receive warnings to beware of nuclear fall-out, pesticides, smog, and even our food, but I try not to think about it.
10. In Frederick Philip Grove's novels he wrote mainly about the Prairies.

11. Macbeth is a complicated and ambiguous hero, and that makes it a good play.
12. In urban redevelopment projects they try to make neighbourhoods safe and attractive.
13. In the nineteenth century you didn't have many options in motorized transportation.
14. It rained for a week, but it is possible that we can save the crop.
15. We argue constantly and he never looks straight at me, which bothers me.

EXERCISE 3

Revise the following paragraph so that each pronoun refers clearly to a single specific and appropriate antecedent.

In Charlotte Brontë's *Jane Eyre* she is a shy young woman that takes a job as governess. Her employer is a rude, brooding man named Rochester. He lives in a mysterious mansion on the English moors, which contributes an eerie quality to Jane's experience. Eerier still are the fires, strange noises, and other unexplained happenings in the house; but Rochester refuses to discuss this. Eventually, they fall in love. On the day they are to be married, however, she learns that he has a wife hidden in the house. She is hopelessly insane and violent and must be guarded at all times, which explains his strange behaviour. Heartbroken, Jane leaves the moors, and many years pass before they are reunited.

ref
12

CHAPTER 13

Shifts

A sentence or a group of related sentences should be consistent: grammatical elements such as tense, mood, voice, person, and number should remain the same unless grammar or meaning requires a shift. Unnecessary shifts in these elements confuse readers and distort meaning.

13a Keep a sentence or related sentences consistent in person and number.

Person in grammar refers to the distinction among the person talking (first person), the person spoken to (second person), and the person, object, or concept being talked about (third person). **Number** refers to the distinction between one (singular) and more than one (plural). Both nouns and personal pronouns change form to show differences in number, but only personal pronouns have distinctive forms for the three persons.

Shifts in person

The most common faulty shifts in person are shifts from second to third and from third to second person. They occur because we can refer to people in general, including our readers, either in the third person (*a person, one*; *people, they*) or in the second person (*you*).

> *People* should not drive when *they* have been drinking.
> *One* should not drive when *he or she* has been drinking.
> *You* should not drive when *you* have been drinking.

297

Although any one of these possibilities is acceptable in an appropriate context, a mixture of them is inconsistent.

INCONSISTENT	If a *person* works hard, *you* can accomplish a great deal.
REVISED	If *you* work hard, *you* can accomplish a great deal.
REVISED	If a *person* works hard, *he or she* can accomplish a great deal.
BETTER	If *people* work hard, *they* can accomplish a great deal.

Shifts in number

shift

13a

Inconsistency in number occurs most often between a pronoun and its antecedent (see 8b).

INCONSISTENT	If a *student* does not understand a problem, *they* should consult the instructor.
REVISED	If a *student* does not understand a problem, *he or she* should consult the instructor.
BETTER	If *students* do not understand a problem, *they* should consult the instructor.

Inconsistency in number can also occur between other words (usually nouns) that relate to each other in meaning.

INCONSISTENT	All the *boys* have a good *reputation*.
REVISED	All the *boys* have good *reputations*.

The consistency in the revised sentence is called **logical agreement** because the number of the nouns is logically consistent.

EXERCISE 1

Revise the following sentences to make them consistent in person and number.

Example:

A plumber will fix burst pipes, but they won't repair water-logged appliances.

Plumbers will fix burst pipes, but they won't repair water-logged appliances.

1. When a student is waiting to hear from university or community college admissions departments, you begin to notice what time the mail carrier arrives.
2. If tourists cannot find the Arts Centre one should ask for directions.

3. When taxpayers do not file their return on time, they may be penalized.
4. If a student misses too many classes, you may fail a course.
5. One should not judge other people's actions unless they know the circumstances.

13b Keep a sentence or related sentences consistent in tense and mood.

shift

13b

Shifts in tense

Certain changes in tense within a sentence or from one sentence to another may be required to indicate changes in actual or relative time (see 7f). For example:

Josef *will graduate* from university twenty-three years after his father *arrived* in Canada. [Josef's graduation is still in the future, but his father arrived in the past.]

But changes that are not required by meaning distract readers. Unnecessary shifts from past to present or from present to past in passages narrating a series of events are particularly confusing.

INCONSISTENT	When British Columbia *joined* Confederation in 1871, the federal government *promised* a transcontinental railway. The CPR *is* finally built and unites the country in 1885. [Tense shifts from past to present.]
REVISED	When British Columbia *joined* Confederation in 1871, the federal government *promised* a transcontinental railway. The CPR *was* finally built and united the country in 1885.

The present tense is used to describe what another author has written, including the action in literature or a film (see also 38b-3).

INCONSISTENT	The main character in the novel *suffers* psychologically because he *has* a clubfoot, but he eventually *triumphed* over his handicap.
REVISED	The main character in the novel *suffers* psychologically because he *has* a clubfoot, but he eventually *triumphs* over his handicap.

Shifts in mood

Shifts in the mood of verbs occur most frequently in directions when the writer moves between the imperative mood (*Unplug the* appliance) and the indicative mood (*You should unplug the appliance*). (See 7g.) Directions are usually clearer and more concise in the imperative, as long as use of the imperative is consistent.

> **INCONSISTENT**   *Cook* the mixture slowly, and *you should stir* it until the sugar is dissolved. [Mood shifts from imperative to indicative.]
>
> **REVISED**   *Cook* the mixture slowly, and *stir* it until the sugar is dissolved. [consistently imperative]

EXERCISE 2

Revise the following sentences to make them consistent in tense and mood.

> *Example:*
>
> Lynn ran to first, rounded the base, and keeps running until she slides into second.
>
> Lynn ran to first, rounded the base, and *kept* running until she *slid* into second.

1. Misunderstandings sometimes occurred when people of one culture do not understand the rules of appropriate behaviour in another culture.
2. Soon after he joined the union, Lester appears at a rally and makes a speech.
3. First sand down any paint that is peeling; then you should paint the bare wood with primer.
4. Rachel was walking down the street, and suddenly she stopped as a shot rings out.
5. To buy a tape deck, find out what features you need and you should decide what you want to pay.

shift

13c

13c Keep a sentence or related sentences consistent in subject and voice.

When a verb is in the active voice, the subject names the actor: *Linda passed the peas*. When a verb is in the passive voice, the subject names the receiver of the action; the actor may not be mentioned or may be mentioned in a prepositional phrase: *The peas were passed (by Linda)*. (See pp. 241–42.)

A shift in voice may sometimes help focus the reader's attention on a single subject, as in *The candidate campaigned vigorously and was nominated on the first ballot*. However, most shifts in subject and voice not only are unnecessary but also may create confusion or error.

INCONSISTENT	In the morning the *children rode* their bicycles; in the afternoon *their skateboards were given* a good workout. [The shift in subject from *children* to *skateboards* is confusing. Without a named actor the second clause implies that people other than the children used the skateboards.]
REVISED	In the morning the *children rode* their bicycles; in the afternoon *they gave* their skateboards a good workout.
INCONSISTENT	As *we looked* out over the ocean, *ships could be seen* in the distance. [Since the main clause does not name an actor, the reader cannot be sure who is looking.]
REVISED	As *we looked* out over the ocean, *we could see* ships in the distance.

shift

13d

EXERCISE 3

Make the following sentences consistent in subject and voice.

Example:

At the reunion they ate hot dogs and volleyball was played.
At the reunion they ate hot dogs and *played volleyball*.

1. Some arrowheads were dug up, and the researchers found some pottery that was almost undamaged.
2. They started the game after some practice drills were run.
3. The tornado ripped off the roof, and it was deposited in a nearby lot.
4. The debate was begun by the cabinet minister when he introduced the new bill.
5. If you learn how to take good notes in class, much extra work will be avoided.

13d Don't shift unnecessarily between indirect and direct quotation.

Direct quotation reports, in quotation marks, the exact words of a speaker: *He said, "I am going."* **Indirect quotation** reports what was said but not necessarily in the speaker's exact words: *He said that he was going.*

INCONSISTENT	Sue asked whether we had repaired the car and "Is anything else likely to happen?"
REVISED	Sue asked, "Have you repaired the car? Is anything else likely to happen?"

REVISED   Sue asked whether we had repaired the car and whether anything else was likely to happen.

shift

13d

EXERCISE 4

Revise each of the following sentences twice, once to make the form of quotation consistently indirect and once to make it consistently direct.

Example:

Jerome asked whether the host had arrived and "Are the cameras ready?"

Jerome asked whether the host had arrived and *whether the cameras were ready.*

Jerome asked, *"Has the host arrived? Are the cameras ready?"*

1. The politician promised that he would balance the budget but "I will not raise taxes and I will not cut back on social assistance programs."
2. Coach Butler said that our timing was terrible and "I would rather cancel the season than watch you play."
3. The report concluded, "Drought is a serious threat" and that we must begin conserving water now.
4. The author claims that adults pass through emotional stages and "No stage can be avoided."
5. My grandfather says, "Gardening keeps me alive" and that, in any event, the exercise helps ease his arthritis.

EXERCISE 5

Revise the following paragraph to eliminate unnecessary shifts in person, number, tense, mood, and voice.

Driving in snow need not be dangerous if you practise a few rules. First, one should avoid fast starts, which prevent the wheels from gaining traction and may result in the car's getting stuck. Second, drive more slowly than usual, and you should pay attention to the feel of the car: if the steering seemed unusually loose or the wheels did not seem to be grabbing the road, slow down. Third, avoid fast stops, which lead to skids. One should be alert for other cars and intersections that may necessitate that the brakes be applied suddenly. If you need to slow down, the car's momentum can be reduced by downshifting as well as by applying the brakes. When braking, don't press the pedal to the floor, but it should be pumped in short bursts. If you feel the car skidding, the brakes should be released and the wheel should be turned into the direction of the skid, and then the brakes should be pumped again. If one repeated these motions, the skid would be stopped and the speed of the car would be reduced.

CHAPTER 14

Misplaced and Dangling Modifiers

In reading a sentence in English, we depend principally on the arrangement of the words to tell us how they are related. In writing, we usually follow unconsciously the arrangements readers expect. But we may create confusion if we fail to connect modifiers to the words they modify.

MISPLACED MODIFIERS

We say that a modifier is **misplaced** if it appears to modify the wrong part of the sentence or if we cannot be certain what part of the sentence the writer intended it to modify. Misplaced modifiers may be awkward, unintentionally amusing, or genuinely confusing.

 Place modifiers where they will clearly modify the words intended.

Readers tend to link a modifying word, phrase, or clause to the nearest word it could modify: *I saw a man in a green hat.* Thus the writer must place the phrase so that it clearly modifies the intended word and not some other.

CONFUSING	She served hamburgers to the men *on paper plates*. [Surely the hamburgers, not the men, were on paper plates.]
CLEAR	She served the men hamburgers *on paper plates*.

CONFUSING	He was unhappy that he failed to break the record *by a narrow margin*. [The sentence implies that he wanted to break the record only by a narrow margin.]
CLEAR	He was unhappy that he failed *by a narrow margin* to break the record.
CONFUSING	According to police records, many dogs are killed by automobiles and trucks *roaming unleashed*. [The phrase appears to modify *automobiles and trucks*.]
CLEAR	According to police records, many dogs *roaming unleashed* are killed by automobiles and trucks.
CONFUSING	The mayor was able to cut the ribbon and then the band played *when someone found scissors*. [The clause appears to modify *the band played*.]
CLEAR	*When someone found scissors*, the mayor was able to cut the ribbon and then the band played.

mm

14a

EXERCISE 1

Revise the following sentences so that prepositional phrases and subordinate clauses clearly modify the words they are intended to modify.

Example:

I came to enjoy flying over time.
Over time I came to enjoy flying.

1. The senator returned to Parliament Hill after a long illness on Monday.
2. I watched a film clip of the accident in my hospital bed.
3. The artist painted a canvas at a summer retreat that imitated Monet's style.
4. The consulate received the letter from a messenger with exotic stamps.
5. Trisha delivered a party platter to the host wrapped in cellophane.
6. The computer needs repair in the library.
7. Marie opened the book given to her last Christmas by Charles Dickens.
8. The bell is an heirloom that you hear chiming.
9. She stared at the people standing nearby with flashing eyes.
10. Southern Ontario gains a huge supply of hydro-electric power from Niagara Falls that will never be exhausted.

14b   Place limiting modifiers carefully.

Limiting modifiers include *almost*, *even*, *exactly*, *hardly*, *just*, *merely*, *nearly*, *only*, *scarcely*, and *simply*. They modify the expressions that immediately follow them. Compare the uses of *just* in the following sentences:

> The instructor *just nodded* to me as he came in.
> The instructor nodded *just to me* as he came in.
> The instructor nodded to me *just as he came in*.

In speech several of these modifiers frequently occur before the verb, regardless of the words they are intended to modify. In writing, however, these modifiers should fall immediately before the word or word group they modify to avoid any ambiguity.

mm
14c

UNCLEAR	They *only* saw each other during meals. [They had eyes only for each other, or they met only during meals?]
CLEAR	They saw *only* each other during meals.
CLEAR	They saw each other *only* during meals.

NOTE: *Only* is acceptable immediately before the verb when it modifies a whole statement.

He *only* wanted his guest to have fun.

EXERCISE 2

Use each of the following limiting modifiers in two versions of the same sentence.

> *Example:*
> only
> He is the *only* one I like.
> He is the one *only* I like.

1. almost
2. even
3. hardly
4. simply
5. nearly

14c   Avoid squinting modifiers.

A **squinting modifier** is one that may refer to either a preceding or a following word, leaving the reader uncertain about what it is intended to modify. A modifier can modify only *one* grammatical element in a sentence. It cannot serve two elements at once.

Squinting	Snipers who fired on the soldiers *often* escaped capture.
Clear	Snipers who *often* fired on the soldiers escaped capture.
Clear	Snipers who fired on the soldiers escaped capture *often*.

When an adverb modifies an entire main clause, as in the last example, it can usually be moved to the beginning of the sentence: *Often, snipers who fired on the soldiers escaped capture.*

EXERCISE 3

Revise each of the following sentences twice so that the squinting modifier applies clearly first to one element and then to the other.

> *Example:*
>
> The work that he hoped would satisfy him completely frustrated him.
>
> The work that he hoped would *completely* satisfy him frustrated him.
>
> The work that he hoped would satisfy him frustrated him *completely*.

1. People who sunbathe frequently can damage their skin.
2. The contestant who answered the first question completely lost his concentration during the second round.
3. The hockey team that wins championships most of the time has excellent goal tending.
4. I told my son when the game was over I would play with him.
5. People who see psychologists occasionally will feel better.

14d Avoid separating a subject from its verb or a verb from its object or complement.

When we read a sentence, we expect the subject, verb, and object or complement to be close to each other. If adjective phrases or clauses separate them, the meaning is usually clear.

> The wreckers who were demolishing the old house discovered a large box of coins. [The subject, *wreckers*, and the verb, *discovered*, are separated by the adjective clause beginning *who*.]

However, if an adverb phrase or clause interrupts the movement from subject to verb to object or complement, the resulting sentence is likely to be awkward and confusing.

AWKWARD	The *wreckers*, soon after they began demolishing the old house, *discovered* a large box of coins. [The clause beginning *soon after* interrupts the movement from subject to verb.]
REVISED	Soon after they began demolishing the old house, the *wreckers discovered* a large box of coins.
AWKWARD	Three of the wreckers *lifted*, with great effort, *the heavy box*. [The phrase beginning *with* interrupts the movement from verb to object.]
REVISED	Three of the wreckers *lifted the heavy box* with great effort.

14e Avoid separating the parts of a verb phrase or the parts of an infinitive.

A verb phrase consists of a helping verb plus a main verb, as in *will call, was going, had been writing*. Such phrases constitute close grammatical units. We regularly insert single-word adverbs in them without causing awkwardness: *Abercrombie had almost completed his assignment*. But when longer word groups interrupt verb phrases, the result is almost always awkward.

AWKWARD	Many students *had*, by spending most of their time on the assignment, *completed* it.
REVISED	By spending most of their time on the assignment, many students *had completed* it.
REVISED	Many students *had completed* the assignment by spending most of their time on it.

Infinitives consist of the marker *to* plus the plain form of a verb: *to produce, to enjoy*. The two parts of the infinitive are widely regarded as a grammatical unit that should not be split.

AWKWARD	Environment Canada expected temperatures *to not rise*.
REVISED	Environment Canada expected temperatures *not to rise*.

Note, however, that a split infinitive may sometimes be natural and preferable, though it may still bother some readers.

> Several Canadian industries expect *to* more than *triple* their use of robots within the next decade.

We could recast the sentence entirely: *Several Canadian industries expect to increase their use of robots by more than 200 percent within the next decade*. But the split construction seems acceptable for economy.

EXERCISE 4

Revise the following sentences to connect separated parts (subject-predicate, verb-object-complement, verb phrase, infinitive).

Example:

Most children have by the time they are seven lost a tooth.
By the time they are seven, most children have lost a tooth.

1. The mail carrier returned, after two weeks, the undelivered letter.
2. The lieutenant had given, although he was later accused of dereliction of duty, the correct orders.
3. The girls loved to daily sun beside the pool.
4. Ballet will, if the present interest continues to grow, be one of the country's most popular arts.
5. The beavers, when the new housing construction began, abandoned their dam.

---

dm

14f

DANGLING MODIFIERS

14f Avoid dangling modifiers.

A **dangling modifier** does not sensibly modify anything in its sentence.

DANGLING *Passing the building*, the vandalism was clearly visible. [The modifying phrase seems to describe *vandalism*. The writer has not said who was passing the building or who saw the vandalism.]

DANGLING *Shortly after leaving home*, the accident occurred. [The modifying phrase seems to describe *accident*. The writer has not said who left home or who was in the accident.]

Dangling modifiers occur most often when certain kinds of modifying word groups precede the main clause of the sentence. These word groups include participial phrases (*passing the building*); infinitive phrases (*to see*); prepositional phrases in which the object of the preposition is a gerund (*after leaving home*); and elliptical clauses in which the subject and perhaps the verb are understood (*while at work*). (See 5c.) These phrases and clauses are about something, but their subjects are not expressed. Thus readers take them to modify the following noun, the subject of the main clause. If they do not sensibly define or describe the following noun, they are dangling modifiers.

IDENTIFYING AND REVISING DANGLING MODIFIERS

1. If the modifier lacks a subject of its own (e.g., *running away*), identify what it describes.
2. Verify that what the modifier describes is in fact the subject of the main clause. If it is not, the modifier is probably dangling.
3. Revise a dangling modifier (*a*) by recasting it with a subject of its own or (*b*) by changing the subject of the main clause.

dm
14f

	MODIFIER DESCRIBES DIGGERS	**SUBJECT IS WATER**
DANGLING	*Having sweltered in the sun*, the water tasted wonderful to the diggers.	
REVISION A	*After the diggers had* sweltered in the sun, the water tasted wonderful.	
REVISION B	Having sweltered in the sun, *the diggers thought* the water tasted wonderful.	

DANGLING	*Being very tired*, Morton's alarm failed to disturb his sleep. [participial phrase]
DANGLING	*To get up on time*, a great effort was needed. [infinitive phrase]
DANGLING	*On rising*, coffee was essential to waken Morton. [prepositional phrase]
DANGLING	*Until completely awake*, work was impossible. [elliptical clause]

These sentences are illogical: alarm clocks don't get tired, effort doesn't get up, coffee doesn't rise, and work doesn't awaken. Note that a modifier may be dangling even when the sentence elsewhere contains a word the modifier might seem to describe, such as *Morton's* and *Morton* in the first and third examples. In addition, a dangling modifier may fall at the end of a sentence:

DANGLING	Work came easily *when finally awake*.

We correct dangling modifiers by recasting the sentences in which they appear. We can change the subject of the main clause to a word the modifier properly defines or describes. Or we can recast the dangling modifier as a complete clause. The following examples illustrate these revisions.

DANGLING	*Being crowded in the car*, the trip was uncomfortable.
REVISED	Being crowded in the car, *we* were uncomfortable. [new subject]
REVISED	*Because we were* crowded in the car, the trip was uncomfortable. [rewritten modifier]
DANGLING	*After unlocking the door*, the cat refused to go out.
REVISED	After *I had unlocked the door*, the cat refused to go out. [rewritten modifier]
DANGLING	*To take sharp action pictures*, the shutter speed should be fast.
REVISED	To take sharp action pictures, *a photographer* should use a fast shutter speed. [new subject]
REVISED	*If a photographer wants* to take sharp action pictures, the shutter speed should be fast. [rewritten modifier]
DANGLING	The stitches were removed from Larry's wound *while still in the hospital*.
REVISED	*Larry* had the stitches removed while still in the hospital. [new subject]
REVISED	The stitches were removed from Larry's wound while *he was* still in the hospital. [rewritten modifier]

dm

14f

EXERCISE 5

Revise the following sentences to eliminate any dangling modifiers. Each item has more than one possible answer.

Example:

Driving north, the vegetation became increasingly sparse.

Driving north, *we noticed* that the vegetation became increasingly sparse.

As we drove north, the vegetation became increasingly sparse.

1. By turning the lights down, the room looked less dingy.
2. To file a formal complaint, a statement must be submitted.
3. Having prepared thoroughly, the exam was easy for me.
4. Though usually energetic, emotional problems had sapped her strength.
5. Staring at the ceiling, the idea became clear.
6. Sagging and needing a new coat of paint, Mr. Preston called the house painter.
7. Monday passed me by without accomplishing anything.
8. To obtain disability income, a doctor must certify that an employee cannot work.

9. When only a ninth grader, my grandmother tried to teach me double-entry bookkeeping.
10. After weighing the alternatives, his decision became clear.

EXERCISE 6

Combine each pair of sentences below into a single sentence by rewriting one as a modifier. Make sure the modifier applies clearly to the appropriate word. You will have to add, delete, and rearrange words, and you may find that more than one answer is possible in each case.

> *Example:*
> Cameron demanded a hearing from the faculty. Cameron wanted to appeal the decision.
>
> *Wanting to appeal the decision*, Cameron demanded a hearing from the faculty.

1. We were taking our seats. The announcer read the line-up.
2. I was rushing to the interview. My shoelace broke.
3. The children crowded into the buses. The children were from the fifth grade.
4. She was trying to cheer Jason up. Her Halloween mask terrified Jason instead.
5. They were holding hands. A man crept up behind them.
6. She rested her bandaged foot on the stool. She was wearing a yellow satin robe.
7. My uncle said he had never received good advice. He was fifty years old then.
8. Several people saw the fugitive. The people had been shopping in town.
9. We reached the end of the road. A vast emptiness surrounded us.
10. Sylvie received a letter announcing she had won. The letter came the day after she returned from vacation.

EXERCISE 7

Revise the following paragraph to eliminate any misplaced or dangling modifiers.

Town legend has it that Mr. Potter was as an infant left on the doorstep of a church in a basket. After a few days he was placed in the care of experienced foster parents along with two other orphans who provided love and strong guidance. Eventually adopted by his foster parents, Mr. Potter's life was seemingly happy and uneventful through law school. His bizarre behaviour only started after his law practice began to completely fail.

mm, d
14

CHAPTER 15

Mixed and Incomplete Sentences

MIXED SENTENCES

A **mixed sentence** contains two or more parts that are incompatible—that is, the parts do not fit together. The misfit may be in grammar or in meaning.

MIXED **GRAMMAR**	After watching television for twelve hours was the reason his head hurt.
MIXED **MEANING**	The work involved in directing the use of resources is the definition of management.

 Be sure that the parts of your sentences, particularly subjects and predicates, fit together grammatically.

Many mixed sentences occur when we start a sentence with one grammatical plan or construction in mind but end it with a different one. Such sentences often result from a confusion between two ways of making a statement.

MIXED	In all her efforts to please others got her into trouble.

In this mixed sentence the writer starts with a modifying prepositional phrase and then tries to make that phrase work as the subject of *got*. But prepositional phrases can very seldom function as sentence subjects. The sentence needs a new subject for *got*.

REVISED	In all her efforts to please others, *she* got into trouble. [The necessary subject *she* is added to the main clause.]
REVISED	*All her efforts* to please others got her into trouble. [The preposition *In* is dropped, leaving the subject *All her efforts.*]

Each group of sentences below illustrates a similar confusion between two sentence plans and gives ideas for revising the subject and sometimes the predicate so that they fit grammatically.

MIXED	Although he was seen with a convicted thief does not make him a thief. [The writer has used an adverb clause, beginning *Although*, as the subject of *does*. An adverb clause cannot serve as a subject.]
REVISED	*That* he was seen with a convicted thief does not make him a thief. [*That* changes the clause into a noun clause, a grammatical subject.]
REVISED	Although he was seen with a convicted thief, *he is* not necessarily a thief. [A new subject and verb are supplied for the main clause.]
MIXED	Among those who pass the entrance examinations, they do not all get admitted to the program. [The modifying phrase beginning *Among* demands a subject that gives an amount, such as *all* or *many*, not the general *they*.]
REVISED	Among those who pass the entrance examinations, *not all* get admitted to the program.
REVISED	Among those who pass the entrance examinations, *many* do not get admitted to the program.
REVISED	*Not all those* who pass the entrance examinations get admitted to the program.

15b Be sure that the subjects and predicates of your sentences fit together in meaning.

The mixed sentences examined above are confusing because their parts do not fit together grammatically. Another kind of mixed sentence fails because its subject and predicate do not fit together in meaning: the subject is said to be or do something it cannot logically be or do. Such a mixture is sometimes called **faulty predication**.

The most common form of faulty predication occurs when the linking verb *be* connects a subject and its complement. Since such a sentence forms a kind of equation, the subject and complement must be items that can be sensibly equated. If they are not, the sentence goes awry.

> **FAULTY**   A *compromise* between the city and the town would be the ideal *place* to live.

In this sentence the subject *compromise* is equated with the complement *place*. Thus the sentence says that *a compromise is a place*, clearly not a sensible statement. Sometimes such mixed sentences seem to result from the writer's effort to compress too many ideas into a single word or phrase. The preceding sentence can be revised to state the writer's meaning more exactly.

mixed
15b

> **REVISED**   A *community* that offered the best qualities of both city and town would be the ideal *place* to live.

A special kind of faulty predication occurs when a clause beginning *when* or *where* follows a form of *be* in a definition, as in *Suffrage is where you have the right to vote*. Though the construction is common in speech, written definitions require nouns or noun clauses on both sides of *be*: *Suffrage is the right to vote*.

> **FAULTY**   *An examination* is *when you are tested* on what you know.
>
> **REVISED**   *An examination is a test* of what you know.
>
> **REVISED**   *In an examination you are tested* on what you know.

A similar kind of faulty predication occurs when a *because* clause follows the subject-verb pattern *The reason is*, as in *The reason is because I don't want to*. This construction is common in speech, but it is redundant since the conjunction *because* means *for the reason that*. The construction should not appear in writing.

> **FAULTY**   The *reason* we were late *is because* we had an accident.
>
> **REVISED**   The *reason* we were late is *that* we had an accident.
>
> **REVISED**   We were late *because* we had an accident.

Faulty predications are not confined to sentences with *be*. In the following sentences the italicized subjects and verbs highlight the misfit between them.

> **FAULTY**   The *use* of emission controls *was created* to reduce air pollution. [The controls, not their use, were created.]

REVISED	Emission *controls were created* to reduce air pollution.
FAULTY	The *area* of financial mismanagement *poses* a threat to small businesses. [Mismanagement, not the area, poses the threat.]
REVISED	Financial *mismanagement poses* a threat to small businesses.

In some mixed sentences the combination of faults is so confusing that the writer has little choice but to start over.

MIXED	My long-range goal is through law school and government work I hope to deal with those problems I deal with more effectively.
POSSIBLE REVISION	My long-range goal is to go to law school and then work in government so that I can deal more effectively with problems I face.

mixed
15b

EXERCISE 1

Revise the following sentences so that their parts fit together both in grammar and in meaning. Each item has more than one possible answer.

Example:

When they found out how expensive pianos are is why they were discouraged.

They were discouraged *because* they found out how expensive pianos are.

When they found out how expensive pianos are, *they* were discouraged.

1. The different accents of students is in where they grew up.
2. Because he believes news programs are misleading is why he does not watch them.
3. By simply increasing the amount of money we spend will not solve the problem of crime.
4. An antique is when an object is one hundred or more years old.
5. Among the polished stones, they were all beyond my price range.
6. Schizophrenia is when a person withdraws from reality and behaves in abnormal ways.
7. Any government that can afford a fleet of nuclear submarines, they should be able to solve their country's social problems too.
8. Needlepoint is where you work with yarn on a mesh canvas.
9. Through the help of his staff is how the mayor got reelected.
10. The reason many people don't accept the theory of evolution is because it goes contrary to their religious beliefs.

INCOMPLETE SENTENCES

The most serious kind of incomplete sentence is the fragment (see Chapter 10). But sentences are also incomplete when the writer omits one or more words needed to make a phrase or clause clear or accurate.

15c	**Be sure that omissions from compound constructions are consistent with grammar or idiom.**

inc

15c

In both speech and writing we commonly use **elliptical constructions**, constructions that omit words necessary for meaning (see 5c-4). In the following sentences the words in parentheses can be omitted without confusing or distracting the reader. Notice that they all involve compound constructions.

> My car has been driven 80 000 km; his (has been driven) only 20 000 km.
>
> Some people heat by oil, some (heat) by gas and some (heat) by electricity.
>
> She had great hopes for her sons and (for) their children.

Such omissions are possible only when the words omitted are common to all the parts of a compound construction. When the parts differ in grammar or idiom, all words must be included in all parts.

> My car *has been driven* 80 000 km; their cars *have been driven* only 20 000 km.
>
> I *am* firm; you *are* stubborn; he *is* pig-headed.
>
> The students *were* invited and *were* happy to go. [Each *were* has a different grammatical function: the first is a helping verb in the passive verb phrase *were invited*; the second is a linking verb with the complement *happy*.]
>
> She had faith *in* and hopes *for* the future. [Idiom requires different prepositions with *faith* and *hopes*, so both must be included.]

Notice that in the sentence *My brother and friend moved to Charlottetown*, the omission of *my* before *friend* indicates that *brother* and *friend* are the same person. If two different persons are meant, the modifier or article must be repeated: *My brother and my friend moved to Charlottetown.*

(See 31b-3 for a list of English idioms and 17a for a discussion of grammatical parallelism.)

15d Be sure that all comparisons are complete and logical.

Comparisons make statements about the relation between two or more things, as in *Dogs are more intelligent than cats* or *Bones was the most intelligent dog we ever had.* To be complete and logical, a comparison must state the relation fully enough to ensure clarity; it must compare only items that can sensibly be compared; and it must include all and only the items being compared.

1 State a comparison fully enough to ensure clarity.

In a comparison such as *Luke likes bowling better than (he likes) tennis*, we can omit *he likes* because only one meaning is possible. But sentences such as *Luke likes bowling better than Jeannette* may mean either "better than he likes Jeanette" or "better than Jeannette likes bowling." Therefore, we must be careful to state such sentences fully enough to prevent any misreading.

UNCLEAR	They worry more about money than their child.
CLEAR	They worry more about money than their child *does*.
CLEAR	They worry more about money than *about* their child.

2 Be sure that the items being compared are in fact comparable.

A comparison is logical only if it compares items that can sensibly be compared. We can compare one food with another or one car with another, but we cannot sensibly compare food with cars. We are likely to make illogical comparisons unintentionally.

ILLOGICAL	The cost of a computer is greater than a calculator. [The writer compares the cost of something with a calculator.]
REVISED	The cost of a computer is greater than *the cost of* (or *that of*) a calculator.

3 In comparing items in the same class, use *other* or *any other*. In comparing items in different classes, use *any*.

When we compare a person or thing with all others in the same group, we form two units: (1) the individual person or thing and (2) all *other* persons or things in the group. The two units need to be distinguished.

> Jess [the individual] was more stubborn than *any other* child in the family [all the others in the group].

ILLOGICAL	Montreal is larger than *any* city in Quebec. [Since Montreal is itself a city in Quebec, the sentence seems to say that Montreal is larger than itself.]
LOGICAL	Montreal is larger than *any other* city in Quebec. [Adding *other* excludes Montreal from the group of the province's other cities.]

inc

15e

When a person or thing is compared with the members of a *different* group, the two units are logically separate.

> Some North American cars [one group] are cheaper than *any* foreign car [a different group].

ILLOGICAL	Montreal is larger than *any other* city in Manitoba. [The cities in Manitoba constitute a group to which Montreal does not belong.]
LOGICAL	Montreal is larger than *any* city in Manitoba. [Omitting the word *other* makes a separate group of the Manitoban cities.]

4 Avoid comparisons that do not state what is being compared.

Brand X gets clothes *whiter*. [Whiter than what?]
Brand Y is so much *better*. [Better than what?]

15e Be careful not to omit articles, prepositions, or other needed words.

In haste or carelessness writers sometimes omit small words such as articles and prepositions that are needed for clarity.

INCOMPLETE	Regular payroll deductions are a type painless savings. You hardly notice missing amounts, and after period of years the contributions can add a large total.
REVISED	Regular payroll deductions are a type *of* painless savings. You hardly notice *the* missing amounts, and after *a* period of years the contributions can add *up to* a large total.

In both speech and writing we often omit *that* when it introduces a noun clause following a verb: *We knew (that) he was coming.* But such an omission can sometimes be confusing.

INCOMPLETE She observed many people who had been invited were missing. [At first reading, *many people* appears to be the object of *observed* rather than the subject of the entire subordinate clause.]

REVISED She observed *that* many people who had been invited were missing.

Attentive proofreading is the only insurance against the kind of omissions described in this section. (See 2d.) *Proofread all your papers carefully.*

inc
15e

EXERCISE 2

Revise the following sentences so that they are complete, logical, and clear. Some items have more than one possible answer.

> *Example:*
> Our house is closer to the courthouse than the subway stop.
> Our house is closer to the courthouse than *it is to* the subway stop.
> Our house is closer to the courthouse than the subway stop *is.*

1. I get along with my parents better than my sister.
2. Our member of Parliament not only believes but works for tax reform.
3. Wally believed people who came to him with their problems were using him.
4. His tip was larger than any customer I ever waited on.
5. With an altitude of 5950 metres, the Yukon's Mount Logan is higher than any mountain in Canada.
6. The largest bookstore Canada stocks two three copies most books in print.
7. The dog is only a puppy; the cats both ten years old.
8. My chemistry text is more interesting to me than any other social science text.
9. Inventors usually have an interest and talent for solving practical problems.
10. The legal question raised by the prosecution was relevant and considered by the judge.

EXERCISE 3

Revise the following paragraph to eliminate mixed or incomplete constructions.

The Halifax Citadel has overlooked city and its natural harbour for over 130 years. When it was being constructed in the nineteenth century was when design problems were discovered. Because they had to deal with structural problems was why the Royal Engineers took almost thirty years to build it. At a cost exceeding £242 000, the Citadel was more expensive than any Canadian fortress. Immediately, however, the introduction of rifled artillery was why the installation became obsolete. The solution of new artillery was installed, and the Citadel housed British garrison until 1906.

15

PART IV

Effective Sentences

CHAPTER 16

Using Co-ordination and Subordination

To communicate effectively, you often need to combine several statements into a single sentence, fitting thoughts together according to their relative importance. You can **co-ordinate** the facts and ideas you wish to emphasize equally, such as the thoughts about insurance in the sentence *Home insurance is costly, but car insurance is almost a luxury*. You can **subordinate** statements of lesser importance to those you wish to emphasize. In the sentence *Because accidents are frequent, car insurance is expensive*, the clause beginning *Because* is grammatically subordinate to the main clause. The information you decide to subordinate may be important to the total meaning of the sentence, providing necessary explanation or support, but readers will almost always see it as less important than that presented in the main clause.

The box on page 323 and the following sections provide guidelines for using co-ordination and subordination effectively in constructing sentences.

16a Co-ordinating to relate equal ideas

Two or more simple sentences in a row will seem roughly equal in importance but distinct, even if they are related in content. Thus readers will have to detect on their own the specific relations among the sentences. By linking sentences and ideas with co-ordinating conjunctions or conjunctive adverbs, a writer can help readers see the relations more easily. Compare the following passages.

We should not rely so heavily on coal, oil, and uranium. We have a substantial energy resource in the moving waters of our rivers.

322

PRINCIPAL WAYS TO CO-ORDINATE AND SUBORDINATE INFORMATION IN SENTENCES

Use **co-ordination** to relate ideas of equal importance (16a).

1. Link main clauses with a comma and a co-ordinating conjunction: *and, but, or, nor, for, so, yet* (5d-1).

   The fortress of Louisbourg is now restored, *but* fifty years ago it was in ruins.

2. Relate main clauses with a semicolon alone or a semicolon and a conjunctive adverb: *however, indeed, thus*, etc. (5d-2).

   The remains of some buildings still existed; *however*, they were piles of stones overgrown with brush.

3. Within clauses, link words and phrases with a co-ordinating conjunction: *and, but, or, nor* (5d-1).

   The people *and* officials of Cape Breton were indifferent to Louisbourg *or* took its ruin for granted.

Use **subordination** to de-emphasize ideas (16b).

1. Use a subordinate clause beginning with a subordinating conjunction: *although, because, if, whereas*, etc. (5c-4).

   Although the fortress of Louisbourg became a national historic site in 1928, there was no public support for reconstruction.

2. Use a subordinate clause beginning with a relative pronoun: *who, whoever, which, that* (5c-4).

   The first strong step was taken by Parks Canada, *which began to rebuild the fortress in 1961*.

3. Use a prepositional, verbal, or absolute phrase.

   Like most national historic sites, Louisbourg is protected by Parks Canada. [Prepositional phrase. See 5c-1.]

   Parks Canada, *supervising many popular tourist sites*, is a highly visible government agency. [Verbal phrase. See 5c-2.]

   Visitors can always learn something at National Parks, *the guides being helpful and informative*. [Absolute phrase. See 5c-3.]

4. Use an appositive (5c-5).

   A branch of the Department of the Environment, Parks Canada also runs Pacific Rim and other wilderness parks.

5. Use a modifying word.

   At the *grey stone* fortress, guides dressed in *eighteenth-century* costumes protect the *reconstructed* Louisbourg from carelessness and vandalism.

co-ord

16a

Smaller streams add to the total volume of water. The resource renews itself. Coal and oil are irreplaceable. Uranium is also irreplaceable. The cost of water does not increase much over time. The costs of coal, oil, and uranium rise dramatically.

We should not rely so heavily on coal, oil, and uranium, for we have a substantial energy resource in the moving waters of our rivers and streams. Coal, oil, and uranium are irreplaceable and thus subject to dramatic cost increases; water, however, is self-renewing and more stable in cost.

The information in both passages is essentially the same, but the second is shorter and considerably easier to read and understand. Whereas the first passage strings ideas together in short, simple sentences without relating them to each other, the second passage builds connections among co-ordinate ideas: the availability of water in rivers and streams (first sentence); the relation between renewal and cost (second sentence); and the contrast between water and the other resources (both sentences).

co-ord
16a

Punctuating co-ordinated words, phrases, and clauses

Most co-ordinated words, phrases, and subordinate clauses are not punctuated with commas (see 21j-2). The exceptions are items in a series and co-ordinate adjectives.

We rely heavily on *coal, oil, and uranium*. [A series; see 21f-1.]

Dusty, dog-eared books littered his rooms. [Co-ordinate adjectives; see 21f-2.]

In a sentence consisting of two main clauses, punctuation depends on whether a co-ordinating conjunction, a conjunctive adverb, or no connecting word links the clauses.

Oil is irreplaceable, *but* water is self-renewing. [See 21a.]
Oil is irreplaceable; *however*, water is self-renewing. [See 22b.]
Oil is irreplaceable; water is self-renewing. [See 22a.]

1   **Avoiding faulty co-ordination**

Faulty co-ordination occurs when no logical connection seems to exist between two co-ordinated statements or when the connection expressed by the co-ordinating conjunction contradicts common sense.

FAULTY   Forecasters had predicted a mild winter, and temperatures were lower than normal.

REVISED   Forecasters had predicted a mild winter, *but* temperatures were lower than normal.

Sometimes faulty co-ordination occurs because the writer omits necessary information, as in the following example.

FAULTY	Nancy is a hairdresser, and she has developed a skin allergy.
REVISED	As a hairdresser, Nancy *must use products containing strong chemicals*; *consequently*, she has developed a skin allergy.
REVISED	*Because* her work as a hairdresser *requires that she use products containing strong chemicals*, Nancy has developed a skin allergy.

Often, as the second revision shows, the intended relation between clauses can be clarified by subordinating one of the ideas if it modifies or explains the other one. The following is another example.

FAULTY	John Stuart Mill was a utilitarian, and he believed that actions should be judged by their usefulness or by the happiness they cause.
REVISED	John Stuart Mill, *a utilitarian*, believed that actions should be judged by their usefulness or by the happiness they cause.

co-ord
16a

2   Avoiding excessive co-ordination

A stringy compound sentence—a sequence of main clauses linked with co-ordinating conjunctions—creates the same effect as a series of simple sentences: it obscures the relative importance of ideas and details.

EXCESSIVE CO-ORDINATION	We were near the end of the trip, and the storm kept getting worse, and the snow and ice covered the windshield, and I could hardly see the road ahead, and I knew I should stop, but I kept on driving, and once I barely missed a truck.

This sentence contains two main assertions: *the storm kept getting worse* and *I kept on driving*. All the rest is detail elaborating on these simple statements. The information in the sentence needs to be recombined using subordination so that the reader can easily distinguish between main assertions and the details that support them.

REVISED	As we neared the end of the trip, *the storm kept getting worse*, covering the windshield with snow and ice until I could barely see the road ahead. Even though I knew I should stop, *I kept on driving*, once barely missing a truck.

Be careful not to overuse *so* as a connecter.

EXCESSIVE   Jim has an examination that day, so he came
CO-ORDINATION home late, so he missed seeing the fire, so he was
not able to describe it to us.

As with other varieties of excessive co-ordination, the best way to revise such sentences is to separate the main statement from dependent details.

REVISED   *Jim was not able to describe the fire to us* because
he had an examination that day and arrived home
too late to see the fire.

Excessive co-ordination is not always as obvious as it is in the two preceding examples. The following passage contains only two compound sentences, but they still connect facts so loosely that the reader is left to distinguish their importance.

EXCESSIVE   A man came out of the liquor store. He wore a pair
COORDINATION of frayed corduroy pants, and he wore a brown
sweater. He started toward a blue car, and the
police arrested him.

In revising this passage, a writer might use subordination to show which ideas are important and which less important. The essential fact that the police arrested the man could become the main clause and all other details part of a single subordinate *when* clause.

REVISED   When a man wearing frayed corduroy pants and a
brown sweater came out of the liquor store and
started toward a blue car, *the police arrested him.*

co-ord
16a

EXERCISE 1

Combine sentences in the following passages to co-ordinate related ideas in the way that seems most effective to you. You will have to supply co-ordinating conjunctions or conjunctive adverbs and the appropriate punctuation.

1. Many chronic misspellers do not have the time to master spelling rules. They may not have the motivation. They rely on dictionaries to catch misspellings. Most dictionaries list words under their correct spellings. One kind of dictionary is designed for chronic misspellers. It lists each word under its common *mis*spellings. It then provides the correct spelling. It also provides the definition.

2. Henry Hudson was an English explorer. He captained ships for the Dutch East India Company. On a voyage in 1610 he

passed by Greenland. He sailed into a great bay in today's northern Canada. He thought he and his sailors could winter there. The cold was terrible. Food ran out. The sailors mutinied. The sailors cast Hudson adrift in a small boat. Eight others were also in the boat. Hudson and his companions perished.

EXERCISE 2

Revise the following sentences to eliminate faulty or excessive co-ordination. Relate ideas effectively by adding or subordinating information or by forming more than one sentence. Each item has more than one possible answer.

Example:

My dog barks, and I have to move out of my apartment.

Because my dog's barking *disturbs my neighbours*, I have to move out of my apartment.

co-ord
16a

1. The candidate was a New Democrat, and she disagreed with both the Conservative and the Liberal.
2. He is almost always cheerful, and he has few friends.
3. The dean was furious, and she let the police know it, but they refused to listen, and they began patrolling the campus anyway.
4. The dogs escaped from the pen because the keeper forgot to secure the latch, and the dogs wanted freedom, and they got it by running away, and it took the rest of the day to find them.
5. The weather in March is cold and rainy, but sometimes it is warm and sunny, and the inconsistency makes it impossible to plan outdoor activities, yet everyone wants to be outdoors after the long winter.
6. The gun sounded, and I froze, but an instant later I was running with a smooth, pumping motion, and I knew I would win the race.
7. The citizens of British Columbia are determined to protect their children, and they have some of the nation's toughest drunk-driving laws.
8. Two days last month were legal holidays, and the school held classes as usual.
9. Registering for classes the first time is confusing, and you have to find your way around, and you have to deal with strangers.
10. Air traffic in and out of major cities increases yearly, and the congestion is becoming dangerous, but the current regulations are inadequate, and they cannot control even the present traffic.

16b Subordinating to distinguish main ideas

Like paragraphs, many sentences consist of a main idea amplified and supported by details. Usually, the main idea appears in the main clause, and the details appear in subordinate structures such as phrases or subordinate clauses. This arrangement helps readers distinguish principal ideas from supporting information. In the following sentence the writer does not provide such assistance.

> In recent years computer prices have dropped, and production costs have dropped more slowly, and computer manufacturers have had to contend with shrinking profits.

The writer gives three facts: computer prices have decreased, production costs have decreased, and profits have shrunk. By loosely co-ordinating these three facts, the writer suggests some relation among them. But *in recent years* and *more slowly* provide the only explicit relations. We do not know which fact the writer considers most important or how the others qualify or support it. Look at the improvement in these revisions.

> *Because* production costs have dropped more slowly than computer prices in recent years, computer manufacturers have had to contend with shrinking profits.
>
> In recent years computer manufacturers have had to contend with shrinking profits *on account of* a slower drop in production costs than in computer prices.
>
> *Faced with* a slower drop in production costs than in computer prices, computer manufacturers have had to contend with shrinking profits in recent years.

In these revisions the words *because, on account of,* and *faced with* indicate specific cause-and-effect relations among the three facts. Each sentence makes clear that computer manufacturers' profits decline when prices fall more quickly than production costs, but the emphasis varies from one version to another.

No rules can specify what information in a sentence you should make primary and what you should subordinate; the decision will depend on your meaning. But, in general, you should consider using subordinate structures for details of time, cause, condition, concession, purpose, and identification (size, location, and the like). Consider the use of subordinate clauses in the following pairs of examples. (Some appropriate subordinating conjunctions and relative pronouns are listed in parentheses.)

> Time (*after, before, since, until, when, while*)
> The mine explosion killed six workers. The owners adopted safety measures.

sub

16b

After the mine explosion killed six workers, the owners adopted safety measures.

CAUSE (*because, since*)

Fletcher has been without work for six months. He is having trouble paying his bills.

Because Fletcher has been without work for six months, he is having trouble paying his bills.

CONDITION (*if, provided, since, unless*)

Bruce attends no lectures and studies infrequently. He has little chance of passing his biology examination.

Since Bruce attends no lectures and studies infrequently, he has little chance of passing his biology examination.

CONCESSION (*although, as if, even though, though*)

The horse looked gentle. It proved high-spirited and hard to manage.

Although the horse looked gentle, it proved high-spirited and hard to manage.

sub

16b

PURPOSE (*in order that, so that, that*)

Parliament passed new immigration laws. Illegal immigrants could not enter Canada.

Parliament passed new immigration laws *so that* illegal immigrants could not enter Canada.

IDENTIFICATION (*that, when, where, which, who*)

The old factory now manufactures automobile transmissions. It stands on the south side of town and covers two hectares.

The old factory, *which* stands on the south side of town and covers two hectares, now manufactures automobile transmissions.

Using subordinate clauses to distinguish main ideas from supporting information is an important strategy for creating effective sentences. But you can use other grammatical constructions as well to indicate the subordinate role of certain statements or information. A verbal or prepositional phrase, an appositive, an absolute phrase, or even a single-word modifier will often be the appropriate choice. In general, a subordinate clause places greatest emphasis on the subordinate information; verbal phrases, appositives, and absolute phrases give less weight; prepositional phrases still less; and single words the least. The following sets of examples illustrate the differences among subordinate constructions.

Old barns are common in Ontario. They are often unpainted. [separate sentences]

Old barns, *which are often unpainted*, are common in Ontario. [subordinate clause]

Old barns, *often unpainted*, are common in Ontario. [verbal phrase]

Old *unpainted* barns are common in Ontario. [single word]

The horse looked gentle. It proved high-spirited and hard to manage. [separate sentences]

Although the horse looked gentle, it proved high-spirited and hard to manage. [subordinate clause]

Despite its gentle appearance, the horse proved high-spirited and hard to manage. [prepositional phrase]

The horse, *a gentle-looking animal*, proved high-spirited and hard to manage. [appositive]

The *gentle-looking* horse proved high-spirited and hard to manage. [single word]

<table>
<tr><td>sub</td></tr>
<tr><td>16b</td></tr>
</table>

Punctuating subordinate constructions

A modifying word, phrase, or clause that introduces a sentence is usually set off from the rest of the sentence with a comma (see 21b).

Fortunately, I got the job.
In a little over six months, the company will open a new plant.
Buffeted by the wind, the boat drifted out to sea.
When the crisis passed, everyone was relieved.

A modifier that interrupts or concludes a main clause is *not* set off with punctuation when it restricts the meaning of a word or words in the clause (see 21c).

Her article *about a bank failure* won a prize.

The article *that won the prize* appeared in the local newspaper.

She wrote the article *because the bank failure affected many residents of the town*.

When an interrupting or concluding modifier does *not* restrict meaning, but simply adds information to the sentence, it *is* set off with punctuation, usually a comma or commas (see 21c).

The bank, *over forty years old*, never reopened.

The bank managers, *who were cleared of any wrongdoing*, all found new jobs.

The customers of the bank never recovered all their money, *although most of them tried to do so*.

Like a modifier, an appositive is set off with punctuation (usually a comma or commas) only when it does *not* restrict the meaning of the word it refers to (see 21c-2).

> The movie, *a science-fiction adventure*, was a huge success.
> The movie *Star Wars* was directed by George Lucas.

A dash or dashes may also be used to set off a non-restrictive appositive, particularly when it contains commas (see 25b-2). A concluding appositive is sometimes set off with a colon (see 25a-1).

1 Avoiding faulty subordination

Faulty subordination occurs when a writer uses a subordinate clause or other subordinate structure for what seems clearly to be the most important idea in the sentence. Often, faulty subordination merely reverses the dependent relation the reader expects.

FAULTY	Ms. Kogawa was in her first year of teaching, although she was a better instructor than others with many years of experience. [The sentence suggests that Ms. Kogawa's inexperience is the main idea, whereas the writer almost certainly intended to stress her skill *despite* her inexperience.]
REVISED	Although Ms. Kogawa was in her first year of teaching, *she was a better instructor than others with many years of experience.*
FAULTY	René's final interview that was to determine his admission to law school began at two o'clock. [Common sense says that the important fact is the interview's purpose, not its time.]
REVISED	*René's final interview*, which began at two o'clock, *was to determine his admission to law school.*

2 Avoiding excessive subordination

Excessive subordination sometimes occurs when a writer tries to cram too much loosely related information into one long sentence.

OVERLOADED	The boats that were moored at the dock when the storm, which was one of the worst in three decades, struck were ripped from their moorings, because the owners had not been adequately prepared, since the weather office had predicted the storm would blow out to sea, which they do at this time of year.

Since such sentences usually have more than one idea that deserves a main clause, they are best revised by sorting their details into more than one sentence.

> **REVISED** Struck by one of the worst storms in three decades, *the boats at the dock were ripped from their moorings. The owners were unprepared,* because the weather office had said that storms at this time of year blow out to sea.

A common form of excessive subordination occurs with a string of adjective clauses beginning *which, who,* or *that,* as in the following:

> **STRING OF** Every Christmas we all try to go to my
> **ADJECTIVE** grandfather's house, which is near Edmonton,
> **CLAUSES** which is an attractive city where my parents now live.

sub
16b

To revise such sentences, consider recasting some of the subordinate clauses as other kinds of modifying structures. In the following revision, for example, the clause *which is near Edmonton* has been reduced to a simple modifier, and the clause *which is an attractive city* has been changed to an appositive.

> **REVISED** Every Christmas we all try to go to my grandfather's house *near Edmonton, an attractive city* where my parents now live.

EXERCISE 3

Combine each of the following pairs of sentences twice, each time using one of the subordinate structures in parentheses to make a single sentence. You will have to add, delete, change, and rearrange words.

Example:

During the late eighteenth century, workers carried beverages in brightly coloured bottles. The bottles had cork stoppers. (*Clause beginning* that. *Phrase beginning* with.)

During the late eighteenth century, workers carried beverages in brightly coloured bottles *that had cork stoppers.*

During the late eighteenth century, workers carried beverages in brightly coloured bottles *with cork stoppers.*

1. Harrods in London is the largest departments store in the world. It consists of over 250 departments. (*Phrase beginning* consisting. *Phrase beginning* with.)

2. The man saw a ship approaching. He fell to his knees. (*Clause beginning* <u>when</u>. *Phrase beginning* <u>seeing</u>.)
3. Highway 1 is the most direct route to school. It is under construction. (*Clause beginning* <u>although</u>. *Appositive beginning* <u>the most</u>.)
4. Ellen Fairclough was the first woman federal cabinet minister in Canada. She was dedicated to equal opportunity for women. (*Phrase beginning* <u>dedicated</u>. *Appositive beginning* <u>the first</u>.)
5. James Joyce is one of the century's most controversial writers. He has been praised as the greatest writer since Milton and condemned as a writer of "latrine literature." (*Clause beginning* <u>who</u>. *Phrase beginning* <u>praised</u>.)
6. The Amish live peaceful but austere lives. Most of them refuse to use modern technology. (*Absolute phrase beginning* <u>most</u>. *Phrase beginning* <u>living</u>.)
7. Hernando de Soto is the legendary European discoverer of the Mississippi River. He supposedly died on the river's banks. (*Clause beginning* <u>who</u>. *Appositive beginning* <u>the legendary</u>.)
8. Computerized newspaper operations speed up and simplify copy preparation. They are favoured by editors and reporters. (*Clause beginning* <u>because</u>. *Phrase beginning* <u>favoured</u>.)
9. John Maclean founded the Maclean Hunter publishing empire. He first published *Canadian Grocer* in 1887. (*Clause beginning* <u>who</u>. *Clause beginning* <u>when</u>.)
10. In World War I, German forces set out to capture Verdun. Verdun was a fortress in northeastern France. (*Clause beginning* <u>which</u>. *Appositive beginning* <u>a fortress</u>.)

sub

16b

EXERCISE 4

Rewrite the following paragraph in the way you think most effective to subordinate the less important ideas to the more important ones. Use subordinate clauses and other subordinate constructions as appropriate.

Many students today are no longer majoring in the liberal arts. I mean by "liberals arts" such subjects as history, English, and the social sciences. Students think a liberal arts degree will not help them get jobs. They are wrong. They may not get practical, job-related experience from the liberal arts, but they will get a broad education, and it will never again be available to them. Many employers look for more than a technical, professional education. They think such an education can make an employee's views too narrow. The employers want open-minded employees. They want employees to think about problems from many angles. The liberal arts curriculum instils such flexibility. The flexibility is vital to the health of our society.

| **EXERCISE 5**

Revise the following sentences to eliminate faulty or excessive subordination by reversing main and subordinate ideas, by co-ordinating ideas, or by making separate sentences. Some items have more than one possible answer.

> *Example:*
>
> Terrified to return home, he had driven his mother's car into a cornfield.
>
> *Having driven his mother's car into a cornfield*, he was terrified to return home.

1. The National Theatre in London is government funded, which means that stand-by and discounted tickets are available for every performance.
2. He had experienced two near air disasters, although he continued to fly.
3. The car that my boss parked in front of the store, which rolled into my bike, was the car that he had just bought.
4. A woman who wants a career in the armed forces is better off now than she used to be because reasonable people no longer think that there's anything wrong with women who want to become career officers, which used to be a problem.
5. The speaker from the Naturalists Club, whom we had invited on short notice when our planned speaker cancelled, nevertheless gave an informative talk about the need to preserve our wilderness areas, which he said were in danger of extinction.

sub
16c

16c   Choosing clear connecters

Most connecting words signal specific and unambiguous relations; for instance, the co-ordinating conjunction *but* clearly indicates contrast, and the subordinating conjunction *because* clearly indicates cause. A few connecters, however, require careful use, either because they are ambiguous in many contexts and may therefore confuse the reader or because they are often misused in current English.

1   Avoiding ambiguous connecters: *as* and *while*.

The subordinating conjunction *as* can indicate several kinds of adverbial relations, including comparison and time.

COMPARISON	He was working *as* rapidly as he could.
TIME	The instructor finally arrived *as* the class was leaving.

As is sometimes used to indicate cause, but in that sense it is often ambiguous and should be avoided.

AMBIGUOUS	*As* I was in town, I visited some old friends. [Time or cause intended?]
CLEAR	*When* I was in town, I visited some old friends. [time]
CLEAR	*Because* I was in town, I visited some old friends. [cause]

The subordinating conjunction *while* can indicate either time or concession. Unless the context makes the meaning of *while* unmistakably clear, choose a more exact connecter.

AMBIGUOUS	*While* we were working nearby, we did not hear the burglars enter. [Time or concession?]
CLEAR	*When* we were working nearby, we did not hear the burglars enter. [time]
CLEAR	*Although* we were working nearby, we did not hear the burglars enter. [concession]

sub

16c

2 Avoiding misused connecters: *as*, *like*, and *while*

The use of *as* as a substitute for *whether* or *that* is nonstandard—that is, it violates the conventions of spoken and written standard English.

| NON-STANDARD | He was not sure *as* he could come. |
| REVISED | He was not sure *whether* (or *that*) he could come. |

Although the preposition *like* is often used as a conjunction in informal speech and in advertising (*Dirt-Away works like a soap should*), writing and formal speech generally require the conjunction *as*, *as if*, or *as though*.

| INFORMAL SPEECH | It seemed *like* the examination would never end. |
| WRITING | It seemed *as if* (*as though*) the examination would never end. |

The subordinating conjunction *while* is sometimes carelessly used in the sense of *and* or *but*, creating false subordination.

| FAULTY | My sister wants to study medicine *while* I want to study law. |
| REVISED | My sister wants to study medicine, *and* I want to study law. |

EXERCISE 6

Substitute a clear or correct connecter in the following sentences where *as*, *while*, and *like* are ambiguous or misused.

Example:

He looked to me like he had slept in his clothes.

He looked to me *as if* he had slept in his clothes.

1. The poet looked like he had never read in public before.
2. Many writers use *he* to denote both males and females, while others avoid the usage.
3. As I was going home for Thanksgiving, my mother cooked a pumpkin pie for me.
4. Some banks now charge for each transaction, like the monthly charge weren't enough of a burden for customers.
5. As teachers and legislators worry about the literacy of high school students, the situation may improve.

sub

16c

EXERCISE 7

The following paragraph consists entirely of simple sentences. Use co-ordination and subordination to combine sentences in the way you think most effective to emphasize main ideas.

Sir Walter Raleigh personified the Elizabethan Age. That was the period of Elizabeth I's rule of England. The period occurred in the last half of the sixteenth century. Raleigh was a courtier and poet. He was also an explorer and entrepreneur. Supposedly, he gained Queen Elizabeth's favour. He did this by throwing his cloak beneath her feet at the right moment. She was just about to step over a puddle. There is no evidence for this story. It does illustrate Raleigh's dramatic and dynamic personality. His energy drew others to him. He was one of Elizabeth's favourites. She supported him. She also dispensed favours to him. However, he lost his queen's good will. Without her permission he seduced one of her maids of honour. He eventually married the maid of honour. Elizabeth died. Then her successor imprisoned Raleigh in the Tower of London. Her successor was James I. Raleigh was charged falsely with treason. He was released after thirteen years. He was arrested again two years later on the old treason charges. At the age of sixty-six he was beheaded.

CHAPTER 17

Using Parallelism

Parallelism is a similarity of grammatical form between two or more co-ordinated elements.

The air is dirtied by	‖ factories	‖ belching	‖ smoke
and	‖ cars	‖ spewing	‖ exhaust.

Parallel structure reinforces and highlights a close relation or a contrast between compound sentence elements, whether they be words, phrases, or entire clauses.

The principle underlying parallelism is that form should reflect meaning: since the parts of compound constructions have the same function and importance, they should have the same grammatical form (see the box on p. 338). For the writer, parallelism is both a way to emphasize related ideas and a grammatical requirement to be observed in constructing sentences. In the following sections we will look at both roles of parallelism.

17a Using parallelism for co-ordinate elements

Parallel structure is necessary wherever co-ordination exists: wherever elements are connected by co-ordinating conjunctions or by correlative conjunctions, wherever elements are compared or contrasted, and wherever items are arranged in a list or outline. The elements should match each other in structure, though they need not match word for word, as the previous sentence of this paragraph illustrates. In the following sentence the co-ordinate prepositional phrases are parallel even though the second phrase contains more words.

We passed *through the town* and *into the vast, barren tundra*.

PATTERNS OF PARALLELISM

PARALLEL WORDS

In 1988 a Greek cyclist, backed up by ‖ engineers,
physiologists,
and ‖ athletes,
broke the world's record for human flight
with neither ‖ a boost
nor ‖ a motor.

PARALLEL PHRASES

‖ Pedalling ‖ a superlight plane
and ‖ sipping ‖ a special nutritious drink,
the pilot made an over-water journey of
‖ more than ‖ one hundred kilometres
in ‖ fewer than ‖ four hours.

To conserve energy, the pilot
both ‖ kept ‖ to the straightest possible course
and ‖ stayed ‖ near the surface of the water.

PARALLEL SUBORDINATE CLAUSES

The plane was escorted by several boats
‖ whose equipment ‖ tracked ‖ the wind
and ‖ whose passengers ‖ monitored ‖ the pilot's health.

PARALLEL MAIN CLAUSES

‖ The plane ‖ alighted ‖ just nine metres offshore,
and ‖ the pilot ‖ swam ‖ to a welcoming crowd.

//
17a

1 Using parallelism for elements linked by co-ordinating conjunctions

The co-ordinating conjunctions *and*, *but*, *or*, *nor*, and *yet* always signal a need for parallelism, as the following sentences show.

Miracle Grill will cook your food *in the kitchen* or *on the patio*.

Political candidates *often explain what they intend to do* but *rarely explain how they are going to do it*.

In Melanie's home, children had to account for *where they had been* and *what they had been doing*.

Sentence elements linked by co-ordinating conjunctions should be parallel in structure; otherwise, their co-ordination will be weakened and the reader distracted.

FAULTY	Three reasons why Canadian wheat farmers are leaving their farms are their debts are too high, they have had poor crops, and international farm subsidy wars.
REVISED	Three reasons why Canadian wheat farmers are leaving their farms are high debts, poor crops, and international farm subsidy wars.

All the words required by idiom or grammar must be stated in compound constructions (see also 15c).

FAULTY	The boy demonstrated an interest and a talent for writing.
REVISED	The boy demonstrated an interest *in* and a talent for writing. [Idiom dictates different prepositions with *interest* and *talent*.]
FAULTY	The thieves were careless and apprehended.
REVISED	The thieves were careless and *were* apprehended. [Each *were* serves a different grammatical function—the first as a linking verb, the second as a helping verb.]

//
17a

Often, the same word must be repeated to avoid confusion.

CONFUSING	James stood up for his principles by not taking drugs and leaving the group. [Did he leave the group or not?]
REVISED	James stood up for his principles by not taking drugs and by leaving the group.

Be sure that clauses beginning *and who* or *and which* are co-ordinated only with preceding *who* and *which* clauses.

FAULTY	Lisa is a young woman of great ability and who wants to be a professor.
REVISED	Lisa is a young woman *who has* great ability and who wants to be a professor.
REVISED	Lisa is a young woman of great ability *who wants* to be a professor.

2 **Using parallelism for elements linked by correlative conjunctions**

Correlative conjunctions are pairs of connecters such as *both . . . and, not only . . . but also*, and *either . . . or* (see 5d-1). They stress equality and balance and thus emphasize the relation between elements, even long phrases and clauses. The elements should be parallel to confirm their relation.

All-terrain vehicles are not only *interrupting the peacefulness of the wilderness* but also *destroying its vegetation*.

At the end of *Fifth Business*, Dunstan Ramsay has both *achieved self-knowledge through his quest* and *learned acceptance of his whole personality*.

Most errors in parallelism with correlative conjunctions occur when the element after the second connecter does not match the element after the first connecter.

NON-PARALLEL	He told the boys either to brush the horse or feed the chickens.
REVISED	He told the boys either to brush the horse or *to* feed the chickens.
NON-PARALLEL	We were warned that we must either pay our rent or we must vacate the apartment.
REVISED	We were warned that we must either pay our rent or *vacate* the apartment.

· //

17a

3   Using parallelism for elements being compared or contrasted

Elements being compared or contrasted should ordinarily be cast in the same grammatical form.

It is better *to live rich* than *to die rich*.   —SAMUEL JOHNSON

WEAK	Anna wanted a job rather than to apply for welfare.
REVISED	Anna wanted a job rather than *welfare payments*.
REVISED	Anna wanted *to find a job* rather than to apply for welfare.

4   Using parallelism for items in lists or outlines

The elements of a list or outline that divides a larger subject are co-ordinate and should be parallel in structure. (See also 1h-2 on outlining.)

FAULTY	**IMPROVED**
The Renaissance in England was marked by	The Renaissance in England was marked by
1. an extension of trade routes	1. the extension of trade routes
2. merchant class became more powerful	2. the increasing power of the merchant class

3. the death of feudalism	3. the death of feudalism
4. upsurging of the arts	4. the upsurge of the arts
5. the sciences were encouraged	5. the encouragement of the sciences
6. religious quarrels began	6. the outbreak of religious quarrels

EXERCISE 1

Identify the parallel elements in the following sentences. How does parallelism contribute to the effectiveness of each sentence?

1. But on St. Urbain, our fathers worked as cutters or pressers or scrap dealers and drifted into cold-water flats, sitting down to supper in their freckled Penman's long winter underwear, clipping their nails at the table.   —MORDECAI RICHLER

2. To enter the United States is a matter of crossing an ocean; to enter Canada is a matter of being silently swallowed by an alien continent.   —NORTHROP FRYE

3. If [the Scotch] boil their salmon and halibut till no taste remains, if they bake out of their haddock the last drop of moisture, if they serve these ruined fish with a dry, grey potato and (for variation) boiled turnips and sprouts, if they offer for dessert soggy rice pudding with bloated raisins bulging out of it, if they equate a distaste for haggis with disloyalty to Scotland herself—let nobody pity them or wonder why they eat as they do.   —HUGH MACLENNAN

4. I don't remember much being made of the sacredness of the life we took, but there was a real emphasis on fair play, much of it codified in law, like shooting game birds only on the wing, like not hunting deer with flashlights at night, like not shooting does.   —JANE RULE

5. [I]t is the character who chooses which parts of the personal past, the family past, and the ancestral past have to be revealed in order for the present to be realized and the future to happen.   —MARGARET LAURENCE

EXERCISE 2

Revise the following sentences to make co-ordinate, compared, or listed elements parallel in structure. Add or delete words or rephrase as necessary to increase the effectiveness of each sentence.

Example:

After emptying her bag, searching the apartment, and having called the library, Jennifer realized she had lost the book.

After emptying her bag, searching the apartment, and *calling* the library, Jennifer realized she had lost the book.

1. The reviews of the play were uniformly positive: unstinting praise for the actors; the director's interpretation was acclaimed; and the reviews applauded the playwright's technique.
2. Her tennis coach taught her how to serve and rushing the net and winning the point.
3. The unprepared student wishes for either a blizzard or to have a blackout on the examination day.
4. Working last summer as a waitress, I learned about choosing wine, how to serve wine, and making small talk while wrestling the cork from the bottle.
5. My favourite winter activities are skiing, reading, and to drink herbal tea by the fire.
6. To receive an A in that class, one must have both a perfect attendance record and academic record.
7. In moving from Winnipeg to Victoria, I was bothered less by the distance than to experience the climate change and especially that Christmases are usually mild and snowless.
8. After a week on a construction job, Leon felt not so much exhausted as that he was invigorated by the physical labour.
9. To lose weight, cut down on what you eat, eat fewer calories in the food you do consume, and you should exercise regularly.
10. Her generosity, sympathetic nature, and the fact that she is able to motivate employees make her an excellent supervisor.

17b   Using parallelism to increase coherence

Parallelism not only ensures similarity of form for co-ordinated structures but also enhances coherence by clearly relating paired or opposed units. Consider this sentence:

> **NON-PARALLEL**   During the early weeks of the term, the course reviews fundamentals, but little emphasis is placed on new material or more advanced concepts.

Here "the course" is doing two things—or doing one thing and not doing the other—and these are opposites. But the non-parallel construction of the sentence (*the course reviews . . . little emphasis is placed*) does not help the reader see the connection quickly.

> **REVISED**   During the early weeks of the term, the course reviews fundamentals but *places little emphasis* on new material or more advanced concepts.

Effective parallelism will enable you to combine in a single, well-ordered sentence related ideas that you might have expressed in two or three separate sentences. Compare the following three sentences with the original single sentence written by H. L. Mencken.

> Slang originates in the effort of ingenious individuals to make language more pungent and picturesque. They increase the store of terse and striking words or widen the boundaries of metaphor. Thus a vocabulary for new shades and differences in meaning is provided by slang.

> Slang originates in the effort of ingenious individuals to make the language more pungent and picturesque—to increase the store of terse and striking words, to widen the boundaries of metaphor, and to provide a vocabulary for new shades and differences in meaning.
> —H. L. MENCKEN

Parallel structure works as well to emphasize the connections among related sentences in a paragraph (see 3b-2).

> Style is an extraordinary thing. It is one of the subtlest secrets of all art.... *In painting, it is* composition, colour-sense, and brushwork. *In sculpture, it is* the treatment of depths and surfaces and the choice of stones and metals. *In music, it is* surely the melodic line, the tone-colour, and the shape of the phrase.... *In prose and poetry, it is* the choice of words, their placing, and the rhythms and melodies of sentence and paragraph.   —GILBERT HIGHET

Here, Highet clarifies and emphasizes his assertion that style is common to all forms of art by casting four successive sentences in the same structure (*In* ..., *it is* ...).

//

17

EXERCISE 3

Combine each group of sentences below into one concise sentence in which parallel elements appear in parallel structures. You will have to add, delete, change, and rearrange words. Each item has more than one possible answer.

Example:

Christin sorted the books neatly into piles. She was efficient about it, too.

Christin sorted the books neatly *and efficiently* into piles.

1. The professor spoke rapidly. Moreover, his voice was almost inaudible.
2. The cyclists finally arrived at their destination. They arrived after riding uphill most of the day. They had also endured a hailstorm.

3. I go to jazz class on Wednesday evenings. Sometimes I attend on Friday afternoons.
4. Finding an apartment requires expenditures of time and energy. It requires paying close attention to newspaper advertisements. It also requires that one learn the city's neighbourhoods.
5. After making several costly mistakes, he stopped to consider the jobs available to him. He thought about his goals for a job.
6. To make a good stew, marinate the meat. There should be plenty of vegetables added. Wine should be included for flavour. Simmer the whole thing for at least two hours.
7. Michel had three desires. First, he wanted money. Second, he wanted to be famous. The third desire was for happiness.
8. The sun looks small at its zenith. But it looks large when it reaches the horizon.
9. Most people who saw the movie were unimpressed with the acting. Or they frankly criticized the acting.
10. We returned from camping very tired. We were dirty. Mosquito bites covered us.

//
17b

EXERCISE 4

Revise the following paragraph to create parallelism wherever it is required for grammar or for coherence.

The great white shark has an undeserved bad reputation. Many people consider the great white not only swift and powerful but also to be a cunning and cruel predator on humans. However, scientists claim that the great white attacks humans not by choice but as a result of chance. To a shark, our behaviour in the water is similar to that of porpoises, seals, and sea lions—the shark's favourite foods. These sea mammals are both agile enough and can move fast enough to evade the shark. Thus the shark must attack with swiftness and noiselessly to surprise the prey and giving it little chance to escape. Humans become the shark's victims not because the shark has any preference or hatred of humans but because humans can neither outswim nor can they outmanoeuvre the shark. If the fish were truly a cruel human-eater, it would prolong the terror of its attacks, perhaps by circling or bumping into its intended victims before they were attacked.

C H A P T E R   18

Emphasizing Main Ideas

Effective writing uses co-ordination, subordination, and parallelism to help readers understand the relationship of ideas and details. It also emphasizes important information by making it readily apparent to readers.

18a Arranging ideas effectively

In arranging ideas within sentences for emphasis, you should keep two principles in mind. First, the beginnings and endings of sentences are the most emphatic positions, and endings are generally more emphatic than beginnings. Second, a parallel series of words, phrases, or clauses will be most emphatic if the elements appear in order of increasing importance.

WAYS TO EMPHASIZE IDEAS

1. Put important ideas in the beginnings or endings of sentences (18a-1).
2. Arrange series items in order of increasing importance (18a-2).
3. Use an occasional balanced sentence (18a-2).
4. Use judicious repetition of key words and phrases (18b).
5. Set off important ideas with punctuation (18c).
6. Use the active voice (18d).
7. Write concisely (18e).

---

1   **Using sentence beginnings and endings**

Readers automatically seek a writer's principal meaning in the basic sentence—that is, in the subject that names a topic and the predicate that comments on the topic (see 5a). Thus you can help ensure that readers understand your intended meaning by controlling the relation of the basic sentence to any other words, phrases, or clauses that modify all or parts of it.

Just as in speech we stress the beginning and the ending of a sentence, so in reading we expect the beginning and the ending to contain important information. Thus the most effective way to call attention to information is to place it first or last in the sentence, reserving the middle for incidentals.

UNEMPHATIC   Education remains the most important single means of economic advancement, in spite of its shortcomings.

REVISED   In spite of its shortcomings, education remains the most important single means of economic advancement.

REVISED   Education remains, in spite of its shortcomings, the most important single means of economic advancement.

emph
18a

The topic (*education*), the comment (*remains . . . advancement*), and the modifier (*in spite . . . shortcomings*) are worded the same in all three sentences. But the first sentence focusses our attention on education's shortcomings, even though the writer clearly wished to emphasize its importance. The first revision stresses the qualifying phrase a bit by placing it at the beginning but emphasizes education's importance by reserving it for the end. The second revision de-emphasizes the qualification by placing it in the middle.

Many sentences begin with the subject and predicate plus their modifiers and then add more modifiers. Such sentences are called **loose** (because they are not tightly structured) or **cumulative** (because they accumulate information as they proceed).

LOOSE   Lars staggered through the doorway, his pants torn, his shirt ripped open, his face scraped.

LOOSE   The Canadian Shield is made up of bare rock, thin soil, and muskeg, in an area extending from Hudson Bay to the Adirondacks and covering about 4.6 million square kilometres, scoured by past glaciers and strewn with countless lakes and rivers.

As these examples illustrate, a loose sentence completes its main statement (topic and comment) and then explains, amplifies, or illustrates it. By thus accumulating information, the sentence parallels the way we naturally think.

The opposite kind of sentence, called **periodic**, saves the main clause until just before the end (the period) of the sentence. Everything before the main clause points toward it.

PERIODIC   His pants torn, his shirt ripped open, his face scraped, Lars staggered through the doorway.

PERIODIC   In an area extending from Hudson Bay to the Adirondacks and covering about 4.6 million square kilometres, scoured by past glaciers and strewn with countless lakes and rivers, the Canadian Shield is made up of bare rock, thin soils, and muskeg.

A variation of the periodic sentence names the subject at the beginning, follows it with a modifier, and then fills in the predicate.

emph

18a

Lars, his pants torn, his shirt ripped open, his face scraped, staggered through the doorway.

Whether the subject comes first or is delayed along with the predicate, the periodic sentence creates suspense for the reader by reserving the important information of the main clause for the end. But it requires careful planning so that the reader can remember all the information leading up to the main clause. Most writers save periodic sentences for when their purpose demands climactic emphasis.

2   **Arranging parallel elements effectively**

Series

Parallelism requires that you express co-ordinate ideas in similar grammatical structures (see Chapter 17). In addition, you should arrange the co-ordinate ideas in order of importance. A series of grammatically parallel elements can be weak if you arrange the elements randomly.

UNEMPHATIC   The storm ripped the roofs off several buildings, killed ten people, and knocked down many trees in town.

In this sentence the most serious damage (*killed ten people*) is buried in the middle. The revised sentence below presents the items in order of increasing importance.

> **EMPHATIC**   The storm knocked down many trees in town, ripped the roofs off several buildings, and killed ten people.

You may want to use an unexpected item at the end of a series for humour or for another special effect.

> Early to bed and early to rise makes a man healthy, wealthy, and dead.   —JAMES THURBER

But be careful not to use such a series unintentionally. The following series seems thoughtlessly random rather than intentionally humorous.

> **UNEMPHATIC**   The painting has subdued tone, great feeling, and a length of about one metre.
>
> **EMPHATIC**   The painting, about one metre long, has subdued tone and great feeling.

emph
18a

Balanced sentences

When the clauses of a compound or complex sentence are parallel, the sentence is **balanced**.

> The fickleness of the women I love is equalled only by the infernal constancy of the women who love me.   —GEORGE BERNARD SHAW

In a pure balanced sentence two main clauses are exactly parallel: they match item for item.

> The love of liberty is the love of others; the love of power is the love of ourselves.   —WILLIAM HAZLITT

But the term is commonly applied to sentences that are only approximately parallel or that have only some parallel parts.

> If thought corrupts language, language can also corrupt thought.   —GEORGE ORWELL

> The secret of learning to act lies not in the study of methods but in the close observation of those who have already learned.

Balanced sentences are heavily emphatic but require thoughtful planning. When used carefully, they can be an especially effective way to alert readers to a strong contrast between two ideas.

EXERCISE 1

Underline the main clause in each of the following sentences, and identify each sentence as loose or periodic. Then rewrite each loose sentence as a periodic one and each periodic sentence as a loose one.

1. Matthew's children worked two years to get him out of jail—writing letters, seeing lawyers, attending meetings—because they knew him to be honest and believed him to be innocent.
2. Aspiring writers can learn much from waiting on tables, eavesdropping on conversations to sharpen their ear for dialogue and to pick up promising story material.
3. Louis Riel was an obvious leader for the Métis, a man educated in law and theology and deeply committed to the welfare of his people.
4. Finally, early in July 1884, at the request of a group of Saskatchewan Métis led by Gabriel Dumont, Riel arrived at Batoche.
5. In 1885, after the court had found him guilty of treason and the federal Cabinet had been swayed by political considerations, Riel was hanged.

emph
18a

EXERCISE 2

Combine each group of sentences below into a single loose sentence and then into a single periodic sentence. You will have to add, delete, change, and rearrange words. Each item has more than two possible answers. Does the loose or the periodic sentence seem more effective to you?

Example:

The woman refused any treatment. She felt that her life was completed. She wished to die.

Loose: The woman refused any treatment, feeling that her life was completed and wishing to die.

Periodic: Feeling that her life was completed and wishing to die, the woman refused any treatment.

1. The lead singer aroused the audience. He was spinning around the stage. He was dancing with the microphone stand.
2. Many writers now use computers. The machines make both revising and editing easier and faster.
3. The swan took flight. Its wings beat against the water. Its neck stretched forward.
4. The abandoned car was a neighbourhood eyesore. Its windows were smashed. Its body was rusted and dented.
5. Carl walked with his back straight. He held his head high. He stared straight ahead. He hid his shame.

EXERCISE 3

Revise the following sentences so that elements in a series or balanced elements are arranged to give maximum emphasis to main ideas.

Example:

The campers were stranded without matches, without food or water, and without a tent.

The campers were stranded without matches, without a tent, and without food or water.

1. Remembering summers at my grandmother's makes me happy, but I get angry when I remember later summers that I spent at camp.
2. Good scientists seek the truth regardless of personal success, whereas for bad scientists personal success is more important than the truth.
3. The car had several problems: the upholstery was torn, the engine was missing, and the left rear window would not open.
4. The explosion at the chemical factory blew up half a city block, killed six workers, and started a fire in a building.
5. In the 1950s Canadians wanted to keep up with the Joneses; keeping up with change is what Canada wants in the 1990s.

emph

18b

18b Repeating ideas

Although careless repetition results in weak and wordy sentences, judicious repetition of key words and phrases can be an effective means of emphasis. Such repetition often combines with parallelism. It may occur in a series of sentences within a paragraph, or it may occur in a series of words, phrases, or clauses within a sentence.

> We shall not flag or fail. We shall fight in France, we shall fight on the seas and oceans, we shall fight with growing confidence and growing strength in the air, we shall defend our island, whatever the cost may be, we shall fight on the beaches, we shall fight on the landing grounds, we shall fight in the fields and in the streets, we shall fight in the hills; we shall never surrender.
> —WINSTON CHURCHILL

> Never in the field of human conflict was so much owed by so many to so few.
> —WINSTON CHURCHILL

18c Separating ideas

When you save important information for the end of a sentence, you can emphasize it even more by setting if off from the rest of the sentence. The second example below illustrates how putting an important idea in a separate sentence can highlight it.

> [A]lthough the questions I have just told you about are the usual ones (and I swear that I have not invented or coloured them), every now and then a student calls who is really excited about literature, who understands what a writer is saying to him, who feels that the literature of his country is a live thing, and who takes writing seriously.

> [A]lthough the questions I have just told you about are the usual ones (and I swear that I have not invented or coloured them), every now and then a student calls who is really excited about literature, who understands what a writer is saying to him, and who feels that the literature of his country is a live thing. He takes writing seriously.   —ROBERTSON DAVIES

emph
18c

You can vary the degree of emphasis by varying the extent to which you separate one idea from the others. A semicolon provides more separation than a comma, and a period provides still more separation. Note the use of all three in the following example.

> This revelation was an even greater shock to me; not only was my country owned, but it was owned by the kind of people who carried tin boats across portages and didn't burn their garbage. One doubted their competence.   —MARGARET ATWOOD

Sometimes a dash or a pair of dashes will isolate and thus emphasize a part of a statement (see also 25b).

> His schemes were always elaborate, ingenious, and exciting—and wholly impractical.

> Athletics—even winning athletics—have never been a profitable university operation in Canada.

EXERCISE 4

Emphasize the main idea in each sentence or group of sentences below by following the instructions in parentheses: either combine sentences so that parallelism and repetition stress the main idea, or place the main idea in a separate sentence. Each item has more than one possible answer.

Example:

I try to listen to other people's opinions. When my mind is closed, I find that other opinions open it. And they can change my mind when it is wrong. (*parallelism and repetition*)

I try to listen to other people's opinions, for they can open my mind when it is closed and they can change my mind when it is wrong.

1. Without funding, the centre will close. The counselling program will end if funding stops. (*parallelism and repetition*)
2. Anil worked harder than usual to win the chemistry prize that his father had won before him, for he could not let his father down. (*separation*)
3. One of the few worthwhile habits is daily reading. One can read for information. One can read for entertainment. Reading can give one a broader view of the world. (*parallelism and repetition*)
4. My parents fear change. They fear change in morals. They are afraid their neighbourhood will change. They are afraid of change in their own children. (*parallelism and repetition*)
5. By the time the rescuers reached the crash site, the wind had nearly covered the small plane with snow and no one had survived. (*separation*)

emph
18d

18d   Preferring the active voice

In the active voice of the verb, the subject acts (*I peeled the onions*). In the passive voice, the subject is acted upon and the actor is either relegated to a phrase (*The onions were peeled by me*) or omitted entirely (*The onions were peeled*). (See Chapter 7, p. 241.) The passive voice is thus indirect because it obscures or removes the actor. The active voice is more direct, vigorous, and emphatic. Further, all sentences turn on their verbs, which give sentences their motion, pushing them along. And active verbs push harder than passive ones.

PASSIVE	For energy conservation it is urged that all lights be turned off when not being used. [Who is urging? Who is to turn the lights off?]
ACTIVE	To save energy, students should turn off all lights they are not using.
PASSIVE	The new outpatient clinic was opened by the hospital administration so that the costs of non-emergency medical care would be reduced.
ACTIVE	The hospital administration opened the new outpatient clinic to reduce the costs of non-emergency medical care.

Sometimes the actor is unknown or unimportant, and much technical writing deliberately omits the actor in order to give impersonal emphasis to what is being acted upon. In these cases the passive voice can be useful.

> Wellington was called the "Iron Duke."
> Thousands of people are killed annually in highway accidents.
> The mixture was then stirred.

Except in these situations, however, rely on the active voice. It is economical and creates movement. (See also 31c-3.)

18e Being concise

Conciseness—brevity of expression—aids emphasis no matter what the sentence structure. Unnecessary words detract from necessary words. They clutter sentences and obscure ideas.

One common structure that may contribute to wordiness is the expletive construction, which inverts the normal subject-verb order by beginning a sentence with *there* or *it* and a form of the verb *be* (see 5e-4).

WEAK	*There are* likely to be thousands of people attending the rally against nuclear arms.
EMPHATIC	*Thousands of people are* likely to attend the rally against nuclear arms.

Some frequently used qualifying phrases such as *in my opinion*, *more or less*, and *for the most part* are also unnecessarily wordy. They can always be reworded more concisely and can often be omitted entirely.

WEAK	*In my opinion*, the competition for grades distracts many students from their goal of obtaining a good education.
EMPHATIC	*I think* the competition for grades distracts many students from their main goal of obtaining a good education.
MORE EMPHATIC	The competition for grades distracts many students from their goal of obtaining a good education.

(See 31c for a longer discussion of concise writing.)

EXERCISE 5

Revise the following sentences to make them more emphatic by converting passive voice to active voice, by eliminating expletive constructions, or by condensing or eliminating wordy phrases. (For additional exercises with the passive voice, see pp. 204, 243, and 487.)

> *Example:*
>
> The problem in this particular situation is that we owe more money than we can afford under present circumstances.
>
> The *problem is* that we owe more money than we can afford.

1. As far as I am concerned, the major weakness of the restaurant in question is that the service is surly, in a manner of speaking.
2. The contestant was seated behind a screen so that she could not be seen by the judges while her performance was heard.
3. After all these years there is still something calling me back to the town where I lived as a child.
4. The protesters were ordered by the police to clear the sidewalk when the motorcade was approaching.
5. There must have been some reason, whether conscious or unconscious, why he acted as he did.

emph
18e

EXERCISE 6

Drawing on the advice in this chapter, rewrite the following paragraph to emphasize main ideas and to de-emphasize less important information.

In preparing pasta, there is a requirement for common sense and imagination rather than for complicated recipes. The key to success in this area is fresh ingredients for the sauce and perfectly cooked pasta. The sauce may be made with just about any fresh fish, meat, cheese, herb, or vegetable. As for the pasta itself, it may be dried or fresh, although fresh pasta is usually more delicate and flavourful, as many experienced cooks have found. Dried pasta is fine with zesty sauces; with light oil and cream sauces fresh pasta is best used. There is a difference in the cooking time for dried and fresh pasta, with dried pasta taking longer. It is important that the package directions be followed by the cook and that the pasta be tested before the cooking time is up. The pasta is done when the texture is neither tough nor mushy but *al dente*, or "firm to the bite," according to the Italians, who ought to know.

CHAPTER 19

Achieving Variety

In a paragraph or an essay, sentences do not stand one by one. Rather, each stands in relation to those before and after it. To make sentences work together effectively, the writer must vary their length, structure, and word order to reflect the importance and complexity of ideas. Although experienced writers generally find that variety takes care of itself as they commit ideas to paper, inexperienced writers often have difficulty achieving variety without guidance and practice.

A series of similar sentences will prove monotonous and ineffective, as the following passage illustrates.

> The armies of the British general James Wolfe and the French general the Marquis de Montcalm fought on 13 September 1759. The battle was on the Plains of Abraham. They were fighting for possession of Quebec City and, ultimately, all of what would become Canada. It was one of the most decisive events in our history. Wolfe and Montcalm were contesting the identity and future of our country. Other battles had yet to be fought. Montreal was not captured by the British until the next year. France did not officially yield its colony to England until 1763. Wolfe had already defeated Montcalm, however, in the battle which claimed both their lives, and, in effect, New France had become British North America.

Individually, these nine sentences are perfectly clear and adequately detailed. But together they do not make pleasant reading, and their relative importance is obscure. Their lengths are roughly the same, they are about equally detailed, and they all consist of one or two main clauses beginning with the subject. At the end of the passage we have a sense of names, dates, and events but no sure sense of how they relate.

WAYS TO ACHIEVE VARIETY AMONG SENTENCES

1. Vary the length and structure of sentences so that important ideas stand out (19a).
2. Vary the beginnings of sentences with modifiers, transitional words and expressions, and occasional expletive constructions (19b).
3. Occasionally, invert the normal order of subject, predicate, and object or complement (19c).
4. Use an occasional command, question, or exclamation (19d).

19

Now compare the preceding passage with a more effective version.

> When the armies of the British general James Wolfe and the French general the Marquis de Montcalm met on the Plains of Abraham, on 13 September 1759, to fight for possession of Quebec City and, ultimately, all of what would become Canada, it was one of the most decisive events in our history.
>
> These generals were contesting the identity and the future of our country. To be sure, other battles had yet to be fought, for Montreal was not captured by the British until the next year, and France did not officially yield its colony to England until 1763. But, when Wolfe defeated Montcalm in the battle which claimed both their lives, New France in effect became British North America.

The information in these two passages is almost identical. The differences lie chiefly in the sentence variety of the second and the sharp focus on the significance of the battle which that variety underscores. The four sentences of the second passage range from twelve to fifty-four words, and only the second sentence begins with its subject. The first sentence brings together in one long *when* clause all the details of place, time, and cause contained in the first three sentences of the first passage. The sentence is periodic (see 18a-1), and the suspense it creates forces us to focus on the significance of the battle described in the main clause at the end. The very brief second sentence, contrasting sharply with the one before it, further develops the importance of the event. The third sentence, a long, loose one (see 18a-1), describes the lingering obstacles to a political resolution. And the fourth sentence, another short one, tersely indicates the full significance of the battle. Together, the four sentences clearly, even dramatically, convey that the battle marked a turning point in Canadian history.

The rest of this chapter suggests how you can vary your sentences for the kind of interest and clarity achieved in the second passage.

19a Varying sentence length and structure

The sentences of a stylistically effective essay will differ most obviously in their length. Further, some sentences will consist only of one main clause with modifiers, others of two main clauses; some will be loose, and a few perhaps will be periodic. (See 18a-1.) This variation in length and structure marks mature writing, making it both readable and clear.

Neither short sentences nor long sentences are intrinsically better. But in most contemporary writing, sentences tend to vary from about ten words on the short side to about forty words on the long, with an average of between fifteen and twenty-five words, depending on the writer's purpose and style. Your sentences generally should not be all at one extreme or the other because if they are, your readers may have difficulty focussing on main ideas and seeing the relations among them. If most of your sentences contain thirty-five words or more, you probably need to break some up into shorter, simpler sentences. If most of your sentences contain fewer than ten or fifteen words, you probably need to add details to them or combine them through co-ordination and subordination. Examine your writing particularly for a common problem: strings of main clauses, subjects first, in either simple or compound sentences.

1 Avoiding strings of brief and simple sentences

A series of brief and simple sentences is both monotonous and hard to understand because it forces the reader to sort out relations among ideas. If you find that you depend on brief, simple sentences, work to increase variety by combining some of them into longer units that emphasize and link new and important ideas while de-emphasizing old or incidental information. (See 16a, 16b, and 18a.)

The following example shows how a string of simple sentences can be revised into an effective piece of writing.

WEAK

The moon is now drifting away from the earth. It moves away at the rate of about three centimetres per year. Our days on earth are getting longer. They grow a thousandth of a second longer every century. A month might become forty-seven of our present days long. We might eventually lose the moon altogether. Such great planetary movement rightly concerns astronomers. It need not worry us. The movement will take 50 million years.

REVISED

The moon is now drifting away from the earth, moving at the rate of about three centimetres per year. And at the rate of a thousandth of a second or so every century, our days on earth are getting longer. Someday, a month will be forty-seven of our present days long, if we don't eventually lose the moon altogether. Such great planetary movement rightly concerns astronomers, but it need not concern us. It will take 50 million years.

In the first passage the choppy movement of the nine successive simple sentences leaves the reader with nine independent facts and a lame conclusion. The revision retains all the facts of the original but compresses them into five sentences that are structured to emphasize main ideas—the moon's movement (sentence 1), our lengthening days (2), and the enormous span of time involved (5)—and to show relations among ideas.

2   Avoiding excessive compounding

Because compound sentences are usually just simple sentences linked with conjunctions, a series of them will be as weak as a series of brief simple sentences, especially if the clauses of the compound sentences are all about the same length.

WEAK

The hotel beach faces the south, and the main street runs along the north side of the hotel. The main street is heavily travelled and often noisy, but the beach is always quiet and sunny. It was Sunday afternoon, and we were on the hotel beach. We lay stretched out on the sand, and the sun poured down on us.

REVISED

The main street, heavily travelled and often noisy, runs along the north side of the hotel. But on the south side the hotel beach is always quiet and sunny. On Sunday we lay there stretched out on the sand, letting the sun pour down on us.

The first passage creates a seesaw effect. The revision, with some main clauses changed into modifiers and repositioned, is both clearer and more emphatic. (See 16a-2 for additional discussion of how to avoid excessive co-ordination within sentences.)

> **EXERCISE 1**
>
> Rewrite the following paragraphs to increase variety so that important ideas receive greater emphasis than supporting information

does. You will have to change some main clauses into modifiers and then combine and reposition the modifiers and the remaining main clauses.

1. Charlotte Perkins Gilman was a leading intellectual in the women's movement during the first decades of this century. She wrote *Women and Economics*. This book challenged Victorian assumptions about differences between the sexes. It explored the economic roots of women's oppression. Gilman wrote little about gaining the vote for women. Many feminists were then preoccupied with this issue. Historians have since focussed their analyses on this issue. As a result, Gilman's contribution to today's women's movement has often been overlooked.

2. Nellie McClung was a Canadian reformer and suffragist, and she was raised in Manitoba. She joined the Winnipeg women's rights movement, and she was welcomed by it because of her witty arguments. She fought for female suffrage in Manitoba and Alberta. Some feminists criticize her support of traditional family values. She was ignored for a decade, but she was rediscovered by the women's movement in the 1960s. Most women's rights advocates now recognize her contribution to the feminist cause.

var
19b

19b Varying sentence beginnings

Most English sentences begin with their subjects.

The defendant's lawyer relentlessly cross-examined the stubborn witness for two successive days.

However, an unbroken sequence of sentences beginning with the subject quickly becomes monotonous, as shown by the altered passage on Wolfe and Montcalm at the start of this chapter (p. 355). Your final arrangement of sentence elements should always depend on two concerns: the relation of a sentence to those preceding and following it and the emphasis required by your meaning. When you do choose to vary the subject-first pattern, you have several options.

Adverb modifiers can often be placed at a variety of spots in a sentence. Consider the different emphases created by moving the adverbs in the basic sentence above.

For two successive days, the defendant's lawyer *relentlessly* cross-examined the stubborn witness.

Relentlessly, the defendant's lawyer cross-examined the stubborn witness *for two successive days*.

Relentlessly, for two successive days, the defendant's lawyer cross-examined the stubborn witness.

Notice that the last sentence, with both modifiers at the beginning, is periodic and thus highly emphatic (see 18a-1).

Beginning a sentence with a participial phrase also postpones the subject and sometimes creates a periodic sentence.

> The lawyer thoroughly cross-examined the witness and then called the defendant herself to testify.
>
> *Having thoroughly cross-examined the witness*, the lawyer called the defendant herself to testify.

When the relation between two successive sentences demands, you may begin the second with a co-ordinating conjunction or with a transitional expression such as *first, for instance, however, in addition, moreover,* or *therefore*. (See 3b-6 for a list of transitional expressions.)

> The witness expected to be dismissed after his first long day of cross-examination. He was not; the defendant's lawyer called him again the second day.
>
> The witness expected to be dismissed after his first long day of cross-examination. *But* he was not; the defendant's lawyer called him again the second day.
>
> The price of clothes has risen astronomically in recent years. The cotton shirt that once cost $6 and now costs $25 is an example.
>
> The price of clothes has risen astronomically in recent years. *For example*, a cotton shirt that once cost $6 now costs $25.

Occasionally, an expletive construction—*it* or *there* plus a form of *be*—may be useful to delay and thus emphasize the subject of the sentence.

> His judgment seems questionable, not his desire.
>
> *It is* his judgment that seems questionable, not his desire.

However, expletive constructions are more likely to flatten writing by adding extra words. You should use them rarely, only when you can justify doing so. (See also 18e.)

EXERCISE 2

Revise each pair of sentences below, following the instructions in parentheses to make a single sentence that begins with an adverb modifier or a participial phrase, or to make one of the two sentences begin with an appropriate co-ordinating conjunction or transitional expression.

Example:
The *Seabird* took first place. It moved quickly in the wind.
(*one sentence with participial phrase beginning* moving)
Moving quickly in the wind, the *Seabird* took first place.

1. The loan application was denied by the bank. The business had to close its doors. (*two sentences with transitional expression*)
2. The school may build a new athletic complex. It will tear down the old field house. (*one sentence with adverb modifier beginning* if)
3. Municipal voting rights for propertied women were established by 1900. Women were not actually given the vote in federal elections until 1918. (*two sentences with co-ordinating conjunction*)
4. Brent had orders to stay in bed. He returned to work immediately. (*one sentence with adverb modifier beginning* although)
5. The rescuers were careful as they handled the ropes. They lowered the frightened climber from the ledge. (*one sentence with participial phrase beginning* carefully)

var
19c

EXERCISE 3

Revise the following paragraph to vary sentence beginnings by using each of the following at least once: an adverb modifier, a participial phrase, a co-ordinating conjunction, and a transitional expression.

The instructor found himself in class alone. He waited patiently for his students to arrive. He went over his lecture notes. He read yesterday's newspaper. No one arrived. He noticed an article on the front page of the paper reminding readers to turn their clocks back one hour. He realized his mistake. He smiled.

19c Inverting the normal word order

Inverted sentences such as *Up came the down* and *Mutton he didn't like* are infrequent in modern prose. Because the word order of subject, verb, and object or complement is so strongly fixed in English, an inverted sentence can be emphatic.

Gino had once been a dog lover. Then his neighbour's barking dogs twice raced through his garden. Now *all dogs*, especially barking dogs, *Gino detests*.

Inverting the normal order of subject, verb, and complement can be useful in two successive sentences when the second expands on the first.

Critics of his economic policies were not kind to Prime Minister R. B. Bennett during the Depression. Particularly *harsh was the term* for cars pulled by horses because the owners could not afford gas: Bennett buggies.

Inverted sentences used without need are artificial. Avoid descriptive sentences such as *Up came Travis and down went Abby's spirits*.

▌19d   Mixing types of sentences

Most written sentences make statements. Occasionally, however, questions, commands, or, more rarely, exclamations may enhance variety. Questions may set the direction of a paragraph, as in *What does a detective do*? or *How is the percentage of unemployed workers calculated*? More often, though, the questions used in exposition or argumentation do not require answers but simply emphasize ideas that readers can be expected to agree with. These **rhetorical questions** are illustrated in the following passage.

Why do our writers keep searching for "the Canadian identity"? Canadians know who they are: they aren't Americans.

Imperative sentences occur frequently in an explanation of a process, particularly in directions, as the following passage on freewriting illustrates.

The goal of freewriting is to discover whatever ideas the topic suggests. Push yourself to keep writing. Don't go back to reread, and don't delete ideas that seem dumb or repetitious. Never stop to edit, to cross out mistakes, or to worry about grammar and spelling.

Notice that these examples use questions and commands not merely to create variety but to achieve some special purpose. Variety occurs because a particular sentence type is effective for the context, not because the writer set out to achieve variety for its own sake.

▌**EXERCISE 4**

Imagine that you are writing an essay either on the parking problem at your university or on the problems of living in a residence. Practise varying sentences by composing a sentence or passage to serve each of the following purposes.

1. Write a question that could open the essay.
2. Write a command that could open the essay.
3. Write an exclamation that could open the essay.
4. For the body of the essay, write an appropriately varied paragraph of at least five sentences, including at least one short and one long sentence beginning with the subject; at least one sentence beginning with an adverb modifier; at least one sentence beginning with a co-ordinating conjunction or transitional expression; and one rhetorical question or command.

EXERCISE 5

The following paragraph consists entirely of simple sentences that begin with their subjects. As appropriate, use the techniques discussed in this chapter to vary sentences so that the paragraph is more readable and its important ideas stand out clearly. You will have to delete, add, change, and rearrange words.

The Italian volcano Vesuvius had been dormant for many years. It then exploded on August 24 in the year A.D. 79. The ash, pumice, and mud from the volcano buried two busy towns. Herculaneum is one. The more famous is Pompeii. The ruins of both towns lay undiscovered for many centuries. Herculaneum and Pompeii were discovered in 1709 and 1748, respectively. The excavation of Pompeii was the more systematic. It was the occasion for initiating modern methods of conservation and restoration. The methods replaced earlier practices. Herculaneum was simply looted of its most valuable finds. It was then left to disintegrate. Pompeii appears much as it did before the eruption. A luxurious house opens onto a lush central garden. An election poster decorates a wall. A dining table is set for breakfast.

var

19

P A R T   V

Punctuation

MAJOR INTERNAL SENTENCE PUNCTUATION
Commas, Semicolons, Colons, Dashes, and Parentheses

(For explanations, consult the sections in parentheses.)

Sentences with two main clauses

The bus stopped, *but* no one got off. (21a)
The bus stopped; no one got off. (22a)
The bus stopped; *however*, no one got off. (22b)
The mechanic replaced the battery, the distributor cap, and the starter; *but* still the car would not start. (22c)
His duty was clear: he had to report the theft. (25a-1)

Introductory elements

MODIFIERS (21b)

After the argument was over, we laughed at ourselves.
Racing over the plain, the gazelle escaped the lion.
To dance in the contest, he had to tape his knee.
Suddenly, the door flew open.
With 125 passengers aboard, the plane was half full.
In 1983 he won the Nobel Prize.

ABSOLUTE PHRASES (21d)

Its wing broken, the bird hopped around on the ground.

Interrupting and concluding elements

NON-RESTRICTIVE MODIFIERS (21c-1)

Jim's car, *which barely runs*, has been impounded.
We consulted the dean, *who had promised to help us*.
The boy, *like his sister*, wants to be a pilot.
They moved across the desert, *shielding their eyes from the sun*.
The men do not speak to each other, *although they share a car*.

NON-RESTRICTIVE APPOSITIVES

The author of "In Flanders Fields," *John McCrae*, served as a medical officer with the Canadian Expeditionary Force during World War I. (21c-2)
The population of the three Prairie provinces—*Alberta, Saskatchewan, and Manitoba*—is approximately 17.5 percent of Canada's total population. (25b-2)
Our father demanded one promise: *that we not lie to him*. (25a-1)

RESTRICTIVE MODIFIERS (21j-3)

The car *that hit mine* was uninsured.
We consulted a teacher *who had promised to help us*.
The boy *in the black hat* is my cousin.
They were surprised to find the desert *teeming with life*.
The men do not speak to each other *because they are feuding*.

Restrictive appositives (21j-3)

Shaw's play *Saint Joan* was performed last year.
Their sons *Tony, William, and Steve* all chose medical careers, leaving only Joe to run the family business.

Parenthetical expressions

We suspect, *however*, that he will not come. (21c-3)
Jan is respected by many people—*including me*. (25b-2)
Brian Macdonald (*b. 14 May 1928*) is a brilliant choreographer. (25c-1)

Absolute phrases (21d)

The bird, *its wing broken*, hopped about on the ground.
The bird hopped about on the ground, *its wing broken*.

Phrases expressing contrast (21e)

The humidity, *not just the heat*, gives me headaches.
My headaches are caused by the humidity, *not just the heat*.

Concluding summaries and explanations

The movie opened to bad notices: *the characters were judged shallow and unrealistic*. (25a-1)
Mrs. McEvoy served us oatcakes, bannocks, and crowberries—*all Cape Breton favourites*. (25b-3)

Items in a series

Three or more items

Chimpanzees, gorillas, orangutans, and gibbons are all apes. (21f-1)
The cities singled out for special praise were *Fredericton, New Brunswick; Thunder Bay, Ontario; and Red Deer, Alberta*. (22d)

Two or more adjectives before a noun or pronoun (21f-2)

Dingy, smelly clothes decorated their room.
The luncheon consisted of *one tiny watercress* sandwich.

Introductory series (25b-3)

Appropriateness, accuracy, and necessity—these criteria should govern your selection of words.

Concluding series

Every word should be *appropriate, accurate, and necessary*. (25a-3)
Every word should meet three criteria: *appropriateness, accuracy, and necessity*. (25a-1)
Pay attention to your words—*to their appropriateness, their accuracy, and their necessity*. (25b-3)

p

CHAPTER 20

End Punctuation

THE PERIOD

 Use the period to end sentences that are statements, mild commands, or indirect questions.

STATEMENTS

These are exciting and trying times.

The airline went bankrupt.

The violins played quietly in the background.

MILD COMMANDS

Please do not smoke.

Think of the possibilities.

Turn to page 146.

If you are unsure whether to use an exclamation point or a period after a command, use a period. The exclamation point should be used only rarely (see 20f).

An **indirect question** reports what someone has asked but not in the original speaker's own words.

INDIRECT QUESTIONS

The judge asked why I had been driving with my lights off in the middle of the night.

Students sometimes wonder whether their teachers read the papers they write.

Abused children eventually stop asking why they are being punished.

20b Use periods with most abbreviations.

Ordinarily, use periods with abbreviations.

p.	B.A.	A.D.	Mr.
U.S.S.R.	Ph.D.	a.m.	Mrs.
M.D.	e.g.	p.m.	Ms.
Dr.	B.C.	c.o.d.	M.

When an abbreviation falls at the end of a sentence, use only one period: *Julius Caesar died in 44 B.C.*

Periods are usually dropped from abbreviations for organizations, corporations, and government agencies when more than two words are abbreviated. For example:

IBM	UBC	CFL	UN

Check a dictionary for the preferred form of such abbreviations, and see Chapter 28 on abbreviations.

Note that **acronyms**—pronounceable words, such as UNESCO, NATO, CUSO, and WHO, formed from the initial letters of the words in a name—never require periods (see 28b).

> **EXERCISE 1**
>
> Revise the following sentences so that periods are used correctly.
> *Example:*
> Several times I wrote to ask when my subscription ended?
> Several times I wrote to ask when my subscription ended.
> 1. The instructor asked when Plato wrote *The Republic*?
> 2. Give the date within one century
> 3. The exact date is not known, but it is thought to be around 370 BC..
> 4. Dr Arn is not an MD; he is a PhD.
> 5. You will find that information on p 256.

?
20c

THE QUESTION MARK

20c Use the question mark after direct questions.

DIRECT QUESTIONS

Who will follow her?
What is the difference between these two people?
Will economists ever really understand the economy?

After indirect questions, use a period: *My mother asked why I came in so late.* (See 20a.)

Questions in a series are each followed by a question mark.

The officer asked how many times the suspect had been arrested. Three times? Four times? More than that?

The use of capital letters for questions in a series is optional (see 26a).

NOTE: Question marks are never combined with other question marks, exclamation points, periods, or commas.

FAULTY	I finally asked myself, "Why are you working at a job you hate?."
REVISED	I finally asked myself, "Why are you working at a job you hate?"

20d Use a question mark within parentheses to indicate doubt about the correctness of a number or date.

The Greek philosopher Socrates was born in 470 (?) B.C. and died in 399 B.C. from drinking poison after having been condemned to death.

NOTE: Don't use a question mark within parentheses to express sarcasm or irony. Express these attitudes through sentence structure and diction. (See Chapters 18 and 31.)

FAULTY	Her friendly (?) criticism did not escape notice.
REVISED	Her criticism, *too rough to be genuinely friendly,* did not escape notice.

EXERCISE 2

Revise the following sentences so that question marks (along with other punctuation marks) are used correctly.

Example:

"When will it end?," cried the man dressed in rags.
"When will it end?" cried the man dressed in rags.

1. In Homer's *Odyssey*, Ulysses took seven years to travel from Troy to Ithaca. Or was it eight years. Or more?
2. Ulysses must have wondered whether he would ever make it home?
3. "What man are you and whence?," asks Ulysses's wife, Penelope.

4. Why does Penelope ask, "Where is your city? Your parents?"?
5. Penelope does not recognize Ulysses and asks who this stranger is?

THE EXCLAMATION POINT

 Use the exclamation point after emphatic statements and interjections, and after strong commands.

No! We must not lose this election!
When she saw her rain-soaked term paper, she gasped, "Oh, no!"
Come here immediately!
"Stop!" he yelled.

Follow mild interjections and commands with commas or periods, as appropriate.

No, the response was not terrific.
To prolong your car's life, change its oil regularly.

NOTE: Exclamation points are never combined with other exclamation points, question marks, periods, or commas.

FAULTY	My father was most emphatic. "I will not give you any more money!," he roared.
REVISED	My father was most emphatic. "I will not give you any more money!" he roared.

!
20f

 Avoid overusing exclamation points.

Don't express sarcasm, irony, or amazement with the exclamation point. Rely on sentence structure and diction to express these attitudes. (See Chapters 18 and 31.)

FAULTY	After travelling almost 2 billion km through space, *Voyager 2* missed its target by 66 km(!).
REVISED	After travelling almost 2 billion km through space, *Voyager 2* missed its target by *a mere* 66 km.

Relying on the exclamation point for emphasis is like crying wolf: the mark loses its power to impress the reader. Frequent exclamation points can also make writing sound overemotional. In the following passage, the writer could have conveyed her ideas more effectively by punctuating sentences with periods.

Our city government is a mess! After just six months in office, the mayor has had to fire four city officials! In the same period the city aldermen have done nothing but argue! And city services decline with each passing day!

EXERCISE 3

Revise the following sentences so that exclamation points (along with other punctuation marks) are used correctly. If a sentence is punctuated correctly as given, circle the number preceding it.

Example:
"Well, now!," he said loudly.
"Well, now!" he said loudly.

1. As the firefighters moved their equipment into place, the police shouted, "Move back!."
2. A child's cries could be heard from above: "Help me. Help."
3. When the child was rescued, the crowd called "Hooray."
4. The rescue was the most exciting event of the day!
5. I can hardly wait to tell you about it.

EXERCISE 4

Insert appropriate punctuation (periods, question marks, or exclamation points) where needed in the following paragraph.

When visitors first arrive in Hawaii, they often encounter an unexpected language barrier Standard English is the language of business and government, but many of the people speak Pidgin English Instead of an excited "Aloha" the visitors may be greeted with an excited Pidgin "Howzit" or asked if they know "how fo' find one good hotel" Many Hawaiians question whether Pidgin will hold children back because it prevents communication with the *haoles*, or Caucasians, who run businesses Yet many others feel that Pidgin is a last defense of ethnic diversity on the islands To those who want to make standard English the official language of the state, these Hawaiians may respond, "Just 'cause I speak Pidgin no mean I dumb" They may ask, "Why you no listen" or, in standard English, "Why don't you listen"

NOTE: See page 440 for a punctuation exercise combining periods with other marks of punctuation such as commas and semicolons.

!
20f

CHAPTER 21

The Comma

The comma is the most frequently used—and misused—mark of internal punctuation. In general, commas function within sentences to separate elements (see the box on the next page). Commas also have several conventional uses, as in dates. Omitting needed commas or inserting needless ones can confuse the reader, as the following sentences show.

COMMA NEEDED	Though very mild-mannered Mackenzie King dominated federal politics for more than twenty years.
REVISED	Though very mild-mannered, Mackenzie King dominated federal politics for more than twenty years.
UNNEEDED COMMAS	The hectic pace of Beirut, broke suddenly into frightening chaos when the city became, the focus of civil war.
REVISED	The hectic pace of Beirut broke suddenly into frightening chaos when the city became the focus of civil war.

 21a Use a comma before a co-ordinating conjunction linking main clauses.

The co-ordinating conjunctions are

for	and	or	so	but	nor	yet

Words or phrases joined by a co-ordinating conjunction are *not* separated by a comma: *Bill plays and sings Irish and English folk songs* (see 21j-2). However, main clauses joined by a co-ordinating

PRINCIPAL USES OF THE COMMA

1. To separate main clauses linked by a co-ordinating conjunction (21a).

The steering was stiff, *but* the car rode smoothly.

2. To set off most introductory elements (21b).

Fortunately, the ride would be comfortable.

3. To set off non-restrictive elements (21c).

We dreaded the trip, *which would take sixteen hours.*

Our destination, *Winnipeg*, was unfamiliar to us.

4. To separate items in a series (21f-1).

We would need *a new home, new schools, and new friends.*

5. To separate co-ordinate adjectives (21f-1).

first adjective, second adjective, word modified

A *bumpy, cramped* ride would have been unbearable.

Other uses of the comma:

To set off absolute phrases (21d).
To set off phrases expressing contrast (21e).
To separate parts of dates, addresses, and long numbers (21g).
To separate quotations and explanatory words (21h).
To prevent misreading (21i).

See also 21j for when *not* to use the comma.

;
21a

conjunction *are* separated by a comma. Main clauses are those which have a subject and a predicate (but no subordinating word at the beginning) and make complete statements (see 5c).

> Montreal has been a strong centre of Canadian poetry since the 1930s, and undoubtedly the English-speaking poets in that city are stimulated to a certain degree by the presence of a vital French-Canadian tradition.   —GEORGE WOODCOCK

> The fact of speaking French and of having inherited French intellectual tradition does make us different, but in daily values we are wholly North American.   —LISE BISSONETTE

> Seventeen years ago this month I quit work, *or*, if you prefer, I retired from business.   —F. SCOTT FITZGERALD

> They made their decision with some uneasiness, *for* they knew that in such places any failure to conform could cause trouble.
> —RICHARD HARRIS

> In putting on trousers a man always inserts the same old leg first. . . . All men do it, *yet* no man thought it out and adopted it of set purpose.   —MARK TWAIN

> Near evening I was too jittery to attend to chores, *so* Bailey volunteered to do all before his bath.   —MAYA ANGELOU

EXCEPTIONS: Some writers prefer to use a semicolon before *so* and *yet*.

> Many people say that the institution of marriage is in decline; *yet* recent evidence suggests that the institution is at least holding steady.

When the main clauses in a sentence are very long or grammatically complicated, or when they contain internal punctuation, a semicolon before the co-ordinating conjunction will clarify the division between clauses (see 22c).

> Life would be dull without its seamier side, its violence, filth, and hatred; *for* otherwise how could we appreciate the joys?
> —ELLEN STEPIK

When main clauses are very short and closely related in meaning, you may omit the comma between them as long as the resulting sentence is clear.

> She opened her mouth *but* no sound came out of it.
> —FLANNERY O'CONNOR

> My heart raced *and* I felt ill.

If you are in doubt about whether to use a comma in such sentences, use it. It will always be correct.

EXERCISE 1

Insert a comma before each co-ordinating conjunction that links main clauses in the following sentences.

Example:

I would have attended the concert and the reception but I had to baby-sit for my niece.

I would have attended the concert and the reception, but I had to baby-sit for my niece.

1. Parents once automatically gave their children the father's surname but some no longer do.
2. Instead, they bestow the mother's name for they believe that the mother's importance should be recognized.
3. The child's surname may be just the mother's or it may link the mother's and the father's with a hyphen.
4. Sometimes the first and third children will have the mother's surname and the second child will have the father's.
5. Occasionally the mother and father combine parts of their names and a new hybrid surname is born.

EXERCISE 2

Combine each group of the following sentences into one sentence that contains only two main clauses connected by the co-ordinating conjunction in parentheses. Separate the main clauses with a comma. You will have to add, delete, and rearrange words.

Example:

The circus had come to town. The children wanted to see it. Their parents wanted to see it. (*and*)

The circus had come to town, *and* the children and their parents wanted to see it.

1. Parents were once legally required to bestow the father's surname on their children. These laws have been contested in court. They have been found invalid. (*but*)
2. Parents may now give their children any surname they choose. The arguments for bestowing the mother's surname are often strong. They are often convincing. (*and*)
3. Critics sometimes question the effects of unusual surnames on children. They wonder how confusing the new surnames will be. They wonder how fleeting the surnames will be. (*or*)
4. Children with surnames different from their parents' may suffer embarrassment. They may suffer identity problems. Giving children their father's surname is still very much the norm. (*for*)
5. Hyphenated names are awkward. They are also difficult to pass on. Some observers think they will die out in the next generation. Or they may die out before. (*so*)

21a

21b   Use a comma to set off most introductory elements.

An introductory element modifies a word or words in the main clause that follows. Such elements include subordinate clauses serving as adverbs (5c-4); participles, infinitives, and participial and infinitive phrases serving as adjectives and adverbs (5c-2); prepositional phrases (5c-1); and sentence modifiers such as *unfortunately*, *certainly*, and *of course*. These elements are usually set off from the rest of the sentence with a comma.

> *When the news was confirmed that the entire force was to be shipped west on the new railroad*, a kind of frenzy seized the country. [subordinate clause]   —PIERRE BERTON
>
> *Exhausted*, the runner collapsed at the finish line. [participle]
>
> *To win the most important race of her career*, she had nearly killed herself. [infinitive phrase]
>
> *From one point of view*, Canada appears to be an unlikely collection of regional and racial polarities. [prepositional phrase]
>
> *Unfortunately*, the diamond was fake. [sentence modifier]

The comma may be omitted following short introductory prepositional and infinitive phrases and subordinate clauses if its omission does not create confusion. (If you are in doubt, however, the comma is always correct.)

21b

CLEAR	*By the year 2000* the world population will be more than 6 billion. [prepositional phrase]
CLEAR	*To write clearly* one must think clearly. [infinitive phrase]
CLEAR	*When snow falls* the city collapses. [subordinate clause]
CONFUSING	At eighteen people are considered young adults.
REVISED	At eighteen, people are considered young adults.

NOTE: Take care to distinguish verbals used as modifiers from verbals used as subjects. The former almost always take a comma; the latter never do.

> *Jogging through the park*, I was unexpectedly caught in a downpour. [participial phrase used as modifier]
>
> *Jogging through the park* has become a popular form of recreation for city dwellers. [gerund phrase used as subject]
>
> *To dance professionally*, he trained for years. [infinitive phrase used as modifier]

To dance professionally is his one desire. [infinitive phrase used as subject]

In addition, do not use a comma to separate a verbal from the noun or pronoun it modifies when the verbal restricts the meaning of the noun or pronoun (see also 21c).

Shuttered houses lined the street. [*Shuttered* restricts *houses*.]

Shuttered, the houses were protected from the elements. [*Shuttered* does not restrict *houses*.]

EXERCISE 3

Insert commas where needed after introductory elements in the following sentences. If a sentence is punctuated correctly as given, circle the number preceding it.

Example:

After the new library opened the old one became a student union.

After the new library opened, the old one became a student union.

1. Veering sharply to the right a large flock of birds neatly avoids a high wall.
2. Moving in a fluid mass is typical of flocks of birds and schools of fish.
3. With the help of complex computer simulations zoologists are learning more about this movement.
4. Because it is sudden and apparently well co-ordinated the movement of flocks and schools has seemed to be directed by a leader.
5. Almost incredibly the group could behave with more intelligence than any individual seemed to possess.
6. However new studies have discovered that flocks and schools are leaderless.
7. Evading danger turns out to be an individual response.
8. When each bird or fish senses a predator it follows individual rules for fleeing.
9. To keep from colliding with its neighbours each bird or fish uses other rules for dodging.
10. Multiplied over hundreds of individuals these responses look as if they have been choreographed.

EXERCISE 4

Combine each of the following pairs of sentences into one sentence that begins with an introductory phrase or clause as specified in parentheses. Follow the introductory element with a comma. You will have to add, delete, change, and rearrange words.

21b

Example:

The girl was humming to herself. She walked upstairs. (*phrase beginning Humming*)

Humming to herself, the girl walked up the stairs.

1. Scientists have made an effort to explain the mysteries of flocks and schools. They have proposed bizarre magnetic fields and telepathy. (*phrase beginning In*)
2. Scientists developed computer models. They have abandoned earlier explanations. (*clause beginning Since*)
3. The movement of a flock or school starts with each individual. It is rapidly and perhaps automatically co-ordinated among individuals. (*phrase beginning Starting*)
4. One zoologist observes that human beings seek coherent patterns. He suggests that investigators saw purpose in the movement of flocks and schools where none existed. (*phrase beginning Observing*)
5. One may want to study the movement of flocks or schools. Then one must abandon a search for purpose or design. (*phrase beginning To*)

21c Use a comma or commas to set off non-restrictive elements.

Restrictive and non-restrictive sentence elements contribute differently to meaning and require different punctuation. A **restrictive element** limits, or restricts, the meaning of the word or words it applies to. Thus it is essential to the meaning of the sentence and cannot be omitted without significantly changing that meaning. Restrictive elements are never set off with punctuation.

RESTRICTIVE ELEMENT

Employees *who work hard* will receive raises.

A **non-restrictive element** gives added information about the word or words it applies to, but it does not limit the word or words. It can be omitted from the sentence without changing the essential meaning. Non-restrictive elements are always set off with punctuation.

NON-RESTRICTIVE ELEMENT

Jacqueline Blanc, *who lives next door*, got a raise.

The relation of restriction and punctuation is an inverse one: when the element is *not* essential, the punctuation *is*; and when the element *is* essential, the punctuation is *not*.

Commas are most commonly used to set off non-restrictive elements, although dashes or parentheses are sometimes used to emphasize or de-emphasize them (see 25b-2 and 25c-1, respectively, and especially the box on p. 432). Whatever punctuation mark you select, be sure to use a pair if the non-restrictive element falls in the middle of a sentence—one *before* and another *after* the element.

A test can help you determine whether a sentence element is restrictive or non-restrictive: Does the fundamental meaning of the sentence change when the element is removed? It does in the restrictive example given for *Employees will receive raises* does not provide the same information about employees as the original sentence did. The employees are no longer defined or limited to a specific group, the ones who work hard, but instead encompass all employees, whatever their work habits. Conversely, *Jacqueline Blanc got a raise* has essentially the same meaning as the original non-restrictive example. No matter where Jacqueline Blanc lives, she still got the raise.

The presence or absence of commas around a sentence element can change the meaning of a single sentence, as the following examples illustrate.

> The band *playing old music* held the audience's attention.
>
> The band, *playing old music*, held the audience's attention.

In the first sentence the absence of commas restricts the subject to a particular band, the one playing old music, and thus implies that more than one band played more than one kind of music. In the second sentence, however, the commas setting off the phrase imply that only one band played, because the phrase does not restrict the subject to a particular band. Which punctuation is correct depends on the writer's intended meaning and on the context in which the sentence appears. For example:

RESTRICTIVE

A new band called Fats made its debut on Saturday night. The band *playing old music* held the audience's attention. The other groups created much less excitement.

NON-RESTRICTIVE

A new band called Fats made its debut on Saturday night. The band, *playing old music*, held the audience's attention. If this performance is typical, the group has a bright future.

21c

1 Use a comma or commas to set off non-restrictive clauses and phrases.

Clauses and phrases serving as adjectives and adverbs may be either non-restrictive or restrictive. Only non-restrictive clauses and phrases are set off with punctuation, as the following examples illustrate.

NON-RESTRICTIVE CLAUSES

Three-year-old Nancy, *whose blue eyes shone with mischief,* had to be rescued more than once from her adventures. [Compare *Three-year-old Nancy had to be rescued more than once from her adventures.* The look of the child's eyes does not restrict the meaning.]

Newfoundland, *which entered Confederation in 1949,* became Canada's tenth province. [Compare *Newfoundland became Canada's tenth province.* The meaning of the subject is unchanged.]

Both traditions were so mature they had become almost decadent, *while Canada herself was still raw.* [Compare *Both traditions were so mature they had become almost decadent.* The meaning of the main clause remains the same.]   —HUGH MACLENNAN

NOTE: Most subordinate clauses serving as adverbs are restrictive because they describe conditions necessary to the main clause. They are set off by a comma only when they introduce sentences (see 21b) and when they are truly non-restrictive, adding incidental information (as in the last example above) or expressing a contrast beginning *although, even though, though, whereas,* and the like.

NON-RESTRICTIVE PHRASES

21c

The Saskatchewan Legislative Building, *at one end of a beautiful floral mall,* is Regina's most dominant landmark. [Compare *The Saskatchewan Legislative Building is Regina's most dominant landmark.* The building's name identifies it; the reference to the floral mall is merely an additional but non-essential detail.]

The library's most valuable book, *bought at an auction in 1962,* is a thirteenth-century Bible. [Compare *The library's most valuable book is a thirteenth-century Bible.* Assuming that a more valuable book was not purchased in some other year, the details of the Bible's purchase do not restrict it further.]

He beat the other runners, *reaching the finish line in record time.* [Compare *He beat the other runners.* The meaning of the main clause remains the same.]

NOTE: When a participial phrase is separated from the noun or pronoun it modifies, as in the last example above, a comma is essential to clarify that the phrase does not modify the word closest to it. Without the comma, the reader automatically connects the phrase to *runners: He beat the other runners reaching the finish line in record time.*

RESTRICTIVE CLAUSES

Every question *that has a reasonable answer* is justifiable. [Compare *Every question is justifiable*, which clearly alters the writer's meaning.] —KONRAD LORENZ

He wore the look of one *who knows he is the victim of a terrible disease and understands his helplessness*. [Compare *He wore the look of one*. Without its modifying clause, *one* is meaningless.] —STEPHEN CRANE

Books fall apart *when they are not well bound*. [Compare *Books fall apart*, which omits the limiting circumstances and thus implies that all books always fall apart. See the note on the preceding page about adverb clauses.]

RESTRICTIVE PHRASES

A student *seeking an easy course* should not enrol *in History 101*. [Compare *A student should not enrol*, which fails to limit the kind of student who should not enrol and does not specify the course to be avoided.]

The ongoing taboo *against women dating men shorter than themselves* is among the strictest of this society. [Compare *The ongoing taboo is among the strictest of this society*, which no longer specifies what taboo.] —RALPH KEYES

The sealed crates *containing the records of my past* were drawn from storage and opened. [Compare *The sealed crates were drawn from storage and opened*. The crates are no longer limited by their contents.] —JOHN GREGORY DUNNE

NOTE: Whereas both non-restrictive and restrictive clauses may begin with *which*, only restrictive clauses begin with *that*. Some writers prefer *that* exclusively for restrictive clauses and *which* exclusively for non-restrictive clauses. See the "Glossary of Usage," page 747, for advice on the use of *that* and *which*.

2 Use a comma or commas to set off non-restrictive appositives.

An **appositive** is a noun or noun substitute that renames and could substitute for another noun immediately preceding it. (See 5c-5.) Many appositives are non-restrictive; thus they are set off, usually with commas. Take care *not* to set off restrictive appositives; like restrictive phrases and clauses, they limit or define the noun or nouns they refer to.

NON-RESTRICTIVE APPOSITIVES

The Chapman lighthouse, *a three-legged thing erect on a mud-flat*, shone strongly. [Compare *The Chapman lighthouse shone strongly*.] —JOSEPH CONRAD

Alice Munro's 1986 book of short stories, *The Progress of Love*, won the Governor General's medal for fiction. [Compare *Alice Munro's 1986 book of short stories won the Governor General's 1986 medal for fiction.*]

RESTRICTIVE APPOSITIVES

Paul Scott's novel *The Jewel in the Crown* is about India under British rule. [Compare *Paul Scott's novel is about India under British rule*, which implies wrongly that Scott wrote only one novel.]

The philosopher *Alfred North Whitehead* once wrote that the history of philosophy was a series of footnotes to Plato. [Compare *The philosopher once wrote that the history of philosophy was a series of footnotes to Plato.*]

Our language has adopted the words *garage, panache, and fanfare* from French. [Compare *Our language has adopted the words from French.*]

3 Use a comma or commas to set off parenthetical expressions.

Parenthetical expressions are explanatory, supplementary, or transitional words or phrases. (Transitional expressions include *however, indeed, consequently, as a result, of course, for example*, and *in fact*; see 3b-6 for a longer list.) Parenthetical expressions are usually set off by a comma or commas.

21c

The Cubist painters, *for example*, were obviously inspired by the families of crystals.   —JACOB BRONOWSKI

The only option, *besides locking him up*, was to release him to his parents' custody.

The film is one of Jewison's best, *according to the judgment of the critics*.

Any writer, *I suppose*, feels that the world into which he was born is nothing less than a conspiracy against the cultivation of his talent.
                                                             —JAMES BALDWIN

(Dashes and parentheses may also set off parenthetical elements. See 25b-2 and 25c-1, respectively, and see especially the box on p. 432.)

4 Use a comma or commas to set off *yes* and *no*, tag questions, words of direct address, and mild interjections.

YES AND NO

Yes, the editorial did have a point.
No, that can never be.

Tag questions

Jones should be allowed to vote, *should he not?*
They don't stop to consider others, *do they?*

Direct address

Cody, please bring me the newspaper.
With all due respect, *sir*, I will not do that.

Mild interjections

Well, you will never know who did it.
Oh, they forgot all about the baby.

(You may want to use exclamation points to set off forceful interjections. See 20e.)

21c

EXERCISE 5

Insert commas in the following sentences to set off non-restrictive elements, and delete any commas that incorrectly set off restrictive elements. If a sentence is correct as given, circle the number preceding it.

Example:

Emily Stowe who was the first Canadian woman to practise medicine in Canada championed women's rights for forty years.

Emily Stowe, who was the first Canadian woman to practise medicine in Canada, championed women's rights for forty years.

1. Italians insist that Marco Polo the thirteenth-century explorer did not import pasta from China.
2. Pasta which consists of flour and water and often egg existed in Italy long before Marco Polo left for his travels.
3. A historian who studied pasta places its origin in the Middle East in the fifth century.
4. Most Italians dispute this account although their evidence is shaky.
5. Wherever it originated, the Italians are now the undisputed masters, in making and cooking pasta.
6. Marcella Hazan, who has written several books on Italian cooking, insists that homemade and hand-rolled pasta is the best.
7. Most cooks must buy dried pasta lacking the time to make their own.

8. The finest pasta is made from semolina, a flour from hard durum wheat.
9. Pasta manufacturers choose hard durum wheat, because it makes firmer cooked pasta than common wheat does.
10. Pasta, made from common wheat, tends to get soggy in boiling water.

EXERCISE 6

Combine each pair of sentences below into one sentence that uses the element described in parentheses. Insert commas as appropriate. You will have to add, delete, change, and rearrange words. Some items have more than one possible answer.

Example:
Mr. Ward's oldest sister helped keep him alive. She was a doctor in the hospital. (*non-restrictive clause beginning* who)
Mr. Ward's oldest sister, *who was a doctor in the hospital*, helped keep him alive.

1. Most sources say it was the Italians. The Italians introduced pasta as a main dish. (*restrictive clause beginning* who)
2. The Italians use the word to mean only tubular pasta. The word is *macaroni*. (*restrictive appositive*)
3. North American manufacturers use *macaroni* to mean all flour-and-water pasta. These manufacturers are unlike the Italians. (*non-restrictive phrase beginning* unlike)
4. North Americans also use *spaghetti* for all flour-and-water pasta. The meaning is "little strings" in Italian. (*non-restrictive phrase beginning* meaning)
5. North American colonists first imported pasta from the English. The English had discovered it as tourists in Italy. (*non-restrictive clause beginning* who)
6. The English returned from their grand tours of Italy. They were called *macaronis* because of their fancy airs. (*restrictive phrase beginning* returning)
7. A hairstyle was also called *macaroni*. It had elaborate curls. (*restrictive phrase beginning* with)
8. The song "Yankee Doodle" refers to this hairdo. It reports that Yankee Doodle "stuck a feather in his cap and called it macaroni." (*restrictive clause beginning* when)
9. The song was actually intended to poke fun at unrefined North American colonists. It was a creation of the English. (*non-restrictive appositive*)
10. The colonists adopted the jolly tune. They turned it to their advantage. (*non-restrictive phrase beginning* turning)

21c

21d Use a comma or commas to set off absolute phrases.

An **absolute phrase** modifies a whole main clause rather than any word or word group in the clause; it is not connected to the rest of the sentence by a conjunction, preposition, or relative pronoun. (See 5c-3.) Absolute phrases usually consist of at least a participle and its subject (a noun or pronoun), as in the following:

Their work finished, the men quit for the day.

Absolute constructions can occur at almost any point in the sentence. Whatever their position, they are always set off by a comma or commas.

Their homework done, the children may watch whatever they want on television.

After reaching Eagle Rock, we pointed our canoes toward shore, *the rapids ahead being rough*.

His clothes, *the fabric tattered and the seams ripped open*, looked like Salvation Army rejects.

EXERCISE 7

Insert commas in the following sentences to set off absolute constructions.

Example:

The recording contract was cancelled the band having broken up.

The recording contract was cancelled, the band having broken up.

1. The election having ended officials felt somewhat secure in their posts.
2. Prices having risen rapidly the government debated a price freeze.
3. A price freeze was no one's perfect solution the measure being always controversial.
4. Businesses their profits otherwise made vulnerable would demand a wage freeze as well.
5. They would threaten employee layoffs their threats carrying some weight with the Prime Minister.
6. A price freeze would be welcomed by labour workers' incomes already suffering from inflation.
7. Workers their real income having been eaten away by rising prices and taxes would resist any wage freeze.
8. The Prime Minister would have to persuade businesses to accept a price freeze his methods depending on their recalcitrance.

9. No doubt the Prime Minister his advisers having urged it would first try a patriotic appeal.
10. Arm-twisting having worked for previous Prime Ministers this one might resort to it.

21e Use a comma or commas to set off phrases expressing contrast.

The essay needs less wit, *more pith*.

His generosity, *not his good looks*, won him friends.

Style is the manner of a sentence, *not its matter*.   —DONALD HALL

It is not light that is needed, *but fire*; it is not the gentle shower, *but thunder*.   —FREDERICK DOUGLASS

NOTE: Writers often omit commas around contrasting phrases beginning *but*.

His life was long *but sadly empty*.   —HERMAN CRATSLEY

EXERCISE 8

Insert commas in the following sentences to set off phrases that express contrast.

Example:
Moira not her sister was the one who attended university in Nova Scotia.

Moira, not her sister, was the one who attended university in Nova Scotia.

1. The expense of heating homes not just the cold makes the winter months difficult in most parts of Canada.
2. Many people must forego necessities not just luxuries to pay their heating bills.
3. People use their gas ovens more for heat less for cooking.
4. Using a gas oven for heat is extremely dangerous not safe as many people believe.
5. The gas fumes not the flames are the source of danger.

21f Use commas between items in a series and between co-ordinate adjectives.

1 Use commas between words, phrases, or clauses forming a series.

Place commas between all elements of a **series**—that is, three or more items of equal importance.

The names *Belial, Beelzebub, and Lucifer* sound ominous.

He felt cut off from them *by age, by understanding, by sensibility, by technology, and by his need to measure himself against the mirror of other men's appreciation.*   —RALPH ELLISON

The ox was *solid black, stood five feet high at the shoulder, had a five-foot span of horns, and must have weighed 1,200 pounds on the hoof.*   —RICHARD B. LEE

Though some writers omit the comma before the co-ordinating conjunction in a series (*Breakfast consisted of coffee, eggs and kippers*), the final comma is never wrong and it always helps the reader see the last two items as separate. Use it consistently and your writing will be clearer, as the following example shows.

> **CONFUSING**   The job involves typing, answering the phone, filing and reading manuscripts.
>
> **CLEAR**   The job involves typing, answering the phone, filing, and reading manuscripts.

EXCEPTION: When items in a series are long and grammatically complicated, they may be separated by semicolons. When the items contain commas, they must be separated by semicolons. (See 22d).

21f   **2**   **Use commas between co-ordinate adjectives not linked by conjunctions.**

Co-ordinate adjectives are two or more adjectives that modify equally the same noun or pronoun. The individual adjectives are separated either by co-ordinating conjunctions or by commas.

> The *sleek* and *shiny* car was a credit to the neighbourhood.
>
> The *dirty, rusty, dented* car was an eyesore.
>
> Nothing is more essential to *intelligent, profitable* reading than sensitivity to connotation.   —RICHARD ALTICK

Adjectives are not co-ordinate—and should *not* be separated by commas—when the one nearer the noun is more closely related to the noun in meaning.

> The house overflowed with *ornate electric* fixtures. [*Ornate* modifies *electric fixtures*.]
>
> The museum's most valuable object is a *sparkling diamond* necklace. [*Sparkling* modifies *diamond necklace*.]

Two tests will help you determine whether adjectives are co-ordinate: (1) Can the adjectives be rearranged without changing the meaning? (2) Can the word *and* be inserted between the adjectives without changing the meaning? If the answer to both these questions is *yes*, then the adjectives are co-ordinate. In the sentence *She was a faithful sincere friend*, the adjectives can be rearranged (*sincere faithful friend*, and they can be separated by *and* (*faithful and sincere friend*). Thus the adjectives are co-ordinate, and a comma belongs between them: *She was a faithful, sincere friend*. However, in the sentence *They are dedicated medical students*, the adjectives cannot be rearranged (*medical dedicated students*) or separated by *and* (*dedicated and medical students*). Thus the adjectives are not co-ordinate, and no comma belongs between them.

Notice that numbers are not co-ordinate with other adjectives.

FAULTY	Among the junk in the attic was *one, lovely* vase.
REVISED	Among the junk in the attic was *one lovely vase.*

Do not use a comma between the final co-ordinate adjective and the noun.

FAULTY	Travelling through the Rockies by train is a stirring, spectacular, experience.
REVISED	Travelling through the Rockies by train is a stirring, spectacular experience.

21f

EXERCISE 9

Insert commas in the following sentences to separate co-ordinate adjectives or elements in a series. Circle the number preceding each sentence whose punctuation is already correct.

Example:

Although quiet by day, the club became a noisy smoky dive at night.

Although quiet by day, the club became a noisy, smoky dive at night.

1. Shoes with high heels originated to protect feet from the mud garbage and animal waste in the streets.
2. The first known high heels worn strictly for fashion appeared in the sixteenth century.
3. The heels were worn by men and made of colourful silk brocades soft suedes or smooth leathers.
4. High-heeled shoes received a boost when the short powerful King Louis XIV of France began wearing them.
5. Louis's influence was so strong that men and women of the court priests and cardinals and even household servants donned high heels.
6. Eventually only wealthy fashionable French women wore high heels.

7. In the seventeenth and eighteenth centuries, French culture represented the one true standard of elegance and refinement.
8. High-heeled shoes for women spread to other courts most European and North American countries and almost all social classes.
9. Now high heels are commonplace, though their heights and shapes undergo wide often baffling swings.
10. A Paris store recently showed a pair of purple satin pumps with tiny jewelled bows and 10-cm stiletto heels.

21g   Use commas according to convention in dates, addresses, and place names.

The items in a date, address, or place name are conventionally separated with commas, as illustrated below. When they appear within sentences, dates, addresses, and place names punctuated with commas are also ended with commas.

DATES

April 17, 1982, was the day Queen Elizabeth II signed the Constitution Act that patriated Canada's constitution.

Canada's declaration of war on Germany on September 10, 1939, occurred more than one week after Britain's declaration.

Commas are not used between the parts of a date in inverted order: *Their anniversary on 15 December 1982 was their fiftieth.* Commas need not be used in dates consisting of a month or season and a year: *Lester B. Pearson served as leader of the Liberal Party from January 1958 to April 1968.*

ADDRESSES AND PLACE NAMES

Use the address 49 Nanook Cres., Kanata, Ontario, for all correspondence.

Send inquiries to Box 72, Corner Brook, Newfoundland.

Brandon, Manitoba, is the location of Assiniboine Community College.

Commas are not used between province names and postal codes in Canadian addresses when these appear on the same line, although two spaces are left preceding postal codes, or between state names and zip codes in U.S. addresses:

Box 124, Abbotsford, BC V2S 4N8, is going to be my new address.
Poetry submissions sent to Box 49, Berkeley, CA 94720, must be postmarked by October 31 at the latest.

EXERCISE 10

Insert commas as needed in the following sentences.

Example:

One fund-raising event will be held on June 24 1992 and the other in late January 1993.

One fund-raising event will be held on June 24, 1992, and the other in late January 1993.

1. The Scotia Festival of Music will hold a benefit dinner and performance on September 24 1992 in Halifax.
2. Performers are expected from as far away as St. John's Newfoundland and Thunder Bay Ontario.
3. All inquiries sent to Scotia Festival of Music 1541 Barrington St. Suite 317 Halifax NS B3J 1Z5 will receive a quick response.
4. The deadline for ordering tickets by mail is Friday August 24, 1992.

 Use commas with quotations according to standard practice.

The words used to explain a quotation (*he said, she replied,* and so on) may come before, after, or in the middle of the quotation. They must always be separated from the quotation by punctuation, usually a comma or commas. (See pp. 420–21 for a summary of conventions regarding quotations.)

21h

1 **Ordinarily, use a comma to separate introductory and concluding explanatory words from quotations.**

General Sherman summed up the attitude of all thoughtful soldiers when he said, "War is hell."

"Knowledge is power," wrote Francis Bacon.

EXCEPTIONS: Do not use a comma when explanatory words follow a quotation ending in an exclamation point or a question mark (see 20c and 20e).

"Claude!" Mrs. Harrison called.

"Why must I come home?" he asked.

Do not use commas with a quotation introduced by *that* or with a short quotation in a sentence that does more than merely introduce or explain the quotation.

The warning that "cigarette smoking is dangerous to your health" has fallen on many deaf ears.

People should always say "Excuse me" when they bump into fellow pedestrians.

Use a colon instead of a comma to separate explanatory words from a quotation when there is an emphatic break between them in meaning or in grammar or when the quotation is very formal or longer than a sentence. (See also 25a.) For instance:

> The 1982 Constitution Act is unequivocal: "English and French are the official languages of Canada and have equality of status and equal rights and privileges as to their use in all institutions of the Parliament and government of Canada."

2 Use a comma after the first part of a quotation interrupted by explanatory words. Follow the explanatory words with the punctuation required by the quotation.

QUOTATION

"When you got nothin', you got nothin' to lose."

EXPLANATORY WORDS

"When you got nothin'," Kris Kristofferson sings, "you got nothin' to lose." [The explanatory words interrupt the quotation at a comma and thus end with a comma.]

QUOTATION

"That part of my life was over; his words had sealed it shut."

EXPLANATORY WORDS

"That part of my life was over," she wrote; "his words had sealed it shut." [The explanatory words interrupt the quotation at a semicolon and thus end with a semicolon.]

QUOTATION

"One of the few shared sentiments of all regions of Canada is an unreasoning dislike of Toronto. Unreasoning, because the Toronto loathed throughout Canada has pretty well ceased to exist."
—KILDARE DOBBS

EXPLANATORY WORDS

"One of the few shared sentiments of all regions of Canada is an unreasoning dislike of Toronto," observed Kildare Dobbs almost twenty-five years ago. "Unreasoning, because the Toronto loathed throughout Canada has pretty well ceased to exist." [The explanatory words interrupt the quotation at the end of a sentence and thus end with a period.]

21h

NOTE: Using a comma instead of a semicolon or a period in the last two examples would result in the error called a comma splice: two main clauses separated only by a comma, without a linking co-ordinating conjunction. (See 11a.)

3 **Place commas that follow quotations within quotation marks.**

"That's my seat," she said coldly.

"You gave it up," I replied evenly, "so you have no right to it."

EXERCISE 11

Insert commas or semicolons in the following sentences to correct punctuation with quotations. Circle the number preceding any sentence whose punctuation is already correct.

> *Example:*
> The shoplifter declared "I didn't steal anything."
> The shoplifter declared, "I didn't steal anything."

1. The writer and writing teacher Peter Elbow suggests that an "open-ended writing process . . . can change you, not just your words."
2. "I think of the open-ended writing process as a voyage in two stages" Elbow says.
3. "The sea voyage is a process of divergence, branching, proliferation, and confusion" Elbow continues "the coming to land is a process of convergence, pruning, centralizing, and clarifying."
4. "Keep up one session of writing long enough to get loosened up and tired" advises Elbow "long enough in fact to make a bit of a voyage."
5. "In coming to new land" Elbow says "you develop a new conception of what you are writing about."

21i

21i **Use commas to prevent misreading.**

The comma tells the reader to pause slightly before moving on. In some sentences words may run together in unintended and confusing ways unless a comma separates them. Use a comma in such sentences even though no rule requires one.

CONFUSING	Soon after she left town for good. [A short introductory phrase does not require a comma, but clarity requires it in this sentence.]
REVISED	Soon after, she left town for good.
CONFUSING	The students who can usually give some money to the United Way. [Without a comma the sentence seems incomplete.]
REVISED	The students who can, usually give some money to the United Way.

EXERCISE 12

Insert commas in the following sentences to prevent misreading.

Example:

To Laura Ann symbolized decadence.

To Laura, Ann symbolized decadence.

1. Though happy people still have moments of self-doubt.
2. In research subjects have reported themselves to be generally happy people.
3. Yet those who have described sufferings as well as joys.
4. Of fifty eight subjects reported bouts of serious depression.
5. For half the preceding year had included at least one personal crisis.

21j

21j Avoid misusing or overusing the comma.

Although commas are useful and often necessary to signal pauses in sentences, they can make sentences choppy and even confusing if they are used more often than needed or in violation of rules 21a through 21h. Examine every sentence you write to be sure you have used commas appropriately.

1 Don't use a comma to separate a subject from its verb, or a verb or a preposition from its object, unless the words between them require punctuation.

| FAULTY | The returning *athletes, expected* a warmer welcome than they received. [separation of subject and verb] |
| REVISED | The returning *athletes expected* a warmer welcome then they received. |

FAULTY	After deciding that she could do one but not both, my sister *chose, to have children* rather than pursue a career. [separation of verb and object]
REVISED	After deciding that she could do one but not both, my sister *chose to have children* rather than pursue a career.
FAULTY	Amazingly, the refund arrived *after, only three weeks*. [separation of preposition and object]
REVISED	Amazingly, the refund arrived *after only three weeks*.

In the following sentence, commas are needed to set off the non-restrictive clause that interrupts subject and verb (see 21c).

Canadians, who are preoccupied with other sports, have not developed a strong interest in supporting professional basketball.

2 Don't use a comma to separate words or phrases joined by co-ordinating conjunctions.

FAULTY	*The defence attorney, and the presiding judge* disagreed with the verdict. [compound subject]
REVISED	*The defence attorney and the presiding judge* disagreed with the verdict.
FAULTY	Television advertising is *expensive, and sometimes very effective*. [compound complement]
REVISED	Television advertising is *expensive and sometimes very effective*.
FAULTY	The use of *cocaine, and other harmful drugs* is increasing alarmingly. [compound object of a preposition]
REVISED	The use of *cocaine and other harmful drugs* is increasing alarmingly.
FAULTY	The boys *hiked up the mountain, and camped for the night* on the summit. [compound predicate]
REVISED	The boys *hiked up the mountain and camped for the night* on the summit.
FAULTY	Banks *could, and should* help older people manage their money. [compound helping verb]
REVISED	Banks *could and should* help older people manage their money.

21j

See 21a and 21f-1, respectively, for the appropriate use of commas with co-ordinating conjunctions when they link main clauses or elements in a series.

3 Don't use commas to set off restrictive elements.

FAULTY	The land, *that both families claim as theirs*, is mostly swamp. [The clause beginning *that* restricts the meaning of the subject *land*.]
REVISED	The land *that both families claim as theirs* is mostly swamp.
FAULTY	Brooke's sentimental romance, *The History of Emily Montague* (1769), is often deemed to be the first Canadian novel. [The title of the novel is essential to distinguish the novel from the rest of Brooke's work.]
REVISED	Brooke's sentimental romance *The History of Emily Montague* (1769) is often deemed to be the first Canadian novel.
FAULTY	Birds, *heading south*, signal the end, *of summer*. [*Heading south* limits *birds*, and *of summer* limits *end*.]
REVISED	Birds *heading south* signal the end *of summer*.
FAULTY	Buckle your seat belt, *whenever you travel by car*. [The clause specifies when to buckle up.]
REVISED	Buckle your seat belt *whenever you travel by car*.

(See 21c for further discussion of identifying and punctuating non-restrictive and restrictive elements in sentences.)

4 Don't use a comma before the first or after the last item in a series unless a rule requires it.

FAULTY	The *forsythia, daffodils, and tulips,* turned the garden into a rush of colour. [The comma after *tulips* separates subject and verb.]
REVISED	The *forsythia, daffodils, and tulips* turned the garden into a rush of colour.
FAULTY	Among other things, the Europeans brought to the New World, *horses, advanced technology, and*

21j

new diseases. [The comma after *World* separates verb and object.]

REVISED   Among other things, the Europeans brought to the New World *horses, advanced technology, and new diseases.*

In the following sentence the commas before and after the series are appropriate because the series is a non-restrictive appositive (see 21c-2).

The three Prairie provinces, *Alberta, Saskatchewan, and Manitoba,* share similar historical and cultural backgrounds.

However, many writers prefer to use dashes rather than commas to set off series functioning as appositives (see 25b-2).

(See 21f-1 for further discussion of punctuating series.)

5   Don't use commas to set off an indirect quotation or a single word unless it is a non-restrictive appositive.

INDIRECT QUOTATION

FAULTY   The students asked, why they had to take a test the day before vacation.

REVISED   The students asked why they had to take a test the day before vacation.

QUOTED OR ITALIZED WORD

FAULTY   James Joyce's story, "Araby," was assigned last year, too. [The story title is a restrictive appositive. The commas imply wrongly that Joyce wrote only one story.]

REVISED   James Joyce's story "Araby" was assigned last year too.

FAULTY   The word, *open,* can be both a verb and an adjective. [*Open* is a restrictive appositive.]

REVISED   The word *open* can be both a verb and an adjective.

The following sentence requires commas because the quoted title is a non-restrictive appositive.

Hugh MacLennan's first published novel, *Barometer Rising,* ushered in a new phase in Canadian literary production.

(See 21c-2 for more on punctuating appositives.)

21j

EXERCISE 13

Revise the following sentences to eliminate needless or misused commas. Circle the number preceding each sentence that is already punctuated correctly.

Example:

The portrait of the founder, that hung in the dining hall, was stolen by pranksters.

The portrait of the founder that hung in the dining hall was stolen by pranksters.

1. In Greek mythology Theseus is protected by the god, Poseidon.
2. Theseus is an adventurer, and a hero of the Athenians.
3. In one of his adventures Theseus sails, to Crete, to kill the Minotaur, which has been devouring young Athenians.
4. The Minotaur, half-bull and half-human, is kept by the king of Crete, Minos, in his maze-like palace.
5. Each year Minos captures fourteen young Athenians, and throws them to the Minotaur in revenge for the death of his son in Athens.
6. When Theseus arrives in Crete, Minos challenges him by, throwing a gold ring into the sea and ordering him to retrieve it.
7. Under the water Theseus meets a woman, who is Poseidon's wife and who hands him the ring to return to Minos.
8. Theseus later meets Minos's only daughter, Ariadne, and she gives him a ball of string so that he can find his way out of the maze.
9. She warns, that the Minotaur's victims have been too exhausted from being lost in the maze to fight for their lives.
10. With a ball of string Theseus can leave a trail behind him, and find his way through, and out of the maze.
11. Theseus does, as Ariadne urges, and conserves the energy, needed to kill the Minotaur.
12. He also rescues some youths, whom the Minotaur has not yet killed.
13. Theseus, the youths, and Ariadne, all flee from Crete in Theseus's ship.
14. They travel to the island, of Naxos, where Theseus deserts Ariadne.
15. One version of the myth explains, that another god, Dionysus, orders Theseus away so that he can have Ariadne for himself.

EXERCISE 14

Insert commas in the following paragraph wherever they are needed, and eliminate any misused or needless commas.

21j

Canadian sport is indebted to the Indian for the toboggan snow-shoe lacrosse stick and canoe. The coureurs de bois and the voyageurs through their close contact with the Indians, helped introduce into European settlements the activities, that resulted from the use of these pieces of equipment. Many Indian games had utilitarian purposes related to survival (e.g., wrestling jousting archery spear-throwing and foot and canoe racing) while activities such as dancing and baggataway . . . had religious significance. The Indians also developed a great variety of games such as awl games ring and pole snow snake cat's cradle dice and birchbark cards partly for the sheer love of play, and sometimes for the purpose of gambling. The games of the Inuit, were similarly related to preparing youth for co-operative existence in a harsh environment where one also needed to know one's tolerance limits. Blanket toss tug-of-war dogsled races drum dances spear-throwing and ball games as well as self-testing games, such as arm-pull hand-wrestling and finger-pull helped to fulfil this purpose. Gambling was common and even useful because it served to redistribute surplus goods.

NOTE: See page 440 for a punctuation exercise combining commas with other marks of punctuation such as semicolons and colons.

21j

CHAPTER 22

The Semicolon

| **22a** | Use a semicolon to separate main clauses not joined by a co-ordinating conjunction. |

Main clauses contain a subject and a predicate and do not begin with a subordinating word (see 5c). They may be linked by a co-ordinating conjunction such as *and* or *but* and then separated by a comma (see 21a). But when no co-ordinating conjunction is present, the clauses should be separated with a semicolon.

> I was not led to the university by conventional middle-class ambitions; my grip on the middle class was more tenuous than that on the school system. —ROBIN FOX

The box opposite distinguishes among the principal uses of three often-confused marks: semicolon, comma, and colon. In choosing among the three marks that separate main clauses—the semicolon, the comma with a co-ordinating conjunction, and the period— you need to decide what effect you want to achieve. A semicolon provides less separation between main clauses than a period and more separation than a comma with a co-ordinating conjunction. Generally, the semicolon is most appropriate when the first clause creates some suspense—some expectation in the reader that an equally important and complementary statement is coming. The semicolon then provides a pause before the second clause fulfils the expectation.

> Directing movies was only one of his ambitions; he also wanted to direct theatrical productions of Shakespeare's plays.

NOTE: If you do not link main clauses with a co-ordinating conjunction and you separate them only with a comma or with no punctuation at all, you will produce a comma splice or a fused sentence. See Chapter 11.

DISTINGUISHING THE COMMA, THE SEMICOLON, AND THE COLON

The **comma** chiefly separates both equal and unequal sentence elements.

—It separates main clauses when they are linked by a co-ordinating conjunction (21a).

An airline once tried to boost sales by advertising the tense alertness of its crews, *but* nervous fliers did not want to hear about pilots' sweaty palms.

—It separates subordinate information that is part of or attached to a main clause, such as a non-restrictive modifier or an introductory element (21b–21h).

Although the airline campaign failed, many advertising agencies, including some clever ones, copied its underlying message.

The **semicolon** chiefly separates equal and balanced sentence elements.

—It separates complementary main clauses that are *not* linked by a co-ordinating conjunction (22a).

The airline campaign had highlighted only half the story; the other half was buried in the copy.

—It separates complementary main clauses that are related by a conjunctive adverb (22b).

The campaign should not have stressed the seller's insecurity; *instead,* the campaign should have stressed the improved performance resulting from that insecurity.

The **colon** chiefly separates unequal sentence elements.

—It separates a main clause from a following explanation or summary, not necessarily a complete main clause (25a).

Many successful advertising campaigns have used this message: anxious seller as harder working and smarter than the competition.

;
22a

EXCEPTION: Writers sometimes use a comma instead of a semicolon between very short and closely parallel main clauses.

The poor live, the rich just exist.

But a semicolon is safer, and it is always correct.

EXERCISE 1

Insert semicolons or substitute them for commas to separate main clauses in the following sentences.

Example:

One man at the auction bid prudently another did not.

One man at the auction bid prudently; another did not.

1. More and more musicians are playing computerized instruments more and more listeners are worrying about the future of acoustic instruments.
2. The computer is not the first new technology in music the pipe organ and saxophone were also technological breakthroughs in their day.
3. Musicians have always experimented with new technology audiences have always resisted the experiments.
4. Most computer musicians are not merely following the latest fad they are discovering new sounds and new ways to manipulate sound.
5. Few musicians have abandoned acoustic instruments most value acoustic sounds as much as electronic sounds.

EXERCISE 2

Combine each set of three sentences below into one sentence containing only two main clauses, and insert a semicolon between the clauses. You will have to add, delete, change, and rearrange words. Most items have more than one possible answer.

Example:

Alex Colville's painting is highly realistic. His subjects are almost always chosen from his immediate environment. Colville's work has dominated the post-war Maritime painting scene.

The subjects of Alex Colville's highly realistic paintings are almost always chosen from his immediate environment; his work has dominated the post-war Maritime painting scene.

1. Electronic instruments are prevalent in jazz. They are also prevalent in rock music. They are less common in classical music.
2. Jazz and rock change rapidly. They nourish experimentation. They nourish improvisation.
3. Traditional classical music does not change. Its notes and instrumentation were established by a composer. The composer was writing decades or centuries ago.
4. Contemporary classical music not only can draw on tradition. It also can respond to innovations. These are innovations such as jazz rhythms and electronic sounds.
5. Much contemporary electronic music is more than just one type of music. It is more than just jazz, rock, or classical. It is a fusion of all three.

;
22a

Use a semicolon to separate main clauses related by a conjunctive adverb.

Conjunctive adverbs include *consequently, hence, however, indeed, instead, nevertheless, otherwise, still, then, therefore,* and *thus.* (See p. 200 for more explanation and a fuller list.) When a conjunctive adverb relates two main clauses, the clauses should be separated by a semicolon.

> The Labour Canada lawyers will be here in a month; *therefore,* the grievance committee should meet as soon as possible.

> For the first time in twenty years, the accident rate in Montreal did not rise; *indeed,* it actually declined.

The position of the semicolon between main clauses never changes, but the conjunctive adverb may move around within a clause. The adverb is usually set off with a comma or commas.

> Gaëtan Boucher won three speed-skating medals for Canada at the 1984 Sarajevo Winter Olympics; *however,* in Calgary four years later he was unable to win any medals at all.

> Gaëtan Boucher won three speed-skating medals for Canada at the 1984 Sarajevo Winter Olympics; in Calgary four years later, *however,* he was unable to win any medals at all.

> Gaëtan Boucher won three speed-skating medals for Canada at the 1984 Sarajevo Winter Olympics; in Calgary four years later he was unable to win any medals at all, *however.*

; 22b

Commas are optional with *thus, hence,* and some other one-syllable conjunctive adverbs; and commas are usually omitted when *therefore, instead,* and a few other adverbs fall inside or at the ends of clauses.

> She skipped first grade; *thus* she is younger than her classmates.

> She skipped first grade; she is *therefore* younger than her classmates.

> I did not buy the book; I borrowed it *instead.*

NOTE: If you use a comma or no punctuation at all between main clauses connected by a conjunctive adverb, you will produce a comma splice or a fused sentence. See Chapter 11.

EXERCISE 3

Insert a semicolon in each of the following sentences to separate main clauses linked by a conjunctive adverb, and insert a comma or commas where needed to set off the adverb.

Example:

He knew that tickets for the concert would be scarce therefore he arrived at the box office hours before it opened.

He knew that tickets for the concert would be scarce; therefore, he arrived at the box office hours before it opened.

1. Music is a form of communication like language the basic elements however are not letters but notes.
2. Computers can process any information that can be represented numerically consequently they can process musical information.
3. A computer's ability to process music depends on what software it can run furthermore it must be connected to a system that converts electrical vibration into sound.
4. Computers and their sound systems can produce many different sounds indeed the number of possible sounds is infinite.
5. The powerful music computers are very expensive they are therefore used only by professional musicians.

EXERCISE 4

Combine each set of three sentences below into one sentence containing only two main clauses. Connect the clauses with the conjunctive adverb in parentheses, and separate them with a semicolon. (Be sure conjunctive adverbs are punctuated appropriately.) You will have to add, delete, change, and rearrange words. Each item has more than one possible answer.

Example:

The Albanians censor their news. We get little news from them. And what we get is unreliable. (*therefore*)

The Albanians censor their news; *therefore*, the little news we get from them is unreliable.

1. Most music computers are too expensive for the average consumer. Digital keyboard instruments can be inexpensive. They are widely available. (*however*)
2. Inside the keyboard is a small computer. The computer controls a sound synthesizer. The instrument can both process and produce music. (*consequently*)
3. The person playing the keyboard presses keys or manipulates other controls such as switches. The computer and synthesizer convert these signals. The signals are converted into vibrations and sounds. (*then*)
4. The inexpensive keyboards can perform only a few functions. To the novice computer musician, the range is exciting. The range includes drum rhythms and simulated instruments. (*still*)
5. Would-be musicians can orchestrate whole songs. They start from just the melody lines. They need never again play *Chopsticks*. (*thus*)

22c   **Use a semicolon to separate main clauses if they are long and complex or if they contain commas, even when they are joined by a co-ordinating conjunction.**

You would normally use a comma with the co-ordinating conjunctions *and*, *but*, *or*, *nor*, and *for* between main clauses. But placing semicolons between clauses punctuated with commas or between long and grammatically complicated clauses makes a sentence easier to read.

> Whatever happens, we shall have to take Layton as he comes and wishes, the good and the bad together; *but* that is better than not having him at all.   —GEORGE WOODCOCK

> The great cliffs about Cape Diamond gave the place superb natural protection; but further up the river, above Cap Rouge, the approaches were more open; *and* below the town nearly as far as the Montmorency River, the low Beauport flats invited attack.
> —DONALD CREIGHTON

Many writers prefer to use a semicolon instead of a comma between main clauses joined by the co-ordinating conjunctions *so* and *yet*, even when the clauses are not complicated or internally punctuated.

> The day was rainy and blustery; *so* the food vendors kept their fruits and vegetables indoors.

> Three truckloads of supplies arrived at the construction site; *yet* we still did not have enough cement.

;
22c

EXERCISE 5

Substitute semicolons for commas in the following sentences to separate main clauses that are long or grammatically complicated or that are internally punctuated.

Example:

She enjoyed dancing to popular music, often joined a group for square dancing, and even danced the fox trot with her father and brothers, but she preferred ballet.

She enjoyed dancing to rock music, often joined a group for square dancing, and even danced the fox trot with her father and brothers; but she preferred ballet.

1. The ushers had been instructed to clear the movie theatre of popcorn boxes, candy wrappers, and beverage containers, yet we found trash all over the floor when we took our seats.

2. Seeking a change after the long, arduous trial, Judge Doucette rented a cottage on a remote, uncrowded island, and there he found the serenity he needed.

3. By evening, having looked at every house on the realtor's list, the Dalys were exhausted and crabby, but they still hadn't found anything they could afford to buy.

4. James did whatever he wanted, without regard for the feelings or welfare of those around him or for the harm he was doing to himself, and eventually he got into trouble.

5. She had a challenging job, a decent income, and good prospects for the future, but she remained miserable.

EXERCISE 6

Combine each set of sentences below into one sentence containing only two main clauses. Link the clauses with the co-ordinating conjunction in parentheses, and separate them with a semicolon. You will have to add, delete, change, and rearrange words. Each item has more than one possible answer.

Example:

The election will be close. Perhaps it will be a tie. The nominees have hardly campaigned. They do not seem worried. (*but*)

The election will be close, perhaps a tie; *but* the nominees have hardly campaigned and do not seem worried.

1. The reform movements of the 1830s had a variety of goals. The goals included the regulation of child labour. They also included equal rights for women. Few of the goals were realized until later. (*but*)

2. Scientists cannot count the stars, planets, and moons in the universe. They do not have the means. They must rely on estimates. (*so*)

3. By 1900 more than a million Canadians resided in the United States. More than half a million Americans had moved to Canada. The forty-ninth parallel had become largely imaginary. (*but*)

4. Most Canadians believe that Revenue Canada reads their tax returns carefully. They believe that the taxation department checks and double-checks all the information they provide. Revenue Canada counts on this belief to keep the taxpayers honest. (*and*)

5. In the office Mrs. Ledo was a tyrant. She expected her subordinates to do exactly as she said. At home she was a push-over. She let her children do whatever they pleased. (*yet*)

;
22c

Use semicolons to separate items in a series if they are long or contain commas.

You normally use commas to separate items in a series (see 21f-1), but use semicolons instead when the items are long or internally punctuated. The semicolons help the reader identify the items.

> The custody case involved Amy Dalton, the child; Ellen and Mark Dalton, the parents; and Ruth and Hal Blum, the grandparents.

> One may even reasonably advance the claim that the sort of communication that really counts, and is therefore embodied into permanent records, is primarily written; that "words fly away, but written messages endure," as the Latin saying put it two thousand years ago; and that there is no basic significance to at least fifty percent of the oral interchange that goes on among all sorts of persons, high and low.   —Mario Pei

EXERCISE 7

Substitute semicolons for commas in the following sentences to separate long or internally punctuated items in a series.

Example:

After graduation he debated whether to settle in Vancouver, which was temperate but far from his parents, Toronto, which was exciting but expensive, or Winnipeg, which was close to home but already familiar.

After graduation he debated whether to settle in Vancouver, which was temperate but far from his parents; Toronto, which was exciting but expensive; or Winnipeg, which was close to home but already familiar.

1. The Indian subcontinent is separated from the rest of the world by clear barriers: the Bay of Bengal and the Arabian Sea to the east and west, respectively, the Indian Ocean to the south, and 2575 km of mountain ranges to the north.

2. For thousands of years the subcontinent attracted immigrants, who fled poverty or oppression in their own lands, invaders, who aimed to conquer and rule the vast territory, and colonizers, who sought to enrich their own countries with India's labour and resources.

3. As a result, India is a nation of ethnic and linguistic diversity, with numerous religions, including Hinduism, Islam, and Christianity, with distinct castes as well as Aryan, Dravidian, and Mongoloid ethnic groups, and with sixteen languages, including the official Hindi and the "associate official" English.

;

22c

4. Between the seventeenth and nineteenth centuries the British colonized most of India, taking control of government and the bureaucracy, running all significant mining, farming, industry, and trade, and assuming a social position above all Indians.

5. During British rule the Indians' own unresolved differences and their frustrations with the British erupted in violent incidents such as the Sepoy Mutiny that began on February 26, 1857, and lasted two years, the Amritsar Massacre on April 13, 1919, and violence between Hindus and Moslems during World War II that resulted in the division of India into India and Pakistan.

EXERCISE 8

Combine each of the following sets of sentences into one sentence that includes a series punctuated with semicolons. As appropriate, rewrite the items in the series into parallel constructions (see 17a). You will have to add, delete, change, and rearrange words. Each item has more than one possible answer.

Example:

He lived in a dream world. It was populated by chauffeurs who drove him about in expensive, fast cars. Servants fulfilled his every wish. Politicians sought his advice and money.

He lived in a dream world populated by chauffeurs who drove him about in expensive, fast cars; servants who fulfilled his every wish; and politicians who sought his advice and money.

1. India's geography is varied. It includes the world's highest mountains, the Himalayas, in the north. Some of the world's most fertile farmland is farther south. And still farther south are unpopulated deserts and tropical rain forests.

2. In the village of Cherrapunji the annual rainfall is 1145 cm. It is one of the highest rainfalls on earth. Raindrops are sometimes as big as marbles. The citizens wear straw armour. They need to protect themselves from wind, rain, and flying debris.

3. Monsoon winds drive India's climate. The winds bring the hot, dry season between October and May. They bring the cool, rainy season between June and September. And they bring the short spells of moderate rain and temperature as the seasons change.

4. India's cultural life and economy are influenced by the monsoon. It may bring just the rain needed for a bountiful harvest. It may deposit unusually long, hard rains. These rains flood and ruin crops. Or it may withhold rain from drought- and famine-stricken lands.

;
22d

5. In ancient Indian religions the moods of the monsoon were attributed to the moods of the gods. One mood was their pleasure with human beings. It brought the good monsoon of moderate rains. Another mood was their anger at human transgressions. It brought scorching drought. And another mood was their grief over still other transgressions. It brought crop-killing rains.

22e Avoid misusing or overusing the semicolon.

1 Don't use a semicolon to separate a subordinate clause or a phrase from a main clause.

The semicolon separates only equal sentence parts: main clauses and sometimes items in series. It does not separate unequal parts: subordinate clauses and main clauses, or phrases and main clauses.

FAULTY	According to African authorities; only about 35 000 Pygmies exist today.
REVISED	According to African authorities, only about 35 000 Pygmies exist today.
FAULTY	The world would be less interesting; if clothes were standardized.
REVISED	The world would be less interesting if clothes were standardized.

Many readers regard a phrase or subordinate clause set off with a semicolon as a sentence fragment. See Chapter 10.

2 Don't use a semicolon to introduce a series.

Colons and dashes, not semicolons, introduce explanations, series, and so forth. (See 25a and 25b.)

FAULTY	The teacher had heard all the students' reasons for doing poorly; psychological problems, family illness, too much work, too little time.
REVISED	The teacher had heard all the students' reasons for doing poorly: psychological problems, family illness, too much work, too little time.

;
22e

REVISED	The teacher had heard all the students' reasons for doing poorly—psychological problems, family illness, too much work, too little time.

3 | **Don't overuse the semicolon.**

Use the semicolon only occasionally. Too many semicolons, even when they are required by rule, often indicate repetitive sentence structure. Compare two versions of the same information.

SEMICOLON OVERUSED

The Make-a-Wish Foundation helps sick children; it grants the wishes of children who are terminally ill. The foundation learns of a child's wish; the information usually comes from parents, friends, or hospital staff; the wish may be for a special toy, perhaps, or a visit to Disneyland. The foundation grants some wishes with its own funds; for other wishes it appeals to those who have what the child desires.

REVISED

The Make-a-Wish Foundation grants the wishes of children who are terminally ill. From parents, friends, or hospital staff, the foundation learns of a child's wish for a special toy, perhaps, or a visit to Disneyland. It grants some wishes with its own funds; for other wishes it appeals to those who have what the child desires.

;
22e

EXERCISE 9

Revise the following sentences or groups of sentences to eliminate misused or overused semicolons, substituting other punctuation as appropriate.

Example:

The doctor gave all her patients the same advice; cut back on salt and fats, don't smoke, and exercise regularly.

The doctor gave all her patients the same advice: cut back on salt and fats, don't smoke, and exercise regularly.

1. The main religion in India is Hinduism; a way of life as well as a theology and philosophy.
2. Unlike Christianity and Judaism; Hinduism is a polytheistic religion; with deities numbering in the hundreds.
3. Hinduism is unlike many other religions; it allows its creeds and practices to vary widely from place to place and person to person. Other religions have churches; Hinduism does not.

Other religions have principal prophets and holy books; Hinduism does not. Other religions are centred on specially trained priests or other leaders; in Hinduism the individual is his or her own priest.

4. In Hindu belief there are four types of people; reflective, emotional, active, and experimental.

5. Each type of person has a different technique for realizing the true, immortal self; which has infinite existence, infinite knowledge, and infinite joy.

EXERCISE 10

Insert semicolons in the following paragraph wherever they are needed. Eliminate any misused or needless semicolons, substituting other punctuation as appropriate.

The set, sounds, and actors in the movie captured the essence of horror films. The set was ideal; dark, deserted streets, trees dipping their branches over the sidewalks, mist hugging the ground and creeping up to meet the trees, looming shadows of unlighted, turreted houses. The sounds, too, were appropriate, especially terrifying was the hard, hollow sound of footsteps echoing throughout the film. But the best feature of the movie was its actors; all of them tall, pale, and thin to the point of emaciation. With one exception, they were dressed uniformly in grey and had grey hair. The exception was an actress who dressed only in black; as if to set off her pale yellow, nearly white, long hair; the only colour in the film. The glinting black eyes of another actor stole almost every scene, indeed, they were the source of all the film's mischief.

;

22e

NOTE: See page 440 for a punctuation exercise combining semicolons with other marks of punctuation such as commas and colons.

CHAPTER 23

The Apostrophe

Unlike other punctuation marks, which separate words, the apostrophe (') appears as *part* of a word to indicate possession, the omission of one or more letters, or (in a few cases) plural number.

23a Use the apostrophe to indicate the possessive case for nouns and indefinite pronouns.

The **possessive case** shows ownership or possession of one person or thing by another (see Chapter 6). Possession may be shown with an *of* phrase (*the hair of the dog*); or it may be shown with the addition of an apostrophe and, usually, an *-s* (*the dog's hair*). The possessive form functions as an adjective does to limit a noun. Keep in mind that the apostrophe or apostrophe plus *-s* is an addition: everything before this addition should spell the name of the owner or owners without dropped or added letters.

1 Add -'s to form the possessive case of singular or plural nouns or indefinite pronouns that do not end in -s.

The *cat's* eyes were pale blue.
Bill *Boughton's* skilful card tricks amaze his friends.
The *children's* parents were *everybody's* friends.

2 Add -'s to form the possessive case of singular words ending in -s.

Henry *James's* novels reward the patient reader.
Doris's term paper was read aloud in our English class.
The *business's* customers filed suit.

USES AND MISUSES OF THE APOSTROPHE

USES	**MISUSES**
Possessives of nouns and indefinite pronouns (23a)	Possessives of personal pronouns (23b)

Chip's	weeks'		**NOT** it's	**BUT** its
Park's	Parks'			your's	yours
everyone's				

Contractions (23c)	Third-person singulars of verbs (23b)

won't	shouldn't		**NOT** swim's	**BUT** swims
they're	it's		go's	goes

Plurals of letters, numbers, and words named as words (23d)	Plurals of nouns (23b)

C's	*6*'s	*if*'s		**NOT** book's	**BUT** books
				Freed's	Freeds

EXCEPTION: We typically do not pronounce the possessive *-s* of a few singular nouns ending in an *s* or *z* sound, especially names with more than one *s* sound (*Moses*), names that sound like plurals (*Rivers*, *Bridges*), and other nouns when they are followed by a word beginning in *s*. In these cases, many writers add only the apostrophe to indicate possession.

> *Moses'* mother concealed him in the bulrushes.
> Sharon *Hutchins'* father served for two years in the UN peacekeeping force in Cyprus.
> For *conscience'* sake she confessed her lie.

However, usage varies widely, and the final *-s* is not wrong with words like these (*Moses's*, *Hutchins's*, *conscience's*).

3 **Add only an apostrophe to form the possessive case of plural words ending in -*s*.**

> The *teachers'* association called a strike.
> *Workers'* incomes have risen over the past decade, but not fast enough.
> She took two *years'* leave from school.
> The *Murphys'* car was stolen.

23a

Note the difference in the possessives of singular and plural words ending in -*s*. The singular form usually takes -'*s*: *James's* (see page 412). The plural takes only the apostrophe: *Smiths'*.

4   Add -'*s* only to the last word to form the possessive case of compound words or word groups.

My *father-in-law's* birthday was yesterday.
The *council president's* address was a bore.
Go bang on *somebody else's* door.

5   When two or more words show individual possession, add -'*s* to them all. If they show joint possession, add -'*s* only to the last word.

INDIVIDUAL POSSESSION

Harry's and Gerry's dentists both use hypnotism. [Harry and Gerry have different dentists.]

JOINT POSSESSION

That living room is an example of *John and Martha's* bad taste. [John and Martha are jointly responsible for the living room.]

23a

EXERCISE 1

Form the possessive case of each word or word group in parentheses.

Example:

The (*men*) blood pressures were higher than the (*women*).
The *men's* blood pressures were higher than the *women's*.

1. In the myths of the ancient Greeks, the (*goddesses*) roles vary widely.
2. (*Demeter*) responsibility is the fruitfulness of the earth.
3. (*Athena*) role is to guard the city of Athens.
4. (*Artemis*) function is to care for wild animals and small children.
5. (*Athena and Artemis*) father, Zeus, is the king of the gods.
6. Even a single (*goddess*) responsibilities are often varied.
7. Over several (*centuries*) time, Athena changes from a (*mariner*) goddess to the patron of crafts.
8. Athena is also concerned with fertility and with (*children*) well-being, since (*Athens*) strength depended on a large and healthy population.
9. Athena often changes into (*birds*) forms.
10. In (*Homer*) Odyssey she assumes a (*sea eagle*) form.

11. In ancient Athens the myths of Athena were part of (*everyone*) knowledge and life.
12. A cherished myth tells how Athena fights to retain possession of her (*people*) land when the god Poseidon wants it.
13. (*Athena and Poseidon*) skills are different, and each promises a special gift to the Athenians.
14. At the (*contest*) conclusion, Poseidon has given water and Athena has given an olive tree, for sustenance.
15. The other gods decide that the (*Athenians*) lives depend more on Athena than on Poseidon.

23b Don't use the apostrophe where it is not required.

Not all words ending in -*s* take an apostrophe. Three kinds of words are especially likely to attract unneeded apostrophes: plural nouns, third-person singular verbs, and the possessives of personal pronouns.

The plurals of nouns are generally formed by adding -*s* or -*es* (*boys*, *Cheungs*, *families*, *Joneses*). Don't mistakenly add an apostrophe to form the plural.

FAULTY   The unleashed *dog's* began travelling in a pack.

REVISED   The unleashed *dogs* began travelling in a pack.

FAULTY   The *Jones'* and *Bass'* are feuding.

REVISED   The *Joneses* and *Basses* are feuding.

Present-tense verbs used with *he*, *she*, *it*, and other third-person singular subjects always end in -*s* and *never* take an apostrophe.

FAULTY   The subway *break's* down less often now.

REVISED   The subway *breaks* down less often now.

His, *hers*, *its*, *ours*, *yours*, *theirs*, and *whose* are possessive forms of the personal pronouns. They do not need apostrophes.

FAULTY   Credit for discovering the house is really *her's*.

REVISED   Credit for discovering the house is really *hers*.

FAULTY   A chameleon is known for *it's* ability to change *it's* skin colour to match *it's* environment.

REVISED   A chameleon is known for *its* ability to change *its* skin colour to match *its* environment.

23b

The personal pronouns are often confused with contractions. See 23c on the next page.

EXERCISE 2

Supply the appropriate form—possessive or plural—of each word given in parentheses. Some answers require apostrophes, and some do not.

Example:

A dozen Hawaiian (*shirt*), each with (*it*) own loud design, hung in the window.

A dozen Hawaiian *shirts*, each with *its* own loud design, hung in the window.

1. Demeter may be the oldest of the Greek (*god*), older than Zeus.
2. Many prehistoric (*culture*) had earth (*goddess*) like Demeter.
3. In myth she is the earth mother, which means that the responsibility for the fertility of both (*animal*) and (*plant*) is (*she*).
4. The (*goddess*) power is so great that the world becomes desolate when she neglects (*it*) care.
5. Her (*trouble*) begin with the kidnapping of her daughter, Kore, by the god Hades.
6. (*Hades*) domain is the underworld.
7. Both Demeter and Hades insist that Kore is rightfully (*they*).
8. Eventually, like divorced (*parent*), Demeter and Hades agree to share Kore.
9. Demeter restores the (*earth*) fruitfulness.
10. The world owes a debt to Zeus, (*who*) mediation encourages Demeter and Hades to compromise.

23c

23c Use an apostrophe to indicate the omission of one or more letters, numbers, or words in a standard contraction.

it is	it's	does not	doesn't
they are	they're	were not	weren't
you are	you're	class of 1990	class of '90
who is	who's	of the clock	o'clock
cannot	can't	madam	ma'am

Contractions of verb phrases (*don't, weren't, isn't*) and of pronoun-verb pairs (*I'll, we're, she's*) are common in speech and in informal writing. They may also be used to relax style in more formal kinds of writing, as they are in this handbook. But be aware that many people disapprove of contractions in any kind of formal writing.

NOTE: Don't confuse the personal pronouns *its*, *their*, *your*, and *whose* with the contractions *it's*, *they're*, *you're*, and *who's*.

FAULTY *It's* messiness is not *you're* problem or *they're* problem. But *whose* going to clean up?

REVISED   *Its* messiness is not *your* problem or *their* problem. But *who's* going to clean up?

EXERCISE 3

Form contractions from each set of words below. Use each contraction in a complete sentence.

Example:

we are
we*'re*
We*'re* open to ideas.

1. she would
2. could not
3. they are
4. he is
5. do not
6. she will
7. hurricane of 1962
8. is not
9. we would
10. will not

EXERCISE 4

Revise the following sentences to correct mistakes in the use of contractions and personal pronouns. Circle the number preceding any sentence that is already correct.

23c

Example:

The company gives it's employees their birthdays off.
The company gives *its* employees their birthdays off.

1. In Greek myth the goddess Demeter has a special fondness for Eleusis, near Athens, and it's people.
2. She finds rest among the people and is touched by their kindness.
3. Arriving in the disguise of an old woman, Demeter cares for a baby who's father is the king.
4. She tries to make the child immortal by laying it in fire to burn away its mortality.
5. Stopped by the baby's mother, the goddess announces, "You're eyes gaze on Demeter."
6. Demeter rewards the Eleusians with the secret for making they're land fruitful.
7. Demeter also presents the Eleusians with corn, and it's they who introduce the new food to the rest of the world.
8. The Eleusians begin a cult in honour of Demeter, whose worshipped in secret ceremonies.
9. At this point the ceremonies leave myth and enter history, for written texts record they're actual occurrence.
10. Yet its unknown what happened in the ceremonies, for no participant ever revealed their rituals.

| **23d** | **Use an apostrophe plus -*s* to form the plurals of letters, numbers, and words named as words.** |

That sentence has too many *but*'s.

At the end of each chapter the author had written two *3*'s.

Remember to dot your *i*'s and cross your *t*'s, or your readers may not be able to distinguish them from *e*'s and *l*'s.

Notice that the letters, numbers, and words are italicized (underlined in typed or handwritten copy) but that the apostrophe and added, -*s*, are not. (See 27d on this use of italics or underlining.)

EXCEPTION: References to the years in a decade are not italicized and usually omit the apostrophe, but either *1960's* or *1960s* is acceptable as long as usage is consistent.

EXERCISE 5

Form the plural of each letter, number, or word by using an apostrophe and -*s* and by underlining (italicizing) appropriately. Use the new plural in a complete sentence.

Example: x

Erase or white-out typing mistakes. Do not use *x*'s.

1. 7   3. if   5. stop
2. q   4. and

EXERCISE 6

Correct any mistakes in the use of the apostrophe or any confusion between personal pronouns and contractions in the following paragraph.

Landlocked Chad is among the worlds most troubled countries. The people's of Chad are poor: they're average per capita income equals $88 a year. No more than 17 percent of Chads population is literate, and every thousand people must share only two teacher's. The natural resources of the nation have never been plentiful, and now, as it's slowly being absorbed into the growing Sahara Desert, even water is scarce. Chads political conflicts go back beyond the turn of the century, when the French colonized the land by brutally subduing it's people. The rule of the French—who's inept government of the colony did nothing to ease tensions among racial, tribal, and religious groups—ended with independence in 1960. But since then the Chadians experience has been one of civil war and oppression, and now their threatened with invasions from they're neighbours.

NOTE: See page 440 for a punctuation exercise involving apostrophes along with other marks of punctuation.

CHAPTER 24

Quotation Marks

The principal function of quotation marks—either double (" ") or single (' ')—is to enclose direct quotations from speech and from writing. The chart on the next two pages summarizes this and other uses. Always use quotation marks in pairs, one at the beginning of a quotation and one at the end.

 Use double quotation marks to enclose direct quotations.

Direct quotations report what someone has said or written in the exact words of the original. Always enclose direct quotations in quotation marks.

Pierre Elliott Trudeau's famous 1967 statement, "There's no place for the state in the bedrooms of the nation," led to a considerable relaxation of Canada's divorce and anti-homosexual laws.

Indirect quotations report what has been said or written, but not in the exact words of the person being quoted. Indirect quotations are *not* enclosed in quotation marks.

Pierre Elliott Trudeau's affirmation that the state has no place in the bedrooms of the nation led to a considerable relaxation of Canada's divorce and anti-homosexual laws.

24b Use single quotation marks to enclose a quotation within a quotation.

When you quote a writer or speaker, use double quotation marks (see 24a). When the material you quote contains yet another
(*Text continues p. 422*)

HANDLING QUOTATIONS FROM SPEECH OR WRITING
(For explanations, consult the sections in parentheses.)

Direct and indirect quotation

DIRECT QUOTATION (24a)

According to Lewis Thomas, "We are, perhaps uniquely among the earth's creatures, the worrying animal. We worry away our lives."

QUOTATION WITHIN QUOTATION (24b)

Quoting a phrase by Lewis Thomas, the author adds, "We are 'the worrying animal.' "

INDIRECT QUOTATION (24a)

Lewis Thomas says that human beings are unique among animals in their worrying.

Quotation marks with other punctuation marks

COMMAS AND PERIODS (24g-1)

Human beings are "the worrying animal," says Thomas. Thomas calls human beings "the worrying animal."

SEMICOLONS AND COLONS (24g-2)

Machiavelli said that "the majority of men live content"; in contrast, Thomas calls us "the worrying animal."

Thomas believes that we are "the worrying animal": we spend our lives afraid and restless.

QUESTION MARKS, EXCLAMATION POINTS, DASHES (24g-3)

When part of your own sentence

Who said that human beings are "the worrying animal"?
Imagine saying that we human beings "worry away our lives"!
Thomas's phrase—"the worrying animal"—seems too narrow.

When part of the original quotation

"Will you discuss this with me?" she asked.
"I demand that you discuss this with me!" she yelled.
"Please, won't you—" She paused.

Altering quotations

BRACKETS FOR ADDITIONS (25d)

"We [human beings] worry away our lives," says Thomas.

BRACKETS FOR ALTERED CAPITALIZATION (26a)

"[T]he worrying animal" is what Thomas calls us. He says that "[w]e worry away our lives."

ELLIPSIS MARKS FOR OMISSIONS (25e)

"We are . . . the worrying animal," says Thomas.

Our worrying places us "uniquely among the earth's creatures. . . . We worry away our lives."

Punctuating explanatory words

INTRODUCTORY EXPLANATORY WORDS (21h-1)

He says, "We worry away our lives."

An answer is in these words by Lewis Thomas: "We are, perhaps uniquely among the earth's creatures, the worrying animal."

Thomas says that "the worrying animal" is afraid and restless.

CONCLUDING EXPLANATORY WORDS (21h-1)

We are "the worrying animal," says Thomas.
"Who says?" she demanded.
"I do!" he shouted.

INTERRUPTING EXPLANATORY WORDS (21h-2)

"We are," says Thomas, "perhaps uniquely among the earth's creatures, the worrying animal."

"I do not like the idea," she said; "however, I agree with it."

We are "the worrying animal," says Thomas. "We worry away our lives."

" "
24a

See also:

SPECIAL KINDS OF QUOTED MATERIAL

Dialogue (3d-4, 24c)
Poetry (24c, 25f)
Prose passages of more than four lines (24c)

USING QUOTATIONS IN YOUR OWN TEXT

Quotations versus paraphrases and summaries (36c)
Avoiding plagiarism when quoting (36d)
Introducing quotations in your text (36f-2)
Citing sources for quotations (36i)

(*Continued from p. 419*)

quotation, distinguish the two by enclosing the second quotation in single quotation marks.

> "[I]n the past century it has come to be generally acknowledged," observed Marshall McLuhan, "that, in the words of Wyndham Lewis, 'The artist is always engaged in writing detailed history of the future because he is the only person aware of the nature of the present.'"

Notice that two different quotation marks appear at the end of the sentence—one single (to finish the interior quotation) and one double (to finish the main quotation).

EXERCISE 1

Insert single and double quotation marks as needed in the following sentences. Circle the number preceding any sentence that is already correct.

> *Example:*
>
> The purpose of this book, explains the preface, is to examine the meaning of the phrase Dance is poetry.
>
> "The purpose of this book," explains the preface, "is to examine the meaning of the phrase 'Dance is poetry.'"

1. Why, the lecturer asked, do we say Bless you! or something else when people sneeze but not acknowledge coughs, hiccups, and other eruptions?
2. She said that sneezes have always been regarded differently.
3. Sneezes feel more uncontrollable than some other eruptions, she said.
4. Unlike coughs and hiccups, she explained, sneezes feel as if they come from inside the head.
5. She concluded, People thus wish to recognize a sneeze, if only with a Gosh.

24c   Set off quotations of dialogue, poetry, and long prose passages according to standard practice.

Dialogue

When quoting conversations, begin a new paragraph for each speaker.

> "What shall I call you? Your name?" Andrews whispered rapidly, as with a high squeak the latch of the door rose.
>
> "Elizabeth," she said. "Elizabeth."
>
> —GRAHAM GREENE, *The Man Within*

NOTE: When you quote a single speaker for more than one paragraph, put quotation marks at the beginning of each paragraph but at the end of only the last paragraph. The absence of quotation marks at the end of each paragraph but the last tells readers that the speech is continuing.

Poetry

When you quote a single line from a poem, song, or verse play, place the line in the running text and enclose it in quotation marks.

> P. K. Page captures the quiet desperation of the stenographers' lives in the line, "In the inch of the noon as they move they are stagnant."

Poetry quotations of two or three lines may be placed in the text or displayed separately. If you place such a quotation in the text, enclose it in quotation marks and separate the lines with a slash surrounded by space (see 25f).

> Lampman's heat-held landscape unexpectedly induces incisive thought rather than mental lethargy when the persona observes, "In the full furnace of this hour / My thoughts grow keen and clear."

Quotations of more than three lines of poetry should always be separated from the text with space and an indention. Do not add quotation marks.

> F. R. Scott's satirical description of the Canadian authors' meeting reaches its climax in the following passage:
>
>> Shall we go round the mulberry bush, or shall
>> We gather at the river, or shall we
>> Appoint a poet laureate this Fall,
>> Or shall we have another cup of tea?

The *MLA Handbook*, the standard guide to manuscript format in English and some other disciplines, recommends the following spacings for displayed quotations: double-space above and below the quotation, indent it ten spaces from the left margin, and double-space the quoted lines. Unless your instructor specifies otherwise, follow these guidelines for your papers, whether typewritten or handwritten. (See Chapter 37, p. 621, for an example of a displayed quotation in a typed paper.)

NOTE: Be careful when quoting poetry to reproduce faithfully all line indentions, space between lines, spelling, capitalization, and punctuation, as in the original.

Long prose passages

Separate a prose quotation of more than four typed or handwritten lines from the body of your paper. Following the guidelines of the *MLA Handbook*, double-space above and below the quotation, indent it ten spaces from the left margin, and double-space the quoted lines. Do not enclose it in quotation marks.

> Pierre Berton draws attention to the effect of the new railroad's efficiency in moving troops to quell the 1885 Métis uprising in Saskatchewan:
>
> > If Riel's rebellion helped change eastern attitudes to the prairies, it also helped change them towards the CPR. Van Horne was later to remark in his dry way that the railway should have erected a statue to the Métis leader. As early as April 6, he was able to tell a friend in Scotland that "there is no more talk about the construction of the Lake Superior line having been a useless expenditure of money, nor about the road having been built too quickly. Most people are inclined to think it would have been better had it been built three or four weeks quicker."

NOTE: The shorter quotation within the long quotation is enclosed within double quotation marks.

24d Do not use a paragraph indention when quoting a single complete paragraph or a part of a paragraph. Use paragraph indentions only when quoting two or more complete paragraphs.

EXERCISE 2

Practise using quotation marks in quoted dialogue, poetry, and long prose passages by completing each of the following exercises.

1. Write a short sketch of dialogue between two people.
2. Write a sentence that quotes a single line of poetry.
3. Write two sentences, each quoting the same two lines of poetry. In one, place the poetry lines in the text. In the other, separate the two lines from the text.
4. Write a sentence introducing a prose passage of more than four lines, and then set up the quotation appropriately.

24d Put quotation marks around titles according to standard practice.

Use quotation marks to enclose the titles of songs, short poems, articles in periodicals, short stories, essays, episodes of television and radio programs, and the subdivisions of books. Use italics (or under-lining) for all other titles, such as books, plays, periodicals, movies, television programs, and works of art. (See 27a.)

NOTE: Use single quotation marks for a quotation within a quoted title, as in the second article in the box below.

See 26b for guidelines on the use of capital letters in titles.

TITLES TO BE ENCLOSED IN QUOTATION MARKS

SONGS

"Yellow Submarine"
"Can't Buy Me Love"

SHORT POEMS

"The Flight of the Geese"
"The Bull Calf"

ARTICLES IN PERIODICALS

"Protecting Coastal Riches"
"D. C. Scott's 'The Height of Land' and the Greater Romantic Lyric"

SHORT STORIES

"Boys and Girls"
One's a Heifer"

ESSAYS

"Politics and the English Language"
"Canadian Wry"

EPISODES OF TELEVISION AND RADIO PROGRAMS

"New Backs for Old" (on *The Nature of Things*)
"Cooking with Clams" (on *Eating In*)

SUBDIVISIONS OF BOOKS

"Voyage to the Houyhnhnms" (Part IV of *Gulliver's Travels*)
"No Fences Make Good Neighbours" (Chapter 3 of *The 49th Paradox*)

" "

24e

 Occasionally, quotation marks may be used to enclose defined words and words used in a special sense.

By "charity," I mean the love of one's neighbour as oneself.
Pardon my pun, but I find that lawyer "appealing."

NOTE: In definitions, italics (or underlining) are more common than quotation marks (see 27d).

By *charity*, I mean the love of one's neighbour as oneself.

EXERCISE 3

Insert quotation marks as needed for titles and words in the following sentences. If quotation marks should be used instead of italics, insert them.

Example:

The students call her professor despite her youth.
The students call her "professor" despite her youth.

1. In Chapter 8, entitled *How to Be Interesting*, the author explains the art of conversation.
2. The Beatles' Let It Be reminds him of his uncle.
3. Doom means simply judgment as well as unhappy destiny.
4. The article that appeared in *Maclean's* was entitled *The Mean Machines*.
5. In my encyclopedia the discussion under Modern Art fills less than a column.

24f Avoid using quotation marks where they are not required.

Don't use quotation marks in the titles of your papers unless they contain or are themselves direct quotations.

Not	"The Nature of Poetic Vision in One Poem by Margaret Avison"
But	The Nature of Poetic Vision in One Poem by Margaret Avison
Or	The Nature of Poetic Vision in Margaret Avison's "Perspective"

Don't use quotation marks to enclose common nicknames or technical terms that are not being defined.

Not	Even as premier of Saskatchewan, "Tommy" Douglas preferred to use his nickname.
But	Even as premier of Saskatchewan, Tommy Douglas preferred to use his nickname.
Not	"Mitosis" in a cell is fascinating to watch.
But	Mitosis in a cell is fascinating to watch.

Don't use quotation marks in an attempt to justify or apologize for slang and trite expressions that are inappropriate to your writing. If slang is appropriate, use it without quotation marks.

Not	It "rained cats and dogs" for the whole week, so we made no "bread" working.
But	It rained hard for the whole week, so we made no money working.

(See 31a-1 and 31b-5 for more on slang and trite expressions.)

24g **Place other marks of punctuation inside or outside quotation marks according to standard practice.**

1 **Place commas and periods inside quotation marks.**

"Your first cheque will come next month," the social worker said.
Without pausing he pointed and said, "That's the man."
Swift uses irony in his essay "A Modest Proposal."

(See 21h for the use of commas to separate quotations from words used to introduce or explain them.)

2 **Place colons and semicolons outside quotation marks.**

A few years ago the slogan in elementary education was "learning by playing"; now educators are concerned with teaching basic skills.

We all know what is meant by "inflation": more money buys less.

3 **Place dashes, question marks, and exclamation points inside quotation marks only if they belong to the quotation.**

When a dash, question mark, or exclamation point is part of the quotation, put it *inside* quotation marks.

"But must you—" Marcia hesitated, afraid of the answer.
Did you say, "Who is she?"
"Go away!" I yelled.

When a dash, question mark, or exclamation point applies only to the larger sentence, not to the quotation, place it *outside* quotation marks.

One of the most evocative lines in English poetry—"After many a summer dies the swan"—was written by Alfred, Lord Tennyson.

Who said, "Now cracks a noble heart"?

That woman called me "stupid"!

EXERCISE 4

Revise the following sentences for the proper use of quotation marks. Insert quotation marks where they are needed, remove them where they are not needed, and be sure that other marks of punctuation are correctly placed inside or outside the quotation

" "
24g

marks. Circle the number preceding any sentence that is already punctuated correctly.

Example:

The award-winning story was entitled How to Say I'm Sorry to a Child.

The award-winning story was entitled "How to Say 'I'm Sorry' to a Child."

1. The course reading included Virginia Woolf's essay The Anatomy of Fiction.
2. No smoking on this bus! the driver shouted.
3. The advertising slogan, The 40% tax bracket has its comforts, is designed to appeal to people in upper-income brackets.
4. Wearing a drab sweater and a bulky wrap-around skirt, she was the epitome of a "plain Jane."
5. How can we answer children who ask, Will there be a nuclear war?
6. In Canada the signs say, Keep off the grass; in England they say, Please refrain from stepping on the lawn.
7. In *King Richard II* Shakespeare calls England This precious stone set in the silver sea.
8. The doctors gave my father an "electrocardiogram" but found nothing wrong.
9. The re-election of Mulroney's Tories—whom Allan Fotheringham calls "The Recessive Convertible Party"—undermined the assumption of many that the Progressive Conservatives are unable to stay in power for more than one term.
10. Must we regard the future with what Kierkegaard called fear and trembling?

EXERCISE 5

Insert quotation marks as needed in the following paragraph.

In one class we talked about two lines from Shakespeare's Sonnet 55:

> Not marble, nor the gilded monuments
> Of princes, shall outlive this powerful rime.

Why is this true? the teacher asked. Why does Shakespeare's powerful rime indeed live longer than the gilded monuments / Of princes? She then asked if the lines were protected only by Shakespeare's status as our greatest writer. No, said one student. It has more to do with the power of the language. Then another student added, Even though paper is less durable than stone, ideas are more durable than monuments to dead princes. The whole discussion was an eye-opener for those of us (including me) who had never given much credit to rhymes or the words that made them.

NOTE: See page 440 for a punctuation exercise involving quotation marks along with other marks of punctuation.

24g

CHAPTER 25

Other Punctuation Marks

THE COLON

25a Use the colon to introduce and to separate.

1 Use a colon to introduce summaries, explanations, series, appositives ending sentences, long or formal quotations, and statements introduced by *the following* or *as follows*.

The colon is primarily a mark of introduction: it tells the reader that the preceding statement is about to be explained, amplified, or summarized; or it signals that a series or quotation follows. A colon is always preceded by a complete main clause, but it need not be followed by a main clause. Thus the colon differs from the semicolon, whose primary function is to separate main clauses expressing complementary and equally important ideas (see 22a, especially the box on p. 401). The colon is often interchangeable with the dash, though the dash is more informal and more abrupt (see 25b).

SUMMARY

They cannot pay their children's post-secondary educational costs because their money is tied up in their house and antique furniture: they are possession-rich and cash-poor.

EXPLANATION

It is a good thing to be old early: to have the fragility and sensitivity of the old, and a bit of wisdom, before the years of planning and building have run out. ——MARTIN GUMBERT

429

SERIES

It is impossible to dissociate language from science or science from language, because every natural science always involves three things: the sequence of phenomena on which the science is based; the abstract concepts which call these phenomena to mind; and the words in which the concepts are expressed.

—ANTOINE LAVOISIER

FINAL APPOSITIVE

Two chief elements make work interesting: first, the exercise of skill, and second, construction.   —BERTRAND RUSSELL

LONG OR FORMAL QUOTATION

He concluded with an ultimatum: "Either improve the mass transit system or anticipate further decay in your downtown area."

STATEMENT INTRODUCED BY *THE FOLLOWING* OR *AS FOLLOWS*

The relation between leisure and income is as follows: the quality of play depends on the quantity of pay.

NOTE: A complete sentence following a colon may begin with a small letter, as above, or with a capital letter.

:

25a

2   Use a colon to separate titles and subtitles, the subdivisions of time, and the parts of biblical citations.

TITLES AND SUBTITLES

Charles Dickens: *An Introduction to His Novels*
The Blue-Eyed Sheiks: *The Canadian Oil Establishment*

TIME	BIBLICAL CITATIONS
08:00	Isaiah 28:1–6
12:26	1 Corinthians 3:6–7

3   Avoid misusing the colon.

Use the colon only at the end of a main clause. Avoid using it between a verb and its object or between a preposition and its object.

NOT	Two thought-provoking docudramas about political extremism in North America are: Paul Schrader's *Patty Hearst* and Paul Donovan's *The Squamish Five*.
BUT	Two thought-provoking docudramas about political extremism in North America are Paul Schrader's *Patty Hearst* and Paul Donovan's *The Squamish Five*.

NOT	Shakespeare showed the qualities of a Renaissance thinker, such as: humanism and a deep interest in classical Greek and Roman literature.
BUT	Shakespeare showed the qualities of a Renaissance thinker, such as humanism and a deep interest in classical Greek and Roman literature.

EXERCISE 1

Insert colons as needed in the following sentences, or delete colons that are misused.

> *Example:*
>
> Mix the ingredients as follows sift the flour and salt together, add the milk, and slowly beat in the egg yolk.
>
> Mix the ingredients as follows: sift the flour and salt together, add the milk, and slowly beat in the egg yolk.

1. In the remote parts of many Third World countries, simple signs mark human habitation a dirt path, a few huts, smoke from a campfire.
2. In the built-up sections of industrialized countries, nature is all but obliterated by signs of human life, such as: houses, factories, skyscrapers, and highways.
3. The spectacle makes many question the words of Ecclesiastes 1:4 "One generation passeth away, and another generation cometh; but the earth abideth forever."
4. Yet many scientists see the future differently they hold that human beings have all the technology necessary to clean up the earth and restore the cycles of nature.
5. All that is needed is: a change in the attitudes of those who use technology.

25b

THE DASH

 25b   **Use a dash or dashes to indicate sudden changes in tone or thought and to set off some sentence elements.**

1   **Use a dash or dashes to indicate sudden shifts in tone, new or unfinished thoughts, and hesitation in dialogue.**

SHIFT IN TONE

He tells us—does he really mean it?—that he will speak the truth from now on.

UNFINISHED THOUGHT

If she found out—he did not want to think what she would do.

HESITATION IN DIALOGUE

"Under certain circumstances"—in spite of his anger, Athanase smiled—"yes, quite good enough." The smile faded. "Listen, Father—you will not dictate to me in the matter of my son's school. That is beyond your authority."   —HUGH MACLENNAN

2 | Use a dash or dashes to emphasize non-restrictive elements.

Dashes may be used in place of commas (21c) or parentheses (25c-1) to set off and emphasize non-restrictive elements such as modifiers, appositives, and parenthetical expressions. (See the box below.) Dashes are especially useful when these elements are internally punctuated. Be sure to use a pair of dashes when the element interrupts a main clause.

APPOSITIVE

The qualities Monet painted—sunlight, rich shadows, deep colours—abounded near the rivers and gardens he used as subjects.

25b

DISTINGUISHING DASHES, COMMAS, AND PARENTHESES

Dashes, commas, and parentheses may all set off non-essential information such as non-restrictive modifiers and parenthetical expressions.

Dashes give the information the greatest emphasis (25b):

Many students—including some employed by the college—disapprove of the new work rules.

Commas are less emphatic (21c):

Many students, including some employed by the college, disapprove of the new work rules.

Parentheses, the least emphatic, signal that the information is just worth a mention (25c-1):

Many students (including some employed by the college) disapprove of the new work rules.

MODIFIER

Though they are close together—separated by only a few blocks—the two neighbourhoods could be in different countries.

PARENTHETICAL EXPRESSION

In some quarters—very small—Canada is represented as one of America's chief liabilities, a kind of chronic headache extending over 3,000 painful miles of frontier.   —BRUCE HUTCHISON

3 Use a dash to set off introductory series and concluding series and explanations.

INTRODUCTORY SERIES

Shortness of breath, skin discoloration or the sudden appearance of moles, persistent indigestion, the presence of small lumps—all these may signify cancer.

A dash sets off concluding series and explanations more informally and more abruptly than a colon does (see 25a-1).

CONCLUDING SERIES

We packed our camping gear—tent, sleeping bags, and stove.

CONCLUDING EXPLANATION

The country was the most beautiful he had seen—green, rolling hills dotted with stands of dark pine and etched with stone walls.

25b

4 Avoid misusing or overusing the dash.

Don't use the dash when commas, semicolons, and periods are more appropriate. And don't use too many dashes. They can create a jumpy or breathy quality in writing.

NOT	In all his life—eighty-seven years—my great-grandfather never allowed his picture to be taken—not even once. He claimed the "black box"—the camera—would steal his soul.
BUT	In all his eighty-seven years my great-grandfather did not allow his picture to be taken even once. He claimed the "black box"—the camera—would steal his soul.

EXERCISE 2

Insert dashes as needed in the following sentences.

> *Example:*
> What would we do if someone like Adolf Hitler that monster appeared among us?
> What would we do if someone like Adolf Hitler—that monster—appeared among us?

1. The movie-theatre business is undergoing dramatic changes changes that may affect what movies are made and shown.
2. The closing of independent theatres, the control of theatres by fewer and fewer owners, and the increasing ownership of theatres by movie studios and distributors these changes may reduce the availability of non-commercial films.
3. Yet at the same time the number of movie screens is increasing primarily in multiscreen complexes so that smaller films may find more outlets.
4. The number of active movie screens that is, screens showing films or booked to do so is higher now than at any time since World War II.
5. The biggest theatre complexes seem to be something else as well art galleries, amusement arcades, restaurants, spectacles.

( )
25c

PARENTHESES

| 25c | Use parentheses to enclose non-essential elements within sentences. |

| 1 | Use parentheses to enclose parenthetical expressions. |

Parenthetical expressions include explanations, facts, digressions, and examples that may be helpful or interesting but are not essential to meaning. They are emphasized least when set off with a pair of parentheses instead of commas or dashes (see the box on p. 432).

> He drove trucks (tractor-trailers, actually) to earn money for technical college tuition.

> The population of Greater Montreal (now just over 1.8 million) has declined since 1966.

> Unlike the creatures (some insects, for instance) that have been unchanged for five, ten, even fifty million years, man has changed over this time-scale out of all recognition.   —JACOB BRONOWSKI

NOTE: Don't put a comma before a parenthetical expression enclosed in parentheses.

NOT   The dungeon, (really the basement) haunted us.

BUT   The dungeon (really the basement) haunted us.

A comma or period falling after a parenthetical expression should be placed outside the closing parenthesis.

> We received numerous complaints (125 to be exact), but most harped on the same old theme (namely, high prices).

When it falls between other complete sentences, a complete sentence enclosed in parentheses has a capital letter and end punctuation.

> In general, coaches will tell you that scouts are just guys who can't coach. (But then, so are brain surgeons.)   —ROY BLOUNT, JR.

---

2   Use parentheses to enclose letters and figures labelling items in lists within sentences.

> My father could not, for his own special reasons, even *like* me. He spent the first twenty-five years of my life acting out that painful fact. Then he arrived at two points in his own life: (1) his last years, and (2) the realization that he had made a tragic mistake.
> —RAY WEATHERLY

( )
25c

When lists are set off from the text, the numbers or letters labelling them are usually not enclosed in parentheses.

EXERCISE 3

Insert parentheses as needed in the following sentences.

Example:

Students can find good-quality, inexpensive furniture for example, desks, tables, chairs, sofas, even beds in junk stores.

Students can find good-quality, inexpensive furniture (for example, desks, tables, chairs, sofas, even beds) in junk stores.

1. Many of those involved in the movie business agree that multiscreen complexes are good for two reasons: 1 they cut the costs of exhibitors; and 2 they offer more choices to audiences.
2. Those who produce and distribute films and not just the big studios argue that the multiscreen theatres give exhibitors too much power.

3. The major studios are buying movie theatres to gain control over important parts of the distribution process what gets shown and for how much money.
4. For twelve years 1938–1950 the federal government forced the studios to sell all their movie theatres.
5. But because they now have more competition television and videocassette recorders, the studios are permitted to own theatres.

BRACKETS

25d   **Use brackets only within quotations to indicate your own comments or changes.**

If you need to explain, clarify or correct the words of the writer you quote, place your additions in a pair of brackets.

> "That Petro-Canada station [just north of Mississauga] is one of the busiest in the nation," said a company spokesperson.

Also use brackets if you need to alter the capitalization of a quotation so that it will fit into your sentence. (See also 26a.)

> "[O]ne of the busiest in the nation" is how a company spokesperson described the station.

You may also use a bracketed word or words to substitute for parts of the original quotation that would otherwise be unclear. In the sentence below, the bracketed word substitutes for *they* in the original.

> "Despite considerable achievements in other areas, [humans] still cannot control the weather and probably will never be able to do so."

The word *sic* (Latin for "in this manner") in brackets indicates that an error in the quotation appeared in the original and was not made by you.

> According to the newspaper report, "The car slammed thru [*sic*] the railing and into oncoming traffic."

But don't use *sic* to make fun of a writer or to note errors in a passage that is clearly non-standard or illiterate.

THE ELLIPSIS MARK

25e Use the ellipsis mark to indicate omissions within quotations.

The **ellipsis mark** consists of three spaced periods (. . .). It is used most often to indicate an omission from a quotation, as illustrated in the following excerpts from this quotation about the Philippines:

ORIGINAL QUOTATION

"It was the Cuba of the future. It was going the way of Iran. It was another Nicaragua, another Cambodia, another Vietnam. But all these places, awesome in their histories, are so different from each other that one couldn't help thinking: this kind of talk was a shorthand for a confusion. All that was being said was that something was happening in the Philippines. Or more plausibly, a lot of different things were happening in the Philippines. And a lot of people were feeling obliged to speak out about it."
— JAMES FENTON, "The Philippine Election"

OMISSION OF PART OF A SENTENCE

"But all of these places . . . are so different from each other that one couldn't help thinking: this kind of talk was a shorthand for a confusion."

"But . . . this kind of talk was a shorthand for a confusion."

OMISSION OF PARTS OF TWO SENTENCES

"All that was being said was that . . . a lot of different things were happening in the Philippines."

OMISSION OF ONE OR MORE SENTENCES

"It was the Cuba of the future. It was going the way of Iran. It was another Nicaragua, another Cambodia, another Vietnam. . . . All that was being said was that something was happening in the Philippines."

Notice that when the ellipsis mark follows a complete sentence, as in the example immediately above, or an incomplete sentence, four equally spaced periods result: the sentence period (closed up to the last word of the sentence) and the three periods of the ellipsis mark. Notice also that although Fenton's essay goes on after the quoted passage, an ellipsis mark is not used at the end of the quotation.

If you omit one or more lines of poetry or paragraphs of prose from a quotation, use a separate line of ellipsis marks across the full width of the quotation to show the omission.

NOTE: Pauses and unfinished statements in quoted speech may be indicated with an ellipsis mark instead of a dash (25b-1).

"I wish . . . " His voice trailed off.

EXERCISE 4

To practise using ellipsis marks to show omissions from quotations, follow each instruction below, using the following paragraph by Kildare Dobbs.

The truth is that the thought "Canada" is impossible to think all at once. Love of country is difficult when, like Aristotle's "creature of vast size," its unity and wholeness are lost to imagination. And so the patriotism of Canadians tends to be—in a perfectly respectable and human sense—provincial, and even parochial.

—KILDARE DOBBS

1. Quote the second sentence from the paragraph, but omit the words *like Aristotle's "creature of vast size"* (and punctuation, as necessary). Show the omission with an ellipsis mark.
2. Quote the third sentence, omitting the words *in a perfectly respectable and human sense* (and punctuation, as necessary). Show the omission with an ellipsis mark.
3. Quote the entire paragraph, omitting the opening words *The truth is that* as well as the concluding *and even parochial*. Show the omissions in the proper way.

THE SLASH

25f Use the slash between options and to separate lines of poetry that are run in to the text.

OPTION

I don't know why some teachers oppose pass/fail courses.

When used between options, the slash is not surrounded by extra space.

NOTE: The options *and/or* and *he/she* should be avoided. (See the Glossary of Usage, pp. 734 and 740.)

POETRY

A. M. Klein's description of a poet as "the nth Adam taking a green inventory / in world but scarcely uttered" captures the essence of his view of the poet's function in society.

When used to separate lines of poetry, the slash in surrounded by space. (See 24c for more on quoting poetry.)

EXERCISE 5

Insert colons, dashes, parentheses, brackets, ellipsis marks, or slashes as needed in the following sentences, or remove them where they are not needed. When different marks would be appropriate in the same place, be able to defend the choice you make. Circle the number preceding any sentence that is already correct.

Example:

The residents of the neighbourhood including many who grew up there signed a petition against further development.

The residents of the neighbourhood—including many who grew up there—signed a petition against further development. [The dashes emphasize the parenthetical expression.]

1. Moderate temperatures, spectacular scenery, and the proximity of the sea these are her favourite characteristics of Vancouver.
2. In the March 1958 federal election, John Diefenbaker (affectionately dubbed "Dief the Chief" by his admirers) led the Conservatives to winning 208 seats in the House of Commons the highest number ever held by a single party in Canada up to that time.
3. He has all the qualities of a fine cook he shops patiently for the freshest ingredients, he prepares the food with imagination and care, and he serves the meal elegantly.
4. From the reviewer's sentence "The acting is amazingly incompetent, given that these actors can be powerful," the advertisement extracted praise by using an ellipsis mark: "The acting is amazingly powerful."
5. The bikers—tattooed and draped in chains look more threatening than they really are.
6. "Buy the new *Universal Dictionary* sic," the ad said. But why would anybody buy a dictionary that can't spell dictionary?
7. James Joyce's *Ulysses* first published in 1922 is a beautiful, shocking novel.
8. In the letter he quoted two lines of poetry that John Donne once wrote in a letter of his own "Sir, more than kisses, letters mingle souls; For thus friends absent speak."
9. Paying taxes one of life's certainties is only a little less painful than the other certainty.
10. Sylvie Bernier's gold medal in diving the first ever for Canada in that sport was probably the highlight for this country at the 1984 Los Angeles Olympics.

/

25t

EXERCISE ON CHAPTERS 20–25
Periods, Commas, Semicolons, Apostrophes, Quotation Marks,
Colons, Dashes, and Parentheses

The following paragraphs are unpunctuated except for end-of-sentence periods. Insert the appropriate punctuation marks where they are required. When different marks would be appropriate in the same place, be able to defend the choice you make.

Brewed coffee is the most widely consumed beverage in the world. The trade in coffee beans alone amounts to well over $6 billion per year and the total volume of beans traded exceeds 4 335 000 t per year. Its believed that the beverage was introduced into Arabia in the fifteenth century AD probably by Ethiopians. By the middle or late sixteenth century the Arabs had introduced the beverage to the Europeans who at first resisted it because of its strong flavor and effect as a mild stimulant. The French Italians and other Europeans incorporated coffee into their diets by the seventeenth century the English however preferred tea which they were then importing from India. Since America was colonized primarily by the English Americans also preferred tea. Only after the Boston Tea Party 1773 did Americans begin drinking coffee in large quantities. The United States is currently the greatest coffee-consuming country in the world approximately 400 million cups per day according to 1985 figures although surprisingly in terms of per capita consumption it ranks only eighth behind Sweden Denmark Finland Norway Switzerland Belgium and the Netherlands in that order. In Canada largely because of this country's British heritage tea-drinking vies with coffee-drinking for popularity although in the period from 1936 to 1976 per capita tea consumption fell by 31 percent whereas coffee consumption rose by around 270 percent. Both American and Canadian coffee consumption has been spurred on by such familiar advertising claims as Good to the last drop Rich hearty aroma Always rich never bitter.

Produced from the fruit of an evergreen tree coffee is grown primarily in Latin America southern Asia and Africa. Coffee trees require a hot climate high humidity rich soil with good drainage and partial shade consequently they thrive on the east or west slopes of tropical volcanic mountains where the soil is laced with potash and drains easily. The coffee beans actually seeds grow inside bright red berries. The berries are picked by hand and the beans are extracted by machine leaving a pulpy fruit residue that can be used for fertilizer. The beans are usually roasted in ovens a chemical process that releases the beans essential oil caffeol which gives coffee its distinctive aroma. More than a hundred different varieties of beans are produced in the world each with a different flavor attributable to three factors the species of plant *Coffea arabia* and *Coffea robusta* are the most common and the soil and climate where the variety was grown.

p

PART VI

Mechanics

CHAPTER 26

Capitals

Experienced writers generally agree on when to use capitals, but the conventions are constantly changing. Consult a recent dictionary if you have any doubt about whether a particular word should be capitalized.

 26a Capitalize the first word of every sentence.

> Every writer should own a good dictionary.
> Will this rain ever stop?
> Watch out!

When quoting other writers, you must reproduce the capital letters beginning their sentences or indicate that you have altered the source. Whenever possible, integrate the quotation into your own sentence so that its capitalization coincides with yours.

> "Psychotherapists often overlook the benefits of self-deception," the author argues.

> The author argues that "the benefits of self-deception" are not always recognized by psychotherapists.

If you need to alter the capitalization in the source, indicate the change with brackets (see 25d).

> "[T]he benefits of self-deception" are not always recognized by psychotherapists, the author argues.

> The author argues that "[p]sychotherapists often overlook the benefits of self-deception."

NOTE: Capitalization of questions in a series is optional. Both of the following examples are correct.

Is the population a hundred? Two hundred? More?
Is the population a hundred? two hundred? more?

Also optional is capitalization of the first word in a complete sentence after a colon (see 25a).

26b Capitalize words in the titles of works according to standard practice.

Capitalize all words in the title of a work *except* articles (*a, an, the*) and prepositions and conjunctions of fewer than five letters. Capitalize even these short words when they are the first or last word in a title or when they fall after a colon or semicolon.

The Sound and the Fury
"Courtship Through the Ages"
Merry England; *Or, the History of a People*

Understanding Media: *The Extensions of Man*
"The Mask of the Bear"
Management: *A New Approach*
"Once Is Not Enough"

NOTE: Always capitalize the prefix or first word in a hyphenated word within a title. Capitalize the second word only if it is a noun or an adjective or is as important as the first word.

"Applying Stage Make-up"
The Pre-Raphaelites

Through the Looking-Glass
"A Poet's-Eye View"

26c Always capitalize the pronoun *I* and the interjection *O*. Don't capitalize *oh* unless it begins a sentence.

I love to stay up at night, but, oh, I hate to get up in the morning.
He who thinks himself wise, O heavens, is a great fool.
—VOLTAIRE

cap
26d

26d Capitalize proper nouns, proper adjectives, and words used as essential parts of proper nouns.

1 Capitalize proper nouns and proper adjectives.

Proper nouns name specific persons, places, and things: *Shakespeare, Alberta, World War I*. **Proper adjectives** are formed from some proper nouns: *Shakespearean, Albertan*. Capitalize all proper nouns and proper adjectives but not the articles (*a, an, the*) that precede them.

PROPER NOUNS AND ADJECTIVES TO BE CAPITALIZED

SPECIFIC PERSONS AND THINGS

Bryan Adams	the Leaning Tower of Pisa
Napoleon Bonaparte	Gardiner Dam
Doris Lessing	Place Ville Marie

SPECIFIC PLACES AND GEOGRAPHICAL REGIONS

Lethbridge	the Mediterranean Sea
China	Lake Victoria
Europe	the Northeast
North America	the Rocky Mountains

DAYS OF THE WEEK, MONTHS, HOLIDAYS

Monday	Yom Kippur
May	Christmas
Thanksgiving	Victoria Day

HISTORICAL EVENTS, DOCUMENTS, PERIODS, MOVEMENTS

World War II	the Middle Ages
the War of 1812	the Age of Reason
the Red River Rebellion	the Renaissance
Meech Lake Accord	the Great Depression
the Constitution Act	the Romantic Movement

GOVERNMENT OFFICES OR DEPARTMENTS AND INSTITUTIONS

House of Commons	The Supreme Court of Canada
Ministry of Education	Royal Columbian Hospital
Public Accounts Committee	Dawson College
Canada Post Corporation	North York Board of Education

POLITICAL, SOCIAL, ATHLETIC, AND OTHER ORGANIZATIONS AND ASSOCIATIONS AND THEIR MEMBERS

New Democratic Party	Rotary Club, Rotarians
Communist Party, Communist	Anglican Church of Canada
Canadian National Institute for the Blind	National Action Committee on the Status of Women
B'nai B'rith	Montreal Canadiens
	Atlantic Symphony Orchestra

RACES, NATIONALITIES, AND THEIR LANGUAGES

Algonquins	Germans
French Canadian, Negro	Métis
Caucasian	Italian
But: blacks, whites	

(continued)

cap
26d

RELIGIONS AND THEIR FOLLOWERS

Christianity, Christians	Judaism, Orthodox Jew
Protestantism, Protestants	Hinduism, Hindu
Catholicism, Catholics	Islam, Moslems *or* Muslims

RELIGIOUS TERMS FOR SACRED PERSONS AND THINGS

God	Buddha
Allah	the Bible (*but* biblical)
Christ	the Koran

NOTE: Capitalization of pronouns referring to God is optional in most contexts, but the capital is often used in religious texts and should be used where necessary to avoid confusion.

AMBIGUOUS	Our minister spoke of God as though *he* loved every member of our congregation.
REVISED	Our minister spoke of God as though *He* loved every member of our congregation.

2 **Capitalize common nouns used as essential parts of proper nouns.**

Common nouns name general classes of persons, places, or things, and they generally are not capitalized. However, capitalize the common nouns *street, avenue, park, river, ocean, lake, company, college, county,* and *memorial* when they are part of proper nouns naming specific places or institutions.

cap
26d

Main Street	Carleton County
Dewdney Avenue	Lake Ontario
Stanley Park	Hudson Bay Company
St. Lawrence River	Medicine Hat College
Pacific Ocean	Surrey Memorial Hospital

3 **Capitalize trade names.**

Trade names identify individual brands of certain products. When a trade name loses its association with a brand and comes to refer to a product in general, it is not capitalized. Refer to a dictionary for current usage when you are in doubt about a name.

Scotch tape	Xerox
Chevrolet	Bunsen burner
But: nylon, thermos	

26e Capitalize titles when they precede proper names but generally not when they follow proper names or are used alone.

Professor Otto Osborne	Otto Osborne, a professor of English
Doctor Jane Covington	Jane Covington, a medical doctor
Senator Duff Roblin	Duff Roblin, a senator from Manitoba
the Reverend Wilma Voss	Wilma Voss, the minister

EXCEPTION: Many writers capitalize a title denoting very high rank even when it follows a proper name or is used alone.

Ramon Hnatyshyn, Governor General of Canada
the Prime Minister of Canada

26f Avoid unnecessary capitalization.

In general, modern writers capitalize fewer words than earlier writers did. Capitalize only when a rule says you must.

1 Don't capitalize common nouns used in place of proper nouns.

UNNECESSARY   I am determined to take an Economics course before I graduate from University.

REVISED   I am determined to take an economics course before I graduate from university.

REVISED   I am determined to take Economics 101 before I graduate from Lakehead University.

cap
26f

2 Don't capitalize compass directions unless they refer to specific geographical areas.

The storm blew in from the northeast and then veered south along the coast. [Here *northeast* and *south* refer to general directions.]

People from the West have trouble adjusting to the East's humid summers. [Here *West* and *East* refer to specific regions.]

3 Don't capitalize the names of seasons or the names of academic years or terms.

spring	autumn	senior year
fall	winter semester	summer term

4 Don't capitalize the names of relationships unless they form part of or substitute for proper names.

my mother   the father of my friend
Makito's brother

BUT

I remember how Father scolded us.

Aunt Ethel, Uncle Jake, and Uncle Irvin died within two months of each other.

EXERCISE

Capitalize words as necessary in the following sentence, or substitute lower-case letters for unnecessary capitals. Consult a dictionary if you are in doubt. If the capitalization in a sentence is already correct, circle the number preceding the sentence.

Example:
The first book on my summer reading list is stephen leacock's *sunshine sketches of a little town.*

The first book on my summer reading list is Stephen Leacock's *Sunshine Sketches of a Little Town.*

1. The new Place des Arts is very imposing. it is made of reinforced concrete and steel.
2. My Grandmother told me stories about my Father and Uncle Gérard.
3. Although Rashid is a moslem, he is very knowledgeable about the bible, especially the old testament.
4. Professor Kellogg recommended that *Sexist and non-sexist language* be a required text for all fall writing courses.
5. The photograph showed senator Davey shaking hands with the Pastor of the largest Church in Toronto.
6. The fraser canyon is in british columbia, between lytton and hope.
7. Colson, the doctor, knew his medicine, but his manner made his patients nervous.
8. Our scavenger-hunt map directed us two blocks Southeast and two blocks Northeast to find an old sink.
9. The Mackenzie river, issuing from the shallow swamps and mud banks of the west arm of Great Slave lake, flows for more than 4000 km through the barren lands of the northwest territories before emptying into the Beaufort sea.
10. The new Roy Thompson hall is an acoustical triumph, but, Oh, it was expensive to build.

cap

26f

CHAPTER 27

Italics

Type that slants upward to the right is known as *italic type*. We use italics to distinguish or emphasize certain words and phrases. In your handwritten or typed papers, *underline* to indicate material that would be italicized if set into type.

27a Underline titles according to standard practice.

Underline the titles of books, long poems, plays, periodicals, pamphlets, published speeches, long musical works, movies, television and radio programs, and works of visual art. (See the box on the facing page.) Use quotation marks for all other titles, such as songs, short poems, short stories, articles in periodicals, essays, and episodes of television and radio programs. (See 24d.)

NOTE: Be careful to underline marks of punctuation only if they are part of the title: *Did you read Survival?* (not *Survival?*). In titles of newspapers underline the name of the city only when it is part of the title.

Manchester Guardian
Winnipeg Free Press

When giving the title of a periodical in your text, you do not need to capitalize or underline the article *the*, even if it is part of the title.

She has the *Winnipeg Free Press* delivered to her in Halifax.

Omit the article entirely in bibliographic references (see Chapter 35, pp. 557–58).

TITLES TO BE UNDERLINED (ITALICIZED)

BOOKS

Survival
War and Peace
The Promise
The Last Spike

PLAYS

Equus
Hamlet
The Ecstasy of Rita Joe
Colours in the Dark

PAMPHLETS

The Truth About Alcoholism
On the Vindication of the Rights of Women

LONG MUSICAL WORKS

Tchaikovsky's *Swan Lake*
Bach's *St. Matthew Passion*
MacMillan's *Two Sketches for Strings*
But: Symphony in C

TELEVISION AND RADIO PROGRAMS

Sportsweekend
Beachcombers
The National

LONG POEMS

Beowulf
The Song of Roland
Paradise Lost
Brebeuf and His Brethren

PERIODICALS

Time
Tamarack Review
Montreal Star
Mechanical Engineering

PUBLISHED SPEECHES

Lincoln's *Gettysburg Address*
Pericle's *Funeral Oration*

MOVIES

Gone with the Wind
Star Wars
The Rowdyman

WORKS OF VISUAL ART

Michelangelo's *David*
the *Mona Lisa*
A. Y. Jackson's *The Northland*

---

ital
27b

EXCEPTIONS: Legal documents, the Bible, and their parts are generally not italicized.

NOT	They register their *deed*.
BUT	They register their deed.
NOT	We studied the *Book of Revelation* in the *Bible*.
BUT	We studied the Book of Revelation in the Bible.

27b **Underline the names of ships, aircraft, spacecraft, and trains.**

Queen Elizabeth II   *Apollo XI*
Spirit of St. Louis   *Orient Express*
Challenger

27c Underline foreign words and phrases that are not part of the English language.

English tends to absorb foreign words and phrases that speakers and writers find useful. The French expression "bon voyage," for example, is now part of our language and need not be underlined. If a foreign word or phrase has not been absorbed into our language, it should be underlined. A dictionary will tell you whether or not the words you wish to use should be underlined.

> The scientific name for the brown trout is *Salmo trutta*. [The scientific names for plants and animals are always underlined.]
>
> What a life he led! He was a true *bon vivant*.
>
> The Latin *De gustibus non est disputandum* translates roughly as "There's no accounting for taste."

27d Underline words, letters, numbers, and phrases named as words.

> Some people pronounce *th*, as in *thought*, with a faint *s* or *f* sound.
>
> Carved into the middle of the column, six metres up, was a mysterious 7.
>
> Try pronouncing *unique North York* ten times fast.

Italics may also be used instead of quotation marks in definitions (see 24e).

> The word *syzygy* refers to a straight line formed by three celestial bodies, as in the alignment of earth, sun, and moon that produces an eclipse.

27e Occasionally, underlining may be used for emphasis.

Compare these sentences:

I thought you had the key.	I *thought* you had the key.
I thought you had the key.	I thought *you* had the key.

In the absence of clues from context, the first sentence doesn't tell us where the emphasis should lie. The three following sentences, however, tell us exactly which word to emphasize, and the different emphases create different meanings. In this way italics (or underlining) can stress an important word or phrase, especially in reporting how someone said something. But such emphasis should be used sparingly. Excessive underlining will make your writing sound immature or hysterical, as the following example illustrates.

> The hunters had *no* food and *no* firewood. But they were *too* tired to do anything more than crawl into their *sopping* sleeping bags. Had it been ten degrees colder, *they might have frozen to death*.

If you find that you rely too much on underlining to achieve emphasis, consult Chapter 18 for other techniques to help you accent your writing.

EXERCISE

Underline (italicize) words and phrases as needed in the following sentences, or circle any words or phrases that are italicized unnecessarily.

Example:
Of Hitchcock's movies, Psycho is the scariest.
Of Hitchcock's movies, <u>Psycho</u> is the scariest.

1. The essay contains many puns and jeux de mots.
2. The author's stories have appeared in such widely diverse periodicals as Saturday Night and Chatelaine.
3. The director warned the writer that the screenplay for The Apprenticeship of Duddy Kravitz had better be finished *tout de suite*.
4. The map was *so* out of date that it didn't even show the *town* Tammy lived in, let alone the *street* her *house* was on.
5. According to Books in Canada, Rudy Wiebe's First and Vital Candle is out of print.
6. At one time Canada's second-largest city had two major English language newspapers, the Montreal Star and the Montreal Gazette.
7. Both the *Old Testament* and the *New Testament* of the *Bible* offer profound lessons in human nature.
8. No matter how many times I say it, the word euphemism comes out wrong.
9. Homo sapiens has evolved further than any other species.
10. Whether he's watching Masterpiece Theatre, Sportsweekend, or the silliest situation comedy, Larry is happy in front of the television.

ital

27e

CHAPTER 28

Abbreviations

All writers use certain standard abbreviations such as *Dr.* and *Ph.D.* because they are convenient and readily understood, and technical writers use a great many other abbreviations (see 28f). Nevertheless, only a few abbreviations are acceptable in general writing. For a list of abbreviations used in source citations, see Chapter 35, p. 570–71.

28a Use standard abbreviations for titles immediately before and after proper names.

BEFORE THE NAME	AFTER THE NAME
Dr. Phillip Hsu	Phillip Hsu, M.D.
Mr., Mrs. Ms., Hon.	D.D.S., D.V.M., Ph.D.
St., Rev., Msgr., Gen.	Ed.D., O.B.E., S.J., Sr., Jr.

(Note that the title *Ms.* is followed by a period, even though it is not actually an abbreviation: *Ms. Judith Boyer*.)

Use abbreviations such as *Rev.*, *Hon.*, *Prof.*, *Sen.*, *Dr.*, and *St.* (for *Saint*) only if they appear with a proper name. Spell them out in the absence of a proper name.

FAULTY	We learned to trust the *Dr.*
REVISED	We learned to trust the *doctor.*
REVISED	We learned to trust *Dr. Kaplan.*

The abbreviations for academic degrees—*Ph.D.*, *M.A.*, *B.A.*, and the like—may be used without a proper name.

My brother took seven years to get his *Ph.D.* It will probably take me just as long to earn my *B.A.*

28b Familiar abbreviations and acronyms for names of organizations, corporations, people, and some countries are acceptable in most writing.

An **acronym** is an abbreviation that spells a pronounceable word, such as WHO, UNESCO, and NATO. These abbreviations, written without periods, are acceptable in most writing as long as they are familiar. So are several familiar abbreviations of the names of organizations, corporations, people, and countries. When these abbreviate three or more words, they are usually written without periods.

ORGANIZATIONS	RCMP, YMCA, CLC
CORPORATIONS	IBM, CTV, CPR
PEOPLE	JFK, LBJ, PET
COUNTRIES	U.K. (or UK), U.S.S.R. (or USSR)

(See 20b for more information on when to use periods in abbreviations.)

NOTE: If a name or term (such as *operating room*) appears often in a piece of writing, then its abbreviation (*O.R.*) can cut down on extra words. Spell out the full term at its first appearance, indicate its abbreviation in parentheses, and use the abbreviation from then on. However, if the term occurs only a few times in a paper, the abbreviation will serve no useful purpose and may even confuse readers. In that case spell out the term each time it occurs.

28c Use *B.C., A.D., a.m., p.m., no.*, and *$* only with specific dates and numbers.

The abbreviation B.C. ("before Christ") always follows a date, whereas A.D. (*anno Domini*, latin for "year of the Lord") precedes a date.

44 B.C.	8:05 p.m. (*or* P.M.)	no. 36 (*or* No. 36)
A.D. 1492	11.26 a.m. (*or* A.M.)	$7.41

FAULTY	Hospital routine is easier to follow in the a.m. than in the p.m.
REVISED	Hospital routine is easier to follow in the *morning* than in the *afternoon or evening*.

NOTE: The preceding capitalized abbreviations are often set in small capital letters in publications: B.C., A.D. In handwriting and keying, use B.C. and A.D. The abbreviation for *number* may either be capitalized or not (No., no.).

28d Generally, reserve common Latin abbreviations such as *i.e.*, *e.g.*, and *etc.* for use in source citations and comments in parentheses.

i.e.	that is (*id est*)
cf.	compare (*confer*)
e.g.	for example (*exempli gratia*)
et al.	and others (*et alii*)
etc.	and so forth (*et cetera*)
N.B.	note well (*nota bene*)

He said he would be gone a fortnight (i.e., two weeks).
Bloom et al., editors, *Anthology of Light Verse*
Trees, too, are susceptible to disease (e.g., Dutch elm disease).

(Note that these abbreviations are generally not italicized or under-lined.) In formal writing use the appropriate English phrases instead of the Latin abbreviations.

FAULTY	The cabs of some modern farm machines—e.g., combines—look like airplane cockpits.
INFORMAL	The cabs of some modern farm machines (e.g., combines) look like airplane cockpits.
FORMAL	The cabs of some modern farm machines (for example, combines) look like airplane cockpits.
FORMAL	The cabs of some modern farm machines—for example, combines—look like airplane cockpits.

ab
28e | **28e** Don't use *Inc.*, *Bros.*, *Co.*, or *&* (for *and*) except when it is part of the official name of a business firm.

FAULTY	*The Block bros.* established a successful realty company.
REVISED	*The Block brothers* established a successful realty company.
REVISED	*Block Bros. Realty Ltd.* has garnered a large share of the Canadian real estate market.
FAULTY	We read about the Hardy Boys & Nancy Drew.
REVISED	We read about the Hardy Boys *and* Nancy Drew.

In most writing don't abbreviate units of
measurement; geographical names; names of
days, months, and holidays; names of people;
courses of instruction; and labels for divisions of
written works.

Units of measurement, geographical names, specialized terms, and other words are often abbreviated in technical writing. In other academic writing and general writing, however, such words should be spelled out.

UNITS OF MEASUREMENT

The dog is seventy *centimetres* (not *cm*) high.
Dig a hole two *metres* (not *m*) deep.

EXCEPTIONS: Long phrases such as *kilometres per hour* (kph) or *cycles per second* (cps) are usually abbreviated, with or without periods: *The speed limit on that road was once* 110 *kph* (or *k.p.h.*).

GEOGRAPHICAL NAMES

The publisher is in *Ontario* (not *Ont.* or *ON*).
He came from Aukland, *New Zealand* (not *N.Z.*).
She lived on *University Boulevard* (not *Blvd.*).

EXCEPTIONS: The United States is often referred to as the U.S.A. (USA) or the U.S., and the Soviet Union as the U.S.S.R. (USSR).

NAMES OF DAYS, MONTHS, AND HOLIDAYS

The truce was signed on *Tuesday* (not *Tues.*), *January* (not *Jan.*) 16.
The *Christmas* (not *Xmas*) holidays were uneventful.

NAMES OF PEOPLE

James (not *Jas.*) Bennett ran for that seat.

Robert (not *Robt.*) Service's "roughneck" verse provides entertaining insight into life in the Yukon at the turn of the century.

COURSES OF INSTRUCTION

I'm majoring in *political science* (not *poli. sci.*).
Economics (not *Econ.*) is a tough course.

LABELS FOR DIVISIONS OF WRITTEN WORKS

The story begins on *page* (not *p.*) 15 in *Volume* (not *Vol.*) 2.
Read *Chapter* (not *Ch.*) 6.

ab
28f

EXERCISE 1

Revise the following sentences as needed to correct faulty use of abbreviations. Circle the number preceding any sentence in which the abbreviations are already correct as written.

Example:

One prof. spent five class hrs. reading from the textbook.

One *professor* spent five class *hours* reading from the textbook.

1. The kite was flying at about fifty m when the line snapped.
2. Old Montreal, a section of the city south of Dorchester Blvd., contains a number of bldgs. dating from the 18th cent.
3. Jet lag—i.e., disruption of sense of time, place, or well-being—often afflicts air travellers.
4. Upon his inauguration on Fri., Jan. 20, 1961, JFK became the first Roman Catholic President in American history.
5. The relationship between the U.S.A. and the U.S.S.R. is one of the most analysed subjects of the century.
6. Mount Vesuvius erupted in *anno Domini* 79 and buried Pompeii.
7. Mr. and Mrs. Harold Marsh, Jr., donated a new wing for the library.
8. The Lynch bros., Wm. & Robt., went bankrupt in the same year.
9. They asked the rev. to marry them on horseback.
10. There, in the middle of Ch. 6 between pp. 128 & 129, was a leaf my mother had pressed as a child.

EXERCISE 2

Spell out all inappropriate abbreviations in the following paragraph. If an abbreviation is appropriate in its context, leave it as is.

The advantages of a grad. degree are not lost on me. With a Ph.D. I might become a university prof., a job that would allow me to work only in the p.m., so I wouldn't have to get up before 11:00 a.m., and only on Tues., Wed., and Thurs., my favourite days. Or I could get an M.D. and become a dr. Though I might have to work long hrs., I could earn plenty of $ and, by serving on a professional association like the CMA, could have a lot of influence. I know about these advantages because my two older bros. are Prof. Giordano and Dr. Giordano. I also know how hard they had to work for their degrees, so I think I'll stick with poli. sci. courses and look for a nice, safe govt. job after I get my B.A.

ab
28f

CHAPTER 29

Numbers

Experienced writers vary in their choice between writing numbers out and using figures. In scientific and technical writing, all numbers are usually written as figures. In business writing, all numbers over ten are usually written as figures. In general writing, numbers are more often spelled out. The following rules give conventions for general writing.

 Use figures for numbers that require more than two words to spell out.

The leap year has *366* days.
In 1986 the population of Moncton, New Brunswick, was *55 468*.

Spell out numbers of one or two words. (See also 29b.)

That hotel can accommodate no more than *seventy-five* people.

The first writing we know of was done more than *six thousand* years ago.

The collection included almost *twelve hundred* drawings and paintings.

A hyphenated number can be considered one word.

The ball game drew *forty-two thousand* people.

EXCEPTION: When you use several numbers together, they should be consistently spelled out or consistently expressed in figures.

INCONSISTENT   Only *ninety-nine* students attended the first lecture, but the audience increased to *126* for the second lecture and *two hundred* for the third.

457

REVISED   Only *99* students attended the first lecture, but the audience increased to *126* for the second lecture and *200* for the third.

29b Use figures instead of words according to standard practice.

Even when a number requires one or two words to spell out, we conventionally use figures for days and years; pages, chapters, volumes, acts, scenes, and lines; decimals, percentages, and fractions; addresses; scores and statistics; exact amounts of money; and the time of day.

DAYS AND YEARS

18 June 1990   A.D. 12   456 B.C.

EXCEPTION: The day of a month may be expressed in words when it is not followed by a year (*June fifth*; *October first*).

PAGES, CHAPTERS, VOLUMES, ACTS, SCENES, LINES	DECIMALS, PERCENTAGES, AND FRACTIONS
Chapter 9, page 123	22.5
Isaiah 28:1 in the Bible	48% (or 48 percent)
Hamlet, Act 5 (*or* V), Scene 3 (*or* iii), lines 35–40	3 1/2

ADDRESSES	SCORES AND STATISTICS
355 Clinton Avenue	21 to 7
419 Stonewall Street	a mean of 26
Brandon, MB R7B 2B3	a ratio of 8 to 1

EXACT AMOUNTS OF MONEY	THE TIME OF DAY
$4.50	9:00 a.m.
$3.5 million (*or* $3,500,000)	3:45 p.m.
$2763 (*or* $2,763)	14:30

EXCEPTIONS: Round dollar or cent amounts of only a few words may be expressed in words: *seventeen dollars*; *fifteen hundred dollars*; *sixty cents*. When the word *o'clock* is used for the time of day, also express the number in words: *two o'clock* (not *2 o'clock*).

29c Always spell out numbers that begin sentences.

We are so accustomed to seeing a capital letter at the beginning of a sentence that a number there can make reading difficult.

Therefore, always spell out any number that begins a sentence. If the number requires more than two words, avoid further awkwardness by rewording the sentence so that the number falls later and can be expressed as a figure.

Awkward	*103* of the opening-night audience asked for a refund.
Awkward	*One hundred and three* of the opening-night audience asked for a refund.
Revised	Of the opening-night audience, *103* asked for a refund.

EXERCISE

Revise the following sentences to correct the use of numbers. Circle the number preceding any sentence in which numbers are already used appropriately.

Example:

Carol paid one hundred and forty-five dollars for a bridesmaid's dress she would never wear again.

Carol paid $145 for a bridesmaid's dress she would never wear again.

1. 1036 Colgate University students played Twister for three and one-half hours on May fifth, 1984, in the largest game on record.
2. I lost a trivia game because I forgot that ten Downing Street is Prime Minister Thatcher's residence.
3. Only 27 percent of the 350 consumers we polled preferred the new product to the old one.
4. The world's tallest free-standing structure, the CN Tower, is 553 m high and cost fifty-two million dollars to build.
5. Covering four hundred and two acres, Angkor Wat in Cambodia is the largest religious building ever constructed.
6. A litre is equal to twenty-two one-hundredths of an imperial gallon.
7. Not until page ninety-nine, in the middle of Chapter five, does the author introduce the main character.
8. I was born on May fifteenth, six days after my dog.
9. Noma Industry's share price rose to twenty-two dollars by the end of 1986.
10. Dominating the town's skyline was a sign that stood ten metres off the ground and measured 37 metres by twelve metres.

num

29c

CHAPTER 30

Word Division

As much as possible, avoid dividing words. If you must divide a word between the end of one line and the beginning of the next, do so only between syllables. Put a hyphen at the end of the first line, never at the beginning of the second. Never divide the last word on a page, because in the act of turning the page the reader may forget the beginning of the word. If you are in doubt about how to break any word into syllables, consult a dictionary. Note, however, that not all syllable breaks are appropriate for word division. Use the following rules to decide when and how to divide words.

 Don't make a division that leaves a single letter at the end of a line or fewer than three letters at the beginning of a line.

FAULTY	A newspaper or television editorial for or *a-gainst* a candidate can sway an election.
REVISED	A newspaper or television editorial for or *against* a candidate can sway an election.
FAULTY	Counselling is required for every child *abus-er*.
REVISED	Counselling is required for every child *abuser*.

 Don't divide one-syllable words.

Since one-syllable words have no break in pronunciation, they should not be divided.

| FAULTY | The shiny, spinning space capsule *drop-ped* suddenly from the clouds. |
| REVISED | The shiny, spinning space capsule *dropped* suddenly from the clouds. |

30c Divide compound words only between the words that form them or at fixed hyphens.

Compound words are made up of two or more words (*draw-back, homecoming*). Their component words may be separated by a hyphen (*well-paying, cross-reference*), in which case the hyphen is called **fixed**. Compound words should be divided only between their component words and at fixed hyphens.

FAULTY	If you want to have friends, be *good-na-tured*.
REVISED	If you want to have friends, be *good-natured*.
FAULTY	Sherlock Holmes exemplifies the *mas-termind*.
REVISED	Sherlock Holmes exemplifies the *master-mind*.

(See 34d for guidelines on when to use hyphens in spelling compound words.)

30d Avoid confusing word divisions.

div
30d

Some word divisions may momentarily confuse the reader because the first or second part by itself forms a pronounceable (or unpronounceable) unit that does not fit with the whole. For example: *poi-gnant, read-dress, in-dict*. Avoid word divisions like these.

CONFUSING	Her walking out of class was an act of *her-oism*.
CLEAR	Her walking out of class was an act of *hero-ism*.
CONFUSING	He claims that stealing never bothered his *con-science*.
CLEAR	He claims that stealing never bothered his *conscience*.

EXERCISE

Revise the following sentences to repair any incorrect word divisions. Consult a dictionary if necessary. Circle the number preceding any sentence in which word division is already correct.

Example:

I thought Guy's joke was sidesplit-
ting, but no one else even smiled.

I thought Guy's joke was *side-
splitting*, but no one else even smiled.

1. After my cousin graduated, she joined the army as an officer.
2. A travel agent booked a seat for me on a charter flight.
3. The tarantella is a vivacious folk dance of southern Italy.
4. He took bad advice from several well-mean-
ing friends.
5. The product inspector detects any surfaces that are not smoothly sanded.
6. Last year I completely forgot to call my father on Father's Day.
7. Each of the twenty-three apartments he looked at was rented before he could make a deposit on it.
8. People find any number of ways to keep from feeling middle-aged.
9. While the photographers snapped pictures, Dan blush-
ed with embarrassment.
10. After the lecture Dotty felt she knew e-
nough about the subject to pass the test.

div
30d

PART VII

Effective Words

CHAPTER 31

Controlling Diction

Diction is the choice and use of words. Controlling your diction will help you express yourself with precision and clarity, so that you affect your readers as you want. You should select words suited to your writing situation—that is, your purpose, your meaning, and your readers backgrounds, interests, and expectations. And you should prune words that make your writing weak or inexact.

No firm rules dictate the proper words for every writing situation, but the following sections offer some guidelines for choosing words. The most useful advice, perhaps, is to suspect the first word that comes to mind and to be willing to search for a more appropriate or precise substitute.

31a Choosing the appropriate word

Words are appropriate when they suit your subject and the purpose of your writing, the role you are assuming, the attitude you want to project, and the readers you are writing for. We all use various kinds of language—various sets of words—depending on the context in which we are speaking or writing. Talking to friends, for example, you might say, *My sister decided to scrap therapy because her shrink seemed even more strung out than she was*. Writing for a general audience, however, you would convey the same information quite differently, perhaps writing, *My sister decided to abandon therapy because her psychiatrist seemed even more disturbed than she was*. In each case the diction fits the occasion. When you talk or write to people you know well and share experiences with, you can relax into colloquial or slang expressions such as *scrap*, *shrink*, and *strung out*.

APPROPRIATE AND INAPPROPRIATE DICTION

Appropriate in all writing situations:
  Standard English

Appropriate in some writing situations:

Slang (31a-1)	Neologisms (31a-5)
Colloquial language (31a-2)	Technical language (31a-6)
Regional words and expressions (31a-3)	Euphemisms (31a-7)

Rarely or never appropriate in writing or speech:

Non-standard language (31a-4)	Pretentious writing (31a-7)
Archaic and obsolete words (31a-5)	Biassed language: sexist, racist, ethnocentric, etc. (31a-8)

Your friends expect such informality. But when you write for a general audience, you must be more formal, using words such as *abandon*, *psychiatrist*, and *disturbed*. These words are more widely understood, and they indicate your respect for your reader's seriousness and intelligence.

Most of your writing in college/university and after will be analysing, explaining, and sometimes defending your understanding and interpretation of facts, events, and ideas. The words appropriate to such writing, like the conventions of grammar and usage described earlier in this handbook, are those of **standard** or **educated English**—that is, the English normally expected and used by educated readers and writers. The vocabulary of standard English is huge, allowing expression of an infinite range of ideas and feelings; but it does exclude words that only limited groups of people use, understand, or find inoffensive. Some of those more limited vocabularies should be avoided altogether; others should be used cautiously and in special situations, as when aiming for a special effect with an audience you know will appreciate it. Whenever you doubt a word's status, consult a dictionary (see 32b-2).

appr
31a

1   **Using slang only when appropriate**

All groups of people—from musicians and computer scientists to vegetarians and golfers—create **slang**, novel and colourful expressions that reflect the group's special experiences and set that group off from others. Slang displays endless inventiveness. Some of it gives new meanings to old words. For example, several decades ago the word *cool* gained a meaning of "pleasing, excellent" (*The movie was cool*), and during the 1970s *into* came to describe personal commitment (*I'm really into plants*). More recently, the word *hacker* has been applied to computer buffs (*Enthusiastic hackers have produced innovative computer games*). Some slang comes from other languages: the word *chow* ("food" or "a meal") comes from the Chinese *chao*, meaning "to stir or fry"; and *schlep* ("to lug" or "a clumsy person") comes from the Yiddish *schleppen*, "to drag." Sometimes the slang of a particular ethnic group is widely adopted by the rest of the population. *Out to lunch*, *put on ice*, and *funky*, for example, are contributions of black slang.

Among those who understand it, slang may be vivid and forceful. It often occurs in dialogue, and an occasional slang expression can enliven an informal essay. Some slang, such as *drop-out* (*she was a high school drop-out*), has proved so useful that it has passed into the general vocabulary.

However, most slang is too flippant and imprecise for effective communication, and it is generally inappropriate for academic or business writing. The writer who says that *many students start out pretty straight but then get weird* deprives her writing of seriousness while failing to specify what happens to the students. Avoiding imprecise slang and including specific, informative language would strengthen the sentence.

2 Using colloquial language only when appropriate

Colloquial language designates the words and expressions appropriate to everyday spoken language. Regardless of our backgrounds and how we live, we all try to *get along with* each other. We sometimes *get together with* our neighbours. We play with *kids*, *go crazy* about one thing, *crab* about something else, and in our worst moments try to *get back at* someone who has made us do the *dirty work*. These italicized words and expressions are not "wrong"; quite the contrary, more formal language might sound stilted and pompous in casual conversation and in some kinds of writing.

appr
31a

When you write informally, colloquial language may be appropriate to achieve the casual, relaxed effect of conversation. An occasional colloquial word dropped into otherwise more formal writing can also help you achieve a desired emphasis. And some formerly colloquial words (*rambunctious*, *trigger* as a verb) have gained acceptance in standard English. But colloquial language does not provide the exactness needed in more formal academic, business, and professional writing. In such writing you should generally avoid any words and expressions labelled "informal" or "colloquial" in your dictionary. Take special care to avoid **mixed diction**, a combination of standard and colloquial words.

> **MIXED DICTION** According to a Native American myth, the Great Creator *had a dog hanging around with him* when he created the earth.
>
> **CONSISTENT** According to a Native American myth, the Great Creator *was accompanied by a dog* when he created the earth.

3 Using regionalisms only when appropriate

Most national languages vary slightly from one geographical area to another. In American English, regional differences are most marked in pronunciation: a Texan overhearing a conversation between a New Yorker and a Georgian will not mistake either for a fellow Texan. Such differences in pronunciation are not as marked in Canada, although the conversation of a fisherman from a Newfoundland outport would sound noticeably different from that of one of his British Columbia counterparts. In a number of instances Canadian pronunciation differs from American, for example, *lieutenant* (Can.: lef ten'ənt, not lü ten'ənt); *been* (rhyming with "bean" rather than "bin"); *shone* (rhyming with "gone," not "bone"); *lever* (as in "beaver," not "sever"); *z* (rhyming with "bed," not "bee"); *route* (rhyming with "suit," not "rout"). (See Walter S. Avis, "Canadian English," reprinted in *Gage Canadian Dictionary*, pp. xi–xiii.) But Canadian regional differences are also reflected in terms of a number of words more or less limited (either in actual word or in unique meaning) to certain areas of the country. Walter Avis gives several examples:

> Other Canadianisms are more or less limited to certain regions—to Newfoundland: *jinker, nunny bag, tickle, tilt*; to the Maritimes: *aboideau, gaspereau, longliner*; to Ontario: *concession road, dew-worm, fire-reels*; to the Prairie Provinces: *bluff* (clump of trees), *grid road, local improvement district*; to British Columbia: *rancherie, skookum, steelhead*; to the Northland: *bush pilot, cat-swing, cheechako* ("Canadian English" xii).

4 Avoiding non-standard language

Words and grammatical forms called **non-standard** are used by many intelligent people who speak dialects other than standard English. In spoken and written standard English, however, these non-

appr
31a

standard forms are considered unacceptable. Examples include *irregardless* or *nowheres*; such pronoun forms as *hisn, hern, hisself*, and *theirselves*; *them* as an adjective, as in *them dishes, them courses*; the expressions *this here* and *that there*, as in *that there elevator*; verb forms such as *knowed, throwed, hadn't ought*, and *could of*; and double negatives such as *didn't never* and *haven't no*. Dictionaries label such expressions "non-standard" or "substandard." Avoid all non-standard expressions in speaking and writing situations calling for standard English.

5   Avoiding obsolete or archaic words and neologisms

Since our surroundings and our lives are constantly changing, some words pass out of use and others appear to fill new needs. **Obsolete** and **archaic** are dictionary labels for words or meanings of words that we never or rarely use but that appear in older documents and literature still read today. Obsolete words or meanings are no longer used at all—for example, *enwheel* ("to encircle") and *cote* ("to pass"). Archaic words or meanings occur now only in special contexts such as poetry—for example, *fast* ("near," as in *fast by the road*) and *belike* ("perhaps"). Both obsolete and archaic words are inappropriate in non-fiction writing for a general audience.

Neologisms are words created (or coined) so recently that they have not come into established use. An example is *prequel* (made up of *pre-*, meaning "before," and the ending of *sequel*), which is a movie or book that takes the story of an existing movie or book back in time. Some neologisms do become accepted as part of our general vocabulary. *Motel*, coined from *motor* and *hotel*, and *brunch*, meaning a combination of breakfast and lunch, are examples. But most neologisms pass quickly from the language. Unless such words serve a special purpose in your writing and are sure to be understood by your readers, you should avoid them.

6   Using technical words with care

All disciplines and professions rely on special words or give common words special meanings. Chemists speak of *esters* and *phosphatides*, geographers and mapmakers refer to *isobars* and *isotherms*, and literary critics write about *motifs* and *subtexts*. Printers use common words like *cut, foul*, and *slug* in special senses. Such technical language allows specialists to communicate precisely and economically with other specialists who share their vocabulary. But without explanation these words are meaningless to the non-specialist. When you are writing for a general audience, avoid unnecessary technical terms. If your subject requires words the reader may not understand, be careful to define them. (See also 31c-4 for a discussion of jargon and overly technical and inflated language.)

7 Avoiding euphemisms and pretentious writing

A **euphemism** is a presumably inoffensive word that a writer or speaker substitutes for a word deemed potentially offensive or too blunt. Writers of media advertising are particularly noted for their use of euphemisms: *dentures* instead of *false teeth*, *bathroom tissue* instead of *toilet paper*, *irregularity* instead of *constipation*, *senior citizens* for *old people*, and *perspire* instead of *sweat*. Because euphemisms usually conceal meaning instead of clarifying it, use them only when you know that blunt, truthful words would needlessly offend members of your audience.

People who write euphemistically also tend to decorate their prose with ornate phrases. Any writing that is more elaborate than its subject requires will sound pretentious or excessively showy. Good writers choose their words for their exactness and economy. Pretentious writers choose them in the belief that fancy words will impress readers. They rarely will.

> **PRETENTIOUS** Many institutions of higher education recognize the need for youth at the threshold of maturity to confront the choice of life's endeavour and thus require students to select a field of concentration.
>
> **REVISED** Many colleges and universities force students to make decisions about their careers by requiring them to select a major.

When either of two words will say what you mean, prefer the small word to the big one, the common word to the uncommon one. If you want to say *It has begun to rain*, say so. Don't say *I perceive that moisture has commenced to precipitate earthward*.

appr
31a

8 Avoiding sexist and other biassed language

Even when we do not mean it to, our language can reflect and perpetuate hurtful prejudices toward groups of people, especially racial, ethnic, religious, age, and gender groups. (See 4d-1 for a discussion of the differences among prejudice, fact, opinion, and belief.) In any kind of speech or writing, a word such as *nigger*, *honky*, *mick*, *kike*, *fag*, *dike*, or *broad*—with or without additionally insulting

ELIMINATING SEXIST LANGUAGE

1. Avoid demeaning and patronizing language.

SEXIST   Pushy broads are entering almost every occupation.

REVISED   *Women* are entering almost every occupation.

SEXIST   Prime Minister Mulroney came to Mila's defence.

REVISED   Prime Minister Mulroney came to *Mrs. Mulroney's* defence.

2. Avoid occupational or social stereotypes.

SEXIST   The caring doctor commends his nurse when she does a good job.

REVISED   Caring *doctors* commend *their nurses* on jobs well done.

SEXIST   Postmen are fairly well paid.

REVISED   *Letter carriers* are fairly well paid.

SEXIST   The grocery shopper should save her coupons.

REVISED   *Grocery shoppers* should save *their* coupons.

3. Avoid using *man* or words containing *man* to refer to all human beings.

SEXIST   Man has not reached the limits of social justice.

REVISED   *Humankind* (or *Humanity*) has not reached the limits of social justice.

SEXIST   The furniture consists entirely of man-made materials.

REVISED   The furniture consists entirely of *synthetic* materials.

4. Avoid using the generic *he* to refer to both genders. (See 8b-3, p. 254.)

SEXIST   The person who studies history knows his roots.

REVISED   The person who studies history knows *his or her* roots.

REVISED   *People* who study history know *their* roots.

adjectives—reflects more poorly on the user than on the person or persons designated. Unbiassed language does not submit to stereotypes. It refers to people as they would wish to be referred to.

Among the most subtle and persistent biassed language is that expressing narrow ideas about men's and women's roles, position, and value in society. This **sexist language** distinguishes needlessly between men and women in such matters as occupation, ability, behaviour, temperament, and maturity. It can wound or irritate readers, and it indicates the writer's thoughtlessness or unfairness. (See the box on the facing page.)

EXERCISE 1

Replace words in the following sentences as needed for standard written English. Consult a dictionary to determine a word's appropriateness and to find suitable substitutes.

Example:

If negotiators get hyper during contract discussions, they may mess up chances for a settlement.

If negotiators *become excited or upset* during contract discussions, they may *harm* chances for a settlement.

1. The food shortages in some parts of Africa are so severe that tens of thousands of people have met their demise.
2. A few stockholders have been down on the company ever since it refused to stop conducting business in South Africa.
3. The most stubborn members of the administration still will not hearken to our pleas for a voice in college doings.
4. They bought a beaut of a Victorian house in a ritzy neighbourhood.
5. A secretary often must support her boss even when she and he disagree.
6. During your first three months on the job, stifle your gripes and showcase your abilities for your boss.
7. Her arm often aches, but she says it doesn't bother her none.
8. Any candidate who understands the finest intricacies of democratic management and can thus covertly persuade the most recalcitrant legislators to do his every bidding could be appointed government house leader faster than you can bat an eye.
9. Too many Little League coaches know lots about baseball but not an awful lot about kids.
10. After every concert the cops hang around the parking lot until all the kids have taken off.

appr

31

31b   Choosing the exact word

Good writers labour to find the words within the large vocabulary of standard English that fit their meaning exactly, with precisely the overtones they intend. Inexact words—wrong, vague, unspecific, or trite—weaken writing and often confuse readers.

1   Using the right word for your meaning

The precise expression of meaning requires understanding both the denotations and connotations of words. A word's **denotation** is the thing or idea it refers to, the meaning listed in the dictionary without reference to the emotional associations it may arouse in a reader. Using words according to their established denotations is essential if readers are to grasp your meaning. The person who writes *Older people must often endure infirmaries* has mistaken *infirmaries* for *infirmities*. In using the wrong word, the writer says something different from what he or she intended, thus either amusing or confusing the reader. The writer who says *The divergence between the estimate and the actual cost is surprising* has also missed the mark, though not as widely. The word needed is *discrepancy*, not *divergence*. The two words are second cousins, but they are not interchangeable. Some mistakes in diction occur because of confusion of **homonyms**, words such as *principle/principal* or *rain/reign/rein* that sound alike but have different spellings and meanings. (See 34a-1 for a list of commonly confused homonyms.) Whenever you are unsure of a word's exact meaning, consult your dictionary.

Writers miss the right word more often by misjudging its connotation than by mistaking its denotation. **Connotation** refers to the associations a word carries with it. Some connotations are personal, deriving from one's particular experiences. A person whose only experience with dogs was being bitten three times will have a different reaction to the word *dog* than will someone who lives with the warm memories of a childhood pet. Such personal associations aside, however, most people agree about the favourable or unfavourable connotations of words. To most readers, the connotations of *love*, *home*, and *peace* are favourable, whereas those of *lust*, *shack*, and *war* are unfavourable. Most of us prefer to hear our tastes described as *inexpensive* rather than *cheap*.

Understanding connotation is especially important in choosing among **synonyms**, words with approximately, but often not exactly, the same meanings. *Cry* and *weep* are similar, both denoting the shedding of tears; but *cry* more than *weep* connotes a sobbing sound

exact
31b

accompanying the tears. *Sob* itself connotes broken, gasping crying, with tears, whereas *wail* connotes sustained sound, rising and falling in pitch, perhaps without tears. Used in the blank in the sentence *We were disturbed by his _____ing*, each of these words would evoke different sounds and images.

Tracking down the word whose connotation is exactly what you want can take time and effort. The most convenient resource is a dictionary, particularly the discussions of synonyms and their shades of meaning at the ends of many entries (see 32b-2 and 33c-2 for samples). Other useful resources are a thesaurus, which lists groups of synonyms, and a dictionary of synonyms, which both lists and defines them. (See 32a-3 for specific titles.)

EXERCISE 2

Revise the following sentences to replace any italicized word that is not used according to its established denotation. If the italicized word in a sentence is used correctly, circle the number preceding the sentence. Consult a dictionary if you are uncertain of a word's precise meaning.

Example:

Sam and Dave are going to Bermuda and Mexico, *respectfully*, for spring vacation.

Sam and Dave are going to Bermuda and Mexico, *respectively*, for spring vacation.

1. The *inference* of the report from the parents is that the school should care for their children in the afternoon.
2. Burning solid waste is not an *economic* way to generate power, but it eliminates the need for new dumping grounds.
3. The jury did not find the defendant's testimony *credible* and so convicted her.
4. Hospital personnel must wear protective clothing when tending a patient with a highly *communicative* disease.
5. I did not attend the lecture on artificial intelligence because I am *disinterested* in computers.
6. We've been without furniture for days, but now the movers are due to arrive *momentously*.
7. To support her argument she *sited* Mead's conclusion that schooling must challenge conventional views of the world.
8. After trying *continually* for two weeks to see my teacher, I finally complained to the dean.
9. One *affect* of the report is that doctors are less willing to order expensive tests for their patients.
10. Having been *deferred* from acting on impulse, she felt paralysed by indecision.

exact

31

EXERCISE 3

Describe how the connotation of each italicized word in the following sentences contributes to the writer's meaning. Give at least one synonym or related word that the writer could have used instead of the italicized word, and describe how the new word would alter the meaning. Consult a dictionary or thesaurus as necessary.

1. [The river] *slumbers* between broad prairies, *kissing* the long meadow grass, and *bathes* the overhanging boughs of elder bushes and willows or the roots of elms and ash trees and clumps of maples. —NATHANIEL HAWTHORNE

2. The new earth, freshly *torn* from its parent sun, was a ball of *whirling gases, intensely* hot, *rushing* through the black spaces of the universe on a path and a speed controlled by *immense* forces. —RACHEL CARSON

3. Summer and winter she *viewed* the town with *sightless* eyes. [The stone angel] was doubly blind, not only stone *unendowed* with even a *pretense* of sight. Whoever carved her had left the eyeballs blank. It seemed strange to me that she should stand above the town, *harking* us all to heaven without knowing who we were at all. —MARGARET LAURENCE

4. Here and there meadow larks *were suddenly upon* straw stacks, telephone wires, fence posts, their song clear with *ineffable exuberance* that *startled and deepened* the prairie silence—each quick and *impudent* climax of notes leaving behind it a vaster, emptier prairie *world*. The sky was *ideal* blue. —W. O MITCHELL

5. Economically, Canada, the old colonial *pussycat*, *doormat* to foreigners *plundering* resources and profits, is fast becoming a *voracious* tiger, especially within the North American economic *scene*. —ANDREW H. MALCOLM

| **2** | **Balancing the abstract and concrete, the general and specific** |

exact

31b

To understand a subject as you understand it, to experience it as you experience it, your readers need ample guidance from your words. When you describe a building as beautiful and nothing more, you force readers to provide their own conceptions of the features that make a building beautiful. If readers trouble to do the work you have assigned them—and they may not—they will call up diverse images of the many beautiful buildings they have seen, not a coherent image of the one you have seen. In evading your responsibility to be exact, you will have failed to communicate your meaning. Effective writing demands that abstract and general words like *beautiful* and *building*, which convey the broad outlines of ideas and objects, be balanced by concrete and specific words that make the ideas and objects sharp and firm. For instance, you might describe a *Victorian brick courthouse faced with stately arched windows and trimmed with ornate sandstone carvings*.

Abstract words name qualities and ideas: *beauty, inflation, depression, labour, management, truth, culture, network, liberal, conservative*. **Concrete words** name things we can know by our five senses of sight, hearing, touch, taste, and smell: *brick, sandstone, arched, bacon, apple, sticky, crisp, hard*.

General words name classes or groups of things, such as *buildings, weather*, or *birds*, and include all the varieties of the class. **Specific words** limit a general class like *buildings* by naming one of its varieties, such as *Victorian courthouse, office tower*, or *hut*. *Weather* includes *sunshine, drought, rain, windstorm*, and *cyclone*. *Birds* include *sparrows, eagles, geese, parrots, bobolinks*, and *vultures*. But *general* and *specific* are relative terms. *Rain* becomes a general word in relation to *drizzle, sprinkle*, and *downpour*, and *downpours* can be *continuous* or *sudden*. You become more and more specific as you move from a general class to a unique item, from *bird* to *pet bird* to *parrot* to *my parrot Moyshe*. (See 1e on distinguishing between the general and specific in shaping ideas.)

Abstract and general words are useful in the broad statements that set the course for your writing.

> The wild horse in North America has a *romantic* history.
>
> We must be *free* from *government interference* in our *affairs*.
>
> *Relations* between the sexes today are only a *little* more *relaxed* than they were in the past.

But these statements must be developed with concrete and specific detail. Writing seldom fails because it lacks abstraction and generality. If often fails because it lacks concrete and specific words to nail down meaning and make the writing vivid, real, and clear. In your own writing choose the concrete and specific word over the general and abstract. Avoid words such as *interesting, nice, area*, and *nature* that are essentially meaningless (see also 31c-1). When your meaning does call for an abstract or general word, make sure you define it, explain it, and narrow it with the concrete and specific words that most precisely reflect your knowledge and experience. Look at how concrete and specific information turns vague sentences into exact ones in the following examples.

exact

31b

VAGUE	The size of his hands made his smallness real. [How big were his hands? How small was he?]
EXACT	Not until I saw his white, doll-like hands did I realize that he stood at least a full head shorter than most other men.

VAGUE   The long flood caused a lot of awful destruction in the town. [How long did the flood last? What destruction did it cause, and why was the destruction awful?]

EXACT   The flood waters, which rose swiftly and then stayed stubbornly high for days, killed at least six townspeople and made life a misery for the hundreds who had to evacuate their ruined homes and stores.

EXERCISE 4

Make the following paragraph vivid by expanding the sentences with appropriate details of your own choosing. Concentrate especially on substituting concrete and specific words for the abstract and general ones in italics.

I remember *clearly* how *awful* I felt the first time I *attended* Mrs. Murphy's second-grade class. I had *recently* moved from a *small* town in Manitoba to a *crowded* suburb of Toronto. My new school looked *big* from the outside and seemed *dark* inside as I *walked* down the *long* corridor toward the classroom. The class was *noisy* as I neared the door; but when I *entered*, *everyone* became *quiet* and *looked* at me. I felt *uncomfortable* and *wanted* a place to hide. However, in a *loud* voice Mrs. Murphy *directed* me to the front of the room to introduce myself.

EXERCISE 5

For each abstract or general word below, give at least two other words or phrases that illustrate increasing specificity or concreteness. Consult a dictionary as needed. Use the most specific or concrete word from each group in a sentence of your own.

   Example:

   tired, *sleepy, droopy-eyed*

   We stopped for the night when I became so *droopy-eyed* that the road blurred.

exact
31b

1. fabric
2. delicious
3. car
4. narrow-minded
5. reach (*verb*)
6. green
7. walk (*verb*)
8. flower
9. serious
10. pretty
11. teacher
12. nice
13. virtue
14. angry
15. crime
16. smile (*verb*)
17. sick
18. desire (*verb*)
19. candy
20. misfortune

3   Using Idioms

Idioms are expressions in any language whose meanings cannot be determined simply from the words in them or whose component words cannot be predicted by any rule of grammar; often, they violate conventional grammar. Examples of English idioms include *put up with*, *plug away at*, and *make off with*. Because they are not governed by rules, idioms usually cause particular difficulty for people learning to speak and write a new language. For instance, those learning English as a second language find it easy to confuse certain prepositions such as *at/in/on* and *of/for*. But English prepositions can cause problems for native speakers of English, too, especially when a preposition is combined with an adjective or a verb. A reference list of some typical idioms with prepositions follows. Check a dictionary if you are unsure of what preposition to use with an idiom (see 32b-2).

abide *by* a rule
abide *in* a place or state

accords *with*
according *to*

accuse *of* a crime

adapt *from* a source
adapt *to* a situation

agree *with* a person
agree *to* a proposal
agree *on* a plan

angry *with*

capable *of*

charge *for* a purchase
charge *with* a crime

compare *to* something in a different class
compare *with* something in the same class

concur *with* a person
concur *in* an opinion

contend *with* a person
contend *for* a principle

differ *with* a person
differ *from* in appearance
differ *about* or *over* a question

identical *with* or *to*

impatient *at* her conduct
impatient *of* restraint
impatient *for* a raise
impatient *with* a person

independent *of*

inferior *to*

infer *from*

oblivious *of* something forgotten
oblivious *of* or *to* one's surroundings

occupied *by* a person
occupied *in* study
occupied *with* a thing

part *from* a person
part *with* a possession

prior *to*

rewarded *by* the judge
rewarded *for* something done
rewarded *with* a gift

superior *to*

wait *at* a place
wait *for* a train, a person
wait *on* a customer

exact

31b

> **EXERCISE 6**
>
> Insert the preposition that correctly completes each idiom in the following sentences. Consult the preceding list or a dictionary as needed.
>
> *Example:*
>
> I disagree _____ many feminists who say women should not be homemakers.
>
> I disagree *with* many feminists who say women should not be homemakers.
>
> 1. He had waited for years, growing impatient _____ her demands and _____ the money that she would leave to him.
> 2. The writer compared gorilla society _____ human society.
> 3. They agreed _____ most things, but they differed consistently _____ how to raise their child.
> 4. I was rewarded _____ my persistence _____ an opportunity to meet the premier.
> 5. He would sooner part _____ his friends than part _____ his Corvette.

4   Using figurative language

Figurative language expresses or implies comparisons between different ideas or objects. The sentence *As I try to write, I can think of nothing to say* is literal. The sentence *As I try to write, my mind is a blank slab of black asphalt* is figurative. The abstract concept of having nothing to say has become concrete, something that readers can understand with their senses as bare, hard, and unyielding.

Figurative language is commonplace. We sprinkle our conversation with figures: having *slept like a log*, we get up to find it *raining cats and dogs*. The sports pages abound in figurative language: the Blue Jays *blank* the Royals, and the Canucks *embark* on another season. Slang, too, is largely figurative: you may think chemistry *stinks*, but you can *get into* physics.

The rapid exchange of speech leaves little time for inventiveness, and most figures of daily conversation, like hastily written news stories, are worn and hackneyed. But writing gives you time to reject the tired figure and to search out the fresh words and phrases that will carry meaning concretely and vividly.

The two most common figures of speech are the **simile** and the **metaphor**. Both compare two things of different classes, often one abstract and the other concrete. A simile makes the comparison explicit and usually begins with *like* or *as*.

> We force their [children's] growth as if they were chicks in a poultry factory.
> —Arnold Toynbee

exact

31b

And then the central volume of the wave rolled on to sea, high and arching and white at the top, its back glossy like the plumage of a bird.   —HUGH MACLENNAN

Instead of stating a comparison, the metaphor implies it, omitting such words as *like* or *as*.

I refuse to accept the notion that nation after nation must spiral down a militaristic stairway into the hell of nuclear war.
—MARTIN LUTHER KING, JR.

A school is a hopper into which children are heaved while they are young and tender; therein they are pressed into certain standard shapes and covered from head to heels with official rubber stamps.
—H. L. MENCKEN

Two other figures of speech, **personification** and **hyperbole**, are less common than metaphor and simile. Personification treats ideas and objects as if they were human.

The economy consumes my money and gives me little in return.

I could hear the whisper of snowflakes, nudging each other as they fell.

Hyperbole deliberately exaggerates.

She appeared in a mile of billowing chiffon, flashing a rhinestone as big as an ostrich egg.

I'm going to cut him up in small cubes and fry him in deep fat.

To be successful, figurative language must be fresh and unstrained, calling attention not to itself but to the writer's meaning. If readers reject your language as trite or overblown, they may reject your message. One kind of figurative language gone wrong is the **mixed metaphor**, in which the writer combines two or more incompatible figures.

| **MIXED** | He often hatched new ideas, using them to unlock the doors of opportunity. |

exact
31b

Since metaphors often generate visual images in the mind of the reader, a mixed metaphor can create a ludicrous scene.

| **MIXED** | Various thorny problems that we try to sweep under the rug continue to bob up all the same. |

To revise a mixed metaphor, follow through consistently with just one image.

| **IMPROVED** | Various thorny problems that we try to weed out continue to thrive all the same. |

EXERCISE 7

Identify each figure of speech in the following sentences as a simile or a metaphor and analyse how it contributes to the writer's meaning.

1. All artists quiver under the lash of adverse criticism.
   —CATHERINE DRINKER BOWEN
2. Louisa spends the entire day in blue, limpid boredom. The caressing sting of it appears to be, for her, like the pleasure of lemon, or the coldness of salt water.
   —ELIZABETH HARDWICK
3. Every writer, in a roomful of writers, wants to be the best, and the judge, or umpire, or referee is soon overwhelmed and shouted down like a chickadee trying to take charge of a caucus of crows.   —JAMES THURBER
4. Canadian soldiers had an ambiguous reputation in England at that time; we were supposed to be loyal, furious, hairy fellows who spat bullets at the enemy, but ate women raw.
   —ROBERTSON DAVIES
5. Western sunset opens its sensational act, turning the uppermost third of the Ferris wheel into a burnished bridge, blinding the roller-coaster cowboys as, whooping up, they slingshot out of the shadowy lower depths.   —JACK LUDWIG

EXERCISE 8

Invent appropriate figurative language of your own (simile, metaphor, hyperbole, or personification) to describe each scene or quality below, and use the figure effectively in a sentence.

Example:
   the attraction of a lake on a hot day
   The small waves *like fingers beckoned* us irresistibly.

1. the sound of a kindergarten classroom
2. people waiting in line to buy tickets to a rock concert
3. the politeness of strangers meeting for the first time
4. a streetlight seen through dense fog
5. the effect of watching television for ten hours straight

exact

31b

5 **Avoiding trite expressions**

Trite expressions or **clichés**, are phrases so old and so often repeated that they become stale. They include worn figures of speech, such as *heavy as lead*, *thin as a rail*, *wise as an owl*; stale scraps from literature, such as *to be or not to be*, *trip the light fantastic*, *gone with the wind*; adjectives and nouns that have become inseparable, such as *acid test*, *crushing blow*, *ripe old age*; and simply overused phrases, such as *point with pride*, *easier said than done*, *better late than never*.

Many of these expressions were probably once fresh and forceful, but constant use has dulled them. Using clichés will weaken your writing by suggesting that you have not thought about what you are saying and have resorted to the easiest phrase. To prevent clichés from sliding into your writing, be wary of any expression you have heard or used before.

The following list contains just a few of the dozens of trite expressions.

add insult to injury	ladder of success
beyond the shadow of a doubt	moving experience
brought back to reality	needle in a haystack
cool, calm, and collected	sadder but wiser
dyed in the wool	sneaking suspicion
face the music	sober as a judge
gentle as a lamb	stand in awe
hard as a rock	strong as an ox
hit the nail on the head	tired but happy
hour of need	tried and true

You can avoid such expressions by substituting fresh words of your own or by restating the idea in plain language.

TRITE   A *motley crowd* of the singer's *ardent admirers* awaited her arrival in *breathless* silence.

REVISED   *Dressed in wild, colourful costumes*, a crowd of the singer's *fans* awaited her arrival in *eager silence*.

EXERCISE 9

Revise the following sentences to eliminate trite expressions.

Example:

The basketball team had almost seized victory, but it faced the test of truth in the last quarter of the game.

The basketball team *seemed about to win*, but the *real test* came in the last quarter of the game.

1. These disastrous consequences of the war have shaken the small nation to its roots.
2. Some say that liberal arts majors face an uphill climb getting jobs in business; others observe that corporations have been looking high and low for liberal arts students.
3. When my father retired from the gas company after thirty long years, he was honoured to receive a large clock in recognition of his valued service.
4. Sam shouldered his way through the crowd, hoping to catch a glimpse of the actress who had become the woman of his dreams.
5. My new car was supposed to be a technological triumph, but the catalytic converter started smelling to high heaven after only a thousand kilometres.

exact
31b

WAYS TO ELIMINATE WORDINESS

1. Cut empty words and phrases (31c-1).

WORDY The highly pressured nature of critical-care nursing is due to the patients' life-threatening illness.

REVISED Critical-care nursing *is highly pressured because* the patients have life-threatening illnesses.

2. Cut unnecessary repetition (31c-2).

WORDY Critical-care nurses must have steady nerves to care for patients who are critically ill.

REVISED Critical-care nurses must have steady nerves to *help very sick* patients.

3. Simplify word groups and sentences (31c-3).

WORDY The nurses must have possession of interpersonal skills and combine them with medical skills.

REVISED The nurses must *possess* interpersonal *and medical* skills.

4. Avoid jargon (31c-4).

WORDY It is considered by most health professionals that the critical-care nurse is an essential component in the improvement of the patient from the status of critical care to that of intermediate care or even that of home care.

REVISED Most health professionals *consider* the critical-care nurse *essential to the patient's improvement* from *critical to intermediate or even home care.*

w
31c

31c Avoiding wordiness

Avoiding wordiness means cutting whatever adds nothing to your meaning or the freshness of your writing. In editing your sentences, locate the forceful and exact words that are essential to your meaning. Cross out all the empty words; cut out repetition that neither clarifies nor emphasizes your meaning; and be sure you have used the most direct grammatical form to express your ideas. Don't sacrifice necessary detail or original expression for mere brevity, however. Concise writing does not waste words but still includes the concrete and specific details that make meaning clear. In concise writing the length of an expression is appropriate to the thought.

1 Cutting empty words and phrases

Writers sometimes resort to empty words and phrases, either thinking that they sound authoritative or leaning on them when solid words will not come. But empty expressions simply fill space, and they should be eliminated in revision.

Filler phrases say in several words what a single word can say as well.

FOR	SUBSTITUTE
at all times	always
at the present time	now
at this point in time	now
in the nature of	like
for the purpose of	for
in order to	to
until such time as	until
for the reason that	because
due to the fact that	because
because of the fact that	because
by virtue of the fact that	because
in the event that	if
by means of	by
in the final analysis	finally

Some filler phrases—such as *all things considered, as far as I'm concerned,* and *for all intents and purposes*—can be cut entirely with no loss in meaning.

**w
31c**

WORDY	*For all intents and purposes*, few women have yet achieved equal pay for equal work.
CONCISE	Few women have yet achieved equal pay for equal work.

All-purpose words, as their name implies, could mean almost anything. They include *angle, area, aspect, case, character, factor, field, kind, situation, thing,* and *type.* Because all-purpose words convey so little information, they almost always clutter and complicate the sentences they appear in.

WORDY	Because I chose the *field* of chemistry as my major, the whole *character* of my attitude toward the *area* of learning has changed.
CONCISE	Majoring in chemistry has changed my attitude toward learning.
WORDY	The *type* of large expenditures on advertising that manufacturers must make is a very important *aspect* of the cost of detergents.
CONCISE	Manufacturers' large advertising expenditures increase the cost of detergents.

EXERCISE 10

Revise the following sentences to achieve conciseness by cutting filler phrases and all-purpose words.

Example:

I came to university because of many factors, but most of all because of the fact that I want a career in medicine.

I came to university *primarily because* I want a career in medicine.

1. Some lawyers still believe that advertising is a thing that will damage their profession.
2. The fact is that most people are too absorbed in their own lives to care much about the situations of others.
3. The baseball situation I like best is when the game seems to be over, for all intents and purposes, and the home team's slugger hits the winning run out of the park.
4. By virtue of their athletic abilities, a few lucky teenagers are able to escape the types of pressures that living in a poverty situation can create.
5. One aspect of majoring in Asian art is a distinct drawback: except for a few rare teaching and curatorial positions, jobs are not available now and probably will not be available for some time to come.

2   Avoiding unnecessary repetition

Deliberately repeating words for parallelism or emphasis may clarify meaning and enhance coherence (see 17b and 18b). But unnecessary repetition weakens sentences. Avoid flabby repetition like that illustrated in the following example.

| **WORDY** | The machine *crushes* the *ore* into fine bits and dumps the *crushed ore* into a bin. |
| **CONCISE** | The machine pulverizes the ore and dumps it into a bin. |

Notice that using one word two different ways within a sentence is especially confusing.

| **CONFUSING** | Preschool instructors play a *role* in the child's understanding of male and female *roles*. |
| **CLEAR** | Preschool instructors contribute to the child's understanding of male and female roles. |

The simplest kind of useless repetition is the **redundant phrase**, a phrase that says the same thing twice, such as *few in number* and *large in size*. Some of the most common redundant phrases are listed below. (The unneeded words are italicized.)

biography *of his life*	*important* (*basic*) essentials
consensus *of opinion*	puzzling *in nature*
co-operate *together*	repeat *again*
final completion	return *again*
frank and honest exchange	square (round) *in shape*
habitual custom	*surrounding* circumstances

A related form of redundancy is repetition of the same idea in slightly different words. In the following sentences, the unneeded phrases are italicized.

| **WORDY** | Theodore Fontane began his writing career late in life *at a relative old age*. |
| **WORDY** | Many unskilled workers *without training in a particular job* are unemployed *and don't have any work*. |

EXERCISE 11

Revise the following sentences to achieve conciseness. Concentrate on eliminating unnecessary or confusing repetition and redundancy.

w
31c

Example:

Because the circumstances surrounding the cancellation of classes were murky and unclear, the editor of the student newspaper assigned a staff reporter to investigate and file a report on the circumstances.

Because the circumstances leading to the cancellation of classes were unclear, the editor of the student newspaper assigned a staffer to investigate and report the story.

1. In today's world in the last quarter of the twentieth century, security has become a more compelling goal than social reform.
2. Deadly nightshade is aptly named. It has small white flowers and deep black fruit. The fruit looks like night, and it also looks like death. The fruit does happen to be poisonous, too.
3. As they embark on the beginning of an operation, all these specialists—the surgeon, the anesthetist, and the operating-room nurses—have specialized tasks to perform.
4. The disastrous drought was devastating to crops, but the farmers co-operated together to help each other out.
5. In deciding whether to choose a career in the field of dentistry, remember that some experts predict a future decline in the incomes of all health professionals.

3   **Simplifying word groups and sentences**

Choose the simplest and most direct grammatical construction that fits your meaning. Don't use a clause if a phrase will do; don't use a phrase if a word will do. *The strength that the panther has*, *the strength of the panther*, and *the panther's strength* mean the same thing. But the first takes six words, the last only three.

WORDY	The figurine, which was carved from a piece of ivory, measured five centimetres.
REVISED	The figurine, carved of ivory, measured five centimetres.
CONCISE	The carved ivory figurine measured five centimetres.
WORDY	People with jobs that are low in pay are more likely to develop problems in their health.
CONCISE	People with low-paying jobs are more likely to develop health problems.

w
31c

(See 16b for advice on the ways to subordinate information.)

You can streamline and strengthen sentences by choosing strong verbs that advance the action rather than weak verbs that merely mark time. Weak verbs and their baggage of extra words flatten sentences just where they should be liveliest, padding them needlessly.

WORDY	The painting *is a glorification of* Queen Victoria.
CONCISE	The painting *glorifies* Queen Victoria.

In the second sentence the direct, evocative verb *glorifies* substitutes for the colourless verb *is*, the long noun *glorification*, and the preposition *of*. Wordy constructions of a weak verb such as *is*, *has*, or *make* plus an adjective or noun commonly clutter writing.

WORDY	I *am desirous* of teaching music to children.
CONCISE	I *want* to teach music to children.
WORDY	He *had the sense* that she would die.
CONCISE	He *sensed* that she would die.
WORDY	Though they *made some advancement* in the next hours, they still failed to reach camp.
CONCISE	Though they *advanced* in the next hours, they still failed to reach camp.

Passive constructions usually contain more words (and much more indirectness) than active constructions. Revise passive constructions by shifting their verbs to the active voice and positioning the actor as the subject. (See also 7h and 18d.)

WORDY	*The building had been designed by the architects* six years earlier, and *the plans had been reviewed by no one* before *construction was begun*.
CONCISE	*The architects had designed the building* six years earlier, and *no one had reviewed the plans* before *construction began*.

Whenever possible, avoid sentences beginning with the expletive constructions *there is* and *there are*. Revise such constructions by removing *there*, moving the subject to the beginning of the sentence, and substituting a strong verb for *is* or *are*. (See also 18e.)

WORDY	*There are several plots that are repeated* in television drama.
CONCISE	*Several plots occur repeatedly* in television drama.

EXERCISE 12

Make the following sentences as concise as possible. Simplify grammatical structures, replace weak verbs with strong ones, and eliminate passive and expletive constructions.

> *Example:*
> He was taking some exercise in the park when several thugs were suddenly ahead in his path.
>
> He was *exercising* (or *jogging* or *strolling*) in the park when several thugs suddenly *loomed* in his path.

1. The new goal posts were torn down by vandals before the first game, and the science building windows were broken.

w
31c

2. The house on Nelson Street that is brightly lighted belongs to a woman who was once a madam.
3. I am aware that most people of about my age are bored by politics, but I myself am becoming more and more interested in the subject.
4. When a social reform is taking root, such as affirmative action in education and business, it is followed by backlash from those for whom the reform is not directly beneficial.
5. The attendance at the conference was lower than we expected, but there is evidence that the results of the meeting have been spread by word of mouth.

4 Avoiding jargon

Jargon is the special vocabulary of any discipline or profession—the terminology that permits doctors, economists, art historians, and others to communicate clearly and efficiently with their colleagues (see 31a-6). But *jargon* also commonly describes any vague, inflated language that states relatively simple ideas in unnecessarily complicated ways. The directions for using a shower head tell us that *this spray system will allow the user to reduce the mean diameter of the spray spectrum* instead of simply saying that *the nozzle will concentrate the spray*. Jargon often sounds as if the writer studied all the guidelines for being exact and concise and then set out to violate every one.

JARGON	The necessity for individuals to become separate entities in their own right may impel children to engage in open rebelliousness against parental authority or against sibling influence, with resultant confusion of those being rebelled against.
TRANSLATION	Children's natural desire to become themselves may make them rebel against bewildered parents or siblings.
JARGON	The weekly social gatherings stimulate networking among members of management from various divisions, with the aim of developing contacts and maximizing the flow of creative information.
TRANSLATION	The weekly parties give managers from different divisions a chance to meet and to share ideas.

w
31c

EXERCISE 13

Make the following passage as concise as possible. Eliminate wordiness by cutting unneeded or repeated words and by simplifying both words and grammatical structures. Consult a dictionary as needed. Be merciless.

Example:

The nursery school teacher education training sessions involve active interfacing with preschool children of the appropriate age as well as intensive peer interaction in the form of role plays.

Training for nursery school teachers involves *interaction* with *preschoolers* and *role-playing with peers*.

At the end of a lengthy line of reasoning, he came to the conclusion that the situation with carcinogens [cancer-causing substances] should be regarded as analogous to the situation with the automobile. Rather than giving in to an irrational fear of cancer, we should consider all aspects of the problem in a balanced and dispassionate frame of mind, making a total of the benefits received from potential carcinogens (plastics, pesticides, and other similar products) and measuring said total against the damage done by such products. This is the nature of most discussions about the automobile. Rather than responding irrationally to the visual, aural, and air pollution caused by automobiles, we have decided to live with them (while simultaneously working to improve on them) for the benefits brought to society as a whole.

w
31c

CHAPTER 32

Using the Dictionary

Consulting a dictionary can strengthen your choice of words. It can show you what words fit your needs (see Chapter 31); it can help you build your vocabulary (see Chapter 33); and it can show you how to spell words (see Chapter 34). It can answer most of the questions about words you may ask. This chapter will show you how to choose a dictionary that suits your purpose, how to read a dictionary without difficulty, and how to work with a dictionary as a flexible, compact, and thorough word reference.

An ordinary dictionary records in an alphabetical list the current usage and meaning of the words of a language. To do this, it includes a word's spelling, syllables, pronunciation, origin, meanings, grammatical functions, and grammatical forms. For some words the dictionary may provide a label indicating the status of the word according to geography, time, style, or subject matter. It may also list other words closely related in meaning and explain the distinctions among them. Some dictionaries include quotations illustrating a word's history or special uses. Many dictionaries include additional reference information, such as an essay on the history of English, a vocabulary of rhymes, names and locations of postsecondary institutions, and tables of weights and measures.

32a Choosing a dictionary

1 Abridged dictionaries

Abridged dictionaries are the most practical for everyday use. Often called desk dictionaries because of their convenient size, they usually list 100 000 to 150 000 words and concentrate on fairly common words and meanings. Though you may sometimes need to consult an unabridged or a more specialized dictionary, a good abridged dictionary will serve most reference needs for writing and reading. Any of the following abridged dictionaries, listed alphabetically, is dependable.

The American Heritage Dictionary, 2nd coll. ed. (1985). This dictionary's most obvious feature is its wealth of illustrations: more than 3000 photographs, drawings, and maps. The dictionary includes foreign words among the main entries and has separate sections on abbreviations and geographical and biographical names. The definitions are arranged in clusters of related meanings, with the most common meaning generally first. Usage labels (*slang, informal*, and so on) are applied liberally. Many words are followed by usage notes, which reflect the consensus of a panel of over 150 writers, editors, and teachers. The dictionary uses as few abbreviations and symbols as practicable. It includes guides to usage, grammar, spelling, and punctuation. Houghton Mifflin (Canada) Ltd. brought out an earlier Canadianized version of this dictionary in 1980, *The Houghton Mifflin Canadian Dictionary of the English Language*, revised to include Canadian words, spellings, maps, biographies, and photographs. It also uses metric units for measurements.

Funk & Wagnalls Canadian College Dictionary, rev. ed. (1989). This dictionary includes lexical and other information pertaining to Canada, including Canadian usage, pronunciation, and spelling, as well as a current list of Canadian universities and colleges, but it is still substantially American in content.

Gage Canadian Dictionary, rev. ed. (1983). As the introduction to this dictionary points out, this is "the only adult-level dictionary currently available that can be said truly to reflect standard Canadian usage throughout." The introductory essay goes on to observe that such usage is often more diverse than that of either Britain or the United States, a factor rarely acknowledged in British or American dictionaries (although these unique differences are not made particularly clear in the dictionary itself). Another limitation of this dictionary is that the number of synonyms for a word rarely if ever exceeds two. The dictionary has also been criticized for not being a broadly representative Canadian lexicon that reflects important regional variations or distinctive elements. *Gage Canadian Dictionary* surpasses all of the other purportedly Canadian dictionaries mentioned in this section, however, in its inclusion of "hundreds of words which are native to Canada or which have meanings peculiar to Canada" (Avis, "Canadian English" xii).

32a

Oxford American Dictionary, (1980). A descendant of the unabridged *Oxford English Dictionary* (see description in 32a-2), this abridged dictionary is somewhat briefer than any of the others listed here. Its pronunciation symbols are particularly straightforward and easy to use. Its word meanings, arranged according to the frequency of their use, are short and simple. The dictionary emphasizes correct American usage, applies usage labels frequently, and includes over 600 usage notes. Unlike most other abridged dictionaries, this one contains no special appendixes and no etymologies, or word histories.

The Random House College Dictionary, rev. ed. (1989). Based on the unabridged *Random House Dictionary of the English Language* (see 32a-2), this dictionary includes abbreviations and biographical and geographical names in the main alphabetical listing. Its list of words is particularly up to date. Appendixes include a manual of style.

Webster's Ninth New Collegiate Dictionary (1989). This dictionary, based on the unabridged *Webster's Third New International Dictionary of the English Language* (see 32a-2), concentrates on standard English and applies usage labels (such as *slang*) less frequently than do other dictionaries. Word definitions are listed in chronological order of their appearance in the language. The main alphabetical listing includes abbreviations. Geographical names and foreign words and phrases appear in appendixes, as does a manual of style. A number of uniquely Canadian words are included.

Webster's New World Dictionary, 3rd coll. ed. (1988). This dictionary includes foreign words, abbreviations, and geographical and biographical names in the main alphabetical listing. The definitions of words are arranged in chronological order. Usage labels (*colloquial*, *slang*, and so on) are applied liberally, and words and phrases of American origin are starred. Appendixes on punctuation and mechanics and on manuscript form are included.

2 Unabridged dictionaries

32a

Unabridged dictionaries are the most scholarly and comprehensive of all dictionaries, sometimes consisting of several volumes. They emphasize the history of words and the variety of their uses. An unabridged dictionary is useful when you are studying a word in depth, reading or writing about the literature of another century, or looking for a quotation containing a particular word. Unfortunately, Canada has no unabridged dictionary of its own at present. The following unabridged dictionaries are available at most libraries.

The Oxford English Dictionary, (*OED*), 2nd ed., 20 volumes (1933–89). The first edition is available in a compact, photographically reduced, three-volume edition (1987), as well as a computerized

CD-ROM format (1989) produced in co-operation with the University of Waterloo in Ontario. This is the greatest dictionary of our language. Its purpose is to show the histories and current meanings of all words. Its entries illustrate the changes in a word's spelling, pronunciation, and meaning with quotations from writers of every century. Some entries span pages. The second edition integrates the original *OED*, the four supplementary volumes published between 1972 and 1986, and approximately 5000 new words and senses of existing words. While basically British, the *OED* does include some American words and meanings.

The Random House Dictionary of the English Language, 2nd ed. (1987). This dictionary is smaller (and less expensive) than many unabridged dictionaries (it has 315 000 entries, compared with 472 000 in *Webster's Third New International*). Its entries and definitions are especially up to date, and it includes hundreds of usage notes. Among its appendixes are short dictionaries of French, Spanish, Italian, and German and a brief atlas with colour maps.

Webster's Third New International Dictionary of the English Language (1986). This dictionary attempts to record the language more as it *is* used than as it *should be* used. Therefore, usage labels (such as *slang*) are minimal. Definitions are given in chronological order or their appearance in the language. Most acceptable spellings and pronunciations are provided. Plentiful illustrative quotations show variations in the uses of words. The dictionary is unusually strong in new scientific and technical terms.

3 Special dictionaries

Special dictionaries limit their attention to a single class of word (for example, slang, engineering terms, abbreviations), to a single kind of information (synonyms, usage, word origins), or to a specific subject (black culture, biography, history), or to a particular country or even region of a country. Thus special dictionaries provide more extensive and complete information about their topics than general dictionaries do.

Special dictionaries on slang or word origins not only can help you locate uncommon information but also can give you a sense of the great richness and variety of language. They often make entertaining reading.

32a

FOR INFORMATION ON SLANG

Partridge, Eric. *A Dictionary of Slang and Unconventional English.* 8th ed. Ed. Paul Beale. 1985.

Wentworth, Harold, and Stuart Berg Flexner. *Dictionary of American Slang.* 2nd supp. ed. 1975.

FOR THE ORIGINS OF WORDS

Oxford Dictionary of English Etymology. Ed. Charles T. Onions et al. 1966.

Partridge, Eric. *Origins: A Short Etymological Dictionary of Modern English*. 1977.

Two kinds of special dictionaries—a usage dictionary and a dictionary of synonyms—are such useful references for everyday writing that you may want one of each on your own reference shelf. A dictionary of usage contains extensive entries for the words, phrases, and constructions that most frequently cause problems and controversy.

FOR GUIDANCE ON ENGLISH USAGE

Follett, Wilson. *Modern American Usage: A Guide*. Ed. Jacques Barzun. 1966.

Fowler, H. W. *A Dictionary of Modern English Usage*. 2nd ed. Rev. and ed. Sir Ernest Gowers. 1987.

Morris, William, and Mary Morris. *Harper Dictionary of Contemporary Usage*. 2nd ed. 1985.

A dictionary of synonyms provides lists of words with closely related meanings. The lists are much more extensive than the usage notes in a general dictionary. Some dictionaries of synonyms contain extended discussions and illustrations of various shades of meaning.

FOR INFORMATION ABOUT SYNONYMS

Lewis, Norman. *The New Roget's Thesaurus of the English Language in Dictionary Form*. 1986.

Webster's New Dictionary of Synonyms. 1984.

FOR INFORMATION ON LANGUAGE USAGE IN A PARTICULAR REGION

Poteet, Lewis J., comp. *The South Shore Phrase Book: A New, Revised and Expanded Nova Scotian Dictionary Complete with Two Appendices*. 2nd ed. 1988.

Pratt, T. K., ed. *Dictionary of Prince Edward Island English*. 1988.

Story, G. M., W. J. Kirwin, and J. D. A. Widdowson, eds. *Dictionary of Newfoundland English*. 1982.

SPECIAL SCHOLARLY DICTIONARY

Avis, Walter S., Patrick D. Drysdale, and Matthew H. Scargill, eds. *Dictionary of Canadianisms on Historical Principles*. 1967.

See 35b for an extensive list of special dictionaries in fields such as literature, business, history, psychology, and science.

32a

32b   Working with a dictionary's contents

1   Finding general information

The dictionary is a convenient reference for information of every sort. Most abridged dictionaries will tell you the atomic weight of oxygen, Napoleon's birth and death dates, the location of Fort Garry, the population of Gambia, what the Red River carts used during pioneer days in the West looked like, the origin and nature of surrealism, or the relation between Canadian and American liquid measures. Finding such information may require a little work—for instance, checking the entry *periodic table* or *element* as well as *oxygen*, or consulting an appendix of biographical names to find Napoleon. But a dictionary is often the quickest and most accessible reference for general information when an encyclopedia, textbook, or other reference book is unavailable or inconvenient to use.

2   Answering specific questions

Dictionaries use abbreviations and symbols to squeeze a lot of information into a relatively small book. This system of condensed information may at first seem difficult to read. But all dictionaries include in their opening pages detailed information on the arrangement of entries, pronunciation symbols, and abbreviations. And the format is quite similar from one dictionary to another, so becoming familiar with the abbreviations and symbols in one dictionary makes reading any dictionary an easy routine. The labelled parts of the two entries on the next page—*conjecture* from the *American Heritage Dictionary* (referred to from now on as *AHD*) and *reckon* from *Webster's Ninth New Collegiate Dictionary*—are discussed in the following sections.

Spelling and word division

The small initial letters for both *conjecture* and *reckon* indicate that these words are not normally capitalized. (In contrast, *Franklin stove* is capitalized in both the *AHD* and *Webster's Collegiate* because *Franklin* is a proper noun.)

The centred periods in **con·jec·ture** and **reck·on** show the divisions of these words into syllables. If you are writing or typing a word of more than one syllable and need to break it at the end of a

32b

line, follow the dictionary's division of the word into syllables. (See also Chapter 30 for general rules about word division.)

THE AMERICAN HERITAGE DICTIONARY

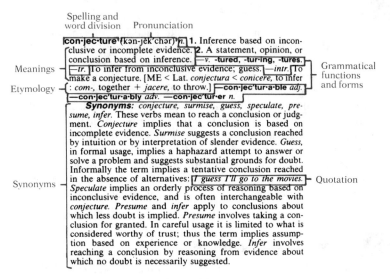

WEBSTER'S NINTH NEW COLLEGIATE DICTIONARY

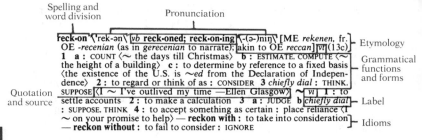

32b

If a word is a hyphenated compound word, such as *cross-question*, a dictionary shows the hyphen as part of the spelling: **cross-question**. The treatment of foreign words such as *joie de vivre* or *ergo*, which are normally italicized (or underlined) in writing, is more varied. *Webster's New World Dictionary* places a special symbol (‡) before each one. *Gage Canadian Dictionary* (referred to hereafter as *GCD*) simply designates them as *French* and *Latin*, respectively, therefore indicating they should be italicized.

Dictionaries provide any variant spellings of a word at the beginning of an entry. Thus, for the word *sulphur*, the *GCD* has "**sul·phur** or **sul·fur**," indicating that either spelling is acceptable.

EXERCISE 1

Check the spelling of the following words in a dictionary. Correct any incorrect spellings, and divide all the words into syllables.

1. England	5. inheritence	9. grievance
2. innoculate	6. over-estimate	10. secretery
3. reccommend	7. depreciation	11. trans-Atlantic
4. methodical	8. excruciating	12. crossreference

Pronunciation

Dictionaries use symbols to indicate how to pronounce a word because the alphabet itself does not record all the sounds in the language. (Listen, for example, to the different sounds of *a* in only three words: *far*, *make*, and *answer*.) Most dictionaries provide a key to the pronunciation symbols at the foot of each page or every two facing pages. In addition to this, the *GCD* puts its "Complete Pronunciation Key" on the inside front and back covers.

The entries for *conjecture* and *reckon* show two slightly different pronunciation systems. In the *AHD's conjecture* the pronunciation appears in parentheses; in *Webster's Collegiate* it appears in reversed slashes (\ \). In both entries the stressed syllable is indicated by an accent mark (′ and `); but in the *AHD* the mark follows the stressed syllable (kən-jĕk′chər), whereas in *Webster's Collegiate* it precedes the stressed syllable (`rek-ən).

Most unabridged and some abridged dictionaries provide variant pronunciations, including regional differences. The *GCD*, for example, provides two pronunciations for the last syllable of *licorice*, and indicates that the word may be pronounced either of three ways: "lĭk′ə rish, lik′rish, or lik′əris."

EXERCISE 2

Consult a dictionary for the correct pronunciation of the following words. Write out the pronunciation as given, using the dictionary's symbols. (If more than one pronunciation is given, write them all out.)

1. crucifixion	5. bathos	9. route
2. mnemonics	6. epitome	10. yacht
3. timorous	7. miserable	11. promenade
4. utilitarian	8. lieutenant	12. insouciance

32b

Grammatical functions and forms

Dictionaries give helpful information about a word's function and forms. The *Webster's Collegiate* entry for *reckon* shows the word to be a verb (*vb*), with the past tense and past participle *reckoned* and the present participle *reckoning*, and with both transitive (*vt*) and intransitive (*vi*) meanings. The *AHD* entry for *conjecture* shows it to be an even more versatile word. It is a noun (*n.*), with separate meanings in that function. And it is also a verb (*v.*): past tense and past participle *conjectured*, present participle *conjecturing*, and third-person singular present-tense *conjectures*. The verb has both transitive (*tr.*) and intransitive (*intr.*) meanings.

Most dictionaries provide not only the principal forms of regular and irregular verbs but also the plural forms of irregular nouns and the comparative and superlative forms of adjectives and adverbs that commonly show degree with *-er* and *-est*. An adjective or adverb without *-er* and *-est* forms in the dictionary requires the addition of *more* and *most* to show the comparative and superlative.

When other parts of speech are formed from the word being defined and have related meanings, those words are grouped at the end of the entry, where they are spelled, divided, accented, and identified by part of speech but not defined. Several of these so-called derivative forms are provided at the end of the *AHD* entry for *conjecture*: *conjecturable* (*adj.*), *conjecturably* (*adv.*), and *conjecturer* (*n.*).

The *Webster's Collegiate* entry for *reckon* ends with two uses of the word in idiomatic expressions (*reckon with* and *reckon without*). These phrases are defined (unlike the related parts of speech of *conjecture*) because, as with all idioms, their meanings cannot be inferred simply from the words they consist of (see 31b-3).

EXERCISE 3

Consult a dictionary to determine the part of speech of each of the following words. If the word functions as more than one part of speech, list them all. If the word is a verb, list its principal parts; if a noun, its plural form; if an adjective or adverb, its comparative and superlative.

1. little	5. machine	9. upset
2. that	6. orient	10. steal
3. study	7. roof	11. manifest
4. happen	8. ring	12. firm

32b

Etymology

Dictionaries provide the **etymology** of a word (its history) to indicate its origin and the evolution of its meanings and forms. The dictionary can compress much information about a word into a small space through symbols, abbreviations, and different typefaces. An explanation of these systems appears in the dictionary's opening pages. The *AHD* traces *conjecture* first to Middle English (ME) (twelfth to fifteenth centuries) and then back to Latin (Lat.). As the entry in *Webster's Collegiate* shows, *reckon* came to English by a different route, arriving from Old English (OE) by way of Middle English (ME). The notation "(13c)" at the end of the second line indicates that the first recorded use of *reckon* to mean "count" occurred in the thirteenth century. (See 33a for a brief history of the English language.)

Sometimes dictionaries do not give the etymology for a word. Their practices differ (and are explained in their opening pages), but in general they omit etymology when it is obvious, unknown, or available elsewhere in the dictionary.

EXERCISE 4

Consult a dictionary for the etymologies of the following words. Use the dictionary's own explanations of abbreviations and symbols to get the fullest history of the word, and write out that history in your own words.

1. grammar	5. penetrate	9. calico
2. engage	6. promote	10. chauvinism
3. leaf	7. retrieve	11. assassin
4. moon	8. toxic	12. water

Meanings

Dictionaries divide the general meaning of a word into particular meanings on the basis of how the word is or has been actually used. They arrange a word's meanings differently, however, explaining the basis of their arrangement in their opening pages. *Webster's Collegiate* and *Webster's New World* list meanings in order of their appearance in the language, earliest first. The *AHD*, *GCD*, and abridged *Random House*, in contrast, usually place the word's most basic or common meaning first and follow it with the other meanings. These different policies will result in roughly the same arrangement of meanings only when the oldest meaning of a word is also the most common. Thus you should be sure you know the system of arrangement used by any dictionary you are consulting. Then read through the entire entry before settling on the meaning that most closely fits the context of what you're reading or writing.

32b

Most dictionaries provide any special technical and scientific meanings of a word in separately numbered entries that are usually labelled. These labels are discussed later in this section.

EXERCISE 5

Consult a dictionary for the meanings of the following words. How many distinct meanings does each word have? How does the dictionary list meanings, chronologically or in order of importance? If chronologically, is the oldest meaning also the most common? What changes have occurred in each word's use over time?

1. weight	5. order	9. prefer
2. recipe	6. apt	10. quit
3. colour	7. astrology	11. spring
4. condition	8. offered	12. sue

Synonyms and antonyms

Synonyms are words whose meanings are approximately the same, such as *small* and *little*. **Antonyms** are words whose meanings are approximately opposite, such as *small* and *big*. When a word has many closely related synonyms that are hard to distinguish, an abridged dictionary may devote a separate paragraph to them. The *AHD* does so in distinguishing the verb *conjecture* from the verbs *surmise*, *guess*, *speculate*, *presume*, and *infer*, each of which can also be looked up in its alphabetical place. *Webster's Collegiate* defines *reckon* with some words in small capital letters (COUNT, ESTIMATE, COMPUTE, and so on). These are both synonyms and cross-references, in that each word may be looked up in its alphabetical place. Dictionaries specify antonyms less often than synonyms, usually with a boldface **ant** at the end of the entry.

Reading through the lists and discussions of synonyms and antonyms for a word can help you locate its meaning in a given context more exactly. (See 33c-2 for a discussion of how to use the synonyms provided by a dictionary to increase your vocabulary.)

32b

EXERCISE 6

Consult a dictionary for the synonyms and antonyms of the following words. Use the word itself and each synonym and antonym appropriately in a sentence of your own.

1. suggest	4. discover	7. kind (*adj.*)
2. plain (*adj.*)	5. change (*v.*)	8. memory
3. high (*adj.*)	6. beautiful	9. serious

Labels

Dictionaries apply labels to words or to particular meanings that have a special status or use. The labels are usually of four kinds: subject, style, region, and time.

Subject labels tell us that a word or one of its meanings has a special use in a field of knowledge or a profession. In its entry for *relaxation*, for instance, the *AHD* presents specialized meanings with the subject labels *physiology*, *physics*, and *mathematics*.

Style labels restrict a word or one of its meanings to a particular level of usage, such as *slang, colloquial* or *informal, non-standard* or *substandard, vulgar*, and *poetic* or *literary*. The label *slang* indicates that a word should be used in writing only for a special effect. For example, most abridged dictionaries label *crumb* as slang when it means "a worthless or despicable person." The label *informal* or *colloquial* is applied to words that are appropriate for conversation and informal writing but not for formal writing. For instance, the *GCD* identifies as informal the use of *sure* in the sentence *That sure is interesting* (the more formal word is *surely*.) The label *non-standard* or *substandard* is applied to words or their meanings that are considered inappropriate for standard speech and writing. The *AHD*, for instance, labels all uses of *ain't* as non-standard. The label *vulgar*, or sometimes *vulgar slang*, is applied to words or their meanings that are normally considered offensive in speech and writing. The label *poetic* or *literary* designates words or their meanings (such as *eve* for *evening* and *o'er* for *over*) used only in poetry or the most formal writing.

Region labels indicate that a particular spelling, pronunciation, or meaning of a word is not national but limited to some area. A regional difference may be indicated by the label *dialect*. The *GCD* labels as *dialect* the use of *critter* to mean "any living creature" or "an animal, especially a cow, raised as livestock" (as in *Get that critter into the barn*). More specific region labels may designate areas of Canada or other countries. The word *bloke* (meaning "fellow") is labelled as British by most dictionaries. And the *GCD* indicates that in Western Canada, *slough* means "a body of fresh water formed by rain or melted snow" or "a soft, deep, muddy place," while on the Pacific coast of Canada *slough* refers to "a shallow or marshy inlet of the sea."

Time labels indicate words or their meanings that the language, in evolving, has discarded. These words and meanings are included in the dictionary primarily to help readers of some older texts that contain them. The label *obsolete* designates words or specific meanings that are no longer used, whereas the label *archaic* designates words or specific meanings that are out of date though still in occasional use.

32b

See 31a for further discussion of levels of usage and their appropriateness in your writing.

EXERCISE 7

Consult at least two dictionaries to determine the status of each of the following words or any one of their meanings according to subject, style, region, or time.

1. impulse	5. goof	9. mad
2. OK	6. jinker	10. sing
3. irregardless	7. lift	11. brief (*n.*)
4. neath	8. potlatch	12. joint

Illustrative quotations

Dictionaries are made by collecting quotations showing actual uses of words in all kinds of speech and writing. Some of these quotations, or others that the dictionary makers invent, may appear in the dictionary's entries as illustrations of how a word may be used. Unabridged dictionaries usually provide many such examples, not only to illustrate a word's current uses but also to show the changes in its meanings over time. Abridged dictionaries use quotations more selectively: to illustrate an unusual meaning of the word, to help distinguish between two closely related meanings of the same word, or to show the differences between synonyms. The *AHD* entry for *conjecture* and the *Webster's Collegiate* entry for *reckon* both employ quotation.

EXERCISE 8

Consult a dictionary to find a quotation illustrating at least one meaning of each word below. Then write an illustrative sentence of your own for each word.

1. jolt	4. ceremonial	7. legitimate
2. articulate	5. sensuous	8. inquire
3. discreet	6. tremble	9. nether

32b

CHAPTER 33

Improving Your Vocabulary

A precise and versatile vocabulary is essential to effective communication. As you gain experience writing, you will want to improve the precision with which you use familiar words (see Chapter 31) and increase the number of words you can use appropriately. To a great extent, you can improve your vocabulary by frequent and inquisitive reading—by troubling to notice and learn the interesting or unfamiliar words used by other writers.

This chapter briefly describes the development of English and explains how words are formed. Then it offers some advice for learning to use new words. The chapter has a twofold purpose: to provide a sense of the potential of English by acquainting you with its history and range of words; and to help you increase the range, versatility, and precision of your own vocabulary.

33a Understanding the sources of English

People change their language as they and their surroundings change. They revise spellings, pronunciation, and syntax, alter meanings, and even add or drop words to keep the language fresh and useful. English changes continuously, but its subtle and complex character stays the same.

English has over 500 000 words, probably more than any other language. This exceptional vocabulary and the power and range of expression that accompany it derive from its special mix of word sources. Unlike many other languages, English has borrowed a large number of words.

How English drew on its several sources and acquired its large vocabulary is the story of historical changes. The ancestor of English,

Indo-European, spoken (but not written) perhaps as far back as 5000 B.C., eventually spread to cover the area from India west to the British Isles. In what is now England, an Indo-European offshoot called Celtic was spoken extensively until the fifth century A.D. But over the next few centuries invaders from the European continent, speaking a dialect of another Indo-European language, Germanic, overran the native Britons. The Germanic dialect became the original source of English.

Old English, spoken from the eighth to the twelfth centuries, was a rugged, guttural language. It used a slightly different alphabet from ours (including the characters ð and þ for *th*), which has been transcribed in the following sample. The sample shows the opening lines of the Lord's Prayer: "Our Father, who art in heaven, hallowed be thy name. Thy kingdom come. Thy will be done on earth as it is in heaven."

> Fæder ure thu the eart on heofonum, si thin nama gehalgod. Tobecume thin rice. Gewurthe thin willa on eorthan swa swa on heofonum.

Many of our nouns, such as *stone*, *word*, *gift*, and *foot*, come from Old English. So do most of our pronouns, prepositions, and conjunctions, some (such as *he*, *under*, and *to*) without any change in spelling. Other Germanic tribes, using a similar dialect but settling on the European continent instead of in England, fostered two other languages, Dutch and German. As a result, Dutch, German, and English are related languages with some similar traits.

In 1066 the Normans, under William the Conqueror, invaded England. The Normans were originally Vikings who had settled in northern France and had forsaken Old Norse for their own dialect of Old French. They made Norman French the language of law, literature, and the ruling class in England. As a result, English acquired many French words, including many military and governmental words such as *authority*, *mayor*, *crime*, *army*, and *guard*. The common English people kept English alive during the Norman occupation, but they adopted many French words intact (*air*, *point*, *place*, *age*). Eventually, the French influence caused the language to shift from Old to Middle English, which lasted from the twelfth through the fifteenth centuries. During this time a great many Latin words also entered English, for Latin formed the background of Norman French and was the language of the Church and of scholars. English words that entered Middle English directly from Latin or from Latin through French include *language*, *luminous*, *memory*, *liberal*, and *sober*.

Middle English, as the following passage from Geoffrey Chaucer's *Canterbury Tales* shows, was much closer to our own language than to Old English.

33a

A clerk there was of Oxenford also,
That unto logyk hadde longe ygo.
As leene was his hors as is a rake,
And he nas nat right fat, I undertake,
But looked holwe, and therto sobrely.

Modern English evolved in the fourteenth and fifteenth centuries as the language's sound and spellings changed. This was the time of the Renaissance in Europe. Ancient Latin and Greek art, learning, and literature were revived, first in Italy and then throughout the continent. English vocabulary expanded rapidly, not only with more Latin and many Greek words (such as *democracy* and *physics*) but also with words from Italian and French. Advances in printing, beginning in the fifteenth century, made publications widely available to an increasingly literate audience. The Modern English used in twentieth-century North America is four centuries and an ocean removed from the Modern English of sixteenth-century England, but the two are fundamentally the same. The differences and the similarities are evident in this passage from the King James Bible, published in 1611:

And the Lord God commanded the man, saying, Of euery tree of the garden thou mayest freely eate. But of the tree of the knowledge of good and euill, thou shalt not eate of it: for in the day that thou eatest thereof, thou shalt surely die.

33b Learning the composition of words

Words can often be divided into meaningful parts. A *handbook*, for instance, is a book you keep at hand (for reference). A *shepherd* herds sheep (or other animals). Knowing what the parts of a word mean by themselves, as you do here, can often help you infer approximately what they mean when combined.

The following explanations of roots, prefixes, and suffixes provide information that can open up the meanings of words whose parts may not be familiar or easy to see. For more information, refer to a dictionary's etymologies, which provide the histories of words (see 32b).

1 Learning roots

A **root** is the unchanging component of words related in origin and usually in meaning. Both *illiterate* ("unable to read and write") and *literal* ("sticking to the facts or to the first and most obvious meaning of an idea") share the root *liter*, derived from *littera*, a Latin word meaning "letter." A person who cannot understand the letters that make up writing is illiterate. A person who wants to understand the primary meaning of the letters (the words) in a contract is seeking the *literal* meaning of that contract.

At least half our words come from Latin and Greek. The list below includes some common Latin and Greek roots, their meanings, and examples of English words containing them.

Root (source)	Meaning	English words
aster, astr (G)	star	astronomy, astrology
audi (L)	to hear	audible, audience
bene (L)	good, well	benefit, benevolent
bio (G)	life	biology, autobiography
dic, dict (L)	to speak	dictator, dictionary
fer (L)	to carry	transfer, referral
fix (L)	to fasten	fix, suffix, prefix
geo (G)	earth	geography, geology
graph (G)	to write	geography, photography
jur, jus (L)	law	jury, justice
log, logue (G)	word, thought, speech	astrology, biology, neologism
luc (L)	light	lucid, translucent
manu (L)	hand	manual, manuscript
meter, metr (G)	measure	metric, thermometer
op, oper (L)	work	operation, operator
path (G)	feeling	pathetic, sympathy
ped (G)	child	pediatrics
phil (G)	love	philosophy, Anglophile
phys (G)	body, nature	physical, physics
psych (G)	soul	psychic, psychology
scrib, script (L)	to write	scribble, manuscript
tele (G)	far off	telephone, television
ter, terr (L)	earth	territory, extra-terrestrial
vac (L)	empty	vacant, vacuum, evacuate
verb (L)	word	verbal, verbose
vid, vis (L)	to see	video, vision, television

33b

EXERCISE 1

Define the following italicized words, using the list of roots above and any clues given by the rest of the sentence. Check the accuracy of your meanings in a dictionary.

1. After guiding me through university, my *benefactor* will help me start a career.
2. Always afraid of leading a *vacuous* life, the heiress immersed herself in volunteer work.
3. The posters *affixed* to the construction wall advertised a pornographic movie.

4. After his *auditory* nerve was damaged, he had trouble catching people's words.
5. The child *empathized* so completely with his mother that he felt pain when she broke her arm.

2 Learning prefixes

Prefixes are standard syllables fastened to the front of a word to modify its meaning. For example, the word *prehistory* is a combination of the word *history*, meaning "based on a written record explaining past events," and the prefix *pre-*, meaning "before." Together, prefix and word mean "before a written record explaining past events," or before events were recorded. Learning standard prefixes can help you improve vocabulary and spelling just as learning word roots can. The following lists group prefixes according to sense so that they are easier to remember. When two or more prefixes have very different spellings but the same meaning, they usually derive from different languages, most often Latin and Greek.

Prefixes showing quantity

MEANING	PREFIXES IN ENGLISH WORDS
half	*semi*-annual; *hemi*sphere
one	*uni*cycle; *mon*arch, *mono*rail
two	*bi*nary, *bi*monthly; *di*lemma, *dicho*tomy
three	*tri*angle, *tri*logy
four	*quad*rangle, *quar*tet
five	*quin*tet; *penta*gon
six	*sex*tuplets; *hexa*meter
seven	*sept*uagenarian; *hept*archy
eight	*octa*ve, *octo*pus
nine	*nona*genarian
ten	*deca*de, *deca*thlon
hundred	*cent*ury; *hecto*litre
thousand	*milli*metre; *kilo*cycle

Prefixes showing negation

MEANING	PREFIXES IN ENGLISH WORDS
without, no, not	*a*sexual; *il*legal, *im*moral, *in*valid, *ir*reverent; *un*skilled
not, absence of, opposing, against	*non*-breakable; *ant*acid, *anti*pathy; *contra*dict
opposite to, complement to	*counter*clockwise, *counter*weight

33b

MEANING	PREFIXES IN ENGLISH WORDS
do the opposite of, remove, reduce	*de*horn, *de*vitalize, *de*value
do the opposite of, deprive of	*dis*establish, *dis*arm
wrongly, bad	*mis*judge, *mis*deed

Prefixes showing time

MEANING	PREFIXES IN ENGLISH WORDS
before	*ante*cedent; *fore*cast; *pre*cede; *pro*logue
after	*post*war
again	*re*write

Prefixes showing direction or position

MEANING	PREFIXES IN ENGLISH WORDS
above, over	*super*vise
across, over	*trans*port
below, under	*infra*sonic; *sub*terranean; *hypo*dermic
in front of	*pro*ceed; *pre*fix
behind	*re*cede
out of	*e*rupt, *ex*plicit; *ec*stasy
into	*in*jection, *im*merse; *en*courage, *em*power
around	*circum*ference; *peri*meter
with	*co*-exist, *col*loquial, *com*municate, *con*sequence, *cor*respond; *sym*pathy, *syn*chronize

---

EXERCISE 2

Provide meanings for the following italicized words, using the lists of prefixes and any clues given by the rest of the sentence. Check the accuracy of your meanings in a dictionary.

1. In 1970 the Hudson's Bay Company, the oldest incorporated joint-stock merchandizing company in the English-speaking world, celebrated its *tricentennial*.
2. Most poems called sonnets consist of fourteen lines divided into an *octave* and a *sestet*.
3. When the Finance Minister raised federal taxes on old-age security and family allowance benefits, the leader of the New Democratic Party proposed the *countermeasure* of increasing corporate tax rates instead.
4. By suggesting an increase in corporate tax rates, the NDP leader hoped to *forestall* what he predicted as the inevitable dismantling of the universality principle underlying this nation's social programs.
5. Ferdinand Magellan, a Portuguese sailor, commanded the first expedition to *circumnavigate* the globe.

33b

3 Learning suffixes

Suffixes are standard syllables fastened to the end of a word to modify its meaning and usually its part of speech. The word *popular* is an adjective. With different suffixes, it becomes a different adjective, an adverb, a noun, and two different verbs.

ADJECTIVE	popular	**NOUN**	popul*ation*
	popul*ous*	**VERB**	popul*ate*
ADVERB	popul*arly*		popul*arize*

Many words change suffixes in the same way. In fact, suffixes help us recognize what parts of speech many words are, as the following examples show.

Noun suffixes

mis*ery*	min*er*	intern*ship*	random*ness*
refer*ence*	base*ment*	presid*ency*	brother*hood*
relev*ance*	national*ist*	discus*sion*	king*dom*
operat*or*	national*ism*	agit*ation*	

Verb suffixes

hard*en*	pur*ify*
national*ize*	agit*ate*

Adjective suffixes

miser*able*	president*ial*	wonder*ful*	use*less*
ed*ible*	gigant*ic*	fibr*ous*	self*ish*
nation*al*	friend*ly*	adop*tive*	flatu*lent*

The only suffix regularly applied to adverbs is *-ly*: *openly*, *selfishly*.

NOTE: Inflectional endings—such as the plural *-s*, the possessive *-'s*, the past tense *-ed*, and the comparative *-er* or *-est*—appear at the ends of words but do not change a word's grammatical function.

33b

> **EXERCISE 3**
>
> Identify the part of speech of each of the following words, and then change it to the part or parts of speech in parentheses by deleting, adding, or changing a suffix. Use the given word and each created word in a sentence. Check a dictionary, if necessary, to be sure suffixes and spellings are correct.

1. magic (*adjective*)
2. durable (*noun; adverb*)
3. refrigerator (*verb*)
4. self-critical (*noun*)
5. differ (*noun; adjective*)
6. equal (*noun; adverb*)
7. conversion (*verb; adjective*)
8. strictly (*adjective; noun*)
9. assist (*noun*)
10. qualification (*verb; adjective*)

33c Learning to use new words

You can learn a new word not only by understanding its composition but also by examining the context in which it appears and by looking it up in a dictionary—both ways to increase your vocabulary by multiplying and varying your experience with language.

1 Examining context

Most people guess the meaning of an unfamiliar word by looking at familiar words around it. Imagine, for example, that you read the following:

> I was so tired I didn't bother with a real bed. I just lay down on the liclac in the living room. As soon as my feet rested at one end and my head at the other, I fell asleep. In the morning I was cramped from pushing against the back of the liclac.

To guess what *liclac* means, you could examine all the familiar words and learn that (1) a liclac isn't a bed, but you can lie on it; (2) it's part of a living room; (3) it's the length of a person; (4) it's narrow and has a back. From these clues you might guess that the nonsense word *liclac* represents a piece of living room furniture similar to a couch or sofa.

Parallelism shows you which ideas line up or go together and can often suggest the meaning of a new word. Watch for parallel ideas in the following sentence.

33c

> The kittens see their mother hunt and kill, and they in turn take up *predatory* behaviour.

If you did not know the word *predatory*, you could put together clues from the context: parallel construction (*kittens see . . . and they . . . take up*); the tip-off phrase *in turn*; and the suggested idea of imitation (kittens watching their mother and taking up her behaviour). These clues produce the correct assumption that predatory behaviour consists of hunting and killing.

The phrase *is called* or the word *is* often signals a definition.

> The point where the light rays come together is called the *focus* of the lens.

Sometimes definitions are enclosed in parentheses or set off by commas or dashes.

> In early childhood these tendencies lead to the development of *schemes* (organized patterns of behaviour).

> Many Chinese practice *Tai Chi*, an ancient method of self-defence performed as exercise in slow, graceful motions.

> At *burnout*—the instant a rocket stops firing—the satellite's path is fixed.

Noticing examples can also help you infer the meaning of a word. The expressions *such as, for example, for instance, to illustrate,* and *including* often precede examples.

> Society often has difficulty understanding *non-conformists* such as criminals, inventors, artists, saints, and political protesters.

The parallel examples help explain *non-conformist* because they all seem to be exceptions, people who go beyond the average or beyond the rules. This is close to an understanding of *non-conformists* as people who do not adapt themselves to the usual standards and customs of society.

Sometimes an example that reveals the meaning of an unfamiliar word is not announced by a phrase.

> During the first weeks of *rehabilitation*, Brian exercised as best he could, took his medicine daily, and thought constantly about the physical condition he once possessed.

Guessing the meaning of *rehabilitation* requires considering what occurred during it: (1) exercising "as best he could," as if Brian had some kind of handicap; (2) taking medicine, as if Brian were ill; and (3) thinking about his past physical condition, as if Brian were wishing for the good shape he used to be in. Putting these examples together suggests that *rehabilitation* is returning to a healthy condition, which is one of its meanings. (The more precise definition is "restoring a former capacity"; and that idea includes reviving a skill as well as recuperation from a sickness.)

33c

EXERCISE 4

Use context to determine the meanings of the following italicized words. Check the accuracy of your guess by consulting a dictionary.

1. [Canada] ought to have been *obliterated* in the War of 1812, but the Americans were *inept*, and more important militarily, half-hearted. —RICHARD GWYN
2. Everything about man is a *paradox*. The *magnanimous* man grown rich becomes mean. The creative artist for whom everything is made easy nods. Every doctrine swears that it will breed men, but none can tell us in advance what sort of men it will breed. —ANTOINE DE SAINT-EXUPÉRY
3. Prime Minister Mackenzie King's World War II slogan, "Conscription if necessary, but not necessarily conscription," is one of the most famous examples of political *obfuscation* on record.
4. As long as there is one upright man, as long as there is one compassionate woman, the *contagion* may spread and the scene is not *desolate*. Hope is the thing that is left to us in a bad time. —E. B. WHITE
5. In a community where public services have failed to keep *abreast* of private consumption, ... in an atmosphere of private *opulence* and public *squalor*, the private goods have full sway. —JOHN KENNETH GALBRAITH

2   Using the dictionary

The dictionary is a quick reference for the meaning of words (see 32b). It can give the precise meaning of a word whose general meaning you have guessed by examining the word's context. It can also help you fix the word in your memory by showing its spelling, pronunciation, grammatical functions and forms, etymology, and synonyms and antonyms.

For example, suppose you did not understand the word *homogeneous* in the following sentence:

Its homogeneous population makes the town stable but dull.

33c

The dictionary gives the meanings of the word: "of the same kind," "of similar composition throughout." Thus the town's population is made up of similar kinds of people. *Homogeneous* comes from the Greek words *hom*, meaning "same," and *genos*, meaning "kind, type." Obviously, the composition of the word reinforces its definitions. Looking down the dictionary's column after the entry for *homogeneous*, you would find a related word, *homogenize*, which might be more familiar because of the common phrase *homogenized milk*. To *homogenize* means "to blend into a smooth mixture" and "to break up the fat globules of milk by forcing them through minute openings." The relation between this familiar word and the other, less familiar one gives added meaning to both words. A similar expansion of meaning could come from examining an antonym of *homogeneous*, such as *heterogeneous*, meaning "consisting of dissimilar ingredients." Thinking of the two opposite words together might fix them both in your memory.

A dictionary of synonyms is the best source for the precise meanings of similar words (see 32a-3). But even an abridged dictionary will supply much information about synonyms (see 32a-1). Most abridged dictionaries list a word's common synonyms and either direct you to the entries for the synonyms or distinguish among them in one place. An example of the latter form is the paragraph below, which follows the main entry for the word *real* in *The American Heritage Dictionary of the English Language*. By drawing on this information as you write, you can avoid overreliance on the word *real* when a more precise word is appropriate.

> **Synonyms:** *real, actual, true, authentic, concrete, existent, genuine, tangible, veritable. Real,* although frequently used interchangeably with the terms that follow, pertains basically to that which is not imaginary but is existent and identifiable as a thing, state, or quality. *Actual* connotes that which is demonstrable. *True* implies belief in that which conforms to fact. *Authentic* implies acceptance of historical or attributable reliability rather than visible proof. *Concrete* implies the reality of actual things. *Existent* applies to concepts or objects existing either in time or space: *existent tensions. Genuine* presupposes evidence or belief that a thing or object is what it is claimed to be. *Tangible* stresses the mind's acceptance of that which can be touched or seen. *Veritable,* which should be used sparingly, applies to persons and things having all the qualities claimed for them.

EXERCISE 5

The preceding dictionary entry lists the following words as synonyms for *real*: *actual, true, authentic, concrete, existent, genuine, tangible,* and *veritable*. Using this entry and consulting another dictionary if necessary, write nine sentences that make precise use of *real* and each of its eight synonyms.

33c

CHAPTER 34

Spelling

Because of the history and complexity of English, spelling English words according to standard usage requires consistent attention. However, learning to spell well is worth the effort because misspelling can make writing seem incompetent or lazy. This chapter will show you how to recognize typical spelling problems, how to follow a handful of rules as a guide to spelling, and how to develop spelling skills through conscious effort.

34a Avoiding typical spelling problems

Spelling well involves recognizing situations that commonly lead to misspelling: pronunciation can mislead you in several ways; different forms of the same word may have different spellings; and some words have more than one acceptable spelling.

1 Avoiding excessive reliance on pronunciation

In English, unlike some languages, pronunciation of words is an unreliable guide to their spelling. The same letter or combination of letters may have different sounds in the pronunciation of different words. For an example, say aloud these different ways of pronouncing the letters *ough*: *tough, dough, cough, through, bough*. Another problem is that some words contain letters that are not pronounced clearly or at all, such as the *ed* in *asked*, the silent *e* in *swipe*, or the unpronounced *gh* in *tight*.

Pronunciation is a particularly unreliable guide to the spelling of **homonyms**, words pronounced the same though they have different spellings and meanings: for example, *great/grate, to/too/two,* *threw/through*, *horse/hoarse*, *board/bored*, *break/brake*. Some commonly confused homonyms and words with very similar pronunciations, such as *accept/except*, are listed in the "Words Commonly Confused" box. (See 34c-4 for some tips on how to use spelling lists.)

WORDS COMMONLY CONFUSED

accept (to receive)
except (other than)

affect (to have an influence on)
effect (result)

all ready (prepared)
already (by this time)

allude (to refer to indirectly)
elude (to avoid)

allusion (indirect reference)
illusion (erroneous belief or
  perception

ascent (a movement up)
assent (agreement)

bare (unclothed)
bear (to carry, or an animal)

board (a plane of wood)
bored (uninterested)

born (brought into life)
borne (carried)

brake (stop)
break (smash)

buy (purchase)
by (next to)

capital (the seat of a
  government)
capitol (the building where a
  state legislature meets)

cite (to quote an authority)
sight (the ability to see)
site (a place)

desert (to abandon)
dessert (after-dinner course)

discreet (reserved, respectful)
discrete (individual or distinct)

elicit (to bring out)
illicit (illegal)

fair (average, or lovely)
fare (a fee for transportation)

forth (forward)
fourth (after *third*)

gorilla (a large primate)
guerrilla (a kind of soldier)

hear (to perceive by ear)
here (in this place)

heard (past tense of *hear*)
herd (a group of animals)

hole (an opening)
whole (complete)

its (possessive of *it*)
it's (contraction of *it is*)

lead (heavy metal)
led (past tense of *lead*)

lessen (to make less)
lesson (something learned)

meat (flesh)
meet (encounter)

no (the opposite of *yes*)
know (to be certain)

passed (past tense of *pass*)
past (after, or a time gone by)

patience (forbearance)
patients (persons under
  medical care)

(continued)

sp

34a

WORDS COMMONLY CONFUSED   (*continued*)

peace (the absence of war)
piece (a portion of something)

plain (clear)
plane (a carpenter's tool, or an airborne vehicle)

presence (the state of being at hand)
presents (gifts)

principal (most important, or the head of a school)
principle (a basic truth or law)

rain (precipitation)
reign (to rule)
rein (a strap for controlling an animal)

raise (to build up)
raze (to tear down)

right (correct)
rite (a religious ceremony)
write (to make letters)

road (a surface for driving)
rode (past tense of *ride*)

scene (where an action occurs)
seen (past participle of *see*)

stationary (unmoving)
stationery (writing paper)

straight (unbending)
strait (a water passageway)

their (possessive of *they*)
there (opposite of *here*)
they're (contraction of *they are*)

to (toward)
too (also)
two (following *one*)

waist (the middle of the body)
waste (discarded material)

weak (not strong)
week (Sunday through Saturday)

which (one of a group)
witch (a sorcerer)

who's (contraction of *who is*)
whose (possessive of *who*)

your (possessive of *you*)
you're (contraction of *you are*)

2   **Distinguishing between different forms of the same word**

sp
34a

Other spelling problems occur when the noun form and the verb form of the same word are spelled differently. For example:

VERB	NOUN	VERB	NOUN
advise	advice	enter	entrance
describe	description	license	licence
practise	practice	marry	marriage
speak	speech	omit	omission

Sometimes the noun and the adjective forms of the same word differ.

NOUN	ADJECTIVE	NOUN	ADJECTIVE
comedy	comic	height	high
courtesy	courteous	Britain	British
generosity	generous		

The principal parts of irregular verbs are usually spelled differently.

begin, began, begun	know, knew, known
break, broke, broken	ring, rang, rung

Irregular nouns change spelling from singular to plural.

child, children	shelf, shelves
goose, geese	tooth, teeth
mouse, mice	woman, women

Notice, too, that the stem of a word may change its spelling in different forms.

four, forty	thief, theft

3 Using preferred spellings

Many words have variant spellings as well as preferred spellings (see 32b-2). Often the variant spellings listed in an American dictionary are British spellings. Because Canadian usage is influenced by the language practices in both the United States and Britain, it is difficult to ascertain which of the two influences is dominant in each instance. The *Gage Canadian Dictionary*, in its attempt to be descriptive rather than prescriptive in this regard, usually lists both American and British alternatives, with the first word being the one perceived to be the spelling preferred by the educated Canadian majority. This situation is complicated by the tendency for Canadian newspapers, periodicals, and publishing houses to opt for American spellings in the interests of both space economy and consistency, whereas educational institutions tend to advocate the retention of British spellings. The following table of comparisons reveals the lack of a strong consensus about which influence should be allowed to determine orthodoxy.

sp
34a

AMERICAN	BRITISH	CANADIAN (preferred)
analyze	analyse	analyse
canceled, labeled, traveled	cancelled, labelled, travelled	cancelled, labelled, travelled
catalog	catalogue	catalogue
center, meter, theater	centre, metre, theatre	centre, metre, theatre

che*ck*	che*que*	che*que*
col*or*, hum*or*, neighb*or*	col*our*, hum*our*, neighb*our*	col*our*, hum*our*, neighb*our*[1]
conne*ction*	conne*xion*	conne*ction*
jail	*gaol*	*jail*
judgment	judg*e*ment	judgment
paraly*z*e	paraly*s*e	paraly*s*e
plo*w*	plo*ugh*	plo*ugh*
reali*z*e	reali*s*e	reali*s*e
ski*ll*ful	ski*l*ful	ski*l*ful
sul*f*ur	sul*ph*ur	sul*ph*ur
wagon	wa*gg*on	wagon
woo*l*en	woo*ll*en	woo*ll*en

Most instructors at Canadian educational institutions would probably look for consistency in their students' spelling practices, but if in doubt, students would be well advised to determine their instructor's preferences before undertaking any writing assignment.

34b Following spelling rules

Misspelling is often a matter of misspelling a syllable rather than the whole word. The following general rules focus on troublesome syllables, with notes for the occasional exceptions.

1 Distinguishing between *ie* and *ei*

Words like *believe* and *receive* sound alike in the second syllable, but the syllable is spelled differently. How do you know which word should have *ie* and which one *ei*? Use the familiar jingle:

I before *e*, except after *c*, or when pronounced "ay" as in *neighbour* and *weigh*.

i BEFORE *e*	believe	bier	hygiene
	grief	thief	friend
	chief	fiend	
ei AFTER *c*	ceiling	conceive	perceive
	receive	deceit	conceit
ei SOUNDED AS "*AY*"	neighbour	freight	beige
	sleigh	eight	heinous
	weight	vein	

[1]At the time of writing, the *GCD* indicates *-or* as the preferred ending for such words, but this is to be changed to *-our* in the next edition of the dictionary.

EXCEPTIONS: In some words an *ei* combination neither follows *c* nor is pronounced *"ay."* These words include *either, neither, foreign, forfeit, height, leisure, weird, seize,* and *seizure.* This sentence might help you remember some of them:

> The weird foreigner neither seizes leisure nor forfeits height.

> **EXERCISE 1**
>
> Insert *ie* or *ei* in the words below. Check doubtful spellings in a dictionary.
>
> 1. br___f
> 2. dec___ve
> 3. rec___pt
> 4. s___ze
> 5. for___gn
>
> 6. pr___st
> 7. gr___vance
> 8. f___nd
> 9. l___surely
> 10. ach___ve
>
> 11. pat___nce
> 12. p___rce
> 13. h___ght
> 14. fr___ght
> 15. f___nt

2   Keeping or dropping a final *e*

Many words end with an unpronounced or silent *e*: for instance, *move, brave, late, rinse.* When adding endings like *-ing* or *-ly* to these words, do you keep the final *e* or drop it? You drop it if the ending begins with a vowel.

> advise + able = advisable
> force + ible = forcible
> surprise + ing = surprising

You keep the final, silent *e* if the ending begins with a consonant.

> advance + ment = advancement
> accurate + ly = accurately
> care + ful = careful

EXCEPTIONS: The silent *e* is sometimes retained before an ending beginning with a vowel. It is kept when *dye* becomes *dyeing*, to avoid confusion with *dying*. It is kept to prevent mispronunciation of words like *shoeing* (not *shoing*) and *mileage* (not *milage*). And the final *e* is often retained after a soft *c* or *g*, to keep the sound of the consonant soft rather than hard.

courageous	changeable	noticeable
outrageous	manageable	embraceable

The silent *e* is also sometimes *dropped* before an ending beginning with a consonant, when the *e* is preceded by another vowel.

> argue + ment = argument
> true + ly = truly
> due + ly = duly

sp
34b

EXERCISE 2

Combine the following words and endings, keeping or dropping final *e*'s as necessary to make correctly spelled words. Check doubtful spellings in a dictionary.

1. malice + ious
2. love + able
3. service + able
4. retire + ment
5. sue + ing
6. virtue + ous
7. note + able
8. battle + ing
9. suspense + ion

3 Keeping or dropping a final *y*

Words ending in *y* often change their spelling when an ending is added to them. The basic rule is to change the *y* to *i* when it follows a consonant.

beauty, beauties	worry, worried	supply, supplier
folly, follies	merry, merrier	deputy, deputize

But keep the *y* when it follows a vowel; when the ending is *-ing*; or when it ends a proper name.

day, days	cry, crying	May, Mays
obey, obeyed	study, studying	Minsky, Minskys

EXERCISE 3

Combine the following words and endings, changing or keeping final *y*'s as necessary to make correctly spelled words. Check doubtful spellings in a dictionary.

1. imply + s
2. messy + er
3. apply + ing
4. delay + ing
5. defy + ance
6. say + s
7. solidify + s
8. Murphy + s
9. supply + ed

4 Doubling consonants

Words ending in a consonant sometimes double the consonant when an ending is added. Whether to double the final consonant depends first on the number of syllables in the word.

In one-syllable words, double the final consonant when a single vowel precedes the final consonant.

slap, slapping	flat, flatter
tip, tipped	pit, pitted

However, *don't* double the final consonant when two vowels or a vowel and another consonant precede the final consonant.

pair, paired	park, parking
real, realize	rent, rented

In words of more than one syllable, double the final consonant when a single vowel precedes the final consonant and the stress falls on the last syllable of the stem once the ending is added.

submit, submitted	refer, referring
occur, occurred	begin, beginning

But *don't* double the final consonant when it is preceded by two vowels or by a vowel and another consonant, or when the stress falls on other than the stem's last syllable once the ending is added, unless the final consonant is -*l*, in which case Canadian practice normally *doubles* that final consonant before the ending.

refer, reference	despair, despairing
relent, relented	beckon, beckoned
label, labelled	travel, travelling

EXERCISE 4

Combine the following words and endings, doubling final consonants as necessary to make correctly spelled words. Check doubtful spellings in a dictionary.

1. repair + ing	4. shop + ed	7. drip + ing
2. admit + ance	5. conceal + ed	8. declaim + ed
3. benefit + ed	6. allot + ed	9. parallel + ing

---

5 Attaching prefixes

Adding prefixes such as *dis-*, *mis-*, *non-*, and *un-* does not change the spelling of a word. When adding a prefix, do not drop a letter from or add a letter to the original word.

uneasy	disappoint	misinform
unnecessary	dissatisfied	misstate
antifreeze	defuse	misspell
anti-intellectual	de-emphasize	non-restrictive

(See also 34d-4 on when to use hyphens with prefixes.)

sp
34b

---

6 Forming plurals

Nouns

Most nouns form plurals by adding -*s* to the singular form.

boy, boys	table, tables	carnival, carnivals

Some nouns ending in *f* or *fe* form the plural by changing the ending to *ve* before adding *-s*.

leaf, leaves   wife, wives
life, lives   yourself, yourselves

Singular nouns ending in *-s*, *-sh*, *-ch*, or *-x* form the plural by adding *-es*.

kiss, kisses   church, churches
wish, wishes   fox, foxes

(Notice that verbs ending in *-s*, *-sh*, *-ch*, or *-x* form the third-person singular in the same way. *Taxes* and *lurches* are examples.)

Nouns ending in *o* preceded by a vowel usually form the plural by adding *-s*.

ratio, ratios   zoo, zoos

Nouns ending in *o* preceded by a consonant usually form the plural by adding *-es*.

hero, heroes   tomato, tomatoes

Some English nouns that were originally Italian, Greek, Latin, or French form the plural according to their original language: *piano, pianos; medium, media; curriculum, curricula; alumna, alumnae; criterion, criteria.*

Compound nouns

Compound nouns form plurals in two ways. An *-s* is added to the last word when the component words are roughly equal in importance, whether or not they are hyphenated.

city-states   bucket seats   breakthroughs
painter-sculptors   booby traps

sp
34b

When the parts of the compound word are not equal—especially when a noun is combined with other parts of speech—then *-s* is added to the noun.

fathers-in-law   passersby

Note, however, that most modern dictionaries give the plural of *spoonful* as *spoonfuls*.

EXERCISE 5

Make correct plurals of the following words. Check doubtful spellings in a dictionary.

1. pile	6. box	11. libretto
2. donkey	7. switch	12. sister-in-law
3. beach	8. rodeo	13. kilometre per hour
4. summary	9. criterion	14. cargo
5. thief	10. cupful	15. hiss

34c Developing spelling skills

The essential steps in improving spelling skills are to cultivate a general wariness about spelling and to make a habit of consulting a dictionary whenever you doubt a spelling. Start by looking up the word as you think it is spelled. Then try different variations based on the pronunciation of the word. Once you think you have found the correct spelling, check the definition to make sure you have the word you want. (Many word processors and computers have built-in spelling checkers that can serve either as ready references or as active monitors of spelling. See Appendix B, p. 731.) In addition to regular use of a dictionary, you can improve spelling in several other ways, as discussed in the following section.

1 Editing and proofreading carefully

If spelling is a problem for you, you will want to give it high priority while editing your writing (see 2c) and again while proofreading, your last chance to catch misspelled words (see 2d). Reading a draft backward, word by word, can help you spot mistakes such as switched or omitted letters in words you know. Because the procedure forces you to consider each word in isolation, it can also highlight spellings you may be less sure of. A sense of uncertainty is crucial in spotting and correcting spelling errors, even for good spellers who make relatively few errors. Listen to your own uncertainty, and let it lead you to the dictionary.

2 Pronouncing carefully

**sp
34c**

Careful pronunciation is not always a reliable guide to spelling (see 34a), but it can keep you from misspelling words that are often mispronounced. For example:

athletics (not ath*e*letics)	nuclear (not nuc*u*lar)
disastrous (not disast*e*rous)	library (not libary)
recognize (not reconize)	mischievous (not mischiev*i*ous)
lightning (not light*e*ning)	stric*t*ly (not stricly)
height (not height*h*)	gover*n*ment (not goverment)
irrelevant (not irre*v*elant)	hist*o*ry (not histry)
perform (not p*r*eform)	represent*a*tive (not representive)

3 Using mnemonics

Mnemonics (pronounced with an initial "*n*" sound) are techniques for assisting your memory. The *er* in *letter* and *paper* can remind you that *stationery* (meaning "writing paper") has an *er* near the end; *stationary* with an *a* means "standing in place." If you identify the words you have trouble spelling, you can take a few minutes to think of your own mnemonics, which may work better for you than someone else's.

4 Studying spelling lists

Learning to spell commonly misspelled words will reduce your spelling errors. Keep a list of all the words you misspell in your papers, and teach yourself tricks to remember their spellings. For general improvement in spelling, work with the following list of commonly misspelled words. Study only six or seven words at a time. If you are unsure of the meaning of a word, look it up in a dictionary and try using it in a sentence. Pronounce the word out loud, syllable by syllable, and write the word out. (The list of similar-sounding words in 34a should be considered an extension of the one below.)

sp
34c

absence	annual	breath	competition
abundance	answer	breathe	complement
acceptable	apology	Britain	compliment
accessible	apparent	bureaucracy	conceive
accidentally	appearance	business	concentrate
accommodate	appetite		concert
accuracy	appreciate	calculator	condemn
accustomed	appropriate	calendar	conquer
achieve	approximately	carrying	conscience
acknowledge	argument	cede	conscious
acquire	arrest	cemetery	consistency
across	ascend	centre	consistent
actually	assassinate	certain	continuous
address	assistance	changeable	controlled
admission	associate	changing	controversial
adolescent	atheist	characteristic	convenience
advice	athlete	chief	convenient
advising	attendance	chocolate	coolly
against	audience	choose	course
aggravate	average	chose	courteous
aggressive		climbed	criticism
all right	bargain	coarse	criticize
all together	basically	colour	crowd
almost	beginning	column	cruelty
although	behaviour	coming	curiosity
altogether	belief	commercial	curious
amateur	believe	commitment	
analysis	beneficial	committed	deceive
analyse	benefited	committee	deception
angel	boundary	competent	decide

decision
definitely
degree
dependant
dependent
descend
descendant
describe
description
desirable
despair
desperate
destroy
determine
develop
device
devise
dictionary
difference
dining
disagree
disappear
disappoint
disapprove
disastrous
discipline
discriminate
discussion
disease
dissatisfied
distinction
divide
divine
division
doctor
drawer

easily
ecstasy
efficiency
efficient
eighth
either
eligible
embarrass
emphasize
empty
endeavour
enemy
entirely
environment
equipped
especially
essential
every
exaggerate
exceed
excellent
exercise
exhaust
existence
expense

experience
experiment
explanation
extremely

familiar
fascinate
favourite
February
finally
focusses
forcibly
foreign
foresee
forty
forward
friend
frightening
fulfil

gauge
generally
government
grammar
grief
guarantee
guard
guidance

happily
harass
height
heroes
hideous
honourable
humorous
hungry
hurriedly
hurrying
hypocrisy
hypocrite

ideally
illogical
imaginary
imagine
imitation
immediately
immigrant
incidentally
incredible
independence
independent
individually
inevitably
influential
initiate
innocuous
inoculate
insistent
integrate
intelligence

interest
interference
interpret
irrelevant
irresistible
irritable
island

jealousy
judgment

knowledge

laboratory
labourer
leisure
length
library
licence
license
lightning
likelihood
literally
livelihood
loneliness
loose
lose
luxury
lying

magazine
maintenance
manageable
marriage
mathematics
meant
medicine
miniature
minor
minutes
mirror
mischievous
missile
misspelled
morale
morals
mournful
muscle
mysterious

naturally
necessary
neighbour
neither
nickel
niece
ninety
ninth
noticeable
nuclear
nuisance
numerous

observer
obstacle
occasion
occasionally
occur
occurrence
odour
official
omission
omit
omitted
opponent
opportunity
opposite
ordinary
originally

paid
panicky
parallelled
particularly
peaceable
peculiar
pedal
perceive
perception
performance
permanent
permissible
persistence
personnel
perspiration
persuade
persuasion
petal
physical
pitiful
planning
pleasant
poison
politician
pollute
possession
possibly
practically
practice
practise
prairie
precede
preference
preferred
prejudice
preparation
prevalent
primitive
privilege
probably
procedure
proceed
process
professor
prominent

sp
34c

pronunciation	resistance	sponsor	tomorrow
psychology	restaurant	stopping	tragedy
purpose	rhythm	strategy	transferred
pursue	ridiculous	strength	truly
pursuit	roommate	strenuous	twelfth
	rumour	stretch	tyranny
quandary		strict	
quantity	sacrifice	studying	unanimous
quiet	sacrilegious	succeed	unconscious
quizzes	safety	successful	undoubtedly
	satellite	sufficient	unnecessary
realistically	savour	summary	until
realize	scarcity	superintendent	usually
really	schedule	supersede	
rebel	science	suppress	vacuum
rebelled	secretary	surely	vegetable
recede	seize	surprise	vengeance
receipt	separate	suspicious	vicious
receive	sergeant		vigorous
recognize	several	technical	villain
recommend	sheriff	technique	visible
reference	shining	temperament	
referred	shoulder	temperature	weather
relief	significance	tendency	Wednesday
relieve	similar	than	weird
religious	sincerely	theatre	wherever
remembrance	skilful	then	whether
reminisce	sophomore	thorough	wholly
renown	source	though	woman
repetition	speak	throughout	women
representative	speech	together	writing
resemblance			

34d Using the hyphen to form compound words

The hyphen (-) is a mark of punctuation used either to divide a word or to form a compound word. Always use a hyphen to divide a word at the end of a line and continue it on the next line as explained in Chapter 30 on word division. Using a hyphen to form compound words is somewhat more complicated.

Compound words express a combination of ideas. They may be written as a single word, like the noun *breakthrough*; as two words, like the noun *decision making*; or as a hyphenated word, like the noun *cover-up*. Sometimes compound words using the same element are spelled differently—for example, *cross-reference*, *cross section*, and *crosswalk*. Several reliable generalizations can be made about using the hyphen for compound words. But if you doubt the spelling of a compound word, consult a dictionary.

1 Forming compound adjectives

When two or more words serve together as a single modifier

before a noun, a hyphen or hyphens form the modifying words clearly into a unit.

> She is a *well-known* actor.
> The conclusions are based on *out-of-date* statistics.
> No *English-speaking* people were in the room.

When the same compound adjectives follow the noun, hyphens are unnecessary and are usually left out.

> The actor is *well known*.
> The statistics were *out of date*.
> Those people are *English speaking*.

Hyphens are also unnecessary in compound modifiers containing an *-ly* adverb, even when these fall before the noun: *clearly defined terms*; *swiftly moving train*.

When part of a compound adjective appears only once in two or more parallel compound adjectives, hyphens indicate which words the reader should mentally join with the missing part.

> Both long- and short-term plans were discussed.

2 Writing fractions and compound numbers

Hyphens join the numerator and denominator of fractions.

three-fourths
one-half

The whole numbers twenty-one to ninety-nine are always hyphenated.

> Eighteen girls and twenty-four boys took the bus.
> The total is eighty-seven.

3 Forming coined compounds

Writers sometimes create (coin) temporary compounds and join the words with hyphens.

> Muhammad Ali gave his opponent a classic come-and-get-me look.

4 Attaching some prefixes and suffixes

Prefixes are usually attached to word stems without hyphens: *predetermine, unnatural, disengage*. However, when the prefix precedes a capitalized word or when a capital letter is combined with a

sp
34d

word, a hyphen usually separates the two: *un-Christian*, *non-European*, *A-frame*. And some prefixes, such as *self-*, *all-*, *non-*, *co-*, and *ex-* (meaning "formerly"), usually require hyphens no matter what follows: *self-control*, *all-inclusive*, *non-renewable*, *co-operate*, *ex-student*. The only suffix that regularly requires a hyphen is *-elect*, as in *president-elect*.

A hyphen is sometimes necessary to prevent misreading, especially when a prefix and stem place the same two vowels together or when a stem and suffix place the same three consonants together.

> deemphasize, de-emphasize
> antiintellectual, anti-intellectual
> trilllike, trill-like

Check a recent dictionary for the current form, particularly for words that join two *e*'s or *i*'s. If the word you seek does not appear in the dictionary, assume that it should be hyphenated.

5 Avoiding confusion

If you wrote the sentence *Doonesbury is a comic strip character*, the reader might stumble briefly over your meaning. Is Doonesbury a character in a comic strip or a comic (funny) character who strips? Presumably you would mean the former, but a hyphen would prevent any possible confusion: *Doonesbury is a comic-strip character*.

Adding prefixes to words can sometimes create ambiguity. *Recreation* (*creation* with the prefix *re-*) could mean either "a new creation" or "diverting, pleasurable activity." Using a hyphen, *re-creation*, limits the word to the first meaning. Without a hyphen the word suggests the second meaning.

EXERCISE 6

Insert hyphens as needed in the following compounds. Circle all compounds that are correct as given. Consult a dictionary as needed.

1. reimburse
2. deescalate
3. forty odd soldiers
4. little known bar
5. seven eighths
6. seventy eight
7. happy go lucky
8. preexisting
9. senator elect
10. postwar
11. two and six person cars
12. ex songwriter
13. V shaped
14. reeducate

sp

34d

PART VIII

Research Writing

CHAPTER 35

Beginning a Research Project

Much of your writing in college or university will lead you to investigate and assess the work of others. So-called research or term papers serve an obvious practical function in training you to use the resources of a library—a valuable skill for many kinds of work and for life outside of work. But this is only one benefit. In research writing you learn to evaluate other people's work and draw on it to formulate, support, and extend your own opinions. You gain expertise as you study a topic in depth. You increase your control over your environment by uncovering, organizing, and contributing to information and ideas in a way that suits your needs and interests.

Your role in writing a research paper will depend on whether you are called upon mainly to report, to interpret, or to analyse sources. In **reporting**, you survey, organize, and present the available evidence about a topic (for instance, how lobbyists influence MP's votes or how three mice responded to sleep deprivation). In **interpreting**, you examine a range of views on a topic in order to draw your own conclusions (for instance, the ethical dilemmas in using humans as experimental subjects), or you search in varied sources for facts and opinions relevant to your thesis (for instance, that adopted children should, or should not, have access to their birth records). In **analysing**, you isolate an unsolved problem or unanswered question (for instance, the failure of an economics theory to explain a change in the economy or the significance of a repeated image in the work of a poet), and then you attempt to reach a solution or answer through critical evaluation (or analysis) of relevant scholarly sources or of texts such as literary works or historical documents. As the examples indicate, reporting generally serves an explanatory purpose, while interpreting and analysing may serve either an explanatory or a persuasive purpose (see 1c).

530

The three operations are not exclusive: for instance, a paper analysing a repeated image in a poet's work would also involve a survey of poems and an interpretation of their meaning. Because the three operations overlap, the research and writing process described in this and the next two chapters can generally serve any one of them. Throughout these chapters we will follow the development of research papers by two students, Mark Shannon and Deborah Wiebe. Shannon's work, emphasizing interpretation, receives somewhat more attention; Wiebe's work, emphasizing historical description and analysis, enters the discussion whenever her process differed significantly from Shannon's. Both students followed the same basic process, however.

35a Planning a research project

Research writing is undeniably complex, and it can be daunting. Most experienced research writers have stories of blindly rushing around the library or spending weeks obsessed with a single source, or perhaps worst of all, freezing in panic before ever beginning work. And most have found the antidote in thoughtful plans and systematic procedures that help them anticipate and follow through on the diverse and overlapping activities of research writing.

As soon as you receive an assignment for a research project, you can begin developing a strategy for completing it. The first step should be making a schedule that apportions the available time to the necessary work. A possible schedule appears in the box on the next page. In it, each item is a step in the process of research writing (discussed in the section given in parentheses). As you complete the schedule, take into account the deadline, the required length of the paper, your other commitments, and your own writing process. Since these factors vary widely, no general guide can tell you how long each step should take. You can, however, anticipate that each segment marked off by a rule will take *roughly* one-quarter of the total time— for example, a week in a four-week assignment or two weeks in an eight-week assignment. The most unpredictable segments are the first two, so it's wise to get started early enough to be able to accommodate the unexpected.

You can probably see that the research-writing process outlined in the box corresponds to the general writing process discussed in Chapters 1–2, with the three stages of planning or developing (steps 1–8), drafting (step 9), and revising and editing (step 10), plus the additional important stage of documenting the sources you use (steps 11–12). Like any other essay, a research paper evolves gradually and incrementally, the steps sometimes overlapping and repeat-

35a

SCHEDULING STEPS IN RESEARCH WRITING

Complete
by:
_____ 1. Planning a research project (35a)
_____ 2. Finding and limiting a researchable topic (35b)
_____ 3. Finding information and refining the topic (35c)
_____ 4. Making a working bibliography (35d)

_____ 5. Scanning and evaluating sources (36a)
_____ 6. Developing a tentative thesis and outline (36b)
_____ 7. Taking notes using summary, paraphrase, and direct
           quotation (36c) and avoiding plagiarism (36d)

_____ 8. Revising the thesis sentence and writing a formal
           outline (36e)
_____ 9. Drafting the paper (36f)

_____ 10. Revising and editing the paper (36g)
_____ 11. Preparing the final list of works cited (36h)
_____ 12. Preparing final source citations (36i)
_____ 13. Preparing and proofreading the final manuscript
           (36j)
_____ Final paper due

ing. For instance, while you do research, your reading leads you to organize ideas; and while you organize ideas, you discover where you need to do more research. You begin to limit your topic as soon as you have chosen it, and you continue to limit it as you progress. The working thesis and outline you develop must later be refined.

Allowing for such inevitable changes while continuing to forge ahead through the steps is one key to successful and rewarding research writing. Another is systematic procedures for locating, collecting, organizing, and using information—procedures that are the focus of this chapter and the next. These procedures will be easier to follow if you acquire some basic research equipment and carry it with you whenever you work on the project.

1. A package of 7.6 cm x 12.7 cm (3″ x 5″) index cards for source information (see 35d).
2. Several packages of 10.2 cm x 15.2 cm (4″ x 6″) index cards for notes from sources (see 36c).
3. At least one pen plus a spare. Some researchers use several pens with different colours of ink to code their notes.
4. Paper clips and rubber bands for organizing notes.
5. Appropriate coins for operating photocopiers.

35a

In addition, carry index cards or a notebook with you at all times to use as a **research journal**, a place to record your activities and ideas. (See 1b-2 on journal keeping.) In the journal's dated entries, you can keep a record of sources you consult, the leads you want to pursue, any dead ends you reach, and most important, your thoughts about sources, leads, dead ends, new directions, relationships, and anything else that strikes you. Notes on what your sources actually say should be taken and organized separately—for instance, on the note cards discussed in 36c. The research journal is the place for tracking and developing your own ideas. You will probably find that the very act of writing in it opens your mind and clarifies your thinking, making your research increasingly productive and rewarding.

35b Finding and limiting a researchable topic

Before reading this section, you may want to review the suggestions given in 1b for finding and limiting an essay topic. Generally, the same procedure applies to writing any kind of research paper: take a subject assigned to you, or think of one that interests you, and narrow it to manageable dimensions by making it specific. However, as this section will show, selecting and limiting a topic for a research paper do present special opportunities and problems.

Mark Shannon and Deborah Wiebe took different approaches to finding and limiting their topics. For a composition course, Shannon's instructor assigned an interpretation with an argumentative purpose but left the selection of subject to the student. Since Shannon was currently enjoying a course in business management, he decided to take that broad subject as his starting point. Using clustering (see 1d-3), he pursued some implications of this subject as illustrated on the next page. An awareness of gender-role stereotyping, developed during a psychology course in high school, encouraged Shannon to give the most thought to the issue of women in management. He posed questions and more questions until he arrived at the one that seemed potentially most interesting and fruitful: "How far do women still have to go in management, and why?"

In developing a topic for an analysis paper assigned in her Canadian history course, Deborah Wiebe followed quite a different procedure. Her instructor had asked the class to investigate the background leading to some controversial development in Canadian history. Having taken all her elementary schooling in Ontario but her high school education in British Columbia, Deborah remembered

Product safety?

Hiring practices?

Different management approaches when profits are/aren't involved?

Ethical issues

Private vs. public sector

Business management

Women in management

Training programs

Effects of women managers?

Particular industries more open to women?

Progress of women in management?

Women mentors?

Difference between 1960s and now?

Who/what to credit for gains?

How far still to go, and why?

how surprised she had been at her classmates' relative ignorance about the rest of Canada as compared with their greater awareness of the western United States. She decided to investigate the factors that had led British Columbians to join forces (long before the geographically closer provinces such as Alberta and Saskatchewan) with the fledgling confederation of eastern provinces known as Canada, rather than allowing themselves to follow the more geographically appropriate, culturally contiguous, and economically advantageous course of union with the United States. Like Shannon, Wiebe framed the issue as a question that would guide her research: "Why did British Columbia join Confederation rather than being annexed to the United States or remaining a colony of Great Britain?"

Though their approaches differed, both Shannon and Wiebe arrived at topics that satisfied four main requirements of a topic for a research paper. First, both students could expect to find ample published sources of information. The topics were not too recent, as the latest medical breakthrough or yesterday's news item would be, so others would have had a chance to produce evidence, weigh it, and publish their conclusions. Nor were the topics so removed geographically that the sources on them would be inaccessible, as they might be for someone in Prince Edward Island writing about a minor event in Alberta history.

Second, each topic promised to encourage research in the kinds and number of sources required by the assignment. Shannon could research his topic in a variety of sources to present the range of facts and opinions necessary for an interpretation. And Wiebe could consult several primary historical sources as well as more recent contemporary interpretations of the issue in order to arrive at a satisfactory answer to her question. In contrast, topics that require only personal opinion and experience, such as "How I see housewives being depicted in detergent commercials," might be suitable for a personal essay but not for any kind of research paper. Nor is a topic suitable if it requires research in only one source. For this reason straight factual biographies of well-known people and how-to topics such as "Making lenses for eyeglasses" generally make poor research subjects. (The only exception is the literary paper in which you analyse a single work such as a novel. But most literary *research* papers require consulting the published opinions of other critics as well. See 38b.)

The third requirement satisfied by Shannon's and Wiebe's topics is that they promised to foster the objective assessment of sources that would lead to defensible conclusions. Even when a research paper is intended to be argumentative, the success of the argument will depend on the balanced presentation of all points of view. Controversial topics that rest on belief, dogma, or prejudice—such as "When human life begins" or "Why women (or men) are superior"—are certainly arguable, but they are risky because the writer's preconceptions can easily slant either the research itself or the conclusions.

Fourth, and finally, Shannon's and Wiebe's topics suited the length of papers they were assigned (1800 to 2300 words, or about six to ten pages) and the amount of time they were given to prepare the papers (four weeks). In four weeks and ten pages, Shannon could not

---

QUALITIES OF A GOOD RESEARCH TOPIC

1. Published sources will be ample: the topic is neither too recent nor too removed.
2. Sources will be diverse: the topic is neither wholly personal nor wholly factual.
3. Sources can be assessed objectively: the topic is not solely a matter of belief, dogma, or prejudice.
4. Sources can be examined thoroughly in the assigned time and length: the topic is not too broad.

35

have given adequate coverage to one of his broader topics, such as "How much progress have women made in management?" For that, he would have had to canvass at least twenty years' data and opinions, and then in his paper he could have given no more than scant attention to the various measures of "progress" and how women have fared against them. The same would be true of the topic Wiebe originally considered: an analysis of the political factors that had led to making the building of the transcontinental railway a condition of British Columbia's entry into Confederation. Such a study simply would have been too broad for the scope of her essay. She would also have been obliged to do much time-consuming research in the *Hansard* records of the contemporary parliamentary debates on this topic, as well as delving into personal correspondence of such figures as John A. Macdonald, W. C. Van Horne, and others.

EXERCISE 1

Choose three of the following subjects and narrow each one to at least one topic suitable for beginning library work on a research paper. Or list and then limit three subjects of your own that you would enjoy investigating. (This exercise can be the first step in a research paper project that continues through Exercises 2 and 5 in this chapter and Exercises 1, 5, 7, 9, 10, and 11 in Chapter 36.)

1. bilingual education
2. the Opium War
3. recent Canadian drama
4. the history of women's suffrage
5. food additives
6. Meech Lake Accord
7. exploration of outer space
8. the nuclear protest movement
9. the effect of television on professional sports
10. child abuse
11. Indian land claims
12. recent developments in cancer research
13. computer piracy
14. Family Allowances
15. the European exploration of North America before Columbus
16. hazardous substances in the workplace
17. television evangelism
18. science fiction
19. the benefits (or costs) of the Free Trade Agreement
20. water pollution
21. women writers
22. the history of child labour practices
23. comic film actors
24. the best work of a prominent writer
25. genetic engineering
26. heroes and heroines in modern fiction
27. computers and the privacy of the individual
28. Gothic or romance novels in the nineteenth and twentieth centuries
29. the social responsibility of business
30. trends in popular music

35b

35c Finding information and refining the topic

When you investigate a topic, you have access to a wide variety of sources, many of them discussed in this section. (See the box entitled "Index to Research Sources.") By far the most abundant are the reference books, periodicals, and general books in the library. Reference books are good sources for either a summary of a topic or information on where to find out about the topic (see the box below). Periodicals (magazines, journals, and newspapers) contain articles that usually provide detailed and current information on the topic. (see p. 545). General books, which constitute the bulk of a library's collection and are usually available for circulation, include literary works, non-fiction surveys, and in-depth studies of a vast range of subjects (see p. 549–50). Your library may also provide computerized indexes that simplify the search for sources (see p. 552).

A TIP FOR RESEARCHERS

If you are unsure of how to locate or use your library's resources, ask a reference librarian. A reference librarian is very familiar with all the library's resources and with general and specialized research techniques, and it is his or her job to help you and others with research. Even very experienced researchers often consult reference librarians.

Much information for a brief research paper will appear in **secondary sources**, works that report and analyse information drawn from other sources. Whenever possible, however, you should also seek **primary sources**, which include works of literature as well as historical documents (letters, diaries, speeches, and the like) that provide eyewitness accounts of an issue, event, or period. Primary sources may also include your own interviews, experiments, observations, or correspondence, as discussed on page 553. (Both Deborah Wiebe and Mark Shannon were able to use primary sources in their research papers. Wiebe used a couple of contemporary newspaper articles commenting on the debate about whether British Columbia should join Confederation, as well as personal letters written by some of the main figures in the discussion, such as Governor James Douglas and Prime Minister John A. Macdonald. Shannon used his own interview with a woman manager. See p. 632.)

35c

1   **Using reference books**

Reference books available in the library include encyclopedias, dictionaries, digests, bibliographies, indexes, atlases, almanacs, and handbooks. Your research *must* go beyond these sources, but they can help you decide whether your topic really interests you and whether it meets the requirements for a research paper (pp. 534–35). Preliminary research in reference books will also direct you to more detailed sources on your topic. For an analysis paper, a specialized encyclopedia or bibliography can identify the main debates in a field and the proponents of each side.

Mark Shannon's use of reference books illustrates how helpful such sources can be as a starting point. Shannon first consulted *The Encyclopedia of Management* (p. 540), in which the section on women

---

INDEX TO RESEARCH SOURCES

in industry summarized women's advances since the American Civil Rights Act of 1964. The encyclopedia also listed several books and articles for Shannon to pursue.

The following list gives the types of reference works and suggests when each may be profitable. Once you have a topic, you can scan this list for a reference book with which to start. If you want a more comprehensive catalogue and explanation of reference works, consult Eugene P. Sheehy, *Guide to Reference Books*, 10th ed. (1986). For Canadian materials see Dorothy E. Ryder, ed., *Canadian Reference Sources: A Selective Guide*, 2nd ed. (1981).

General encyclopedias

General encyclopedias give brief overviews and brief bibliographies. Because they try to cover all fields, they are a convenient, but very limited, starting point. Be sure to consult the most recent edition.

> *The Canadian Encyclopedia.* 2nd ed. 4 vols. 1988.
> *Collier's Encyclopedia.* 24 vols. 1981.
> *Encyclopedia Americana.* 30 vols. 1988.
> *Encyclopedia International.* 20 vols. 1982.
> *The New Columbia Encyclopedia.* 1975.
> *The New Encyclopaedia Britannica.* 32 vols. 1986.
> *Random House Encyclopedia.* Rev. ed. 1983.

Specialized encyclopedias, dictionaries, bibliographies

A specialized encyclopedia, dictionary, or bibliography generally covers an entire field or subject. These works will give you more detailed and more technical information than a general reference book will, and many of them (especially bibliographies) will direct you to particular books and articles on your subject. One general reference work providing information on sources in many of the fields below is the *Essay and General Literature Index* (published since 1900 and now updated semi-annually). It lists tens of thousands of articles and essays that appear in books (rather than periodicals) and that might not be listed elsewhere.

BUSINESS AND ECONOMICS

> Brown, Barbara E., ed./redactrice. *Canadian Business and Economics: A Guide to Sources of Information/Économique et commerce au Canada: sources d'information.* New ed. 1984.
> Buell, Victor P., ed. *Handbook of Modern Marketing.* 2nd ed. 1986.

35c

Eatwell, John, Murray Milgate, and Peter Newman, eds. *The New Palgrave: A Dictionary of Economics*. 4 vols. 1987.

Graham, Irvin. *Encyclopedia of Advertising*. 2nd ed. 1969.

Greenwald, Douglas. *The McGraw-Hill Dictionary of Modern Economics*. 3rd ed. 1983.

Heyel, Carl. *The Encyclopedia of Management*. 3rd ed. 1982.

Munn, Glenn G. *Encyclopedia of Banking and Finance*. 8th ed. Ed. Ferdinand L. Garcia and Glenn G. Munn. 1983.

Seidler, Lee L., and Douglas R. Carmichael. *Accountant's Handbook*. 6th ed. 2 vols. 1981.

Sloan, Harold S., and Arnold Zurcher. *A Dictionary of Economics*. 5th ed. 1970.

HISTORY

American Historical Association. *Guide to Historical Literature*. 1961.

Binder, Leonard, ed. *The Study of the Middle East: Research and Scholarship in the Humanities and Social Sciences*. 1976.

Cambridge Ancient History. 12 vols. 1923–39. Revision in progress.

Cambridge Mediaeval History. 8 vols. in 9. 2nd ed. 1966–69.

Fairbank, John K., and Denis Twitchett. *Cambridge History of China*. 14 vols. 1978–. In progress.

Freidel, Frank, and Richard K. Showman, eds. *Harvard Guide to American History*. Rev. ed. 2 vols. 1974.

Hammond, N. G. L., and H. H. Scullard. *Oxford Classical Dictionary*. 2nd ed. 1970.

Martin, Michael R., et al. *An Encyclopedia of Latin-American History*. Rev. ed. 1981.

New Cambridge Modern History. 14 vols. 1957–80.

LITERATURE, THEATRE, FILM, AND TELEVISION

Adelman, Irving, and R. Dworkin. *Modern Drama: A Checklist of Critical Literature on Twentieth Century Plays*. 1967.

Bukalski, Peter J. *Film Research: A Critical Bibliography with Annotations and Essays*. 1972.

Drabble, Margaret, ed. *The Oxford Companion to English Literature*. 5th ed. 1985.

Gerther, Richard, ed. *International Television Almanac*. Published annually since 1956.

Gohdes, Clarence L. F., and Sandford E. Marovitz. *Bibliographical Guide to the Study of the Literature of the U.S.A.* 5th ed. 1984.

Hart, James D., ed. *The Oxford Companion to American Literature*. 5th ed. 1983.

35c

Hartnoll, Phyllis, ed. *The Oxford Companion to the Theatre*. 4th ed. 1983.

Holman, C. Hugh, and William Harmon. *A Handbook to Literature*. 5th ed. 1986.

Klinck, Carl F., ed. *Literary History of Canada: Canadian Literature in English*. 2nd ed. 3 vols. 1976.

Lecker, Robert, and Jack David, eds. *The Annotated Bibliography of Canada's Major Authors*. 8 vols. 1979–88.

MLA International Bibliography of Books and Articles on the Modern Languages and Literatures. Published annually since 1922.

Moss, John. *A Reader's Guide to the Canadian Novel*. 2nd ed. 1987.

Schweik, Robert C., and Dieter Riesner. *Reference Sources in English and American Literature: An Annotated Bibliography*. 1977.

Toye, William, ed. *The Oxford Companion to Canadian Literature*. 1983.

Ward, A. W., and A. R. Waller, eds. *The Cambridge History of English Literature*. 15 vols. 1907–33.

Watson, G., ed. *New Cambridge Bibliography of English Literature*. 5 vols. 1969–77.

MUSIC AND THE VISUAL ARTS

Apel, Willi. *The Harvard Dictionary of Music*. 2nd rev. ed. 1972.

Beattie, Eleanor. *A Handbook of Canadian Film*. 2nd ed. 1977.

Chujoy, Anatole, and P. W. Manchester. *The Dance Encyclopedia*. 1978.

Encyclopedia of World Art. 17 vols. 1959–68.

Kallmann, Helmut, Gilles Potvin, and Kenneth Winters, eds. *Encyclopedia of Music in Canada*. 1981.

MacDonald, Colin S. *A Dictionary of Canadian Artists*. 7 vols. 1977–87.

Maillard, Robert, ed. *New Dictionary of Modern Sculpture*. Trans. Bettina Wadia. 1971.

Moore, Frank L. *Crowell's Handbook of World Opera*. 1974.

Sadie, Stanley, ed. *The New Grove Dictionary of Music and Musicians*. 20 vols. 6th ed. 1980.

Stambler, Irwin. *Encyclopedia of Pop, Rock, and Soul*. Rev. ed 1989.

Thompson, Oscar. *International Cyclopedia of Music and Musicians*. 11th ed. 1985.

Trachtenberg, Marvin, and Isabelle Hyman. *Architecture: From Pre-History to Post-Modernism*. 1986.

35c

PHILOSOPHY AND RELIGION

Broderick, Robert, ed. *The Catholic Encyclopedia*. Rev. ed. 1987.

Buttrick, George Arthur, and Keith R. Crim. *The Interpreter's Dictionary of the Bible*. 5 vols. 1976.

Cross, F. L., and Elizabeth A. Livingstone. *The Oxford Dictionary of the Christian Church*. 2nd ed. 1974.

Eliade, Mircea, ed. *The Encyclopedia of Religion*. 16 vols. 1987.

Ferm, Vergilius, ed. *An Encyclopedia of Religion*. 1976.

Rice, Edward. *Eastern Definitions: A Short Encyclopedia of Religions of the Orient*. 1978.

Roth, Cecil, and Geoffrey Wigoder, eds. *The New Standard Jewish Encyclopedia*. 5th ed. 1977.

SCIENCES

Belzer, Jack, et al., eds. *Encyclopedia of Computer Science and Technology*. 15 vols. 1975–80.

Considine, Douglas, ed. *The Encyclopedia of Chemistry*. 4th ed. 1984.

Fairbridge, Rhodes W., ed. *The Encyclopedia of Oceanography*. 1966.

Gray, Peter. *The Encyclopedia of Biological Sciences*. 2nd ed. 1981.

Jobes, Gertrude, and James Jobes. *Outer Space: Myths, Name Meanings, Calendars from the Emergence of History to the Present Day*. 1980.

The Larousse Encyclopedia of Animal Life. 1967.

The McGraw-Hill Encyclopedia of Science and Technology. 5th ed. 15 vols. 1982.

Sarton, George. *An Introduction to the History of Science*. 5 vols. 1927–75.

Thewlis, J., ed. *Encyclopaedic Dictionary of Physics*. 9 vols. plus supplements. 1961–75.

SOCIAL SCIENCES

Brock, Clifton. *The Literature of Political Science*. 1969.

Cersini, Raymond J., And Bonnie D. Ozaki, eds. *Encyclopedia of Psychology*. 4 vols. 1984.

Foreign Affairs Bibliography. 5 vols. 1960–76.

Leach, Maria, and Jerome Fried, eds. *Funk and Wagnalls Standard Dictionary of Folklore, Mythology and Legends*. 2 vols. 1984.

Mitchell, G. Duncan, ed. *A New Dictionary of the Social Sciences*. 1979.

Mitzel, Harold, ed. *Encyclopedia of Educational Research*. 5th ed. 4 vols. 1982.

35c

Samuda, Ronald, J., John W. Berry, and Michel Laferriere, eds. *Multiculturalism in Canada: Social and Educational Perspective*. 1984.

Sills, David L., ed. *International Encyclopedia of the Social Sciences*. 17 vols. plus supplement. 1968–79.

UNESCO International Committee for Social Science Documentation, ed. *International Bibliography of the Social Sciences*. 1960–86.

Webb, William H. *Sources of Information in the Social Sciences: A Guide to the Literature*. 3rd ed. 1986.

Winick, Charles. *Dictionary of Anthropology*. 1977.

Unabridged dictionaries and special dictionaries on language

Unabridged dictionaries are more comprehensive than abridged or college dictionaries. Special dictionaries give authoritative information on individual aspects of language. (See Chapter 32 for more on the kinds of dictionaries and how to use them.)

UNABRIDGED DICTIONARIES

The Oxford English Dictionary. 20 vols. 1989. *The Compact Edition*, 3 vols., was issued in 1987. CD-ROM format appeared in 1989.

The Random House Dictionary of the English Language. 2nd ed. 1989.

Webster's Third New International Dictionary of the English Language. 1986.

SPECIAL DICTIONARIES

Avis, Walter S., Patrick D. Drysdale, and Matthew H. Scargill, eds. *A Dictionary of Canadianisms on Historical Principles*. 1967.

Follett, Wilson. *Modern American Usage: A Guide*. Ed. Jacques Barzun. 1966.

Fowler, H. W. *A Dictionary of Modern English Usage*. 2nd ed. Rev. and ed. Sir Ernest Gowers. 1987.

Lewis, Norman. *The New Roget's Thesaurus of the English Language in Dictionary Form*. 1986.

Morris, William, and Mary Morris. *Harper Dictionary of Contemporary Usage*. 2nd ed. 1985.

Onions, Charles T., et al., eds. *The Oxford Dictionary of English Etymology*. 1966.

Partridge, Eric. *A Dictionary of Slang and Unconventional English*. 8th ed. Ed. Paul Beale. 1985.

35c

Partridge, Eric. *Origins: A Short Etymological Dictionary of Modern English*. 1977.

Webster's New Dictionary of Synonyms. 1984.

Biographical reference works

If you want to learn about someone's life, achievements, credentials, or position, or if you want to learn the significance of a name you've come across, consult one of the following reference works. Note, in addition, that more specialized biographical sources are available in fields such as law, health care, and art.

American Men and Women of Science. 17th ed. 8 vols. 1989.

Bannerman, Jean. *Leading Ladies—Canada 1639–1967*. 1967.

Contemporary Authors. 123 vols. Published since 1967 and updated regularly.

Creative Canada: A Biographical Dictionary of Twentieth-Century Creative and Performing Artists. 2 vols. 1971–72.

Current Biography. Published annually since 1940.

Dictionary of Literary Biography. 48 vols. plus supplements. Published since 1978 and frequently updated and enlarged.

Dictionary of National Biography (British). 22 vols. plus supplements. 1882–1986.

Halpenny, Francess G., et al., eds. *Dictionary of Canadian Biography*. Vols. 1–11 (1000–1890). 1966–85.

James, Edward T., and Janet W. James, eds. *Notable American Women*. 3 vols. 1971–80.

Webster's Biographical Dictionary. 1972.

Who's Who in Canada. Published biennially since 1911.

Atlases and gazetteers

Atlases are bound collections of maps; gazetteers are geographical dictionaries.

Atlas and Gazetteer of Canada. 1969.

Columbia Lippincott Gazetteer of the World. 1962.

Cosmopolitan World Atlas. 1981.

Encyclopaedia Britannica World Atlas International. 1969.

The National Atlas of Canada. 4th ed., revised. 1974.

National Geographic Atlas of the World. 5th ed. 1981.

The Times Atlas of the World. 2nd rev. ed. 1983.

35c

Almanacs and yearbooks

Both almanacs and yearbooks are annual compilations of facts.

Yearbooks record information about the previous year. Almanacs give facts and statistics about a variety of fields.

Britannica Book of the Year. Published annually since 1938.

Canada Year Book. Published annually since 1905 (except for 1970).

Canadian Almanac and Directory. Published annually since 1848.

Facts on File Yearbook. Published annually since 1940.

U.S. Bureau of the Census. *Statistical Abstract of the United States*. Published annually since 1878.

World Almanac and Book of Facts. Published annually since 1868.

2   Using periodicals

Periodicals—journals, magazines, and newspapers—are invaluable sources of information in research. The difference between journals and magazines lies primarily in their content, readership, frequency of issue, and page numbering. Magazines, such as *Psychology Today*, *Maclean's*, and *Saturday Night*, are non-specialist publications intended for diverse readers. Most magazines appear weekly or monthly. Journals, in contrast, often appear quarterly and contain specialized information intended for readers in a particular field. Examples include *Queen's Quarterly*, *The Canadian Historical Review*, and *Journal of Chemical Education*. In most magazines the page numbering begins anew with each issue. Many journals also page each issue separately, but others do not. Instead, the issues for an entire year make up an annual volume, and the pages are numbered continuously throughout the volume, so that issue number 3 (the third issue of the year) may open on page 327. (The method of pagination determines how you cite a journal article in a list of works cited and, if you use them, in footnotes or endnotes; see pp. 563 and 611.)

Using indexes to periodicals

Several guides provide information on the articles in journals, magazines, and newspapers. The contents, formats, and systems of abbreviation in these guides vary widely, and they can be intimidating at first glance. But each one includes in its opening pages an introduction and explanation to aid the inexperienced user. (See also p. 552 on using computerized databases for locating articles in periodicals.)

35c

A typical and general periodical guide is the *Readers' Guide to Periodical Literature*, published since 1900 and updated semi-monthly. It lists—by author, title, and subject—articles published each year in more than a hundred popular magazines. For a paper on a current topic you should consult at least several years' *Readers' Guide* volumes. Mark Shannon, checking a quarterly cumulative volume from 1987, found these possible sources under "Women executives."

Women executives
>   *See also*
>   Clothing and dress—Businesswomen
>   Women entrepreneurs
> Assertiveness breeds contempt [male vs. female evaluations of assertive female managers; study by David L. Mathison] V. Bozzi. *Psychol Today* 21:15 S '87
> Like father, like daughter [father-daughter corporations] R. Rooney. il *Good Housekeep* 204:108-9+ Je '87
> Where women are succeeding. A. B. Fisher. il *Fortune* 116:78-80+ Ag 3 '87

Other general indexes to periodicals include the following:

Canadian News Index. Published 1977–79 (vols. 1–3) as *Canadian Newspaper Index*; new title initiated in 1980 as volume 4. Published monthly, with annual accumulations.

Canadian Periodical Index. Published eleven times per year since 1948.

The New York Times Index. Published annually since 1913. This index to the most complete U.S. newspaper can serve as a guide to national and international events and can indicate what issues of unindexed newspapers to consult for local reactions to such events.

Poole's Index to Periodical Literature. 1802–1907. An index by subject to British, Canadian, and U.S. periodicals of the nineteenth century.

Popular Periodicals Index. Published annually since 1973. An index to about twenty-five contemporary, popular periodicals not listed in major indexes.

Wall Street Journal Index. An index to the leading business newspapers and to *Barron's*. Published monthly since 1958.

35c

For scholarly journals, most libraries have a variety of specialized indexes. Shannon also consulted one of these, the *Social Sciences Index*. The following is approximately one-third of its listings under "Leadership" for the year April 1984 through March 1985. At least five entries held some promise for Shannon.

Leadership
> *See also*
> Authority
> Charisma
> Consensus (Social sciences)
> Cooptation
> Elite (Social sciences)
> Paternalism
> Political leadership
> Supervisors

Are women invisible as leaders? N. Porter and others, bibl *Sex Roles* 9:1035-49 O '83

Australian managers' leadership beliefs. 1970/82. B. W. Stening and P. S. K. Wong. *Psychol Rep* 53:274 Ag '83

Cooperative and competitive relationships between leaders and subordinates. D. Tjosvold and others. bibl *Hum Relat* 36:1111-24 D '83

Determinants of management styles in business and nonbusiness organizations. G. Chitayat and I. Venezia. bibl *J Appl Psychol* 69:437-47 Ag '84

Effective leadership in geography: the role of the department chairperson. S. Khan and G. Vuicich. bibl *Prof Geogr* 36:158-64 My '84

The effects of competent behavior on interpersonal attraction and task leadership. J. W. Rhue and others. bibl *Sex Roles* 10:925-37 Je '84

Effects of leader warmth and directiveness on subordinate performance on a subsequent task. D. Tjosvold. bibl *J Appl Psychol* 69:422-7 Ag '84

Effects of psychological gender and sex-incongruent behavior on evaluations of leadership. M. Remland and others. bibl *Percept Mot Skills* 57 ptl:783-9 D '83

Emergent leadership as a function of sex and task type. D. K. Wentworth and L. R. Anderson. bibl *Sex Roles* 11:513-24 S '84

An estimate of variance due to traits in leadership. D. A. Kenny and S. J. Zaccaro. bibl *J Appl Psychol* 68:678-85 N '83

The factor structure of "most preferred co-worker", and "assumed similarity of opposites" scores. G. Shouksmith. *Psychol Rep* 53:255-8 Ag '83

Group process and sex differences. L. S. Kahn. bibl *Psychol Women Q* 8:261-81 Spr '84

Leader legitimacy. Leader-follower interaction, and followers' ratings of the leader. O. Ben-Yoav and others. *J Soc Psychol* 121:111-15 O '83

Leader sex, leader success, and leadership process: two field studies. R. W. Rice and others. bibl *J Appl Psychol* 69:12-31 F '84

The following is a partial list of scholarly indexes:

America: History and Life. Published three times a year since 1955.

Applied Science and Technology Index. Published monthly since 1958. From 1913 to 1957 this work was combined with the *Business Periodicals Index* in the *Industrial Arts Index*.

35c

Art Index. Published quarterly since 1929.

Biological and Agricultural Index. Published monthly since

1964. From 1916 to 1963 this work was called the *Agricultural Index*.

Business Periodicals Index. Published annually since 1958. From 1913 to 1957 this work was combined with the *Applied Science and Technology Index* in the *Industrial Arts Index*.

Canadian Business Periodical Index. Published monthly since 1975.

Canadian Education Index/Répertoire canadien sur l'éducation. Published quarterly since 1965.

Christian Periodical Index. Published monthly since 1948.

The Education Index. Published monthly since 1929.

ERIC (Education Resources Information Center). *Current Index to Journals in Education*. Published monthly since 1969.

General Sciences Index. Published monthly since 1978.

Humanities Index. Published quarterly since 1974. From 1965 to 1974 this author and subject index was combined with the *Social Sciences Index* in the *Social Sciences and Humanities Index*. From 1907 to 1965 the combined volume was called the *International Index*.

Index Medicus. Published monthly since 1960. From 1927 to 1959 this work was called *Quarterly Cumulative Index Medicus*. From 1899 to 1926 it was *Index Medicus*.

MLA International Bibliography of Books and Articles in the Modern Languages and Literatures. Published annually since 1922.

Music Index. Published monthly since 1950.

Philosopher's Index. Published quarterly since 1967.

Religion Index One: Periodicals and *Religion Index Two: Multi-Author Works*. Now published semi-annually. Formerly published biannually, from 1949–76, as *Index to Religious Periodical Literature*. (*Religion Index Two* began in 1960.)

Social Sciences Index. Published quarterly since 1974. From 1965 to 1974 this author and subject index was combined with the *Humanities Index* in the *Social Sciences and Humanities Index*. From 1907 to 1965 the combined volume was called the *International Index*.

Using abstracts and citation indexes

35c

Consulting a collection of article summaries—or **abstracts**—can tell you in advance whether you want to pursue a particular article further. Such collections are published in many academic disciplines. For example:

Abstracts of English Studies. Published quarterly since 1958.

America: History and Life (U.S. and Canadian history). Published three times a year since 1955.

Biological Abstracts. Published semimonthly since 1926.

Chemical Abstracts. Published weekly since 1907.

Communications Abstracts. Published quarterly since 1982.

Dissertation Abstracts International (doctoral dissertations). Published monthly since 1938. Before 1969, the title was *Dissertation Abstracts*.

Historical Abstracts (world history). Published since 1955.

Psychological Abstracts. Published monthly since 1927.

Sociological Abstracts. Published five times a year since 1952.

When you want to trace what has been written *about* an article or book you are consulting, use a **citation index**. This resource lists references to written works after they are published, as when one scientific article comments on an earlier article. The following is a partial list:

Arts and Humanities Citation Index. Published bimonthly since 1978.

Science Citation Index. Published bimonthly since 1955.

Social Science Citation Index. Published bimonthly since 1969.

Finding and using periodicals

Every library lists its complete periodical holdings either in the main catalogue or in a separate catalogue. The listing for each periodical tells how far back the issues go and where and in what form the issues are stored. The recent issues of a periodical are usually held in the library's periodical room. Back issues are usually stored elsewhere, in one of three forms: in bound volumes; on **microfilm**, a filmstrip showing pages side by side; or on **microfiche**, a sheet of film with pages arranged in rows and columns. Consulting periodicals stored on microfilm or microfiche requires using a special machine, or "reader," which locates and enlarges the page and projects it on a screen. Any member of the library's staff will demonstrate how to operate the reader.

3   Using guides to books

35c

The library catalogue

The library's catalogue lists books alphabetically by authors' names, titles of books, and subjects. (In some catalogues, authors and titles are alphabetized together and subjects are alphabetized separately.) If you are starting research on a subject you don't know very well, begin by looking under subject headings. If you know of an expert in the field and you want to find his or her books, look under the author's name. If you know the title of a relevant book but not the author's name, look for the title.

The library's catalogue may be the familiar card file, cabinets of drawers containing 7.6 cm x 12.7 cm (3″ x 5″) cards. But to save space and time, many libraries have converted their catalogues to other forms. A printed catalogue in bound volumes contains small reproductions of the cards traditionally found in drawers. A catalogue on microfilm or microfiche shows the library's collection on film viewed with a special reader. Increasingly, libraries are computerizing their catalogues: the user gains access to the computer's memory by keying a code, and a screen displays the requested information. (With many computerized catalogues, the user can conduct a customized search through the library's holdings. See p. 552.) If you are uncertain about the location, form, or use of your library's catalogue, seek help from a member of the library's staff.

Though the storage systems vary, all book catalogues contain similar information and follow a similar organization. By far the most widely used catalogue format is that of the Library of Congress card. Samples of author, title, and subject cards appear on the opposite page.

The more systematically you approach the library's catalogue, the more efficient and productive your search will be. The multivolume *Library of Congress Subject Headings* (*LCSH*) is a list of the various headings under which the Library of Congress catalogues books. Consulting this source and following its system of cross-references and headings at different levels of specificity, you will be able to discover the headings most likely to lead to appropriate sources. Mark Shannon, for instance, used *LCSH* to eliminate the heading of "Women—Employment," which was much too broad for his needs. He isolated the narrower "Women executives," with subcategories such as "Attitudes" and "Employment." Note that *LCSH* does not include most proper names of people, places, corporations, associations, government bodies, and the like.

35c

References to books

Two types of reference books can help you identify general books that have information about your topic: publishing bibliographies and digests. Publishing bibliographies tell whether a book is still in print, whether a paperback edition is available, what books were published on a certain topic in a certain year, and so on. These bibliographies include the following:

> *Books in Print*. Published and supplemented annually since 1873. Books indexed by author, title, and subject.
>
> *Canadian Books in Print*. Published annually with quarterly microfiche editions. Books indexed by author and title in one volume and by subject in a separate volume.
>
> *Cumulative Book Index*. Published monthly since 1898.
>
> *Paperbound Books in Print*. Published semi-annually since 1955.

You might, for example, want to know if the author of an encyclopedia article has published any relevant books since the date of the encyclopedia. You could look up the author's name in the latest *Books in Print* to find out.

If you want to evaluate a book's relevance to your topic before you search for it, a review index such as the following will direct you to published reviews of the book.

35c

Book Review Digest. Published annually since 1905. Summar-
izes *and* indexes reviews of books.
Book Review Index. Published annually since 1965.
Index to Book Reviews in the Humanities. Published since 1960.
Recent Publications in the Social and Behavioral Sciences. Pub-
lished annually.
Technical Book Review Index. Published monthly since 1935.

4 Using computerized databases

Libraries that use computers to store information about their
holdings often provide researchers with a quick and effective way to
find relevant sources. Either alone or with the aid of a staff member,
the researcher gives the computer one or more key words about the
topic, and the computer then consults its database (its entire list of
references) to produce a customized list of sources that have been
indexed under the key word or words.

The kinds of computerized databases and the specific search
procedures vary widely from library to library. In some libraries only
the catalogue of general books can be used for a key-word search. The
researcher can generally work unaided, following simple instructions on the computer screen. Other libraries have additional, more
specialized databases that index articles in periodicals, government
documents, unpublished materials, and other resources. To search
these databases, the researcher often must enlist the help of a staff
member, and the library may charge a fee for the service. Ask at your
library to learn the resources available to you and the procedures you
must follow.

The efficiency and reliability of a database search will be
determined largely by the key word or words you give the computer.
If a term is too general, it may turn up a long list of sources with only
a tiny proportion relevant to your topic. If the term is too specific, it
may turn up a too-short list or nothing at all. If Mark Shannon
searched a computerized book catalogue using the general word
"women," the computer would show him every book in the library
indexed under the word—a very long list. If, in contrast, he used the
specific phrase "women executives," the computer would show him
only the sources it could find that were indexed under both important
words in the phrase.

35c

A good source for appropriate key words is the *Library of
Congress Subject Headings* (see p. 550). This reference can help with
searches in other databases besides a book catalogue. Note, however,
that some databases have indexes of their own.

5   Generating your own sources

As noted on page 537, most of the sources you consult for a research project—and most of the resources of the library—are likely to be secondary sources in which the authors draw their information from other authors. However, academic writing will also require you to consult primary sources and to conduct primary research in which you generate information of your own. In many papers this primary research will be the sole basis for your writing, as when you analyse a poem or report on an experiment you conducted. In other papers you will be expected to use your research to support, extend, or refute the ideas of others.

Chapter 38 discusses the textual analyses, observations, experiments, and other primary sources you may use in writing for various academic disciplines. One primary source not covered there is the personal interview with an expert in the topic you are researching. Because of the give-and-take of an interview, you can obtain answers to questions precisely geared to your topic, and you can follow up instantly on points of confusion and unexpected leads. In addition, quotations and paraphrases from an interview can give your paper added immediacy and authority. Mark Shannon used just such an interview in his paper on women executives (see pp. 632–33).

A few precautions will help you get the maximum information from an interview with the minimum disruption to the person you are interviewing.

1. If you do not already know whom to consult for an interview, ask a teacher in the field or do some telephone or library research. Likely sources, depending on your topic, are those who have written about your topic or something closely related, officials in government, businesspeople, even your own aunt, if she is an expert in your topic because of experience, scholarship, or both.
2. In-person interviews are often easier and more productive than telephone interviews. But use the phone rather than forego a valuable source.
3. Call or write for an appointment. Tell the person exactly why you are calling, what you want to discuss, and how long you expect the interview to take. Be true to your word on all points.
4. Prepare a list of open-ended questions to ask—perhaps ten or twelve for a one-hour interview. Listen to your subject's answers so that you can ask appropriate follow-up questions and pick up on unexpected but worthwhile points.
5. Take careful notes; or, if you have the equipment and your subject agrees, tape-record the interview. Before you quote

35c

your subject in your paper, check with him or her that the quotations are accurate.

6. Send a thank-you note immediately after the interview. Promise your subject a copy of your finished paper, and send the paper promptly.

EXERCISE 2

List at least five sources you can consult for further leads on each of the three topics you produced in Exercise 1 (p. 536) or for three other topics. Use the information provided in the preceding section and additional information at your library.

35d Making a working bibliography

1 Keeping systematic records of sources

Trying to pursue every source lead as you came across it would prove inefficient and probably ineffective. Instead, you'll want to find out what is available before deciding which leads to follow, and that requires systematically keeping track of where information is and what it is. You can keep track of sources by making a **working bibliography**, a file of the books, articles, and other sources you believe will help you. When you have a substantial file, you can decide which sources seem most promising and look them up first.

A working bibliography is your opportunity to record all the information you need to find your sources. You can use whatever system you like to keep track of information, but many experienced researchers find a card file safer and more flexible than, say, self-stick notes or pages of lists. Writing each source on an individual 7.6 cm x 12.7 cm (3″ x 5″) card will allow you to arrange your sources alphabetically by author, to discard irrelevant sources without disrupting your list, and later to transfer the information easily to your final list of sources.

Make a bibliography card for each source you think may be useful, whether you find it in the card catalogue, in a reference book, or in an index to periodicals. Include all the information you will need for your final list of sources, using standard formats such as those discussed later in this section. Getting all the information the first time will save you from having to retrace your steps later. For sources you find in the catalogue of books, list every letter and number of the call number on the bibliography card to save time later. (However, you will not transfer the call number to the final list of sources.) Here are two examples of bibliography cards, the first for a book and the second for a periodical.

HD
6054.3
.L63

Loden, Marilyn. Feminine Leadership, or,
How to Succeed in Business Without
Being One of the Boys. New York:
Times, 1985.

Bozzi, Vincent. "Assertiveness Breeds
Contempt." Psychology Today
Sept. 1987: 15.

When you turn in your paper, you will have to attach a list of the sources you have used (see 36h). So that readers can check or follow up on your sources, your list must include all the information needed to find the sources, in a format readers can understand. The following are two general guides to bibliographic formats that you can consult if your instructor does not specify a style to follow.

The Chicago Manual of Style. 13th ed. 1982.
Turabian, Kate L. *A Manual for Writers of Term Papers, Theses, and Dissertations.* 5th ed. Rev. and exp. Bonnie Birtwistle Honigsblum. 1987.

Editors and teachers in most academic disciplines require special formats in their scholarly journals and in student papers— formats that differ in the amount, arrangement, and punctuation of information. Chapter 38 lists the format guides published for psy-

bib

35d

chology, biology, and several other disciplines; and the chapter illustrates some required formats. (See pp. 682 and 700.)

The following section discusses and illustrates the bibliographic formats of the *MLA Handbook for Writers of Research Papers*, 3rd ed. (1988). This book is published by the Modern Language Association and describes standard practice for courses and journals in composition, literature, foreign languages, and many other disciplines.

2 Using MLA bibliographic formats

The bibliographic models that follow are based on the *MLA Handbook*. Use the index opposite to find the page numbers of the models you need. Note that models may have to be combined; for example, in citing an article by four authors appearing in a biweekly periodical, you will need to draw on the models labelled "A book with more than three authors" and "A signed article in a weekly or biweekly periodical."

Books

The basic format for a book includes the following information:

Gilligan, Carol. ① In a Different Voice: Psychological ②
Theory and Women's Development. Cambridge: Harvard UP, 1982. ③

1. The author's full name: the last name first, followed by a comma, and then the first name and any middle name or initial. Omit any title or degree attached to the author's name on the source, such as Dr. or Ph.D. End the name with a period and two spaces.
2. The full title of the book, including any subtitle. Underline the complete title, capitalize all important words (see 26b), separate the main title and the subtitle with a colon and one space, and end the title with a period and two spaces.
3. The publication information: the city of publication, followed by a colon and one space; then the name of the publisher, followed by a comma; and finally the date of publication, ending with a period. All this information can be found on the title page of the book or on the page after the title page. Shorten

INDEX TO MLA BIBLIOGRAPHIC MODELS

most publishers' name—in many cases to a single word. For instance, use "Knopf" for Alfred A. Knopf and "Gage" for Gage Educational Publishing Company. For university presses, use the abbreviation "UP," as in the example on the opposite page.

bib
35d

When other information is required for a reference, it is generally placed either between the author's name and the title or between the title and the publication information, as specified in the following models.

A BOOK WITH ONE AUTHOR

Gilligan, Carol.   In a Different Voice: Psychological

Theory and Women's Development.   Cambridge: Har-

vard UP, 1982.

A BOOK WITH TWO OR THREE AUTHORS

Wimsatt, William K., and Cleanth Brooks.   Literary

Criticism: A Short History.   Chicago: U of Chi-

cago P, 1978.

Give the authors' names in the order provided on the title page. Reverse the first and last names of the first author *only*, and separate the authors' names with a comma.

A BOOK WITH MORE THAN THREE AUTHORS

Lopez, Robert S., et al.   Civilizations: Western and

World.   Boston: Little, 1975.

You may, but need not, give all authors' names if the work has more than three authors. If you choose not to give all names, provide the name of the first author only, and follow the name with a comma and the abbreviation "et al." (for the Latin *et alii*, meaning "and others").

A BOOK WITH AN EDITOR

Ruitenbeek, Hendrick, ed.   Freud as We Knew Him.

Detroit: Wayne State UP, 1973.

The abbreviation "ed.," separated from the name by a comma, identifies Ruitenbeek as the editor of the work.

A BOOK WITH AN AUTHOR AND AN EDITOR

Davies, Robertson.   Hunting Stuart and Other Plays.

Ed. Brian Parker. Toronto: New Press, 1972.

When citing the work of the author, give his or her name first, and give the editor's name after the title, preceded by "Ed." ("Edited by"). When citing the work of the editor, use the form above for a book with an editor, and give the author's name after the title preceded by "By": "Parker, Brian, ed. *Hunting Stuart and Other Plays*. By Robertson Davies."

A TRANSLATION

```
Alighieri, Dante.   The Inferno.   Trans. John Ciardi.

    New York: NAL, 1971.
```

When citing the work of the author, give his or her name first, and give the translator's name after the title, preceded by "Trans." ("Translated by"). When citing the work of the translator, give his or her name first, followed by a comma and "trans.," and give the author's name after the title preceded by "By": "Ciardi, John, trans. *The Inferno*. By Dante Alighieri."

A BOOK WITH CORPORATE AUTHORSHIP

```
Editors of The Progressive.   The Crisis of Survival.

    Glenview: Scott, 1970.
```

List the name of the corporation, institution, or other body as author.

AN ANONYMOUS BOOK

```
Atlas of Canada.   Montreal: Reader's Digest Ass'n.,

    1981.
```

List the book under its title. Do not use "anonymous" or "anon."

A LATER EDITION

```
Bollinger, Dwight L.   Aspects of Language.   2nd ed.

    New York: Harcourt, 1975.
```

For any edition after the first, place the edition number between the title and the publication information. Use the appropriate designation for editions that are named or dated rather than numbered—for instance, "Rev. ed." for "Revised edition."

A REPUBLISHED BOOK

```
James, Henry.   The Golden Bowl.   1904.   London:

    Penguin, 1966.
```

Place the original date of publication (but not the place of publication or the publisher's name) after the title, and then provide the full publication information for the source you are using.

A WORK IN MORE THAN ONE VOLUME

```
Schaff, Philip.   History of the Christian Church.

    3rd ed., rev. 1910.   8 vols.   Grand Rapids, MI:

    Eerdmans, 1963.

Schaff, Philip.   History of the Christian Church.

    3rd ed., rev. 1910.   8 vols.   Grand Rapids, MI:

    Eerdmans, 1963.   Vol. 2.
```

For a work published in more than one volume, give the total number of volumes regardless of how many you are using. Use an Arabic numeral and the abbreviation "vols.," and place the information after the title (see "8 vols." in the first example). If you use only one volume, add that information at the very end of the entry (see "Vol. 2" in the second example).

A WORK IN A SERIES

```
Wilson, Ethel.   The Innocent Traveller.   No. 170,

    New Canadian Library Series.   Toronto: McClel-

    land & Stewart, 1982.
```

Place the name of the series (no quotation marks or underlining) after the title. Indicate the item number in the series, if available.

A SELECTION FROM AN ANTHOLOGY

```
Herbert, George.   "The Pilgrimage."   The Norton

    Anthology of English Literature.   Ed. M. H.

    Abrams et al.   2 vols.   5th ed.   New York: Nor-

    ton, 1986.   Vol. I.   1348-49.
```

Give the author and the title of the selection you are citing, placing the title in quotation marks and ending it with a period. Then give the title of the anthology and the name of the editor(s) preceded by "Ed." ("Edited by"). At the end of the entry give the inclusive page numbers for the entire selection, but do not include the abbreviation "pp." The preceding entry includes total number of volumes, edition number, and specific volume number as well.

TWO OR MORE SELECTIONS FROM THE SAME ANTHOLOGY

Grey, J. David. ed. The Jane Austen Companion. New

York: Macmillan, 1986.

Southam, Brian. "Janeites and Anti-Janeites."

Grey 237-43.

---. "Persuasion: The Cancelled Chapters." Grey

322-23.

When citing more than one selection from the same source, avoid unnecessary repetition by giving the source in full (as in the first entry) and then simply cross-referencing it in entries for the works you used. Thus instead of full bibliographic information for the two Southam articles, give Grey's name and the appropriate pages in his book.

Note that the last two entries also illustrate how to handle two or more works by the same author when you are preparing your final list of works cited: in the second and subsequent entries, replace the author's name with three hyphens followed by a period. This format is discussed more fully on page 598.

AN ARTICLE OR ESSAY FROM A REPRINTED COLLECTION

Gibian, George. "Traditional Symbolism in Crime and

Punishment." PMLA 70 (1955): 979-96. Rpt. in

Crime and Punishment. By Feodor Dostoevsky.

Ed. George Gibian. Norton Critical Editions.

New York: Norton, 1964. 575-92.

Provide the author and title of the article or essay you are using, placing the title in quotation marks and ending it with a period. Then, unless your instructor specifies otherwise, provide the complete information for the earlier publication of the piece, followed by "Rpt. in"("Reprinted in") and the information for the source in which you found the piece. If you are not required to provide the earlier publication information, use the format for a selection from an anthology.

bib

35c

AN INTRODUCTION, PREFACE, FOREWORD, OR AFTERWORD

```
Donaldson, Norman. Introduction.  The Claverings.

    By Anthony Trollope.  New York: Dover, 1977.

    vii-xv.
```

An introduction, foreword, or afterword is often written by someone other than the book's author. When citing such a work, give its name without quotation marks or underlining. Follow the title of the book with its author's name preceded by "By." Give the inclusive page numbers of the part you cite. (In the example above, the small Roman numerals indicate that the cited work is in the front matter of the book, before page 1.)

When the author of a preface or introduction is the same as the author of the book, give only the last name after the title:

```
Gould, Stephen Jay.  Prologue.  The Flamingo's

    Smile: Reflections in Natural History.  By

    Gould.  New York: Norton, 1985.  13-20.
```

AN ENCYCLOPEDIA OR ALMANAC

```
Mark, Herman F.  "Polymers."  Encyclopedia Britan-

    nica: Macropaedia.  1974.

Morley, J. T.  "Social Credit."  The Canadian

    Encyclopedia.  1988.
```

Give the name of an author only when the article is signed; otherwise, give the title first. If the articles are alphabetized in the reference work, you needn't list the editors of the work itself or any page numbers. For familiar sources like those in the examples, provide only the edition number (if there is one) and the year of publication.

Periodicals: journals, magazines, and newspapers

The basic format for an article from a periodical includes the following information:

bib
35d

```
    ┌──①──┐    ┌────────②────────┐
Lever, Janet.  "Sex Differences in the Games Chil-

    dren Play."  Social Problems 23 (1976): 478-87.
                 └─────────③─────────┘
```

1. The author's full name: last name first, followed by a comma, and then the first name and any middle name or initial. Omit any title or degree attached to the author's name on the source, such as Dr. or Ph.D. End the name with a period and two spaces.
2. The full title of the article, including any subtitle. Place the title in quotation marks, capitalize all important words in the title (see 26b), and end the title with a period (inside the final quotation mark) and two spaces.
3. The publication information: the underlined title of the periodical (minus any *A*, *An*, or *The* at the beginning); the volume or issue number (in Arabic numerals); the date of publication, followed by a colon and a space; and the inclusive page numbers of the article (without the abbreviation "pp."). The treatment of volume and issue numbers and publication dates varies depending on the kind of periodical being cited, as the following examples indicate.

A SIGNED ARTICLE IN A JOURNAL WITH CONTINUOUS PAGINATION THROUGHOUT THE ANNUAL VOLUME

```
Lever, Janet.   "Sex Differences in the Games Chil-

     dren Play."   Social Problems 23 (1976): 478-87.
```

Some journals number the pages of issues consecutively throughout a year, so that each issue after the first in a year begins numbering where the previous issue left off—for example, at page 132 or 416. For that kind of journal, give the volume number after the title ("23" in the example above) and place the year of publication in parentheses. The page numbers will be enough to guide readers to the appropriate issue.

A SIGNED ARTICLE IN A JOURNAL THAT PAGES ISSUES SEPARATELY OR THAT NUMBERS ONLY ISSUES, NOT VOLUMES

```
Boyd, Sarah.   "Nuclear Terror."   Adaptation to

     Change 7.4 (1981): 20-23.
```

Some journals page each issue separately (starting each issue at page 1). For these journals, use the same format as for the Lever article above, but give the volume number, a period, and the issue number (as in "7.4" in the Boyd entry). Then readers know which issue of the periodical to consult. When citing an article in a journal that numbers only issues, not annual volumes, treat the issue number as if it were a volume number (as in the Lever citation above).

```
Davidson, Arnold E.   "As Birds Bring Forth the

     Story: The Elusive Art of Alistair MacLeod."

     Canadian Literature 119 (1988): 32-42.
```

A SIGNED ARTICLE IN A MONTHLY OR BIMONTHLY PERIODICAL

```
Wright, Richard.   "The Reluctant Athlete."   Satur-

     day Night Sept. 1988: 79-82.
```

Follow the periodical title with the month (abbreviated) and the year of publication. Don't place the date in parentheses, and don't provide a volume or issue number.

A SIGNED ARTICLE IN A WEEKLY OR BIWEEKLY PERIODICAL

```
Laver, Ross.   "The Tax Squeeze."   Maclean's 8 May

     1989: 10-12.
```

Follow the periodical title with the day, the month (abbreviated if multisyllabic), and the year of publication. Don't place the date in parentheses, and don't provide a volume or issue number.

A SIGNED ARTICLE IN A DAILY NEWSPAPER

```
Picard, André.   "Quebec NDP Opts for Autonomy."

     Globe and Mail 1 May 1981: A1.
```

Give the name of the newspaper as it appears on the first page (but without *A*, *An*, or *The*). Then follow the same format as that above for a weekly or biweekly periodical, with one exception: if the newspaper is divided into lettered or numbered sections, with each section page separately, provide the section designation before the page number when the newspaper does the same (as in "A1" above), or provide the section designation before the colon when the newspaper does not combine the two in its numbering (e.g., "sec. 1: 1 +." The page number "1 +" indicates that the article does not run on consecutive pages but starts on page 1 and continues later in the issue.)

AN UNSIGNED ARTICLE

```
"The Right to Die."   Time 11 Oct. 1976: 101.

"Hundreds of Chinese Reported Defecting."

     Vancouver Sun 17 June 1989: A1.
```

Begin the entry for an unsigned article with the title of the article.

AN EDITORIAL, A LETTER TO THE EDITOR, OR A REVIEW

Doern, Bruce.   "Breaking the U.S. Monopoly in the

Subsidy-defining Game." Editorial.   <u>Financial</u>

<u>Times of Canada</u> June 5-11, 1989: 44.

Don't use quotation marks or underlining for the word "Editorial."
For an unsigned editorial, give the title first.

Dowding,   Michael.   Letter.   <u>Economist</u>   5-11   Jan.

1985: 4.

Don't use quotation marks or underlining for the word "Letter."

Kanfer, Stefan.   "Time Arrested."   Rev. of <u>Cat's</u>

<u>Eye</u>, by Margaret Atwood.   <u>Time</u> 6 Feb. 1989: 70.

"Rev." is an abbreviation for "Review." The name of the author of the
work being reviewed follows the title of the work, a comma, and "by."
If the review has no title of its own, then "Rev. of ... " (without
quotation marks) immediately follows the name of the reviewer.

AN ABSTRACT OF A DISSERTATION

Steciw, Steven K.   "Alterations to the Pessac Proj-

ect of Le Corbusier."   <u>DAI</u> 46 (1986):

565C.   Cambridge U, England.

For an abstract appearing in *Dissertation Abstracts* (*DA*) or *Dissertation Abstracts International* (*DAI*), give the author's name and the title
as for any article. Then give publication information for the source
and the name of the institution granting the author's degree.

Other Sources

A PAMPHLET OR GOVERNMENT DOCUMENT

<u>The Canada-U.S. Trade Agreement in Brief</u>.   2nd ed.

Ottawa: Minister of Supply and Services Canada,

1988.

Most pamphlets can be treated as books. In the preceding example, the pamphlet has no listed author, so the title comes first.

> British Columbia.   Ministry of Education.   <u>Policy</u>
>
>   <u>Directions: A Response to the Sullivan Royal</u>
>
>   <u>Commission on Education by the Government of</u>
>
>   <u>British Columbia</u>.   Vancouver, BC: BC Ministry of
>
>   Education, 1989.
>
> Canada.   Continuing Federal-Provincial-Territorial
>
>   Committee of Officials Responsible for Human
>
>   Rights, Secretary of State.   <u>Convention on the</u>
>
>   <u>Elimination of All Forms of Discrimination</u>
>
>   <u>Against Women: Reference Document</u>.   Ottawa:
>
>   Supply and Services Canada, 1986.

Unless an author is listed for a government document, give the appropriate agency as author. Provide information in the order illustrated, separating elements with a period and two spaces: the name of the government, the name of the agency (which may be abbreviated), and the title and publication information.

AN UNPUBLISHED DISSERTATION OR THESIS

> Spigelman, Martin Samuel.   "The Acadian Renaissance
>
>   and the Development of Acadien-Canadien Rela-
>
>   tions, 1864-1912: des frères trop longtemps
>
>   séparés."   Ph.D. diss. Dalhousie, 1976.

The title is quoted rather than underlined. "diss." stands for "dissertation." "Dalhousie" is the degree-granting institution.

A MUSICAL COMPOSITION OR WORK OF ART

> Mozart, Wolfgang Amadeus.   Piano Concerto No. 20 in D
>
>   Minor, K. 466.

Don't underline musical compositions identified only by form, number, and key. Do underline titled operas, ballets, and compositions (*Carmen, Sleeping Beauty*).

Odjig, Daphne. <u>The Indian in Transition</u>. National

Museum of Man, Ottawa.

Underline the title of a work of art. Include the name and location of the institution housing the work.

A FILM OR TELEVISION PROGRAM

<u>Love Letters: A Dance Fantasy</u>. Members of the

National Ballet of Canada. Choreographed by Ann

Ditchburn. Music by Kate Bush, Laurie Anderson,

Buffy Sainte-Marie, André Gagnon, and Jennifer

Warnes. Cameo appearance by Leonard Cohen.

A & E, 21 May 1989.

Donovan, Paul, dir. <u>The Squamish Five</u>. Bernard

Zukerman, prod. With Robyn Stevan, Michael

McManus, Nicky Guadagni, and David McLeod.

Written by Ken Gass and Terence McKenna. CBC

Enterprises, 1988.

Generally, place the underlined title first (as in the first example), unless you are citing the work of an individual (second example). After the title, give additional information (writer, lead actors, and so on) as seems appropriate. For a television program, give the series title (if any), the network, and the local station, city, and date. For a film, give the distributor and the date.

A PERFORMANCE

<u>Man and Superman</u>. By George Bernard Shaw. Dir.

Christopher Newton. Shaw Festival Theatre,

Niagara-on-the-Lake, ON. 24 May 1989.

McCoppin, Peter, cond. Vancouver Symphony Orchestra

Concert. Featuring Viktoria Mullova, violin.

The Orpheum Theatre, Vancouver. 23 Oct. 1989.

bib
35d

As with films and television programs, the title generally comes first unless you are citing the work of an individual (second example). Provide additional information about participants after the title, as well as the theatre, city, and date. Note that the orchestra concert in the second example is neither quoted nor underlined.

A RECORDING

```
Murray, Anne, et al.   Canadian Content.   Capitol

     Records (Canada) Ltd., SL-6854, n.d.

Brahms, Johannes.   Concerto no. 2 in B-flat, op. 83.

     Perf. Artur Rubinstein.   Cond. Eugene Ormandy.

     Philadelphia Orch.   RCA, RK-1243, 1972.
```

Begin with the name of the individual whose work you are citing. Then provide the title of the recording (first example) or the title of the work recorded (second example), the names of any artists not already listed, the manufacturer of the recording, the catalogue number, and the date.

A LETTER

```
McLennan, Hugh.   Letter to John Gray.   7 December

     1950.   In Elspeth Cameron, Hugh MacLennan:

     A Writer's Life.   Toronto: U. of Toronto

     P., 1981.   253-54.
```

A published letter is listed under the writer's name. Specify that the source is a letter and to whom it was addressed, and give the date on which it was written. The remaining information is treated like that for an edited book. (See also p. 565 for the format of a letter to the editor of a periodical.)

```
James, Jonathan E.   Letter to his sister.   16 Apr.

     1970.   Jonathan E. James Papers.   South Dakota

     State Archive, Pierre.
```

bib
35d

For a letter in the collection of a library or archive, specify the writer, recipient, and date, as above, and give the name and location of the archive as well.

```
Packer, Ann E.   Letter to the author.   15 June 1988.
```

For a letter you receive, give the name of the writer, note the fact that the letter was sent to you, and provide the date of the letter.

A LECTURE OR ADDRESS

```
Carlone, Dennis J.   "Urban Design in the 1990s."

     Sixth Symposium on Urban Issues.   City of Cam-

     bridge.   Cambridge, 16 Oct. 1988.
```

Give the speaker's name, the title if known (in quotation marks), the title of the meeting, the name of the sponsoring organization, the location of the lecture, and the date. If you do not know the title, replace it with "Lecture" or "Address" but *not* in quotation marks.

AN INTERVIEW

```
Smithson, Councilman John.   Personal interview.

     6 Sept. 1985.

Rushton, David.   Interview re: Fraser Valley

     Symphony.  Contact.   Richard Dettman, inter-

     viewer.   CFVR, Abbotsford, BC.   8 June 1989.
```

Begin with the name of the person interviewed. Then specify "Personal interview" (if you conducted the interview in person), "Telephone interview" (if you conducted the interview over the phone), or "Interview" (if you did not conduct the interview)—without quotation marks or underlining. Finally, provide a date (first example) or other bibliographic information and then a date (second example).

AN INFORMATION OR COMPUTER SERVICE

```
Jolson, Maria K.   Music Education for Preschoolers.

     ERIC, 1981.   ED 264 488.

Palfry, Andrew.   "Choice of Mates in Identical

     Twins."  Modern Psychology Jan. 1979: 16-27.

     Dialog file 261, item 5206341.
```

bib
35d

A source you get from an information or computer service should be treated like a book or a periodical article, as appropriate, with the author's name and then the title. If the source has not been published before, simply name the service (ERIC in the Jolson entry on the preceding page), and give the year of release and the service's identifying number. If the source has been published before, give full publication information and then the name of the service and its identifying numbers, as in the Palfry entry.

COMPUTER SOFTWARE

<u>Project Scheduler 5000</u>.   Computer software.   Scitor,

1988.   MS-DOS, 256 KB, disk.

Include the title of the software, the name of the writer (if known), the name of the distributor, and the date. As in this example, you may also provide information about the computer or operating system for which the software is designed, the amount of computer memory it requires, and its format.

3 Abbreviations

The preceding bibliographic formats eliminate many abbreviations. However, they still use some, and you may encounter many more in your reading. The most common abbreviations found in references and source citations are as follows.

anon.	anonymous
bk., bks.,	book(s)
c., ca.	*circa* ("about"), used with approximate dates
cf.	*confer* ("compare")
ch., chs.	chapter(s)
col., cols.	columns(s)
comp., comps.	compiled by, compiler(s)
diss.	dissertation
ed., eds.	edited by, edition(s), editor(s)
et al.	*et alii* ("and others")
ff.	and the following pages, as in pages 17 ff.
ibid.	*ibidem* ("in the same place")
illus.	illustrated by, illustrator, illustration(s)
l., ll.	line(s)
loc. cit.	*loco citato* ("in the place cited")
ms., mss.	manuscript(s)
n., nn.	note(s), as in p. 24, n. 2
n.d.	no date (of publication)
no., nos.	number(s)
n.p.	no place (of publication), no publisher
n. pag.	no pagination

op. cit.	*opere citato* ("in the work cited")
P	Press (UP = University Press)
p., pp.	page(s)
passim	throughout
q.v.	*quod vide* ("which see")
rev.	revised, revision, revised by, review
rpt.	reprint, reprinted
sec.	section
supp., supps.	supplement(s)
trans.	translator, translated by
univ., U	university (UP = University Press)
vol., vols.	volume(s)

EXERCISE 3

Prepare bibliography entries from the following information. Follow the models of the *MLA Handbook* given on pages 556–70 unless your instructor specifies a different style.

1. The second edition of a book called *The Structure of Canadian History*, by J. L. Finlay and D. N. Sprague, published in 1984 by Prentice-Hall in Scarborough, Ontario.
2. An article by Terry Goldie in *English Studies in Canada*, volume 14, number 1, March 1988 issue. The article, entitled "Getting it Right" and subtitled "The Image of Indigenous Peoples in Canadian Fiction in the Eighties," appeared on pages 64–81. The journal is paged continuously throughout the annual volume.
3. The fifth volume of *The History of Technology*, published in 1958 in London by Oxford University Press, written by Charles Singer, E. J. Holmroyd, A. R. Hall, and Trevor I. Williams.
4. A pamphlet entitled *A Triple E Senate is Essential for Canada*, published in Calgary in 1987 by the Canadian Committee for a Triple E Senate.
5. A book by John Bartlett called *Familiar Quotations*, in its fifteenth edition, which was edited by Emily Morison Beck, published in 1980 by Little, Brown and Company in Boston, Massachusetts.

EXERCISE 4

Prepare a working bibliography of at least ten sources for a research paper on one of the following people or on someone of your own choosing. Begin by limiting the subject to a manageable size, focussing on a particular characteristic or achievement of the person. Then consult reference books, periodical indexes, and the library's catalogue of books. Record bibliographic information on note cards, using the models of the *MLA Handbook* unless your instructor specifies a different style.

bib

35d

1. Gordon Lightfoot, or another performer
2. Bertha Wilson, or another Supreme Court justice
3. Rudy Wiebe, or another writer
4. Ben Johnson, or another sports figure
5. Ken Danby, or another artist

EXERCISE 5

Using one of the topics and the possible references for it from Exercise 2 (p. 554), or starting with a different topic and references, prepare a working bibliography of at least ten sources for your developing research paper. List on 7.6 cm x 12.7 cm (3″ x 5″) cards the complete bibliographic information for each source. Use the formats of the *MLA Handbook* unless your instructor specifies a different style.

CHAPTER 36

Working with Sources and Writing the Paper

The previous chapter led you through laying the groundwork for a research project. This chapter takes you into the most personal, most intensive, and most rewarding parts of research writing: reading, evaluating, and taking notes from sources; focussing and shaping your ideas; and drafting and revising the paper. In these stages you probe your topic deeply and make it your own.

As before, the work of Mark Shannon and Deborah Wiebe will illustrate the activity and thought that go into research writing.

36a Scanning and evaluating sources

When to stop looking *for* sources and start looking *at* them depends, of course, on the assigned length of the paper and on the complexity of your subject. You are probably ready to begin reading when your working bibliography suggests that you have explored most aspects of your topic and have found at least some sources that deal directly with your central concern. For a paper of 1800 to 2300 words, ten to fifteen promising titles should give you a good base.

1 Evaluating sources and reading for ideas

Once you have a satisfactory working bibliography, scan your cards for the sources that are most likely to give you an overview of your topic, and consult those sources first. Mark Shannon, for instance, began investigating titles that indicated a focus on the progress of women in upper corporate management. Deborah Wiebe began by looking first at an early history of British Columbia published in 1894 as well as a very full collection of documents—letters, newspaper articles, and the texts of political speeches—from the period of British Columbian history she was investigating: 1860–71. Wiebe's earlier preliminary perusal of these two books had confirmed that they would be the best sources for giving her the flavour of contemporary debate that raged back and forth concerning the three possible directions British Columbia could go: remain a British colony, be annexed to the United States, or become another province in the Dominion of Canada.

As you glance through your sources, your purpose is to evaluate their usefulness and to shape your thinking, not to collect information. A source is potentially useful to you if it is relevant to your topic and if it is reliable. Both relevance and reliability can be determined in part by consulting works *about* the source you are considering— that is, the works listed in citation indexes (p. 548) or book review indexes (p. 551–52). But unless you can dismiss the source on the basis of citations or reviews, you will also need to evaluate it yourself.

Scanning the introductions to books and articles and the tables of contents and indexes of books can help you determine whether a source is relevant. Reliability can be more difficult to judge. If you haven't already done so, read Chapter 4, which includes specific advice for evaluating the writing of others. When scanning potential sources, think critically, looking for sound reasoning, ample evidence, a fair presentation of opposing views, and other features discussed in Chapter 4. In addition, look for information about the author's background to satisfy yourself that the author has sufficient expertise in your subject. Then try to determine whether he or she might be biassed. For instance, a book on parapsychology by someone identified as the president of the National Organization of Psychics may contain an authoritative explanation of psychic powers, but the author's view is likely to be biassed. It should be balanced by research in other sources whose authors are more sceptical of psychic powers.

This balance or opposition is important. You probably will not find harmony among sources, for reasonable people often disagree in their opinions (see 4d-1). Thus you must deal honestly with the gaps and conflicts in sources. Old sources, superficial ones, slanted ones— these should be offset in your research and your writing by sources that are newer, more thorough, or more objective.

Read your sources quickly and selectively to obtain an overview of your topic so that your thesis encompasses the range of available information and represents your informed view. Don't allow yourself to get bogged down in taking very detailed notes at this stage. Without a sense of what information is pertinent, you may not leave time to cover all the potentially relevant sources.

However, do write down general ideas that seem fundamental to your topic. Be especially careful to record ideas of your own, such

36a

as a connection between statements by two different writers, because these may not occur to you later. Use your research journal (see 35a).

36b Developing a tentative thesis and outline

1 Writing a tentative thesis sentence

When you have a fairly good grasp of the range of views on your topic, the information available, and your own opinion, try to develop a thesis in a tentative thesis sentence. (See 1g.) In your thesis sentence (or sentences, if you need two or three at this stage), you should state your general idea and the perspective you take. Although the sentence will undoubtedly need revising as you gather more information, drafting it early can help keep you focussed as you do further research.

For his paper on women in management, Mark Shannon wrote the following tentative thesis sentence:

> Although women have come a long way in their journey to the top of the corporate ladder, they still have a number of obstacles to overcome before they can consider themselves to have arrived.

This thesis sentence stated Shannon's central idea that women still have not overcome all obstacles to upper management. As we will see, Shannon had to revise his thesis sentence later to reflect his further research and to ensure that it adequately communicated his topic and perspective to readers. But this tentative thesis gave him a focus and a way to organize his work.

To frame a tentative thesis sentence for her paper on the factors that led British Columbian politicians to choose confederation with Canada over other options, Deborah Wiebe first had to draw a tentative conclusion on why the confederation advocates were able to persuade the British Columbian populace to overlook their feelings of distrust for Eastern Canada as well as their sense of geographical, economic, and cultural identity with the United States by supporting union with the Dominion of Canada. Wiebe's preliminary reading had given her the impression that the promise of a transcontinental railway as a source of relief to British Columbia's economic crisis was a large factor in the province's eventual decision to join Confederation, but she had also read that the prospect of being able to retain ties to Great Britain by establishing a transcontinental union of provinces, as well as the sheer fact of inadequate American desire and initiative in promoting annexation of British Columbia, both

36b

contributed to the final outcome in Canada's favour as well. She formulated the following tentative thesis sentence:

> While annexation to the United States seemed the most rational and practical solution to British Columbia's economic woes in the late 1860s, the prospect of retaining their ties with Great Britain by being a part of a continent-wide confederation of provinces caught the imagination of British Columbians and led them to support political union with the rest of Canada.

Wiebe recognized that her preliminary thesis sentence was rather unwieldy, but she believed that this initial approach would guide her attempt to capture the essence of that critical debate concerning British Columbia's future. She recognized that this thesis sentence would without doubt have to be considerably refined as she pursued her investigation further.

2   Preparing an informal outline

Having written a tentative thesis for your paper, you will be ready to prepare an **informal outline** that will guide your subsequent research. Like the informal outline for an essay (see 1h-2), the outline should show the main divisions of your paper, in the order you think you will cover them, and it should include the important supporting ideas for each division. Shannon's informal outline, below, is probably sufficient. Notice that the organization corresponds to the arrangement of ideas in the thesis sentence: Shannon first covers women's progress to date and then explores the obstacles that remain.

How far women have come
— American Civil Rights Act of 1964
— Canadian Employment Equity Act and Federal Contractors Program
— 1970s workplace vs. present
Gains made since 1970s
— Success: percentage of women in middle and upper management
— Availability of mentors
— Rise of high-tech and service industries
Obstacles
— Statistics on women at the top
— Breaking the "glass ceiling"
— Last bastion for males
— Conservatism at the top
— "Queen bees" and male clones
— Masculine management style

If you feel that you don't have enough information to complete an informal outline or that some of your ideas lack support, consult sources in your working bibliography that you skipped before, or reexamine the ones you skimmed. Even if you believe your information is adequate for an outline, you may need to experiment with several arrangements of material to produce one that seems satisfactory. But don't try to construct a detailed, final outline at this stage. Both your organization and your thesis will undoubtedly change as you do more research.

EXERCISE 1

Read through the sources in the working bibliography you made in Chapter 35, Exercise 5 (p. 572). Jot down the main ideas related to your topic. Draft a thesis sentence based on those ideas that both states the topic and implies your perspective on it. Finally, construct an informal outline that contains your main divisions and several supporting ideas for each, returning to your sources as needed.

36c Taking notes using summary, paraphrase, and direct quotation

After you have written a thesis sentence and prepared an informal outline, you are ready to gather, interpret, and analyse information. To begin this stage, take detailed notes from your sources to verify and expand your ideas and to record supporting evidence.

Keep a copy of your informal outline with you in the library as a guide to give order to your search. Try to research the headings and subheadings of your outline one at a time. But don't let the outline constrain your thinking. As you learn more about your topic, you will probably revise your outline by changing a heading, by dropping or adding one, or by rearranging headings. Revising is an inevitable, necessary, and beneficial part of research writing.

The most efficient method of reading secondary sources during research is skimming, reading quickly to look for pertinent information. (Primary sources usually need to be read more carefully, especially when they are the focus of your paper.) When skimming, you do not read randomly in hopes of hitting what you want. Rather, you read with a specific question in mind. Consult the table of contents or

36c

index to find what you want, and concentrate on headings and main ideas, skipping material unrelated to the specific question you are researching. Then, when you find something relevant, read slowly and carefully to achieve a clear understanding of what the author is saying and to interpret and evaluate the material in the context of your own and others' opinions.

If it is effective, your final paper will show that you have digested and interpreted the information in your sources—work that can be performed most efficiently in note taking. Taking notes is not a mechanical process of copying from books and periodicals. Rather, as you read and take notes you assess and organize the information in your sources according to your thesis and outline. Thus your notes both prompt and preserve your thoughts.

Using a system for taking notes helps simplify the process and later makes writing the paper easier. The most common method involves note cards: 10.2 cm × 15.2 cm (4″ × 6″) cards allow more room than 7.6 cm × 12.7 cm (3″ × 5″). (Using photocopies from sources is discussed on p. 582.) Write only one fact or idea on a card so that you can easily rearrange information when you want to. (Such rearrangement is extremely difficult when notes are combined on sheets of paper.) If the same source gives you more than one idea or fact, make more than one card. At the top of every card, write the author's last name and the page number(s) of the source so that you will always know where the note came from. (Write a shortened form of the title as well if you are using two or more sources by the author.) In addition, write the outline heading that this note belongs under so that you can remember what you intended to do with it. This format is illustrated in this section by several note cards.

You can use four kinds of notes: summary, paraphrase, direct quotation, and a combination of these methods. When you **summarize**, you condense an extended idea or argument into a sentence or more in your own words. A full discussion of summary appears in 4a, and you should read that section if you have not already. Mark Shannon summarized the following quotation from one of his sources, Ann Hughey and Eric Gelman, "Managing the Woman's Way," *Newsweek*, p. 47:

36c

> Generalizing about male and female styles of management is a tricky business, because stereotypes have traditionally been used to keep women down. Not too long ago it was a widely accepted truth that women were unstable, indecisive, temperamental and manipulative and weren't good team members because they'd never played football. In fighting off these prejudices many women simply tried to adopt masculine traits in the office.

Compare this passage with Shannon's one-sentence summary, which picks out the kernel of Hughey and Gelman's idea:

Masc. and fem. management styles

Hughey and Gelman, p. 47

Rather than be labelled with the un-flattering stereotypes that prevented their promotions, many women adopted masculine qualities.

Summary is most useful when you want to record the gist of an author's idea without the background or supporting evidence.

When you **paraphrase**, you follow much more closely the author's original presentation, but you still restate it in your own words. Paraphrase is most useful when you want to reconstruct an author's line of reasoning but don't feel the original words merit direct quotation. The note card below shows how Shannon might have paraphrased the passage by Hughey and Gelman.

Masc. and. fem. management styles

Hughey and Gelman, p. 47

Because of the risk of stereotyping, which has served as a tool to keep women out of management, it is difficult to characterize a feminine management style. Women have been cited for their emotionality, instability, and lack of team spirit, among other qualities. Many women have defended themselves at work by adopting the qualities of men.

36c

Notice how the paraphrase uses different sentence structures and different words to express Hughey and Gelman's idea:

HUGHEY AND GELMAN'S WORDS	SHANNON'S PARAPHRASE
Generalizing about male and female styles of management is a tricky business, because stereotypes have traditionally been used to keep women down.	Because of the risk of stereotyping, which has served as a tool to keep women out of management, it is difficult to characterize a feminine management style.
Not too long ago it was a widely accepted truth that women were unstable, indecisive, temperamental and manipulative and weren't good team members because they'd never played football.	Women have been cited for their emotionality, instability, and lack of team spirit, among other qualities.
In fighting off these prejudices many women simply tried to adopt masculine traits in the office.	Many women defended themselves at work by adopting the qualities of men.

As you summarize and paraphrase, be careful not to distort the author's meaning, but don't feel you have to put down in new words the whole passage or all the details. Select what is pertinent and restate only that. In this way you will be developing your thoughts about the topic as you read and take notes. (For more on paraphrasing and summarizing, see 36d.)

Summary and paraphrase may be the methods you use most often in taking notes from secondary sources. But you will also want to use **direct quotation** from secondary sources when you feel an author's words give a special effect you want to include, when you want to give impact to an expert's opinion, or when you plan to use a graph, table, or diagram from a source. And in a paper analysing primary sources such as literary works, you will use direct quotation extensively to illustrate and support your analysis.

When taking a quotation from a source, copy the material *carefully*. Take down the author's exact wording, spelling, capitalization, and punctuation. Proofread every direct quotation *at least twice*, and be sure you have supplied big quotation marks so that later you won't confuse the direct quotation with a paraphrase or summary. If you want to add words for clarity, use brackets (see 25d). If you want to omit irrelevant words or sentences, use ellipsis marks, usually three spaced periods (see 25e). The following note card shows how Shannon might have quoted rather than summarized Hughey and Gelman, using ellipses and brackets to make the quotation more concise and specific.

36c

> *Masc. and fem. management styles*
> Hughey and Gelman, p. 47
> "Generalizing about male and female styles of
> management is a tricky business.... Not too long
> ago it was a widely accepted truth that women
> were unstable, indecisive, temperamental and
> manipulative and weren't good team members
> because they'd never played football. In fighting
> off these prejudices many women simply tried
> to adopt masculine traits [such as steadi-
> ness and sportsmanship] in the office."

Using quotation in combination with summary or paraphrase can help you shape the material to suit your purposes (although you must be careful not to distort the author's meaning.) The card below shows how Shannon might have used a combination of quotation and paraphrase to record the statement by Hughey and Gelman. Notice that the quotation marks are clearly visible and that the quotations are absolutely exact.

> *Masc. and fem. management styles*
> Hughey and Gelman, p. 47
>
> It is difficult to characterize a feminine style
> of management "because stereotypes have
> traditionally been used to keep women
> down." Women have been cited as "unstable,
> indecisive, temperamental and manipulative"
> and have been accused of not being "good team
> members." Many women defended themselves
> at work by adopting the qualities of men.

If the material you are quoting, summarizing, or paraphrasing runs from one page to the next in the source, make a mark (such as a check mark or a slash) at the exact spot where one page ends and the next begins. When writing your paper, you may want to use only a part of the material (perhaps the first or second half). The mark will save you from having to go back to your source to find the page on which the material actually appeared.

36c

A note on photocopying

To ensure accuracy of quotations and also to save time, researchers often photocopy sources. (All libraries provide one or more copying machines for this purpose.) But just running pages through a copier does not generate the creative, interpretive, and analytical thinking about sources that is so crucial in taking notes. If you do use a copier, turn to the photocopy soon after you make it, when you still have your hand on the original source and your thoughts about it are still fresh in your mind. At the top of the copy, write a heading from your outline, the author's name, the source title, and the page number, as you would on a note card. Then circle or underline the relevant passages and make notes in the margin about their significance to your topic. To make it possible to integrate photocopied notes with your notes on cards, you might want to paste or tape the copy on a note card of the same size you are using for your handwritten notes. If the photocopy won't fit on one card, cut it apart and paste it on two or more cards. Be sure to write the appropriate source information at the top of each card so that you don't lose track of where the copy, or a part of it, came from.

EXERCISE 2

Prepare two note cards, one containing a summary of the entire following paragraph and the other containing a paraphrase of the first two sentences (ending with the word *land*). Use the format for a note card provided in the preceding section, omitting only the outline heading.

Thus, an integral part of the history of Canada's federal government is a long series of attempts, both fruitful and fruitless, to overcome the geographic and economic disparities that plague that land. From the official beginning in 1867, a foundation stone of the Canadian Confederation has been the government's professed desire and goal to equalize the different legacies of the land. One of the first such efforts was the new country's promise to British Columbia to overcome its physical separation from the rest of Canada by building a transcontinental railroad through the formidable Rocky Mountains; a century later Pierre Elliott Trudeau, campaigning to become prime minister again, was seeking western Canadian votes by promising to double-track the same single rail line through the same mountains.
—Andrew H. Malcolm, *The Canadians*, p. 27

36c

EXERCISE 3

Prepare a note card containing a combination of paraphrase or summary and direct quotation that states the major idea of the following passage. Use the format for a note card provided in the preceding section, omitting only the outline heading.

> Most speakers unconsciously duel even during seemingly casual conversations, as can often be observed at social gatherings where they show less concern for exchanging information with other guests than for asserting their own dominance. Their verbal duelling often employs very subtle weapons like mumbling, a hostile act which defeats the listener's desire to understand what the speaker claims he is trying to say (but is really not saying because he is mumbling!). Or the verbal dueler may keep talking after someone has passed out of hearing range—which is often an aggressive challenge to the listener to return and acknowledge the dominance of the speaker.   —PETER K. FARB, *Word Play*, p. 107

36d Avoiding plagiarism

Plagiarism (from a Latin word for "kidnapper") is the presentation of someone else's ideas or words as your own. You plagiarize deliberately if you copy a sentence from a book and pass it off as your writing, if you summarize or paraphrase someone else's ideas without acknowledging your debt, or if you buy a term paper to hand in as your own. You plagiarize accidentally if you carelessly forget quotation marks around another writer's words or mistakenly omit a source citation for another's idea because you are unaware of the need to acknowledge the idea. Whether deliberate or accidental, plagiarism is a serious and often punishable offence.

You do not plagiarize, however, when you draw on other writers' material and acknowledge your sources. That procedure is a crucial part of honest research writing, as we have seen. This section shows you how to avoid plagiarism by acknowledging sources when necessary and by using them accurately and fairly.

1 Knowing what to acknowledge

When you write a research paper, you co-ordinate information from three kinds of sources: (1) your independent thoughts and experiences; (2) common knowledge, the basic knowledge people share; and (3) other people's independent thoughts and experiences. Of the three, you *must* acknowledge the third, the work of others.

36d

Your independent material

You need not acknowledge your own independent material— your thoughts, compilations of facts, or experimental results, expressed in your words or format—to avoid plagiarism. Such material includes observations from your experience (for example, a conclusion you draw about crowd behaviour by watching crowds at concerts) as well as diagrams you construct from information you gather yourself. Though you generally should describe the basis for your conclusions so that readers can evaluate your thinking, you need not cite sources for them. However, someone else's ideas and facts are not yours; even when you express them entirely in your words and format, they require acknowledgment.

Common knowledge

Common knowledge consists of the standard information of a field of study as well as folk literature and common-sense observations. Standard information includes, for instance, the major facts of history. The dates of Charlemagne's rule as emperor of Rome (800–814) and the fact that his reign was accompanied by a revival of learning—both facts available in many reference books—do not need to be acknowledged, even if you have to look up the information. However, an interpretation of facts (for instance, a theory of how writing began) or a specialist's observation (for instance, an Asian historian's opinion of the effects of Chinese wall posters) is considered independent, not common, knowledge and must be documented.

Folk literature, which is popularly known and cannot be traced to particular writers, is considered common knowledge. Mother Goose nursery rhymes and fairy tales like "Snow White" are examples. However, all literature traceable to a particular writer should be acknowledged. Even a familiar phrase like "miles to go before I sleep" (from Robert Frost's poem "Stopping by Woods on a Snowy Evening") is literature, not folk literature, and requires acknowledgment.

Common-sense observations, such as the idea that weather affects people's spirits or that inflation is most troublesome for people with low and fixed incomes, are considered common knowledge and do not require acknowledgment, even when they also appear in someone else's writing. But a scientist's findings about the effects of high humidity on people with high blood pressure, or an economist's argument about the effects of inflation on immigrants from China, will require acknowledgment.

You may treat common knowledge as your own, even if you have to look it up in a reference book. You may not know, for example, the dates of the French Revolution or the standard definition of *photosynthesis*, although these are considered common knowledge. If you do not know a subject well enough to determine whether a piece of information is common knowledge, make a record of the source as you would for any other quotation, paraphrase, or

36d

CHECKLIST FOR AVOIDING PLAGIARISM

1. What type of source are you using: your own independent material, common knowledge, or someone else's independent material? You must acknowledge someone else's material.
2. If you are quoting someone else's material, is the quotation exact? Have you inserted quotation marks around quotations run into the text? Have you shown omissions with ellipses and additions with brackets?
3. If you are paraphrasing or summarizing someone else's material, have you used your own words and sentence structures? Does your paraphrase or summary employ quotation marks when you resort to the author's exact language? Have you represented the author's meaning without distortion?
4. Is each use of someone else's material acknowledged in your text? Are all your source citations complete and accurate? (See 36i.)
5. Does your list of works cited include all the sources you have drawn from in writing your paper? (See 36h.)

summary. As you read more about the subject, the information may come up repeatedly without acknowledgment, in which case it is probably common knowledge. But if you are still in doubt when you finish your research, always acknowledge the source.

Someone else's independent material

You must always acknowledge other people's independent material—that is, any facts or ideas that are not common knowledge or your own. The source may be anything, including a book, an article, a movie, an interview, a microfilmed document, or a computer program. You must acknowledge not only ideas or facts themselves but also the language and format in which the ideas or facts appear, if you use them. That is, the wording, sentence structures, arrangement of thoughts, and special graphic format (such as a table or diagram) created by another writer belong to that writer just as his or her ideas do. The following example baldly plagiarizes the original quotation from Jessica Mitford's *Kind and Usual Punishment*, p. 9.

ORIGINAL	The character and mentality of the keepers may be of more importance in understanding prisons than the character and mentality of the kept.
PLAGIARISM	But the character and mentality of prison officials (the keepers) is of more importance in understanding prisons than the character and mentality of prisoners (the kept).

36d

Though the writer has made some changes in Mitford's original and even altered the meaning slightly (by changing *may be* to *is*), she has plagiarized on several counts. She has copied key words (*character, mentality, keepers, kept*), duplicated the entire sentence structure, and lifted the idea—all without acknowledging the source. As illustrated in the following section, the writer must either enclose the exact quotation in quotation marks or state the idea in her own words and in her own sentence. Whichever she does, she *must* acknowledge Mitford as the source.

You need to acknowledge another's material no matter how you use it, how much of it you use, or how often you use it. Whether you are quoting a single important word, paraphrasing a single sentence, or summarizing three paragraphs, and whether you are using the source only once or a dozen times, you must acknowledge the original author every time. See 36i for discussion and examples of how to acknowledge sources in your text.

If you read someone else's material during your research but do not include any of that material in your final draft, you need not acknowledge the source with a note because you have not actually used the material. However, your instructor may ask you to include such sources in your list of works consulted (see 36h).

2 Quoting, summarizing, and paraphrasing honestly

When using direct quotation, be sure to copy the material from the source accurately and with clear quotation marks. Use the quotation marks in the running text of your paper even if you are quoting only a single word that the original author used in a special or central way. (See 24c for the style to use with poetry and long quotations, which are set off from the text and not enclosed in quotation marks.) Acknowledge the source in the manner appropriate for the documentation style you are using. (See 36i for the MLA citation style.)

To correct the plagiarism of Mitford's sentence above, the writer would place Mitford's exact words in quotation marks and cite the source properly (in this case, in MLA style).

> **QUOTATION**   According to one critic of the penal system, "The character and mentality of the keepers may be of more importance in understanding prisons than the character and mentality of the kept" (Mitford 9).

36d

When you summarize or paraphrase, you do not use quotation marks, because the words are your own. However, you must acknowledge the author of the idea. Here is a paraphrase of the Mitford quotation above (with the source citation again in MLA style).

PARAPHRASE   One critic of the penal system maintains that we may be able to learn more about prisons from the psychology of the prison officials than from that of the prisoners (Mitford 9).

If you adopt the source's sentence pattern and simply substitute synonyms for key words, or if you use the original words and merely change the sentence pattern, you are not paraphrasing but plagiarizing, even if you acknowledge the source, because both methods use someone else's expression without quotation marks. The inadequate paraphrase below plagiarizes the original source, Frederick C. Crew's *The Tragedy of Manners: Moral Drama in the Later Novels of Henry James*, page 8.

ORIGINAL   In each case I have tried to show that all the action in a "Jamesian novel" may be taken as a result of philosophical differences of opinion among the principal characters, and that these differences in turn are explainable by reference to the characters' differing social backgrounds.

PLAGIARISM   According to Crews, the action in a "Jamesian novel" comes from philosophical differences of opinion between characters, differences that can be explained by examining the characters' differing social backgrounds (8).

The plagiarized passage lifts several expressions verbatim from the source, without change and without quotation marks: *action in a "Jamesian novel"*; *philosophical differences of opinion*; *the characters' differing social backgrounds*. Thus, even though the writer acknowledges the author's work (by giving Crews's name and the parenthetical page number, 8), he plagiarizes because he does not also acknowledge the author's words with quotation marks. The following paraphrase both conveys and acknowledges the author's meaning without stealing his manner of expression.

PARAPHRASE   According to Crews, the characters in Henry James's novels live out philosophies acquired from their upbringing and their place in society (8).

In this paraphrase, although the writer retains Crews's essential meaning, he restates that meaning in a sentence that he himself has clearly constructed and designed to fit his larger purpose.

36d

In paraphrasing or summarizing you must not only devise your own form of expression (or place quotation marks around the author's expressions) but also represent the author's meaning exactly, without distorting it. In the following inaccurate summary the writer has avoided plagiarism but has stated a meaning exactly opposite that of the original. The original quotation, from the artist Henri Matisse, appears in Jack D. Flam, *Matisse on Art*, page 148.

ORIGINAL   For the artist creation begins with vision. To see is itself a creative operation, requiring an effort. Everything that we see in our daily life is more or less distorted by acquired habits, and this is perhaps more evident in an age like ours when cinema posters and magazines present us every day with a flood of ready-made images which are to the eye what prejudices are to the mind.

INACCURATE SUMMARY   Matisse said that the artist can learn how to see by looking at posters and magazines (qtd. in Flam 148).

The revision below combines summary and quotation to represent the author's meaning exactly.

IMPROVED SUMMARY   Matisse said that the artist must overcome visual "habits" and "prejudices," particularly those developed in response to popular cultural images (qtd. in Flam 148).

To be sure you acknowledge sources fairly and do not plagiarize, review the checklist on page 585 both before beginning to write your paper and again after you have completed your first draft.

EXERCISE 4

The numbered items below show various attempts to quote or paraphrase the following passage. Carefully compare each attempt with the original passage. Which are plagiarized, inaccurate, or both, and which are acceptable? Why?

I would agree with the sociologists that psychiatric labeling is dangerous. Society can inflict terrible wounds by discrimination, and by confusing health with disease and disease with badness.
—GEORGE E. VAILLANT, *Adaptation to Life*, p. 361

1. According to George Vaillant, society often inflicts wounds by using psychiatric labelling, confusing health, disease, and badness (361).

2. According to George Vaillant, "psychiatric labeling [such as 'homosexual' or 'schizophrenic'] is dangerous. Society can inflict terrible wounds by . . . confusing health with disease and disease with badness" (361).

3. According to George Vaillant, when psychiatric labelling discriminates between health and disease or between disease and badness, it can inflict wounds on those labelled (361).

4. Psychiatric labels can badly hurt those labelled, says George Vaillant, because they fail to distinguish among health, illness, and immorality (361).

36d

5. Labels such as "homosexual" and "schizophrenic" can be hurtful when they fail to distinguish among health, illness, and immorality.
6. "I would agree with the sociologists that society can inflict terrible wounds by discrimination, and by confusing health with disease and disease with badness" (Vaillant 361).

EXERCISE 5

Continuing from Exercise 1 (p. 577), as the next step in preparing a research paper, make notes of specific information from your sources. Use summary, paraphrase, direct quotation, or a combination as seems appropriate. Be careful to avoid plagiarism or inaccuracy. Mark each card (or photocopy) with the author's name, title, and page number as well as with your outline heading.

36e Revising the thesis sentence and writing a formal outline

As you take notes, you will almost inevitably find reasons to revise your thesis sentence and informal outline. These revisions are the focus of most of the next stage in writing a research paper.

After investigating your topic thoroughly through reading and note taking, you will want to evaluate your thesis sentence in light of what you now know. In his research, for example, Mark Shannon discovered that women seemed to have broken most barriers into middle and upper management but still could not penetrate a "glass ceiling" between themselves and the top jobs, corporate directorships. Many of his sources focussed on the differences in managerial styles between men and women. Accordingly, Shannon altered his thesis to reflect the research and his growing conviction that the masculine management style was key in preventing women from breaking through to top management. At the same time, a lack of space, time, and interest led Shannon to abandon his original plan to cover the progress of women in recent decades (see his informal outline, p. 576). This change is reflected in the openings of his tentative and revised thesis sentences.

Tentative thesis sentence

Although women have come a long way in their journey to the top of the corporate ladder, they still have a number of obstacles to overcome before they can consider themselves to have arrived.

Revised thesis sentence

If women are ever to break through the glass ceiling in significant

36e

numbers, business attitudes will have to change, particularly the definition of successful management styles.

Deborah Wiebe's reading and note taking persuaded her that the factors leading to British Columbia's eventual decision to join the Canadian Confederation were many and varied. Rather than trying to highlight in her thesis sentence the principal reasons for this decision, she decided instead to write her paper as an explication and analysis of these various factors and options. She was thus able to simplify her thesis sentence considerably and at the same time arouse the reader's interest in her topic by means of a very brief description of her intentions.

TENTATIVE THESIS SENTENCE

While annexation to the United States seemed the most rational and practical solution to British Columbia's economic woes in the late 1860s, the prospect of retaining their ties with Great Britain by being a part of a continent-wide confederation of provinces caught the imagination of British Columbians and led them to support political union with the rest of Canada.

REVISED THESIS SENTENCE

British Columbia entered the Canadian Confederation only after other options had been seriously considered and eventually rejected.

After revising your thesis sentence, you may want or be required to prepare a detailed outline from which to write your paper. This **formal outline**, like the formal outline for a brief essay (see 1h-2), is more complete than an informal outline and arranges ideas in a logical way. Inadequate coverage of the thesis, overlapping ideas, ideas that are not parallel yet are in parallel positions, and imprecise phrasing—all of these can be corrected in the process of writing a formal outline. The goal is to produce an outline that presents your ideas in a sensible and persuasive sequence and that supports ideas at each level with enough explanation and evidence.

Before beginning work on your formal outline, you should group your note cards according to their headings, which are also the headings of your informal outline. You can begin revising your outline by rearranging and retitling cards to reflect your changed ideas and the sense of your revised thesis sentence. This is a good time to review your research journal. If you have kept it dutifully, it will undoubtedly contain connections between sources, ideas about sources, and other thoughts that can help you organize your paper. As you move back and forth between specific notes and linking ideas, a complete outline will gradually evolve.

36e

A formal outline is usually written either in phrases—a **topic outline**—or in sentences—a **sentence outline**. A complete topic outline is illustrated in Chapter 1, page 46. A complete sentence outline accompanies Mark Shannon's research paper on pages 619–20. Either is suitable for a research paper, though a sentence outline, because it requires complete statements, conveys more information. The example on the next page shows the formal outline's format and schematic content.

I. First main idea
  A. First subordinate idea
    1. First evidence for subordinate idea
      a. First detail of evidence
      b. Second detail of evidence
    2. Second evidence for subordinate idea
  B. Second subordinate idea
II. Second main idea

In this model main ideas are labelled with Roman numerals, the first sublevel with capital letters, the second with Arabic numerals, and the third with small letters. (A fourth sublevel, if needed, is labelled with Arabic numerals enclosed in parentheses.) Each level of the outline is indented farther than the one it supports.

To be an effective organizer for your thoughts, a formal outline should be detailed and should adhere to several principles of logical arrangement, clarity, balance, and completeness. These are discussed in detail and illustrated in Chapter 1, pages 46–48. Briefly: (1) The outline should divide material into groups that indicate which ideas are primary and, under them, which subordinate. A long, undivided list of parallel items probably needs to be subdivided. (2) Parallel headings should represent ideas of parallel importance and should not overlap one another. (3) Single sublevels should be avoided because they illogically imply that something is divided into only one part.

If you compare Mark Shannon's sentence outline on pages 619–20 with his informal outline on page 576, you can see that the formal outline has more information and a tighter, more logical arrangement of ideas and details.

EXERCISE 6

Identify the flaws in the following partial outline for a research paper. Check especially for departures from formal outline form, including illogical subdivision of topics, inconsistent wording of items, and non-parallel placement of ideas of parallel importance.

36e

THESIS SENTENCE

Food additives, which aid in processing foods and in preserving them or improving their appearance, are more useful to us than they are dangerous.

FORMAL OUTLINE

I. Processing, preservation, appearance
   A. Processing
      1. Leavening agents
      2. Antifoaming agents
      3. Emulsifiers
         a. Bind ingredients together
   B. Preservation
      1. Protect from internal destruction
         a. Natural enzymes can cause discoloration or overripening
         b. Must remove or disable enzymes
      2. External destruction
         a. Bacteria
         b. Fungus
      3. Environment
         a. Heat, moisture, humidity
         b. Humectants protect foods from excess moisture
   C. Appearance
      1. Glazing agents
      2. Foaming agents cause bubbles to appear in hot chocolate
      3. Firming agents
         a. Keep fruits and vegetables firm in cans
         b. Thickeners
            1. Prevent ice crystal formation, as in ice cream
            2. Improve texture
      4. Sequestrants prevent discoloration

EXERCISE 7

Consulting your research journal and using the note cards you prepared in Exercise 5 (p. 589), revise the thesis sentence from Exercise 1 (p. 577) and construct a formal sentence or topic outline (as specified by your instructor) from which to write a paper.

36f

36f

36f **Drafting the paper**

Many writers begin drafting a research paper early, even before they have finished reading, as a means of testing their ideas and finding direction for further research. If you have not yet begun drafting, however, you should be ready to do so after you have taken notes from your sources, revised your thesis as necessary, and written a formal outline for your paper. Take time to organize your notes carefully according to your formal outline. Once you have arranged your notes, go through them slowly, considering which of your ideas each note supports, how you will link the evidence in one note with that in others, and how you will move from one idea and block of evidence to the next. Unless you have done so already, consult your research journal for insights and connections that can help you get started and keep moving.

1 Writing the first draft

Beginning a draft of what will be a relatively long and complicated paper can be difficult, so it may help to remember that you do not have to proceed methodically from beginning to end. To get your juices flowing and give yourself a sense of direction, try writing a quick two- or three-paragraph summary of what the paper will be about. (Pretend you're writing to a friend if that will help loosen you up). Then, when you turn to the paper itself, skip any parts that scare you or give you undue trouble, even the introduction. Try starting with the section that you feel most confident about. Move from there to other sections of the paper, attempting to fit the sections together only after you begin to see the draft take shape.

In writing sections of your draft, remember that a primary reason for doing a research paper is learning how to evaluate and interpret the evidence in sources, draw your own conclusions from the evidence, and weave the two together in a convincing whole. The weaving will be easier if you view each principal idea in your outline as a unit. Depending on the importance of the idea to your scheme, on its complexity, and on the amount of evidence needed to support it, a unit may require a single paragraph or a block of two or three paragraphs.

Begin each unit by stating the idea, which should be a conclusion you have drawn from reading and taking notes. Follow the statement with specific support from your notes: facts and examples; summaries, paraphrases, or quotations of secondary sources; quotations of passages from primary sources with your analysis; and so on. If your research focusses on or has uncovered a disagreement among experts, present the disagreement fairly and give the evidence that leads you to side with one expert or another. As much as possible, try to remain open to new interpretations or new arrangements of ideas that occur to you.

As you draft your paper, insert the source of each summary, paraphrase, and quotation in parentheses in the text—for instance,

36f

"(Hughey and Gelman 47)," referring to page 47 in a work by Hughey and Gelman. If you are conscientious about inserting these notes and carrying them through successive drafts, you will be less likely to plagiarize accidentally and you will have little difficulty citing your sources in the final paper. (Citing sources is discussed on pp. 599–616.)

TIPS FOR DRAFTING A RESEARCH PAPER

1. As a warm-up, write a quick, brief summary of the paper.
2. Start wherever you like.
3. Work in chunks, one unit or principal idea at a time.
4. Insert source information (author's name and page number) into the draft as you quote, paraphrase, or summarize.

---

2 Introducing summaries, paraphrases, and quotations

One of your challenges in writing a research paper will be deciding when, where, and how to introduce summaries, paraphrases, and quotations from your sources into your text. Whether you summarize, paraphrase, or quote, make others' facts and opinions serve your ideas; don't allow them to overwhelm your own point of view. Except when you are analysing literature or other primary sources, favour paraphrases and summaries over quotations. Quote secondary sources only when the original wording is essential to understanding the exact meaning or is particularly succinct, forceful, or otherwise interesting (for instance, a bold statement from an acknowledged authority or an inventive comparison). Keep quotations short by eliminating sentences and phrases that are not essential to the intended meaning and that do not contribute to your purpose. Most papers of six to ten pages should not need more than two to four quotations that are longer than a few lines. More than that may bury rather than enhance your argument.

When using summaries, paraphrases, and quotations, be careful to integrate them into your own sentences and at the same time explain why you are using them. A quotation, summary, or paraphrase that is dumped in readers' laps is unlikely to achieve what you intend it to, as the following example illustrates:

36f

A DUMPED QUOTATION

In short, many news editors and reporters maintain that it is impossible and perhaps not even desirable to keep personal opinions from influencing the selection and presentation of facts. "True, news reporters, like everyone else, form impressions of what they see and hear. However, a good reporter does not fail to separate his opinions from his facts" (Lyman 52).

The writer of this passage provides no clues that the quotation contradicts the first sentence; instead, she forces us to figure that out for ourselves. In addition, she loses an opportunity to explain who Lyman is and why his opinion is worthwhile; consequently, we aren't likely to see the quotation as very strong evidence.

With some rewriting, the quotation above can be smoothly integrated into the writer's sentences so that the contradiction and the reason for quoting Lyman are both clear:

AN INTEGRATED QUOTATION

In short, many news editors and reporters maintain that it is impossible and perhaps not even desirable to keep personal opinions from influencing the selection and presentation of facts. Yet not all authorities agree with this view. Harold Lyman, a newspaper editor for more than forty years, grants that "news reporters, like everyone else, form impressions of what they see and hear." But, Lyman insists, "a good reporter does not fail to separate his opinions from his facts" (52).

In this passage the second sentence and the writer's words *grants*, *But*, and *insists* tell us what to expect in the quotation. (A list of verbs for introducing borrowed material appears in the "Verbs for Introducing Summaries, Paraphrases, and Quotations" box.) And the phrase identifying Lyman, *a newspaper editor for more than forty years*, tells us why Lyman is quoted and why we should value his opinion.

It is not always necessary to name your sources and indicate their credentials in your running text. In fact, such introductions may get in the way when you are simply establishing facts or weaving together facts and opinions from varied sources. In the following passage from Deborah Wiebe's paper, the information is more important than the source, so the name of the source is confined to a parenthetical acknowledgment:

The most prominent group to feel this way was the government led by Governor Seymour. It desired neither union with Canada nor annexation with the United States; it simply wanted to remain loyal to Britain and retain independent colonial status (Careless and Brown 40).

36f

(See pp. 600–06 for an explanation of the parenthetical form of citation used in this passage and the ones above.)

VERBS FOR INTRODUCING SUMMARIES, PARAPHRASES, AND QUOTATIONS

Introduce borrowed material with a verb that conveys information about the source author's attitude or approach to what he or she is saying. In the sentence *King _____ that the flood might have been disastrous*, filling the blank with *observes*, *finds*, or *insists* would create different meanings.

AUTHOR IS NEUTRAL	**AUTHOR INFERS OR SUGGESTS**	**AUTHOR ARGUES**	**AUTHOR IS UNEASY OR DISPARAGING**
comments	analyses	alleges	
describes	asks	claims	belittles
explains	assesses	contends	bemoans
illustrates	concludes	defends	complains
notes	considers	disagrees	condemns
observes	finds	holds	deplores
points out	predicts	insists	deprecates
records	proposes	maintains	derides
relates	reveals	**AUTHOR AGREES**	laments
reports	shows	admits	warns
says	speculates	agrees	
sees	suggests	concedes	
thinks	supposes	concurs	
writes		grants	

In papers analysing literature, historical documents, and other sources, quotations will often be both the target of your analysis and the chief support for your ideas. You may need to quote many brief passages, integrated into your sentences, and then comment on the quotations to clarify your analysis and win readers' agreement with it. An example of such extensive quotation can be seen in the literary analysis in Chapter 38 (pp. 673–75).

If you need guidance in the mechanics of quotation, see 21h (punctuating explanatory words such as *he insists*), 24c (quoting poetry and long prose passages), and 25d and 25e (using brackets and ellipsis marks for additions to and deletions from quotations).

36f

EXERCISE 8

Drawing on the ideas in the following paragraph and using examples from your own observations and experiences, write a paragraph about anxiety. Integrate at least one direct quotation and one paraphrase from the following paragraph into your own sentences. In your paragraph identify the author by name and give his credentials: he is a professor of psychiatry and a practising psychoanalyst.

There are so many ways in which man is unique from all the lower forms of animals, and almost all of them make us uniquely susceptible to feelings of anxiousness. Our imagination and reasoning powers facilitate anxiety; the anxious feeling is precipitated not by an absolute impending threat—such as the worry about an examination, a speech, travel—but rather by the symbolic and often unconscious representations. We do not have to be experiencing a potential danger. We can experience something related to it. We can recall, through our incredible memories, the original symbolic sense of vulnerability in childhood and suffer the feeling attached to that. We can even forget the original memory and still be stuck with the emotion—which is then compounded by its seemingly irrational quality at this time. It is not just the fear of death which pains us, but the anticipation of it; or the anniversary of a specific death; or a street, a hospital, a time of day, a color, a flower, a symbol associated with a death.

—WILLARD GAYLIN, "Feeling Anxious," p. 23

36g Revising and editing the paper

When you have written a first draft, take a break for at least a day so that you can gain some objectivity about your work and read the draft critically when you begin to revise. Then evaluate your first draft according to the advice and revision checklist in 2b (p. 57). Be especially attentive to the following.

1. Ensure that your thesis sentence accurately describes your topic and your perspective as they emerged during drafting, so that the paper is unified and coherent.
2. Be alert for major structural problems that may not have been apparent in your outline:
   —illogical arrangements of ideas;
   —inadequate emphasis of important points and over-emphasis of minor points;
   —imbalance between the views of others (support) and your own views (interpretation or analysis).
3. Hunt out irrelevant ideas and facts that crept in just because you had notes on them.
4. Look for places where supporting evidence is weak.
5. Examine your explanations to be sure your readers will understand them. Define terms and clarify concepts that readers may be unfamiliar with.

When you complete your revision, retype the new draft if possible so that you have a clean copy to edit. For editing, consult the advice and checklist in 2c (p. 65). Try to read the paper from the point of view of someone who has not spent hours planning and research-ing but instead has come fresh to the paper. Look for lapses in sense, awkward passages, poor transitions between ideas and evidence, unnecessary repetitions, wrong or misspelled words, errors in gram-mar, punctuation, or mechanics—in short, anything that is likely to interfere with a reader's understanding of your meaning.

When you finish editing your paper, but before you prepare and proofread the final draft, you need to prepare your list of sources and insert the final source citations into the next. Preparing the list and citing sources are the subjects of the next two sections.

EXERCISE 9

Write the research paper you have been preparing in Chapter 35, Exercises 1, 2, and 5, and this chapter, Exercises 1, 5, and 7. Before beginning the first draft, study your research journal and your notes. While writing, follow your note cards (Exercise 5) and formal outline (Exercise 7) as closely as you need to, but stay open to new ideas, associations, and arrangements. Then revise and edit thoroughly and carefully, working to improve not only your presen-tation of ideas but also, if necessary, the ideas themselves.

|36h| Preparing the final list of works cited

When you finish editing your paper, prepare a final list of the sources you used in it. Include in your list all the sources you quoted, paraphrased, or summarized. Unless your instructor requests it, don't include sources you examined but did not actually use in your paper.

If you are following the guidelines of the *MLA Handbook*, title your list of sources "Works Cited." (Use the title "Works Consulted" if your instructor asks you to include all the sources you examined as well as those you actually used.) Type the information about sources in the formats given on pages 556–70, and arrange them in alphabeti-cal order by the last name of the author or, if an author is not given, by the first main word of the title (excluding *A*, *An*, or *The*). Double-space the entire list (within and between entries), and indent the second and subsequent lines of each entry five spaces from the left. Place the list at the end of your paper. See the lists of works cited in the papers by Mark Shannon (pp. 638–39) and Deborah Wiebe (p. 663–64) and the comments on Shannon's list (pp. 647–48) for the form to follow in typing this section.

The *MLA Handbook* gives a special format for listing two or more works by the same author:

```
Gardner, Howard.   The Arts and Human Development.  New

     York: Wiley, 1973.

---.    The Quest for Mind: Piaget, Lévi-Strauss, and

     the Structuralist Movement.   New York: Knopf,

     1973.
```

The author's name is given only in the first entry. For the second and any subsequent works by the same author, substitute three hyphens for the author's name, followed by a period. Arrange the sources alphabetically by the first main word of the title. Note that the three hyphens stand for *exactly* the same name or names. If the second source above were by Gardner and somebody else, both names would have to be given in full.

Guidelines for source lists in other disciplines are given in Chapter 38 (pp. 682 and 700).

> **EXERCISE 10**
>
> Prepare the final list of works cited for the research paper you wrote and revised in Exercise 9 (p. 598). Follow the *MLA Handbook* models on pages 556–70 unless your instructor specifies a different format.

36i Preparing final source citations

Every time you borrow the words, facts, or ideas of others, you must acknowledge the source in your text so that readers know you borrowed the material and know where you borrowed it from. You do not need to acknowledge your own ideas or ideas that are considered common knowledge when you express these in your own words. But you must acknowledge direct quotations, illustrations, and summaries or paraphrases of others' ideas, facts that aren't common knowledge, and associations between them—no matter what their length or how often you have already cited the source (see 36d for a full discussion of what to acknowledge).

As you drafted your paper, you should have inserted the sources for all your quotations, summaries, and paraphrases (see p. 593). Now, as you read through your paper, recheck these inserts against your note cards. Make sure each summary, paraphrase, and quotation has a citation, proofread every quotation a final time, and then locate the corresponding entry in your list of works cited. The page numbers recorded in your draft and the information on your list of works cited give you everything you need to write final source citations.

cit
36i

The format of source acknowledgments differs from discipline to discipline. The next two sections explain and illustrate the parenthetical style recommended by the *MLA Handbook* (below) and footnotes or endnotes (p. 600). Chapter 38 explains and illustrates the systems in other disciplines. Your instructor will tell you which format to follow.

1 Using the MLA style of parenthetical reference

The documentation system of the *MLA Handbook* employs brief parenthetical references within the text that direct readers to the list of works cited. For example:

```
Only one article mentions this discrepancy (Wolfe 62).
```

The name Wolfe directs readers to the article by Wolfe in the list of works cited, and the page number 62 specifies the page in the article on which the cited material appears.

The following pages describe this documentation system: what must be included in a reference (below), where to place references (p. 605), and when to use footnotes or endnotes in addition to parenthetical references (p. 606).

What to include in a parenthetical reference

The in-text references to sources must include (1) just enough information for the reader to locate the appropriate source in your list of works cited and (2) just enough information for the reader to locate the place in the source where the borrowed material appears. Usually, you can meet these requirements by providing the author's last name and the page(s) in the source on which the material appears. The reader can find the source in your list of works cited and find the borrowed material in the source itself. Refer to the index on the opposite page to find the form of reference for the kind of source and citation you are using.

AUTHOR NOT NAMED IN THE TEXT

When you have not already named the author in your sentence, provide the author's last name and the page number(s), with no punctuation between them, in parentheses.

```
One researcher concludes that "women impose a dis-

tinctive construction on moral problems, seeing moral

dilemmas in terms of conflicting responsibilities"

(Gilligan 105).
```

AUTHOR NAMED IN THE TEXT

If the author's name is already given in your text, you need not repeat it in the parenthetical reference. The reference just gives the page number(s).

```
One researcher, Carol Gilligan, concludes that "women

impose a distinctive construction on moral problems,

seeing moral dilemmas in terms of conflicting respon-

sibilities" (105).
```

A WORK WITH TWO OR THREE AUTHORS

If the source has two or three authors, give all their names in the text or in the reference:

```
Wimsatt and Brooks note the power of Tolstoy's "wal-

loping caricatures of metropolitan fashionable cul-

ture" (464).

Tolstoy wrote "walloping caricatures of metropolitan

fashionable culture" (Wimsatt and Brooks 464).
```

A WORK WITH MORE THAN THREE AUTHORS

If the source has more than three authors, you may list all their last names or use only the first author's name followed by "et al." (the abbreviation for the Latin "and others"). The choice depends on what you do in your list of works cited (see p. 558).

cit
36i

```
It took the combined forces of the Americans, Europe-

ans, and Japanese to break the rebel siege of Peking

in 1900 (Lopez et al. 362).
```

```
It took the combined forces of the Americans, Europe-

ans, and Japanese to break the rebel siege of Peking

in 1900 (Lopez, Blum, Cameron, and Barnes 362).
```

AN ENTIRE WORK (NO PAGE NUMBERS)

When you cite an entire work rather than a part of it, the reference will not include any page number. If the author's name appears in the text, no parenthetical reference is needed. But remember that the source must appear in the list of works cited.

```
Boyd deals with the need to acknowledge and come to

terms with our fear of nuclear technology.
```

A MULTIVOLUME WORK

If you used only one volume of a multivolume work, your list of works cited can indicate that by giving the appropriate volume in the entry (see the second entry for Schaff on p. 560). However, if you used and listed all the volumes, your parenthetical reference must specify which volume you are referring to.

```
The highly regarded historian of Christianity, Philip

Schaff, describing the second-century church father

Justin Martyr as one of the first Christian thinkers,

comments that he was "not a man of genius and accu-

rate scholarship, but of respectable talent, exten-

sive reading, and enormous memory" (2: 715).
```

The number 2 indicates the volume from which the quotation was taken; the number 715 indicates the page number in that volume. If you are referring generally to an entire volume of a multivolume work and are not citing specific page numbers, add the abbreviation "vol." before the volume number, as in "(vol. 5)." Then readers will not misinterpret the volume number as a page number.

A WORK BY AN AUTHOR OF TWO OR MORE WORKS

If your list of works cited includes two or more works by the same author, then your reference must tell the reader which of the author's works you are citing. Use the appropriate title or a shortened version of it in the parenthetical reference.

```
At about age seven, most children begin to tell sto-

ries accurately, describe scenes realistically, and

use appropriate gestures to reinforce their story

(Gardner, Arts 144-45).
```

The title *Arts* is shortened from Gardner's full title, *The Arts and Human Development* (see the entry for this book on p. 599). Often, as here, the first main word in the title is enough to direct the reader to the appropriate source.

AN UNSIGNED WORK

Anonymous works are alphabetized by title in the list of works cited. In the text they are referred to by full or shortened title.

```
One article notes that a death-row inmate may demand

his own execution to achieve a fleeting notoriety

("Right").
```

This reference is to an unsigned article entitled "The Right to Die." A page reference is unnecessary because the article is no longer than a page (see the entry for the article on p. 564).

A GOVERNMENT DOCUMENT OR A WORK WITH A CORPORATE AUTHOR

If the author of the work is listed as a government body or a corporation, cite the work by the name given as the author's. If the name is long, work it into the text to avoid an intrusive reference.

```
The BC Ministry of Education's response to the 1989

Sullivan Royal Commission Report on Education pro-

poses the elimination of grade distinctions during

the primary years (32).
```

AN INDIRECT SOURCE

When you quote or paraphrase one source's quotation of another source, your reference must indicate as much. In the following reference "qtd. in" ("quoted in") says that Davino was quoted by Boyd.

cit
36i

```
George Davino maintains that children as young as

three "are experiencing nightmares about nuclear

war" (qtd. in Boyd 22).
```

A LITERARY WORK

Novels, plays, and poems are often available in many editions, so your instructor may ask you to provide information that will help readers find the passage you cite no matter what edition they consult. For novels, the page number comes first, followed by a semicolon and then information on the appropriate part or chapter of the work.

```
Toward the end of James's novel, Maggie suddenly

feels "the thick breath of the definite--which was

the intimate, the immediate, the familiar, as she

hadn't had them for so long" (535; pt. 6, ch. 41).
```

For verse plays and poems, you can omit the page number and instead cite the appropriate part or act (and scene, if any) plus the line number(s). Use Arabic numerals for acts and scenes ("3.4") unless your instructor specifies Roman numerals("III.iv").

```
Later in King Lear Shakespeare has the disguised

Edgar say, "The prince of darkness is a gentleman"

(3.4.147).
```

For prose plays, provide the page number followed by the act and scene, if any (see the reference to *Death of a Salesman* opposite).

MORE THAN ONE WORK

If you use a parenthetical reference to cite more than a single work, separate the citations by a semicolon.

```
Two recent articles urge small businesses not to rush

to buy a personal computer, even an inexpensive one,

on the grounds that a computer badly used is less

efficient than no computer at all (Richards 162;

Gough and Hall 201).
```

Since long references in the text can distract the reader, you may choose to cite several or more works in an endnote or footnote rather than in the text. See page 606.

Where to place parenthetical references

Generally, place a parenthetical reference at the end of the sentence in which you summarize, paraphrase, or quote a work. The reference should follow a closing quotation mark but precede the sentence punctuation. (See the examples in the previous section.) When a reference pertains to only part of a sentence, place the reference after the material being cited and at the least intrusive point—usually at the end of a clause.

> Although David Frum argues that because of the 1982
> Charter of Rights "the sexy issues that were once
> politicked will now be litigated instead" (57), it
> remains to be seen whether the Supreme Court of
> Canada will permanently assume a more dominant role
> than Parliament in shaping the character of Canadian
> society.

When a reference appears at the end of a quotation set off from the text, place it two spaces *after* the punctuation ending the quotation.

> In Arthur Miller's <u>Death of a Salesman</u>, the most
> poignant defence of Willie Loman comes from his wife,
> Linda:
>
> > He's not the finest character that ever
> > lived. But he's a human being, and a
> > terrible thing is happening to him. So
> > attention must be paid. He's not to be
> > allowed to fall into his grave like an old
> > dog. Attention, attention must finally be
> > paid to such a person. (56; act 1)

(The reference includes the act number as well as the page number. See "A literary work" on the opposite page.)

See the two sample research papers starting on pages 618 and 649 for further examples of placing parenthetical references.

cit
36i

Using footnotes or endnotes in special circumstances

Occasionally, you may want to use footnotes or endnotes in place of·parenthetical references. If you need to cite several sources at once, listing them in a long parenthetical reference could be intrusive. In that case, signal the citation with a numeral raised above the appropriate line of text and write a note with the same numeral to cite the sources:

TEXT   At least five subsequent studies have confirmed these results.[1]

NOTE   [1] Abbott and Winger 266-68; Casner 27; Hoyenga 78-79; Marino 36; Tripp, Tripp, and Walk 179-83.

You may also use a footnote or endnote to comment on a source or provide information that does not fit easily in the text:

TEXT   So far, no one has succeeded in confirming these results.[2]

NOTE   [2] Manter reports spending nearly a year trying to replicate the experiment, but he was never able to produce the high temperatures reported by the original experimenters (616).

In a note the raised numeral is indented five spaces and followed by a space. If the note appears as a footnote, place it at the bottom of the page on which the citation appears, set it off from the text with quadruple spacing, and single-space the note itself. If the note appears as an endnote, place it in numerical order with the other endnotes on a page between the text and the list of works cited; double-space all the endnotes. (See pp. 636–37, 646 for examples of endnotes and the format to use in typing a page of endnotes.)

2   Using footnotes or endnotes to document sources

Until 1984, the *MLA Handbook* recommended using footnotes and endnotes to cite sources, and the current edition continues to provide an explanation and illustrations of this reference system for those who want or are required to use it.

When you document sources with notes (either footnotes or endnotes), you place a raised numeral (^{1}) in the text at the end of the material you are acknowledging, and you number the citations consecutively throughout the paper. The notes themselves then fall in the same order. Footnotes are placed at the bottoms of appropriate pages; endnotes are collected on separate pages between the end of the paper and the list of works cited.

The following is a passage from Mark Shannon's paper showing the use of note numbers in the text.

> In a 1983 test of people's reactions to videotapes of male and female leaders, the psychologists Virginia Brown and Florence Geis found that "[a]lthough both leaders used the same script, the woman was faulted more than the man for being too dominating, cold, and insensitive."[6] Such results reveal that while sex-role stereotyping may not be as obvious as it was in a 1971 study,[7] it remains pervasive in our society.

For footnotes, begin the first entry four lines below the last line of text (two double spaces), single-space each footnote, and double-space between notes. For endnotes, double-space within and between notes, as in the following sample:

> [6] Virginian Brown and Florence Geis, "Turning Lead into Gold: Evaluations of Women and Men Leaders and the Alchemy of Social Consensus," <u>Journal of Personality and Social Psychology</u> 46 (1984): 822.
>
> [7] I. K. Broverman et al., "Sex-Role Stereotypes: A Current Appraisal," <u>Journal of Social Issues</u> 28.2. (1971): 59-78.

See pages 636–37, 646 for the heading, spacing, and other elements of a page of endnotes.

The format for a note differs from that for an entry in the list of works cited.

fn 36i

LIST OF WORKS CITED

Wimsatt, William K., and Cleanth Brooks. <u>Literary</u>

  <u>Criticism: A Short History</u>. Chicago: U of Chi-

  cago P, 1978.

NOTE

  ² William K. Wimsatt and Cleanth Brooks, <u>Lit-</u>

<u>erary Criticism: A Short History</u> (Chicago: U of Chi-

cago P, 1978) 312.

In the works cited entry you start the first line at the left margin and indent the second and subsequent lines five spaces; but in the note you indent the first line and not the others. The note is intended to be read as a sentence, so a period appears only at the end while the body of the note is punctuated with commas and colons. In the note, unlike the works cited entry, you enclose the publication information (place of publication, publisher, date of publication) in parentheses. Whereas you start the works cited entry with the first author's last name, to make it easier to find the name in an alphabetical listing, in the note you give the author's name in normal order. And in the note you include the specific page number(s) in the source from which the summary, paraphrase, or quotation is taken (but without "p." or "pp.").

The following note models use the same sources as those in the bibliographic models on pages 558–70, and the explanations on those pages point out the special information that must be included for each kind of source. Like bibliographic models, note models may be combined if necessary; for example, the model for a book with an editor may be combined with that for a multivolume book if your source is a multivolume edited work. The following note models are for first reference to a source. When you acknowledge the same source more than once in the same paper, you should use the shortened form of reference given on page 615.

Books

A BOOK WITH ONE AUTHOR

  ¹ Carol Gilligan, <u>In a Different Voice: Psycho-</u>

<u>logical Theory and Women's Development</u> (Cambridge:

Harvard UP, 1982) 27.

fn
36i

A BOOK WITH TWO OR THREE AUTHORS

2   William K. Wimsatt and Cleanth Brooks,
Literary Criticism: A Short History (Chicago: U of
Chicago P, 1978) 312.

A BOOK WITH MORE THAN THREE AUTHORS

3   Robert S. Lopez et al., Civilizations:
Western and World (Boston: Little, 1975) 281-82.

A BOOK WITH AN EDITOR

4   Hendrick Ruitenbeek, ed., Freud as We
Knew Him (Detroit: Wayne State UP, 1973) 64.

A BOOK WITH AN AUTHOR AND AN EDITOR

5   Robertson Davies, Hunting Stuart and Other
Plays, ed. Brian Parker (Toronto: New Press, 1972)
17.

A TRANSLATION

6   Dante Alighieri, The Inferno, trans. John
Ciardi (New York: NAL, 1971) 73-74.

A BOOK WITH CORPORATE AUTHORSHIP

7   Editors of The Progressive, The Crisis of
Survival (Glenview: Scott, 1970) 61.

AN ANONYMOUS BOOK

8   Atlas of Canada (Montreal: Reader's Digest
Ass'n., 1981) 27.

A LATER EDITION

9   Dwight L. Bollinger, Aspects of Language, 2nd
ed. (New York: Harcourt, 1975) 20.

fn
36i

A REPUBLISHED BOOK

10   Henry James, The Golden Bowl (1904; London: Penguin, 1966) 163.

A WORK IN MORE THAN ONE VOLUME

11   Philip Schaff, History of the Christian Church, 8 vols., 3rd ed., rev. (1910; Grand Rapids, MI: Eerdmans, 1963) 2: 711.

A WORK IN A SERIES

12   Ethel Wilson, The Innocent Traveller, No. 170, New Canadian Library Series (Toronto: McClelland & Stewart, 1982) 118.

A SELECTION FROM AN ANTHOLOGY

13   George Herbert, "The Pilgrimage," The Norton Anthology of English Literature, ed. M. H. Abrams et al., 2 vols., 5th ed. (New York: Norton, 1986) 1: 1348.

AN ARTICLE OR ESSAY FROM A REPRINTED COLLECTION

14   George Gibian, "Traditional Symbolism in Crime and Punishment," PMLA 70 (1955): 979-96, rpt. in Crime and Punishment, by Feodor Dostoevsky, ed. George Gibian, Norton Critical Editions (New York: Norton, 1964) 577.

AN INTRODUCTION, PREFACE, FOREWORD, OR AFTERWORD

15   Norman Donaldson, introduction, The Claverings, by Anthony Trollope (New York: Dover, 1977) viii.

16   Stephen Jay Gould, prologue, The Flamingo's Smile: Reflections in Natural History, by Gould (New York: Norton, 1985) 16.

AN ENCYCLOPEDIA OR ALMANAC

17   J.T. Morley, "Social Credit," The Canadian Encyclopedia, 1988 ed.

18   Herman F. Mark, "Polymers," Encyclopaedia Britannica: Macropaedia, 1974.

Periodicals: journals, magazines, and newspapers

A SIGNED ARTICLE IN A JOURNAL WITH CONTINUOUS PAGINATION THROUGHOUT THE ANNUAL VOLUME

19   Janet Lever, "Sex Differences in the Games Children Play," Social Problems 23 (1976): 482.

A SIGNED ARTICLE IN A JOURNAL THAT PAGES ISSUES SEPARATELY OR THAT NUMBERS ONLY ISSUES, NOT VOLUMES

20   Sarah Boyd, "Nuclear Terror," Adaptation to Change 7.4 (1981): 20-21.

A SIGNED ARTICLE IN A MONTHLY OR BIMONTHLY PERIODICAL

21   Richard Wright, "The Reluctant Athlete," Saturday Night Sept. 1988: 80.

A SIGNED ARTICLE IN A WEEKLY OR BIWEEKLY PERIODICAL

22   Ross Laver, "The Tax Squeeze," Maclean's 8 May 1989: 12.

A SIGNED ARTICLE IN A DAILY NEWSPAPER

23   André Picard, "Quebec NDP Opts for Autonomy," Globe and Mail 1 May 1981: A1.

fn
36i

AN UNSIGNED ARTICLE

24 "The Right to Die," <u>Time</u> 11 Oct. 1976: 101.

25 "Hundreds of Chinese Reported Defecting,"
<u>Vancouver Sun</u> 17 June 1989: A1.

AN EDITORIAL, A LETTER TO THE EDITOR, OR A REVIEW

26 Bruce Doern, "Breaking the U.S. Monopoly in
the Subsidy-defining Game," editorial, <u>Financial
Times of Canada</u> June 5-11, 1989: 44.

27 Michael Dowding, letter, <u>Economist</u> 5-11 Jan.
1985: 4.

28 Stefan Kanfer, "Time Arrested," rev. of
<u>Cat's Eye</u>, by Margaret Atwood, <u>Time</u> 6 Feb. 1989: 70.

AN ABSTRACT OF A DISSERTATION

29 Steven K. Steciw, "Alterations to the Pessac
Project of Le Corbusier," <u>DAI</u> 46 (1986): 565C
(Cambridge U, England).

Other sources

A PAMPHLET OR GOVERNMENT DOCUMENT

30 <u>The Canada-U.S. Trade Agreement in Brief</u>,
2nd ed. (Ottawa: Minister of Supply and Services Canada, 1988) 22.

31 British Columbia, Ministry of Education,
<u>Policy Directions: A Response to the Sullivan Royal
Commission on Education by the Government of
British Columbia</u> (Vancouver: BC Ministry of
Education, 1989) 14.

**fn
36i**

32 Canada, Continuing Federal-Provincial-
Territorial Committee of Officials Responsible for
Human Rights, Secretary of State, Convention on the
Elimination of All Forms of Discrimination Against
Women: Reference Document (Ottawa: Supply and Ser-
vices Canada, 1986) 9.

AN UNPUBLISHED DISSERTATION OR THESIS

33 Martin S. Spigelman, "The Acadian Renaissance and the Development of Acadien-Canadien Relations, 1864-1912: des frères trop longtemps séparés,"
Ph.D. diss., Dalhousie U., 1976, 184.

A MUSICAL COMPOSITION OR WORK OF ART

34 Wolfgang Amadeus Mozart, Piano Concerto no.
21 in D Minor, K. 466.

35 Daphne Odjig, The Indian in Transition,
National Museum of Man, Ottawa.

A FILM OR TELEVISION PROGRAM

36 Love Letters: A Dance Fantasy, with members
of the National Ballet of Canada, choreographed by
Ann Ditchburn, music by Kate Bush, Laurie Anderson,
Buffy Sainte-Marie, André Gagnon, and Jennifer
Warnes, cameo appearance by Leonard Cohen, A & E, 21
May 1989.

37 Paul Donovan, dir., The Squamish Five, prod.
by Bernard Zukerman, with Robyn Stevan, Michael
McManus, Nicky Guadagni, and David McLeod, written by
Ken Gass and Terence McKenna, CBC Enterprises, 1988.

fn
36i

A PERFORMANCE

[38] <u>Man and Superman</u>, by George Bernard Shaw, dir. Christopher Newton, Shaw Festival Theatre, Niagara-on-the-Lake, ON, 24 May 1989.

[39] Peter McCoppin, cond., Vancouver Symphony Orchestra Concert, The Orpheum Theatre, Vancouver, 23 Oct. 1989.

A RECORDING

[40] Anne Murray et al., <u>Canadian Content</u>, Capitol Records (Canada) Ltd., SL-6854, n.d.

[41] Johannes Brahms, Concerto no. 2 in B-flat, op. 83, perf. Artur Rubinstein, cond. Eugene Ormandy, Philadelphia Orch., RCA, RK-1243, 1972.

A LETTER

[42] Hugh MacLennan, letter to John Gray, 7 Dec. 1950, in Elspeth Cameron, <u>Hugh MacLennan: A Writer's Life</u> (Toronto: U. of Toronto P., 1981) 253.

[43] Jonathan E. James, letter to his sister, 16 Apr. 1970, Jonathan E. James Papers, South Dakota State Archive, Pierre.

[44] Ann E. Packer, letter to the author, 15 June 1988.

A LECTURE OR ADDRESS

[45] Dennis J. Carlone, "Urban Design in the 1990s," Sixth Symposium on Urban Issues, City of Cambridge, Cambridge, 16 Oct. 1988.

AN INTERVIEW

[46] Councilman John Smithson, personal interview, 6 Sept. 1985.

fn
36i

⁴⁷ David Rushton, interview re: Fraser Valley
Symphony, Contact, Richard Dettman, interviewer,
CFVR, Abbotsford, BC, 8 June 1989.

AN INFORMATION OR COMPUTER SERVICE

⁴⁸ Maria K. Jolson, Music Education for
Preschoolers (ERIC, 1981) 16 (ED 264 488).

⁴⁹ Andrew Palfry, "Choice of Mates in Identical
Twins," Modern Psychology Jan. 1979: 19 (Dialog file
261, item 5206341).

COMPUTER SOFTWARE

⁵⁰ Project Scheduler 5000, computer software,
Scitor, 1988, MS-DOS, 256 KB, disk.

Subsequent references to the same source

To minimize clutter in notes and to give readers a quick sense of how often you acknowledge a source, you should use a shortened form for subsequent references to a source you have already cited fully. When you refer to only one source by the author cited (or only one source bearing the title cited if there is no author), the *MLA Handbook* recommends that subsequent references carry only the author's name (or a short form of the title) and the page reference appropriate for the later citation. The following are two examples, preceded by the full citations.

⁵ Robertson Davies, Hunting Stuart and Other
Plays, ed. Brian Parker (Toronto: New Press, 1972)
17.

⁵¹ Davies 41.

²⁴ "The Right to Die," Time 11 Oct. 1976: 101.

⁵² "Right" 101.

fn
36i

However, if two of your sources are by the same author, give a shortened form of the appropriate title so there can be no confusion about which work you are citing (see the following example).

¹ Carol Gilligan, In a Different Voice:

Psychological Theory and Women's Development (Cam-

bridge: Harvard UP, 1982) 27.

⁵³ Carol Gilligan, "Moral Development in the

College Years," The Modern American College, ed. A.

Chickering (San Francisco: Jossey-Bass, 1981) 286.

⁵⁴ Gilligan, "Moral" 288.

NOTE: The *MLA Handbook* discourages use of the Latin abbreviation "ibid." (in the same place") as a means of indicating that a citation refers to the source in the preceding note.

> **EXERCISE 11**
>
> Add the final source citations to the research paper you wrote and revised in Exercise 9 (p. 598), using the list of works cited that you prepared in Exercise 10 (p. 599). Use the style of parenthetical reference recommended by the *MLA Handbook* (pp. 600–606) unless your instructor specifies a different style.

36j Preparing and proofreading the final manuscript

Most instructors expect research papers to be neatly typed with clear titling, double spacing, standard margins, and minimal handwritten corrections. The *MLA Handbook* recommends a format for manuscripts that is spelled out in Appendix A of this book and illustrated in the research papers of Mark Shannon and Deborah Wiebe, starting on page 618. The format is not difficult to follow, and it will make your paper professional looking and easy to read.

Before you submit your paper, proofread it carefully for typographical errors, misspellings, and other slight errors. (See 2d for proofreading tips.) Unless the errors are very numerous (more than several on a page), you can correct them by whiting out or crossing out (neatly) and inserting the correction (neatly) in ink. (See Appendix A, p. 724, for an example.) Don't let the pressure of a deadline prevent you from proofreading, for even minor errors can impair clarity or annoy readers and thus negate some of the hard work you have put into your project.

36j

CHAPTER 37

Two Sample Research Papers

The following pages show the research papers of Mark Shannon and Deborah Wiebe, whose work we followed in the last two chapters. (Shannon's paper begins on page 618, Wiebe's on p. 649.) Both students used the bibliographic formats and the style of parenthetical reference recommended by the *MLA Handbook*, and both typed their papers following the advice on manuscript format in Appendix A of this handbook. At the end of Shannon's paper are comments, keyed by number, that explain the format of his manuscript and some of the decisions he made in moving from research to writing. Comments in the margins of Wiebe's paper note the distinctive features of her analysis.

Breaking the Glass Ceiling   1

By

Mark Shannon

English 101, Section B

Prof. C. Mahoney

February 28, 1989

37

Shannon i

Outline

<u>Thesis sentence</u>: If women are ever to break through the glass ceiling in significant numbers, business attitudes will have to change, particularly the definition of successful management styles.

I. Women face resistance from both men and women in top management.

    A. Women are in a double bind: they are expected to act like men, but are criticized when they do.

    B. Women also face resistance from "queen bees," other women who are already executives.

        1. Queen bees feel that younger women should not have it any easier than they did.

        2. Queen bees interfere with working conditions, morale, and promotions.

II. Business favours a masculine management style over a feminine style.

    A. Kates reports on a 1988 Toronto conference that attempted to come to critical terms with this general trend.

Shannon ii

B. Women are usually not given the option
to exercise their own style.

C. When women imitate men, they are subject to sex-role stereotyping and
alienation.

1. Brown and Geis found stereotyping
in their study.

2. Woman executives pass around a
humorous list of characteristics of
businessmen versus businesswomen.

3. Loden says that women are less
effective when they imitate men.

III. A feminine management style must be
accepted in business if women are to make
it into top management.

A. An interview with a female manager
illustrates a feminine style of
co-operation and participation.

B. Loden and others emphasize that a feminine management style takes account
of people's emotions, an important
part of their lives.

C. A feminine style of management will
help not only women but business
itself.

Shannon 1

Breaking the Glass Ceiling

"You've come a long way, baby." Most
people will recognize this slogan from popular
cigarette advertisements, but its meaning goes
beyond women's freedom to smoke in public.
Nowhere are women's gains more clear than in
the business world. In the United States, the
Civil Rights Act of 1964 made it illegal to
discriminate against women in employment.
Twenty years later, women had established
themselves firmly in corporations on a number
of management levels. Their progress can be
measured by what is expected of companies with
regard to their treatment of women employees.
According to <u>Business Week</u>'s Irene Pave:

> Back in 1966 the mark of a good
> company [for women to work in] was
> women in at least entry-level
> management and other non-clerical
> jobs. In 1976 it was women in middle
> management. Today a good company
> has women above that level or in
> jobs that have remained male turf in
> most companies. (75)

Canada lagged more than twenty years

Shannon 2

behind its U.S. federal counterparts in developing legislation to enhance business opportunities for women. The Employment Equity Act of 1986 required "all federally regulated companies (banks and transport and communication companies) to set up employment equity programs and to file annual reports on the demographic composition of their workforce" (Kates 60). The first reports were due June 1, 1988. A second government initiative was the Federal Contractors Program, established about the same time, which required every company with 100 or more employees that wanted to bid on any federal contract over $200 000 "to prove its commitment to gender and minority equity in terms of hiring, training, salary and promotions. No employee equity plan, no federal contract" (Kates 60).

Largely as a result of developments elsewhere, however, particularly in the United States, notable growth in the opportunities for Canadian women to move into management positions had already begun some years earlier. A 1988 paper by analyst Gladys Symons entitled "Women in Power: The Real Threat to

Corporate Culture" reported that the percentage of women in management rose from 15 percent in 1971 to 32.3 percent by 1985. The rate
of rise in numbers of senior managers was
somewhat slower, moving from 3.7 percent in
1971 to just 6.4 percent in 1981 (reported in
Collins 151). Another sociological analysis,
this one by Dorothy Mikolachki, also appearing
in 1988, gave more recent figures that confirmed the trend described in Symons' article:
"In Canada," Mikolachki noted, "the proportion of women who are in managerial and administrative jobs rose to 8.3 percent from 7.5
percent between 1984 and 1985," adding
"Hardly an upheaval but evidence that women
continue to join the managerial ranks--in
spite of an often unfavorable climate for
them" (42).

　　　Clearly, women have come far in business.
But have they come far enough? The fact is,
women are still rare in the highest executive
positions. In the United States, they represented only about 3 percent of all corporate
directors in 1984 (Lewin). Pave notes that
"no one cites 'equal numbers of men and women

Shannon 4

in top management positions' as the mark of a
good company for women. No company would
qualify" (76). The situation in Canada is
just as grim. In an article appearing at the
end of 1988, James Fleming made the following
observation and prediction:

> . . . the business elite contains
> fewer women than any other ruling
> elite with the exception, perhaps,
> of the Catholic Church. It will be
> at least 10 or 15 years before a
> woman runs one of our 50 largest
> corporations--and that's an optimis-
> tic estimate. (54)

Despite women's persistence in both countries,
a "glass ceiling," or invisible barrier,
seemingly continues to separate women in
middle and upper management from positions in
top management.[1] If women are ever to break
through the glass ceiling in significant
numbers, business attitudes will have to
change, particularly the definition of successful management styles.

 Most experts agree that the main reason
women have not broken through the glass ceil-

ing is, quite simply, that they are women.
Often these women find themselves in a double
bind. On the one hand, they face resistance   17
from male executives who want their successors
to be just like themselves and who therefore
will not consider women for top-management
positions (Pave 78). On the other hand,
resistance sometimes comes from men who do not
want to see women acting the role of executive. According to Felice Schwartz, the founder and president of Catalyst, a firm that
conducts research on corporate women, "It
goes against the grain of most senior executives to encourage and welcome the women, so
unlike their wives, who put career before marriage and rearing children" (185). Thus some   18
women are held back if they behave too much
like women, while others are held back because
they behave too much like men.

As if these two problems were not enough,
women also encounter resistance from the few
women who have made it to the top. These successful women should be acting as mentors for
those coming up behind them, serving as role   19
models and providing guidance. Instead, many

Shannon 6

do just the opposite. David Mathison, an associate professor of business administration at
Loyola Marymount University, identifies the
"queen bee syndrome": a successful woman
feels threatened by the success of other women
and resists them as "intrusions" into her
territory (qtd. in Bozzi).   20

In a 1986 survey of executive women,
Edith Gilson, with Susan Kane, found that the   21
"queen bee" was thriving in American business: 68 percent of those responding to a
questionnaire felt that "their female colleagues were 'unnecessarily competitive' with
one another." Some of the respondents exhibited signs of the "queen bee syndrome." One
woman declared, "I managed to climb to my
position without any special help. . . .   It   22
was tough, but if I did it, why can't other
women?" (184-86).   23

Gilson and Kane emphatically warn against
the dangers of this attitude among women.

> Women's undue competitiveness is a
> major stumbling block to their suc-
> cess. It keeps them awash in anger
> and fear when their energies could

Shannon 7

be used more constructively; sets a
negative example for lower-level
women; creates difficult working
conditions for the women who are its
targets; diminishes the effectiveness of teamwork; and, in some
cases, <u>actively inhibits career</u>
<u>progress</u>. (186-87; emphasis added)

24

Like the male executive's reluctance to pro-

25

mote women, the "queen bee syndrome" must
change before women can make serious inroads
into top management.

Even more significant than the attitudes

26

described above, however, is the preference
for a masculine rather than feminine management style. The feminine management styles
seem to have succeeded quite well at the
middle-management level. But the continued
prevalence of the masculine style of management at top levels, along with the apparent
resistance of top managers to changing that
style, is the single most significant obstacle
to women seeking executive positions.

Characterizing the managerial style of

27

most American industrial corporations, Ann

37

Hughey and Eric Gelman of <u>Newsweek</u> refer to a
"paramilitary form of organization" enforced
by "rigid, drill-sergeant managers" (46).
Marilyn Loden, the author of <u>Feminine Leadership, or, How to Succeed in Business Without
Being One of the Boys</u>, borrows a term from the
feminist writer Betty Friedan in noting the
"masculinism" of the traditional managerial
style (23). Its basic premise, Loden says, is
competition: the successful manager must conquer his corporate enemies, just as he was
trained for victory on the football field or
the battlefield; and strategic thinking must
take precedence over emotion (24-26). It is no
wonder that women--who have been reared to be
emotional, co-operative, and generous--
encounter difficulties when attempting to
adapt to this style.

Despite the difficulties, women are
encouraged to imitate men if they want to succeed. Loden surveyed "how to" books written
during the 1970s and discovered that virtually
all of them gave women exactly that advice
(28). Yet women who acquire more masculine
traits are then subject to stereotyping. In a

28

37

Shannon 9

1983 test of people's reactions to videotapes
of male and female leaders, the psychologists
Virginia Brown and Florence Geis found that
"[a]lthough both leaders used the same
script, the woman was faulted more than the
man for being too dominating, cold, and insen-
sitive" (822). Such results reveal that while
sex-role stereotyping may not be as obvious as
it was in a 1971 study (Broverman et al.), it
remains pervasive.

Rona Maynard calls similar attention to
this dilemma of the contradictory expectations
often faced by senior women executives. In a
study of what had happened after ten years to
33 female 1978 MBA graduates from the University of Western Ontario, she discovered that a
number of these women had chosen either to
drop out of the executive rat race or to
accept a more modest position in the organization concerned. She summarizes this conflicting pressure on senior women managers as follows: "On the one hand, they must demonstrate
such 'masculine' traits as toughness and independence. But if they go too far, their lack
of 'feminine' submissiveness will unnerve

29

30

37

co-workers" (29). Maynard, noting that one of
her subjects actually gave up her management
position because it required her to deny her
feminine identity, concludes, "In her struggle to keep up with men, she felt she was
denying her feminine side--the side that tuned
in to others' feelings and resisted the ruth-
lessness that can be required at the top. She
already hated to fire people" (29). For similar reasons only one of the ten top Canadian
female executives interviewed by Anne Collins
aspired to the CEO position in her company
(37).

Another dimension of sex stereotyping is
examined in a recent book by Nina Colwill,
professor of business administration at the
University of Manitoba, entitled The New Part-
nership: Women and Men in Organizations.
Colwill observes that women in business tend
to be typecast into one of four traditional
roles: mother (the nurturer), seductress (the
sex object), pet (the precocious child), or
iron maiden (the tough asexual) (described in
Kates 63). Colwill remarks that these
"guises" may make the woman executive accept-

Shannon 11

able to men, but it detracts from her competency and effectiveness.

The dilemma of women is also illustrated
in a list comparing businessmen and businesswomen that made the round of women executives
several years ago.

> *A businessman is aggressive; a
> businesswoman is pushy.
>
> *A businessman is good on details;
> she's picky.
>
> *He loses his temper at times
> because he's so involved in
> his work; she's temperamental.
>
> *He knows how to follow through;
> she doesn't know when to
> quit. (qtd. in Loden 38)

The humour here underlines a serious
problem. Loden observes that if a woman tries
to adapt to male business culture without
retaining any of her feminine traits, she will
end up feeling more rather than less alienated
(22). But this is precisely what many women
have been expected to do--and in fact have
done--in order to succeed. Loden explains that
"fraternity pledging"--the term she uses for

31

32

33

37

Shannon 12

the first stage of the adaptation process--
"causes women to gradually deny what they
truly think and feel" (32). Thus rigid
insistence on a masculine managerial style is
not only detrimental in preventing many women
from making it to the top but also harmful in
causing those women who do make it to manage
less effectively than they might.

It seems clear that if business is going
to benefit from women's talents, it must
accommodate a feminine managerial style. As
Hughey and Gelman observe, "the very qualities that men have traditionally denigrated as
feminine--sympathy, sensitivity, a lack of the
killer instinct--may often be advantages when
it comes to getting the best out of people"
(46).

A case in point is a story from a woman I
interviewed, Nora Crisi, who is a manager
responsible for several departments in a
retail organization. A subordinate of hers,
Susan, refused to use the guidelines in the
company manual to train her own subordinates.
In debating how to handle the situation, Crisi
says:

Shannon 13

My only real role model was my own
boss, a man who kept everyone in
line like a drill instructor. He
would have called Susan in and given
her a stern lecture, complete with
threats. I knew I couldn't pull that
off; it wasn't my nature.

Instead, Crisi explained to Susan the necessity for common training practices and encouraged the young supervisor to offer suggestions
for revising the manual if she found problems
with it. Then Crisi emphasized that she would
not tolerate any refusal to adhere to company
policy. The result was surprising: "You know
what? She thanked me! I'd been expecting a
fight, but I think Susan saw that I respected
her, and she appreciated not being treated
like a schoolgirl." Crisi's reliance on her   36
sensitivity, coupled with some of the firmness
she had learned from her own boss, served her
well in a conflict that is common between
managers and subordinates.

Crisi's encouragement of feedback on the
company's policy illustrates another advantage
of a feminine management style: such "parti-

37

Shannon 14

cipative management," as it is commonly
called, permits both emotional and rational
assessments of and responses to business
situations.[2] Acknowledgment of the importance
of emotion has long been absent from traditional management styles. But, in the words of
Antonia Shusta, an executive with Citibank,
"Business is all people and people in large
degree are very emotional. . . . If you don't
understand emotion, you're missing out on a
lot" (qtd. in Hughey and Gelman 47).

According to Marilyn Loden, "Feminine
leaders see the world through two different
lenses concurrently and, as a result, respond
to situations on both the thinking and the
feeling levels" (61). Loden does not advocate
substituting the feminine management style for
the masculine style (5). Rather, she argues
that business must adopt both styles. Only
then, she claims, will women achieve true
equality in the top levels of management
(277).

North American business has been operating on a masculine model since the industrial
revolution. But times have changed, and so has

the business population. Now women as well as men must be encouraged to break through into top management. In order for that to happen, the "old-boy network" must be penetrated, the "queen bee syndrome" must be cured, and old prejudices--women's as well as men's--must be abandoned. Even more important, for women and for business itself, is the adaptation to a more flexible, feminine style of management. Only when these changes are made will that glass ceiling finally be broken.

37

Shannon 16

Notes

41

[1] "Glass ceiling" is commonly used in articles and books about women in management. Although I was unable to find any information on the origins of the term, it appears to have been coined just to describe the situation of women (not men). One of the best-known recent examples of a work employing this term, frequently referred to by both Canadian and American analysts, is Breaking the Glass Ceiling: Can Women Reach the Top of America's Largest Corporations? (1987), by research staff at the Center for Creative Leadership in Greensboro, NC. The book was the product of an in-depth study of factors contributing to the success or failure of 76 women executives selected from the 100 leading companies in the United States. Canadian commentator Anne Collins summarized the primary conclusion of this well-researched study by stating that women executives faced three conditions not experienced by their male counterparts: (1) they had to be better than good, better than a man, at extremely complicated jobs; (2) they had to be role models, to prove their commit-

42

ment to work and to succeed for all women; and
(3) they still carried the largest responsibility for children and for the success of
their marriages, the result being that many of
them had been divorced at least once.

[2] For further information on women and
participative management, see "Special
Talents."

43

37

Shannon 18

Works Cited | 44

Bozzi, Vincent. "Assertiveness Breeds Con- | 45
    tempt." <u>Psychology Today</u> Sept. 1987: 15.

Broverman, I. K., et al. "Sex-Role Stereo- | 46
    types: A Current Appraisal." <u>Journal</u>
    <u>of Social Issues</u> 28.2 (1972): 59-78.

Brown, Virginia, and Florence Geis. "Turning | 47
    Lead into Gold: Evaluations of Women and
    Men Leaders and the Alchemy of Social
    Consensus." <u>Journal of Personality and</u>
    <u>Social Psychology</u> 46 (1984): 811-24.

Collins, Anne. "'Why We're Not Number One': | 48
    A Position Paper from Canada's Top Corpo-
    rate Women." <u>Can. Business</u> Nov. 1988:
    32-39, 141+.

Crisi, Nora. Personal interview. 17 February | 49
    1989.

Fleming, James. "Powerful Women." <u>Report</u>
    <u>on Business Mag.</u> Dec. 1988: 54.

Gilson, Edith, with Susan Kane. <u>Unnecessary</u> | 50
    <u>Choices: The Hidden Life of the Execu-</u>
    <u>tive Woman</u>. New York: Morrow, 1987.

Hughey, Ann, and Eric Gelman. "Managing the | 51
    Woman's Way." <u>Newsweek</u> 17 Mar. 1986:
    46-47.

37

Shannon 19

Kates, Joanne. "Quiet Revolution." <u>Report
on Business Mag.</u> June 1988: 58-64.

Lewin, Tamar. "Women in Board Rooms Are
Still the Exceptions." <u>New York Times</u>
5 July 1984: C1.

Loden, Marilyn. <u>Feminine Leadership, or, How
to Succeed in Business Without Being One
of the Boys</u>. New York: Times, 1985.

Maynard, Rona. "Thanks But No Thanks: Ten
Years Ago. . . . " <u>Report on Business Mag.</u>
Feb. 1988: 26-32, 34.

Mikolachki, Dorothy. "Women Managers Are Not
Dropping Out, but Moving Up." Editorial. <u>Financial Times of Canada</u> 6 June
1988: 42.

Pave, Irene. "A Woman's Place Is at GE, Federal Express, P&G. . . . " <u>Business Week</u>
23 June 1986: 75+.

Schwartz, Felice N. "Don't Write Women Off
as Leaders." <u>Fortune</u> 8 June 1987:
185+.

"The Special Talents Women Bring to Participative Management." <u>International Man-
agement</u> Aug. 1986: 60.

1. **Title page format**. Provide a separate title page if your instructor requests it or if you are required to submit an outline with your paper. On his title page Shannon includes the title of his paper about a third of the way down the page, his own name (preceded by "By") about 2.5 cm (1″) below the title, and, starting about the same distance below his name, some identifying information requested by his instructor (course number, section label, and instructor's name) and the date. He centres all lines in the width of the page and separates them from each other with at least one line of space. If your instructor does not require a title page for your paper, place your name, the identifying information, and the date on the first page of the paper. See Deborah Wiebe's paper (p. 649) for this alternative format.

2. **Outline format**. If your instructor asks you to include your final outline, place it between the title page and the text, as Shannon does on the following pages. Number the pages with small Roman numerals (i, ii), and place your name just before the page numbers in case the pages of your paper become separated. Place the heading "Outline" 2.5 cm from the top of the first page, and double-space under the heading.

3. **Outline content**. Shannon includes his final thesis sentence as part of his outline so that his instructor can see how the parts relate to the whole.

4. Shannon casts his final outline in full sentences. Some instructors request topic outlines, in which ideas appear in phrases instead of in sentences and do not end with periods.

5. Notice that each main division (numbered with Roman numerals) relates to the thesis sentence and that all the subdivisions relate to their main division.

6. **Title**. Shannon has chosen an intriguing title, just ambiguous enough to make his audience want to read further. A more descriptive title, such as "Why Women Are Still Rare in Top Corporate Management," would also have been appropriate but less interesting. **Paper format**. The margins of the paper are 2.5 cm (1″) all around. The title appears on the first page of the paper even if a title page is used. The title is typed 2.5 cm from the top of the page, and it is neither placed in quotation marks nor underlined. The first line of text is typed two lines (double space) below the title. (See Deborah Wiebe's paper, p. 649, for the format of the first page when a title page is not required.)

7. **Introduction**. Shannon begins with a familiar sentence that calls to mind the strides women have made in the past century. He delays presenting his thesis (end of fourth full paragraph) in

order to establish some background: women have indeed made inroads into some levels of management, both in the United States (this paragraph) and Canada (next two paragraphs), yet not into the highest levels (fourth paragraph). The question opening the fourth paragraph sets up the thesis at the end of that paragraph. Note that this introductory material, while quite extensive, is not summarized in the outline.

8. **Common knowledge**. Shannon did not know about the American Civil Rights Act before he began his research, but he found it referred to without documentation in a number of sources. When he realized that it was considered common knowledge, he chose, correctly, not to document it. (See 36d for further discussion of common knowledge.)

9. **Introducing quotations**. Here and elsewhere, Shannon effectively introduces his quotations: he establishes the credentials of each source in an identifying phrase; and he summarizes each source's point of view. (For an additional example, see p. 625. See 36f-2 for a discussion of introducing quotations.)

10. **Format of long quotations**. The Pave quotation exceeds four typed lines, so Shannon sets it off from the text. Such a displayed quotation is set off by double-spacing above and below, is itself double-spaced, and is indented ten spaces from the left margin.

11. **Adding to quotations**. Shannon inserts a clarifying phrase so that readers will understand what Pave means by a "good company." The brackets tell the reader that the phrase is added (see 25d).

12. **Reference when the author is named in the text**. Shannon has already mentioned Pave's name in the text, so he does not repeat it in the reference. **Reference with displayed quotation**. The parenthetical reference after the quotation falls *outside* the sentence period and is separated from the period by two spaces.

13. **Paraphrasing**. Shannon paraphrases Lewin because it is the statistic rather than the author's presentation of it that is important. For other instances of paraphrasing, see "Citing a paraphrase" (next page) and pages 628 and 631. **Reference when the author is not named in the text**. Because Shannon has not used Lewin's name in the text, he provides it in the reference. **Reference to a one-page article**. Lewin's article appears on only one page of the newspaper it is in, and Shannon gives that page number in the list of works cited (see p. 639). Thus he does not need to repeat the page number in the reference.

37

14. **Quotation within a quotation**. Since he must enclose Pave's words in double quotation marks, Shannon encloses her quotation in single quotation marks (see 24b).

15. **Using an endnote for supplementary information**. Here Shannon helps his readers by briefly defining a key term, "glass ceiling." He provides additional information about the term in a note at the end of the paper. (See p. 636.)

16. **Relation to outline**. This paragraph begins part I of Shannon's outline (see p. 619). Part II begins on page 627 and part III on page 632.

17. **Paraphrase**. Shannon paraphrases part of a quotation from Pave. His note card is shown below.

> <u>Sexual stereotypes</u>
>
> Pave, p. 78
>
> "Male chauvinism is most crippling to women at the great divide between upper and top management. Senior managers who always pick men for top spots want clones... — so women always get locked out."

Citing a paraphrase. Shannon includes Pave's name in the reference (page 625) because it is not used in the text. In contrast, the reference later in the paragraph to Schwartz does *not* include the name because the text *does*.

18. **Interpreting sources**. In this summary sentence Shannon pulls together information from the two sources cited earlier in the paragraph and shows how the information relates to his point about the double bind women are in. Thus he does not force his readers to guess why he paraphrases and quotes sources, and he clears the way for the next point.

19. **Defining terms**. Shannon slips in a definition of "mentors" after the comma in this sentence. Since his audience would consist of his classmates as well as his instructor, he thought it likely that at least a few readers would not know the term. Yet he opted to abbreviate and downplay the definition in order not to offend any readers who already understood the term. The following is Shannon's edited draft of this passage.

37

These successful women should be acting as mentors/ *for these coming up behind them, serving as* ~~A mentor is usually an older and professionally more~~

~~advanced person who acts as a~~ role model*s* and pro-

ing ~~vides~~ guidance. *Instead, many do just the* ~~to a younger colleague who is usually~~

opposite. ~~younger and subordinate. Yet often these successful~~

~~women are the opposite of mentors.~~

20. **Reference to an indirect source**. With the use of "qtd. in," Shannon indicates correctly that he obtained the information on Mathison from the article by Bozzi. **Indirect sources**. The Mathison study is important for Shannon's paper, and the information in Bozzi's article clearly indicated that it had been published in a readily available journal. Instead of relying on a brief summary in a magazine, Shannon should have gone directly to Mathison's article. Use indirect sources (and "qtd. in") only when the original material is not available for you to consult. See, for example, page 631 and comment 32, page 645.

21. **Reference to a book written with an assistant**. The word "with" appears before Kane's name on the cover and title page of the Gilson and Kane book. It indicates that Kane assisted Gilson, the researcher and principal author, probably by helping with the writing. Shannon makes this clear to his readers by using "with" as well. (See also the list of works cited, p. 638, and comment 49, p. 648.) **Introducing and citing a discussion of one work**. By mentioning the names of Gilson and Kane at the beginning of the discussion, Shannon makes it clear that what follows is from their work. The page reference at the very end of the paragraph announces that the citation covers all the intervening material. If, instead, Shannon had placed both parts of the citation together (the page reference in the first sentence or the authors' names in the last sentence), readers might be unsure of how much material the citation covered. **Mixing summary, paraphrase, and quotation**. In the rest of this paragraph, Shannon summarizes, paraphrases, and quotes from several pages of Gilson and Kane's book to give the reader a good sense of one of Gilson's findings.

22. **Editing quotations**. Shannon uses an ellipsis mark to show that he has eliminated irrelevant material from the quotation (see 25e). The ellipsis itself consists of three spaced periods. It is preceded by a sentence period closed up to the last word in the sentence, and it is followed by two spaces.

37

23. **Placing and punctuating parenthetical references**. The page reference for all the Gilson and Kane material in this paragraph falls at the end of the paragraph (see comment 21). Since the final quotation ends in a question mark, the reference is followed by a separate period.

24. **Adding emphasis to quotations**. Shannon underlines certain words in the quotation that reinforce his thesis especially clearly. He acknowledges this change inside the parenthetical reference, separated by a semicolon from the page number.

25. **Summary statement**. For three paragraphs Shannon has been discussing the single idea of how sex discrimination by both sexes holds women back. This concluding statement ties the paragraphs together in preparation for a new section of the paper.

26. **Relation to outline**. With this paragraph Shannon begins part II of his outline (see p. 619). **Transitional paragraph**. Shannon devotes a whole paragraph to the shift in direction, briefly summing up the preceding section and then introducing his final and most important point.

27. **Using sources effectively**. In this paragraph Shannon combines material from two sources to support a single point about corporate managerial style. The two sources reinforce each other and strengthen Shannon's conclusion at the end of the paragraph.

28. **Drawing conclusions**. Shannon correctly places the page reference for Loden after the paraphrase but before the conclusion he draws from the evidence. His conclusion not only spells out the significance of the preceding paragraph but also prepares for the next paragraph. However, Shannon should have found and offered evidence for his understanding that women are "reared to be emotional, co-operative, and generous." The statement may seem self-evident, but many readers would justly criticize it as just the kind of stereotype that Shannon himself is criticizing (see 4b-4).

29. **Altering capitalization in quotations**. In the source the word "although" began a sentence and was capitalized. To fit the quotation smoothly into his own sentence, Shannon wanted to use a small letter. The brackets indicate that he altered the capitalization. (See 26a).

30. **Reference to a work with more than three authors**. Here and in the list of works cited (see p. 638), Shannon uses "et al." ("and others") to indicate that the work had at least three other authors besides the one named. Shannon could have given all of the authors' names, too. Either form is correct as long as the list of works cited and the text references are consistent.

37

31. **Reproduction of list**. By indenting the list ten spaces like any other long quotation, Shannon indicates that it is indeed a quotation.

32. **Reference to an indirect source**. Shannon's use of "qtd. in" indicates that Loden herself quoted the list. In this case, unlike on pages 625 and 626, the use of an indirect source is appropriate because the list was available only in Loden's book, not also in another readily available source. (See comment 20, p. 634.)

33. **Selective quotation**. Throughout this paragraph, Shannon chooses quotations carefully. Since he is relying heavily on Loden in this section, he does not simply report what she says but rather uses her ideas and words selectively to support his thesis.

34. **Relation to outline**. At this paragraph Shannon begins part III of his outline (see p. 620).

35. **Primary source: personal interview**. Shannon has tested his ideas by interviewing a woman in a management position. He weaves together paraphrases and quotations from the interview, which he tape-recorded after obtaining Crisi's permission. He does not use a parenthetical reference because all the necessary information (Crisi's name) appears in the text.

36. **Drawing conclusions**. Again, Shannon does not force readers to figure out the significance of his evidence but states plainly what he got from the interview (and what he wants readers to get).

37. **Using an endnote for supplementary information**. Shannon did not want to do more than mention the term "participative management," whose meaning he thought was clear enough from the words themselves. For readers who might want more information, he provides an endnote with a source to consult.

38. **Selecting supporting evidence**. Shannon uses two separate sources here to develop his point, mixing the views of a practitioner and an expert.

39. **From note cards to paper**. Shannon wanted to use material from two widely separated passages in Loden's book, both of which he had quoted on his note cards (see the next page). In the paper, however, he opted for paraphrases of the quotations because he did not want to quote excessively and because he could fit the paraphrases together more smoothly than he could the quotations.

40. **Conclusion**. In his final paragraph Shannon summarizes the main points of his argument in a way that reminds readers of both what holds women back and what he thinks needs to change. The last sentence—by referring to the title and providing a vivid image—gives the paper a dramatic finish.

37

> *Adapting management styles*
> Loden, p. 5
>
> "[T]he feminine style of leadership is not a replacement of the traditional style."

> *Adapting management styles*
> Loden, p. 277
>
> "Equality will be achieved only when organizations acknowledge feminine leadership as an acceptable alternative to the traditional style of management."

41. **Format of notes**. The word "Notes" is centred 2.5 cm (1") from the top of the page. (The heading would be singular—"Note"— if Shannon had not had more than one note.) The notes begin two lines (one double space) below the heading. The notes themselves are double-spaced. The first line of each is indented five spaces and preceded by a raised number corresponding to the number used in the text. A space separates the number and the note.

42. **Endnotes for additional relevant information**. Shannon's first note provides readers with background information on a definition. He also provides some additional interesting information on an important book that uses this term, showing that while the book was based on American experience, it has had a strong impact on Canadian thinking as well. His second note refers interested readers to an article on participative management.

43. **Reference to an unsigned article**. Since Shannon is referring to an unsigned article, he uses a shortened form of the title for his citation. Since the article is only one page, he does not include the page number. See the entry for this work in the list of works cited, page 639.

37

44. **Format of list of works cited**. The heading "Works Cited" is centred 2.5 cm (1″) from the top of the page. The first entry is typed two lines (one double space) below the heading, and the entire list is double-spaced. The first line of each entry begins at the left margin; subsequent lines of the same entry are indented five spaces. The entries are alphabetized. **Note:** Some instructors ask students to use the heading "Works Consulted" rather than "Works Cited." Such a list would include all of the sources used with profit during the course of the research project, not just the ones to which the student had directly referred in the paper.

45. Entry for a **signed article in a monthly periodical**.

46. Entry for an **article with more than three authors**. A source with more than three authors may be listed with all authors' names or just with the first author's name followed by "et al." ("and others"). As his bibliography card indicates below, Shannon had all the names but opted not to use them. His text reference to the Broverman et al. article is consistent with this decision (see p. 629).

> Broverman, I. K., S. R. Vogel, D. M. Broverman, F. E. Clarkson, and P. S. Rosenkrantz. "Sex-Role Stereotypes: A Current Appraisal." *Journal of Social Issues* 28.2 (1972): 59-78.

The Broverman entry also illustrates a **signed article in a journal that pages issues separately** (see p. 563.)

47. Entry for a **signed article in a journal with continuous pagination throughout an annual volume** (see p. 563).

48. Entry for an **article in which pagination is not consecutive**. The "+" indicates that the article does not continue on page 142 but farther back in the issue.

37

49. Entry for a **personal interview**.
50. Entry for a **book written with an assistant**. See the discussion of this source in comment 21, p. 643. Note that this entry differs from one for a source with two authors, such as the Hughey and Gelman entry below.
51. Entry for a **signed article in a weekly periodical**.
52. Entry for a **signed article in a daily newspaper**.
53. Entry for a **book with one author**.
54. Entry for an **unsigned article**. The source is alphabetized in the list of works cited by the first main word of its title, "Special." Here is Shannon's bibliography card for this source:

> "The Special Talents Women Bring to Participative Management."
> <u>International Management</u> Aug. 1986: 60.

Weibe 1

Deborah Wiebe

Dr. Burkinshaw

HIST 236

March 16, 1989 British Columbia at the

Crossroads:

Colony, State, or Province?

In 1871 British Columbia entered Confederation and John A. Macdonald's dream of a
Canada that stretched from coast to coast
finally was realized. The events that led up
to this climax did not occur naturally and
smoothly, however. Prior to the agreement several options were open to British Columbia,
each of which would have had a profound effect
on her future. The people in British Columbia
had varying opinions on these options and did
not hesitate to make themselves heard. British
Columbia entered the Canadian Confederation
only after other options had been seriously
considered and eventually rejected.

By 1868, after Canada had become a
nation, three major options were available
with respect to British Columbia's future.

Format of heading when no title page is required

Statement of process to be discussed

37

Wiebe 2

These alternatives were reflected in the opinions of the British Columbia populace. Each
group argued for the option that it felt would
best serve British Columbians in the future.
The two most prevalent views were those held

Three options
stated

by the group favouring annexation with the
United States and the group favouring union
with the Dominion of Canada. The third view,
held for a period of time by many governing
officials especially, though not engendering
nearly as much public support, was for British
Columbia to remain a colony of Great Britain.

Although Vancouver Island had united with
British Columbia in 1866, the territory
remained in need of further change. At the
time, the population was about ten thousand.
British Columbia didn't have responsible government, although it did have representative
institutions such as legislative assembly
(Hopkins 175). After the gold rushes of the
late 1850s and 1860s, British Columbia had
severe financial problems in the form of huge
debts and unfinished projects. The whole economy was in a state of depression and in need

Wiebe 3

of a real boost--either more political independence, annexation by the United States, or
union with Canada. To clarify why union with
Canada was not the only option, I will examine
the three options, assess the influence of
each, and then explain why British Columbia
finally chose to enter Confederation.

Structure
of essay
described

First, an element of British Columbia's
population desired the territory to remain as
it was--a colony of the British Empire. The
most prominent group to feel this way was the
government led by Governor Seymour. It desired
neither union with Canada nor annexation with
the United States; it simply wanted to remain
loyal to Britain and retain independent colonial status (Careless and Brown 40). However,
in the late 1860s, Britain increasingly began
to seem like a mother country indifferent to
the fate of her colonies. "Many people in
England regarded the colonies as expensive
dependencies and urged the government to grant
them their independence" (Hou and Morgan 37).
In 1869 James Douglas, former governor first
of Vancouver Island and then British Columbia

First
option

37

Wiebe 4

after 1866, wrote in a personal letter: "I
fear British Columbia is not much valued in
England and that we may ere long be dropped
into the lap of the United States. . . . "
(Smith 120). The British Colonist, a British
Columbia newspaper, complained in its
April 25, 1867, issue: " . . . we are treated
very indifferently, and every day we are told
we are a burden and source of continual annoy-
ance to our old mother [Britain]" (Hou and
Morgan 35).

Another reason it appeared British Columbia could not remain a colony of Britain was
that there was growing pressure from both the
United States and Canada as they came to recognize the value of the addition of this territory. At the same time, it was becoming
increasingly clear that British Columbia would
remain stagnant and in a depressed state
unless there was some change.

By 1866 the future of British Columbia
had become a heated issue, and annexation by
the United States was seen as a very real
option. The Dominion of Canada had very little

[Margin notes:]
Quotation to illustrate perceived British attitude toward BC

Second option

37

Wiebe 5

influence on the colony, whereas the American
presence was far more tangible and real. For
example, by April 1865, there was telegraph
communication with Washington, DC, whereas it
took two months for a letter to come from
Britain (Waite 316). British Columbia did a
large percentage of its business with Americans, and a significant proportion of the population was American. The Fourth of July was
considered a holiday in British Columbia--
shops were closed and fireworks were set off
(Waite 316). For some, annexation was simply a
way out of their present state of "poverty
and wretchedness" (Waite 317).

In 1870 J. S. Helmcken, later to become
one of the representatives to Ottawa, said,
"The United States . . . is the Nation by which
we exist . . . which has made this colony what
it is. . . . " (Waite 317). British Columbia
wanted to become part of a larger country, and
to many, the United States seemed the natural
choice. On October 28, 1867, the <u>Chicago Tri-
bune</u> published a letter written by a U.S.
businessman in Victoria which contained the
following excerpt:

Two quotations
of contemporary
opinion supporting
annexation

37

> The people of the Colony . . .
> Englishmen and all, saving the offi-
> cials, are hoping, praying, and
> working to be attached to the United
> States. A petition to her Majesty is
> now being circulated and signed by
> the loyal subjects of Great Britain
> for annexation to the United States,
> as the only means of preventing the
> country [British Columbia] from
> relapsing into its preventative
> condition.   (Hou and Morgan 34)

P. B. Waite, an author on the subject of Confederation, observed, "British Columbia was
like a British colony, but it was becoming
like Oregon before the Treaty of 1846: full of
Americans, envious of American power and
energy, ready to fall into the lap of the
United States. . . . " (Waite 316). Thus there
was sufficient interest in annexation in British Columbia to warrant close consideration.
But it is also important to consider annexation from an American point of view.

Although American interest in acquiring
British Columbia was limited, it was not

Wiebe 7

insignificant. Following the American purchase
of Alaska from the Russians in 1867, many
assumed that British Columbia would eventually
be American territory. The apparently declin-
ing British interest in the colony only
enhanced the assumption. The following is
an excerpt from a Victoria newspaper of
September 15, 1867: " . . . there is a reality
in the statements that the American Government
desires the acquisition of British Columbia,
and that the British Government feel disposed
to entertain the proposition favourably. . . . "
(Hou and Morgan 36).

The most specific American interest in
annexation was shown just prior to 1871 by
the American Secretary of State, William Henry
Seward. It was revealed that he had planned to
use British Columbia in a reparations claim
against Britain. This claim concerned Confed-
erate cruisers that had been built in England
during the American Civil War, in violation of
international law. This matter was referred to
as "The Alabama Claims" because Alabama was
the name of one of the ships involved. Seward
intended to make annexation of British

Paraphrase of
historians'
interesting
speculation

37

Wiebe 8

Columbia one of the terms of settlement. Nothing came of this, however. It is speculated
that Britain did not want to lose its Royal
Navy base on Vancouver Island. Seward later
officially dismissed as a rumour the statement
that he was hoping to accept the colony as an
offset to the <u>Alabama</u> Claims (Akrigg and
Akrigg 347).

As reports of American interest in
acquiring British Columbia began to circulate
in both British Columbia and Canada, awareness
that the colony was at a crossroads in its
political history began to intensify. The
Canadian government became more conscious of
the American threat to its dream of a transcontinental Canada, and renewed interest was
kindled in having British Columbia join Confederation (Akrigg and Akrigg 347). By 1868
there were growing feelings of optimism and
ambition regarding the West. This had not
always been so. In 1865 John A. Macdonald
would gladly have had nothing to do with the
West. He remarked, "I would be quite willing,
personally, to leave that whole country [the
North-West] a wilderness for the next half-

Third
option

Wiebe 9

century, but I fear if Englishmen do not go there, Yankees will. . . . " (Waite 307). An article appeared in the <u>Montreal Gazette</u> on May 24, 1867, which stated, "If the United States desire to outflank us in the West, we must . . . lay our hand on British Columbia. . . . " (Waite 306). However, this task would not be easy. In many ways British Columbia had more in common with and more ties to the United States than it did with the confedera- tion of eastern provinces known as Canada. There had long been in British Columbia a feeling of isolation from and resentment toward Canada. If Canada truly desired British Columbia, she would have to plan a careful strategy in order to acquire it.

First, however, it would be valuable to review why there was opposition in British Columbia to this idea and what turned the tide to result in the entry of British Columbia into Confederation. Frederick Seymour, gover- nor of British Columbia from 1864 to 1869, was initially opposed to British Columbia's enter- ing Confederation, but in 1868 he began to shift his opinion. In a speech at the opening

Reasons for changes in public opinion in BC regarding Confederation option

37

First reason

of the Legislative Council at New Westminster
on March 13, 1868, it was evident that he had
changed his mind: " . . . the possibility alone
of something arising out of [British Columbia's entering Confederation] to promote an
overland communication with Canada was enough
to induce me to support [the union]. . . . "
(Begg 375). Other factors opposing union with
Canada have been discussed already: the sense
of isolation, fear, and resentment felt by
many British Columbians toward Canada, and the
perceived benefits of the annexation with the
U.S. option. But slowly the tide began to turn
in favour of British Columbia becoming the
newest province in the Dominion of Canada.

By Spring 1867, the depression in British
Columbia was severe. Nothing was really hap-
pening with regard to annexation to the United
States, and Confederationists from the East
began to be regarded seriously by British
Columbians as representing an option worth
their careful consideration (Waite 318). The
Confederationists in British Columbia, led by
James Trimble and Amor de Cosmos, began to
publicize the advantages of Confederation

Second
reason

37

Wiebe 11

(Careless and Brown 40). On May 21, 1868, the
Confederation League was formed. Its objective
was " . . . to effect Confederation as speedily
as possible, and secure representative institutions for the colony and thus get rid of the
present one-man government with its huge staff
of overpaid and do-nothing officials" (Begg
379).

Some historians believe that the depression in British Columbia was the key catalyst
to the desire for union with the Dominion of
Canada (Akrigg and Akrigg 345). After the gold
rush was over in 1865, prosperity had begun to
dwindle and the two separate colonies of British Columbia and Vancouver Island had begun to
slide toward bankruptcy. In an attempt to prevent the economy from deteriorating any further, the decision to unite the two colonies
was made in July 1866. However, within six
months British Columbia was on the edge of
bankruptcy once more (Waite 311). When Canada
offered to assume British Columbia's debt, the
opportunity seemed too good to pass up.

Thirdly, Governor Anthony Musgrave   Third
                                           reason
provided the impetus for taking the final

37

steps toward union with Canada. After Governor
Seymour died an 1869, Musgrave, former
lieutenant-governor of Newfoundland and a sup-
porter of Confederation, was appointed by the
colonial office in Britain to replace him. On
March 6, 1868, the Privy Council in Ottawa had
submitted a report to the Duke of Buckingham
in Britain, informing him that " . . . the Government of Canada will be prepared to submit
to [British] Parliament a proposal for the
admission of British Columbia into the Union
[of Canada] . . . " and asking him to move
British Columbia's Legislative Council to take
further action (Begg 379). It would appear
that Britain's appointment of Musgrave was the
response Ottawa desired. Shortly following
Musgrave's appointment, he persuaded the Legislative Council to draw up terms for union
with Canada that they would find acceptable
(Careless and Brown 41). In 1870 former governor James Douglas wrote in a private letter
that "Confederation with Canada is now one of
the ruling manias, and my impression is that
it will not long be delayed" (Smith 120).

    After British Columbia's Legislative

Resolution
of debate
regarding
Confederation

Council devised terms for union which it
deemed acceptable, it sent delegates to Ottawa
to negotiate. On July 7, 1870, Ottawa and
British Columbia agreed on the terms. It is
interesting to note here that John A. Macdonald was not directly involved in the process by which his dream of a coast-to-coast
Canada was achieved. At the time he was suffering from a breakdown and G. E. Cartier was
acting prime minister. Since by now Canada
wanted British Columbia badly, the terms were
very much in the latter's favour.

The guarantee of a transcontinental railway to be started within two years and completed in ten was probably the most important
term of the agreement (Careless and Brown 41).
The British Imperial Government was even willing to guarantee its completion within ten
years (Begg 397). Following the agreement on
the terms, the Legislative Council submitted a
request for Crown approval for the admittance
of British Columbia as a province. This was a
mere formality, however, and British Columbia
was given legal provincial status on May 16,
1871. It was not until July 20, 1871, however,

Wiebe 14

that Canada's sixth province officially joined
the union (Careless and Brown 41). Yet, even
after British Columbia's entry into Confederation had been accomplished officially, it took
a period of time before a sense of collective
national identity would emerge and a feeling
of nationhood would stretch to include British
Columbia (Waite 321). British Columbia still
struggles to this very day with occasional
feelings of isolation from Eastern Canada.

Thus, it was never a foregone conclusion
that British Columbia would eventually join
the rest of Canada. For a while, annexation to
the United States was a very real possibility,
and many people assumed it was inevitable.
Even today, in some ways British Columbia
seems more influenced by the United States
than by Ottawa. But, by virtue of British
Columbia's entry into Confederation in 1871,
Macdonald's vision of a transcontinental
Canada was fulfilled and British Columbia's
political future was changed forever.

Recapitulation
of main
thesis

37

Wiebe 15

Works Cited

Akrigg, G. P. V., and Helen B. Akrigg.
    British Columbia Chronicle (1847-1871):
    Gold and Colonists. Vancouver: Discovery
    Press, 1977.

Begg, Alexander. History of British Columbia:
    From Its Earliest Discovery to the Pres-
    ent Time. 1894. Toronto: McGraw-Hill
    Ryerson, 1972.

Careless, J. M. S., and R. Craig Brown, eds.
    The Canadians: 1867-1967. Toronto: Mac-
    millan of Canada, 1967.

Friesen, J., and H. K. Ralston, eds. Histori-
    cal Essays on British Columbia. Toronto:
    Gage, 1980.

Hopkins, E. Russell. Confederation at the
    Crossroads. Toronto: McClelland & Stew-
    art, 1968.

Hou, Charles, and Marlena Morgan. The Destiny
    of British Columbia: Confederation or
    Annexation? 1866-1871. Vancouver: B.C.
    Teachers' Federation, 1984.

37

Wiebe 16

Johnson, Patricia M. <u>Canada's Pacific Province: Selected Sources from Early Times
to the Present.</u>   Toronto: McClelland &
Stewart. 1966

Lower, J. A. <u>Canada: An Outline History</u>.
Toronto: McGraw-Hill Ryerson, 1973.

MacBeth, R. G. <u>The Making of the Canadian
West</u>. Toronto: Coles Publishing Co.,
1973.

Ormsby, Margaret A. <u>British Columbia: A His-
tory</u>. Vancouver: Macmillan of Canada,
1971.

Reid, J. H. Stewart, Kenneth McNaught, and
Harry S. Crowe, eds. <u>A Source-book of
Canadian History: Selected Documents and
Personal Papers</u>. Toronto: Longmans
Canada, 1967.

Smith, Dorothy Blakey. <u>James Douglas: Father
of British Columbia</u>. Toronto: Oxford UP,
1971.

Waite, P. B. <u>The Life and Times of Confederation 1864-1867</u>. Toronto: U of Toronto
P, 1962.

37

Writing in the Disciplines

Writing in the academic disciplines you study in college and university helps you learn concepts, focus ideas, reflect on assumptions, answer questions, interpret patterns, and analyse data. Learning is thus an important reason for writing: when you write a paper for a course in history, anthropology, or biology, you demonstrate your understanding of concepts and explain how you arrived at that understanding.

This chapter explains how to adapt the writing strategies explained in Chapters 1–2 on the writing process and Chapters 35–37 on research writing to academic writing in general (38a) and, more specifically, to the writing situations you will encounter in the humanities (38b), the social sciences (38c), and the natural applied sciences (38d). For each field or group of related disciplines, the chapter introduces the basic information needed to follow the guidelines below.

GUIDELINES FOR ACADEMIC WRITERS

1. For the discipline you are writing in, understand the methodology and the kinds of evidence considered appropriate and valid.
2. Analyse the special demands of the assignment—the kind of research and sources you need. The questions you set out to answer, the assertions you wish to support, will govern how you choose your sources and evidence.
3. Know the specialized tools and language of the discipline.
4. Use the style of documentation and the manuscript format customarily used by writers in the discipline.

38a Understanding the goals and requirements of the disciplines

1 Methods and evidence

The **methodology** of a discipline is the way its practitioners study their subjects—that is, how they proceed when investigating the answers to questions. Academic or scholarly writers do not compose directly out of their personal experience. Rather, they collect and organize the kinds of evidence appropriate to the discipline, and they base any opinions on that evidence. The evidence comes from research like that described in the last three chapters: it may come from the researcher's own close observations and analysis of a text or experiment; or it may come from sources, most likely those located in a library.

When you conduct original research, you generate your own evidence. You might analyse the images in a poem and then use examples as evidence for your interpretation of the poem. Or you might conduct a survey of fellow students and then use data from the survey to support your conclusions about students' attitudes. Either of these kinds of evidence would be a **primary source**, a first-hand or original account that does not rely on others' sources. Additional examples of primary sources include historical documents such as letters and diaries, works of art such as paintings or photographs, and reports on experiments that the writer has conducted. The research papers in the preceding chapter both use primary sources: Mark Shannon's paper includes the results of an interview he conducted, and Deborah Wiebe's includes excerpts from contemporary politicians' letters, speeches, and reports concerning British Columbia's entry into the Canadian Confederation. The sample papers in this chapter also depend on primary sources.

As the examples of primary sources indicate, many are to be found in the library. But more prevalent among a library's holdings are **secondary sources**, books and articles written *about* primary sources. Much academic writing requires that you use such sources to spark, extend, or support your own ideas, as when you review the published opinions and information on your subject before contributing conclusions from your original research.

2 Assignments

For most academic writing, your primary purpose will be either to explain something to your readers or to persuade them to accept your conclusions. (See 1c on purpose.) To achieve your purpose, you will adapt your writing process to the writing situation, particularly to the kinds of evidence required by the assignment and to the kinds of thinking you are expected to do. Most assignments will contain key words that tell you what these expectations are—words such as *compare*, *define*, *analyse*, and *illustrate* that express customary ways of thinking about and organizing a vast range of subjects. Sections 1d-6 and 3c-2 explore these so-called patterns of development. You should be aware of them and alert to the wording in assignments that directs you to use them. In addition, if you have not already done so, you should read Chapter 4 on critical reading and writing, skills fundamental to completing almost any academic writing assignment.

3 Tools and language

When you write in an academic discipline, you use the scholarly tools of that discipline, including specialized references such as periodical indexes, abstracts, and computerized databases. (See 35c for helpful lists of references.) In addition, you may use the aids developed by practitioners of the discipline for efficiently and effectively approaching research, conducting it, and recording the findings. Many of these aids, such as a system of note cards for recording evidence from sources, are discussed in Chapters 35 and 36 and can be adapted to any discipline. Other aids are discussed in later sections of this chapter.

Pay close attention to the texts assigned in a course and any materials given out in class, for these items may introduce you to valuable references and other research aids, and they will use the specialized language of the discipline. This specialized language allows practitioners to write to each other both efficiently and precisely. It also furthers certain concerns of the discipline, such as accuracy and objectivity. Scientists, for example, prefer the verb *indicate* rather than *prove* in discussing their conclusions, because all results are provisional. Some of the language conventions like this one are discussed in the following sections. As you gain experience in a particular discipline, keep alert for such conventions and train yourself to follow them.

4 Documentation and format

Most disciplines publish journals that require authors to use a certain documentation style and manuscript format. In turn, most instructors in a discipline require the same of students writing papers for their courses.

When you document your sources, you tell readers which ideas and information you borrowed and where they can find your sources. Thus documentation indicates how much knowledge you have and how broad and deep your research was. It also helps you avoid **plagiarism**, the serious offence of presenting the words, ideas, and data of others as if they were your own. (See 36d on avoiding plagiarism.)

Manuscript format includes such features as margins and the placement of the title. But it also extends to special elements of the manuscript, such as tables or an abstract, that may be required by the discipline.

The following sections direct you to the style guides published by different disciplines and outline the basic requirements of the ones used most often. If your instructor does not require a particular style, consult one of the general guides listed on page 555, or use the style of the Modern Language Association, which is described and illustrated at length in 35d-2 (p. 556), 36i-1 (p. 600), and Appendix A (p. 720).

38b Writing in the humanities

The humanities, sometimes known as the reconstructive and speculative disciplines, include the arts, film, literature, history, and philosophy. The texts in these disciplines record and speculate about the growth, ideas, and emotions of human beings. Writing in the humanities explains, interprets, analyses, and reconstructs, based on the evidence in both primary and secondary sources.

This section concentrates on writing about literature and about history and concludes with two sample literary papers (see p. 674). The other disciplines mentioned have their own concerns, of course, but share many important goals and methods with literature and history.

1 Methods and evidence in the humanities

Literature

As a reader and a student of literature, you read a work and interpret and analyse its implications. You make inferences or draw conclusions from the writer's written words (the text).

A literary analysis is often based only on the text or texts themselves, without recourse to secondary sources. Your assignment may, however, ask you to augment your own inferences with those of other critics who have written about the work(s). (See pp. 674 and 676 for examples of both kinds of literary analysis.)

When analysing a literary work, you can use the list on the next page to track the elements of the work and ask questions about them.

History

History as a discipline attempts to reconstruct the past. In Greek the word for history means "to inquire": historians inquire into the past to understand the events of the past. Then they report, explain, analyse, and evaluate those events in their context, asking such questions as what happened before or after the events or how the events were related to the existing political and social structures.

Historians' reconstructions of the past—their conclusions about what happened and why—are always supported with reference to the written record. The evidence of history is mainly primary sources, such as eyewitness accounts and contemporary documents, letters, commercial records, and the like. For history papers, you might also be asked to support your conclusions with those in secondary sources.

In reading historical sources, you need to weigh and evaluate their evidence. If, for example, you find conflicting accounts of the same event, you need to consider the possible biases of the authors or their sources so that you can reject unreliable sources or balance opposing evidence. In general, the more a historian's conclusions are supported by public records such as deeds, marriage licences, and newspaper accounts, the more reliable the conclusions are likely to be.

2 Assignments in the humanities

Papers in the humanities generally perform one or more of the following operations: analysis, explanation, interpretation, evaluation, and synthesis. Using **analysis**, you might examine the elements of a story or painting or break down the causes and effects of a historical event. Using **explanation**, you might show how a film director created a particular sequence, or you might clarify a general's role in a battle. Using **interpretation**, you might infer the meaning of a poem from its images. Using **evaluation**, you might weigh the merits of a historian's conclusions or of an architect's design. Using **synthesis**, you might create a sense of a historical period based on an archive of contemporary letters. Most likely, you will use these operations in combination—say, interpreting and explaining the meaning of a painting before evaluating the merits of the work.

38b

QUESTIONS FOR A LITERARY ANALYSIS

Plot: the relationships and patterns of events in a short story, novel, or play.

What actions happen?
How are the events connected?
How do the actions begin or end?

Character: the people the author creates.

Who are the principal people in the story, play, or poem?
How do they stay the same? Why?
How do they change? Why?

Point of view: the perspective or attitude of the speaker in a poem or the voice who tells a story. The point of view of a narrator may be **first person** (*I*) or **third person** (*he, she, it, they*). If third person, it may be **omniscient** (able to see and hear everything both inside and outside all characters), **limited** (able to see and hear what is inside only the main character), or **objective** (able only to see and hear what is external to the characters—what they do and say).

Who is the narrator? Is he or she identified?
What are the significance and effect of the author's choice of narrator and point of view?
Is the narrator subjective or objective? Is he or she trustworthy?

Tone: the feelings conveyed; the predominant attitude.

Do the words sound sad? happy? something else?
Does the narrator have an ironic tone, saying one thing and meaning another?
What does the tone say about the author's attitudes and intentions?

Images: word pictures or visual details.

What images does the writer use? What pictures do they evoke?
What is the significance of images in conveying the author's meaning?

Setting: the place where the action happens.

What is the principal setting, and what does it contribute to the author's meaning?
When the scene shifts, why does it?

Theme: the main idea or general meaning of the work

What do all the other elements point to as the author's intended meaning?

38b

3 Tools and language in the humanities

Literature

Analysing a work of literature (or any work of art) requires looking closely at its elements. As you read, pose questions about the text, such as why a character speaks with a lisp or why images of water recur in a poem. One helpful way of staying sharp and curious while reading is to make notes in a **reading journal**, a log of questions, reactions, and insights in any form you can reread and use later for writing. (It's a good idea to note the page numbers of the text in your journal so that you can always find the appropriate passages.) If you own your copy of the text, you can also underline key passages and use the margins for comments and questions. The point is to interact with the text—talk back to it, ask questions of it, analyse it.

When you write about a literary work, you explicate or unfold its meaning or the meaning of devices employed by the author. Your evidence is mainly direct quotations from the work, although you will occasionally use paraphrase and summary as well (see 36c). When using quotations, keep the following guidelines in mind.

GUIDELINES FOR USING QUOTATIONS IN LITERARY ANALYSIS

1. Choose quotations that clearly support your assertions. Don't use your own words merely to explain quotations, and don't use quotations just to use quotations. Instead, make quotations serve your ideas.
2. When you use a quotation, specify how it relates to your idea. Introduce it, and draw a conclusion from it.
3. Work quotations into your own prose. Avoid dumping quotations in readers' laps (See 36f-2.)
4. Reproduce spelling, punctuation, capitalization, and all other features exactly as they appear in the source. (See 25d for the use of brackets when you need to add something to a quotation; and see 25e for the use of an ellipsis mark when you need to omit something from a quotation.)
5. Document your sources. (See p. 672.)

Generally, literary analysts avoid claiming absolute certainty about an author's meaning, saying that the author *suggests* or *implies* (rather than *means* or *intends*) to convey that they are making inferences. Note also that it is conventional in writing about literature to use the present tense of verbs in describing both the author's work and the action in the work. For example:

38b

On the surface, the poet *addresses* a young child, Margaret, who *mourns* the falling of the gold-coloured leaves in a grove.

Margaret *represents* the stage of childhood in which we first become aware that "nature imitates man's mortality."

These passages come from the literary papers on pages 674 and 676, which also illustrate the other features discussed here.

History

The historian's tools are those of any thorough and efficient researcher, as discussed in Chapters 35 and 36: a system for finding and tracking sources (35c, 35d); methodical examination of sources, including evaluation of their biases (36a); a system for taking notes from sources (36c); and a separate system, such as a research journal, for tracking one's own evolving thoughts (35a).

When writing about history, it's important to remain as objective as possible. Historians strive for precision and logic; they do not guess about what happened or speculate about "what if." They avoid trying to influence readers' opinions with words having strongly negative or positive connotations, such as *stupid* or *brilliant* (see 31b-1). Instead, they show the evidence and draw conclusions from that. Generally, they avoid using *I*: it tends to draw attention away from the evidence and toward the writer, and it may imply a bias even when there is none.

Writing about history demands some attention to the tenses of verbs to maintain consistency. (See also 31b.) Generally, historians use the past tense to refer to events that occurred in the past. They reserve the present tense only for statements about the present or statements of general truths (see 7e-1). For example:

> During its five years in power, Prime Minister Lester Pearson's Liberal government *seemed* to stumble from one crisis to another, but when he *resigned* in 1968 he *left* behind a record of legislative accomplishment—including the Canada Pension Plan, a national universal medicare plan, and the adoption of a new flag—that *continues* to have a profound impact on Canadian society.

4 Documentation and format

Most writers in the humanities follow the guidelines for documentation and manuscript format established by the Modern Language Association (MLA) and set forth in the *MLA Handbook for Writers of Research Papers*, 3rd ed. (1988). In the MLA documentation style, parenthetical citations in the text of a paper refer to a list of works cited at the end. The system is thoroughly explained and illustrated in Chapters 35 and 36: bibliographic formats in 35d (p. 556), the list of works cited in 36h (p. 598), and parenthetical citations in 36i-1 (p. 600).

You should be aware that some literature instructors and practitioners of other disciplines in the humanities prefer an earlier MLA style of endnotes or footnotes rather than parenthetical references. This earlier style is explained and illustrated in 36i-2 (pp. 606–07). Some historians and philosophers may prefer a different style of endnotes or footnotes or a different style of parenthetical references (such as that of the American Psychological Association; see pp. 682–89). Clearly, your first move in deciding what documentation style to use is to ask your instructor.

The MLA guidelines for manuscript format are given in Appendix A of this book (p. 720) and illustrated in the two sample research papers in Chapter 37 (pp. 618 and 649). Consult Appendix A if you are in doubt about matters of format, and ask your instructor if he or she has any special requirements not mentioned there.

5 Two sample literary papers

The following sample papers illustrate two kinds of literary analysis, one based solely on the literary work itself (see the Gerard Manley Hopkins poem), and one drawing as well on secondary sources (p. 676). Both papers are by the same student and take as their subject the following poem.

GERARD MANLEY HOPKINS
Spring and Fall
To a Young Child

Margaret, are you grieving
Over Goldengrove unleaving?
Leaves, like the things of man, you
With your fresh thoughts care for, can you?
Ah! as the heart grows older
It will come to such sights colder
By and by, nor spare a sigh
Though worlds of wanwood leafmeal lie;
And yet you will weep and know why.
Now no matter, child, the name:
Sorrow's springs are the same.
Nor mouth had, no nor mind, expressed
What heart heard of, ghost guessed:
It is the blight man was born for,
It is Margaret you mourn for.

38b

A literary analysis (no secondary sources)

John D. Teehan

Professor Roche

English 203

October 29, 1988

Death and Resurrection in Hopkins's

"Spring and Fall"

In Gerard Manley Hopkins's poem "Spring and Fall: To a Young Child," a duality presents itself through the poet's address to a young child: namely, death and resurrection.

On the surface, the poet addresses a young child, Margaret, who mourns the falling of the gold-coloured leaves in a grove. As a child, the poet implies, Margaret may not yet understand that mortal things such as leaves or "things of man" (line 3) all eventually come to an end. They are born, they live, and they die. The poet then goes on to explain that as one grows older, one becomes accustomed to such routine cycles as the falling of leaves or decaying trees and even comes "to such sights colder / By and by" (6-7). This cycle of death, decomposition, rebirth, life, and back to death is inevitable.

Humans, too, as part of this natural process, are born to die. Margaret has no conception of this fact, but the poet, being older and less innocent, recognizes that she mourns the leaves in anticipation of her own death: "It [death] is the blight man was born for, / It is Margaret you mourn for" (14-15). Eventually she "will weep and know why" (9). She can escape neither her own

38b

death nor an awareness of it. And that awareness will always form "Sorrow's springs" (11).

But death can also lead to resurrection. For Hopkins as a Christian, and more especially as a priest, all humans and human-born Christ inevitably come to death, just as the leaves on a tree must inevitably fall; but then they are reborn. Hopkins omits any explicit reference to resurrection in this rather bleak poem. Yet it permeates the whole because of the person to whom this bleakness is addressed: the innocent Margaret. It may be, as Hopkins says, that the aging heart grows increasingly cold to death and does not "spare a sigh / Though worlds of wanwood leafmeal lie" (7-8). Margaret, however, with her "fresh thoughts" (4), is proof that innocence may be reborn. And, in that, she is proof of the rebirth of all living things. Even as Margaret comes to the realization of the inevitability of death and her part in it, other innocents will take her place to prove the equal inevitability of new life.

Thus this poem about death also seems to be about life. The young child heads unaware to her own end, but briefly, at least, she signifies immortality.

[New page.]

Work Cited

Hopkins, Gerard Manley. "Spring and Fall: To a Young
    Child." The Poems of Gerard Manley Hopkins.
    Ed. W. H. Gardner and N. H. Mackenzie. 4th ed.
    London: Oxford UP, 1967.

38b

A literary analysis with secondary sources

John D. Teehan

Professor Roche

English 203

November 16, 1988

Death and Resurrection in Hopkins's

"Spring and Fall"

In Gerard Manley Hopkins's poem "Spring and Fall: To
a Young Child," a duality presents itself through the
poet's address to a young child: namely, death and
resurrection.

On the surface, the poet addresses a young child,
Margaret, who mourns the falling of the gold-coloured
leaves in a grove. As a child, the poet implies, Margaret
may not yet understand that mortal things such as leaves
or "things of man" (line 3) all eventually come to an
end. They are born, they live, and they die. The poet then
goes on to explain that as one grows older, one becomes
accustomed to such routine cycles as the falling of leaves
or decaying trees and even comes "to such sights
colder / By and by" (6-7). This cycle of death, decomposition, rebirth, life, and back to death is inevitable.

Margaret represents the stage of childhood in which
we first become aware that "nature imitates man's mortality" (Mackenzie 143). Humans, too, are born to die.
Margaret has no conception of this fact, but the poet,
being older and less innocent, recognizes that she mourns
the leaves in anticipation of her own death: "It [death]

is the blight man was born for, / It is Margaret you mourn for" (14-15). Eventually she "will weep and know why" (9). She can escape neither her own death nor an awareness of it. And that awareness will always form "Sorrow's springs" (11).

But death can also lead to resurrection. According to his biographer, W. H. Gardner, Hopkins destroyed all the poems he had written before becoming a Jesuit novitiate (68). Once a priest, he imbued his poetry with a religious faith, so it is reasonable to seek evidence of such faith even in this rather bleak poem.

For Hopkins as a Christian, and more especially as a priest, all humans and human-born Christ inevitably come to death, just as the leaves on a tree must inevitably fall; but then they are reborn. Though Hopkins omits any explicit reference to resurrection, it permeates the whole because of the person to whom he addresses his seemingly bleak view: the innocent Margaret.

The word "Spring" in the title of the poem "has the reader see the young girl as a representative of that fresh season" (Mackenzie 142)--a representative not only of spring's newness but also of its sinlessness, its purity (Gardner 161). It may be, as Hopkins says, that the aging heart grows increasingly cold to death and does not "spare a sigh / Though worlds of wanwood leafmeal lie" (7-8). As Norman Weyand points out, Hopkins seems to be expressing the human longing for lasting, unspoiled beauty, a state before the original sin (64). Margaret, with her "fresh thoughts" (4), is proof that such a state of innocence may be reborn. And, in that, she is proof of the rebirth of all living things. Even as Margaret comes to the realization of the inevitability of death and her part in it, other innocents will take her place to prove the equal inevitability of life.

Thus this poem about decay and death also seems to be about purity and life. The young child heads unaware to her own end, but briefly, at least, she signifies immortality.

[New page.]

Works Cited

Gardner, W. H.   Gerard Manley Hopkins (1844-1889).   New Haven: Yale UP, 1948.

Hopkins, Gerard Manley.   "Spring and Fall: To a Young Child."   The Poems of Gerard Manley Hopkins.   Ed. W. H. Gardner and N. H. Mackenzie.   London: Oxford UP, 1967.

Mackenzie, Norman H.   A Reader's Guide to Gerard Manley Hopkins.   Ithaca: Cornell UP, 1981.

Weyand, Norman, ed.   Immortal Diamond: Studies in Gerard Manley Hopkins.   New York: Octagon, 1969.

38c   Writing in the social sciences

The social sciences—including anthropology, economics, education, management, political science, psychology, and sociology—focus on the study of human behaviour. As the name implies, the social sciences examine the way human beings relate to themselves, to their environment, and to each other.

1 Methods and evidence in the social sciences

Researchers in the social sciences systematically pose a question, formulate a **hypothesis** (a generalization that can be tested), collect data, analyse those data, and draw conclusions to support or disprove their hypothesis. This is the scientific method developed in the natural sciences (see p. 698). Social scientists gather data in several ways. They make first-hand observations of human behaviour and record the observations in writing or on audiotape or videotape. They interview subjects about their attitudes and behaviour, recording responses in writing or on tape. (See 35c-5, p. 553, for guidelines on conducting an interview.) They conduct broader surveys using questionnaires that ask people about their attitudes and behaviour. (See the box below.) And they conduct controlled experiments, structuring an environment in which to encourage and measure a specific behaviour. In their writing, social scientists explain their own research or analyse and evaluate others' research.

The research methods of social science generate two kinds of data: quantitative and qualitative. **Quantitative data** are numerical, such as statistical evidence based on surveys, polls, tests, and experi-

---

CONDUCTING A SURVEY

1. Decide what you want to find out—what your hypothesis is. The questions you ask should be dictated by your purpose.
2. Define your population. Think about the kinds of people your hypothesis is about—for instance, college men, or five-year-old children. Plan to sample this population so that your findings will be representative.
3. Write your questions. Surveys may contain closed questions that direct the respondent's answers (checklists and multiple-choice, true/false, or yes/no questions) or open-ended questions allowing brief, descriptive answers. Avoid loaded questions that reveal your own biases or make assumptions about subjects' answers, such as "Do you think the Premier of Quebec should restore language equality in that province?" or "How much more money does your father make than your mother?"
4. Test your questions on a few respondents with whom you can discuss the answers. Eliminate or recast questions that respondents find unclear, discomforting, or unanswerable.
5. Tally the results in actual numbers of answers, including any non-answers.
6. Seek patterns in the raw data that confirm or conflict with your hypothesis. Revise the hypothesis or conduct additional research if necessary.

38c

ments. When public-opinion pollsters announce that 47 percent of Canadians polled approved of the Prime Minister's leadership, they are offering quantitative data gained from a survey. Social science writers present quantitative data in graphs, charts, and other illustrations that accompany their text. (See pp. 690–91.)

Qualitative data are not numerical but more subjective: they are based on interviews, first-hand observations, and inferences, taking into account the subjective nature of human experience. An example is the work of the anthropologist Margaret Mead, whose experiences among the people of Samoa led to an important description of how adolescent Samoans become aware of adult concerns and rituals. Mead's book, *Coming of Age in Samoa*, contains few numbers; the data are qualitative.

2   Assignments in the social sciences

Depending on what social science courses you take, you may be asked to complete a variety of assignments. The **summary or review of research** reports on the available research literature on a subject such as infant perception of colour. The **case analysis** explains the components of a phenomenon such as a factory closing. The **problem-solving analysis** explains the components of a problem, such as unreported child abuse, and suggests ways to solve it. The **research paper** interprets and sometimes analyses the writings of other social scientists about a subject such as the effect of national appeals in advertising. The **research report** explains the author's own original research or attempt to replicate someone else's research. A research paper appears in Chapter 37, page 618. Excerpts from a problem-solving analysis appear at the end of this section, on page 691.

Most social science disciplines have special requirements for the content and organization of each kind of paper. The requirements appear in the style guides of the disciplines, such as the *Publication Manual of the American Psychological Association* (APA), 3rd ed. (1983). (Guides for other disciplines are listed on p. 682.) The APA manual specifies the following outline for the text of a research report.

1. *Abstract:* a summary (about 100 words) of the subject, the research method, the findings, and the conclusions.
2. *Introduction:* a presentation of the problem researched, the research method used, the background (such as other relevant studies), the purpose of the research, and the hypothesis tested.
3. *Method:* detailed discussion of how the research was conducted, including a description of the research subjects, any

38c

materials or tools used (such as questionnaires), and the procedure followed.

4. *Results:* a summary of the data collected and how they were statistically analysed, along with a detailed presentation of the data, often in tables, graphs, or charts.

5. *Discussion:* an interpretation of the data and presentation of conclusions, related to the original hypothesis. (When the discussion is brief, it may be combined with the previous section under the heading "Results and Discussion.")

To this basic text are added a title page and a list of references (the latter is described on pp. 682–83).

Because of the differences among disciplines and even among different kinds of papers in the same discipline, you should always ask your instructor what he or she requires for an assignment.

3　Tools and language in the social sciences

Although a research journal or log may not be required in undergraduate courses, such a notebook can be very helpful. Use it to pose preliminary questions as you begin formulating a hypothesis. In the field (that is, when conducting research), use the journal to react to the evidence you are collecting, to record changes in your perceptions and ideas, and to assess your progress. To avoid confusing reflections on evidence with the evidence itself, keep records of actual data—notes from interviews, observations, surveys, and experiments—separately from the field journal.

Each social science discipline has specialized terminology for concepts basic to the discipline. In sociology, for example, the words *mechanism*, *identity*, and *deviance* have specific meanings different from those of everyday usage. And *identity* means something different in sociology, where it applies to groups of people, than in psychology, where it applies to the individual. Social scientists also use precise terms to describe or interpret research. For instance, they say *The subject expressed a feeling of* rather than *The subject felt* because human feelings and intentions are not knowable for certain; or they say *These studies indicate* rather than *These studies prove* because conclusions are only tentative.

Just as in their research social scientists strive for objectivity, so in their writing they strive to demonstrate their objectivity through language. They avoid expressions such as *I think* in order to focus attention on what the evidence shows rather than on the researcher's opinions. (However, many social scientists prefer *I* to the artificial *the researcher* when they refer to their own actions, as in *I then interviewed the subjects*. Ask your instructor for his or her preferences.) Social scientists also avoid direct or indirect expression of their

38c

personal biases or emotions, either in discussions of other research-ers' work or in descriptions of research subjects. Thus, one social scientist does not call another's work *sloppy* or *immaculate* and does not refer to his or her own subjects as *drunks* or *innocent victims*. Instead, the writer uses neutral language and ties conclusions strictly to the data.

4   Documentation and format

As mentioned earlier, many of the social sciences publish style guides that advise practitioners how to organize, document, and type papers. The following is a partial list.

> American Psychological Association. *Publication Manual of the American Psychological Association*. 3rd ed. 1983.
> American Sociological Association. "Notice to Contributors." Immediately following the table of contents in each issue of *American Sociological Review*.
> American Anthropological Association. "Style Guide and Information for Authors." *American Anthropologist* 81 (1979): 226–31.

By far the most detailed and often-used guide in the social sciences is the *Publication Manual of the American Psychological Association* (APA). Its documentation system of in-text parenthetical references and a reference list and its manuscript format are observed in many disciplines besides psychology, and they are similar to the styles in anthropology, sociology, economics, and other disciplines. By all means, ask your instructor in any discipline what style you should use. If, as is likely, the preferred style is the APA's, then you can use the following explanation and models.

The APA reference list

The APA documentation style is like that of the Modern Language Association in that in-text parenthetical citations (see p. 687) refer the reader to a list of sources at the end of the paper. The list of sources is titled "References" and includes full publication information on every source cited in the paper. The sources are arranged alphabetically by the author's last name or, if there is no author, by the first main word of the title. In the models that follow for various sources, observe these features:

38c

1. Double-space all entries. Type the first line of each entry at the left margin, and indent all subsequent lines three spaces.
2. List all authors last-name first, separating names and parts of names with commas. Use initials for first and middle names.

Use an ampersand (&) rather than "and" before the last author's name.

3. In titles of books and articles, capitalize only the first word of the title, the first word of the subtitle, and proper names; all other words begin with small letters. In titles of journals, capitalize all significant words. Underline the titles of books and journals. Do not underline or use quotation marks around the titles of articles.

4. Give full names of publishers, excluding "Co.," "Inc.," and the like.

5. Use the abbreviation "p." or "pp." before page numbers in books, magazines, and newspapers, but *not* for scholarly journals.

Additional features are noted below.

A BOOK WITH A SINGLE AUTHOR

Rodriguez, R. (1982). <u>A hunger of memory: The educa-tion of Richard Rodriguez.</u> Boston: David R. Godine.

A BOOK WITH TWO OR MORE AUTHORS

Nesselroade, J. R., & Baltes, P. B. (1979). <u>Longi-tudinal research in the study of behavioral development.</u> New York: Academic Press.

A BOOK WITH AN EDITOR

Dohrenwend, B. S., & Dohrenwend, B. P. (Eds.). (1974). <u>Stressful life events: Their nature and effects.</u> New York: John Wiley.

List the editors' names as if they were authors, but follow the last name with "(Eds.)."—or "(Ed.)." with only one editor. Note the periods inside and outside the final parenthesis.

A BOOK WITH A TRANSLATOR

Trajan, P. D. (1927). <u>Psychology of animals.</u> (H. Simone, Trans.). Washington, DC: Halperin & Bros.

38c

The name of the translator appears in parentheses after the title, followed by a comma, "Trans.," a closing parenthesis, and a final period. Note also the absence of periods in "DC."

A BOOK WITH A CORPORATE AUTHOR

```
Editors of The Progressive.  (1970).  The crisis of

    survival.  Glenview: Scott, Foresman.
```

For works without named individuals as authors—such as a book with a corporate or group author (above) or an anonymous book (below)—begin the entry with the corporate or group name or the work's title, respectively. In the reference list, alphabetize the work as if the first main word (excluding *The, A,* and *An*) were an author's last name.

AN ANONYMOUS BOOK

```
Atlas of Canada.  (1981).  Montreal: Reader's Digest

    Ass'n.
```

TWO OR MORE WORKS BY THE SAME AUTHOR(S)

```
Gardner, H. (1973a).  The arts and human development.

    New York: John Wiley.

Gardner, H. (1973b).  The quest for mind: Piaget,

    Lévi-Strauss, and the structuralist movement.

    New York: Alfred A. Knopf.
```

When citing two or more works by exactly the same author(s), arrange the sources in order of their publication dates, earliest first. When citing two or more works by exactly the same author(s), published in the same year—as in the examples above—arrange them alphabetically by the first main word of the title and distinguish the sources by adding a letter to the date. Both the date *and* the letter are used in citing the source in the text (see p. 689).

A LATER EDITION

38c

```
Bollinger, D. L. (1975).  Aspects of language (2nd

    ed.).  New York: Harcourt Brace Jovanovich.
```

The edition number in parentheses follows the title and is followed by a period.

A WORK IN MORE THAN ONE VOLUME

```
Graham, R. (1963).  Arthur Meighen: A biography.

    (Vol. 2).   Toronto: Clarke, Irwin.

Graham, R. (1963).  Arthur Meighen: A biography.

    (Vols. 1-3).  Toronto: Clarke, Irwin.
```

The first entry cites a single volume (2) in the three-volume set. The second cites all three volumes. Use the abbreviation "Vol." within the parentheses, and follow the closing parenthesis with a period. (In the absence of an editor's name, the description of volumes would follow the title without intervening punctuation.)

AN ARTICLE OR CHAPTER IN AN EDITED BOOK

```
Paykel, E. S. (1974).  Life stress and psychiatric

    disorder: Applications of the clinical approach.

    In B. S. Dohrenwend & B. P. Dohrenwend (Eds.),

    Stressful life events: Their nature and effects

    (pp. 239-264).  New York: John Wiley.
```

The publication date of the collection (1974) is given as the publication date of the article or chapter. Following the article or chapter title and a period, information on the collection begins with "In," then the editors' names (in normal order), then "(Eds.)" and a comma, and then the title of the collection and the page numbers of the article in parentheses.

AN ARTICLE IN A JOURNAL WITH CONTINUOUS PAGINATION THROUGHOUT THE ANNUAL VOLUME

```
Emery, R. E. (1982).  Marital turmoil: Interpersonal

    conflict and the children of discord and

    divorce.  Psychological Bulletin, 92, 310-330.
```

See page 563 for an explanation of journal pagination. Note that the article title is not placed in quotation marks and that only the first words of the title and subtitle are capitalized. The journal title, in contrast, is underlined, and all significant words are capitalized. The volume number is separated from the title by a comma and is underlined. No "pp." precedes the page numbers.

38c

AN ARTICLE IN A JOURNAL THAT PAGES ISSUES SEPARATELY

```
Boyd, S. (1981).  Nuclear Terror.  Adaptation to

     Change, 7(4), 20-23.
```

Again, consult page 563 for an explanation of journal pagination. In this case, the issue number in parentheses follows the volume number without intervening space. The issue number is *not* underlined.

AN ARTICLE IN A MAGAZINE

```
Van Gelder, L.  (1986, December).  Countdown to

     motherhood: When should you have a baby?  Ms.,

     pp. 37-39, 74.
```

In the absence of a volume number, give the month of publication after the year, separating them with a comma. Give all page numbers even when the article appears on discontinuous pages. Use "pp." before the page numbers.

AN ARTICLE IN A NEWSPAPER

```
Wagstyl, S.  (1989, June 26).  Bigger proportion of

     old people will mean financial, social strains.

     The Globe and Mail, sec. C, p. 7.
```

Give month *and* date along with year of publication. Use *The* in the newspaper name if the paper itself does.

AN UNSIGNED ARTICLE

```
The right to die.  (1976, October 11).  Time, p. 101.
```

A REVIEW

```
Moore, C.  (1988, November).  Of ice and men.

     [Review of P. Berton, The Arctic grail: The

     quest for the North West Passage and the North

     Pole, 1818-1909].  Books in Canada, p. 30.
```

If the review is not titled, use the bracketed information as the title, keeping the brackets.

38c

A FILM, VIDEOTAPE, OR OTHER NON-PRINT SOURCE

Winkler, D. (Director) & Daly, T. (Producer).

    (1981). <u>Earle Birney: Portrait of a poet</u> [16 mm

    film]. Montreal: National Film Board of Canada.

The names of major contributors are followed by parenthetical designation of their function. The medium is specified in brackets after the title, with no intervening punctuation. Other non-print sources include films, slides, artworks, and musical performances.

COMPUTER SOFTWARE

<u>Microsoft word: Version IV</u>. (1987). [Computer pro-

    gram]. Bellevue, WA: Microsoft.

APA parenthetical citations

In the APA style, parenthetical citations within the text of a paper direct readers to the list of references. The citations contain a minimum of information: the author's last name, the date of publication (a key difference from MLA style), and the page number from which material is borrowed.

AUTHOR NOT NAMED IN THE TEXT

One critic of Milgram's experiments insisted that the

subjects should have been fully informed of the pos-

sible effects on them (Baumrind, 1968, p. 34).

When you do not name the author in your text, place in parentheses the author's name, the date of the source, and the page number(s) preceded by "p." or "pp." Separate the elements with commas. Position the reference so that it is clear what material is being documented *and* so that the reference fits as smoothly as possible into your sentence structure. The following would also be correct:

In the view of one critic of Milgram's experiments

(Baumrind, 1968, p. 34), the subjects should have

been fully informed of the possible effects on them.

38c

AUTHOR NAMED IN THE TEXT

Baumrind (1968, p. 34) insisted that the subjects in

```
Milgram's study should have been fully informed of

the possible effects on them.
```

When you use the author's name in the text, do not repeat it in the reference. Position the reference next to the author's name. If you cite the same source again in the paragraph, you need not repeat the reference as long as the page number (if any) is the same and it is clear that you are using the same source. The following is a later sentence from the paragraph in which the preceding example appears:

```
Baumrind also criticized the experimenters' ratio-

nale.
```

A WORK WITH TWO AUTHORS

```
Pepinsky and DeStefano (1977) demonstrate that a

teacher's language often reveals hidden biases.
```

```
One study (Pepinsky & DeStefano, 1977) demonstrated

the hidden biases often revealed in a teacher's lan-

guage.
```

When given in the text, two authors' names are connected by "and." In a parenthetical reference, they are connected by an ampersand, "&."

A WORK WITH THREE TO SIX AUTHORS

```
Pepinsky, Dunn, Rentl, and Corson (1973) further dem-

onstrated the biases evident in gestures.
```

In the first citation of a work with three to six authors, name all the authors, as in the example above. In the second and subsequent references to a work with three to six authors, give only the first author's name, followed by "et al." (Latin for "and others"):

```
In the work of Pepinsky et al. (1973), the loaded

gestures included head shakes and eye contact.
```

A WORK WITH MORE THAN SIX AUTHORS

```
One study (Rutter et al., 1976) attempts to explain

these geographical differences in adolescent

experience.
```

38c

For more than six authors, even in the first citation of the work, give only the first author's name, followed by "et al."

A CORPORATE AUTHOR

```
An earlier prediction was even more somber (Editors

of The Progressive, 1970).
```

AN ANONYMOUS WORK

```
One article ("Right to Die," 1976) noted that a

death-row inmate may crave notoriety.
```

For an anonymous or unsigned work, use the first two or three words of the title in place of an author's name, excluding an initial *The, A,* or *An.* Unlike in the reference list, the title of an article is placed in quotation marks. (Compare the citation above with the reference on p. 686.) Book and journal titles are underlined, as in the reference list. In all titles cited in the text—not just journal titles, as in the reference list—the significant words are capitalized.

ONE OF TWO OR MORE WORKS BY THE SAME AUTHOR(S)

```
At about age seven, most children begin to use appro-

priate gestures to reinforce their stories (Gardner,

1973a, pp. 144-145).
```

When you cite one of two or more works by the same author(s), the date will tell readers which source you mean—as long as your reference list includes only one source published by the author(s) in that year. If your reference list includes two or more works published by the same author(s) in the same year, the works should be lettered as explained on page 684. Then your parenthetical citation should include the appropriate letter, as in the preceding example.

TWO OR MORE WORKS BY DIFFERENT AUTHORS

```
Two studies (Herskowitz, 1974; Marconi & Hamblen,

1980) found that periodic safety instruction can dra-

matically reduce employees' accidents.
```

38c

List the sources in alphabetical order by the first author's name. Insert a semicolon between sources.

APA manuscript format

In general, the guidelines of the APA for manuscript format coincide with those of the MLA, explained in Appendix A of this book (p. 720). There are, however, some important differences and additions:

1. Use a 4-cm (1½-inch) margin on the left and 2.5-cm (1-inch) margins on the other three sides.
2. Number pages consecutively, starting with the title page. Identify each page (including the title page) with a shortened version of the title as well as a page number. For instance:

```
                                      Dating Violence

                                                    4

violence to include what he called "psychological"

abuse (insults or swearing, spiteful comments, or
```

3. Put the abstract (if there is one) on a page by itself immediately after the title page, with the heading "Abstract" centred at the top of the page.
4. Run into your text all quotations of fewer than forty words, and enclose them in quotation marks. For quotations of more than forty words, set them off from your text by indenting all lines five spaces, double-spacing above and below, and double-spacing the quotation itself. Do not use quotation marks around a quotation displayed in this way.
5. Do not label the introduction with a heading. For other main sections of your paper, such as "Method" and "Results," centre the heading, type it in capital and small letters, do not underline it, and double-space above and below it. (Do not start new pages for these sections.) If you use another level of heading below the main level, begin at the left margin, use capital and small letters, and underline the heading. See page 694 for examples of both headings.
6. Present data in tables and figures (graphs or charts), as appropriate. (See the sample on p. 695 for a clear format to follow.) Begin each illustration on a separate page. Number each kind of illustration consecutively and separately from the other (Table 1, Table 2, etc., and Figure 1, Figure 2, etc.). Refer to all illustrations in your text—for instance, "(See Figure 3.)." Either place illustrations immediately after the text references to them, or, if there are many illustrations, collect them at the end of the paper, after the reference list. (See p. 702 for more information on illustrations.)

38c

7. The reference list starts a new page after the last page of the text, with the heading "References" centred at the top of the page and the entire list typed double-space. (See also p. 697.)

Because many departments and instructors have their own preferences for manuscript format, you should ask your instructor for his or her wishes before preparing your final draft.

5 A sample social science paper

On the following pages are excerpts from a sociology paper. The student followed the organization described on pages 680–81 in both establishing the background for her study and explaining her own research. She also followed the APA style of documentation and manuscript format, although page borders, most page breaks, and other features have been omitted here.

Excerpts from a problem-solving analysis (sociology)

[Title page: centre vertically and horizontally.]

An Assessment of

Dating Violence on Campus

Karen M. Tarczyk

Sociology 213

Dr. Durkan

May 6, 1989

[New page.]

Abstract

Little research has examined the patterns of abuse and violence occurring between couples during courtship. With a questionnaire administered to a sample of university students, the extent and nature of such abuse and violence were investigated. The results, some interpretations, and implications for further research are discussed.

38c

An Assessment of

Dating Violence on Campus

In recent years, a great deal of attention has been devoted to family violence. Numerous studies have been done on spouse and child abuse. However, violent behaviour occurs in dating relationships as well. The problem of dating violence has been relatively ignored by sociological research. It should be examined further since the pre-marital relationship is one context in which individuals learn and adopt behaviours that surface later in marriage.

The American sociologist James Makepeace (1981) contends that courtship violence is a "potential mediating link" between violence in one's family of orientation and violence in one's later family of procreation. His provocative study examining dating behaviours at Bemidji State University in Minnesota caused a controversy. Makepeace reported that one-fifth of the 202 respondents had had at least one encounter with dating violence. He concluded by extending these percentages to students across the United States, suggesting the existence of a major hidden social problem.

Sociologist Walter DeKeseredy (1988) did the first recorded Canadian study of courtship violence among university students. His discoveries were based on questionnaires completed by 333 male undergraduates (single or married less than twelve months) attending 1987 summer or fall classes at York University, the University of Guelph, the University of Toronto, and McMaster University. Having broadened Makepeace's (1981) definition of courtship

38c

violence to include what he called "psychological" abuse (insults or swearing, spiteful comments, or threats of physical violence) as well as sexual abuse itself (the threat to secure sexual compliance as well as the actual use of such force), DeKeseredy made the astonishing discovery that more than 70 percent of his respondents admitted to initiating at least <u>one</u> of these forms of abuse in a dating relationship within the previous twelve months. DeKeseredy also learned that male peer support reinforced such courtship violence to a statistically significant extent.

Even more astonishing, a study of dating abuse by Shirley Mercer (1988) among 304 secondary school students (217 female, 87 male) from four metropolitan Toronto high schools not only revealed that approximately 20 percent of the female respondents had experienced one form of physical, verbal, or sexual abuse in a dating relationship, but also indicated that almost 10 percent of the student population sample checked off attitudinal statements that "condoned, excused, or tolerated male abusive behaviour toward women" (19), including 7.8 percent of the females!

[The introduction continues.]

All these studies indicate a problem that is being neglected. The present study's objectives were (a) to gather more information on the extent and nature of premarital violence, (b) to discover some of the reasons for such violence (something not emphasized in other studies), and (c) to discuss some possible interpretations.

Method

Sample

I conducted a survey of 200 students (134 females, 66
males) at a large Canadian university. The sample consisted of students enrolled in an introductory sociology
course. The mean age of the respondents was 19.35 years,
ranging from 18 to 31. Predominantly, most students
(87.8%) resided in campus residences, not at home or in
their own apartments. Moreover, the majority of the sample
(93.5%) were single and not self-supporting.

The Questionnaire

A questionnaire exploring the personal dynamics of
relationships was distributed during regularly scheduled
class. Questions were answered anonymously in a thirty-
minute time period. The survey consisted of three sections: section 1 and section 2 were filled out by all
respondents; section 3 was filled out only by students
currently dating someone (123 of 200 students).
[The explanation of method continues.]

Section 3 required participants to provide information about their current dating relationships. Levels of
stress and frustration, communication between partners,
and patterns of decision making were examined. These variables were expected to influence the amount of violence in
a relationship. The next part of the survey was adopted
from Murray Strauss's Conflict Tactics Scales (1982).
These scales contain 19 items designed to measure conflict
and the means of conflict resolution, including reasoning,
verbal aggression, and actual violence. The final page of

the questionnaire contained general questions on the couple's use of alcohol, sexual activity, and overall satisfaction with the relationship.

Results

The incidence of verbal aggression and threatened and
actual dating violence was examined. A high prevalence of
students, 53 percent (76 of 123 subjects), reported that
they had been the victims of verbal abuse, either being
insulted or sworn at. In addition, 15 percent (18 of 123)
of respondents admitted being threatened with some type of
violence. Low percentages were reported for the various
types of actual physical violence. (See Table 1.)

[The explanation of results continues.]

[Table on a page by itself.]

Table 1

Incidence of Courtship Violence

Type of Violence	Number of Students Reporting	Percentage of Sample
Insulted or swore	62	53.0
Threatened to hit or throw something	17	14.0
Threw something	8	6.6
Pushed, grabbed, or shoved	18	14.9
Slapped	8	6.6
Kicked, bit, or hit with fist	7	6.0
Hit or tried to hit with something	2	1.6
Threatened with a knife or gun	1	0.8
Used a knife or gun	1	0.8

38

Discussion

Violence within premarital relationships has been relatively ignored. The results of the present study indicate that abuse and force do occur in dating relationships. Although the percentages are small, so was the sample. Extending them to the entire campus population would mean significant numbers. For example, if the 6% incidence of being kicked, bitten, or hit with a fist is typical, then 300 students of a 5000-member student body might have experienced this type of violence.

[The discussion continues.]

If the courtship period is characterized by abuse and violence, what accounts for it? The other sections of the survey examined some variables that appear to influence the nature of the relationship. Level of stress and frustration, both within the relationship and in the respondent's life, was one such variable. The communication level between partners, both the frequency of discussion and the frequency of agreement, was also seen to have an influence on the nature of the relationship.

[The discussion continues.]

The method of analysing the data in this study, utilizing frequency distributions, provided a clear overview. However, more tests of significance and correlation need to be done. A closer look at the social and individual variables affecting the relationship is warranted. The courtship period may set the stage for patterns of married life. It merits more attention.

38c

[New page.]

References

Cates, R. L., Rutter, C. H., Karl, J., Linton, M., & Smith, K. (1982). Premarital abuse: A social psychological perspective. <u>Journal of Family Issues</u>, <u>3</u>(1), 79-90.

DeKeseredy, W. S. (1988). <u>Woman abuse in dating relationships: The role of male peer support</u>. Toronto: Canadian Scholars' Press Inc.

Glaser, R., and Rutter, C. H. (Eds.). (1984). Familial violence [Special issue]. <u>Family Relations</u>, <u>33</u>(3).

Laner, M. (1983). Recent increases in dating violence. <u>Social Problems</u>, <u>22</u>, 152-166.

Makepeace, J. M. (1981). Courtship violence among college students. <u>Family Relations</u>, <u>30</u>, 97-102.

Mercer, S. L. (1988). Not a pretty picture: An exploratory study of violence against women in high school dating relationships. <u>Resources for Feminist Research/Documentation sur la recherche féministe</u>, <u>17</u>(2), 5-23.

Socko performance on campus. (1981, June 7). <u>Time</u>, 66-67.

Strauss, M. L. (1982). <u>Conflict tactics scales</u>. New York: Sociological Tests.

38d Writing in the natural and applied sciences

The natural and applied sciences include biology, chemistry, physics, mathematics, engineering, computer science, and their branches. Their purpose is to understand natural and technological phenomena. (A *phenomenon* is a fact or event that can be known by the senses.) Scientists conduct experiments and write to explain the step-by-step processes in their methods of inquiry and discovery.

1   Methods and evidence in the sciences

Scientists investigate phenomena by the **scientific method**, a process of continual testing and refinement. (See below.) Scientific evidence is almost always quantitative—that is, it consists of numerical data obtained from the measurement of phenomena. These data are called **empirical** (from a Greek word for "experience"): they result from observation and experience, generally in a controlled laboratory setting but also (as sometimes in astronomy or biology) in the natural world. Often the empirical evidence for scientific writing comes from library research into other people's reports of their investigations. Surveys of known data or existing literature are common in scientific writing.

THE SCIENTIFIC METHOD

1. Observe carefully. Accurately note all details of the phenomenon being researched.
2. Ask questions about the observations.
3. Formulate a **hypothesis**, or preliminary generalization, that explains the observed facts.
4. Test the hypothesis with additional observation or controlled experiments.
5. If the hypothesis proves accurate, formulate a **theory**, or unified model, that explains *why*. If the hypothesis is disproved, revise it or start anew.

---

2   Assignments in the sciences

No matter what your assignment, you will be expected to document and explain your evidence carefully so that anyone reading can check your sources and replicate your research. It is important for your reader to know the context of your research—both the previous experimentation and research on your particular subject (acknowledged in the survey of the literature) and the physical conditions and other variables surrounding your own work.

38d

Assignments in the natural and applied sciences include a **summary**, which distils the essence of a research article in brief, concise form; a **critique**, which summarizes and critically evaluates a scientific report; a **laboratory report**, which explains the procedure and results of an experiment conducted by the writer; a **research report**, which reports on the experimental research of other scientists and reports the writer's own methods, findings, and conclusions; and a **research proposal**, which reviews the relevant literature and explains a plan for further research. Summary is discussed at length in 4a (p. 131). A laboratory report in biology begins on page 703.

A laboratory report has four or five major sections:

1. *Abstract:* a summary of the report. (See p. 703.)
2. *Introduction* or *Objective:* a review of why the study was undertaken, a summary of the background of the study, and a statement of the problem being studied.
3. *Method* or *Procedure:* a detailed explanation of how the study was conducted, including any statistical analysis.
4. *Results:* an explanation of the major findings (including unexpected results) and a summary of the data presented in graphs and tables.
5. *Discussion:* an interpretation of the results and an explanation of how they relate to the goals of the experiment. This section also describes new hypotheses that might be tested as a result of the experiment. If the section is brief, it may be combined with the previous section in a single section of *Conclusions*.

In addition, laboratory or research reports may include a list of references (if other sources were consulted). They almost always include tables and figures (graphs and charts) containing the data from the research (see p. 704).

3 Tools and language in the sciences

Keeping a journal or notebook can help you reflect on and rethink your ideas for writing, pose and answer questions, or explore your changing attitudes about a subject. In the sciences, a **lab notebook** or **scientific journal** is almost indispensable for accurately recording the empirical data from observations and experiments. Use such a notebook or journal for the following purposes:

1. Record observations from reading, from class, or from the lab.
2. Ask questions and refine hypotheses.
3. Record procedures.
4. Record results.
5. Keep an ongoing record of ideas and findings and how they change as data accumulate.
6. Sequence and organize your material as you compile your findings and write your report.

38d

When writing in your notebook, try to observe as well the special conventions of language in the sciences. The main convention is the use of objective language that removes the writer as a character in the situation and events being explained, except as the impersonal agent of change, the experimenter. Accordingly, scientists rarely use *I* in their reports and evaluations, and they often resort to the passive voice of verbs, as in *The mixture <u>was</u> then <u>subjected</u> to centrifugal force.* This conscious objectivity focusses attention (including the writer's) on the empirical data and what they show. It discourages the writer from, say, ascribing motives and will to animals and plants. For instance, instead of asserting that the sea tortoise *evolved* its hard shell *to protect* its body, a scientist would write only what could be observed: that the hard shell *covers and thus protects* the tortoise's body.

As in the social sciences, each discipline in the natural and applied sciences has a specialized vocabulary that permits precise, accurate, and efficient communication. Some of these terms, such as *pressure* in physics, have different meanings in the common language and must be handled carefully in science writing. Others, such as *enthalpy* in chemistry, have no meanings in the common language and must simply be learned and used correctly.

4 Documentation and format in the sciences

Within the natural and applied sciences, the scholars and teachers of each discipline use a slightly different style of documentation and manuscript format. Following are some of the style guides most often consulted:

> American Chemical Society. *Handbook for Authors of Papers in American Chemical Society Publications*. 1978.
> American Institute of Physics. *Style Manual for Guidance in the Preparation of Papers*. 3rd ed. 1978.
> American Mathematical Society. *A Manual for Authors of Mathematical Papers*. 8th ed. 1980.
> Council of Biology Editors. *CBE Style Manual: A Guide for Authors, Editors, and Publishers in the Biological Sciences*. 5th ed. 1983.

Documentation

Some documentation styles in the sciences closely resemble other styles discussed in this chapter and Chapter 36: the APA system of in-text parenthetical citations and a separate reference list (see pp. 682–89) and the system of in-text raised numerals referring to separate footnotes or endnotes described in the *MLA Handbook* (see pp. 606–616). In a third style (described briefly below), in-text numbers in parentheses or brackets refer to a list of correspondingly numbered references. Obviously, you must ask your instructor's preference for style and consult the appropriate style guide before preparing a final manuscript.

38d

In a style recommended by the Council of Biology Editors (CBE), the list of references (entitled "References") arranges and numbers sources in the order in which they were cited in the text of the paper. For example:

```
1.  Hepburn, P. X.; Tatin, J. M.   Human physiology.   New
    York: Columbia University Press; 1975.

2.  Jonson, P., editor.   Anatomy yearbook.   Los Angeles:
    Anatco; 1987.

3.  Ancino, R.; Carter, K. V.; Elwin, D. J.   Factors con-
    tributing to viral immunity: a review of the research.
    Developmental Biology 30:156-169; 1983.
```

Note that since the sources are arranged in order of citation, they are not in alphabetical order. Also note the key features of the bibliographic formats as outlined below. (Compare these formats with those of the APA, pp. 683–87, which differ especially in punctuation and the handling of titles.)

1. Each entry begins a new line and is numbered. The number is followed by a period and two spaces. Subsequent lines of each entry then begin directly under the first word of the first line.
2. Authors' first and middle names are represented by initials.
3. Authors' names are separated by semicolons (references 1 and 3).
4. No titles are underlined or placed in quotation marks.
5. Only in journal titles (reference 3) is any but the first word of a title capitalized. In book and article titles and subtitles, all words after the first word begin with small letters (references 1–3).
6. The name of the publisher is separated from the date of publication by a semicolon (references 1 and 2).
7. No punctuation falls between a journal's title and volume number (reference 3). Page numbers are connected to the volume number with an unspaced colon. The date of publication then follows a semicolon and a space.

When citing sources in the text, use only the numbers from the reference list, plus any page number(s). For example:

```
These forms of immunity have been extensively
researched (3).


Two standard references (1, 2) use this term.
```

38d

```
According to one report (3, p. 160), research into

some forms of viral immunity is almost non-existent.


Hepburn and Tatin (1) do not discuss this project.
```

Manuscript format

As with documentation style, the science disciplines each have their own preferred manuscript formats with subtle differences among them. The CBE format closely resembles that of the APA (see pp. 690–91). Again, ask your instructor for his or her preferences.

Undoubtedly, the most troublesome aspects of manuscript preparation in the sciences are equations or formulas and illustrations (tables and figures). When typing equations or formulas, be careful to reproduce alignments, indentions, underlining, and characters accurately. If your typewriter or word processor lacks special characters, write them in by hand. (Stationery and art-supply stores also have sheets of transfer-type special characters in different sizes that can be applied to your manuscript by rubbing.)

Because you will be expected to share your data with your readers, most of your writing for the sciences is likely to require illustrations to present the data in concise, readable form. Tables usually summarize raw data (see p. 704 for an example), whereas figures (mainly charts and graphs) recast the data to show noteworthy comparisons or changes. Follow these guidelines in preparing and positioning illustrations:

1. Give each illustration a clear label. Number tables and figures separately (Table 1, Table 2, etc.; Figure 1, Figure 2, etc.).
2. Give each illustration a clear title so that readers know what to look for in it. (Generally, a table's label and title are placed above the illustration, whereas a figure's label and title are placed under the illustration.)
3. Provide clear labels for all the parts of illustrations, such as columns in a table and bars in a bar graph. Unless your instructor specifically requests abbreviations, avoid them in the interest of clarity.
4. If you borrow the data or the whole illustration from another source, provide a source note under the illustration. For instance:

```
Source: Ann Menaker. Spectroscopy of plasmas. New

York: Van Nostrand, 1981.
```

5. Refer to each illustration ("See Figure 6") at the point(s) in the text where readers will benefit by consulting it.

38d

6. If your paper includes many illustrations, collect them at the end of the paper, after the reference list. If it includes only a few illustrations, place each one on a page by itself immediately after the page that refers to it.

5 A sample science paper

The following excerpts from a laboratory report in genetics, a branch of biology, illustrate many of the features described in the preceding pages. Some elements, such as page borders and identifiers have been omitted, but otherwise the format illustrates that recommended by the Council of Biology Editors (CBE). (The paper is based entirely on the student's own laboratory experiment and thus does not include text citations or a reference list.)

Excerpts from a laboratory report (biology)

[Title page: centre title vertically and horizontally.]

```
                    Demonstration:

              Genetic Engineering




                              Lynn Treacy
                              Genetics
                              Dr. Smith
                              March 29, 1988
```

[New page.]

```
                      Abstract

     The transfer of the conjugative plasmid for chlora-

phenicol resistance from the donor, E. coli HT-99, to a

suitable recipient, E. coli J-53R, was demonstrated using

in vitro techniques.
```

[New page.]

```
          Demonstration: Genetic Engineering

                      Objective

     The purpose of this experiment was to illustrate the

basic goal of genetic engineering through a demonstra-
```

38d

tion/experiment. In this experiment, a donor, E. coli HT-99, which is resistant to chloraphenicol and sensitive to rifampicin, and a host cell, E. coli J-53R, which is resistant to rifampicin and sensitive to chloraphenicol, were mated. The donor cell contained a chimera, a plasmid of the E. coli donor that had the gene for resistance to the antibody, chloraphenicol, that would serve as a marker for the detection of a successful conjugation.

Procedure

The results of the experiment were gathered from the observance of growth or of lack of growth of the donor, host, and suspected exconjugant on nutrient agar plates containing (1) rifampicin; (2) chloraphenicol; and (3) both rifampicin and chloraphenicol.

[The explanation of procedure continues.]

[Table on a page by itself.]

Table 1. Growth (+) or Non-Growth (−) of Donor, Host, and Exconjugant

| Organism | Growth on Plates Containing | | |
	Rifampicin	Chloraphenicol	Rifampicin and Chloraphenicol
Donor	−	+	−
Host	+	−	−
Exconjugant, 4h	NA	NA	−
Exconjugant, 18h	NA	NA	+

NA = not applicable because not tested for.

38d

Conclusions

The HT-99 cells will grow in the presence of chloraphenicol, because they contain the genes to make them resistant to chloraphenicol, whereas they will not grow in the presence of rifampicin (either alone or containing chloraphenicol). After successful conjugation the exconjugant cells should grow on both plates since the cells possess the genes coding for resistance to rifampicin, and they also have the genes for resistance to chloraphenicol contained in a plasmid. The first test of the exconjugant was negative because the constant agitation of the shaker did not allow conjugation to occur (interrupted the mating between the cells.) After the mixture sat overnight, the exconjugant cells were found, since successful conjugation had occurred.

[The conclusions continue.]

Successful conjugation is easily detected by the use of nutrient agar plates containing the antibiotics chloraphenicol and rifampicin; the simple observation of growth and of no growth is all that is needed to signal a successful or unsuccessful mating.

38d

PART IX

Practical Writing

CHAPTER 39

Essay Examinations

In writing an essay for an examination, you summarize or analyse a topic, usually in several paragraphs or more and usually within a time limit. An essay question not only tests your knowledge of a subject (as short-answer and objective questions do) but also tests your control and synthesis of that knowledge and helps you see it in a new way (as other kinds of questions usually cannot do).

39a Preparing for an essay examination

Taking lecture notes, thoughtfully reading the assigned texts or articles, and reviewing regularly will help you prepare for any kind of examination. In addition, for an essay examination you can practise synthesizing what you know by creating summaries that help you recast others' ideas in your own words and extract the meaning from notes and texts (see the extensive discussion of summary in 4a). And you can prepare outlines that reorganize the course material. For instance, in a business course you could evaluate the advantages and disadvantages of several approaches to management. In a short-story course you could look for a theme running through all the stories you have read by a certain author or from a certain period. In a psychology course you could contrast various theorists' views of what causes a disorder like schizophrenia. Any one of these is a likely topic for an essay question. Thinking of such categories not only can help you anticipate the kinds of questions you may be asked but also can increase your mastery of the material.

39b   Planning your time and your answer

When you first look at your examination, always read it all the way through at least once before you start answering any questions. As you scan the examination, determine which questions seem most important, which ones are going to be most difficult for you, and approximately how much time you'll need for each question. (Your instructor may help by assigning a point value to each question as a guide to its importance or by suggesting an amount of time for you to spend on each question.) You will want to provide your best answer for every question, so this initial planning is important.

To avoid straying from an essay question or answering only part of it, read it at least twice. Examine the words and consider their implications. Look especially for words like *describe*, *define*, *explain*, *summarize*, *analyse*, *evaluate*, and *interpret*, each of which requires a different kind of response. For instance, the instruction *Define dyslexia and compare and contrast it with two other learning disabilities* contains important clues for how an essay should be written. *Define dyslexia* tells you to specify the meaning of the term. A description of how children with dyslexia feel about their disability, however well done, would be irrelevant. Instead, you should say what dyslexia is—a perceptual impairment causing a reader to reverse or scramble letters—and extend the definition by providing distinctive characteristics, ways the impairment seems to work, examples of its effects, and so on. The words *compare and contrast it with two other learning disabilities* tell you to analyse not only its similarities to but also its differences from the other disabilities. Answering this part of the question thus involves thinking of categories for comparison, such as causes, treatments, frequency of occurrence, and severity of effect. An essay that described only similarities or only differences would not answer the question completely.

After you're sure you understand the question, make a brief outline of the main ideas you want to include in your essay. Use the back of the test sheet or exam booklet for scratch paper. Write a brief thesis sentence for your essay that responds directly to the question and represents your view of the topic. (If you are unsure of how to write a thesis sentence, see 1g.) Include key phrases that you can expand with supporting evidence for your view. This stage is much like the planning of an essay or a research paper. Though you don't have as much time to refine and rearrange your ideas, planning will help make your essay unified, coherent, well supported, and concise.

|39c| Starting the essay

A well-constructed thesis sentence will contribute much to an examination essay. Drawing on the brief thesis you devised during planning, you can begin an essay effectively by stating your thesis immediately and including in it an overview of the rest of your essay. Such a capsule version of your answer tells your reader (and grader) generally how much command you have and also how you plan to develop your answer. It also gets you off to a good start.

The opening statement should address the question directly and exactly. The following thesis sentence, in response to the question below, does *not* meet these criteria.

QUESTION

Given humans' natural and historical curiosity about themselves, why did a scientific discipline of anthropology not arise until the twentieth century? Explain, citing specific details.

TENTATIVE THESIS SENTENCE

The discipline of anthropology, the study of humans, actually began in the early nineteenth century and was strengthened by the Darwinian revolution, but the discipline did not begin to take shape until people like Franz Boas and Alfred Kroeber began doing scientific research among non-industrialized cultures.

This tentative thesis sentence says nothing about *why* anthropology did not arise as a scientific discipline until the twentieth century. Instead, it supplies an unspecific (and unrequested) definition of anthropology, vaguely reasserts the truth implied by the question, and adds irrelevant details about the history of anthropology. The following thesis sentence—revised to address the question directly, to state the writer's view, and to preview the essay—begins the answer more effectively.

REVISED THESIS SENTENCE

Anthropology did not emerge as a scientific discipline until the twentieth century because nineteenth-century Westerners' limited contact with remote peoples and the corresponding failure to see those other people as human combined to overcome natural curiosity and to prevent objective study of different cultures.

This thesis sentence specifies the writer's view of the two main causes of the slow emergence of anthropology—limited contact with remote peoples and, related to that, a narrow definition of humanity—that she will analyse in her essay.

39d Developing the essay

You develop your essay by supporting your thesis sentence with sound generalizations, which you support in turn with *specific* evidence. (See 4e). Avoid filling out your essay by repetition. Avoid substituting purely subjective feelings about the topic for real analysis of it. (It may help to abolish the word *I* from your essay.)

The student answering the anthropology question must show that contact between Western and non-Western cultures was limited and must specify how the limitations dulled curiosity, prevented objective study, and hampered the development of anthropology. She also needs to demonstrate how a consequently narrow definition of humanity had the same results. And she *must* support her assertions with concrete evidence. For instance, she might cite nineteenth-century writings that illustrate feelings of superiority toward distant peoples.

The student would not be providing effective evidence if she introduced unsupported generalizations or substituted her subjective feelings for an objective analysis of the problem. For instance, a blanket statement that all nineteenth-century Westerners were narrow-minded or a paragraph condemning their narrowness would only pad the essay.

39e Rereading the essay

The time limit on an essay examination does not allow for the careful rethinking and revision you would give an essay or research paper. You need to write clearly and concisely the first time. If you do have a few minutes after you have finished the entire exam, reread the essay (or essays) to correct illegible passages, misspellings, grammatical mistakes, and accidental omissions. Verify that your thesis is accurate—that it does, in fact, introduce what you ended up writing about. Check to ensure that you have supported all your generalizations thoroughly. Cross out irrelevant ideas and details, and add any information that now seems important. (Write on another page, if necessary, keying the addition to the page on which it belongs.)

CHAPTER 40

Business Writing

When you write a letter to request information, to complain about a product or bill, or to apply for a job, or when you write a memo or report to someone you work with, you are addressing busy people who want to see quickly why you are writing and how they should respond to you. A wordy, incoherent letter or memo full of errors in grammar and spelling may prevent you from getting what you want, either because the reader cannot understand your wish or because you present yourself so poorly. In business writing, state your purpose at the very start. Be straightforward, clear, objective, and courteous, and don't hesitate to be insistent if the situation warrants it. Observe conventions of grammar and usage, for these not only make your writing clear but also impress a reader with your care.

40a Writing business letters and job applications

1 Using a standard form

Business correspondence customarily adheres to one of several acceptable forms. Use either unlined white paper measuring at least 14 cm x 21.5 cm (5½″ x 8½″) or what is called letterhead stationery with your address printed at the top of the sheet. Type the letter if possible, single-spaced, on only one side of a sheet. Follow a standard form for each of the letter's parts. (The form described in this section and illustrated on the facing page is one common model.)

The return-address heading of the letter gives your address (but not your name) and the date. (If you're using letterhead stationery,

Return address heading —
┌ 124 Lake Wapta Rise S.E.
│ Calgary, AB
│ T2J 2N1
└ December 29, 1989

Mrs. Gerda Fandrich ┐
Circulation Supervisor
Sporting Life   Inside address
1320 Saginaw Crescent
Mississauga, ON
L5H 1X5 ┘

Dear Mrs. Fandrich: ⏋——— Salutation

Thank you for your letter of December 20,
which notifies me that Sporting Life will
resume my subscription after stopping it in
error after I had received the July issue.
Since I missed at least five months' issues
because of the magazine's error, I expected my
subscription to be extended for five months
after it would have lapsed--that is, through
June 1990. Instead, you tell me that the magazine will send me the back issues that it
failed to send and that the January issue
(which I have not received) will complete my
current subscription.

Body

I have no interest in receiving the back
issues of Sporting Life because the magazine
is not useful or interesting unless it is current. Since Sporting Life erred in stopping my
subscription prematurely, I still expect it to
make up the difference on the other end of my
subscription.

Unless I hear otherwise from you, I will count
on your extending my subscription at least
through June 1990. If Sporting Life cannot
compensate for its error in this way, I will
cancel my subscription and request a refund.

Close ——— Sincerely,

Signature ——— *Sharon A. Hoskyn*

Sharon A. Hoskyn

you need add only the date.) Align the lines of the heading on the left, and place the whole heading on the right of the page, allowing enough space above it to centre the entire letter vertically on the page. The postal code should be placed on a separate line.

The inside address shows the name, title, and complete address of the person you are writing to, just as this information will appear on the envelope. Begin the address a few lines below the heading at the left side of the page.

The salutation greets the addressee. Place it two lines below the address and two lines above the body of the letter. Always follow it with a colon, not a comma or dash. If you are not addressing a particular person, use a general salutation such as *Dear Sir or Madam* or *Dear Smythe Shoes* (the company name). Use *Ms.* as the title for a woman when she has no other title, when you don't know how she prefers to be addressed, or when you know that she prefers to be addressed as *Ms.* If you know a woman prefers to be addressed as *Mrs.* or *Miss*, use the appropriate title.

The body of the letter, containing its substance, begins at the left margin. You may either indent paragraphs, or you may place an extra line of space between them so that they are readily visible, starting each paragraph at the left margin.

The letter's close begins two lines below the last line of the body and aligns at the left with the heading at the top of the page. Typical closes include *Yours truly* and *Sincerely*. Only the first word is capitalized, and the close is followed by a comma.

The signature of a business letter has two parts: a typed one, four lines below the close, and a handwritten one filling in the space. The signature should consist only of your name, as you sign cheques and school documents.

Below the signature, at the left margin, you may want to include additional information such as *Enc.* (something is enclosed with the letter); *c: Margaret Newton* (a copy is being sent to the person named); or *CHC/enp* (the initials of the author/the initials of the typist).

The envelope for the letter (see facing page) should show your name and address in the upper left corner and the addressee's name, title, and address in the centre. Use an envelope that is the same width as your stationery and about a third the height. Fold the letter horizontally, in thirds.

2 Writing requests and complaints

Letters requesting something—for instance, a pamphlet, information about a product, a T-shirt advertised in a magazine—must be specific and accurate about the item you are requesting. The letter

```
Sharon A. Hoskyn
124 Lake Wapta Rise S.E.
Calgary, AB
T2J 2N1


                    Mrs. Gerda Fandrich
                    Circulation Supervisor
                    Sporting Life
                    1320 Saginaw Cres.
                    Mississauga, ON
                    L5H 1X5
```

40a

should describe the item completely and, if applicable, include a copy or description of the advertisement or other source that prompted your request.

Letters complaining about a product or a service (such as a wrong billing from the telephone company) should be written in a reasonable but firm tone. (See the sample letter on p. 713.) Assume that the addressee is willing to resolve the problem when he or she has the relevant information. In the first sentence of the letter, state what you are writing about. Then provide as much background as needed, including any relevant details from past correspondence (as in the sample letter). Describe exactly what you see as the problem, sticking to facts and avoiding discourses on the company's social responsibility or your low opinion of its management. In the clearest possible words and sentences, proceed directly from one point to the next without repeating yourself. Always include your opinion of how the problem can be solved. Many companies are required by law to establish a specific procedure for complaints about products and services. If you know of such a procedure, be sure to follow it.

3   Writing a job application and résumé

In writing to apply for a job or to request a job interview, you should announce at the outset what job you desire and how you heard about it. (See the sample letter on the next page.) Then summarize your qualifications for the job, including facts about your education and employment history. Include only the relevant facts, mentioning that additional information appears in an accompanying résumé. Include any special reason you have for applying, such as a specific career goal. At the end of the letter, mention that you are available for an interview at the convenience of the addressee, or specify when you will be available (for instance, when your current job or classes leave you free, or when you could travel to the employer's city).

40a

The résumé that you enclose with your letter of application should contain your education, your employment history, and information about how to obtain your references. (See the sample résumé on the facing page.) In preparing your résumé, you may wish to

---

3820 Harwood Crescent
Abbotsford, BC
V2S 6W8
March 15, 1989

Mr. David Meyer
Human Resources Manager
The Vancouver Sun
2250 Granville Street
Vancouver, BC
V6H 3G2

Dear Sir or Madam:

In response to your posting in the English department of Fraser Valley College, I am applying for the summer job of part-time editorial assistant for the Vancouver Sun.

I am now enrolled at Fraser Valley College as a second-year student, with a dual major in English literature and journalism. As the enclosed résumé shows, I have worked on the college newspaper for nearly two years. I have published articles in my hometown newspaper, and I worked a summer there as a copy aid. My goal is a career in journalism. I believe my educational background and my work experience qualify me for the opening you have.

I am available for an interview at any time and would be happy to show samples of my newspaper work. My telephone number is 852-2379. Messages can be left for me at that number.

Sincerely,

D. Roy Daly

D. Roy Daly

Enc.

RÉSUMÉ

D. Roy Daly
3820 Harwood Crescent
Abbotsford, BC
V2S 6W8
(604) 852-2379

Position desired
Part-time editorial assistant

Education
1987 to present
Fraser Valley College
Current standing: Second year
Major: English literature and journalism

1983-87
Mouat Secondary School
Graduated from academic program

Experience
1987 to present
Reporter on the Daily Campus, student news-
    paper of Fraser Valley College.
Responsibilities include writing feature
    stories and sports coverage.

Summer 1988
House painter and free-lance writer. Published
    two articles in the ASM News.

Summer 1987
Copy aid at ASM News. Responsible for copy
    routing. Monitored teleprinter, ran
    errands, assisted reporters.

References

Academic: Placement Office
                   Fraser Valley College
                   Abbotsford, BC
                   V2S 4N2

Employment: Ms. Janice Janzen
                   ASM News
                   34375 Cyril St.
                   Abbotsford, BC
                   V2S 2H5

Personal: Mr. Gary Hanik
                   2367 Broadway St.
                   Clearbrook, BC
                   V2T 3G6

consult one of the many books devoted to application letters, résumés, and other elements of a job search. Three helpful guides are Richard N. Bolles, *What Color Is Your Parachute? A Practical Manual for Job-Hunters and Career Changers* (1988), Catherine V. Davison and L. Glen Tippett (Employment Immigration Canada), *A Job Search Guide* (1977), and Tom Jackson, *The Perfect Résumé* (1981).

40b Writing business memos

Unlike business letters, which address people in other organizations, business memorandums (memos, for short) address people within the same organization. A memo can be quite long, but more often it reports briefly and directly on a very specific topic: an answer to a question, a progress report, an evaluation. Both the form and the structure of a memo are designed to get to the point and dispose of it quickly.

The memo has no return address, inside address, salutation, or close. Instead, as shown in the sample memo on the facing page, the heading typically consists of the date, the addressee's name, the writer's name, and a subject description or title. (If you are sending copies of the memo to someone besides the addressee, give his or her name after *c*, meaning "copy," as shown in the sample memo. Type the body of the memo as you would the body of a business letter: single-spaced, and either double-spaced between paragraphs with no paragraph indentions, or single-spaced between paragraphs, indenting the paragraphs. Never sign a business memo, though you may initial your name in the heading.

Immerse your reader in your subject at the very beginning of the memo. State your reason for writing in the first sentence, but do not waste words with expressions like "The purpose of this memo is. . . . " Devote the first paragraph to a succinct presentation of your answer, conclusion, or evaluation. In the rest of the memo explain how you arrived at your answer, the facts on which you base your conclusion, and your method of evaluation. The paragraphs may be numbered so that the main divisions of your message are easy to see.

A business memo can be more informal in tone than a business letter, particularly if you know the addressee; but it should not be wordy. Use technical terms if your reader will understand them, but otherwise keep your language simple and use short sentences. Provide only the information that your reader needs to know.

The sample memo from a sales representative to her district manager, illustrates these guidelines. Notice especially the form of the memo, the writer's immediate statement of her purpose, the clear structure provided by the three numbered paragraphs, and the direct tone of the whole.

December 20, 1989

To: Chuck Tufts
c: Paul Forrest
From: Becky Gough
Subject: 1989 sales of Quick Wax in territory 12

Since it was introduced in January of this
year, Quick Wax has been unsuccessful in my
territory and has not affected sales of our
Easy Shine. Discussions with customers and my
own analysis of Quick Wax suggest three reasons for its failure to compete with our
product.

1. Quick Wax has not received the promotion
    necessary for a new product. Advertising--
    primarily on radio--has been sporadic
    and has not developed a clear, consistent
    image for the product. In addition, the
    Quick Wax sales rep in this territory is
    new and inexperienced; he is not known to
    customers, and his sales pitch (which I
    once overheard) is weak. As far as I can
    tell, his efforts are not supported by
    phone calls or mailings from his home
    office.

2. When Quick Wax does make it to the store
    shelves, buyers do not choose it over our
    product. Though priced competitively with
    our product, Quick Wax is poorly pack-
    aged. The container seems smaller than
    ours, though in fact it holds the same
    225 g. The lettering on the Quick Wax
    package (red on blue) is difficult to
    read, in contrast to the white-on-green
    lettering on our package.

3. Our special-purchase offers and my
    increased efforts to serve existing cus-
    tomers have had the intended effect of
    keeping customers satisfied with our
    product and reducing their inclination to
    stock something new.

Preparing a Manuscript

A legible, consistent, and attractive manuscript is a service to readers because it makes reading easier. This appendix discusses the materials necessary for manuscript preparation and some conventions of format adapted from the *MLA Handbook*, 3rd. ed. (Most of these guidelines are standard, but your instructor may request that you follow different conventions in some matters.)

A1 Choosing the appropriate materials

a Handwritten papers

For handwritten papers, you can use regular white paper, 21.5 cm × 28 cm (8½″ × 11″), with horizontal lines spaced between ½ cm and 1 cm apart. Don't use paper torn from a notebook, unlined paper, paper with narrow lines, coloured paper, or paper other than 21.5 cm × 28 cm (such as legal or stenographer's pads). Use the same type of paper throughout a project. Write on only one side of a sheet.

Use black or blue ink, not pencil. If possible, use an ink eraser or eradicator to correct mistakes. If you must cross out material, draw a single line through it. Don't scribble over or black out a mistake, and don't write corrections on top of mistakes.

b Typewritten papers

For typewritten papers, use 21.5 cm × 28 cm white bond paper of sixteen- or twenty-pound weight. Some instructors also accept the same size surface-coated bond paper (called "erasable" or "corrasable"), but ink smears easily on such paper. Onionskin sheets, paper torn from notebooks, coloured paper, and paper smaller or larger than 21.5 cm × 28 cm are unacceptable. Use the same type of paper throughout a project. Type on only one side of a sheet.

Use a black ribbon that is fresh enough to make a dark impression, and make sure the keys of the typewriter are clean. To avoid smudging the page when correcting mistakes, use a liquid correction fluid or a correction tape. Don't use hyphens or *x*'s to cross out mistakes, and don't type corrections (strikeovers) on top of mistakes.

c Papers produced on a word processor

Two kinds of printers are used with most computerized word processors. Letter-quality printers (including daisywheel and laser printers), like a regular typewriter, produce characters with solid lines. Dot-matrix printers form characters out of tiny dots, and the legibility of their type varies considerably. If you use a word processor with a dot-matrix printer, make sure the dots are close enough together to produce legible characters. In addition, make sure the tails on letters such as *j*, *p*, and *y* descend below the line of type, as they do in the typeface used here. Resist the temptation to use any of the unusual type sizes or styles that your printer may be capable of producing, for such embellishments can clutter your manuscript and distract readers from what you are saying. Before you submit a paper printed on a dot-matrix printer, show your instructor a sample of the type to be sure it is acceptable.

Be sure the printer ribbon is fresh so that it leaves a dark impression. Use standard-sized 21.5 cm × 28 cm (8½″ × 11″) white bond paper of sixteen- or twenty-pound weight, not the lightweight green-striped paper associated with computer printouts. If you use continuous paper folded like a fan at perforations, it will also come with a row of holes along each side for feeding the paper into the printer. Before submitting your paper, remove these strips of holes along the perforations and separate the pages at the folds.

A2 Following a standard format

A consistent physical format makes the script, margins, paging, title, and identification visually effective and avoids the illegibility and the confusion of inconsistencies. See the sample research papers in Chapter 37 (pp. 618 and 649) for examples of the items that are discussed in this section. (For the special formats of source citations and a list of works cited, which are not discussed here, see 36h and 36i.)

a Script

Handwritten script should be reasonably uniform and clear. Be sure letters are easily distinguishable. Cross all *t*'s; dot all *i*'s with dots, not circles; form the loops of letters carefully. Make capital letters and small letters clearly different. Space consistently between words and between sentences. If your handwriting is difficult to read, submit a typed paper if possible. If you don't have access to a typewriter and your handwriting is illegible or unusual in size, decoration, or slant, make it more legible or conventional when writing the final manuscript. Indent the first line of every paragraph about 2.5 cm (1"). Write on every line or every other line as specified by your instructor.

In script produced on a typewriter or word processor, indent the first line of every paragraph five spaces and double-space throughout. Leave one space between words. Type punctuation as indicated in the box on the facing page. Use handwriting to make any symbols that are not on your keyboard, leaving three or four spaces and then inserting the symbol in ink.

For both typed and handwritten script, try to avoid breaking words at the ends of lines. If you must break a word, follow the guidelines provided in Chapter 30. Don't start a line with any mark of punctuation other than a dash, an opening parenthesis, an opening quotation mark, or an ellipsis mark when one of these is called for.

Set off quotations of more than four lines of prose or three lines of poetry; two- or three-line poetry quotations may be set off or placed in the text (see 24c). In handwritten copy, indent all lines of a displayed quotation 2.5 cm from the left margin. In typewritten copy, indent all lines ten spaces. Double-space above and below each quotation, and double-space the quotation itself. (See 24c.)

b   Margins

Use 2.5-cm margins on all sides of each page. The top margin will contain the page number, as discussed next. If the right margin is uneven, it should be no narrower than 2.5 cm. If you have a word processor or electronic typewriter that produces an even (or justified) right margin, use the feature only if it does not leave wide spaces between words and thus interfere with readability. When using a word processor, be sure to instruct the computer to set appropriate margins. Don't let the lines of type run across the perforations on continuous fanfold paper.

c   Paging

Whether or not you provide a separate title page, begin numbering your paper on the first text page, and number consecutively through the end. Use Arabic numerals (1, 2, 3), and do not add periods, parentheses, hyphens, or the abbreviation "p." However, for every page after the first, place your last name before the page

FORMING AND SPACING PUNCTUATION

ONE SPACE AFTER

Comma	dog, and
Semicolon	dog; and
Colon	dog: its
Apostrophe ending word	dogs' toys
Closing quotation mark	
Double	"dog" and
Single	'dog' and (use apostrophe)
Closing parenthesis	(dog) and
Closing bracket	[dog] and (or leave space and handwrite: ⌈dog⌉)

TWO SPACES AFTER

Sentence period	dog. The
Question mark	dog? The
Exclamation point	dog! The (or type an apostrophe over a period)

NO SPACE EITHER SIDE

Dash (two hyphens)	dog--its
Hyphen	one-half
Apostrophe within word	dog's

ONE SPACE BEFORE AND AFTER

Ellipsis mark within sentence	dog . . . in

EXCEPTIONS

Two spaces after closing quotation mark, parenthesis, or bracket after the end of a sentence:

   dog."   The
   dog.)   The
   dog.]   The

When an ellipsis mark ends a sentence, one space after the sentence period and two spaces after the ellipsis mark:

   dog. . . .   The

No space between two or more adjacent punctuation marks:

   "Who knows the word 'anoxia'?"
   (The dog finally came home.)

ms
A2

number in case the pages become separated after you submit your paper. (See p. 619 for an example.) Align the page number with the right margin, and position it about 1.5 cm (½″) from the top of the page, at least two lines above the first line of text.

d Title and identification

If you do not use a separate title page for an essay, provide your name and the date, plus any other information requested by your instructor, on the first text page. Place this identification 2.5 cm (1″) from the top of the page, aligned with the left margin and double-spaced. Double-space again, and centre the title. Don't underline the title or place quotation marks around it, and capitalize the words in the title according to the guidelines in 26b. Double-space between the title and the first line of text. (See p. 649 for an example of this format.)

For a research paper, your instructor may ask you to provide a separate title page. If so, follow the guidelines and example on pages 618 and 640. On page 1 of the paper repeat the title, centred 2.5 cm from the top of the page, and double-space between the title and the first line of text. (See p. 621 for an example.)

A3 Proofreading, correcting, and submitting the final manuscript

Proofread each page of your paper carefully, concentrating on spelling, punctuation, mechanics, grammar, and manuscript format. (See 2d for proofreading tips and a proofreading exercise.) If a page has several errors, retype or rewrite the page. If it has one or two errors and you can't eradicate them, correct them in ink. Draw a single line through a word you want to delete. Don't try to correct a misspelled word without crossing out and rewriting the whole word. To replace a word or mark of punctuation, draw a line through the item, place a caret (∧) underneath it, and write the new word or mark in the space above the old one. To add words or marks of punctuation, place a caret underneath the line at the point where you wish to insert the word or mark; then centre the word or mark over the caret in the space above the line.

```
                                      organisms
    An ecosystem is a community of  organisms  interacting
                                            ∧
                           the
    with each other and with ∧ environment.
```

If you have to add more words than will fit between the lines of text, rewrite or retype the page.

When you submit your final paper, be sure the pages will stay together when the paper is shuffled in with others. Depending on the wishes of your instructor, you may fold the paper in half lengthwise, paperclip or staple the pages in the upper left corner, or place the paper in a special binder.

APPENDIX B

Writing with a Word Processor

Writing with a word processor can save time and make writing easier. The advantage of word processing is that you can perform such operations as adding to notes, rearranging outlines, and rewriting first drafts without having to cut pages apart or rekey entire pages. The machine will not think for you, but it may leave you more time for the important work of thinking, exploring ideas, focussing and organizing material, and improving content and clarity. This appendix explains how you can incorporate a word processor into your writing process, following the stages of development, drafting, and revising discussed in Chapters 1 and 2.

Using a word processor does not require an understanding of computers or expert keying skills. All it takes is a little perseverance and a few hours of practice. If you do not have your own word processor, find out what's available at your school since many academic institutions have computers available for student use. When you begin using a word processor, carefully read the system's **documentation**—the materials that explain the system, such as a user's manual, tutorial, and reference manual. Study the keyboard carefully, and make a list of the basic keystrokes you need to perform important commands, such as inserting, deleting, saving, and printing text. Be adventurous: experiment with commands, and learn by trial and error. Your play will not hurt the machine, and it will help you.

You may have heard of writers losing all their work because their word processor somehow failed or "crashed." It is possible to lose text accidentally, but a few precautions will prevent permanent loss of your work. These are spelled out in the box on the next page.

B1

TIPS FOR SUCCESSFUL WORD PROCESSING

1. Save your work frequently by using the **save** or **file** command. Then your text will be permanently stored—usually on a magnetic disk that you can remove from the computer for safekeeping.
2. Think of each computer disk as a separate file drawer containing electronic copies of your papers. Label each paper with its own **file** or **document name** for easy retrieval.
3. Make a **back-up** or duplicate disk of your work at the end of each word-processing session as insurance against the loss or damage of your working disk.
4. Keep your disks in dust covers, and store them safely away from heat, cold, or sources of magnetism such as the computer itself or a stereo or television.
5. Regularly print paper copies of your work. They serve as second back-up copies and, more important, they give you something to work on when you revise and edit.

B1   Using a word processor for development

All word processors can aid the initial steps of the writing process (see Chapter 1). You can generate ideas on the computer, expand and reorganize them, and then transfer usable material directly into your draft or revision.

a   Finding a topic and generating ideas

A word processor is an excellent medium for freewriting (see 1b-5 and 1d-1). Most computer monitors, or screens, have a dial that controls the brightness of the images on the screen. While freewriting, you can turn the brightness all the way down so that the screen appears blank. The computer will record what you write but keep it from you and thus prevent you from tinkering with your prose. This **invisible writing** can free the mind for very creative results. When you're finished freewriting, simply turn up the brightness control to read what you've written and then save or revise it as you see fit. Later, you can transfer some or all of your freewriting into your draft.

The computer is also useful for listing ideas or brainstorming (see 1d-2). You may actually find that you can generate more ideas faster with a computer than with a pen or a typewriter. When you're finished, delete weak ideas and expand strong ones. As you exhaust your topic, save your list and print it for further consideration. Later, you can develop it further by adding, deleting, and rearranging. You can also freewrite from the list, exploring items that seem promising.

b   Making notes

Keeping an electronic journal is a good way to build a file of ideas. Write and save regular entries, just as you would in a paper journal (see 1b-2). Then you can move blocks of it into another discovery exercise or a draft.

The computer can also help you take notes from your reading or create notes according to your own structure. For example, you can key passages underlined or marked in your reading into the computer—as long as you are careful to protect against plagiarism by using quotation marks and keeping a record of the author, source, and page number(s) (see 36d). When you are ready to do so, you can transfer the best quotations (and the citations for them) into your draft.

To develop your own notes, try using the journalist's questions (see 1d-5) or the questions derived from the patterns of development (1d-6). Key either list of questions into the computer and save it. Then for each writing project, duplicate the list in a new file and insert possible answers. Print out your notes so that you can select material from them for future drafts.

c   Considering audience and organizing ideas

You can create a standard file of questions for considering audience by keying the "Questions About Audience" from page 27 into your computer and saving them. For each assignment, duplicate the file and insert appropriate answers between the questions. Save the answers under a new file name, and print a copy for future reference.

The ease of adding, deleting, and rearranging on a word processor makes it the ideal tool for shaping and organizing material (see 1h). Beginning with just a list of ideas, you can isolate the more general points and then use the computer's tab settings to indent the more specific material. Unusable ideas can be deleted; redundant ideas can be merged. Print out each version of your outline to work on or use as a guide to planning, drafting, or revising. The outline in memory can be called up and revised as needed to reflect changes in your thinking and writing.

Many word processors can display two separate files on the screen at the same time, one on the top of the screen and one on the bottom. (The two slots are sometimes called **windows**.) To organize notes with this feature, start with a blank screen on the top, retrieve a file of notes at the bottom, and transfer selected copy (such as a thesis statement and general ideas) to the top. Or convert an informal outline to a formal one by transferring details from notes at the bottom of the screen to an informal outline at the top, inserting appropriate indentions, numbers, and letters for different levels of generality.

B2 Using a word processor for drafting

Many writers find that a word processor eases the transition from developing ideas to drafting. You can retrieve notes to the screen and rewrite, delete, or insert as needed. You can expand your outline into a draft by composing paragraphs directly under headings, deleting the remnants of the outline and adding transitions as you go along. Or you can freewrite a first draft, starting with a blank screen and letting the words flow until you're ready to consult your notes or outline for new material. If you're borrowing material from other writers, be sure to transfer source information as well as quotations from your notes to your draft so that you don't plagiarize, even accidentally. (The split-screen capability can help with documentation if you write your draft on one half and retrieve quotations and source citations from notes on the other half.)

Whatever your drafting style, take advantage of the word processor's speed and flexibility. Don't stop to correct errors or rewrite—both of which the computer will help you handle easily in a later draft. Put alternative ideas or phrasings in brackets so that you can consider them later without getting sidetracked now. Use an asterisk (*) or some other symbol to mark places where you feel blocked or very uncertain. Later, you can find these places quickly by instructing the computer to search for the symbol. If it helps, use invisible writing just to keep moving through a draft (see p. 726).

Frequently save or file the text you're drafting—at least once every twenty minutes or every few pages and every time you take a break or leave the computer for any reason. When you finish a drafting session, save your work, make a back-up copy on a separate disk, and print a paper copy in case anything happens to your disks. You will need the paper copy for revising and editing.

B3 Using a word processor for revising and editing

The convenience of extensive revision and editing is the greatest advantage of word processing. The machine eliminates the tedious, often messy labour of keying or writing out successive drafts or pieces of drafts. Instead, working on a copy of the most recent draft stored in the computer, you can add, delete, and move words, lines, and whole passages with a few keystrokes. If you want to compare, for example, two different organizations or ways of explaining an important point, you can work on two duplicates of the latest draft, print both, and read them side by side. (A split-screen word processor allows this function on the screen as long as the passages are fairly short.)

Like most writers, you may find that you revise and edit more on a word processor than you do on a typewriter or in handwriting. It's important, though, that you not let the ease of revision lure you into obsessive rewriting—a kind of wheel-spinning in which changes cease to have a marked effect on meaning or clarity and may in fact sap the writing of energy. In addition, you need to think beyond the confines of the screen so that larger issues of meaning and structure are not lost to superficial matters such as word choice and sentence arrangement.

Here are some guidelines for using a word processor as an effective revision tool.

1. Deal with major revisions first: see the revision checklist on page 58. Save editing, formatting the manuscript, and proofreading for later drafts.
2. Use commands for deleting and moving blocks of copy as you would cut and paste a handwritten draft.
3. Save earlier drafts under their own file names in case you need to consult them for ideas or phrasings. Make a duplicate of any draft you want to revise, and work on the duplicate.
4. If you tend to rewrite excessively when working on the computer or have trouble finding your focus or organizing your paper, print a copy of your draft and work on it. Many writers prefer to work on paper copy (also called **hard copy**) because it is easier to read and allows a view of the whole not permitted on the computer screen. It is an easy matter to transfer changes from printed copy to computer.

The word processor is also an excellent tool for editing and proofreading—tightening, clarifying, refining, and correcting. (See the editing checklist on p. 66.) The following guidelines will help you make the most of the machine.

1. Save your drafts on the computer, print your work, and do your editing on a paper copy. Most people find it much harder to spot errors on the computer screen than on paper. And paper copy may discourage you from overediting to the point where you say less with less life. You can easily transfer the editing changes from paper to the computer.

2. After editing, return to the draft in the computer. Either work through the draft line by line or use the **search command** to find the places you want to change. The search command directs the computer to locate any words or phrases you specify.

3. Use the search command as well to find misused words or stylistic problems that tend to crop up in your writing. Such problems might include *there are*, *it is*, and other expletive constructions (see 5e-4); *the fact that* and other wordy phrases (31c-1); and *is*, *are*, and other forms of *be*, which often occur in wordy constructions (31c-3) and passive sentences (7h).

4. Make sure that you neither omit needed words nor leave in unneeded words when deleting or inserting text on the computer.

5. Resist the temptation to view the final draft coming out of the printer as perfect simply because the copy is clean. Always proofread your final draft *carefully*. (See 2d for proofreading tips.)

A note on manuscript format

Most word processors provide automatic settings for margins, tabs, indentions, and other features of manuscript format. Use these settings to produce a manuscript that coincides with the format described in Appendix A or any format requested by your instructor. Appendix A also contains advice about print styles, paper, and other aspects of word processing (see especially A1-c and A2-b).

B4   Using optional programs on a word processor

Many word processors either come with optional programs such as spelling checkers or are compatible with other packages that provide these programs. The following list describes the kinds of programs you're most likely to see.

1. *Invention or discovery programs* help you develop a topic by prompting you with a structured set of questions or by providing creative analogies that help you think imaginatively. These programs can help you get started and develop new insights.

2. *Outlining programs* help you organize your work by providing automatic indentions, easy resequencing, and other features.

3. *Style-checking programs* help you find and correct wordy and awkward phrases and faulty grammar and punctuation. These programs are usually limited because they cannot identify the context of a possible flaw or error. Consult this book whenever you are unsure of a style checker's advice.

4. *Thesaurus programs* help with word choices by responding to your word with a display of several synonyms (words with similar meanings) and sometimes antonyms (words with opposite meanings). A single keystroke allows you to replace your word with a displayed word. (However, you should always consult a dictionary for the meaning of any word you are not sure of.)

5. *Spell-checking programs* help you find typographical errors and misspelled words, and they display correct spellings on the screen. They can be valuable proofreading aids. However, they are limited because they cannot store every possible word and thus may identify a word you use as misspelled even though it is correct. In addition, they are unreliable because they cannot identify errors such as a confusion among *there*, *their*, and *they're*. Maintain a file of your frequent misspellings and use the search command to check them yourself.

B4

Glossary of Usage

This glossary provides notes on words or phrases that often cause problems for writers. The recommendations for standard written English are based on current dictionaries and usage guides like the ones listed in 32a. Items labelled **non-standard** should be avoided in speech and especially in writing. Those labelled **colloquial** and **slang** occur in speech and in some informal writing but are best avoided in the more formal writing usually expected in college/university and business. (Words and phrases labelled *colloquial* include those labelled by many dictionaries with the equivalent term *informal*.) See Chapter 31 for further discussion of word choice and for exercises in usage. See 32b-2 for a description of dictionary labels. Also see 34a-1 for a list of commonly confused words that are pronounced the same or similarly. The words and definitions provided there supplement this glossary.

The glossary is necessarily brief. Keep a dictionary handy for all your writing, and make a habit of referring to it whenever you doubt the appropriateness of a word or phrase.

a, an   Use *a* before words beginning with consonant sounds, including those spelled with an initial pronounced *h* and those spelled with vowels that are sounded as consonants: *a historian, a one-o'clock class, a university.* Use *an* before words that begin with vowel sounds, including those spelled with an initial silent *h*: *an orgy, an L, an honour.*

When you use an abbreviation or acronym in writing (see 28b), the article that precedes it depends on how the abbreviation is to be read: *He was once an NFB producer.* (*NFB* is to be read as three separate letters, and *n* is pronounced "en.") *Many Americans opposed a SALT treaty.* (*SALT* is to be read as one word, *salt.*)

accept, except   *Accept* is a verb meaning "receive." *Except* is usually a preposition or conjunction meaning "but for" or "other than"; when it is used as a verb, it means "leave out." *I can accept all your suggestions except the last one. I'm sorry you excepted my last suggestion from your list.*

adverse, averse   *Adverse* and *averse* are both adjectives, and both mean "opposed" or "hostile." But *averse* describes the subject's opposition to something, whereas *adverse* describes something opposed to the subject: *The premier was averse to adverse criticism.*

advice, advise   *Advice* is a noun, and *advise* is a verb: *Take my advice; do as I advise you.*

affect, effect   Usually *affect* is a verb, meaning "to influence," and *effect* is a noun, meaning "result": *The drug did not affect his driving; in fact, it seemed to have no effect at all.* But *effect* occasionally is used as a verb meaning "to bring about": *Her efforts effected a change.* And *affect* is used in psychology as a noun meaning "feeling or emotion": *One can infer much about affect from behaviour.*

aggravate   *Aggravate* should not be used in its colloquial meaning of "irritate" or "exasperate" (for example, *We were aggravated by her constant arguing*). *Aggravate* means "make worse": *The Prime Minister was irritated by the Senate's stubbornness because he feared any delay might aggravate the West's disenchantment with Ottawa.*

agree to, agree with   *Agree to* means "consent to," and *agree with* means "be in accord with": *How can they agree to a treaty when they don't agree with each other about the terms?*

ain't   Non-standard for *am not, isn't,* or *aren't.*

all, all of   Usually *all* is sufficient to modify a noun: *all my loving, all the things you are.* Before a pronoun or proper noun, *all of* is usually appropriate: *all of me , in all of France.*

all ready, already   *All ready* means "completely prepared," and *already* means "by now" or "before now": *We were all ready to go to the movie, but it had already started.*

all right   *All right* is always two words. *Alright* is a common misspelling.

all together, altogether   *All together* means "in unison," or "gathered in one place." *Altogether* means "entirely." *It's not altogether true that our family never spends vacations all together.*

allusion, illusion   An *allusion* is an indirect reference, and an *illusion* is a deceptive appearance: *Paul's constant allusions to Shakespeare created the illusion that he was an intellectual.*

almost, most   *Almost* is an adverb meaning "nearly"; *most* is an adjective meaning "the greater number (or part) of." In formal writing, *most* should not be used as a substitute for *almost*: *We see each other almost* (not *most*) *every day.*

a lot   *A lot* is always two words, used informally to mean "many." *Alot* is a common misspelling.

among, between   In general, *among* is used for relationships involving more than two people or things. *Between* is used for relationships involving only two or for comparing one thing to a group to which it belongs. *The four of them agreed among themselves that the choice was between Montreal and Vancouver.* Increasingly, though, *between* is used for relationships involving three or more comparable people or things: *Let's keep this just between the three of us, shall we?*

amongst   Although sometimes used by Canadian or British writers, *amongst* is an overrefined substitute for *among.*

amount, number   *Amount* refers to a quantity of something (a singular noun) that cannot be counted. *Number* refers to countable items (a plural noun). *The amount of leftover ice we can save depends on the number of containers we have to put it in.*

gl/us

an, and   *An* is an article (see *a, an*). *And* is a co-ordinating conjunction. Do not carelessly omit the *d* from *and*.

and etc.   *Et cetera* (*etc.*) means "and the rest"; *and etc.* therefore is redundant. See also *et al.*, *etc.*

and/or   *And/or* is awkward and often confusing. A sentence such as *The decision is made by the mayor and/or the council* implies that one or the other or both make the decision. If you mean both, use *and*; if you mean either, use *or*. Use *and/or* only when you mean three options.

and which, and who   When *which* or *who* is used to introduce a relative clause, *and* is superfluous: *CFCF is my favourite AM radio station, which* (not *and which*) *I listen to every morning*. *And which* or *and who* is correct only when used to introduce a second clause beginning with the same relative pronoun: *Shaila is my cousin who goes to school here and who always calls me at seven in the morning*.

ante-, anti-   The prefix *ante-* means "before" (*antedate, antediluvian*); *anti-* means "against" (*antiwar, antinuclear*). Before a capital letter or a vowel, *anti-* takes a hyphen: *anti-Freudian, anti-isolationist*.

anxious, eager   *Anxious* means "nervous" or "worried" and is usually followed by *about*. *Eager* means "looking forward" and is usually followed by *to*. *I've been anxious about getting blisters*. *I'm eager* (not *anxious*) *to get new running shoes*.

anybody, any body; anyone, any one   *Anybody* and *anyone* are indefinite pronouns; *any body* is a noun modified by an adjective; *any one* is a pronoun or adjective modified by *any*. *How can anybody communicate with any body of government? Can anyone help Amy? She has more work than any one person can handle*.

any more, anymore   *Any more* is used in negative constructions to mean "no more." *Anymore*, an adverb meaning "now," is also used in negative constructions. *He doesn't want any more*. *She doesn't live here anymore*.

anyplace   Colloquial for *anywhere*.

anyways, anywheres   Non-standard for *anyway* and *anywhere*.

apt, liable, likely   *Apt* and *likely* are interchangeable. Strictly speaking, though, *apt* means "having a tendency to": *Horace is apt to forget his lunch in the morning*. *Likely* means "probably going to": *Horace is leaving so early today that he's likely to catch the first bus*.

Liable is normally used to mean "in danger of" and should be confined to situations with undesirable consequences: *If Horace doesn't watch out, he is liable to trip over that lawn sprinkler*. In the strictest sense, *liable* means "responsible" or "exposed to": *If Horace trips over that lawn sprinkler, the owner will be liable for damages*.

as   *As* is often used to mean *because, since, while, whether*, or *who*. It may be vague or ambiguous in these senses: *As we were stopping to rest, we decided to eat lunch*. (Does *as* mean "while" or "because"?) Usually a more precise word is preferable. See also 16c.

As never should be used as a substitute for *whether* or *who*. *I'm not sure whether* (not *as*) *we can make it*. *That's the man who* (not *as*) *gave me directions*.

as, like In formal speech and writing, *as* may be either a preposition or a conjunction; *like* functions as a preposition only. Thus, if the construction being introduced is a full clause rather than a word or phrase, the preferred choice is *as* or *as if* (see 16c): *The plan succeeded as* (not *like*) *we hoped. It seemed as if* (not *like*) *it might fail. Other plans like it have failed.*

When *as* serves as a preposition, the distinction between *as* and *like* depends on meaning. *As* suggests that the subject is equivalent or identical to the description: *She was hired as an engineer. Like* suggests resemblance but not identity: *People like her do well in such jobs.* See also *like, such as.*

as, than In comparisons, *as* and *than* may be followed by either subjective- or objective-case pronouns: *You are as tall as he* (subjective). *They treated you better than him* (objective). The case depends on whether the pronoun is the subject or object of a verb: *I love you more than he* (*loves you*) (*he* is the subject of the missing verb *loves*). *I love you more than* (*I love*) *him* (*him* is the object of the missing verb *love*). See also 6e.

gl/us

assure, ensure, insure *Assure* means "to promise": *He assured us that if we left early, we would miss the traffic. Ensure* and *insure* are sometimes used interchangeably to mean "make certain," but most reserve *insure* for matters of legal and financial protection and use *ensure* for more general meanings: *We left early to ensure that we would miss the traffic. It's expensive to insure yourself against floods.*

as to A stuffy substitute for *about*: *The suspect was questioned about* (not *as to*) *her actions.*

at The use of *at* after *where* is wordy and should be avoided: *Where are you meeting him?* is preferable to *Where are you meeting him at?*

at this point in time Wordy for *now, at this point,* or *at this time.*

averse, adverse See *adverse, averse.*

awful, awfully Strictly speaking, *awful* means "awe-inspiring." As intensifiers meaning "very" or "extremely" (*He tried awfully hard*), *awful* and *awfully* are colloquial and should not be used in formal speech or writing.

a while, awhile *Awhile* is an adverb; *a while* is an article and a noun. Thus *awhile* can modify a verb but cannot serve as the object of a preposition, and *a while* is just the opposite: *I will be gone awhile* (not *a while*). *I will be gone for a while* (not *awhile*).

bad, badly In formal speech and writing, *bad* should be used only as an adjective; the adverb is *badly. He felt bad because his tooth ached badly.* In *He felt bad,* the verb *felt* is a linking verb and the adjective *bad* is a subject complement. See also 9b.

being as, being that Colloquial for *because,* the preferable word in formal speech or writing: *Because* (not *Being as*) *the world is round, Columbus never did fall off the edge.*

beside, besides *Beside* is a preposition meaning "next to." *Besides* is a preposition meaning "except" or "in addition to" as well as an adverb meaning "in addition." *Besides, several other people besides you want to sit beside Dr. Christensen.*

better, had better *Had better* (meaning "ought to") is a verb modified by an adverb. The verb is necessary and should not be omitted: *You had better* (not *better*) *go.*

between, among See *among, between.*

bring, take Use *bring* only for movement from a farther place to a nearer one and *take* for any other movement. *First, take these books to the library for renewal, then take them to Mr. Daniels. Bring them back to me when he's finished.*

bunch In formal speech and writing, *bunch* (as a noun) should be used only to refer to clusters of things growing or fastened together, such as bananas and grapes. Its use to mean a group of items or people is colloquial: *crowd* or *group* is preferable.

burst, bursted; bust, busted *Burst* is a standard verb form meaning "to fly apart suddenly" (principal parts *burst, burst, burst*). The past-tense form *bursted* is non-standard. The verb *bust* (*busted*) is slang.

but, hardly, scarcely These words are negative in their own right; using *not* with any of them produces a double negative (see 9f). *We have but an hour* (not *We haven't got but an hour*) *before our plane leaves. I could hardly* (not *I couldn't hardly*) *make out her face in the dark.*

but however, but yet These and similar expressions, in which *but* is combined with another conjunction, are redundant and should be avoided: *He said he had finished, yet* (not *but yet*) *he continued.*

but that, but what These wordy substitutes for *that* and *what* should be avoided: *I don't doubt that* (not *but that*) *you are right.*

calculate, figure, reckon As substitutes for *expect* or *imagine* (*I figure I'll go*), these words are colloquial.

can, may Strictly, *can* indicates capacity or ability, and *may* indicates permission: *If I may talk with you a moment, I believe I can solve your problem.*

can't help but This idiom is common but redundant. Either *I can't help wishing* or the more formal *I cannot but wish* is preferable to *I can't help but wish.*

case, instance, line Expressions such as *in the case of, in the instance of,* and *along the lines of* are usually unnecessary padding in a sentence and should be avoided.

censor, censure To *censor* is to edit or remove from public view on moral or some other grounds; to *censure* is to give a formal scolding. *The lieutenant was censured by Major Theriault for censoring the letters the recruits wrote home from basic training camp.*

centre around *Centre on* is generally considered more logical than, and preferable to, *centre around.*

climatic, climactic *Climatic* comes from *climate* and refers to weather: *Last winter's low temperatures may indicate a climatic change. Climactic* comes from *climax* and refers to a dramatic high point: *During the climactic duel between Hamlet and Laertes, Gertrude drinks poisoned wine.*

complement, compliment   To *complement* something is to add to, complete, or reinforce it: *Her yellow blouse complemented her black hair.* To *compliment* something is to make a flattering remark about it: *He complimented her hair. Complimentary* can also mean "free": *a complimentary sample of our new product*; complimentary *tickets*.

conscience, conscious   *Conscience* is a noun meaning "a sense of right and wrong"; *conscious* is an adjective meaning "aware" or "awake." *Though I was barely conscious, my conscience told me to confess.*

contact   Often used imprecisely as a verb when a more exact word such as *consult, talk with, telephone,* or *write to* would be appropriate.

continual, continuous   *Continual* means "constantly recurring": *Most movies on television are continually interrupted by commercials. Continuous* means "unceasing": *Cable television often presents movies continuously without commercials.*

convince, persuade   In the strictest sense, to *convince* someone means to change his or her opinion; to *persuade* someone means to move him or her to action. *Convince* thus is properly followed by *of* or *that*, whereas *persuade* is followed by *to*: *Once he convinced Othello of Desdemona's infidelity, Iago easily persuaded him to kill her.*

could of   See *have, of.*

couple of   Used colloquially to mean "a few" or "several."

credible, creditable, credulous   *Credible* means "believable": *It's a strange story, but it seems credible to me. Creditable* means "deserving of credit" or "worthy": *Asked to play "Red River Valley," Steve gave a creditable performance. Credulous* means "gullible": *The credulous Claire believed Tim's statement that he was quitting school.* See also *incredible, incredulous.*

criteria   The plural of *criterion* (meaning "standard for judgment"): *Of all our criteria for picking a roommate, the most important criterion is a sense of humour.*

data   The plural of *datum* (meaning "fact"): *Out of all the data generated by these experiments, not one datum supports our hypothesis.* Usually, a more common term like *fact, result,* or *figure* is preferred to *datum.* Though *data* is very often used as a singular noun, it is still treated as plural in much formal speech and writing: *The data fail* (not *fails*) *to support the hypothesis.*

device, devise   *Device* is the noun, and *devise* is the verb: *Can you devise some device for getting his attention?*

differ from, differ with   To *differ from* is to be unlike: *The twins differ from each other only in their hairstyles.* To *differ with* is to disagree with: *I have to differ with you on that point.*

different from, different than   *Different from* is preferred: *His purpose is different from mine.* But *different than* is widely accepted when a clause follows, particularly when a construction using *from* would be wordy: *I'm a different person now than I used to be* is preferable to *I'm a different person now from the person I used to be.*

gl/us

discreet, discrete   *Discreet* (noun form *discretion*) means "tactful": *What's a discreet way of telling Maud to be quiet? Discrete* (noun form *discreteness*) means "separate and distinct": *Within a computer's memory are millions of discrete bits of information.*

disinterested, uninterested   *Disinterested* means "impartial": *We chose Pete, as a disinterested third party, to decide who was right. Uninterested* means "bored" or "lacking interest": *Unfortunately, Pete was completely uninterested in the question.*

don't   *Don't* is the contraction for *do not*, not for *does not*: *I don't care, you don't care*, but *he doesn't* (not *don't*) *care.*

due to   *Due* is an adjective or noun; thus *due to* is always acceptable as a subject complement: *His gray hairs were due to age.* Many object to *due to* as a preposition meaning "because of" (*Due to the holiday, class was cancelled*). A rule of thumb is that *due to* is always correct after a form of the verb *be* but questionable otherwise.

due to the fact that   Wordy for *because*.

each and every   Wordy for *each* or *every*. Write *each one of us* or *every one of us*, not *each and every one of us*.

eager, anxious   See *anxious, eager*.

effect   See *affect, effect*.

elicit, illicit   *Elicit* is a verb meaning "bring out" or "call forth"; *illicit* is an adjective meaning "unlawful." *The crime elicited an outcry against illicit drugs.*

ensure   See *assure, ensure, insure*.

enthused   Used colloquially as an adjective meaning "showing enthusiasm." The preferred adjective is *enthusiastic*: *The coach was enthusiastic* (not *enthused*) *about the team's victory.*

especially, specially   *Especially* means "particularly" or "more than other things"; *specially* means "for a specific reason." *I especially treasure my boots. They were made specially for me.*

et al., etc.   *Et al.*, the Latin abbreviation for "and other people," is often used in source references for works with more than three authors: *Jones et al.* (see 35d-2, 36i-1). *Etc.*, the Latin abbreviation for "and other things," should not be used to refer to people. *Etc.* should be avoided in formal writing. When used, it should not substitute for precision, as in *The government provides health care, etc.* See also *and etc.*

everybody, every body; everyone, every one   *Everybody* and *everyone* are indefinite pronouns: *Everybody* (*everyone*) *knows Tom steals. Every one* is a pronoun modified by *every*; *every body* a noun modified by *every*. Both refer to each thing or person of a specific group and are typically followed by *of*: *The game commissioner has stocked every body of fresh water in the state with fish, and now every one of our rivers is a potential trout stream.*

everyday, every day   *Every day* is a noun modified by *every*; *everyday* is an adjective meaning "used daily" or "common": *Every day she had to cope with everyday problems.*

everywheres   Non-standard for *everywhere*.

except   See *accept, except*.

except for the fact that   Wordy for *except that*.

explicit, implicit   *Explicit* means "stated outright": *I left explicit instructions. The movie contains explicit sex. Implicit* means "implied, unstated": *We had an implicit understanding. I trust Marcia implicitly*.

farther, further   *Farther* refers to additional distance (*How much farther is it to the beach?*), and *further* refers to additional time, amount, or other abstract matters (*I don't want to discuss this any further*).

fewer, less   *Fewer* refers to individual countable items (a plural noun), *less* to general amounts (a singular noun): *Skim milk has fewer calories than whole milk. We have less milk left than I thought*.

field   The phrase *the field of* is wordy and generally unnecessary: *Margaret plans to specialize in* (not *in the field of*) *family medicine*.

figure   See *calculate, figure, reckon*.

fixing to   Avoid this colloquial substitute for "intend to": *The school intends* (not *is fixing*) *to build a new library*.

flaunt, flout   *Flaunt* means "show off": *If you have style, flaunt it. Flout* means "scorn" or "defy": *Hester Prynne flouted convention and paid the price*.

flunk   A colloquial substitute for *fail*.

former, latter   *Former* refers to the first-named of two things, *latter* to the second-named: *I like both skiing and swimming, the former in the winter and the latter all year round*. To refer to the first- or last-named of three or more things, say *first* or *last*: *I like jogging, swimming, and hang gliding, but the last is inconvenient in the city*.

fun   An an adjective, *fun* is colloquial and should be avoided in most writing: *It was a pleasurable* (not *fun*) *evening*.

further   See *farther, further*.

get   This common verb is used in many slang and colloquial expressions: *get lost, get with it, get your act together, that really gets me, getting on. Get* is easy to overuse; watch out for it in expressions like *it's getting better* (substitute *it's improving*) and *we got done* (substitute *we finished*).

good, well   *Good* is an adjective, and *well* is nearly always an adverb: *Larry's a good dancer. He and Linda dance well together. Well* is properly used as an adjective only to refer to health: *You don't look well. Aren't you feeling well?* (*You look good*, in contrast, means "Your appearance is pleasing.")

good and   Colloquial for "very": *I was very* (not *good and*) *tired*.

had better   See *better, had better*.

had ought   The *had* is unnecessary and should be omitted: *He ought* (not *had ought*) *to listen to his mother*.

half   Either *half a* or *a half* is appropriate usage, but *a half a* is redundant: *Half a loaf* (not *A half a loaf*) *is better than none. I'd like a half-gallon* (not *a half a gallon*) *of mineral water, please*.

gl/us

hanged, hung Though both are past-tense forms of *hang, hanged* is used to refer to executions and *hung* is used for all other meanings: *Louis Riel was <u>hanged</u>* (not <u>*hung*</u>) *in a Regina jail. I <u>hung</u>* (not <u>*hanged*</u>) *the picture you gave me.*

hardly See *but, hardly, scarcely.*

have, of Use *have,* not *of,* after helping verbs such as *could, should, would, may,* and *might: You should have* (not <u>*should of*</u>) *told me.*

he, she; he/she The pronouns *he* and *she* refer to male and female antecedents, respectively. In the past, when the antecedent could be either male or female, convention allowed the use of *he* to mean "he or she": *After the infant learns to crawl, <u>he</u> progresses to creeping.* However, many people today object to this use of *he* because readers tend to think of *he* as male, whether or not that is the writer's intention. The construction *he/she,* one substitute for *he,* is awkward and objectionable to most readers. The better choice is to use *he or she,* to make the pronoun plural, or to rephrase. For instance: *After the infant learns to crawl, <u>he or she</u> progresses to creeping. After <u>infants</u> learn to crawl, <u>they</u> progress to creeping. After learning to crawl, <u>the infant</u> progresses to creeping.* See also 8b-3 and 31a-8.

gl/us

herself, himself See *myself, herself, himself, yourself.*

hisself Non-standard for *himself.*

hopefully *Hopefully* means "with hope": *Freddy waited <u>hopefully</u> for a glimpse of Eliza.* The use of *hopefully* to mean "it is to be hoped," "I hope," or "let's hope" is now very common; but since many readers continue to object strongly to the usage, you should avoid it. *<u>I hope</u>* (not <u>*Hopefully*</u>) *Eliza will be here soon.*

idea, ideal An *idea* is a thought or conception. An *ideal* (noun) is a model of perfection or a goal. *Ideal* should not be used in place of *idea: The <u>idea</u>* (not <u>*ideal*</u>) *of the play is that our <u>ideals</u> often sustain us.*

if, whether For clarity, begin a subordinate clause with *whether* rather than *if* when the clause expresses an alternative: *<u>If</u> I laugh hard, people can't tell <u>whether</u> I'm crying.*

illicit See *elicit, illicit.*

illusion See *allusion, illusion.*

impact Careful writers use both the noun and the verb *impact* to connote forceful or even violent collision. Avoid the increasingly common diluted meanings of *impact:* "an effect" (noun) or "to have an effect on" (verb). The diluted verb (*The budget cuts <u>impacted</u> social science research*) is bureaucratic jargon.

implicit See *explicit, implicit.*

imply, infer Writers or speakers *imply,* meaning "suggest": *Jim's letter <u>implies</u> he's having too good a time to miss us.* Readers or listeners *infer,* meaning "conclude": *From Jim's letter I <u>infer</u> he's having too good a time to miss us.*

in, into *In* indicates location or condition: *He was <u>in</u> the garage. She was <u>in</u> a coma. Into* indicates movement or a change in condition: *He went* *into the garage. She fell into a coma. Into* is also slang for "interested in" or "involved in": *I am into Zen.*

in . . .   A number of phrases beginning with *in* are unnecessarily wordy and should be avoided: *in the event that* (for *if*); *in the neighbourhood of* (for *approximately* or *about*); *in this day and age* (for *now* or *nowadays*); *in spite of the fact that* (for *although* or *even though*); and *in view of the fact that* (for *because* or *considering that*). Certain other *in* phrases are nothing but padding and can be omitted entirely: *in the case of, in nature, in number, in reality, in terms of,* and *in a very real sense.* See also 31c.

incredible, incredulous   *Incredible* means "unbelievable"; *incredulous* means "unbelieving": *When Nancy heard Dennis's incredible story, she was frankly incredulous.* See also *credible, creditable, credulous.*

individual, person, party   *Individual* should refer to a single human being in contrast to a group or should stress uniqueness: *The Canadian Charter of Rights and Freedoms places strong emphasis on the rights of the individual.* For other meanings *person* is preferable: *What person* (not *individual*) *wouldn't want the security promised in that advertisement? Party* means "group" (*Can you seat a party of four for dinner?*) and should not be used to refer to an individual except in legal documents.

infer   See *imply.*

in regards to   Non-standard for *in regard to* (or *as regards* or *regarding*). See also *regarding.*

inside of, outside of   The *of* is unnecessary when *inside* and *outside* are used as prepositions: *Stay inside* (not *inside of*) *the house. The decision is outside* (not *outside of*) *my authority. Inside of* may refer colloquially to time, though in formal English *within* is preferred: *The law was passed within* (not *inside of*) *a year.*

instance   See *case, instance, line.*

insure   See *assure, ensure, insure.*

irregardless   Non-standard for *regardless.*

is because   See *reason is because.*

is when, is where   These are mixed constructions (faulty predication; see 15b) in sentences that define: *Adolescence is a stage* (not *is when a person is*) *between childhood and adulthood. Socialism is a system in which* (not *is where*) *government owns the means of production.*

its, it's   *Its* is a possessive pronoun: *That plant is losing its leaves. It's* is a contraction for *it is: It's likely to die if you don't water it.* Many people confuse *it's* and *its* because possessives are most often formed with *-'s*; but the possessive *its,* like *his* and *hers,* never takes an apostrophe.

-ize, -wise   The suffix *-ize* is frequently used to change a noun or adjective into a verb: *revolutionize, immunize.* The suffix *-wise* commonly changes a noun or adjective into an adverb: *clockwise, otherwise, likewise.* But the two suffixes are used excessively and often unnecessarily, especially in bureaucratic writing. Avoid their use except in established words: *The two nations are ready to settle on* (not *finalize*) *an agreement. I'm highly sensitive* (not *sensitized*) *to that kind of criticism. From a financial standpoint* (not *Moneywise*), *it's a good time to buy real estate.*

gl/us

kind of, sort of, type of   In formal speech and writing, avoid using *kind of* or *sort of* to mean "somewhat": *He was rather* (not *kind of*) *tall.*

Kind, sort and *type* are singular and take singular modifiers and verbs: *This kind of dog is easily trained.* Agreement errors often occur when these singular nouns are combined with the plural demonstrative adjectives *these* and *those*: *These kinds* (not *kind*) *of dogs are easily trained. Kind, sort,* and *type* should be followed by *of* but not by *a*: *I don't know what type of* (not *type* or *type of a*) *dog that is.*

Use *kind of, sort of,* or *type of* only when the word *kind, sort,* or *type* is important: *That was a strange* (not *strange sort of*) *statement. He's a funny* (not *funny kind of*) *guy.*

later, latter   *Later* refers to time; *latter* refers to the second-named of two items. See also *former, latter.*

gl/us

lay, lie   *Lay* is a transitive verb (principal parts *lay, laid, laid*) that means "put" or "place" and takes a direct object. *If we lay this tablecloth in the sun next to the shirt Sandy laid out there this morning, it should dry quickly. Lie* is an intransitive verb (principal parts *lie, lay, lain*) that means "recline" or "be situated": *I lay awake all night last night, just as I had lain the night before. The town lies east of the river.* See also 7b.

leave, let   *Leave* and *let* are interchangeable only when followed by *alone; leave me alone* is the same as *let me alone.* Otherwise, *leave* means "depart" and *let* means "allow": *Julia would not let Susan leave.*

less   See *fewer, less.*

let   See *leave, let.*

liable   See *apt, liable, likely.*

lie, lay   See *lay, lie.*

like, as   See *as, like.*

like, such as   When you are giving an example of something, use *such as* to indicate that the example is a representative of the thing mentioned, and use *like* to compare the example to the thing mentioned: *Steve has recordings of many great saxophonists such as Ben Webster, Coleman Hawkins, and Lee Konitz. Steve wants to be a great jazz saxophonist like Ben Webster, Coleman Hawkins, and Lee Konitz.*

Most writers prefer to keep *such* and *as* together: *Steve admires saxophonists such as* rather than *Steve admires such saxophonists as.*

likely   See *apt, liable, likely.*

line   See *case, instance, line.*

literally   This adverb means "actually" or "just as the words say," and it should not be used to qualify or intensify expressions whose words are not to be taken at face value. The sentence *He was literally climbing the walls* describes a person behaving like an insect, not a person who is restless or anxious. For the latter meaning, *literally* should be omitted.

lose, loose   *Lose* is a verb meaning "mislay": *Did you lose a brown glove? Loose* is an adjective meaning "unrestrained" or "not tight": *Don't open the door; Ann's canary got loose. Loose* also can function as a verb meaning "let loose": *They loose the dogs as soon as they spot the bear.*

lots, lots of   Colloquial substitutes for *very many, a great many,* or *much.* Avoid *lots* and *lots of* in academic or business writing. When you use either one informally, be careful to maintain subject-verb agreement: *There are* (not *is*) *lots of fish in the pond.*

may, can   See *can, may.*

may be, maybe   *May be* is a verb, and *maybe* is an adverb meaning "perhaps": *Tuesday may be a legal holiday. Maybe we won't have classes.*

may of   See *have, of.*

media   *Media* is the plural of *medium* and takes a plural verb: *All the news media are increasingly visual.*

might of   See *have, of.*

moral, morale   As a noun, *moral* means "ethical conclusion" or "lesson": *The moral of the story escapes me. Morale* means "spirit" or "state of mind": *Victory improved the team's morale.*

most, almost   See *almost, most.*

must of   See *have, of.*

myself, herself, himself, yourself   The *-self* pronouns are reflexive or intensive, which means they refer to or intensify an antecedent (see 5a-2): *Paul and I did it ourselves*; *Jill herself said so.* Though the *-self* pronouns often are used colloquially in place of personal pronouns, especially as objects of prepositions, they should be avoided in formal speech and writing unless the noun or pronoun they refer to is also present: *No one except me* (not *myself*) *saw the accident. Our delegates will be Susan and you* (not *yourself*).

nohow   Non-standard for *in no way* or *in any way.*

nothing like, nowhere near   As colloquial substitutes for *not nearly,* these idioms are best avoided in formal speech and writing: *The human bones found in Europe are not nearly* (not *nowhere near*) *as old as those found in Africa.*

nowheres   Non-standard for *nowhere.*

number   See *amount, number.*

of, have   See *have, of.*

off of   *Of* is unnecessary. Use *off* or *from* rather than *off of*: *He jumped off* (or *from,* not *off of*) *the roof.*

OK, O.K., okay   All three spellings are acceptable, but avoid this colloquial term in formal speech and writing.

on, upon   In modern English, *upon* is usually just a stuffy way of saying *on.* Unless you need a formal effect, use *on*: *We decided on* (not *upon*) *a location for our next meeting.*

on account of   Wordy for *because of.*

on the other hand   This transitional expression of contrast should be preceded by its mate, *on the one hand*: *On the one hand, we hoped for snow. On the other hand, we feared that it would harm the animals.*

However, the two combined can be unwieldy, and a simple *but*, *however*, *yet*, or *in contrast* often suffices: *We hoped for snow.* <u>*Yet*</u> *we feared that it would harm the animals.*

outside of See *inside of, outside of.*

owing to the fact that Wordy for *because.*

party See *individual, person, party.*

people, persons In formal usage, *people* refers to a general group: *We the <u>people</u> of Canada.* . . . *Persons* refers to a collection of individuals: *Will the person or <u>persons</u> who saw the accident please notify.* . . . Except when emphasizing individuals, prefer *people* to *persons.*

per Except in technical writing, an English equivalent is usually preferable to the Latin *per*: *$10 <u>an</u>* (not *<u>per</u>*) *hour*; *sent <u>by</u>* (not *<u>per</u>*) *parcel post*; *requested <u>in</u>* (not *<u>per</u>* or *<u>as per</u>*) *your letter.*

percent (per cent), percentage Both of these terms refer to fractions of one hundred and should be avoided except when specifying actual statistics. Use an expression such as *part of*, *a number of*, or *a large* (or *small*) *proportion of* when you mean simply "part."

    Percent always follows a numeral (*40 percent of the voters*), and the word should be used instead of the symbol (%) in general writing. *Percentage* usually follows an adjective (*a high percentage*).

person See *individual, person, party.*

persons See *people, persons.*

persuade See *convince, persuade.*

phenomena The plural of *phenomenon* (meaning "perceivable fact" or "unusual occurrence"): *The Centre for Short-Lived <u>Phenomena</u> judged that the <u>phenomenon</u> we had witnessed was not a flying saucer.*

plenty A colloquial substitute for *very*: *He was going <u>very</u>* (not *<u>plenty</u>*) *fast when he hit that tree.*

plus *Plus* is standard as a preposition meaning *in addition to*: *His income <u>plus</u> mine is sufficient.* But *plus* is colloquial as a conjunctive adverb: *Our organization is larger than theirs; <u>moreover</u>* (not *<u>plus</u>*), *we have more money.*

practicable, practical *Practicable* means "capable of being put into practice"; *practical* means "useful" or "sensible": *We figured out a <u>practical</u> new design for our kitchen, but it was too expensive to be <u>practicable</u>.*

precede, proceed The verb *precede* means "come before": *My name <u>precedes</u> yours in the alphabet.* The verb *proceed* means "move on": *We were told to <u>proceed</u> to the waiting room.*

prejudice, prejudiced *Prejudice* is a noun; *prejudiced* is an adjective. Do not drop the *-d* from *prejudiced*: *I was fortunate my parents were not <u>prejudiced</u>* (not *<u>prejudice</u>*).

pretty Overworked as an adverb meaning "rather" or "somewhat": *He was <u>somewhat</u>* (not *<u>pretty</u>*) *irked at the suggestion.*

previous to, prior to Wordy for *before.*

principal, principle *Principal* is a noun meaning "chief official" or, in finance, "capital sum." As an adjective, *principal* means "foremost" or "major." *Principle* is a noun only, meaning "rule" or "axiom." *Her principal reasons for confessing were her principles of right and wrong.*

proceed, precede See *precede, proceed.*

provided, providing *Provided* may serve as a subordinating conjunction meaning "on the condition (that)"; *providing* may not. *The grocer will begin providing food for the soup kitchen provided* (not *providing*) *we find a suitable space.*

question of whether, question as to whether Wordy for *whether.*

raise, rise *Raise* is a transitive verb that takes a direct object, and *rise* is an intransitive verb that does not take an object: *The Kirks have to rise at dawn because they raise cows.*

real, really In formal speech and writing, *real* should not be used as an adverb; *really* is the adverb and *real* an adjective. *Popular reaction to the announcement was really* (not *real*) *enthusiastic.*

reason is because Mixed construction (faulty predication; see 15b). Although the expression is colloquially common, formal speech and writing require a *that* clause after *reason is*: *The reason he is absent is that* (not *is because*) *he is sick.* Or: *He is absent because he is sick.*

reckon See *calculate, figure, reckon.*

regarding, in regard to, with regard to, relating to, relative to, with respect to, respecting Stuffy substitutes for *on, about,* or *concerning*: *Mr. McGee spoke about* (not *with regard to*) *the plans for the merger.*

respectful, respective *Respectful* means "full of (or showing) respect": *If you want respect, be respectful of other people. Respective* means "separate": *After a joint Christmas celebration, the French and the Germans returned to their respective trenches.*

rise, raise See *raise, rise.*

scarcely See *but, hardly, scarcely.*

sensual, sensuous *Sensual* suggests sexuality; *sensuous* means "pleasing to the senses." *Stirred by the sensuous scent of meadow grass and flowers, Cheryl and Paul found their thoughts growing increasingly sensual.*

set, sit *Set* is a transitive verb (principal parts *set, set, set*) that describes something a person does to an object: *He set the pitcher down. Sit* is an intransitive verb (principal parts *sit, sat, sat*) that describes something done by a person who is tired of standing: *She sits on the sofa.* See also 7b.

shall, will *Will*, originally reserved for the second and third persons, is now generally accepted as the future-tense helping verb for all three persons: *I will go, you will go, they will go.* The main use of *shall* is for first-person questions requesting an opinion or consent: *Shall I order a pizza? Shall we dance?* (Questions that merely inquire about the future use *will*: *When will I see you again?*) *Shall* can also be used for the first person when a formal effect is desired (*I shall expect you around three*), and it is occasionally used with the second or third person to express the speaker's determination (*You shall do as I say*).

should, would *Should* expresses obligation for first, second, and third persons: *I should fix dinner. You should set the table. Jack should wash the dishes.* *Would* expresses a wish or hypothetical condition for all three persons: *I would do it. Wouldn't you? Wouldn't anybody?* When the context is formal, however, *should* is sometimes used instead of *would* in the first person: *We should be delighted to accept your kind invitation.*

should of See *have, of.*

since *Since* is often used to mean "because": *Since you ask, I'll tell you.* Its primary meaning, however, relates to time: *I've been waiting since noon.* To avoid confusion, some writers prefer to use *since* only in contexts involving time. If you do use *since* in both senses, watch out for ambiguous constructions, such as *Since you left, my life is empty,* where *since* could mean either "because" or "ever since."

sit, set See *set, sit.*

situation Often unnecessary, as in *The situation is that we have to get some help* (revise to *We have to get some help*) or *The team was faced with a punting situation* (revise to *The team was faced with punting* or *The team had to punt*).

so Avoid using *so* alone as a vague intensifier: *He was so late. So* needs to be followed by *that* and a clause that states a result: *He was so late that I left without him.*

some *Some* is colloquial as an adverb meaning "somewhat" or "to some extent" and as an adjective meaning "remarkable": *We'll have to hurry somewhat* (not *some*) *to get there in time. Those are remarkable* (not *some*) *photographs.*

somebody, some body; someone, some one *Somebody* and *someone* are indefinite pronouns; *some body* is a noun modified by an adjective; and *some one* is a pronoun or an adjective modified by *some. Somebody ought to invent a shampoo that will give hair some body. Someone told Janine she should choose some one plan and stick with it.*

someplace Informal for *somewhere.*

sometime, sometimes, some time *Sometime* means "at an indefinite time in the future": *Why don't you come up and see me sometime?* *Sometimes* means "now and then": *I still see my old friend Joe sometimes.* *Some time* means "span of time": *I need some time to make the payments.*

somewheres Non-standard for *somewhere.*

sort of, sort of a See *kind of, sort of, type of.*

specially See *especially, specially.*

such Avoid using *such* as a vague intensifier: *It was such a cold winter. Such* should be followed by *that* and a clause that states a result: *It was such a cold winter that Napoleon's troops had to turn back.*

such as See *like, such as.*

supposed to, used to In both these expressions, the *-d* is essential: *I used to* (not *use to*) *think so. He's supposed to* (not *suppose to*) *meet us.*

sure Colloquial when used as an adverb meaning *surely*: *The Calgary Flames sure played well in the Stanley Cup finals.* If you merely want to be emphatic, use *certainly*: *The Calgary Flames certainly played well.* If your goal is to convince a possibly reluctant reader, use *surely*: *The Calgary Flames surely played well. Surely the Calgary Flames played well.*

sure and, sure to; try and, try to *Sure to* and *try to* are the preferred forms: *Be sure to* (not *sure and*) *buy milk. Try to* (not *Try and*) *find some decent tomatoes.*

take, bring See *bring, take.*

than, as See *as, than.*

than, then *Than* is a conjunction used in comparisons, *then* an adverb indicating time: *Holmes knew then that Moriarty was wilier than he had thought.*

gl/us

that, which *That* always introduces restrictive clauses: *We should use the lettuce that Marita bought* (*that Marita bought* identifies the specific lettuce being referred to). *Which* can introduce both restrictive and nonrestrictive clauses, but many writers reserve *which* only for clauses: *The leftover lettuce, which is in the refrigerator, would make a good salad* (*which is in the refrigerator* simply provides more information about the lettuce). See also 21c.

their, there, they're *Their* is the possessive form of *they*: *Give them their money. There* indicates place (*I saw her standing there*) or functions as an expletive (*There is a hole behind you*). *They're* is a contraction for *they are*: *They're going fast.*

theirselves Non-standard for *themselves.*

then, than See *than, then.*

these kind, these sort, these type, those kind See *kind of, sort of, type of.*

this here, these here, that there, them there Non-standard for *this, these, that,* or *those.*

thusly A mistaken form of *thus.*

till, until, 'til *Till* and *until* have the same meaning; both are acceptable. *'Til*, a contraction of *until*, is an old form that has been replaced by *till*.

time period Since a *period* is an interval of time, this expression is redundant: *They did not see each other for a long time* (not *time period*). *Six accidents occurred in a three-week period* (not *time period*).

to, too, two *To* is a preposition; *too* is an adverb meaning "also" or "excessively"; and *two* is a number. *I too have been to Europe two times.*

too Avoid using *too* as an intensifier meaning "very": *Monkeys are too mean.* If you do use *too*, explain the consequences of the excessive quality: *Monkeys are too mean to make good pets.*

toward, towards Both are acceptable, though *toward* is preferred. Use one or the other consistently.

try and , try to See *sure and, sure to; try and, try to.*

type of See *kind of, sort of, type of.* Don't use *type* without *of: It was a family type of* (not *type*) *restaurant.* Or, better: *It was a family restaurant.*

uninterested See *disinterested, uninterested.*

unique As an absolute adjective (see 9e-5), *unique* cannot sensibly be modified with words such as *very* or *most: That was a unique* (not *a very* or *the most unique*) *movie.*

until See *till, until, 'til.*

upon, on See *on, upon.*

usage, use *Usage* refers to conventions, most often those of a language: *Is "hadn't ought" proper usage? Usage* is often misused in place of the noun *use: Wise use* (not *usage*) *of insulation can save fuel.*

use, utilize *Utilize* means "make use of": *We should utilize Emil's talent for mimicry in our play.* In most contexts, *use* is equally or more acceptable and much less stuffy.

used to See *supposed to, used to.*

wait for, wait on In formal speech and writing, *wait for* means "await" (*I'm waiting for Paul*), and *wait on* means "serve" (*The owner of the store herself waited on us*).

ways Colloquial as a substitute for *way: We have only a little way* (not *ways*) *to go.*

well See *good, well.*

whether, if See *if, whether.*

which See *that, which.*

which, who *Which* never refers to people. Use *who* or sometimes *that* for a person or persons and *which* or *that* for a thing or things: *The baby, who was left behind, opened the door, which we had closed.* See also 12f.

who's, whose *Who's* is the contraction of *who is: Who's at the door? Whose* is the possessive form of *who: Whose book is that?*

will, shall See *shall, will.*

-wise See *-ize, -wise.*

with regard to, with respect to See *regarding.*

would See *should, would.*

would have Avoid this construction in place of *had* in clauses that begin *if* and state a condition contrary to fact: *If the tree had* (not *would have*) *withstood the fire, it would have been the oldest in town.* (See also 7g-2).

would of See *have, of.*

your, you're *Your* is the possessive form of *you: Your dinner is ready. You're* is the contraction of *you are: You're bound to be late.*

yourself See *myself, herself, himself, yourself.*

Index

Inde

Index

Index

Acknowledgments

Photograph, page 15: Claude Lupien. Courtesy of the National Gallery of Canada.

We wish to thank the following for permission to reprint excerpts from copyrighted materials:

Addison Wesley, U.S.—William Ouchi, from *Theory Z: How American Business Can Meet the Japanese Challenge*. Copyright © 1981 by William Ouchi.

Atwood, Margaret, from "True North," *Saturday Night*, Jan. 1987:146. Copyright © 1987 by Margaret Atwood.

Berton, Pierre, from *The Last Spike*, Toronto: McClelland and Stewart, 1971. Copyright © 1971 by Pierre Berton.

Boston Globe—David Chandler, from "Air Bags—Life Saving and Unavailable," *Sci/Tech*, March 1985.

Britt Jordan, Suzanne, from "That Lean and Hungry Look," *Newsweek*, 9 Oct. 1978. Copyright © 1978 by Suzanne Britt.

Canada, Minister of Supply and Services, 1989 from "Constitution Act, 1982," (Justice Canada).

Careless, Prof. J.M.S., from *Canada: A Story of Challenge*, Toronto: Macmillan of Canada, 1963. Copyright © 1963 by Prof. J.M.S. Careless.

Clarke, Arthur C. and Scott Meredith Literary Agency, New York, from *The Star of the Magi*. Copyright © 1972 by Arthur C. Clark.

Cohen, Carl, from *Civil Disobedience*, University of Columbia Press, 1971. Copyright © 1971 by Carl Cohen.

College English Association, Inc.—Laurence Perrine, from "Fifteen Ways to Write Five Hundred Words," *The CEA Critic*, Nov. 1962. Copyright © 1962.

Curtis Brown, Ltd.—Gilbert Highet, from "Poets in a Landscape," *Poets in a Landscape*. Copyright © 1957 by Gilbert Highet.

Doubleday & Company, Inc. and Blassingame, McCauley & Wood—Edward T. Hall, from *The Hidden Dimension*. Copyright © 1966 by Edward T. Hall.

Drucker, Peter F., from "How Best to Protect the Environment," *Harper's* Magazine, Jan. 1972. Copyright © 1971 by Minneapolis Star and Tribune Co., Inc.

Encyclopaedia Britannica—René Dubos, from *Man, Medicine and Environment*. Copyright © 1968 by Encyclopaedia Britannica.

Fitzhenry & Whiteside—Andrew Malcolm, from *The Canadians*. Copyright © 1985 by Fitzhenry & Whiteside, Toronto, ON.

Fotheringham, Allan, from "Cromwell Rules in the Nation's Capital," *Maclean's*, 3 April, 1989:68. Copyright © 1989 by Allan Fotheringham.

Fulford, Robert, from "Charter of Wrongs," *Saturday Night*, Dec. 1986:7. Copyright © 1986 by Robert Fulford.

Garson, Barbara, from *All the Livelong Day*. Copyright © 1972, 1975 by Barbara Garson.

Godine, David R., Publisher, Inc.—Donald Hall, from *String Too Short to Be Saved*. Copyright © 1960, 1961, 1979 by Donald Hall.

Harper & Row, Publishers, Inc.—Annie Dillard, from "Sojourner," *Teaching a Stone to Talk: Expeditions and Encounters*. Copyright © 1982 by Annie Dillard.—Freeman J. Dyson, from *Disturbing the Universe*. Copyright © 1979 by Freeman J. Dyson.—Willard Gaylin, from "Feeling Used," *Feelings: Our Vital Signs*. Copyright © 1979 by Willard Gaylin.—E.B. White, from "Poetry," *One Man's Meat*. Copyright © 1944 by E.B. White.

Holt, Rinehart and Winston—Judith Wax, from *Starting in the Middle*. Copyright 1979 by Judith Wax.

Houghton Mifflin Company—definition of "conjecture" and synonym for "real" from *The American Heritage Dictionary, Second College Edition*. Copyright © 1985 by Houghton Mifflin Company.

Hurtig Publishers Ltd.—George Woodcock, from "Various Americas," *The New Romans: Candid Canadian Opinions of the U.S.*, Al Purdy, ed. Copyright © 1968 by Hurtig Publishers Ltd.

Kidder, Tracy & John, from *The Soul of a New Machine*. Copyright © 1981 by John Tracy Kidder.

Little, Brown and Company, Inc.—Buller, Lynn M., from "The Encyclopedia Game," *Lifestyle: Diversity in American Society*, Saul D. Feldman and Gerald W. Thielbar, eds. Copyright © 1977 by Little, Brown and Company, Inc.—Frederick J. Dockstader, from *Indian Art in America*. Published in 1966 by the New York Graphic Society. (A New York Graphic Society Book.)

PLAN OF THE BOOK AND GUIDE TO CORRECTION CODE AND SYMBOLS